Preface

The renewed move to EMU became operational on 1 July 1990 when Stage I of the process proposed in the Delors Committee Report was begun. In December 1990 the European Community will begin an intergovernmental conference to negotiate new Treaty provisions that will lay the constitutional foundations of economic and monetary union (EMU). The European Council has agreed that the new Treaty provisions should be drawn up, ratified by all Member States and available for use before 1 January 1993. It has also decided that a second intergovernmental conference should work at the same time on further Treaty provisions to adapt the institutions of the Community to the requirements of the political union for efficient and democratic decision-making.

The Community has thus established its agenda with clarity and precision. It is an agenda of historic importance.

While the content of the agenda is both economic and political, the whole process will stand or fall on the basis of the functional qualities of the economic and monetary union.

This is why the Commission decided to prepare a thorough economic appraisal of the likely economic effects — costs as well as benefits — of the move to EMU. In so doing it was asking its own staff in the Directorate-General for Economic and Financial Affairs to build a bridge between the political negotiators on the one hand, and the community of academic economists on the other, and to stimulate a two-way process of motivation of economic research and supply of economic advice. The findings of the research have been summarized in the proposal on economic and monetary union submitted in August 1990 to the Council and Parliament as the Commission's contribution to the work of the forthcoming intergovernmental conference. The systemic proposals contained in that document are thus supported by detailed economic analysis.

The present volume is the analysis of the Commission's staff. Another volume of papers, to be published later in European Economy, will offer a cross-section of academic analysis of principal features of the EMU challenge.

With the 1992 programme to complete the internal market, the Commission has acquired some experience of the interaction between policy analysis and policy implementation. In 'The economics of 1992', published in European Economy in March 1988, the Commission presented its economic analysis underlying the Cecchini Report on the potential gains from completing the internal market. That study helped the Commission clarify its priorities in implementing the 1992 programme, and also to establish the credibility of 1992 in the eyes of business opinion.

Although methodologically quite different, the present study on EMU is in some respects a sequel to this earlier work on 1992. It appears at a particularly important time. While not pretending to resolve all the uncertainties, the study offers to those concerned with preparation of the EMU Treaty provisions a handbook on the economic implications of their possible choices. The main actors in the economy — businesses, trade unions, governments — are offered a reference study which should help them prepare their strategies to exploit to the full the potential benefits of EMU and minimize its possible costs.

While the past few years have been extremely positive for the Community, both in terms of its actual economic trends and its systemic developments, the onset of the Gulf crisis in the summer of 1990 announces a more difficult period ahead. Already the oil price increase is approaching in magnitude those experienced in the 1970s. How does this affect the EMU project? The present study has much to say on this. While it makes no attempt to discuss short-run questions, a pervasive theme is how best the European economy may be equipped to absorb major external economic shocks in order to minimize the cost of their impact. The major conclusion is that a strongly unified European economic and monetary system can indeed lower these costs, compared to a poorly coordinated or disparate response.

Stage I of the movement towards EMU provides the framework within which a resolute and well-coordinated Community response to the current tensions in the international economy can be arrived at. To complete the membership of the exchange rate mechanism of the EMS has always been regarded as a vital element of the programme for Stage I. It is therefore encouraging that Spain (on 20 June 1989) and the United Kingdom (on 8 October 1990) have now joined the eight original members of the exchange rate mechanism. The two newcomers are due, moreover, to move from the broad to the narrow fluctuation margins during Stage I after a transitional period. This extension of participation in the exchange rate mechanism means that over 90 % of the Community economy is now managed under the influence of a continuously operating and powerful mechanism of monetary policy coordination. This is a good augury for the further convergence sought for the remainder of Stage I, in parallel with the negotiations of the forthcoming intergovernmental conference.

Jacques Delors
President

Henning Christophersen
Vice-President

Brussels, 10 October 1990

The present study was directed by Michael Emerson, Director for the economic evaluation of Community policies, with the support of a task force of economists of the Directorate-General for Economic and Financial Affairs. Two economic advisers of the Directorate-General, Daniel Gros and Jean Pisani-Ferry, made major contributions. The task force was based on the division for integration economics, headed by Horst Reichenbach, with Alexander Italianer (head of sector), Stefan Lehner and Marc Vanheukelen. The econometric modelling work was undertaken by Jean Pisani-Ferry, Alexander Italianer and Andries Brandsma. The research on transaction costs was undertaken by Marc Vanheukelen. Valuable contributions were made also by the directorate for national economies, notably its director, Jorge Braga de Macedo with Joan Pearce and Jürgen Kröger; by Antonio Cabral and Pedro Santos of the directorate for the evaluation of Community policies; and by Christian Ghymers of the monetary directorate.

The work of the task force benefited from the guidance of a steering group consisting of the Director-General — successively Antonio Costa and Giovanni Ravasio — Heinrich Matthes, Michael Emerson, Jean-François Pons, Jorge Braga de Macedo, Horst Reichenbach and Hervé Carré.

The task force received valuable support from Rudy Druine, Rod Meiklejohn, Marc Nelissen, Rui Pericao, José Secades; Verena Barwig, Anna-Maria Dürr, Brigitte Devereux, Kathrine Kaad Jacobsen, and especially Carine Collard who coordinated the preparation of the final text.

Helpful advice is acknowledged from several economists outside the Commission, including Michel Aglietta, Richard Baldwin, Peter Bofinger, Anton Brender, Ralph Bryant, Jean-Michel Charpin, Alex Cukierman, Andrew Hughes-Hallet, Peter Kenen, Willem Molle, Manfred Neumann, Richard Portes, André Sapir, Niels Thygesen, Frederik van der Ploeg, Paul Van Rompuy and Charles Wyplosz.

Certain organizations have also provided valuable assistance by way of data or survey results. These included several central banking institutions; the Banca d'Italia, the Banque de France, the Deutsche Bundesbank, the Institut Belgo-Luxembourgeois de Change, the Bank of International Settlements; and a considerable number of private financial institutions, as well as the Association for the Monetary Union of Europe and the Bureau européen des consommateurs.

Appreciation is also expressed to the International Monetary Fund for permission to make use of the Multimod model, and in particular to Paul Masson and Stephan Symansky of the staff for helpful support and suggestions.

Summary of contents

Abbreviations and symbols used

Countries

B	Belgium
DK	Denmark
D	Federal Republic of Germany
GR	Greece
E	Spain
F	France
IRL	Ireland
I	Italy
L	Luxembourg
NL	The Netherlands
P	Portugal
UK	United Kingdom
EUR 9	European Community excluding Greece, Spain and Portugal
EUR 10	European Community excluding Spain and Portugal
EUR 12	European Community, 12 Member States

Currencies

ECU	European currency unit
BFR	Belgian franc
DKR	Danish krone
DM	Deutschmark
DR	Greek drachma
ESC	Portuguese escudo
FF	French franc
HFL	Dutch guilder
IRL	Irish pound (punt)
LFR	Luxembourg franc
LIT	Italian lira
PTA	Spanish peseta
UKL	Pound sterling
USD	US dollar
SFR	Swiss franc
YEN	Japanese yen
CAD	Canadian dollar
ÖS	Austrian schilling

Other abbreviations

ACP	African, Caribbean and Pacific countries having signed the Lomé Convention
ECSC	European Coal and Steel Community
EDF	European Development Fund
EIB	European Investment Bank
EMCF	European Monetary Cooperation Fund
EMS	European Monetary System
ERDF	European Regional Development Fund
Euratom	European Atomic Energy Community
Eurostat	Statistical Office of the European Communities
GDP (GNP)	Gross domestic (national) product
GFCF	Gross fixed capital formation
LDCs	Less-developed countries
Mio	Million
Mrd	1 000 million
NCI	New Community Instrument
OCTs	Overseas countries and territories
OECD	Organization for Economic Cooperation and Development
OPEC	Organization of Petroleum Exporting Countries
PPS	Purchasing power standard
SMEs	Small and medium-sized enterprises
SOEC	Statistical Office of the European Communities
toe	Tonne of oil equivalent
:	Not available

ONE MARKET ONE MONEY

An Evaluation of the Potential
Benefits and Costs of Forming
an Economic and Monetary Union

MICHAEL EMERSON
DANIEL GROS
ALEXANDER ITALIANER
JEAN PISANI-FERRY
HORST REICHENBACH

OXFORD UNIVERSITY PRESS
1992

Oxford University Press, Walton Street, Oxford OX2 6DP
Oxford New York Toronto
Delhi Bombay Calcutta Madras Karachi
Petaling Jaya Singapore Hong Kong Tokyo
Nairobi Dar es Salaam Cape Town
Melbourne Auckland
and associated companies in
Berlin Ibadan

Oxford is a trade mark of Oxford University Press

Published in the United States
by Oxford University Press, New York

British Library Cataloguing in Publication Data
Data available

Library of Congress Cataloging in Publication Data
Data available
ISBN 0–19–877323–4
ISBN 0–19–877324–2 (Pbk)

Printed in Great Britain by
the Alden Press, Oxford

Executive summary

Summarized in terms of the three major objectives of economic policy, the likely impact of EMU is:

(i) *Microeconomic efficiency: sure advantages, as a single currency and economic union complement the single market and add to its impact. One market needs one money. Economic analysis supports the perceptions of industrialists that the benefits could substantially reinforce the gains being obtained from 1992 — see Graph 1.1.*

(ii) *Macroeconomic stability: sure advantages as regards better overall price stability (i.e. both very low in-*

flation on average, and low variability) assuming that the issues of institutional central bank design are handled well, and probably some gain also in terms of the stability of the real economy (lesser fluctuations in output and employment) — see Graph 1.2.

(iii) *Equity as between countries and regions: opportunities and risks for all regions, and no a priori balance of relative advantage for the original or newer Member States. The least-favoured regions have a real opportunity for rapid catch-up. EMU, like 1992, is a positive-sum game.*

The present study evaluates the benefits and costs of forming an economic and monetary union (EMU) in the European Community.

Economic principles

Defining EMU and its alternatives. Monetary union can consist of either a fixed exchange rate regime or a single currency. While both are possible, a single currency is found to offer a better benefit-cost result in economic terms, and so is the main focus of the analysis.

Economic union consists of a single market for goods, services, capital and labour, complemented by common policies and coordination in several structural, micro- and macroeconomic domains. An efficient economic union requires much less centralization of policy competences than monetary union.

For the purpose of comparison with a future EMU, thus defined, the point of departure is assumed to be a Community which has completed the internal market according to the 1992 programme, combined with the European Monetary System in which all Member States take part (1992 + EMS).

If the Community were not to move ahead to EMU, would '1992 + EMS' be a stable alternative? This is not sure, since complete capital liberalization requires virtually a unified monetary policy if exchange rates are to be stable. Other alternatives to EMU might therefore be 1992 with less than a completed EMS, or a completed EMS with less than a

fully integrated single market. The net benefits of EMU would be correspondingly greater in relation to these alternatives.

The economic mechanisms in play. The macroeconomic performance of the Community is at stake. The impacts of EMU will go to the heart of the determinants of the rate of inflation, growth, public finance trends and even the management of the world economy.

Because of these different types of impact (e.g. both growth and stability) an aggregate, quantified estimate of the potential impact of EMU is not feasible. However many individual effects can be assessed empirically and this is done throughout the study. For example, savings in monetary transaction costs with EMU would be comparable to savings in frontier costs with 1992. In both cases these relatively small direct gains are no more than a small part of the indirect and further dynamic gains.

This view is supported in surveys of industrialists' opinions, undertaken by independent research organizations, from which it appears that the addition of a single currency to the single market more than doubles the number who would expect a very positive impact on the European business climate.

The larger part of the potential economic gains would not be the automatic results of the institutional changes. The full gains would require the concerted commitment of national governments, employers and employees as well as the Community itself to what amounts to a change of economic system. This is because the systemic changes deliver only part of their economic benefits directly; in a larger measure the benefits would flow indirectly from policy changes in-

Two views of EMU

GRAPH 1.1: **A business perception of the microeconomic impact of EMU**

Opinions on the prospects for the business climate become very much more positive when a single currency complements the single market.

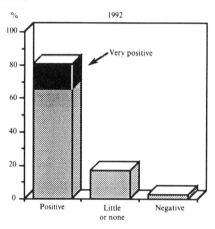 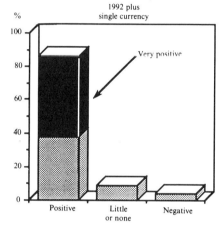

Source: Business survey undertaken for the Commission by Ernst & Young.

GRAPH 1.2: **An economist's perception of the macroeconomic impact of EMU**

Compared to a floating exchange-rate regime, EMU improves greatly on the stability of inflation and real economic activity; it also improves on the EMS especially as regards the stability of real economic activity.

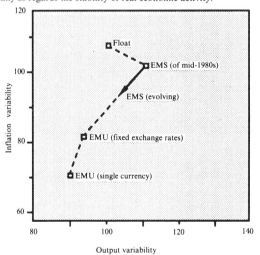

Source: Simulations of IMF Multimod model undertaken by the Commission staff.

duced by the new institutions and rules, and changed behaviour in the private economy (Graph 1.3 illustrates this point).

In order to mobilize expectations and to begin to induce these indirect effects in anticipation of EMU, it is vital that the intention of the Community to establish the definitive EMU within a relevant time-horizon be credible. While the precise means of making such commitments credible is one of the tasks of the forthcoming intergovernmental conference (rather than the present study), it is possible in some degree to model how the economy will respond to a fully credible EMU. Simulations presented in this study suggest that the economy would be not only more efficient and less inflationary, but also subject to less variability of prices and output levels.

The main benefits and costs

The main chapters of the study organize the analysis and findings along the following lines:

(i) *Efficiency and growth.* Elimination of exchange rate uncertainty and transaction costs, and further refinements to the single market are sure to yield gains in efficiency. Through improving the risk-adjusted rate of return on capital and the business climate more generally there are good chances that a credible commitment to achieving EMU in the not-too-distant future will help further strengthen the trend of investment and growth.

(ii) *Price stability.* This is a generally accepted objective, and beneficial economically in its own right. The problem is that of attaining price stability at least cost, and then maintaining it. The Community has the opportunity of being able to build its monetary union on the basis of the reputation for monetary stability of its least inflationary Member States. Given the paramount importance of credibility and expectations in winning the continuous fight against inflation at least cost, this is a great advantage.

(iii) *Public finance.* A new framework of incentives and constraints will condition national budgetary policies, for which the key-words will be autonomy (to respond to country-specific problems), discipline (to avoid excessive deficits) and coordination (to assure an appropriate overall policy-mix in the Community). EMU will also bring valuable gains for many countries' national budgets through reductions in interest rates, as inflation

and exchange risk premiums are eliminated. These benefits will very probably outweigh the loss of seigniorage revenue to be experienced by some countries.

(iv) *Adjusting to economic shocks.* The main potential cost of EMU is that represented by the loss of monetary and exchange rate policy as an instrument of economic adjustment at the national level. This loss should not be exaggerated since exchange rate changes by the Community in relation to the rest of the world will remain possible, whereas within the EMS the nominal exchange rate instrument is already largely abandoned, and EMU will reduce the incidence of country-specific shocks. Relative real labour costs will still be able to change; budgetary policies at national and Community levels will also absorb shocks and aid adjustment, and the external current account constraint will disappear.

Moreover, model simulations suggest that with EMU, compared to other regimes, the Community would have been able to absorb the major economic shocks of the last two decades with less disturbance in terms of the rate of inflation and, to some extent also, the level of real activity. This is of renewed relevance, given that the Gulf crisis of summer 1990 once again subjects the Community to a potentially damaging economic shock.

(v) *The international system.* With the ecu becoming a major international currency, there will be advantages for the Community as banks and enterprises conduct more of their international business in their own currency; moreover the monetary authorities will be able to economize in external reserves and achieve some international seigniorage gains. EMU will also mean that the Community will be better placed, through its unity, to secure its interests in international coordination processes and negotiate for a balanced multipolar system.

The impact through time and space

(vi) *Transitional costs and benefits.* The costs of the transition to EMU (in disinflating, reducing budget deficits), for the countries not yet fully prepared, would be greatly reduced by the setting of clear political commitments to the definitive EMU at a not-too-distant time in the future. If economic agents (public authorities, companies, trade unions, individuals) perceive these commitments to be credible, they will anticipate EMU in their economic strategies and behaviour. Such a process

GRAPH 1.3: **Simplified schema of the effects of EMU**

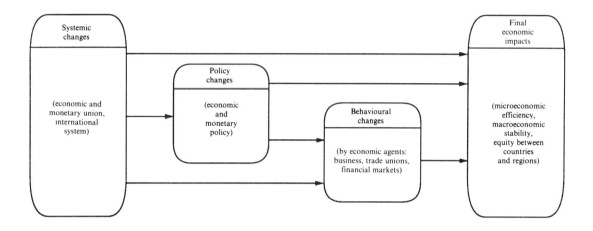

Note: See Graph 1.4 for greater detail.

has already been at work to advantage with the 1992 programme, and a similar strategy could be equally beneficial for EMU, if not more so.

Since most of the costs of moving to EMU arise in the preparatory stages of the process (as set out in the Delors Committee report), whereas some of the important benefits (elimination of exchange rate uncertainty and transaction costs) arise only in the definitive regime with a single currency, there is a clear economic case for a relatively short duration for the transitional period.

(vii)   *Impact on the regions.* As regards the regional distribution of the impact, which is relevant to the objective of longer-term convergence of economic performance, there are no a priori grounds for predicting the pattern of relative gains and losses. There are risks and opportunities of different types affecting both categories of regions. Policies are already at work to reduce lo-

cational disadvantages of the least favoured and geographically peripheral regions. However, the key to the catching-up process lies in obtaining synergies between Community and national efforts to upgrade the least favoured regional economies. The fixing of clear policy objectives, such as for the single market and EMU, are also highly relevant here for mobilizing such efforts.

(viii) *Convergence.* About half the Community (D, F, B, NL, L, DK, IRL) could proceed now to EMU with little difficulty, notably given their advanced degree of convergence in terms of inflation and cost trends. Three other countries (I, E, UK) have some adjustments to make still, but these are surely feasible within a few years. The two remaining countries (GR, P) have larger adjustments to make, but these countries too could, with political will, set their sights on participation in the full EMU, at the same date as the rest of the Community.

Key points relevant to the forthcoming intergovernmental conference, which will prepare Treaty provisions for EMU, are:

(i)   the case for a single currency as the first-best form of monetary union is supported on economic grounds, since only in this way can exchange uncertainty and transaction costs be completely eliminated and the benefits of full credibility of the union fully secured;

(ii) the case for the central bank to be granted a clear mandate to secure price stability and institutional independence is also supported, and indeed necessary to secure the full potential gains of a single currency;

(iii) the case for centralized powers over budgetary policy is much weaker, but the future regime will still have to conciliate the need for a common standard of discipline over deficits and debt with that for flexible response at the national level to country-specific shocks;

(iv) the transitional adjustment of private and public sectors to the disciplines of EMU will be made more rapidly and at less cost if the final objectives for EMU are the subject of credible commitments by the public authorities for completing the monetary union at a not-too-distant time in the future.

Further conditions for a successful functioning of EMU are:

(i)   an effective economic policy coordination function will be required, built presumably around the powers of the Council of Ministers for Economics and Finance;

(ii) this coordination function will have to concern the overall macroeconomic policy mix of the Community, and thus require concertation with EuroFed and a unified Community participation in international economic and monetary cooperation;

(iii) Member States will be largely responsible for managing national budget deficits at the low levels consistent with a high standard of monetary stability, since Community rules in this area should not establish a precise centralized control;

(iv) the costs of absorbing country-specific economic shocks will be minimized if labour costs adjust relatively flexibly;

(v)   the catch-up process of the least-developed countries and regions depends critically on securing synergies between on the one hand national development and stabilization efforts, and on the other hand the Community's policies for the single market and EMU.

Part A

Synthesis and economic principles

Chapter 1

Synthesis

The present study is an evaluation by the staff of the Commission of the potential economic impact of forming an economic and monetary union (EMU) in the European Community. It provides an analytical background to the proposals which the Commission addressed to the Council and Parliament in August 1990 entitled 'Economic and monetary union'.

1.1. What alternative regimes are to be compared?

The processes of completing the single market by 1992 and now of achieving EMU are continuous ones. To make an analysis of their benefits and costs requires that the points of comparison be clear, which is not itself such a simple matter.

The end-point of the process must be defined, as also the alternative regime which would otherwise be assumed to prevail at that time.

As regards the end-point, the Delors Committee report identifies the definitive monetary regime as consisting either of a fixed exchange rate system or a single currency system. There are significant economic and political differences between the two, with the single currency emerging as the first-best economic system. The latter is therefore the principal reference for the end-point, although the comparison with the fixed exchange rate alternative is thoroughly discussed (Chapters 2, 8).

Economic union is a less clear-cut concept than monetary union. A completed internal market for goods, services, labour and capital is a large and necessary feature of economic union. Beyond that, however, there is a wide spectrum of conceivable possibilities. These range between adding rather little to 1992 to examples of federal economic unions such as in the United States, with a very large federal budget and associated responsibilities for public expenditure functions and taxation.

The approach of the present study is to follow the principle of 'subsidiarity' that is increasingly advocated by the Community institutions. According to this principle only those economic policy functions which can be more efficiently discharged at the Community level are transferred from the national level. The list of policies that qualify on these

grounds is likely to evolve gradually over time as increasing interdependence makes various policies more difficult to manage efficiently at the national level. Indeed, the increase in Community competences assumed for the purpose of the present study, to be added to 1992 and so to constitute the economic union, are basically evolutionary in nature (see Chapters 2, 3 and 5).

As regards the alternative regime, as a first approximation this might be the status quo in the first half of 1990, just before the beginning of Stage I of the EMU process, but, as will be seen, this is not entirely satisfactory.

The status quo of the first half of 1990 sees the legislative programme for completing the internal market as a little over half adopted. There were already, however, signs that the economy has been anticipating 1992, both at the level of business decisions and national economic policies. Moreover the economic impact of 1992 has earlier been the subject of detailed evaluations in the Cecchini report and associated literature (see 'The economics of 1992' in *European Economy* No 35 of March 1988). For these reasons the status quo may be more suitably defined as assuming completion of the 1992 programme.

On the monetary side the status quo of 1990 sees eight countries adhering to the narrow-band variant of the exchange rate mechanism (ERM) of the European Monetary System (EMS). Two countries (Spain and the United Kingdom) joined the broader band of the ERM recently (on 20 June 1989 and 8 October 1990 respectively), and two countries (Greece and Portugal), remain outside the ERM. However, all Member States are committed to joining the narrow band of the ERM as well as completing the liberalization of capital movements. While the timing of these remaining actions to complete the EMS is not fixed, it is agreed that this will take place in Stage I of the EMU process which began on 1 July 1990.

The present study concentrates therefore on comparing the net advantage of moving from a Community that had completed the single market and membership of the EMS (1992 + EMS) to an EMU comprising a monetary union with a single currency and an economic union possessing a minimum of competences.

In one important respect, however, this approach may well err on the side of underestimating the net advantages of moving to EMU. This is because the advantages of 1992 + EMS may not all be sustainable without the clear prospect of further movement to the definitive EMU. The economic advantages of 1992 are certainly not fully achievable without a single currency, especially in the field of financial market integration. In addition the EMS in its present stage of development may not be compatible with complete capital market liberalization as required by 1992. The status quo may not, therefore, be a stable one. If the move to EMU were not to take place, it is quite likely that either the EMS would become a less stable arrangement or capital market liberalization would not be fully achieved or maintained. For these reasons it can be argued that the alternative regime for the benefit-cost analysis should be something less advanced in terms of integration than either the full 1992 programme or the present EMS or both (these alternatives are discussed more thoroughly in Chapter 2). In essence, the alternative to progress is regress, rather than the status quo. If this argument is accepted, it logically strengthens the economic case for moving ahead to EMU.

Intermediate stages of monetary integration which are intended to be transitional are not substantially analysed, since their overall economic consequences are hard to evaluate, for reasons commented on below (Chapter 8). This is true both of the Stage II of the Delors Committee report, and the alternative Stage II proposed by the British Government.

1.2. The conceptual framework

EMU will have a very pervasive impact on the workings of the economy. Many different mechanisms will come into play and interact. It is therefore particularly important to establish a clearly structured conceptual framework within which to discuss the detail.

The impact of EMU may be viewed schematically (in a simplified form in Graph 1.3 above) as a chain of cause and effect that passes through successive phases: first systemic changes, these leading to actual policy changes, and then on to behavioural changes in the economy, before emergence of the final economic impacts in terms of the objectives of public policy. Thus, more precisely:

(i) the definitive EMU represents initially a set of systemic changes, or changes to the economic constitution. This involves the new single currency (the ecu) in its domestic and international role, the new central bank (EuroFed), the completed single market (1992) and a changed role for national budgets (budget rules);

(ii) the policy changes occur in both the monetary and economic branches. The introduction of a single currency and the EuroFed institution has a profound impact on the management of monetary policy. For example, the commitment of monetary policy to price stability should acquire decisively strengthened qualities of unity and credibility. Economic policy-makers will also

find themselves operating within the constraints of new disciplines and responsibilities as regards budgetary policy;

(iii) the behavioural changes of economic agents concern enterprises, trade unions, households and financial markets. They come to recognize that the systemic changes not only affect them directly through the single market and single currency, but also indirectly through the policy-makers (monetary and budgetary policies, for example, become less accommodating with respect to non-competitive costs and prices);

(iv) the final economic impacts may be identified in terms of the three conventional objectives of economic policy: microeconomic efficiency in resource allocation and economic growth, macroeconomic stability with regard both to inflation and output and employment, and equity with respect to the distribution of impacts between countries and regions. The systemic, policy and behavioural changes all culminate in impacts that fall under one or more of these objectives.

However, as was suggested in Graph 1.3, some of the impacts of the systemic changes deliver benefits directly, such as when the single currency eliminates transaction costs, without passing indirectly through policy and behavioural changes. Similarly for policy changes, there is a mix of direct and indirect impacts.

Moreover there are some important interactions between these final impacts. For example, lower inflation contributes to higher efficiency; and faster economic growth contributes to the catch-up of backward regions.

This schema of analysis, in its simplified form, is not yet sufficiently precise to identify the economic mechanisms that actually deliver the final benefits and costs. Greater detail is therefore given in Graph 1.4, in which the mechanisms are identified and these form the core structure to the study as a whole. Each of these mechanisms is discussed individually later in this chapter, and they are also summarized as a check-list in Box 1 at the end of this chapter.

Sixteen mechanisms may appear complicated, but this represents the reality that the impacts of EMU will be both complex and heterogeneous in nature. There will be costs as well as benefits, direct as well as indirect effects, automatic as well as conditional effects. Compared to the economic impact of 1992, which essentially improves the efficiency of the economy, EMU will in addition have an important impact in lowering the average rate of inflation, as well as in lowering the variability of both the level of output and inflation. All of these impacts correspond to distinct objectives of economic policy. However reliable quantification is only possible for some of them. For this reason, quite apart from the problems of weighting together heterogeneous impacts, no overall quantitative estimate of the potential net benefits of EMU is presented. This difference with the Commission's earlier study on the impact of 1992 does not mean that EMU is any less far-reaching in its implications, on the contrary. The economic methodology used to assess these various types of impact is explained in Chapter 2, with further detail in supporting chapters and annexes.

While the individual mechanisms at work may be numerous and complex, the overall picture becomes clear when it is observed that they all converge in their effects upon one or more of the three classic objectives of economic policy: efficiency, stability and equity.

Thus:

(i) Efficiency: the addition of a single currency to a single market will perfect the resource allocation function of the price mechanism at the level of the Community as a whole. Without a completely transparent and sure rule of the law of one price for tradable goods and services, which only a single currency can provide, the single market cannot be expected to yield its full benefits — static and dynamic. With 'one market and one money', the Community economy could confidently be expected to improve further its underlying economic performance. This already appears in the views of industrialists recorded in surveys, according to which the addition of a single currency to the single market would more than double the number of enterprises expecting

GRAPH 1.4: **Detailed schema of the effects of EMU**

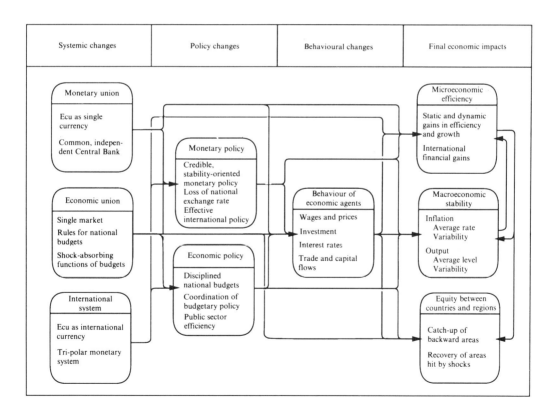

a 'very positive' impact on the business climate in the Community — as was shown in Graph 1.1.

(ii) Stability: governments aim to secure a favourable combination of two main macroeconomic equilibria — the price level and real economic activity (output and employment). More precisely, the objectives are to achieve low inflation and unemployment levels in terms of their equilibrium rates, and also minimum variability in both cases. EMU, with a well designed institutional structure building on an inherited reputation for price stability, is a highly probable means of securing the price stability objective. The growth effects of extra induced investment could also, possibly, reduce the underlying unemployment rate. The prospects of securing a reduced variability of inflation and output may be less self-evident, but evidence from new methods of model simulation suggest that a favourable outcome can be secured here too, as was shown in Graph 1.2. These simulations replicate the typical economic shocks experienced in the last two decades such as the oil shocks. They suggest that under EMU the Community would have absorbed these shocks at less cost than was the case under less unified monetary regimes. (Correspondingly, the new oil shock of 1990 could be better handled if EMU were already in place.)

(iii) Equity: the main focus here is between regions and countries whose initial conditions differ markedly, for example advanced versus less-developed. There are arguments that go in off-setting directions, for example economy of scale advantages of the centre versus lower labour costs and faster potential productivity gains in the least favoured regions. There are no grounds for expecting the net balance of relative advantage to fall systematically in one direction or the other. Community policy instruments are addressed to making good weaknesses in basic resource endowment where possible. But the major determinant of the desired catch-up process will be whether the public authorities and economic agents of the regions and countries concerned can secure synergies between Community strategies for 1992 and EMU and domestic development efforts.

1.3. The main benefits and costs

The 16 mechanisms already announced are now explained sufficiently to indicate their most important features, with a full account given in supporting chapters.

These mechanisms are presented in groups (five in all, corresponding to Chapters 3 to 7). The first two, concerning microeconomic efficiency and price stability and monetary policy, introduce the most important direct effects of economic and monetary union.

The next two groups, concerning public finance and the problem of adjusting the economy without changes in the nominal exchange rate, introduce important indirect impacts for both the stability and efficiency of the economy, and also concern conditions for a successful functioning of EMU.

The final category concerns impacts on the international economic and monetary system. This has implications for macroeconomic stability and, at the microeconomic level, for business and banking through the role of the ecu as an international currency.

1.3.1. Concerning efficiency and growth

EMU will result in an amplification of the type of economic benefits that follow from the 1992 programme. Indeed only a single currency allows the full potential benefits of a single market to be achieved. For this reason it is no coincidence that they are historically observed to go together. The economic literature also now points out how the static efficiency gains from market and monetary integration should also translate into dynamic gains in terms of the rate of economic growth for a medium-term period at least.

Exit exchange rate variability and uncertainty (mechanism 1)

The EMS has observed a considerable reduction in nominal exchange rate variability between the ERM participants, but this is not the case for currencies outside the ERM. In recent experience (1987-89) the average monthly variability of individual EC currencies against all other EC currencies has been 0,7 % for ERM currencies and 1,9 % for non-ERM currencies. These are therefore the degrees of variability that EMU could eliminate.

The reduction of real exchange rate variability has been less pronounced. However, as argued further below, some real flexibility (i.e. in relative labour costs and competitiveness) is actually desirable.

Exchange rate uncertainty is as damaging to the economy as variability if not more so. Uncertainty, as revealed by exchange risk premiums in interest rate differentials, can persist well beyond the actual stabilization of the exchange rate. This is why moves from the present EMS to monetary union would be highly beneficial to the business environment, even if the recent stability of EMS exchange rates has been impressive.

There is evidence that foreign direct investment responds positively to exchange rate stability. Recent surveys show that exchange rate stability is generally highly valued by industrialists. Econometric evidence on the impact on trade is weak, but the impact through the efficiency and volume of investment seems likely to be more important.

Exit transaction costs (mechanism 2)

These typically range from the very small for inter-bank transactions (0,1 %), to the more substantial for commercial transactions (0,3 % for an ECU 100 000 transfer, 0,5 % for ECU 10 000), to the very costly for small bank transfers (12 % for ECU 100). The cost of exchanging bank-notes between major and minor currencies can be an extremely high 25 %. In addition companies incur in-house costs, which case studies indicate can amount to around 4 % of the profits on sales in other EC markets.

Overall transaction costs can be conservatively estimated to amount to around 1/2 % of GDP (ECU 13 to 19 billion per year) for the Community as a whole, which is to be compared to the 1/4 % of GDP estimated in the Cecchini report for border costs for the circulation of goods. Both appear to be only a small part of the overall market-segmenting influences. On the monetary side the combination of risk factors and transaction costs has a particularly damaging impact on efficient resource allocation.

Transaction costs are particularly high (1 % of GDP) for some of the Member States which have small and very open economies or weak currencies that are little used internationally.

Apart from foreign exchange transaction costs, cross-border transactions bear additional costs (bank charges and commissions, delays) due to the present inefficiency of international payments systems. Only the combination of 1992 and a single currency can offer the prospect of reducing these costs to a minimum, such as within the United States.

In a fixed exchange rate system the authorities could conceivably impose a 'par-clearing' practice on banks, as was the case at one stage in the United States: (i.e. no bid-offer margins and no special exchange transaction costs would be permitted). But this would still presumably require monetary reforms, so as to give all currencies of the system the same par value, which practically amounts to moving to a single currency.

Building on 1992 (mechanism 3)

The 1992 programme will achieve the essential breakthrough for market integration. However, there are several respects in which microeconomic policies of the Community should be able to secure further economic benefits beyond those following from implementation of the 1985 White Paper. These include deeper liberalization of energy and transport markets than provided for in the White Paper. European infrastructural investments for cross-border traffic, including high-speed trains and better air traffic control, will complement market-opening policies. Competition policies for reducing subsidies and controlling undesirable concentrations have a large agenda for action ahead. Increasing integration will call for some tax harmonization initiatives to avoid inefficient market distortions. The R&D policies of the Community could be further developed to profit from economy of scale advantages for many projects. The current expansion of the structural Funds, in the course of being doubled between 1988 and 1992, will have to be evaluated and adapted to the needs of economic union.

From static to dynamic gains (mechanism 4)

The gains from 1992 and monetary integration have traditonally been analysed in terms of step improvements in economic efficiency and welfare, i.e. a once and for all gain, even if this is achieved only progressively over a period of years. Actual experience of how the 1992 process seems to affect the economy and recent developments in the economic literature have drawn attention to how a major impetus, such as 1992 or EMU or both together, may also trigger an increase in the underlying rate of growth of the economy. Two features of this analysis may be highlighted.

First, if the productivity of factors of production is improved (as through the 1992 programme) or if the risk-adjusted rate of return is increased (as through EMU in diminishing exchange rate risk), then investment will increase and so carry with it the rate of economic growth at least in the medium run. Estimates show that if EMU reduced the risk premium in the required rate of return by a moderate amount (0,5 percentage points) there could be a substantial growth offered over the long run, accumulating to perhaps 5 % of GDP.

Second, analysis of the European unemployment problem has recently given attention to the 'hysteresis' effect, according to which alternative equilibrium rates of unemployment are possible, with the actual one heavily influenced by recent history or inertial factors. According to this interpretation an impetus that creates more optimistic expectations in the economy may effectively shift the economy onto a higher performance trajectory, with a dynamic adjustment from one equilibrium unemployment rate to a second more favourable one. More optimistic expectations, initiated by a credible policy deemed favourable to the business environment, may thus become self-fulfilling.

Although such arguments may still be speculative, they bear comparison with the rise of business confidence and investment in the Community since the time when the 1992 programme became credible. Given the very positive business opinions on EMU reported above, it is quite conceivable that the addition of EMU to 1992 could indeed carry the economy onto a still stronger trend performance.

1.3.2. Concerning price stability

Since it is proposed that the Community's future central bank (EuroFed) be given the statutory duty to secure price stability as its priority objective, it is important to be clear of the economic justification for this choice, and why monetary union could achieve it at least cost.

The benefits of price stability (mechanism 5)

Taking the macroeconomic record of the industrialized countries in terms of inflation, growth, unemployment and income per capita levels over medium- to long-run periods, there is no evidence that higher inflation can be exploited as a means of securing the other economic policy objectives mentioned. The old theory that there is a trade-off between high inflation and low unemployment is now unsupported as a matter of theory or empirical analysis, except for short-run periods. On the contrary there is some (statistically weak) positive relationship between low inflation and high real economic performance. The post-war macroeconomic experience of the industrialized world suggests that, on average, high inflation countries have a higher unemployment rate and a lower income per capita.

To identify more precisely why this should be so, economic analysis makes the distinction between anticipated and unanticipated inflation.

Anticipated inflation imposes costs on the holders of money, and on producers in the need to change price lists. It does, however, give quasi-tax revenues to the government (seigniorage), which is only an advantage to the extent governments cannot collect taxes efficiently.

Unanticipated inflation may allow governments to benefit in the short run by depreciating the public debt in real terms; but in the long run this becomes a disadvantage since markets impose an inflation risk premium on governments which do not earn a reputation for stability-oriented policy.

High inflation rates are also more variable and uncertain, and cause more relative price variability. This makes the price mechanism less efficient in its resource allocation function. At the macroeconomic level it results in 'stop and go' policies, which make efficient business strategies extremely difficult.

Institutional factors conducive to price stability (mechanism 6)

While any government and central bank can in principle secure price stability, there are reasons to expect this objective to be achieved with a higher probability and minimal cost by an independent central bank which is given this objective as its statutory duty.

Political science recognizes, in this context, the importance of the different incentive structures of central banks and governments. Governments typically have electoral cycles which may at times make it attractive to exploit short-term gains against longer-term costs. Monetary policy is vulnerable in this situation, unless the central bank has political independence, board members with long and secure tenure, and statutes establishing an explicit duty to give priority to price stability.

In practice these factors appear responsible for the observed correlation between institutional independence of the central bank and price stability, with Germany and Switzerland representing the most positive examples.

Thus there are sound reasons for the design of EuroFed to follow these examples, more than some average central banking constitution.

The costs of disinflation (mechanism 7)

The reduction of inflation is usually resisted because it involves transitional costs. These arise for two reasons: wage and price rigidity and the difficulty of securing credibility for the stabilization objective.

These two factors are related, and both can be strongly influenced by institutional strategies. This has already been observed in the processes of convergence in the EMS, with the linkage of the exchange rate of countries whose stabilization strategies were initially weak in credibility to those with strong credibility. Political commitment to a central banking system, which itself has a reputation for price stability, is thus a key to minimizing the transitional costs of disinflation. Expectations are at the heart of the inflation process. This is why disinflation costs could be reduced by agreement in the Community on a suitable institutional design of Euro-Fed, and clear commitments to its full entry into operation at a fixed date.

Such a date should be just long enough to allow for necessary adjustments, but not so distant as to appear irrelevant to economic agents.

1.3.3. Concerning public finance

The public finances of Member States will be deeply affected by the move to EMU. This will involve direct benefits, as well as some costs, for the budgets of some countries in the transitional period. But more important will be the recasting of the role of national budget policies in the monetary union, and the intensified competitive pressure in due course on national public expenditure and tax systems.

Revision of the framework for macroeconomic budgetary policy (mechanism 8)

Loss of the monetary policy and exchange rate instrument at the national level will place new demands on budgetary policy at the national level for stabilization and adjustment purposes in the case of country-specific disturbances. This requires flexibility and autonomy, at least within a normal range of sustainable public deficit and debt levels.

However, a high standard of monetary stability implies that unsustainable public deficits and debt cannot be monetized anymore. Budgetary discipline, in order to avoid excessively high deficits, will need to be intensified, and the Community is discussing proposals to this effect. Measures to this effect would be justified because it is not self-evident whether monetary union will itself have the automatic effect of enhancing budget discipline at the national level. While monetization will cease to be possible, financial market integration will make available a larger source of savings to national authorities and the external current account will disappear as a direct financial constraint.

Increased economic interdependence between Member States will also warrant more intensified coordination of budgetary policies and mutual surveillance, especially in relation to the overall monetary-budgetary policy-mix and the Community's external current account.

Direct impacts on expenditures and revenues (mechanism 9)

In EMU the profits from the issue of currency will naturally be collected at the Community level, and these seigniorage revenues will in some way be returned to the national economies (central bank profits are usually transferred to the budget), and to this extent there will be no loss of seigniorage. Countries with the highest inflation rates may suffer net seigniorage losses, but not greater than 1/2 to 1 % of GDP, given that the 1992 programme will already induce through competitive pressures a reduction in the very high reserve requirements imposed in some countries by the central bank.

On the other hand countries with high interest rates will benefit as these come down to the rates prevailing in countries with the lowest inflation rates. In part these reductions will only be in the nominal interest rate, offset by a lower erosion by inflation of the real value of the public debt. Even this, however, is not without significance, since a lower nominal interest rate would help reduce the apparent budget deficit automatically, and imply less need to cut real public expenditure programmes that might seem necessary. However, real interest rates could also be reduced where these carry at present a significant premium reflecting market perceptions of expected depreciation and exchange-rate risk.

This margin is in several countries 2 % or more. While these premiums are transitional in nature, they are typically large compared to the likely net loss of seigniorage in the case of Community countries which are already embarked on the transition towards monetary stability. (Seigniorage is only really important for countries that have permanently very high inflation rates and poorly developed tax systems).

Indirect impact on expenditures and taxation (mechanism 10)

EMU will intensify competitive pressures on certain public expenditures and taxes on mobile factors. As a general spur to public sector efficiency these pressures are to be welcomed, for example to improve education systems and economic infrastructure, and avoid social security systems imposing unnecessarily heavy taxes on employment. However care will also need to be taken to avoid under-provision of public goods whose benefits spread across frontiers, or the erosion of taxation on tax bases that can easily migrate. This is the economic justification for acts of harmonization or establishment of minimum standards of public goods or tax rates in appropriate cases.

1.3.4. Concerning adjustment without exchange rate changes

The principal risk in forming a monetary union is that involved in losing the possibility to change the nominal exchange rate. This section evaluates that risk, and the alternative instruments for adjusting economies in circumstances when nominal exchange rate changes might otherwise be made. The chief uses of exchange rate changes are to improve labour cost competitiveness (e.g. devalue to protect employment) or control inflation better (e.g. revalue to reduce prices). The inflation issue has already been discussed above, and so the present section focuses on the uses for the exchange rate for purposes of preserving employment and regional balance in the case of adverse economic shocks.

Loss of the nominal exchange rate instrument (mechanism 11)

The loss of the nominal exchange rate instrument implied by EMU is the most important economic cost involved, but this should not be exaggerated for several reasons. First, the nominal exchange rate of the ecu, in relation to the rest of the world, will still be variable. Secondly, participants in the ERM have already forgone nominal exchange rate changes to a high degree, and even those currencies outside the ERM pursue 'firm' exchange rate policies to avoid risks of higher inflation. Thirdly, changes in nominal exchange rates have been no ultimate guide to real exchange rate changes (i.e. relative labour costs and competitiveness) between EC countries in the last decade; a correlation is only observed for an initial period. They therefore chiefly serve only to offset differences in inflation rates. Exchange rate changes can help for an initial period to protect employment from the effects of an adverse economic shock, but at the cost of poorer results in terms of inflation and also, in the medium term, dissipation of the employment gains too. (Simulation results are given in Chapter 6 and Annex D.)

Real adjustments in competitiveness (mechanism 12)

Real exchange rate changes remain possible in EMU, since some important prices can change still between regions (e.g. those of housing and commercial property) as well as wage costs. Some federations (e.g. Canada) have seen as large real adjustments between provinces as the EC national economies observed between themselves in the last decade. While adjustments to adverse shocks need to remain possible, the evidence of the last two decades within the EC shows that trend changes in real exchange rates have not explained differences in growth rates at all. Persistent real devaluation strategies do not seem to buy faster growth, at least not in Western Europe.

EMU will reduce country-specific shocks (mechanism 13)

The case for exchange rate changes relates mainly to the incidence of country-specific shocks that cause losses of

demand for a country's typical products, or of competitiveness for its producers. While the possible occurrence of country-specific shocks cannot be eliminated, they are likely to become less probable for three reasons. First, integration as a result of 1992 and EMU leads to changes in industrial structures in the direction of deeper 'intra-industry' trade and investment relations, which means that most countries become involved in both exporting and importing the products of many industries. Old-style comparative advantage, in which countries specialize their production in distinct commodities, becomes less important. As a result sector-specific shocks become to a lesser degree country-specific in their impact. Secondly, a credible monetary union will affect the behaviour of wage-bargainers. They will be more careful about risking becoming uncompetitive, given that devaluation will not be an option. Thirdly, EMU will eliminate an important category of country-specific shocks which originate in exchange rate movements themselves and imperfectly coordinated monetary policy. Recent methods of model simulation suggest that EMU could as a result significantly reduce the variability of inflation and also to some extent output (see Chapter 6 and Annex E). These results apply also to the costs of asymmetric responses by Member States to common economic shocks, of which oil price rises are the major example (recurring in 1990 for the third time in recent history).

Financial flows will be available to absorb shocks (mechanism 14)

A major effect of EMU is that balance of payments constraints will disappear in the way they are experienced in international relations. Private markets will finance all viable borrowers, and savings and investment balances will no longer be constraints at the national level. National budgets will, as mentioned, retain their capacity to respond to national and regional shocks through the mechanisms of social security and other policies. The Community's structural policies have a complementary role, and may be further developed in response to needs.

1.3.5. Concerning the international system

The primary aim of EMU is to strengthen the integration of the Community and improve its economic performance. However, due to its weight in the world economy, EMU will necessarily have far-reaching implications for the international economic and monetary system. Care will have to be taken to avoid some potential problems, and to make the changes a positive-sum game for the international community as a whole.

The ecu as a major international currency (mechanism 15)

As the single currency of the Community, the ecu will compete as an international vehicular currency with the dollar and yen on an equal footing. The ecu would no doubt increase its international market share as a numeraire for trade and contract thus saving around 0,05 % of GDP to the Community in transaction costs; also as a means of payment and store of value in the denomination of assets and liabilities, perhaps to the extent of a conservative 5 % of the total world portfolio. Community enterprises and banks would have the advantage of doing more of their business in their own currency. The economy would be less subject to short-term variability in its terms of trade as a result. Seigniorage gains from the use of ecu banknotes in other countries would develop, gradually accumulating perhaps to around USD 35 billion (as a one-time gain, not annually). EMU would also be beneficial to those partner countries, mainly in the rest of Europe presumably, which were to choose to peg their currencies to the ecu. International reserve holdings of ecu-denominated assets outside the Community will probably increase, but since these will bear market interest rates they represent little direct gain. The Community itself would be able to economize in external reserve assets, perhaps by as much as one half, or USD 200 billion. The various portfolio shifts into ecus could conceivably cause an unintended exchange rate appreciation, but this would not necessarily happen since borrowers and lenders might increase their demand for ecus in parallel, and the movement could be a gradual one over many years.

International cooperation (mechanism 16)

EMU would effectively unify and strengthen the Community's presence in international forums. As the Community and its Member States would speak with one voice, a reduction in the number of players (e.g. from G7 to G4) should facilitate the coordination process. The Community could intervene more effectively to encourage developments of the world policy-mix that would be advantageous to its interests. In terms of systemic developments EMU could be a decisive building block for establishing a balanced tri-polar monetary regime.

1.4. The impact through time and space

While the ultimate impact of these many consequences of moving to EMU is highly likely to be exceedingly beneficial there are further dimensions to be evaluated. For the Community as a whole there is the question how the flow of

benefits and costs will develop over time through the stages proposed in the Delors Committee report. This will influence the optimal speed of the move towards the single currency. For each Member State there is the question how it in particular stands to be affected, given differences in economic structure at the outset. A preoccupation of several countries is how the economically least-favoured regions are likely to be affected. (These issues are examined in Chapters 8 to 10).

1.4.1. Transitional issues

The optimal speed of the move to the definitive EMU will depend on three inter-related factors: first, how benefits and costs of EMU develop stage by stage, secondly, whether the intermediate stages will face risks of instability, and thirdly, the progress made by Member States in the convergence of their economic performance. The overall conclusion points to the advantages of relatively rapid moves through to the single currency, but taking sufficient time to foster greater convergence for several countries. There is a strong economic case for setting fixed and credible time-tables, to spur convergence and encourage anticipatory adjustments on the part of governments and businesses.

Benefits and costs by stages

Exchange rate variability within the ERM has already been reduced by three-quarters of what preceded establishment of the EMS, and this will presumably be the experience also of new ERM participating currencies as its membership is generalized in Stage I. Correspondingly, a large part of the costs of adjustment to exchange rate stability have already been borne, or will be so in Stage I. However, exchange rate uncertainty, and associated interest rate costs may remain a good deal longer.

The benefits from achieving fully credible monetary stability (internal and external) can only be achieved by a single currency, since exchange rate fixity can be affirmed but not proved. A single currency would be for all enterprises, trade unions and individuals sign of a genuine regime change, and would help ensure that they adapt to the required wage and price discipline. In addition transaction costs will only be eliminated with a single currency. International advantages will also accrue especially with a single currency.

The costs of doing without exchange rate changes as an adjustment instrument will gradually diminish over time as economic integration becomes deeper.

Overall the adjustment costs of EMU mostly arise early in the transition, and the benefits are harvested to a considerable extent only at the end of the process, as is illustrated by Table 1.1 for the 16 mechanisms discussed above. The single currency is clearly the first-best solution economically.

Possible instability in the transition

The complete openness and increasing integration of financial markets resulting from the 1992 programme will increase the potential for currency substitution. Speculative attacks on individual currencies could be of enormous power if financial markets are given any reason to doubt the commitment of the authorities to defend the fluctuation margins of the ERM. The transition will also have to manage smoothly the change of monetary policy leadership from one based on Germany to that of the independent EuroFed. These factors favour a short Stage II while EuroFed becomes established but does not have full responsibility. It also points to the advantages of the single currency as the definitive regime, in preference to fixed exchange rates, in terms of clarity, credibility and therefore stability.

Table 1.1

Economic mechanisms generating benefits and costs, by stages of EMU, as in the Delors Committee Report

	Stage I	Stage IIIa (fixed exchange rates)	Stage IIIb (single currency)
Efficiency and growth			
1. Exchange-rate variability and uncertainty	+	+ +	+ +
2. Exchange transaction costs	•	+	+ +
3. Extending 1992 to economic union	•	+	+
4. Dynamic gains	•	+	+ +
Price stability			
5. Price discipline	+	+ +	+ +
6. Institutions conducive to stability-oriented monetary policy	•	+	+ +
7. Transitional costs of disinflation	− −	−	−
Public finance			
8. Autonomy, discipline, coordination	− / +	− / +	− / +
9. Lower interest-rate costs (less seigniorage losses)	− / +	+	+ +
10. Public sector efficiency	+	+	+
Adjustment without exchange-rate changes			
11. Loss of nominal exchange-rate instrument	−	− −	− −
12. Adjustment of real wage levels	− / +	− / +	− / +
13. Lesser country-specific shocks	+	+ +	+ +
14. Removal of external constraints	•	+	+ +
International system			
15. Ecu as international currency	•	+	+ +
16. Improved international coordination	•	+	+ +

Note: + benefit, − costs, • insignificant or uncertain. The comparisons are between the stages and a baseline case that assumes completion of the single market and membership of the European Monetary System's exchange-rate mechanism.

Convergence requirements

Monetary union requires virtually complete convergence of inflation. At the limit, with perfect markets it imposes the law of one price on all tradable goods and services. Monetary unions nevertheless often sustain persistent divergences in relative wage levels, in line with productivity and competitivity differences. In the case of countries catching up in level of productivity and incomes, there will as a result be some margin (possibly around 1 to 2% per year) for consumer prices on average to rise a little faster than in the Community as a whole as the prices of non-tradable services converge on the levels found in high income countries.

Budget balances and current account balances can diverge even more substantially, as the Dutch example of high budget deficits and current account surpluses and the reverse British example suggest. The essential requirements for budgetary policy is sustainability of the public debt without recource to monetary financing.

It is therefore important that a reasonable degree of convergence of price inflation, and reduction of excessive budget deficits are achieved before a locking of the exchange rates. However, the convergence of price and cost performance and budgetary policies will be strongly influenced by the credibility of commitments to a given future monetary regime, so long as the time-horizon is not too long. For this reason commitments to the later stages of EMU should not be held up until the ultimately required degree of convergence is already achieved.

Of the existing ERM countries, Germany, France, Belgium, Luxembourg, the Netherlands, Denmark and Ireland are already sufficiently convergent for monetary union as regards price inflation. The other large Member States — Italy, Spain and the United Kingdom — are not so far behind and adequate convergence should be attainable within a few years. Even if Portugal and Greece have a bigger adjustment to make, these countries could, with a major effort of political will, sufficiently catch up on the rest of the Community so as to join the definitive EMU at the outset.

1.4.2. Regional impact

Neither economic theory nor the current experiences of the least favoured and geographically peripheral regions of the Community point to a bias in the sense that these regions might systematically profit either more or less from EMU than the average. While the economic centre of the Community benefits from economy of scale advantages, it is not evident that these relative advantages are destined to grow. The least favoured regions still have other advantages. While the latter may fear the economic power of the large corporations of the centre, the trade unions of the centre fear the competition of low cost locations in the periphery. Companies are quite willing to relocate to the periphery, according to business surveys, if competitive advantage within the internal market is offered.

The Community's policies are already addressed to reducing the locational disadvantages and weaknesses in resource endowment of the western and southern periphery. This is done both in the 1992 programme and the structural Funds (for example in the transport and telecommunications sectors). The structural Funds also aim to improve basic resource endowment of weaker regions through manpower training and investment.

The diverse experiences of Ireland, Spain, Portugal, Greece and the Italian south point to the possibilities of a successful catching-up process, but also to this being far from inevitable and to be conditioned essentially by the extent of the commitment of the countries and regions concerned to generalized modernization. Such modernization has to extend very deeply, and to acquire socio-political as well as purely economic dimensions. The Community of 1992 and EMU clearly offers a framework for such efforts, which may amount to a thorough regime change for society as well as the economy. This will be even more emphatically illustrated in the case of the Community's newest region, East Germany.

1.4.3. Benefits and costs by country

As regards the benefits of achieving price stability, EMU clearly offers most at this point to the five Member States (Italy, Spain, United Kingdom, Portugal, Greece) with inflation rates above the 2 to 3% standard encompassing the other seven countries. The adjustment costs of disinflation should be lessened as these countries enter into commitments to join progressively more ambitious stages of the EMU process (indeed, Italy and Spain have both given examples of this in the last year in respectively moving into the narrow and broad bands of the ERM).

Germany is apprehensive over the risk that EuroFed's monetary policy might not keep to the highest stability standard. While this issue should be resolved in deciding the statutes of EuroFed, a broader perspective suggests positive advantage also for Germany. In the absence of the move to EMU it is unlikely that Germany's partners would be so committed to price stability, and the risks of importing inflation from them would be correspondingly greater given also that the theoretical option of a floating exchange rate is now excluded in practice.

While the extent of the remaining exchange rate variability still to be reduced is closely related to present ERM commitments, significant costs of exchange rate uncertainty (as incorporated in interest rate premiums) are borne by most ERM countries. In particular, all ERM countries except Germany and the Netherlands stand to gain from lower real interest rates in passing to a fully credible EMU. Non-ERM countries would also secure such advantages at a comparable stage in the stabilization process. These interest rate savings will benefit public budgets as well as private investment.

The elimination of transaction costs in passing to a single currency will especially benefit the countries with poorly developed financial markets and traditionally weak currencies. These costs are particularly heavy for the tourist sectors of the southern Member States.

All Member States should benefit from the improved business climate created by EMU, and by the stronger international presence of the ecu and the Community.

1.5. The Community as an advantageous monetary area

One way of drawing together the arguments set out above is to consider how they relate to the traditional arguments of the economic literature concerning the 'optimal currency area'. The present study has made use of the main insights of this theory. However, there are further relevant arguments, especially in the case of the Community, that need to be brought into account in order to guide the overall and policy-relevant judgement, which is whether EMU could indeed be advantageous when all benefits and costs are considered together. (The optimal currency area theory was originally developed to define the optimal geographic jurisdiction of a given money; the Community more nearly faces the inverse task of defining the optimum economic and monetary competences of a given geographic jurisdiction.)

The two original insights of work on the optimal currency area were:

(i) labour and capital should be sufficiently mobile across the regions of the union to permit adjustment to region-specific economic shocks to take place without too serious costs, especially in terms of unemployment (see Chapter 6);

(ii) monetary union would be beneficial in eliminating transaction costs in exchanging currencies (Chapter 3).

The formation of currency areas would depend then on the actual trade-off between these two factors. Since in the Community labour mobility is still limited, the net balance of advantage might on these grounds alone be uncertain.

Subsequent developments to the theory added two more considerations that already make the benefit-cost balance more favourable in the case of the Community:

(i) if the States concerned are individually small and open, then exchange rate changes will cause significant disturbances to price stability (Chapter 4);

(ii) if an economy has a diversified industrial structure, with more intra-industry trade than narrow specializations in particular commodities, then the likely incidence of economic shocks warranting exchange rate changes would be less (Chapter 6).

Further branches of economic analysis and empirical facts particularly relevant to the Community push the probable benefit-cost ratio much further still in favour of EMU in the Community:

(i)   the analysis of inflation and efficient price stabilization strategies has come to attach increased importance to expectations, the credibility of policy commitments, and the reputation of institutions. When these analytical developments are combined with the actual possibility in the Community of building the monetary union around the stability standard established by its least inflationary members, an important argument for EMU is added (Chapter 4);

(ii) moreover recent methods of macroeconomic model simulation, incorporating the effect of forward-looking expectations, provide evidence that the overall stability properties of the economy, of both price and to some extent real activity levels, would be improved under EMU (Chapter 6);

(iii) related considerations arise in political economy literature on problems of 'government failure' in budgetary as well as monetary policy. EMU offers also an opportunity to correct problems of this nature experienced by some Member States with a new institutional structure and set of incentives and constraints for national authorities. In the extreme cases this amounts effectively to a 'regime change', which is being achieved over a period of years in the newer Member States, and more suddenly now in the case of East Germany (Chapters 9 and 10 and Annex C);

(iv) recent developments in the theory of economic growth suggest that the static efficiency gains of 1992 and EMU could well translate also into dynamic gains in the rate of growth (Chapter 3);

(v) finally, the Community is a special case in that its large size means that formation of EMU will not leave the international system unaffected (as would, for example, a Benelux EMU), but offers further advantages through causing changes in that system (Chapter 7).

The overall results of the benefit-cost analysis of the Community facing the prospect of EMU may therefore be summarized as follows. Old economic theory guiding judgment on the formation of monetary unions might have suggested, for the Community, that the trade-off between the two arguments then considered relevant were of uncertain advantage. New economic theory and particular features of the Community's actual structure and situation add seven further arguments, all pointing to benefits for EMU in the Community. On these grounds the economic case becomes strongly advantageous. Political union objectives may further be added. But the case can stand powerfully on economic criteria alone.

Box 1.1: Check-list of economic impacts of EMU

Impacts relating to efficiency and growth

1. EMU would completely eliminate nominal exchange rate variability which in recent years has averaged 0,7% per month for ERM currencies and 1,9% for non-ERM currencies (each currency against all other EC currencies). It would also eliminate uncertainty (which interest rate premiums show to be considerable even where actual exchange rates have been stable).

2. Only a single currency completely eliminates the transaction costs of exchanging currencies. These costs are non-trivial for many businesses, and can be sizeable for small transactions between persons and for tourists. They amount to at least ½% of GDP per year (ECU 13-19 billion) for the EC as a whole, and up to 1% for smaller Member States.

3. Going beyond the single market measures of the 1985 White Paper, additional economic advantages can be secured by further measures in such fields as energy, transport, competition, R&D, environmental and taxation policies.

4. The combination of the 1992 programme and EMU could well translate into not only considerable 'static' once and for all efficiency gains, but also 'dynamic' gains (i.e. a higher sustainable rate of economic growth). Estimates show that a moderate reduction in the riskiness of investment (e.g. exchange rate uncertainty) could have a substantial growth effect in the long run.

Impacts relating to price stability

5. Price stability is itself advantageous for efficient resources allocation. While difficult to measure, this is borne out in macro- and microeconomic evidence.

6. EuroFed will be most likely to secure price stability if its statutes establish this as its priority duty and grant it political independence to fulfil this duty. The actual price stability performance of independent central banks is clearly positive.

7. The reduction of inflation to a common very low rate could be achieved at minimal transitional cost through clear political commitment to a EuroFed of this design, to become fully operational at a not too distant date.

Impacts relating to public finance

8. The role of national budgetary policies will be substantially revised, with new needs for autonomy to permit flexibility com-

bined with enhanced discipline over excessive deficits and coordination to ensure an appropriate policy-mix for the Community.

9. The most inflationary countries will lose seigniorage revenues up to 1% of GDP but against this there will often be interest rate savings of larger size, notably where these comprise a significant exchange rate risk premium.

10. Competitive pressures should increase the efficiency of public expenditures and taxation, but in some cases the Community may have to establish minimum tax rates and cooperate in the provision of public goods to avoid inefficient outcomes.

Adjustment without exchange rate changes

11. The main cost of EMU is the loss of the national monetary and exchange rate instrument. This cost should not be exaggerated, since it has already largely been renounced within the ERM, while changes will remain possible for the Community as a whole in relation to the rest of the world.

12. Changes in real exchange rates (competitiveness) remain possible and desirable within EMUs, and examples from federations show that this is not just a theoretical possibility. This is why wage and price flexibility is a necessary condition of success.

13. EMU will reduce the incidence of country-specific shocks that warrant real exchange rate changes, as a result of changes in industrial structure and wage bargaining. Also shocks resulting from exchange rate instability and uncoordinated monetary policy will be eliminated, and so the variability of output and inflation reduced.

14. Financial flows will be available to absorb economic shocks. Monetary union will remove external financial constraints, and national and Community budgets will also help absorb shocks.

Impacts on the international system

15. As the Community's single currency, the ecu will develop into a major international currency, resulting in several kinds of financial advantage for the Community's economy: less transaction costs in international trade, more ecu-dominated financial issues managed by European banks, smaller needs for external currency reserves, seigniorage gains on foreign holdings of ecu notes.

16. EMU should facilitate international coordination, and give more weight to the Community in encouraging developments of the world policy-mix favourable to its interest. It should also facilitate establishment of a balanced tri-polar regime.

Chapter 2

The economics of EMU

This chapter presents the main economic assumptions and the theoretical and methodological tools upon which the study is based. Section 2.1 is devoted to a discussion of the content of EMU and of the alternatives against which its effects are assessed, whereas Section 2.2 presents the underpinnings and methods of the cost/benefit approach.

The main conclusions are the following.

Economic union will increase the degree of integration of capital, goods and labour markets across the Community, but not to the degree of integration reached by national economies. This will differentiate EMU from existing economic and monetary unions consisting of federal States, where labour mobility across States is higher than will be the case in the Community.

Already with irrevocably fixed exchange rates, monetary union implies complete equalization of nominal interest rates on equivalent assets, almost perfect substitutability of national currencies when these remain in a fixed exchange rate system with monetary policy in the hands of a single institution. A single currency does not increase the macroeconomic constraints imposed by EMU. It offers, however, a number of additional advantages. This study concentrates, therefore, on the benefits and costs of a full EMU with a single currency.

The experience of monetary unions suggests that in EMU inflation convergence will not need to be perfect. Moreover, as the catching-up of less advanced Member States proceeds, their real exchange rate should appreciate through a slightly higher inflation rate, due to the catch-up in the relative price of non-tradable products. Rough calculations suggest these differentials might in some cases exceed 1 % and even 2 % per annum. The same applies to wages and labour costs as a whole, for which differentials may be even larger.

The gains from EMU are evaluated with respect to a '1992 + Stage I' baseline in which realignments would still be possible, but in practice only in the case of shocks. It is assumed that Stage I would remain as asymmetric as the present EMS, and would also lead to further convergence in inflation rates. Since it cannot be taken for granted that Stage I could remain stable indefinitely, consideration has also to be given to the gains from EMU with respect to alternative exchange rate regimes.

There is no ready-to-use theory for assessing the costs and benefits of EMU. Despite its early insights, the 'theory of optimum currency areas' provides a too narrow and somewhat outdated framework of analysis. Recent developments in both

micro- and macroeconomics have not yet led to a unified theory of monetary unions. However they provide building blocks for a comprehensive analysis of EMU.

Four major categories of permanent effects can be expected from EMU:

(i)   microeconomic efficiency gains, which arise from the elimination of exchange rate uncertainty and transaction costs, and lead to a permanent increase in output;

(ii) macroeconomic stability effects, which arise both from the elimination of intra-Community exchange rates and from policy discipline in the monetary and fiscal fields, and impact on the variability of output, prices, and other macroeconomic variables;

(iii) regional equity effects, which concern the distribution of costs and benefits of EMU among Member States and regions;

(iv) external effects, through a wider international role of the ecu, tighter international policy coordination, and possibly changes in the international monetary regime.

In addition, important macroeconomic effects should arise in the transition towards EMU:

(i)   Both the lack of a unified theory and the diversity of effects involved imply that an attempt to make an overall quantitative assessment of EMU would be meaningless. However, partial quantifications are provided when possible in this report.

(ii) In comparison to alternative benchmark exchange rate regimes, i.e. financial market autarky and free float, EMU can be expected to yield significant benefits. Thus, in so far as the risks of instability in Stage I could lead the system to revert to some mix of capital controls and crawling peg as in the early EMS, the net benefit of EMU would only be greater.

2.1. EMU and alternatives

The basic definition of EMU is institutional and legal. Section 2.1.1 first discusses its economic content, which is necessary for an assessment of its costs and benefits. Section 2.1.2 then discusses the economic content of the reference cases against which the costs and benefits of EMU are assessed, namely a 'Stage I + 1992' baseline, and alternative exchange rate regimes.

2.1.1. The economic content of EMU

The Madrid meeting of the European Council of June 1989 endorsed the approach to EMU proposed by the report of the Committee for the Study of Economic and Monetary Union (the Delors Report), and as decided by the European Council the first stage of the realization of EMU began on 1 July 1990.

The economic definition of EMU given by the Delors Report is now widely accepted. For monetary union, it uses as a definition the three conditions stated in the Werner Report (1970), namely:

(i)   total and irreversible convertibility of currencies;

(ii) complete liberalization of capital transactions and full integration of banking and financial markets;

(iii) elimination of margins of fluctuation and irrevocable locking of exchange rate parities.

As mentioned in the Report, the first two conditions have already been met, or will be with the completion of the internal market programme. [1] Therefore, the decisive step towards full monetary union appears to be the irrevocable locking of exchange rates, which implies the creation of a single central bank (EuroFed). As discussed in more detail below, the adoption of a single currency would then be highly desirable. Since membership in the exchange rate mechanism (ERM) of the EMS is presently narrower than Community membership, it would be important that all its Member States participate in the ERM beforehand.

The definition of economic union is less clear-cut since it involves measures relating to different fields. It is also, by nature, more open-ended than monetary union. The Delors Report describes it in terms of four basic elements:

(i)   the single market within which persons, goods, services and capital can move freely;

(ii) competition policy and other measures aimed at strengthening market mechanisms;

(iii) common policies aimed at structural change and regional development;

(iv) macroeconomic policy coordination, including binding rules for budgetary policies.

The precise contents and implications of these measures and policies are discussed below and analysed in various sections of this study. Table 2.1 below gives a synthetic presentation of the features of EMU compared to those of the single market programme.

Table 2.1

Major features of 1992 and EMU

	'1992'	Stage I EMU	Final EMU
Monetary union			
Convertibility	X	X	X
Free capital movements	X	X	X
Irrevocable parities/single currency			X
All Member States in the ERM/EMU		X	X
Economic union			
Single market	X	X	X
Competition policy	P	P	E
Regional and structural policies	P	P	E
Macroeconomic coordination		P	E

P = partially. E = enhanced.

General principles

The above presentation makes clear that the overall conception of EMU aims at a certain balance in the progress towards monetary union on the one hand, and economic union on the other. This approach is called parallelism and was stressed by the European Council meeting of Madrid. Other principles to be followed in the design of EMU are subsidiarity and the necessity to allow for specific situations.

Subsidiarity is an important criterion for assigning tasks to the different levels of government in a multi-level government system. In its most general form, it states that tasks should be assigned to the lowest level of government, unless welfare gains can be reaped by assigning it to a higher level. [2] It is therefore a principle which aims at the decentralization of government functions as long as this is justified on efficiency grounds. In the Community context, the application of this principle should ensure that a policy function is assigned to the Community level only when it can be performed in a more efficient way at that level than by national or local governments.

Application of the principle of subsidiarity in the economic field can be based on the two familiar criteria of cross-country spill-overs and economies of scale as discussed in Box 2.1.

---

[1]   Capital markets liberalization is effective in most Member States. Only Spain, Portugal and Greece still maintain exchange controls and these will be progressively removed by 1992. In some cases the phasing-out may be extended until 1995.

[2]   This definition follows Van Rompuy, Abrahams and Heremans (1990), to which the reader can refer for a detailed discussion of economic federalism.

Box 2.1: The economic meaning of the principle of subsidiarity: assigning tasks to the Community on efficiency grounds

Two economic criteria can be used as necessary conditions for assigning on efficiency grounds a particular policy function to the Community:

(i) assignment of a policy function at the national level is inefficient because of the existence of cross-country spill-overs giving rise to externalities; since national governments do not take fully into account the consequences of their actions on the rest of the Community, they are bound to take suboptimal decisions;

(ii) the management of a policy function involves indivisibilities and/or economies of scale, which imply that productivity and effectiveness are improved when it is performed at a higher level.

For both criteria it is essential that externalities or economies of scale are significant at the Community level. Environmental effects (e.g. acid rain) provide classic cases of externalities; other examples can also be found in macroeconomic policy. Community-wide economies of scale are apparent in certain R&D investments (e.g. space programmes).

For the assignment to the Community level to be an adequate response, it is however necessary that two additional conditions are met:

(a) this assignment is demonstrated to yield net benefits after administrative costs and the balance of government versus market failures are taken into account, and

(b) *ad hoc* coordination among national governments is not sufficient to correct for inefficiencies.

Other motives of assignment of tasks to the Community level can stem from distributional or citizenship considerations, which are not discussed here.

The necessity of taking into account the diversity of specific situations refers to the fact that all Member States are not at present in the same economic condition, given for example different inflation rates or levels of development. This issue is taken up where necessary in the analytical chapters below, and on a country-by-country basis in Chapters 9 and 10.

The remainder of this section analyses the economic content of EMU and presents the related assumptions upon which this study is based.

Economic union

The economic consequences of 1992 have been evaluated in detail in the study *The economics of 1992* (Commission of the EC, 1988). Table 2.1 summarizes the elements of economic union which were not, or only partially, part of the single market programme: mainly regional and structural policy on the one hand, and macroeconomic coordination on the other.

An important issue for the analysis of EMU is the extent of the integration effects that can be expected from the completion of the internal market. Although persons, goods and services, and capital will be allowed to move freely across frontiers, this does not mean that integration will be perfect from the outset. Effective integration can be expected to lag somewhat behind *de jure* integration. However, a distinction has to be made in this respect between the mobility of capital, goods, and persons.

1. Capital mobility across countries can be expected to be almost perfect once exchange controls are removed in the narrow sense that arbitrage equalizes interest rates corrected

for the forward exchange discount. This condition, known as covered interest rate parity, means that it becomes theoretically equivalent to borrow in the home currency or to borrow in a foreign currency and to hedge against exchange rate variations. As pointed out in Chapter 6, covered interest rate parity already holds for countries which have removed exchange controls.

Nevertheless, this only means that agents throughout the Community have equal access to lending or borrowing in the same currency whichever currency they choose. But covered interest rate parity does not imply that neither nominal nor real interest rates are equalized across currencies nor that capital circulates across the EC in the same way as within the United States. Without monetary union, agents would still form expectations of exchange rate changes and/or ask for risk premiums when they lend in a foreign currency, with the consequence that real interest rates differ across the Community and that cross-country financing is limited by the exchange rate risk. The importance of this remaining barrier is a matter of theoretical and empirical discussion which is taken up in Chapters 3, 5 and 6, but its existence is indisputable.

Since monetary union would remove this last barrier, it can be assumed that perfect capital mobility would be achieved. Government bonds of the same maturity and risk would become perfect substitutes across the Community. However, domestic and foreign stocks would still be imperfect substitutes due to a different degree of information on domestic and foreign firms. To that extent, some segmentation of capital markets would remain even in EMU.[3]

---

3   See, for example, Artus (1990).

2. Integration of the markets for goods and services can be expected to increase in the course of the progress towards the single market. Nevertheless, this will be a lengthy process because obstacles to perfect integration not only arise from legal or technical barriers but also from habits of consumers and the behaviour of firms, especially in the service sector where so-called 'non-tradables' account for a large part of the production. Even for typical manufactured tradables, integration is far from complete since goods produced in two different Member States are imperfect substitutes and consumption structures are still biased towards home goods. [4] This imperfect integration is apparent at the macro-economic level as the marginal propensity to spend on home country goods is much higher than the marginal propensity to import in most Member States (exceptions being the smallest, very open economies).

Imperfect integration has important consequences for the design and properties of an economic and monetary union. [5] First, goods market integration cannot be expected to arbitrage away differences in price levels as would be the case for homogeneous commodities, which means that changes in real exchange rates (i.e. price competitiveness) are still possible within the Community whatever the exchange rate regime. As documented below, the experience of existing monetary unions indicates that, although nominal exchange rates are fixed, real exchange rates can be affected by differentiated movements in domestic prices. Moreover, and secondly, such real exchange rate changes remain a necessary component of the national adjustment to policy or non-policy shocks of a domestic or external origin. Thirdly, country-specific shocks can arise in product markets (e.g. a fall in the demand for goods from a given country) or the effects of global shocks can differ across countries. These issues are taken up in Chapter 6.

3. Labour mobility within the Community can also be expected to increase but is bound to remain limited, except for specific skills, due to cultural and linguistic barriers. Even within Member States or within the United States, mobility is actually far from perfect as exemplified by differences in regional unemployment rates. Therefore, at least in the decades ahead labour market integration will remain limited and, except for certain well-established migration flows, labour mobility between countries cannot be expected to act

as a significant equilibrating mechanism within EMU. This issue is further developed in Chapter 6.

A reasonable assumption for EMU is therefore that the degree of integration of markets will be high for capital, still limited but increasing for goods and services, and low for labour. This is an important characteristic which will, at least in the years existing ahead, differentiate the Community from economic and monetary unions such as the federal States, whose degree of integration is higher.

Another major difference between EMU and existing monetary unions in federal States will be the degree of centralization of public finance. In modern federal States like the United States, Canada, Australia or Germany, federal government expenditures account for at least half of total government expenditures. [6] This gives to the federal budget, first, the role of reducing automatically regional income differentials (through progressive income taxation and social transfers), and second, enough weight to be used in aggregate macroeconomic management. Since the Community budget only amounts to 2 % of total EC government expenditures, neither its interregional nor its global function can be compared to that of federal budgets. In so far as shocks affect incomes of Member States in an asymmetric way, other adjustment mechanisms will have to take the place of a central budget as an automatic stabilizer. To the extent that aggregate fiscal policy measures are required, most if not all of this policy will have to be implemented through coordination among Member States.

Monetary union with irrevocably fixed exchange rates

When a monetary union has the form of irrevocably fixed exchange rates, the logical consequences of this definition have to be made clear in order to avoid misunderstandings. 'Irrevocability' of exchange rates has to be taken literally if monetary union is to mean something else than a mere hardening of the EMS.

Three propositions can be made in order to characterize the macroeconomic effects of a monetary union:

(i) *Irrevocably fixed exchange rates imply nominal interest rates equalization.* With perfect capital mobility, nominal interest rates on assets of the same nature, maturity and specific risk can only differ because of (a) expected depreciation and (b) exchange risk premiums. Both can only arise to the extent that their irrevocability is not fully credible in the eyes of the markets. Thus, truly irrevocable exchange rates imply the same interest rates

---

4   Markets for automobiles are a good example.
5   The importance of imperfect integration of goods markets for the analysis of exchange rate regimes has been stressed by Baldwin and Krugman (1987) and Krugman (1989) in response to the 'global monetarist' approach of McKinnon. For an attempt to measure macroeconomically this integration in the Community, see Aglietta, Coudert and Delessy (1990).
6   The minimum is 45 % for Canada. See Chapter 6, Section 6.7.

across the union.[7] This is a direct consequence of the incompatibility of fixed exchange rates, full capital mobility and autonomy of monetary policies already underlined by the Padoa-Schioppa Report (1987).

(ii) *Irrevocably fixed exchange rates require that national currencies become almost perfect substitutes.* Since interest rates are equalized and conversion rates are fixed, the only differences between holding currency x or y are that (a) the acceptability of x and y for transactions differ on their respective territories (in particular due to legal tender provisions), and (b) conversion of x into y entails transaction costs as long as par-clearing is not established. From a macroeconomic point of view, irrevocably fixed exchange rates are equivalent to a single currency except that the rate of conversion is not one for one.

(iii) *Irrevocably fixed exchange rates imply that monetary policy is put under the control of a single institution.* Exchange rates can only be deemed irrevocable if all official monetary institutions within the Community guarantee without limits the conversion of any currency of the system into another at the given rate. Indeed without this multilateral guarantee there would be no difference between monetary union and the unilateral commitments to exchange rate fixity that are already made within the ERM, albeit whose credibility is hard to achieve and always subject to changes in the judgment of the markets. But this requires giving the responsibility for monetary policy to a single institution, since in the absence of this centralization any creation of money by a national central bank would impact throughout the union without any possibility for another Member State to shelter from its consequences. Without a central institution, the system would therefore incorporate a strong incentive for countries to 'free ride' at the expense of their neighbours, i.e. to expand money supply and seigniorage gains excessively at home without bearing the full associated inflation costs.[8] Even the 'anchor country' of the ERM would lose its monetary autonomy since irrevocably fixed exchange rates would remove all asymmetries within the system.

The macroeconomic implications of a monetary union with irrevocably fixed exchange rates are therefore the same as those of a single currency. In spite of the persistence of national monetary symbols whose denominations and values differ, these in fact become different images of the same currency. In consequence, the discipline imposed upon monetary policy is exactly the same in both cases: there is no room for decentralization and differences in the conduct of monetary policy.[9]

The above propositions are based on the assumption that all agents believe in the irrevocability of exchange rates. However, the nature of the commitments which could lead agents to rule out any possibility of parity changes is not easy to define. Exchange rate credibility can either be achieved through the building of a reputation or through commitments whose breach would be very costly in political and/or economic terms.

Experience shows that reputation-building is a lengthy process, and that even long-lasting exchange rate stability does not necessarily lead to the complete disappearance of bond rate differentials. Two relevant experiences are those of the Netherlands, which since 1983 has maintained a fixed central rate within the ERM with respect to the Deutschmark, and that of Austria, which at least since 1981 has pegged its currency to the DM.[10] Although both countries benefited from particularly good starting conditions because of their size, their economic links with Germany, their inflation record and the autonomy of their central banks, the convergence of bond rates in both cases took several years to be achieved. Moreover, the option of a permanent and unilateral Deutschmark peg is not really available for larger Member States like France, Italy, Spain and the United Kingdom for obvious economic and political reasons.

Credibility is a direct function of the strength of the commitment to exchange rate fixity and of the difficulty of seceding from the union: tying one's hand, in the words of Giavazzi and Pagano (1988), yields benefits to the country which makes this commitment. In an EMU, an externality is also at work since credibility is a property of the system which is shared by all its members. Commitment can never be absolute, since whatever its technicalities monetary union is the result of a treaty among sovereign States which can always be renounced. However the institutional setting of a monetary union affects its credibility. As long as currencies as well as national money and bond markets remain distinct — which would be the case with irrevocably fixed rates but not the single currency — it is still possible to leave the system at a moderate economic cost. Moreover, since the existence of separate markets for bonds denominated in

---

7   Strictly speaking, this is only true if currencies are exchanged at par since in the presence of transaction costs, interest rate arbitrage is not perfect, and short-term interest rate differentials can therefore appear.

8   This is shown for example by Casella (1990) and Krugman (1990).

9   This only refers to macroeconomic policy. Other functions of central banks, like supervision, may be more decentralized, but are not discussed here.

10   On the Dutch experience, see Annex B. The Austrian experience is analysed by Genberg (1989) and Hochreiter and Törnqvist (1990).

different currencies provides a measure of credibility through yield differentials for assets of the same category and risk, the irrevocability of the exchange rates can always be questioned by market forces.

Monetary union with a single currency

Since a strong and binding commitment to exchange rate fixity is a necessary condition of the success of EMU, the question arises how institutional devices could enhance the credibility of this commitment. A natural candidate is the adoption of a single currency which would replace existing national currencies. [11] Starting with the Werner report, the choice of a single currency has been considered an alternative definition of monetary union, and it has been argued above that both definitions are macroeconomically equivalent, provided fixed exchange rates are indeed irrevocable. However a single currency has a number of additional advantages which are discussed throughout this report and summarized in Box 2.2. The only cost it entails, apart from to the cost of introducing it, is in effect a benefit: it makes exit from the union very difficult. An early move to a single currency would therefore increase the net benefit of EMU.

The nature of this single currency has to be discussed briefly in order to avoid misunderstandings. Two major questions are, first its relation to existing national currencies, and second its relation to the present ecu.

Box 2.2: Six differences between a single currency and irrevocably fixed exchange rates

1. *Transaction costs:* a single currency would eliminate all the costs arising to firms and individuals from conversions from one Community currency into another (Chapter 3).

2. *Transparency of prices:* as goods and services would be priced in the same currency, this would further strengthen the pro-competitive effect of the single market (Chapter 3).

3. *Economies of scale:* a single currency would lead markets for the same categories of financial instruments to merge, yielding benefits in terms of market depth and efficiency (Chapter 3).

4. *Credibility:* a single currency gives from the outset maximum credibility to monetary union (Chapter 4).

5. *Visibility:* a single currency would be for all Community agents a visible sign of the creation of EMU and would make those agents more conscious of the associated wage and price discipline (Chapter 6).

6. *External benefits:* only with a single currency can the EMU lead to a recasting of international currencies and to a more balanced international monetary regime (Chapter 7).

As to the relation to existing national currencies, the introduction of a single currency (the ecu) would necessitate in each country a change in the unit of account. The new unit of account could be used for all bank notes and coin in the Community, which would no doubt continue to bear different national symbols (as in the Belgian and Luxembourg francs, or English and Scottish pounds). Alternatively notes and coin could continue to bear their traditional names in each country, but would be exchanged one to one for ecus. Therefore, 1 franc would be equivalent to 1 lira or 1 mark, which would be different names for the ecu. A further alternative is that notes and coins could be denominated in ecu on one side and the national currency name on the other, so long as the same quantity was indicated. There would be no significant economic differences between these alternatives.

As to the relation between the present private ecu and future ecus, they would be different in that the new ecu would be a full currency instead of a mere financial instrument. Its supply would be under the control of a single institution instead of being the result of separate policies governing the

---

[11]   The term 'common currency' is ambiguous: it sometimes refers to a single currency, which would replace the national currencies, and sometimes to a parallel currency, which would be issued in addition to existing ones. It is therefore not used throughout this report. See also below on the hard ecu proposal.

value of the national currencies constituting the basket ecu. In spite of this difference, however, the choice of the same unit of account could ensure that at the outset of the monetary union both would have the same value. There would be no change in ecu denominated contracts.

This study concentrates on the benefits and costs of a full EMU with a single currency. However, specific differences between the single currency and a fixed exchange rate system are discussed throughout the text.

Macroeconomic convergence in EMU

Since EMU will be characterized on the one hand by imperfect economic integration and on the other by a single monetary policy, the issue arises of what degree of price and more generally macroeconomic convergence is required for the stability of EMU.

In existing federal States, inflation can frequently diverge in the short run by a few percentage points. Table 2.2 presents aggregate evidence drawn from the Canadian experience. Due to different local conditions, consumer price inflation varies across cities, while GDP deflators exhibit large spreads across provinces because of different industrial structures (some provinces being heavily specialized in the production of oil and raw materials). In fact, real exchange rate variability is sometimes even higher within Canada than across ERM countries. [12]

Table 2.2

Indicators of city and regional inflation divergence within Canada

Annual rates	1971Q1-1979Q4	1980Q1-1987Q4
Relative city-consumer prices (8 cities/Toronto)	.	
(i) average standard deviation	1,1	1,6
(ii) maximum standard deviation	2,2	2,2
Relative provincial GDP deflators (9 provinces/Ontario)		
(i) average	8,6	4,1
(ii) maximum	33,6	11,3

Source: adapted from Poloz (1990).
Note: based on standard deviations of relative price levels with respect to Toronto for city-CPIs (8 cities), and to the Province of Ontario for provincial GDP deflators (9 provinces).

---

[12] See Poloz (1990) for details.

In the long run, however, price inflation does not in general diverge by more than a fraction of one percentage point per year across States or regions. In Europe the monetary unions between Ireland and the United Kingdom, and Belgium and Luxembourg, for example, led to almost complete convergence in inflation rates over the long run. From 1950 until 1978 (when the Irish pound ceased to be linked to the UK pound and joined the EMS), the average difference in annual consumer price inflation between Ireland and the UK was less than 0,4 %. Similarly, between Luxembourg and Belgium the average difference over the period 1950-88 was about 0,3 % per annum.

However, even these small differences in rates of growth of consumer prices can lead to considerable differences in price levels. For the Ireland/UK case the cumulative difference was about 10 % (over 28 years) and for the Belgian/Luxembourg case it was about 15 % (over 38 years). Between Germany and the Netherlands there was even a cumulative difference of about 20 % for the 19 years (from 1950 to 1969) during which the exchange rate was fixed. However, this lack of convergence, which became stronger towards the end of the period, might have led to the cut in the link after 1969 (Graph 2.1).

GRAPH 2.1: **Evolution of relative consumer prices in three monetary unions, 1950-88**

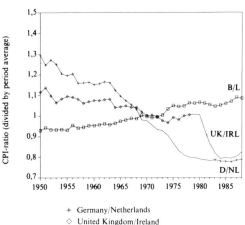

+ Germany/Netherlands
◇ United Kingdom/Ireland
□ Belgium/Luxembourg

Base period average = 1. Lines with symbols represent periods with constant nominal exchange rates. Lines without symbols represent periods with variable exchange rates.

Long-run convergence in inflation is the result of arbitrage in tradable goods whose price, although not equalized, cannot permanently diverge. There is, however, no equivalent mechanism to foster convergence in the price of non-tradable goods. Movements of factors of production, i.e. capital and labour, impose some limits to divergences in the price of non-tradables, but experience shows that this process is very slow. Real estate prices, for example, can diverge considerably inside a monetary union if local growth conditions differ. Convergence does not have to be perfect therefore in terms of consumer price inflation and certainly not in terms of the level of consumer prices. [13]

Inflation differentials can even arise from equilibrating mechanisms, when the starting point is one of divergence. A well-known example of such mechanism is the real appreciation of the exchange rate generally experienced by catching-up countries. [14] Although such figures are surrounded with considerable uncertainty, comparison of price levels indicate that in 1989 consumer prices were about 40 % below the Community average in Portugal and some 20 % below average in Spain. [15] As catching-up proceeds, this gap will narrow through higher inflation in these countries than in the rest of the EC. Assuming, for example, full catching-up and equalization of price levels in 20 years, this would mean that recorded consumer price inflation would each year be 2,5 percentage points higher in Portugal, and about 1 % higher in Spain than in the whole Community. It must be stressed, of course, that such differentials would only be warranted to the extent that they went hand-in-hand with higher productivity gains and growth.

Labour costs also require convergence. But in this area there are even more reasons for national differences in the short and long run since differences in productivity growth rates should be approximately reflected in the growth of real wages. Actually, convergence in labour costs without convergence in productivity could only lead to regional pockets of unemployment and stagnation. It is therefore of paramount importance that regional labour costs remain in line with productivity differentials.

The experience of the three European monetary unions already examined can again be used to illustrate this. The relative wage levels displayed in Graph 2.2 suggest that real wages could diverge by as much as one percentage point per year over long periods of time. This is almost three times higher than the corresponding figure for differences in consumer price inflation mentioned above. For example, wages in Ireland have increased by about 40 percentage points more than in the UK during the period 1950-78, an average difference of more than 1% p.a. over this 28 years period. The difference in the degree of convergence of wages and consumer prices can be seen by comparing Graphs 2.1 and 2.2, showing that wages typically diverged more than consumer prices in three cases of intra-European monetary unions.

GRAPH 2.2: **Evolution of relative wage levels in three monetary unions, 1950-88**

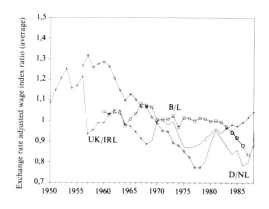

◇ Germany/Netherlands
+ United Kingdom/Ireland
□ Belgium/Luxembourg

Base period average = 1. Lines with symbols represent periods with constant nominal exchange rates. Lines without symbols represent periods with variable exchange rates.

Since EMU will comprise a group of countries with large initial differences in labour productivity levels, nominal wage increases should diverge as long as productivity grows at different rates. Present GDP per employed person (a rough measure of labour productivity) is estimated to be about

[13] Even prices of tradables can exhibit wide divergence in level terms. A recent survey by Runzheimer Mitchell Europe shows that both before and after tax retail prices of typical standardized manufactured goods of the same brand name often vary by 100% or more across the Community. Arguably, price transparency within EMU could reduce these variations, but some divergence would surely remain. See *The Financial Times*, 9 July 1990.
[14] The standard rationale behind this phenomenon is that as catching-up proceeds, the relative price of non-tradables, for which productivity gains are lower, increases with respect to that of tradables. Assuming purchasing power parity in the traded-goods sector, this leads to real exchange rate appreciation. The analysis of mechanisms of this type goes back to Ricardo. For a modern restatement, see Balassa (1964).
[15] *Source:* Eurostat, *Indice des prix à la consommation,* supplément 1, 1990.

50 % of the Community average in Portugal.[16] If this gap were closed in 20 years, real wages could rise annually by 3,5 % more in Portugal than in the Community as a whole. German reunification provides an even more striking example: if East German labour productivity were before reunification about 50 % of the West German level, a catch up in about 10 years could see wage increases by 7% more each year in East Germany.

The need for convergence in public budget imbalances is more difficult to assess since in existing federal States national or regional deficits (or surpluses) do not in general converge to a common value. Moreover, Member States should retain a large autonomy as regards short-run budgetary policy. However, excessive deficits that lead to exploding public debts are not compatible with EMU, essentially because the policy of price stability of the EuroFed might be jeopardized if individual member countries run up excessive public debts or deficits. Coordination of fiscal policies among Member States would also be required. Chapter 5 discusses in detail the desirable properties of the budgetary regime of EMU.

The necessary degree of convergence in terms of external current account imbalances is also difficult to assess. Since the current account is identically equal to the difference between overall savings and investment, it is clear that a balanced current account is not always a desirable result. As discussed in Chapter 6, economies with a low capital/labour ratio and therefore with a relatively large potential for investment would actually gain from being able to partially finance investment through foreign savings, thus running current account deficits. This implies that current account imbalances should not be a cause for concern if they reflect patterns of this type and are financed automatically through private capital flows, which is in principle the case in a well functioning EMU with a single currency. However, in the transitional stages current account imbalances will still remain highly visible and might at times signal the need for policy adjustments. It is difficult to decide, a priori, whether current accounts disappear as an issue already when capital markets are completely integrated and exchange rate fixity becomes credible, or only when there is a single currency. Chapter 6 further discusses these matters.

A well functioning EMU does not need only convergence in the macroeconomic performance of its member countries. An efficient management of macroeconomic policy for the union also requires that there is convergence in the policy

preferences, or at least agreement on the policy objectives, and therefore on the weighting of targets and the choice of instruments of economic policy. For example, if there is a large, common, inflationary shock, such as an increase in the price of oil, member countries should have a reasonable degree of convergence regarding the desirable degree of smoothing of the consequences of the shock on output and inflation. Otherwise, some countries might for example decide to suppress its inflationary consequences using price controls. This would inevitably lead to distortions within the single market. However, the same requirement for convergence implies policy autonomy in the use of domestic (e.g. budgetary) instruments while facing asymmetric shocks.

The common goal of price stability is therefore not sufficient by itself to lead to full convergence and ensure a stable EMU. It would need to be underpinned by other fundamental ground rules, such as the 1992 rules for market competition, and rules on fiscal discipline. Inside a consistent set of such ground rules (which together may be termed 'Ordnungspolitik' in German) there would then be room for subsidiarity and competitive processes at the firm and government level. Without a common framework for economic policy, national reactions to large shocks might be fundamentally different and endanger the cohesion of the union.

Stages of EMU

The three-stage approach outlined in the Delors Report provides a blueprint for the realization of EMU. Therefore, the precise economic content and implications of each of these stages has to be made explicit. Table 2.3 presents in a simplified fashion the major features of each of those stages. Since Stage III is identical to monetary union as already described, the comments below concentrate on Stages I and II.

The major decisions to be taken in Stage I are already effective since in the economic field the internal market programme is on track, the reform of the structural Funds is in operation and the new decision governing coordination and surveillance was finalized in early 1990. In the monetary field capital market liberalization is effective in most Member States and monetary coordination is being strengthened within the framework of the Committee of Central Bank Governors. The remaining aspects mainly relate to country-specific adjustments, i.e. participation in the ERM, further convergence towards low inflation, and budgetary adjustments.

In contrast to Stage I, which is basically defined in economic terms, Stage II is mainly institutional in nature. It is meant

---

[16] GDP per employed person, at standard purchasing power exchange rates. *Source:* Eurostat.

Table 2.3

Major features of the three EMU stages

Economic	Monetary
Stage I	
• Completion of the internal market	• Capital market liberalization
• Strengthened competition policy	• Enhanced monetary and exchange rate coordination
• Full implementation of the reform of the structural Funds	• Realignments possible, but infrequent
• Enhanced coordination and surveillance	• All EC currencies in the narrow-band ERM
• Budgetary adjustments in high debt/deficit countries	• Extended use of the ecu
Stage II	
• Evaluation and adaptation of Stage I policies	• Establishment of EuroFed
• Review of national macroeconomic adjustments	• Possible narrowing of EMS bands
Stage III	
• Definitive budgetary coordination system	• EuroFed in charge of monetary policy
• Possible strengthening of structural and regional policies	• Irrevocably fixed exchange rates or ecu as single currency

to be a transitional stage only. The Delors Report placed emphasis on the gradual transfer in Stage II of responsibility for monetary policy. After discussion, the emphasis has since been placed more on the technical preparation of the EuroFed institution in Stage II, on the grounds that policy responsibility must be clear-cut. For this reason it is now widely considered that Stage II should be quite short.

The economic logic of Stage II is that of a transition between an asymmetric system where monetary policy is coordinated through the exchange markets and a system in which monetary policy is set at the Community level and exchange markets lose their coordination function. The single most important step in this process is the irrevocable fixing of parities at the outset of Stage III.

The economic and monetary content of Stage III has already been described. On the economic side application of the principle of subsidiarity results in an evolutionary set of policy responsibilities, with considerable room for debate and experimentation over the best regime at any one time. This concerns especially the rules and competences of national and EC budgets, which Chapter 5 discusses in more detail.

The timing of the transition through the Stages is largely a matter for political choice, although as developed in Chapter 8 pure cost/benefit considerations tend to argue in favour of a rapid move toward full EMU. The degree of convergence of inflation, budget deficits and other variables needed

in the move to the definitive EMU is discussed in Chapter 8. However, the speed of this convergence will depend heavily on the timing and credibility of the political commitments to move to Stages II and III.

2.1.2. Alternatives to EMU

Against what benchmark situation should the effects of EMU be assessed? This question is less obvious than it seems at first sight since the situation of today cannot be taken as a stable point of reference for two reasons: first, decisions have been taken whose effects are not yet visible, e.g. regarding the completion of the internal market and capital market liberalization; second, commitments have been made which are not yet translated into effective decisions, e.g. the British commitment to participate in the ERM during Stage I. The present situation can therefore only be viewed as a snapshot in an ongoing process. Choosing this situation as a baseline would not be satisfactory. It would in addition introduce somewhat artificial differences among Member States depending on their present situation within or with respect to the ERM. This section reviews the alternative baselines against which EMU can be evaluated.

Stage I as a baseline

A natural starting point for comparisons is Stage I, or a 'EMS + 1992' hypothetical baseline, which is assumed to incorporate all the effects of decisions and commitments described in the first panel of Table 2.3. This is the basic hypothesis which is retained throughout this study, although comparisons are in some cases also made with alternative baselines. Given the importance of the 1992 programme in this regard, a relatively large part of economic union effects are therefore already present. Most of the additional gains from EMU would thus arise from progress in the monetary field, whose effects may be evaluated against a clear and uniform benchmark.

Since Stage I is not yet observed, assumptions have to be made regarding its functioning. Major issues regard (1) its basic monetary logic, (2) the practice of realignments and (3) the micro and macroeconomic effects of capital market liberalization.

1. As to its basic monetary logic, Stage I would not be very different from the EMS of the late 1980s. Like in any other fixed-but-adjustable exchange rate system, one can assume that it will remain asymmetric in the sense that one particular national central bank acts as a *de facto* leader. Whether this 'anchor country' would be Germany as in the 1980s, or whether a competition for the leadership might arise is an open issue (see Chapter 8). Whichever the leader, however, the logic of such a system is that overall monetary policy is set by a particular central bank, while the policy of the $(N-1)$ other members is devoted to the peg of the exchange rate. Therefore, as long as central parities remain fixed, the only room for manoeuvre for autonomous monetary policies is provided by the possibility of exchange rate movements within the bands.

This relates to the monetary logic of a fixed-but-adjustable exchange rate system without capital controls. Admittedly, monetary policy coordination could become more symmetric in the perspective of EMU through informal cooperation among central banks, as a preparation for Stages II and III. However, for the evaluation of EMU, Stage I has to be regarded as much as possible as a steady state, setting aside features that would stem from future developments of EMU.

2. The most uncertain issue concerning the evolution of the EMS in Stage I concerns the practice of realignments. Two extreme models are (a) some kind of loosely defined soft EMS, and (b) a *de facto* monetary union where realignments would become exceptional, an image of which can be provided by the present situation between Germany and the Netherlands.[17] Capital market liberalization within the con-

text of a fixed-but-adjustable exchange rate system points in the direction of the second model: realignments would still be possible, but since anticipated realignments can give rise to potentially unlimited capital movements, one cannot assume that this instrument could be used by governments systematically.

Realignments come onto the agenda either when countries are characterized by different inflation trends or subject to country-specific shocks. Whether or not significant differences in inflation trends could still be compensated by periodic realignments in Stage I is in principle an open issue. The disciplinary effect of the EMS has proven effective since the second half of the 1980s when realignments became rare and compensated only half of the inflation differentials (Table 2.4). This is widely considered to be a major factor of inflation convergence within the narrow-band ERM. This record should continue with the removal of the last capital controls, for the only way to discourage speculative attacks is (i) to make the realignments rare and randomly distributed, (ii) to offset only partially inflation differentials, and (iii) to avoid discrete jumps in the market exchange rate, i.e. to realign inside the band. Since the first two are costly in terms of relative prices while the third either implies a renunciation of the EMS (if bands are so wide than the system becomes closer to a flexible rate system) or frequent realignments, these techniques cannot really accommodate large and permanent inflation differentials. This is the reason for expecting further inflation convergence in Stage I.[18] Actually, there is already a clear tendency within the core ERM towards a *de facto* narrowing of the bands of fluctuation *vis-à-vis* the Deutschmark.[19]

An opposite strand of arguments states that capital controls, by allowing for delayed realignments and therefore real exchange rate appreciations in the more inflationary countries, were a key component of inflation discipline in the EMS. Another argument states that exchange rate credibility would lead to a decrease in nominal interest rates in inflationary countries, thereby leading to low real interest rates and a weakening of inflation discipline.[20] Those arguments, however, can only be considered of some validity in the short run. They do not demonstrate how large differences in trend inflation could be accommodated at low cost within a Stage I EMU without leading to speculative attacks. There-

[17] In May 1990, Belgium announced its intention to commit itself to exchange rate stability *vis-à-vis* the Deutschmark. The French Government has also repeatedly stressed its intention to rule out devaluations.

[18] The requirements for a realignment rule in an EMS without capital controls are discussed by Driffill (1988) and Obstfeld (1988). See also Annex E.
[19] See Annex E.
[20] See Giavazzi and Giovannini (1989), Giavazzi and Spaventa (1990).

Table 2.4

Realignments in the EMS, 1979-89

(*vis-à-vis* the Deutschmark)

	B/L	DK	F	IRL	I	NL	Narrow band	ERM
1979-83								
Number of realignments	5	7	4	4	5	2	22	27
Average size (%)	4,9	4,4	7,1	5,2	6,3	2	5,1	5,3
Average cumulated price differential	1,65	3,1	6,7	12,0	9,8	1,0	5,0	5,9
Degree of offsetting (%)	296,6	139,8	105,4	43,5	64,4	203,2	101,2	89,7
1984-87								
Number of realignments	2	2	2	3	3	—	9	12
Average size (%)	1,5	2,5	4,5	4,7	4,7	—	3,5	3,8
Average cumulated price differential	5,3	6,8	8,3	6,1	9,3	—	6,6	7,3
Degree of offsetting (%)	28,5	36,5	54,5	77,2	50,7	—	52,7	52,1

Note: All data refer to bilateral Deutschmark exchange rates. Cumulated price differentials (CPI, monthly data) are measured between two realignments. Offsetting of inflation differentials is measured by the ratio of central rate variation to the price differential by the time of the realignment.
Source: Commission services.

fore it can be considered that regarding inflation discipline, the implications of Stage I would not be very different from those of a full EMU.

However realignments might still be possible in the case of country-specific shocks, provided those shocks are unexpected. A country hit, for example, by a fall in the demand for its exports (a demand shock) or a surge in nominal wages (a supply shock) could use the exchange rate instrument in order to modify its real exchange rate or to accommodate the inflationary shock. As discussed in Chapter 6, this is where Stage I would retain nominal exchange rate flexibility that would be lost in the full EMU.

3. Capital market liberalization is already in effect for most countries, however its full impact is not yet observed. It will not only affect potential short-term capital movements, but also the integration of financial markets. One can expect therefore, the supply of financial products to increase, presumably providing larger hedging opportunities, and also, some reduction in transaction and hedging costs because of economies of scale, technological change, and greater competition.[21] Although the extent of these microeconomic effects cannot be assessed with precision, they have to be

taken into account in the cost-benefit evaluation of EMU (Chapter 3).[22]

Summing up, the following hypotheses are made regarding Stage I:

(i)   The working of the exchange rate system will remain asymmetric, with an anchor country setting the overall monetary policy while the (N-1) others are coordinated through the exchange markets.

(ii)   Exchange rate discipline in Stage I will see further convergence towards low inflation, practically eliminating trend differences in inflation rates which do not arise from equilibrating mechanisms. However, realignments would still be an available instrument in the case of unexpected country-specific shocks.

(iii)   The removal of capital controls will yield savings in transaction and hedging costs as well as a closer integration of capital markets, but fall short of what a genuine EMU would bring.

---

[21]   See the special issue of *European Economy* (1988b), and Gros (1990).

[22]   Other effects of the removal of capital controls concern the allocation of savings, i.e. the micro and macroeconomic effects of capital markets integration which are discussed in Chapters 3 and 6. Here also the removal of capital controls is expected to yield some benefits, although this is incomplete as long as exchange rate risk remains a barrier to capital mobility.

The above characterization of Stage I is based on the assumption that it is stable, at least as a transitional stage. However, this stability has been questioned by a number of authors, either directly or with reference to the 'evolutionary approach to EMU', proposed in 1989 by the British Government (HM Treasury, 1989), which bears close resemblance to a protracted Stage I. The issue of stability in the transition is taken up in Chapter 8, where it is argued that Stage I can be considered stable as long as economic policies in the Member States are consistent with the constraints of the system, but that 'systemic instability' could arise from a refusal of the asymmetric character of the system or from a competition for leadership. Indeed, the stability of a Stage I lasting for a few years and considered to be a transition towards full EMU, and that of the same system without the prospect of moving on to the definitive EMU are two different issues: as long as governments and agents expect a new regime to be established in the near future, their behaviour is conditioned accordingly. Historically, the coexistence of fixed exchange rates and completely free capital movements never lasted for very long.[23] It cannot be taken for granted that a renunciation of EMU would not lead, sooner or later, some countries to opt for more exchange rate flexibility or, alternatively, to reintroduce some capital controls. Therefore, the costs and benefits of EMU have to be discussed in the wider context of the possible alternative choices of exchange rate regimes.

Alternative exchange rate regimes

The well-known inconsistency between financial integration, fixed exchange rates and monetary policy autonomy provides an appropriate starting point for the discussion of the alternatives to EMU. All three objectives are legitimate, the first two because of the economic benefits they yield, and the third because policy autonomy is, *ceteris paribus,* desirable on subsidiarity grounds. A tri-dimensional trade-off is therefore at work, which can be represented by Graph 2.3.[24] The three objectives are represented along the three axes of the figure. Any point within the triangle can therefore be characterized by the degree to which each of these objectives is fulfilled. The three sides of the triangle are each characterized by complete fulfilment of one particular condition. Its three corners correspond to situations where two conditions are simultaneously fulfilled, the third being excluded:

(i)   financial market autarky (complete fixity of exchange rate and policy autonomy, but total control of capital

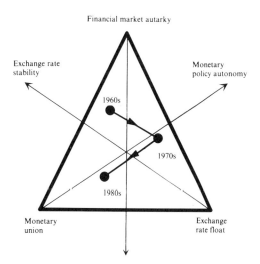

GRAPH 2.3: **A graphical representation of alternative exchange rate regimes**

movements; current account imbalances are settled through official bilateral capital transactions);

(ii)   exchange rate float (complete financial integration and autonomy, with exchange rate determined by the market without any unsterilized intervention);

(iii) monetary union (complete financial integration and exchange rate fixity, with zero policy autonomy).

The evolution of the exchange rate regimes within the Community can be illustrated on the figure. The compromise of the 1960s was characterized by low financial integration due to widespread capital controls and high exchange rate stability. The breakdown of the Bretton Woods system led to greater autonomy at the expense of exchange rate stability, and while the 1970s witnessed to some extent greater financial integration, some countries reverted to capital controls to prevent exchange rate crisis. The creation of the EMS in 1979 has been a reaction to this experience as well as a statement of preference for exchange rate stability, and the 1980s have been characterized by both greater exchange rate fixity and greater financial integration (at the expense of autonomy). Stage I basically represents a continuation of this trend. This is also the case for full EMU.

---

[23]   See Carli (1989) and Giovannini (1989).
[24]   Adapted from Aglietta (1988).

Neither financial autarky nor a clean float represent real alternatives to EMU. It is hard to imagine why and how European governments would choose to renounce the benefits of a Community-wide financial market, or to abandon their aim of exchange rate stability after the successes of the EMS. Both moves would represent a dramatic reversal of the historical trend. However, the two cases are useful benchmarks for a discussion of the costs and benefits of EMU.

The 'hard ecu' proposal

Another proposal which has been put forward in the summer of 1990 as an alternative to the Delors Committee approach is the 'hard ecu' of the UK Chancellor of the Exchequer.

In this case the ecu would be developed as a parallel currency managed by a new institution, which could be called the European Monetary Fund (EMF). As a first step, the Chancellor proposes setting up a new institution (the EMF) to act as a currency board and provide ecu bank notes on demand for Community currencies. To ensure no new money creation, EMF ecu notes would have to be fully backed by its own holdings of component currencies. The ecu would remain a basket currency, with its interest and exchange rates being determined as now.

A further step would involve a switch from a basket ecu to a 'hard ecu', managed by the EMF, which would fully feature in the EMS on equal terms with other currencies, staying within ERM margins and never being devalued at realignments in relation to any Community currency. The EMF would issue hard ecu deposits in the Community only in return for national currencies. Any excess of national currencies held by the EMF would have to be repurchased by the central banks concerned for hard currencies. The hard ecu is intended specifically to strengthen the pressures for anti-inflationary convergence in the Community by putting it at the centre of the EMS.

The hard ecu plan represents a considerable development of the previous position expressed by the Treasury (*An evolutionary approach to EMU*, HM Treasury, 1989): it acknowledges the need for a new Community monetary institution and allows for the possibility of a single currency at the end of the process.

An assessment of the benefits and costs of the hard ecu proposal must take into account its uncertain evolution. To its proponent, this uncertainty is one of its main attractions, since it stems from the freedom of choice over whether to use the hard ecu, which is left to the markets. This means that, in relation to the existing situation, no economic agent has to undergo extra costs by using the hard ecu, since

national currencies remain as alternatives. On the other hand, this uncertainty also means unpredictable currency substitution possibilities. This could have costs in terms of macroeconomic stability, with monetary control made more difficult.

As regards the hard ecu's likely economic impact, this would of course depend on whether it was actually taken up and used in macroeconomically significant amounts: clearly, if the amounts used were small, the effects would be very slight.

If, however, the hard ecu were to become widely used, its impact may be considered in terms of the effects discussed in this study. To the extent that the hard ecu were used for international commerce and achieved the economies of scale observed with major currencies, there could be savings in transaction costs for some users. However, these costs would not be eliminated as with a single currency. Similarly some exchange rate uncertainty would remain. While the mechanism contains an incentive in favour of stability-oriented macroeconomic policies, it is not clear that this would add to the disciplines already experienced by currencies that participate in the narrow-band of the exchange rate mechanism of the EMS (or the incentive to be faced by the other Community countries when they put their currencies into the narrow band). It is likely to be in the least convergent countries that the use of the hard ecu would grow fastest. If in some countries the hard ecu acquired a significant market share in relation to the national currency, there would arise the question of what the denominator would be for domestic wage and price contracts. Presumably this transitional stage would also mean considerable uncertainty for economic agents, until the time came for the switch to a single currency. Externally, the hard ecu could take on a wider international role, but not to the extent that would a single Community currency.

2.2. The economic impact of EMU

The aim of the present section is to outline the costs and benefits of EMU as well as to discuss the methods and techniques of their evaluation: Subsection 2.2.1 reviews the theoretical aspects, and Subsection 2.2.2 the nature of costs and benefits, together with the more technical questions of economic evaluation and measurement.

The basic message of this investigation is that both because of the present state of the theory of monetary unification and because of the diversity of the effects involved, an overall quantitative evaluation of the gains from EMU would be both out of reach and inappropriate. The present study has accordingly the more modest aim to propose a framework for the analysis of the economics of EMU and to provide some partial quantifications. However, qualitative conclusions can be drawn from a comprehensive approach to the costs and benefits of EMU.

2.2.1. Building blocks for the analysis of EMU

In contrast to the trade field, where standard economic theory has for long offered straightforward arguments in favour of trade liberalization and economic integration more generally, the analysis of EMU cannot be based on a simple, unified, ready-to-use theory of the benefits of monetary integration. The two issues of economic integration and monetary integration are indeed treated very differently in economic theory. The case for economic integration is based on a unified and secure microeconomic approach since whatever the latest developments in the theory of international trade, the basic rationale for the internal market programme is still rooted in the approaches of Adam Smith and David Ricardo.[25] Monetary integration, however, immediately raises a more complex set of theoretical and empirical issues.[26]

This may seem paradoxical since, as pointed out by various authors,[27] the use of a single money seems to be as essential to the unification of the US internal market as the absence of any direct or indirect trade barriers. Though the diversity of industrial structures among US states or regions is as great as among the Member States of the Community, the idea of appreciating the Texas dollar when the price of oil rises, or depreciating the Michigan dollar when Detroit is outpriced by Japanese car exports, sounds as pointless as introducing custom duties inside the US market. The same applies to other federal States, which without exception have chosen to have a single currency. History also shows that monetary unification has most frequently gone hand in hand with trade integration.[28] One could therefore expect economic theory to provide the rationale for these empirical observations.

There is indeed a theory whose aim is to aid the analysis of monetary integration: the theory of optimum currency areas developed in the 1960s by Robert Mundell, Ronald McKinnon and others. The basic insight of this approach is that the adoption of a single currency involves a trade-off between, on the one hand, the benefits arising from monetary integration and, on the other hand, the costs incurred when the exchange rate is lost as an adjustment instrument. This insight remains valid and is taken as a basis for the present study. However, a precise and comprehensive identification of those costs and benefits is not provided by the theory of optimum currency areas, since (i) some of the benefits associated with monetary unification are assumed without further investigation, while others are simply omitted, and (ii) the framework for the analysis of costs is rather limited and outdated. The most well-known conclusion of this approach, namely that labour mobility across an area is the essential criterion for deciding whether monetary union is desirable, appears to be largely overstated in early formulations of the theory, at least as regards the EC. Moreover, economic theory has evolved substantially in several relevant branches since the early 1960s (Box 2.3), but the revision of the theory of optimal currency areas has not kept up with this. Thus, the analysis of EMU does not need to be limited to this rather narrow approach.

Recent developments in several branches of economics provide elements of a comprehensive approach to the costs and benefits of EMU.

1. Although almost no recent reserch has been specifically devoted to the microeconomics of monetary union — except the contribution by R. Baldwin, some recent developments in the microeconomics of imperfect markets (i.e. in presence of externalities, or adjustment and information costs) lead to a better if still incomplete understanding of the channels through which the adoption of a single currency would provide output and welfare gains.[29]

2. A large body of literature has been devoted to the question of the choice of an optimal exchange rate policy for a small economy in a stochastic environment, and thus in an environment of random disturbances.[30] The issue is which monetary and exchange rate policy performs best for reduc-

---

[25] However, as pointed out by Ingram (1973), most estimates of the benefits of the Common Market, made in advance of the economic realities, were close to zero.

[26] Paul Krugman (1990) states: 'The economics of international money, by contrast [to those of trade integration], are not at all well understood: they hinge crucially not only on sophisticated and ambiguous issues like credibility and coordination, but on even deeper issues like transaction costs and bounded rationality'.

[27] For example Krugman (1990), Baldwin (1990).

[28] A classic example is that of the German monetary unification in the nineteenth century, which followed a few years after the trade and economic unification under the Zollverein. See Holtfrerich (1989).

---

[29] See Chapter 3 and Baldwin (1990).

[30] See, for example, Marston (1985), Aizenman and Frenkel (1985). For a recent survey, see Argy (1990).

Box 2.3: EMU and the theory of optimum currency areas

The theory of optimum currency areas was developed in the 1960s in order to determine what should be the appropriate domain within which exchange rates are fixed.[31]

The question relates to the debate at that time between the proponents of exchange rate fixity and those of floating exchange rates. The basic argument for floating was twofold: first that exchange rate changes were a less costly way of correcting current account imbalances, and more generally of adjusting relative prices between two countries when prices are sticky, and second that it would allow countries to pursue independent macroeconomic policies (e.g. to choose different inflation rates).[32]

The optimum currency areas approach uses an implicit stabilization framework and introduces the issues of asymmetries and alternative adjustment channels when countries face exogenous shocks. Mundell (1961) points out that exchange rate flexibility is of no use between the US and Canada if, due to a shock to the industrial structure, both countries are hurt by a shift in the relative economic conditions of their eastern and western parts. What is needed instead is a change in the relative prices of eastern and western products. Therefore, the right criterion for designing a currency area should be the degree of factor (capital, i.e. physical investment, and labour) mobility within the region, since a high degree of factor mobility would provide the adjustment channel which is lost in a fixed exchange rate regime. It was precisely because of a low labour mobility within Europe that Meade (1957) argued that exchange rates should remain flexible within that zone. It became conventional wisdom to say that Europe was *not* an optimum currency area.

Although the overall approach remains a useful starting point, this conclusion only holds within a specific and rather limited framework whose adequacy for today's analysis is questionable. First, the microeconomic benefits of a monetary union are simply assumed without further exploration: in Mundell's words, 'money is a convenience and this restricts the optimum number of currencies'. Second, although labour mobility across Europe remains low — but it is also limited within the United States — the mobility of both physical and especially financial capital is now much higher than in the early 1960s. As pointed out by Ingram (1959, 1973), the degree of international financial integration has to be introduced as a specific criterion and the alternative adjustment channel of cross-country financing has

therefore to be taken into account. Third, Mundell's implicit framework is a world of rigid wages and prices. Although wage/price stickiness is still a fact of life, their rigidity could be less than in Mundell's framework, and the possibility of market adjustments has to be considered. Fourth, there is the implicit assumption that no inefficiencies arise from flexible exchange rates, such as because of instability in the exchange markets and non-cooperative or suboptimal policies. Obviously this can no longer be considered an acceptable hypothesis in the light of recent experience.

Fifth, the whole approach ignores policy credibility issues which have been stressed by recent macroeconomic theory. Six, the theory of optimum currency treats the whole area as a small country within a given world and thus it ignores the external effects of monetary integration.

The approaches of McKinnon (1963) and Kenen (1969) to this same topic are different. McKinnon points out that if exchange rate changes are used to offset the effects of domestic demand shocks on the current account, price instability is bound to increase in line with the degree of openness (or the share of tradables in production) in a floating rates regime. This is particularly relevant within the EC and is a major reason behind the long-standing choice of a peg system by smaller open economies like the Netherlands and Belgium. Moreover, Krugman (1990), building on this argument, argues that the costs of monetary union decrease and the benefits increase with the intensity of trade within the currency area. Kenen focuses on the degree of product diversification and argues that countries characterized by a low degree of diversification should retain exchange rate flexibility in order to offset product-specific shocks, while a high degree of product diversification, by averaging product-specific shocks, could compensate for low labour mobility. In practice EC countries typically have highly diversified industrial structures. The general issue of the impact of different industrial structures is discussed in Chapter 6.

Summing up, the optimum currency area approach provides useful insights but cannot be considered a comprehensive framework in which the costs and benefits of EMU can be analysed. Empirical applications of this approach are scarce and hardly conclusive.

---

[31] Major contributions include Mundell (1961), Mc Kinnon (1963), and Kenen (1969). For more recent surveys, see Ishiyama (1975), and Wihlborg and Willett (1990).
[32] See, for example, Friedman (1953).

ing aggregate macroeconomic variability, i.e. insulates better the economy from the effects of shocks. This line of research has established (i) that the choice between exchange rate regimes not only depends on the pattern of shocks (domestic or foreign, real or monetary) affecting the economy, but also on the degree of wage-price indexation; and that with full and instantaneous indexation, there is no difference whatsoever between fixed and floating rates, [33] and (ii) that neither fixed nor floating exchange rates are generally optimal, but rather that some country-dependent mix of the two regimes is preferable. [34]

3. Applications of game theory in the field of macro-economic policy have led to emphasize issues in the choice of an exchange rate regime which had been for long stressed by policymakers but were largely ignored by the literature of the 1960s. This approach leads to questioning the standard policy autonomy argument in favour of flexible exchange rates from two different angles. First, this autonomy might not be optimal from a political economy point of view, e.g. if domestic monetary authorities suffer from low credibility. [35] In such instances, policy discipline through the pegging of the exchange rate to a hard currency can be a short cut to a long and painful reputation-building. This line of research appears to be especially relevant in the European case, since for several countries, membership of the ERM has been perceived as a way to borrow the credibility of the Bundesbank. [36] Second, the risks of suboptimal outcomes when monetary policies separately aim at contradictory results have been stressed by the literature on policy coordination. [37]

4. Another domain of research concerns the relative performance of alternative monetary arrangements at the world level. Two decades of disappointing experience with floating exchange rates have stimulated new research on the causes of exchange rate instability and on possible remedies. [38] This research is of special relevance in the European case since the creation of EMU would bring more symmetry in the international monetary system and could therefore be a building block for wider changes in this system.

5. Last but not least, there is already a substantial and growing body of research on the economics of EMU which draws on all the above theories, and of which the papers presented in 'The economics of EMU' (*European Economy* (1990)) offer an up-to-date sample.

These developments in economic research do not yet provide an integrated approach to monetary union. One might doubt they ever will, since very different fields of economic theory are involved in the analysis of EMU: microeconomic efficiency has little to do with stability in a stochastic environment or with the rules-versus-discretion debate in macroeconomic policy. Recent contributions which, in the spirit of the optimum currency area approach, attempt to isolate a trade-off in the choice for or against EMU (seigniorage versus transaction costs, or insulation from shocks versus time-inconsistency [39]) only highlight partial aspects of the choice problem raised by EMU. In any case, much more research has to be done before these different branches can be linked together within a unified model of the welfare effects of international money.

However, empirical analysis can obtain results from these various fields as building blocks for a comprehensive approach to EMU. As detailed below, it turns out that this approach leads to basing the case for EMU on a much broader framework of analysis than that provided by the theory of optimal currency areas. While this report has no theoretical pretensions, the nature of the effects discussed in the analytical chapters can be taken as an indication of the scope that a full theory of monetary unions would have to encompass.

Before turning in more detail to the nature of costs and benefits, three important methodological points have to be made:

(i)   A number of questions arise whose answers rely on different paradigms. The use of a single currency yields efficiency gains which are much of the same nature as those arising from the elimination of physical and technical barriers to trade. The natural framework for

---

[33]   See Annex D for an analysis of the links between the speed of indexation and the cost of losing the exchange rate as an instrument.

[34]   Another, related approach stresses the relative information content of exchange rate regimes in rational expectation models. The emphasis is on the degree to which prices provide the right information to agents regarding the nature of the shocks affecting the economy under alternative exchange rate regimes. No strong result in favour of one regime or another emerges from this literature. See Wihlborg and Willett (1990) for a survey.

[35]   This might arise from public choice considerations, but also from the time-inconsistency argument. See Kydland and Prescott (1977), Barro and Gordon (1983).

[36]   See, for example, Giavazzi and Pagano (1988), and several contributions to Giavazzi, Micossi and Miller (1989).

[37]   For a recent survey, see Currie, Holtham and Hughes Hallett (1989).

[38]   See, for example, Williamson (1985), McKinnon (1988), Krugman (1990).

[39]   On the first aspect, see Canzioneri and Rogers (1989). On the second, see, for example, Van der Ploeg (1990).

the analysis of these effects is the classical microeconomic paradigm of competitive markets and flexible prices. The costs of losing the exchange rate instrument, however, only arises in a world of imperfect integration and sticky prices, i.e. within a Keynesian paradigm, since the whole macroeconomic issue of choice of an exchange rate regime is irrelevant if markets are perfectly integrated and prices fully flexible. Finally, the analysis of the credibility of EMU and of its effects for inflation discipline has to be based on a third paradigm, where considerations of political economy play an important role, together with theories of expectations and strategic behaviour. In all, therefore, one has to accept a somewhat eclectic approach.

(ii) Due to the present state of the theory, an attempt to make an overall quantitative evaluation of the costs and benefits of EMU would hardly be meaningful. Some of the effects that can be expected from EMU cannot be yet quantified, and others would only be evaluated with a considerable margin of uncertainty. For example, few results are available regarding the welfare costs of inflation, despite the fact that most economists and policymakers agree on the importance of these effects. Moreover, the lack of a unified theory would raise problems of inconsistency in the aggregation of effects of a different nature. This does not preclude partial quantifications, and indeed several such assessments of specific effects are given throughout this report.

(iii) Reliance on the most recent literature has the advantage of bringing in the most recent insights of current research, but also has its cost: results can be model-dependent, and are therefore less secure and widely accepted than with established theories. Empirical assessments also remain fragile and frequently disappointing.

2.2.2. Costs and benefits

According to the method sketched out above, the present costs-benefit analysis of EMU is based on the combination of different approaches. Major categories of effects have been presented in Chapter 1. The aim of this section is to present in more detail the categorization of effects and the methodology of the present study.

Direct and indirect effects of EMU

As presented in Graph 1.2 of Chapter 1, the final economic impacts of EMU will arise both directly from changes in the economic system of the Community, and indirectly through policy and behavioural changes induced by the systemic

changes. Although this is not a water-tight distinction since any change immediately impacts on the system as a whole, it is important to sort out indirect effects from direct ones since the latter are unconditional while the former are conditional on the policy stance of EuroFed and national fiscal authorities, and on the modifications in the behaviour of private agents that can be expected from both systemic and policy changes. For example, savings in transaction costs are an unconditional consequence of the adoption of a single currency which directly affects economic efficiency, while price stability is conditional on the policy of EuroFed and on wage and price discipline.

It could be argued that those effects which are conditional on the quality of economic policies should not be assessed as arising from EMU *per se*: whatever the institutional design of the system, it cannot be taken for granted that it will lead to more appropriate policies. However, as discussed above, policy discipline effects cannot be ignored as they are an integral part of the motives behind the choice of EMU. Indeed, it is well known that any exchange rate regime has disciplinary effects on economic policies, and this has for long been considered one of the prominent aspects of the choice of an exchange rate regime.

What can be expected is that an adequate design of the institutional system, notably in the statutes of EuroFed, or in the framework for budgetary policies, will yield benefits either because of a greater effectiveness of Community and national policies, or through a removal of the inefficiencies associated with low policy credibility, which have a strong impact on expectations and risk premiums incorporated in interest rates and other financial variables. As discussed in Chapter 4, an independent EuroFed with a clear mandate to achieve price stability would inherit the reputation of the most stability-oriented central banks of the Community. As to the budgetary regime, governments should retain fiscal flexibility for stabilization and adjustment purposes, but as public debt monetization would be ruled out, the avoidance of unsustainable fiscal positions would become an absolute requirement. There would also be a strengthening of coordination and surveillance procedures.

Throughout this study, it has been assumed that EuroFed would fulfil its mandate to aim at price stability. Regarding budgetary policies, it is generally assumed that Member States would not depart from disciplined policies. As the importance of these and of other explicit policy assumptions is highlighted when needed in the text, the reader should be able to distinguish between direct and indirect effects of EMU.

The same kind of issues arise for behavioural changes. It is well known that the behaviour of private agents cannot be supposed to remain invariant with respect to systemic or policy regime changes. Wage bargaining and price-setting behaviours, for example, are not independent from the policy of the central bank. However, there is no sure way to identify precisely the consequences of EMU on agents' behaviour, and excessive reliance on behavioural changes could also be misleading.

In most of this study, behaviour has only been supposed to be affected through the impact of the exchange rate and monetary policy regime on expectations. This means for example that wage-setting behaviour is supposed to be changed in so far as price expectations would be modified by the exchange rate and policy regime. [40] This assumption is warranted since EMU will not be a mere unilateral commitment to exchange rate stability, but rather an institutional change whose impact should be clear for all agents (especially with the adoption of a single currency). It has also been assumed that the policy of EuroFed would be as credible to the public as the policy of the more stability-oriented central banks of the Community. The possibility of deeper changes in behaviour is discussed (for example in Chapter 6 as regards wage and price flexibility), but the assessment of EMU does not rely upon this type of assumption.

The distinction between direct and indirect effects, which refers to the channels of action, should not be mistaken for that between static and dynamic effects, which refers to the time dimension. Static effects are supposed to arise at the outset of EMU, or possibly with some lag. These are for instance savings on transaction costs or the benefits of stable prices. Dynamic effects are those which only build up progressively over time, because capital accumulation or other stock adjustments are involved. They translate into an increase in the rate of economic growth for a substantial period. This is the case for the effects of a lower riskiness of investment, but it also arises when hysteresis is at work, as for example in the emergence of the ecu as a major international currency. [41]

Costs and benefits in outline

Regarding the permanent effects of EMU, three major categories of final impacts have been distinguished in Chapter 1, which relate to microeconomic efficiency, macroeconomic stability, and regional equity. In addition, EMU will give rise to important transitional effects, mainly of a macroeconomic nature. Costs and benefits of EMU, grouped in these four major categories, are summarized in Table 2.5. For the sake of clarity, external effects resulting from the consequences of EMU for the Community's relations with the rest of the world are presented separately from purely internal effects, although they have the same type of final impact.

The major costs and benefits of EMU are discussed in the chapters of Part B below together with some associated policy issues. As this analysis does not follow the above categorization, but rather isolates groups of policy issues (the 5 domains and 16 mechanisms detailed in Chapter 1), Table 2.5 gives a summary presentation of the main effects with reference to the chapters in which they are discussed.

(a) Microeconomic efficiency effects, which are presented in Chapter 3, are basically of the same nature as those arising from the completion of the internal market. [42] They proceed from two microeconomic phenomena in the monetary field (the disappearance of exchange rate uncertainty and transaction costs) and one in the economic field (measures to strengthen the internal market, e.g. competition policy). Although, as detailed in Chapter 3 and in Baldwin (1990), the microeconomics of monetary union raise difficult technical issues, the basic logic is straightforward: EMU yields (i) direct benefits arising from savings on transaction and hedging costs; (ii) indirect benefits due to the impact on trade, cross-border investment and capital flows of the disappearance of exchange rate barriers; and (iii) further dynamic benefits due to the impact on domestic investment decisions of an overall reduction in uncertainty (conditional on the stability gains brought by EuroFed policy).

Efficiency gains are microeconomic in nature but would obviously translate into macroeconomic effects. They can ultimately be expected to raise permanently the level of output and real income in the Community because of a higher overall factor productivity and a higher capital stock, in the same way as the completion of the internal market is expected to yield output and income gains. During the transition to this higher steady-state, growth would be increased. According to 'new growth models', there is even the possibility of a sustained rise in the GDP growth rate of the Community. This remains, however, a conjecture. [43]

---

[40]   The exact definition of a behavioural change depends on the model which is used to represent behaviours. For example, changes in the reaction of wages to an inflationary shock as a consequence of monetary union would be assessed as an exogenous change in behaviour in a model with adaptive expectations, though it would only be an endogenous reaction to the regime change in a model with forward-looking expectations. See Annex E for further discussion.

[41]   There is a slight difference in terminology on this point between this study and the Report on the economics of 1992 in *European Economy* (1988a).

[42]   See *European Economy* (1988a).

[43]   See Chapter 3 and Baldwin and Lyons (1990).

Table 2.5

Major categories of effects of EMU

	Nature of the final impact	Main channels of action	
		Direct	Indirect
Microeconomic efficiency	Steady state level of output and income in the Community	Savings in transaction and hedging costs[3]	Strengthening of the internal market[3]
		Disappearance of exchange rate uncertainty and instability[3, 6]	Integration of goods and capital markets[3]
			Effects of lower uncertainty on the riskiness of investment[3]
			Induced dynamic effects[3]
			Seigniorage revenue losses for some Member States[5]
			Effects on taxation and provision of public goods[5]
Macroeconomic stability	Steady state rate of inflation Variability of output and inflation, with associated consequences for welfare	Loss of an adjustment instrument for asymmetric shocks[6]	Price stability as consequence of EuroFed policy[4]
		Disappearance of non-cooperative exchange rate policies[6]	Sound, coordinated fiscal policies[5]
		Greater availability of external financing[6]	
Regional equity	Distributional effects among Member States and regions	Spatial distribution of direct micro and macro gains[9, 10]	Differentiated impacts of EMU depending on initial macroeconomic conditions and economic policy strategies[9, 10]
External effects	Both micro and macro effects for the Community	Additional savings on transaction costs, revenues from international seigniorage and reduction in the need for exchange reserves[7]	Better coordination internationally[7] Changes in the international monetary system[7]
Transitional effects	Changes in the macroeconomic transition path towards EMU	Disinflation costs[8] Costs of fiscal adjustment[5, 8]	Drop in real interest rates[5] Effects on the dollar/ecu exchange rate[7]

Note: numbers in brackets refer to the chapters of this study.

As for any efficiency gains, there will also be temporary negative effects and adjustments in the short run, for example as the foreign exchange activities of banks decrease.

To a large extent, gains of this category are not conditional on macroeconomic policies. Some would nevertheless disappear if inadequate policies were to give rise to macroeconomic instability. In addition, for EMU to yield efficiency gains in the medium run, real exchange rate levels within the Community have to be consistent with economic fundamentals. Although an initial misalignment could be eventually corrected through relative price movements without changing the nominal exchange rate, it could in the meantime have severe welfare-reducing effects. It is therefore important that initial levels are in line with fundamentals. This assumption is maintained throughout this study.

In addition to its effects on the private sector, EMU will also affect taxation and the provision of public goods, and more generally public sector efficiency. This topic is discussed in Chapter 5.

(b) Macroeconomic stability effects, which are discussed in Chapters 4 and 6, are of a different nature. These effects concern the variability of macroeconomic variables, both nominal and real. Variability arises as a consequence of policy and non-policy shocks of a domestic (e.g. non-permanent changes in the behaviour of private agents) or external (e.g. a change in a partner country's economic policy) origin. This is an important topic for two reasons. First, variability in macroeconomic variables like the price level, inflation, [44] GDP and employment is welfare-reducing *per se* for risk-adverse agents, even if their average level remains unaffected (see Box 2.4). Second, aggregate variability also permanently influences the level of output, at least if it goes with greater uncertainty, because it reduces the information content of prices and leads to an increase in risk premiums.[45]

Regarding stability, EMU yields both permanent costs and benefits. The net impact in terms of macroeconomic stability in EMU is therefore an empirical issue. The main costs arise from the loss of a policy instrument for stabilization (Chapter 6). Once exchange rates are irrevocably fixed, national monetary policies can no longer be used to cushion the effects of asymmetric disturbances, either through market adjustments (as in a floating rate regime) or through discretionary exchange rate adjustments (as in the EMS). In this respect the loss of the monetary and exchange rate policy at the national level has to be considered a cost as long as wages and prices do not fully and instantaneously respond to a disequilibrium in the labour or goods markets. This is the basic optimum currency area argument, which obviously only applies to relativities, since the common monetary policy can be used to cushion the impact of common shocks.

In addition to the benefits already discussed resulting from the extension of price stability to all Member States (Chapter 4), significant gains would arise from the removal of inefficiencies associated with exchange rate flexibility (Chapter 6). Exchange rate instability, i.e. that part of its variability which does not result from fundamental changes in policies or in the economy more generally is harmful, because it impacts on macroeconomic variables like inflation and output, therefore increasing their variability.[46] The re-

moval of this market failure would be stabilizing.[47] Another effect concerns failures of governments and authorities to act in a cooperative fashion. Non-cooperative monetary and exchange rate policies are welfare-reducing, for example if each government separately aims to export the adverse consequences of a common inflationary shock through exchange rate appreciation. This risk would disappear in EMU. In addition, the alternative adjustment mechanism of external financing exists, and its availability is increased by exchange rate fixity.

Admittedly, the EMS already removes at least part of exchange rate instability, and reduces the risk of non-cooperative policies since realignments are not unilaterally decided but negotiated. The same would hold in Stage I. This is a clear benefit, but this also goes with a cost because of asymmetry in monetary policy. As long as one national central bank sets the pace for monetary policy in the Community as a whole, policy reactions to asymmetric shocks are unlikely to be optimal since the legitimate objective of the national central bank is to seek the stability of domestic prices in its national economy. For example, if the French economy were hit by an inflationary shock there would be no case for the Bundesbank to tighten its policy.[48] In EMU, the policy of EuroFed would be more symmetric and would only react to country-specific developments which affect price stability in the Community as a whole.[49]

(c) Regional equity effects concern the distribution of costs and benefits among Member States and regions. Differences in industrial structure, size and level of development, or foreign trade patterns can significantly affect the balance of costs and benefits across Member States. For example, the analysis of transaction costs shows that these are higher for smaller countries, which rarely use their own currency in trade invoicing and whose financial markets lack depth. Initial macroeconomic conditions are also an important factor to take into account, as differences in inflation rates or fiscal conditions can alter the extent of policy changes brought about by EMU, at least transitionally. These issues are taken up Chapters 9 and 10. The specific role of the Community budget is discussed in Chapter 6.

(d) External effects which are the topic of Chapter 7 originate in the large size of the Community in the world economy. Due to its size, the effects of EMU would not be

---

[44] Variability in prices, i.e. inflation, has to be distinguished from variability in inflation, i.e. in the change in the rate of increase of prices. Theoretically prices can be rising while the rate of inflation is stable. However, in practice inflation and its variability are correlated (see Chapter 4).
[45] See Chapter 3 and Baldwin (1990).
[46] Exchange rate instability has to be distinguished from variability and uncertainty. Variability refers to the observed changes in exchange rates. Uncertainty refers to the unanticipated component of these changes. Instability refers to that part of variability which cannot be explained by changes in policies or other economic fundamentals.

[47] Obviously, this is only true in so far as the variability of other variables (e.g. the dollar exchange rate) does not increase as a consequence of intra-Community exchange-rate fixity. This issue is discussed in Chapter 3.
[48] Except for offsetting the effects of spill-overs of French inflation on Germany.
[49] See Chapter 6, especially the results from stochastic simulation.

limited to the Community but would also have an impact on the international monetary and economic system. First, the ecu would become one of the major world currencies alongside the dollar and the yen, and could acquire a vehicular role in trade and finance for EC residents as well as non-residents. This could bring additional savings on transaction costs, yield some revenues from international seigniorage, and impact on macroeconomic stability. Second, the Community would be able to engage more effectively in international policy coordination and to speak with a single voice in international monetary affairs. More generally, policy coordination at the G7 level would be transformed as the number of large players would be basically reduced to three. This would also impact on macroeconomic stability. Finally, both moves could ultimately induce wide-ranging changes in the international monetary system.

(e) Transitional effects are discussed in the analytical chapters and summarized in Chapter 8. These effects differ from permanent ones which arise in comparing a steady-state EMU to an alternative steady-state, generally assumed to be '1992 + EMS' (but alternative baselines are also discussed). Only these effects represent the durable benefits and costs of EMU. However, since the starting point may not be a steady state, and indeed is surely not such for some countries, the costs and benefits of a relatively rapid move towards EMU have to be considered compared to those which would arise from a lengthy convergence within the framework of Stage I. In particular, as discussed in Chapter 5, a number of Member States still suffer from low exchange rate and monetary policy credibility, and therefore from relatively high real *ex-post* interest rates. Although most if not all of these phenomena would disappear in the due course in a steady-state Stage I, experience shows this is a lengthy process. A more prompt move towards EMU could significantly affect the balance of macroeconomic costs and benefits in the transition towards low inflation and budgetary positions (Chapter 8). Transitional issues also arise in the external field, as an increase in the demand for ecu assets could lead to an appreciation of the Community currency (Chapter 7).

Methodology of evaluations

Strictly speaking, the effects of EMU should only be deemed positive or negative with respect to an explicit welfare function. Aggregation of these effects would also imply the choice of a common yardstick, which as discussed in Box 2.4 could only rest on some rather arbitrary assumptions. In practice, this has not been necessary, since no overall quantitative evaluation has been attempted. However, as several partial evaluations are given in this study, issues of comparability and relative importance arise. Table 2.6 attempts to summarize the major elements which contribute to this evaluation.

The categories of effects distinguished above relate to different fields of economic theory, and to some extent to different paradigms, as summarized in the first two columns of Table 2.6. This has consequences for the methods and instruments of evaluation that are available and on the possibility of quantifying the different effects.

(a) For microeconomic efficiency effects, the natural focus is on their permanent impact on the levels of output and welfare. The associated framework of analysis is therefore the classical full employment/flexible prices model, since these assumptions are standard for the long run.[51] However in the textbook versions of the standard microeconomic model, where transaction costs are zero and adjustments are costless, and where all agents have perfect information and no aversion towards risk, exchange rate regimes are neutral. Gains from a move towards monetary union arise when these oversimplifying assumptions are relaxed, which frequently implies using recent insights from research in progress.

Evaluation techniques are diverse. Gains from the elimination of transaction costs can be directly assessed using surveys and data on bank balance sheets, provided assumptions are made regarding the respective effects of capital market liberalization and the adoption of a single currency. The assessment of indirect effects is more partial and tentative since, firstly, only some aspects are quantified, and secondly evaluations with present models are bound to provide orders of magnitude, rather than precise figures. Dynamic gains are evaluated using either calibrated standard growth models, or the more recent endogenous growth models.

The time horizon corresponding to these effects is short for the most direct ones, like the elimination of transaction and hedging costs. Indirect and dynamic effects can normally be expected to accrue over many years if not decades, but the experience with the internal market tends to show that favourable expectations can lead firms to increase investment even before the policy measures are effectively implemented.

(b) The basic framework of analysis for macroeconomic stability effects is that of neo-Keynesian models, which are characterized by sticky wages and prices in the short run. Only in this kind of model can the loss of the exchange rate instrument be assessed. However, this framework has to be extended to encompass also policy discipline effects.

---

51 'Full employment' does not mean that there is indeed full employment in the baseline, but only that the long run refers to the horizon where short-term unemployment effects of efficiency gains are eliminated.

Box 2.4: Measurement issues in the cost/benefits analysis

EMU will have three concurrent types of impact:

(i)   on the level of output in the steady-state and the path towards this new equilibrium;

(ii) on its variability in a stochastic environment (i.e. characterized by the occurrence of random economic shocks);

(iii) inflation and other macroeconomic variables are also affected in both the foregoing ways.

(i) Effects which impact on the level of output (mostly efficiency effects) can be measured either in terms of output or in terms of welfare. The output measure can be related directly to usual macroeconomic statistics (GDP), but it is 'gross', since it does not take into account the cost of forgoing present consumption in order to accumulate capital. The welfare measure, which is derived from microeconomic utility considerations, is theoretically more appropriate. However it is less easy to grasp and rests on assumptions concerning among other things the rate of time preference. Both measures are close to each other in the case of direct, static efficiency gains, but can differ widely as soon as intertemporal issues are involved.

(ii) Variability in macroeconomic variables raises in addition the issue of risk aversion. Only for risk-neutral individuals and firms would temporary deviations from equilibrium not be welfare-reducing, provided they are averaged over time. The welfare cost of variability *per se* is however not of the same nature as the welfare cost of, for example, a permanent income loss. Aggregation of level and variability effects could only rest on a measure of risk aversion.

(iii) Taking into account other macroeconomic variables implies relying on a weighting of these variables. Due to the non-availability of a social welfare function derived from the utility functions of individuals, economists usually use macroeconomic welfare functions that are supposed to reflect policy preferences (and the welfare of the general public, provided policymakers express the preferences of this public). Here also, evaluations have to rest on some rather arbitrary quantitative assumptions regarding the weighting of deviations of output and inflation from their optimal level. [50]

An overall measurement of the effects of EMU would have been vulnerable to changes in technical assumptions regarding the parameters discussed above. For the partial quantifications which are given in this study, reliance is placed mostly on usual statistics, i.e. output rather than welfare, and generally to discuss the results of macroeconomic model simulations in terms of changes in familiar variables rather than on the basis of a macro welfare function.

[50]   A specific problem is that the weight of inflation in usual macro welfare functions (which attempts to reflect the preferences of policymakers) cannot be based on micro-economic grounds. See Blanchard and Fisher (1989), Chapter 11.

Table 2.6

Assumptions and methods of quantitative evaluations of EMU

	Underlying theories	Main assumptions	Methods and instruments	Quantitative assessment
Microeconomic efficiency	Microeconomics of imperfect markets	Flexible prices and full employment (long run)	Direct evaluations and surveys (transaction costs)	Substantial for direct effects
	Growth theory ('old' and 'new')	Information and adjustment costs, risk aversion	Computations with calibrated growth models	Partial and tentative for indirect and dynamic effects
Macroeconomic stability	Macroeconomic theory	Sticky prices and underemployment (short run)	Econometric techniques	Partial evaluation for analytical purposes
	Game-theoretic approach to economic policy	Imperfect credibility	Deterministic simulations with macro models	Attempt at a synthetic quantification through stochastic simulations
	Political economy		Stochastic simulations	
Regional equity	Both micro and macro approaches	As for micro and macro	No specific instrument	No quantitative assessment for individual Member States
	Theory of economic integration			
External	International monetary economics	Relaxation of the 'small country' assumption	No specific instrument	Only for specific effects
	Theory of international policy coordination			
Transitional effects	As for macro stability	As for macro stability	No specific instrument	Only for specific effects

The degree of wage-price rigidity, and the associated costs of losing the exchange rate instrument, can be evaluated using econometric techniques or the estimates incorporated in empirical macroeconomic models (Box 2.5). However standard methods can provide only some analytical elements rather than comprehensive assessment, since (i) deterministic simulations only evaluate the effects of single, specific shocks, and (ii) the impact of a change in the monetary regime on the behaviour of agents is not taken into account. Both limitations can be overcome through stochastic simulations with a model incorporating forward-looking features. The results of these simulations represent the average behaviour of an economy facing randomly distributed shocks, under different exchange rate regimes. They provide therefore a synthetic assessment. But this also is not fully comprehensive as some other gains resulting from the availability of alternative adjustment mechanisms or from the elimination of non-cooperative exchange rate behaviour are not taken into account.

Generally speaking, this type of macroeconomic stability effects will arise as soon as exchange rates are irrevocably fixed. The time horizon corresponding to this category of effects can be assessed to be about five years for specific shocks since as discussed in Chapter 6, the real effects of nominal exchange rates changes do not last longer.

Policy discipline effects also concern macroeconomic stability, but instead of focusing on the availability and effectiveness of policy instruments, the approach here focuses on their possible misuses. As already mentioned, the corresponding analytical framework stresses both the nature of economic policies that monetary authorities and governments can be expected to follow within a given framework of incentives and their interaction with private agents who form expectations regarding future policies.

Quantification of such effects is difficult since (i) the effectiveness of the EMU policy framework can only be a matter of judgment, (ii) there is only a weak causal link between a given framework of incentives and the policies which are effectively followed, and (iii) credibility varies over time and cannot generally be directly observed. Experience with the EMS provides a good reference since the system has evolved from merely an exchange rate stabilizing device into a very effective disciplinary device without major institutional changes. Only partial computations are therefore given (mostly as regards transitional aspects), which aim at indicating orders of magnitude; they do not represent a comprehensive assessment of the policy discipline effects of EMU. Model simulations are also provided for illustrative purposes.

It is difficult to establish which part of policy discipline effects can be expected to be reaped at the outset of Stage III, and which part will only arise after the reputation of EuroFed is established and fiscal coordination and surveillance procedures have proven effective.

(c) The evaluation of regional equity effects relies on the same approaches as micro and macroeconomic evaluations, supplemented by insights from the theory of economic integration. Conclusions regarding the regional impact of EMU are drawn from this analysis, but no specific attempt at a country-by-country quantitative evaluation has been made. The time horizon for these effects is the same as for micro and macroeconomic effects.

(d) The analysis of external effects rests on the standard framework for the study of international monetary regimes. Data are provided to give an assessment of possible changes in the international use of currencies, but no quantitative evaluations of the associated gains are given except for very direct and specific effects like the reduction on transaction costs or the revenues from international seigniorage. Indeed, a large part of the gains one can expect in this field depends on the behaviour of third countries, since EMU will only create opportunities for change in international monetary cooperation.

A large part of the external effects of EMU can be expected to arise only in the medium to long run, because of hysteresis in the international role of currencies and of the delays required for systemic changes in international monetary relations.

(e) Transitional effects are basically of a macroeconomic nature. The same approaches have been used as for evaluating macroeconomic stability effects, especially as regards issues of credibility and policy discipline.

Costs and benefits of alternative exchange rate regimes

It has been argued in Section 2.1.1 that for comprehensiveness, benefits and costs of EMU should not only be assessed with respect to the '1992 + EMS' baseline but also in comparison to alternative exchange rate regimes. Since this is obviously a very wide issue, only the main arguments will be given here. For this purpose, Table 2.7 gives in a schematic fashion the costs and benefits of the three 'pure' regimes of Graph 2.3: financial markets autarky, free float and EMU.

The costs of financial autarky are immediately apparent: microeconomic efficiency is bound to be low due to a complete segmentation of capital markets; no significant external influence can be expected for the Community as priority is given to autonomy over coordination and collective influ

Box 2.5: Macroeconomic models for EMU simulations

Two different multi-country macroeconomic models have been used for evaluating some of the effects of EMU.

The Quest model of the Commission's services is a medium-sized quarterly model in the neo-Keynesian tradition. As a structural model, it involves a complete representation of the national economies and of their trade linkages. The 1989 version which has been used for this study incorporates individual structural models of four Member States (France, Germany, Italy, United Kingdom) and the US. [52] Exchange rates in Quest are exogenous, i.e. the exchange rate is considered as a policy instrument. This approximates to the situation within the EMS, as a country facing an adverse shock can settle upon a realignment in order to offset the impact of the shock. Simulations therefore provide some assessment of the cost of losing this instrument.

Quest, however, cannot be used for an evaluation of the macroeconomic stability properties of alternative exchange rate regimes (including float), for such an evaluation requires, first, that exchange rates are endogenous, and second that the model takes into account that a change of regime impacts on the behaviour of agents. This second requirement originates in the 'Lucas critique' of policy evaluation with econometric models, according to which changes in policy regime alter the behavioural parameters of the model. [53] Its theoretical relevance in the case of a regime change like EMU is indisputable, especially for the adoption of a single currency, since the nature of this change, its permanent character and the associated constraints would be highly visible for and credible to all agents. The extent of these changes in behaviour is however an empirical issue.

The Multimod model developed at the IMF responds to a large extent to these two problems. [54] The forward-looking financial block of this small annual model of the G7 economies involves an endogenous determination of exchange rates through a financial arbitrage condition (under the assumptions of perfect capital mobility, complete asset substitutability, and perfect foresight), whereas the real sector incorporates in a simplified fashion both backward- and forward-looking features. When simulating the effects of shocks under different regimes, it is assumed that agents have full knowledge of the structure of the economy and

therefore of the consequences of the shock. [55] However, wage-price stickiness (which can be due to multi-year contracts) and liquidity constraints imply short-term departures from equilibrium in the Keynesian tradition.

The specific features of Multimod make it a suitable instrument for an examination of macroeconomic stability in EMU, either through deterministic simulations which attempt at evaluating the effects of the same shock under alternative regimes, or through stochastic simulations whose aim is to provide an overall quantitative assessment of these regimes in an environment of random disturbances. However Multimod has its weak points too. First, it is a highly aggregated model which sometimes rests on simplifying assumptions, especially when compared to structural models like Quest. Second, the estimation strategy followed by the IMF team has been to incorporate only significant parameter differences across countries, which is both a strength (because of the uncertainty surrounding these asymmetries) and a weakness (because the precision of individual equations is reduced). Third, as a forward-looking model Multimod tends to exhibit much less nominal rigidity than standard macro models, and more generally a stronger tendency to revert to the baseline equilibrium. Since the estimation of forward-looking models raises a number of technical difficulties, there is a certain degree of uncertainty in this field too. Fourth and conversely, although regime changes impact on behaviour through expectations, it is still possible that some genuine behavioural changes regarding, for example, investment or wage behaviours arising from EMU, are ignored.

Due to the different characteristics of the two models, it has been chosen to specialize each in a certain type of simulations. The main purpose of the Quest simulations is to evaluate the cost of losing the exchange rate as an instrument in a standard target-instrument policy framework, whereas Multimod simulations are devoted to the overall assessment of the consequences of EMU for macroeconomic stability. However, results from both models can also be considered as representing the uncertainty surrounding the true model of the economy and therefore the range of possible effects of EMU.

Model simulations are presented in Chapters 5 and 6. Detailed results, methodology and technical elements are given in Annexes D and E.

---

[52] For an overall presentation of Quest, from which the version used in this study however differs in some respects, see Bekx, Bucher, Italianer and Mors (1989). Models for other EC Member States and Japan are under development. In the present Quest model, feedbacks from the rest of the world are however incorporated in a reduced form.
[53] See Lucas (1976).
[54] Commission services are grateful to the IMF for providing the latest version of Multimod as well as technical support, but the simulations have been carried out under their sole responsibility. Neither the results nor possible errors should be attributed in any way to the IMF.

[55] Technically, expectations are model-consistent, which means that in deterministic simulations future values of variables and the impact on the behaviour of agents are known (obviously, this is not the case for unanticipated shocks). For a general presentation of Multimod, see Masson, Symansky and Meredith (1990). The version used in this study differs from the one presented in this paper, due to minor changes introduced in the version used at the Commission.

Table 2.7

A schematic presentation of costs and benefits of alternative exchange rate regimes

	Financial autarky	Free float	EMU
Microeconomic efficiency	low	medium	high
Macroeconomic stability:			
(a) In the presence of shocks			
Asymmetric shocks	low	high	low
Symmetric shocks	medium	low	high
Exchange rate instability	high	low	high
(b) Resulting from policy discipline			
Monetary credibility	medium	country-dependent	high
Fiscal discipline	country-dependent	medium	medium
External influence	low	low	high

ence-building. The average macroeconomic performance can also be expected to be poor in a regime characterized by the need for each country to achieve external balance: asymmetric shocks but also symmetric ones, if policy reactions differ, would give rise to balance-of-payment crises as in the 1970s. Only for shocks that arise from exchange rate instability can this regime achieve a fair performance. Finally, policy discipline is not high in such a regime since external pressures only arise when the country experiences a current account deficit. As past experience consistently shows, this is at most a second best since current account deficits exhibit only a weak and at least delayed correlation with either monetary or fiscal mismanagement.

The arguments for free float are well known: each country has maximum policy autonomy and, provided wage-price indexation is not complete in the short run, exchange-rate changes can cushion asymmetric shocks. In spite of these arguments, however, the performance of flexible exchange rates is generally considered disappointing for several reasons. First, exchange rate variability is an obstacle to microeconomic efficiency: as shown by the recent US experience, wide exchange rate swings degrade the quality of price signals and lead firms to adopt 'wait and see' attitudes;[56] moreover, exchange rate misalignments imply significant welfare losses, especially when adjustment costs are important. Secondly, stabilizing properties of floating exchange rates are only apparent while facing country-specific, i.e. asymmetric real shocks; symmetric shocks, especially supply shocks, give rise to beggar-thy-neighbour exchange rate poli-

cies as each country tries to export inflation or unemployment; moreover, monetary shocks to the exchange rate itself, which arise from failures in the international financial markets, are a source of instability. Thirdly, policy autonomy in a floating rates regime implies that no strong effects on policy discipline can be expected. Finally, individual participation of Member States in a floating rates regime cannot be expected to increase the influence of the Community as a whole.

Over the whole range of effects considered in Table 2.7, the only important disadvantage of EMU concerns macroeconomic stability in the presence of asymmetric shocks. This is indeed a well-known argument and has unambiguously to be considered a cost, but one that should be weighted against the clear advantages EMU yields in other fields.

Although for most Member States neither a pure floating regime nor financial autarky are real alternatives to EMU, the qualitative framework of arguments presented points to the basic features of its costs and benefits when compared to hybrid regimes that could represent possible alternatives. As already discussed, an important methodological choice of the present study is to assess the costs and benefits of EMU as compared to a '1992 + EMS' baseline, in spite of the rather hypothetical character of some of its features and of the diversity of present situations among Member States regarding their participation in the ERM. In so far as the risk of systemic instability in Stage I could lead the system to a reversion to some kind of pre-Stage I regime (i.e. some loosely defined mix of capital controls and crawling peg as in the early EMS), it is apparent that the net benefit of EMU could only be greater.

---

[56]   See Baldwin (1988), Dixit (1989), and for a general discussion Krugman (1989 b).

References

Aglietta, M. (1988), 'Régimes monétaires, monnaie supranationale, monnaie commune'. Communication à la Conférence internationale de Barcelone sur la théorie de la régulation, June.

Aglietta, M., Coudert, V. and Delessy, H. (1990), 'Politiques budgétaires et ajustements macro-économiques dans la perspective de l'intégration monétaire européenne', in *Lectures critiques du rapport Delors*, De Pecunia Vol. II, No 2-3, Brussels, September.

Aizenman, J. and Frenkel, J.A.(1985), 'Optimal wage indexation, foreign exchange intervention, and monetary policy', *American Economic Review*, Vol. 75, No 3, June.

Argy, V. (1989), 'Choice of exchange rate regime for a smaller economy — A survey of some key issues', in *Choosing an exchange rate regime: the challenge for smaller industrial countries*, edited by V. Argy and P. De Grauwe, CEPS/IMF.

Artus, P. (1990), 'Epargne nationale, investissement et intégration internationale', Document de travail 1990-17/T, Caisse des Dépôts et Consignations.

Backus and Drifill, J., (1985), 'Inflation and reputation', *American Economic Review*, June.

Balassa, B. (1964), 'The purchasing power parity doctrine: a reappraisal', *Journal of Political Economy*, December.

Baldwin, R. (1988), 'Hysteresis in import prices: the beachhead effect', *American Economic Review*, Vol. 78, No 4, September.

Baldwin, R. (1990), 'On the microeconomics of EMU', in *European Economy* (1990).

Baldwin, R. and Krugman, P. (1987), 'The persistence of the US trade deficit', *Brookings Papers on Economic Activity* No 1.

Baldwin, R. and Lyons, R. (1990), 'External economics and European integration: the potential for self-fulfilling expectations', in *European Economy* (1990).

Barro, R.J. and Gordon, D. (1983), 'A critical theory of monetary policy in a natural rate model', *Journal of Political Economy*, 91, pp. 589-610, August.

Bekx, P., Bucher, A, Italianer, A. and Mors, M. (1989), 'The Quest model (version 1988)', *EC Economic Papers* No 75, March.

Blanchard, O. J. and Fisher, S. (1989), *Lectures on macroeconomics*, MIT Press, Cambridge.

Canzoneri, M. and Rogers, C. A. (1989), 'Is the European Community an optimal currency area? Optimal taxation versus the cost of multiple currencies', *American Economic Review*, November.

Carli, G. (1989), *The evolution towards economic and monetary union: a response to the HM Treasury Paper*, Ministerio del Tesoro, December.

Casella, A. (1990), 'Participation in a monetary union', NBER Working Paper No 3220, January.

Currie, A., Holtham, G. and Hughes Hallett, A. (1989), 'The theory and practice of international policy coordination: does coordination pay?' in *Macroeconomic policies in an interdependent world*, edited by R. Bryant, D. Currie, R. Portes, CEPR/The Brookings Institution/IMF.

Dixit, A. (1989), 'Entry and exit decisions under uncertainty', *Journal of Political Economy*, Vol. 97, pp. 620ff.

Driffill, J. (1988), 'The stability and sustainability of the European Monetary System with perfect capital markets', in *The European Monetary System*, edited by F. Giavazzi, S. Micossi and M. Miller, Banca d'Italia/CEPR.

European Economy (1988a), 'The economics of 1992', No 35, March.

European Economy (1988b), 'Creation of a European financial area', Special issue No 36, May.

European Economy (1990), 'The economics of EMU', special issue.

Flood, R., Bhandari, J. and Horne, J. (1989), 'Evolution of exchange rate regimes', *IMF Staff Papers*, Vol. 36, No 4, December.

Friedman, M. (1953), 'The case for flexible exchange rates', in *Essays in Positive Economics*, The University of Chicago Press.

Genberg, H. (1989), 'In the shadow of the mark: exchange rate and monetary policy in Austria and Switzerland'. in

Choosing an exchange rate regime: the challenge for smaller industrial countries, edited by V. Argy and P. De Grauwe, CEPS/IMF.

Giavazzi, F. and Giovannini, A. (1989), *The European Monetary System*, MIT Press, Cambridge.

Giavazzi, F., Micossi, S. and Miller, M, eds (1988), *The European Monetary System*, Cambridge University Press.

Giavazzi, F. and Spaventa, L. (1990), 'The new EMS', CEPR Discussion Paper No 369, January

Giavazzi, F. and Pagano, M. (1988), 'The advantage of tying one's hands', *European Economic Review*, June.

Giovannini A. (1989), 'How do fixed exchange rate regimes work? Evidence from the gold standard Bretton Woods and the EMS', *Blueprints for exchange rate management*, January.

Gros, D. (1990), 'The EMS without capital controls', *Ecu Newsletter*, No 30, pp. 22-26, October.

HM Treasury (1989), *An evolutionary approach to economic and monetary union*, London, November.

Hochreiter, E. and Törnqvist, A. (1990), 'Austria's monetary and exchange rate policy — Some comparative remarks with respect to Sweden', in *Lectures critiques du rapport Delors*, De Pecunia Vol. II, No 2-3, Brussels, September.

Holtfrerich, C. L. (1989), 'The monetary unification process in nineteenth-century Germany: relevance and lessons for Europe today', in *A European Central Bank?*, edited by M. De Cecco and A. Giovannini, IPMG/CEPR, Cambridge University Press.

Ingram, J. C. (1959), 'State and regional payments mechanisms', *Quarterly Journal of Economics* No 73, November, pp. 619-632.

Ingram, J. C. (1973), 'The case for European monetary integration', *Princeton essays in international finance*, No 98, Princeton University, April.

Ishiyama, Y. (1975), 'The theory of optimum currency areas: a survey', *IMF Staff Papers* 22.

Kenen, P. B. (1969), 'The theory of optimum currency areas: an eclectic view', in *Monetary problems of the international economy*, edited by R. A. Mundell and A. K. Swoboda, University of Chicago Press.

Krugman, P. (1989a), *Exchange rate instability*, MIT Press, Cambridge, Massachussetts.

Krugman, P. (1989b), 'Policy problems of a monetary union', paper prepared for the CEPR/Bank of Greece Conference on the EMS in the 1990s.

Kydland, F. E. and Prescott, E.C. (1977), 'Rules rather than discretion: the inconsistency of optimal plans'. *Journal of Political Economy*, Vol. 85, No 3.

Lucas, R. E. (1976), 'Econometric policy evaluation: a critique', in Brunner, K. and Meltzer, A. H. (eds), *The Phillips curve and labor markets*, Carnegie-Rochester Conference Series on Public Policy 1, pp. 19-46.

Marston, R. C. (1984), 'Exchange rate unions as an alternative to flexible rates: the effects of real and monetary disturbances', in J. O. Bilson and R. C. Marston (eds), *Exchange rate theory and practice*, NBER/University of Chicago Press.

Marston, R. C. (1985), 'Stabilization policies in open economies', in *Handbook of international economics*, Vol. II, edited by R. Jones and P. Kenen, Elsevier Science Publishers.

Masson, P., Symansky, S., and Meredith, G. (1990), 'Multimod Mark II: A revised and extended model', IMF Occasional Paper No 71, July.

McKinnon, R. I. (1963), 'Optimum currency areas', *American Economic Review*, Vol. 53, pp 717-725, September.

McKinnon, R. I. (1988), 'Monetary and exchange rate policies for international financial stability: a proposal', *Journal of Economic Perspectives*, Vol. 2, No 1, winter.

Meade, J. E. (1957), 'The balance-of-payments problems of a European free-trade area', *Economic Journal*, Vol. 67, pp. 379-396, September.

Mundell, R. A. (1961), 'A theory of optimum currency areas', *American Economic Review*, September.

Obstfeld, M., (1988), 'Competitiveness, realignment, and speculation: the role of financial markets', in *The European Monetary System*, edited by F. Giavazzi, S. Micossi and M. Miller, Banca d'Italia/CEPR.

Padoa-Schioppa, T. (1987), *Efficiency, stability, equity*, Oxford University Press, Oxford.

Poloz, S. (1990) 'Real exchange rate adjustment between regions in a common currency area', mimeo, Bank of Canada, February.

Van der Ploeg, F. (1990), 'Macroeconomic policy coordination during the various phases of economic and monetary integration in Europe', in *European Economy* (1990).

Van Rompuy, P., Abrahams, F. and Heremans, D. (1990), 'Economic federalism and the EMU', in *European Economy* (1990).

Wihlborg, C. and Willett, T. (1990), 'Optimum currency areas revisited', mimeo, April.

Williamson (1985), *The exchange rate system*, Institute for International Economics, Washington.

Part B

The main benefits and costs

Chapter 3

Efficiency gains

This chapter discusses and estimates the gains in terms of economic efficiency from EMU, in particular those arising in the private sector (i.e. to business and households). The public sector will also reap efficiency gains, but these are discussed in Chapters 5 and 7 below.

Since the efficiency gains from monetary union are easier to estimate than those of economic union the chapter discusses first, in Sections 1 and 2, the two main sources for direct efficiency gains from monetary union which are the elimination of exchange rate related transaction costs and the suppression of exchange rate uncertainty. The gains from building on 1992 in moving towards economic union are then discussed in Section 3. However, an economic and monetary union will also have a number of further indirect and dynamic effects which cannot be measured with the same precision as the more direct and static effect of the suppression of exchange rate variability and transaction costs. These indirect and dynamic effects are therefore discussed separately in Section 4 of this chapter. Section 5 concludes by discussing how improved business expectations because of EMU could reignite growth and thus reduce unemployment.

The main findings of this chapter are:

(a) A single currency eliminates the present cost associated with converting one EC currency into another. The resulting savings can be estimated at more than ECU 15 billion per annum, or about 0,4% of Community GDP. The larger part of these gains are 'financial', consisting of the disappearance of the exchange margin and commission fees paid to banks. The other gains take the form of reductions in costs and inefficiencies inside firms.

(b) Transaction cost savings differ strongly from country to country. The gains for the larger Member States whose currency is extensively used as a means of international payments and belongs to the ERM may be of the order of between 0,1% and 0,2% of national GDP. In contrast, the small open and the less developed economies of the Community may stand to gain around 1% of their GDP.

(c) Transaction costs are more harmful to small and medium-sized enterprises engaged in intra-EC trade than to large multinational companies. Whereas total transaction costs incurred by firms can be estimated to amount on average to some 15% of their profits on turnover in other EC countries, they can easily be twice as great in the case of

small firms, in particular when they are located in non-ERM countries.

(d) When accompanied by measures that remove the technical barriers which currently complicate international bank settlements, a single currency will also enable significant cuts to be made in other banking costs in connection with cross-border payments.

(e) EMU would eliminate nominal exchange rate variability among Community currencies. However, some variability in national price levels might remain. Comparisons with other monetary unions indicate that the level of real exchange rate (the nominal exchange rate adjusted for movements in the prices) variability existing at present inside the original narrow band ERM members is not far from what one could expect in EMU. However, aside from this group of countries, EMU should lead to a sharp reduction in real exchange rate variability.

(f) The gains from the suppression of exchange rate variability in terms of increased trade and capital movements are difficult to measure because firms can in many cases insure against this risk using sophisticated foreign exchange market operations. However, business surveys provide strong evidence that despite this possibility, which is in itself costly, foreign exchange risk is still considered a major obstacle to trade. The suppression of exchange rate variability will be more important for small firms and countries with less-developed financial markets that do not have access to sophisticated hedging techniques.

(g) The gains from economic union consist mainly in a better formulation and implementation of Community policies in areas where there are Community-wide external effects or economies of scale and Community action is therefore justified under the principle of subsidiarity. These gains can be shown to be potentially important in a number of policy areas.

(h) A potentially very important gain arises if EMU reduces the overall uncertainty for investors associated with the existence of national currencies and independent monetary policies. A reduction in overall uncertainty could lower the risk premium firms have to pay on equity and would greatly increase investment. Preliminary estimates show that even a reduction in the risk premium of only 0,5 percentage points could raise income in the Community significantly, possibly up to 5-10% in the long run.

(i) Recent research suggests that by improving the expectations of business EMU could lead the Community to a new growth path along which unemployment could be reduced decisively.

(j) In fact, opinion surveys of European industrialists indicate that business leaders do expect significant gains from a single currency. As shown in the introduction to this study, the addition of a single currency to the single market increases the share of industrialists expecting a very positive impact on the business climate from 10 to 45 %.

3.1. Exit exchange rate transaction costs

With the introduction of a single currency all exchange rate related conversion costs disappear on intra-Community transactions.

These costs can be split into two parts. First, there are the direct transaction costs households and firms pay to the financial sector in the form of foreign exchange commissions and the difference between buying and selling rates. Second, there are the costs borne inside companies, arising for instance from the need to allocate personnel and equipment to foreign exchange management. These latter costs might be called 'in house' costs to distinguish them from the former that are more visible since they arise in transactions with the financial sector and might therefore be called external or 'financial' costs.

A recent strand of research in economics (see Akerlof and Yelen (1989)) suggests that even small transaction or information costs can have significant economic effects. This research would imply that the economic losses from exchange rate transaction costs are much larger than the direct costs themselves that are estimated in this section. An illustration of the large indirect effects of even small transaction and information costs is provided by de Jonquières (1990) where it is shown that even for goods to which there are no trade barriers in the Community prices can diverge by as much as 100% (with a range going from 40 to 170%) from one country to another. These price differences imply considerable welfare losses which should be reduced and may be even eliminated under a single currency because with a single currency consumers will immediately be able to compare prices. These additional potential gains are, however, not taken into account in this study since they cannot be quantified with any precision.

3.1.1. External or financial costs

The financial costs Community firms and individuals incur owing to the absence of a single currency can be measured in several ways. The most direct way would be to ascertain the income financial institutions obtain from their customers for foreign exchange services, or, what amounts to the same thing under competitive conditions, to measure the foreign exchange related resource costs of banks. A more indirect approach is to determine the foreign exchange costs banks charge their customers and combine this information with data on the total volume of foreign exchange transactions between EC currencies on behalf of non-bank enterprises and individuals. These data can be derived either from survey results on the turnover on EC foreign exchange markets or from Member States' current and capital account related receipts and payments in EC currency other than the domestic money.

In the present study both the direct and indirect approaches were followed. They lead to very similar estimates of overall financial costs. A detailed presentation of the basic data, working hypotheses and calculations underlying these estimates is given in Annex A of this report. The presentation here is limited to a discussion of the chief findings.

Foreign exchange related revenues for banks

This approach relies on confidential data collected by the Commission services on the foreign exchange related revenues of banks in the Community. Since only information on total foreign exchange revenues is available it was assumed that one half is attributable to foreign exchange between EC currencies. This can be justified by the fact that the value of Member States' current account related payments and receipts denominated in foreign EC currencies clearly exceeds the value in non-EC currencies. The bank revenue data suggest that the total external transactions costs that could be saved by a single currency are about 0,25% of the GDP of the Community. This results from the estimate that a little less than 5% of bank revenues come from foreign exchange activities between EC currencies and that the banking sector accounts for about 6% of the GDP of the Community.

Firms' and households' financial costs of foreign exchange

Approaching the question of quantifying exchange transaction costs from the viewpoint of the buyers of foreign exchange, it is necessary to know the prices banks charge for their intermediation services as well as the total value of transactions in foreign EC currency these prices should be applied to.

Bank foreign exchange charges vary considerably, depending on the currency of exchange, the nature of the foreign exchange 'product' (spot, forward, swaps, options...), the size of the transaction and, as in any other market, the importance of the bank customer.

Box 3.1: Bid-ask spreads and exchange rate variability

While it is apparent that the introduction of a single currency will eliminate all exchange rate related conversion costs it is not clear a priori to what extent these costs will already decline as exchange rates become increasingly fixed.

The available evidence on bid-ask spreads, which are a major component of overall exchange rate conversion costs, indicates that lower exchange rate variability might not have a strong impact on conversion costs. (See for example Boyd, Gielens and Gros (1990) and Black (1989).) Whether the irrevocable fixing of exchange rates would decisively lower the costs of exchanging currencies is difficult to decide since there are only very few historical examples that could be used as a guide. The extent to which this might happen depends on the degree to which operators consider different currencies just different units of account. For example, the exchange rate between the Belgian and the Luxembourg franc has been fixed at one to one for over 50 years and the probability that it might change in the future is

considered very small. Belgian and Luxembourg francs can therefore be exchanged without any conversion costs. However, it is unlikely that the same would occur for the other Community currencies for which it would be more difficult to achieve the same degree of credibility in the irrevocable nature of the exchange rate and for which the actual conversion rates would not be round numbers. It is therefore likely that financial institutions could consider Community currencies as distinct and would charge fees for converting one into another even if exchange rates are declared to be irrevocably fixed by the authorities.

It has been suggested by Dornbusch (1990) that conversion costs for the corporate sector could be eliminated even in a system with separate national currencies through a system of 'par clearing', in which financial institutions would be forced to exchange balances in Community currencies at par, i.e. without a bid-ask spread and without charging foreign exchange fees. Provided national payments and clearing systems are made compatible, such a scheme would therefore create a close substitute for a single currency, at least in terms of transactions costs savings.

(a) Transactions by households

The highest transaction costs arise when exchanging cash. These costs were illustrated vividly by the admittedly theoretical example worked out by Bureau Européen des Unions de Consommateurs[1] (BEUC) in 1988. A traveller is assumed to start out with 40 000 Belgian francs in Brussels embarking on a clockwise tour of all Community capitals (except Luxembourg and Dublin). At the end of the journey the accumulated loss is about 47% if he exchanges his cash at each leg of the roundtrip into local banknotes. Table 3.1. shows how much he would lose at each of his 10 consecutive conversions. The largest losses (14 and 21%) occur when buying or selling in countries with strong currencies the banknotes of weak currencies, like the drachma or the escudo. It will be argued in Annex A that a weighted average of the cost of banknote conversion in the Community is likely to amount to about 2,5%. Using the latter percentage, total banknote transaction costs that will be eliminated by a single EC currency can be estimated to lie between ECU 1,3 and 2 billion, depending on the hypotheses retained to make up for missing data on the volume of banknote conversions in some Member States.

---
[1] See BEUC (1988b).

The exchange margin for traveller's cheques is usually smaller than for cash but there is a 1 % commission charge. Eurocheques, which in many Member States are free of charge (upon the payment of a fixed fee) when used domestically, cost normally between 2 and 3 % when written in a foreign currency. In the case of international credit cards foreign currency costs vary between 1,5 and 2,5 %. With around 40 million international eurocheques in the EC for an average value of ECU 125, a reasonable estimate of the cost savings a single currency would allow for present eurocheque users is between ECU 100 and 150 million per annum. The gains with respect to EC currency denominated traveller's cheques, of which the annual sales in the Community represent a value of around ECU 5 billion, can also be put at around 150 million. The total foreign EC currency payments volume by means of credit cards can be roughly estimated at ECU 10 billion per year. The associated economies a single currency would allow are therefore likely to lie between ECU 150-200 million.

(b) Transactions by the corporate sector

Given the relatively high minimum fee, bank transfers tend to be a relatively costly international payments instrument for small amounts. They are the standard means of international settlements between enterprises, with bank charges being a function of the amount and the currency.

Table 3.1

Currency transaction losses in a (hypothetical) round-trip through 10 countries

Exchanged in on 1 March 1988	Exchange rate applied in local currency			Amounts after exchange transaction	In ecu[1]	Loss in %
B (begin)				BFR 40 000	925,18	
UK	UKL 1	=	BFR 64,95	UKL 615,86	891,30	− 3,66[2]
F	FF 9,8065	=	UKL 1	FF 6039,43	863,55	− 3,11[2]
E	PTA 19,47	=	FF 1	PTA 117 587,49	843.69	− 2,30[2]
P	ESC 1,18	=	PTA 1	ESC 138 753,49	820,35	− 2,77
I	LIT 7,75	=	ESC 1	LIT 1 075 339,52	706,43	− 13,89[2]
GR	DR 10,575	=	LIT 100	DR 113 717,15	686,97	− 2,75
D	DM 0,98	=	DR 100	DM 1 114,43	539,42	− 21,46[2]
DK	DKR 378,44	=	DM 100	DKR 4 217,45	534,42	− 0,95[2]
NL	HFL 27,75	=	DKR 100	HFL 1 170,34	504,71	− 5,56[2]
B (end)	BFR 18,14	=	HFL 1	BFR 21 300	492,66	− 2,39
Total						− 46,75

[1] Official exchange rate published in the *Official Journal of the European Communities*, 1 March 1988.
[2] Additional bank charges can occur.
Source: BEUC (1988b).

Bankers' replies to a questionnaire submitted by the Commission services suggest that when the amount involved is equivalent to ECU 10 000, foreign EC currency bought on the spot market costs around 0,5 %, with reported extremes ranging from 0,1 to 2,5 %. Foreign currency conversion of an amount equivalent to ECU 100 000 was reported to cost about 0,3 %; nevertheless foreign exchange charges very often still exceed 1 % for payments in reputedly weak currencies that are hardly used in international transactions, like the drachma or escudo. Very large amounts, equivalent to ECU 5 million or more, involve costs of the order of 0,05 and 0,1 %, which is the size of the spread that can be observed in the interbank market for foreign exchange.

Bank charges declining with the amount to be converted, an estimate of average exchange transaction costs for firms requires also information on the size distribution of foreign currency payments and receipts. Such data exist for a number of Member States and show that in- and outflows with a value equivalent to ECU 100 000 or more claim about 55 % of the total value of current account transactions in foreign EC currency. For capital account transactions by the non-bank sector this figure climbs to more than 90 %.

As explained in Annex A, combining these figures with the aforementioned information on the banking sector's prices for foreign exchange services allows one to advance the rough estimate that converting the domestic currency into another EC currency costs non-bank firms on average about 0,3-0,35 % as far as current account transactions are con-

cerned; for capital account transactions this percentage can be thought to diminish to about 0,1-0,15 %, leading to an overall average of 0,15-0,2 %.

(c) Grossing up financial costs

The BIS survey in April 1989 on foreign exchange markets suggests that the total net turnover on EC foreign exchange markets arising from the foreign currency needs of the non-bank sector equals some USD 13 000 billion per annum. Depending on assumptions (see Annex A) 34 to 43 % of this turnover can be thought to be directly or indirectly between EC currencies, representing an amount between ECU 4 100 and 5 200 billion. Applying the just mentioned overall cost average of 0,15-0,2 % to the latter values, this would mean that in 1989 exchange transaction costs were situated between ECU 6,2 and 10,4 billion.

To these figures must be added the costs associated with converting banknotes, travellers' cheques and eurocheques as the latter were not taken into account in the BIS survey. Consequently, 'financial' transaction costs borne by the EC economy due to the absence of a single currency can be estimated to range in 1990 from ECU 8 to 13 billion, or from 0,17 to 0,27 % of EC GDP, which is very similar to the aggregate estimate derived from the banking revenue data. [2]

---

[2] The economics literature has so far not come up yet with well-founded transaction cost estimates. Cukierman (1990) provides a back-of-the-envelope assessment, putting financial transaction costs as high as 1 % of Community GDP.

An alternative method of arriving at the transaction volume in EC currency other than the domestic money is to determine, on the basis of balance of payments statistics, each individual Member State's gross current and capital account flows in foreign currency and to isolate the EC component. Unfortunately, the necessary data are not available for all countries. However, the available evidence permits to shed light on the fact that in relative terms the transaction cost savings will be distributed unevenly over the Member States.

These potential savings grow larger:

(i) the lesser the use of the national currency as a means of international payment;

(ii) the more intense the trade in goods, services and assets with other Member States;

(iii) the lower the technical and price efficiency of domestic foreign exchange services;

(iv) the greater the variability of the national currency's exchange rate as it necessitates more systematic hedging (see Section 3.2.4.) and causes bankers' margins to widen.

Small open economies with 'small' currencies like Belgium-Luxembourg, Denmark, Ireland and, to a lesser extent, the Netherlands, or countries with as yet unsophisticated financial markets like Greece, Portugal and Spain will benefit relatively more from the elimination of transaction costs than Germany and France whose currency belongs to the ERM and is a well-accepted means of international settlements. The available material indicates that whereas the exchange transaction cost savings for the latter Member States is likely to oscillate between 0,1 and 0,2 % of GDP, for the small open and less developed economies the gain could be as high as 0,9 %.

Reductions in cost and time of cross-border payments

Apart from eliminating exchange transaction costs, a single currency could also make an important contribution to cutting the present expenses and delays associated with cross-border bank payments.

In comparison to the situation in the USA, where a coast-to-coast cheque costs a fixed money transfer fee of 20 to 50 US cents and takes two working days, these costs and delays are substantial in the Community. A recent study by BEUC [3] found that a bank transfer from one Member State to another of ECU 100 in the beneficiary's money cost on average more than 12 % — of which less than 25 % was

---

[3]   BEUC (1988a).

caused directly by currency conversion — and took generally five working days.

The creation of a single currency and a single system of central banks will permit a major simplification of banks' treasury management, accounting and reporting to monetary authorities. When flanked by internal market measures to remove the technical barriers that still complicate the processing of international bank transfers, these simplifications could make cross-border payments as fast and cheap as domestic ones today.

With an estimated number of 220 million cross-border bank transfers in the Community per year and the difference in fixed processing fee between a domestic and an international settlement (net of exchange transaction costs) around ECU 6 the potential supplementary gain could be set at ECU 1.3 billion.

3.1.2. In-house costs

The existence of different currencies leads also to costs that are internal to the non-financial corporate sector. These costs arise for a variety of reasons. First, multiple currencies render the treasury and accounting functions more complicated so that firms need to devote more personnel to these tasks. They also raise the managerial complexity in transnational firms in that they complicate central management's task of control and evaluation. Second, multiple currencies fragment cash management and thereby lead to company cash being poorly remunerated or, conversely, to interest costs on debit positions. Third, they lengthen the delay between debiting and crediting bank accounts. Fourth, firms may incur opportunity costs in their attempt to avoid, rather than manage, exposure to foreign exchange risk.

These costs are difficult to measure with any precision, since the sources of costs are distributed over a wide number of different departments inside each corporation. They could, in principle, be quantified for each corporation through a careful audit which could determine the resources that could be saved through the introduction of a single currency. Since it would clearly be impossible to do this for a significant number of corporations it was necessary to rely on a sample of case studies.

As explained in Annex A, these case studies suggest a lower bound estimate for these in-house costs equals 0,2 % of firms' turnover from business in other EC countries. Small and medium-sized enterprises tend to suffer relatively larger costs because of the overhead nature of these expenses. Given that value added represents by and large 55 % of corporate turnover and that intra-EC exports of goods and services equal around 16 % of EC value added or GDP, these in-house costs amount to 0,1 % of EC GDP ((0,2 % × 0,16)/0,55).

3.1.3. Summary evaluation of transaction cost savings

This section has estimated the savings in transaction costs that will arise from the introduction of a single currency. Two approaches to estimate the costs of the conversion services performed by banks yielded similar results, namely that the total cost of these services is equivalent to about 0,25 % of the GDP of the Community. To these costs it is necessary to add the in-house costs, of the order of 0,1 % of GDP, which the corporate sector faces. Moreover, a single currency is also a necessary condition for a reduction in cost and time of international bank transfers, which could yield another ECU 1.3 billion.

As shown in Table 3.2, the total quantifiable savings in terms of transaction costs are therefore around 0,3 to 0,4 % of the GDP of the Community or about ECU 13 to 19 billion per annum.

Table 3.2

Cost savings on intra-EC settlements by single EC currency

(in billion ECU, 1990)

		Estimated range	
1. Financial transaction costs			
Bank transfers		6,4	10,6
Banknotes, eurocheques, traveller's cheques, credit cards		1,8	2,5
	Total	8,2	13,1
2. In-house costs		3,6	4,8
3. Reduction of cross-border payments cost		1,3	1,3
	Total	13,1	19,2

Note: Exchange transaction costs associated with several sources of in-house costs are not included in this table.

The latter figures relate only to the direct 'mechanical' expenses occasioned by the need to convert currencies and cover against exchange risk. They do not take into account the implicit tax on cross-border business, hence the fragmentation of markets which the existence of a multitude of EC currencies gives rise to due to the heightened complexity and uncertainty it induces.

The direct costs to households and cross-border shoppers are large in proportional terms, but their total cannot be estimated very accurately. The costs with respect to banknotes and eurocheques can be set at around ECU 2 billion. Under the plausible assumption that these expenses are incurred by households, the total 'financial' and in-house cost firms undergo with regard to their current account transactions with other Member States can be estimated at ECU 7 to 8 billion. As this represents about 1 % of the total value of intra-EC exports of goods and services and profits amount on average to 5-6 % of exports, transaction costs borne by firms are equal to more than 15 % of their profits on exports to other Member States.

Against these efficiency gains one would have to set the cost of introducing the single currency. However, since this is of a once-and-for-all nature it should be small relative to the efficiency gains from a single currency which can be reaped for the indefinite future.

Besides, the Community's banking sector will need to go through an adjustment phase as its resources that have become redundant following the introduction of a single currency are redeployed. These resources could be directed towards the expanding financial intermediation activities in ecu-denominated assets. As argued in Chapter 7, both the world supply of and demand for such assets are likely to increase significantly upon the creation of a single currency.

3.2. Exit exchange rate uncertainty

Monetary union obviously eliminates exchange rate movements and hence uncertainty about intra-EC exchange rates which should stimulate trade and investment. In order to estimate the gains which the suppression of exchange rate variability brings, this section presents first some data about intra-EC exchange rate variability to indicate the reduction in exchange rate variability member countries can expect. However, the economic welfare gains that should result from this are difficult to measure because economic theory has not come to definite results concerning the relationship between exchange rate uncertainty and trade (or investment). The theoretical arguments are therefore examined before proceeding with a discussion of the empirical research on the impact of exchange rate uncertainty on trade and capital flows.

Before going into the measurement of exchange rate uncertainty it is necessary to clarify four general points:

(i) At the theoretical level it is clear that only *unexpected changes* in exchange rates constitute exchange rate uncertainty. However, since a large body of empirical literature [4] has demonstrated that most short run (i.e. over a quarter or a year) changes in exchange rate are unexpected, the variability in actual exchange rates is a good proxy for exchange rate uncertainty. In the remainder of this section the terms 'exchange rate uncertainty' and 'exchange rate variability' will therefore be used interchangeably and will be taken to refer to short run changes in exchange rates.

(ii) It is apparent that a monetary union eliminates only variability in *nominal* exchange rates. Changes in real exchange rates (i.e. the nominal rate corrected by some price index) are still possible, and at times even desirable, if economic conditions and therefore prices develop differently in the regions that are part of the union. The theoretical and empirical literature on exchange rate variability indicates, however, that both nominal and real exchange rate variability may be important. For floating exchange rates this distinction has usually not been important since short run (up to a year) changes in nominal rates are usually equivalent to changes in the real exchange rate, given that national price levels move much more slowly than exchange rates.

For floating exchange rates it is therefore approximately true that a reduction in nominal exchange rate variability is equivalent to a reduction in real exchange rate variability. However, this does not apply to the tightly managed exchange rates that belong to the ERM. Indeed there are some data that suggest that the low degree of real exchange rate variability achieved in the ERM corresponds to the level one could expect to find even inside a monetary union consisting of rather diverse regions as would be the case for the Community. [5] This section will therefore concentrate on the effects of (short run) nominal exchange rate variability although this is only partially equivalent to real exchange rate variability.

Even in EMU long run movements in real exchange rates can occur through movements in wages and prices (see Chapter 2). However, these long run movements are generally not unexpected and should therefore not have the same impact on trade and investment as the largely unexpected short run changes. Economic benefits can therefore be expected only from the suppression of the short run exchange rate variability defined above. [6]

Table 3.3 below illustrates these points with data on the variability of the DM *vis-à-vis* four other currencies: the two extremes are formed by the Dutch guilder and the US dollar. [7] For the US dollar nominal and real exchange rate variability are very high, and about equal in size for all subperiods. For the Dutch guilder nominal and real variability are very low, but the variability of the real rate is much higher especially during the last subperiod. Indeed for 1987-89 the variability of the real DM/HFL rate is of the same order of magnitude as the variability of the real DM/LIT rate, although the variability of the nominal DM/LIT rate is about six times as high as that of the DM/HFL rate. Finally, the DM/DR exchange rate is, for the period 1979-89, over twice as variable as the DM/LIT rate in nominal and real terms, attaining almost the level of the DM/USD rate.

Table 3.3

Bilateral exchange rates

Variability as standard deviation of monthly percentage changes

	1974-78	1979-89	1979-83	1984-86	1987-89
DM/HFL nominal	0,64	0,32	0,46	0,13	0,11
DM/HFL real	0,85	0,52	0,59	0,38	0,52
DM/LIT nominal	2,40	0,85	0,96	0,77	0,69
DM/LIT real	2,32	0,91	1,04	0,78	0,72
DM/DR nominal	1,8	2,15	2,33	2,56	0,75
DM/DR real	2,15	2,33	2,60	2,53	1,41
DM/USD nominal	2,31	2,93	2,64	3,11	2,93
DM/USD real	2,41	2,97	2,68	3,10	2,97

(iii) Any judgement about the impact of an elimination of exchange rate variability on trade, investment and finally economic welfare must be based on the assumption that the existing exchange rate variability is not warranted by variability in underlying economic conditions. If most changes in exchange rates could be regarded as an efficient adjustment to changes in productivity, investment opportunities or other so-called fundamental factors, the suppression of this adjustment mechanism (by irrevocably fixing exchange rates) might actually lower welfare. [8]

---

[4] See Mussa (1986) for a survey.
[5] See Poloz (1990).
[6] This section does not consider separately the issue of medium-term misalignments in exchange rates since they are generally taken not to play an important role among Community currencies, especially those that belong to the ERM.

[7] All the tables in this chapter refer to monthly averages of exchange rates obtained from Commission sources.
[8] Mussa (1986) also offers a cautious assessment of the welfare consequences of exchange rate variability.

However, there is considerable evidence that, in a regime of free float, most exchange rate variability is not related to variability in fundamental factors such as productivity or investment opportunities. It has been impossible so far to relate systematically the evolution of the so-called fundamentals to exchange rate movements (see for example Meese and Rogoff (1983) and Gros (1989)).

Among the currencies participating in the EMS no such overshooting seems to occur and the remaining fluctuations inside the bands just offset short run differences in the stance of monetary policy. However, even though there might be no overshooting among ERM currencies, the remaining intra-ERM exchange rate variability is caused mainly by differences in national monetary policy stances and hence is not related to the fundamental real factors that determine investment and trade, such as productivity and comparative advantage. One could therefore argue that even for EMS currencies the remaining exchange rate variability is not warranted by policy-independent fundamental factors that operate even in EMU. This does not imply that fixing exchange rates involves no economic costs, indeed Chapter 6 below discusses the costs that arise when the adjustment in labour and goods markets is slower than in the foreign exchange market. However, this section concentrates on the gains that might arise from the suppression of exchange rate variability.

(iv) Any positive effect of the suppression of exchange rate variability among Community currencies on intra-EC trade and investment can be considered a benefit of EMU only if there are no side-effects on the variability of the system of Community currencies *vis-à-vis* the other major currencies. If the elimination of intra-EC exchange rate changes leads to more variability among the three remaining currency areas (dollar, yen and ecu) there might be an offsetting negative effect and vice versa if EMU leads to a more stable international monetary system. Since the external and internal trade of the Community are about equal in size this potential offsetting or reinforcing effect could alter substantially the size of the benefits that can be expected from more stable exchange rates within the Community.

The impact of EMU on the global monetary system is discussed in more detail in Chapter 7 of this study, where it is argued that it is difficult to predict a priori what effect the creation of EMU will have on the stability of the global monetary system. This section therefore assumes that the formation of EMU will at least not increase uncertainty in the global monetary system. [9]

3.2.1. Exchange rate variability in the Community

As discussed in the introduction to this section the variability in short run changes in nominal exchange rates is the appropriate measure of exchange rate variability for the purpose of measuring the benefits of irrevocably fixing exchange rates. The exact meaning of 'variability' and of 'short run changes' are always subject to discussion on technical grounds. However, the following tables use the most widely accepted measure of variability, namely the standard deviation of percentage changes in monthly nominal exchange rates. The large literature on the effects of the EMS on exchange rate variability shows that the choice of the exact measure of exchange rate variability is largely arbitrary and does not influence the results since most measures lead to the same conclusion. [10]

Table 3.4 shows the overall variability of the Community currencies (plus the US dollar, the yen and the Swiss franc) using nominal exchange rates. Table 3.5 displays the variability of the currencies considered against Community currencies only. For Community currencies this measures intra-Community variability. Finally, Table 3.6 displays the variability against ERM currencies only. For ERM members [11] this measures intra-ERM variability. These tables show only averages for the pre-EMS and selected post-EMS periods. The study by Weber (1990) also analyses exchange rate variability in some detail.

It is apparent from these tables that global exchange rate variability exceeds intra-Community variability, which, in turn, exceeds intra-ERM variability. EMU will, however, eliminate only intra-Community exchange rate variability. The effect of EMU can therefore be read from Table 3.5 which indicates that the main benefit from irrevocably fixing exchange rates is to reduce the average variability (as measured by the standard deviation) of Community currencies against each other from at present (i.e. 1987-89) 0,8 % (per month) to zero.

As can be seen from Table 3.4 this average hides large differences among member countries. For the UK the reduction would be almost two times as high (1,6 %) and for Belgium it would only be 0,5 % . For the original members of the ERM the average in 1987/89 (and therefore the reduction through irrevocably fixing exchange rates) was only 0,7 %; whereas the other member countries start from

---

[9]   The stochastic simulations presented in Annex E suggest that the variability among the remaining major three currencies would not change substantially.

[10]   See Ungerer *et al.* (1986) and Artis and Taylor (1988) for more references.
[11]   Since Spain did not participate in the ERM until 20 June 1989 and the United Kingdom until 8 October 1990, these two countries are not considered ERM members in the calculations in the present chapter.

Table 3.4

Bilateral nominal exchange rates against 20 industrialized countries

Variability as weighted sum of standard deviation of monthly percentage changes

	1974-78	1979-89	1979-83	1984-86	1987-89	EMU
B/L	1,5	1,4	1,6	1,1	0,9	0,05
DK	1,6	1,5	1,7	1,3	1,2	0,08
D	1,8	1,5	1,6	1,4	1,2	0,09
GR	1,9	2,3	2,5	2,7	1,0	0,05
E	2,9	1,9	2,1	1,4	1,5	0,07
F	2,1	1,5	1,7	1,4	1,1	0,07
IRL	1,7	1,6	1,6	1,7	1,2	0,06
I	2,3	1,5	1,6	1,5	1,2	0,07
NL	1,4	1,2	1,3	1,0	0,9	0,05
P	2,9	1,8	2,3	1,3	1,0	0,05
UK	2,1	2,4	2,4	2,5	1,9	0,10
USA	2,1	2,5	2,3	2,6	2,4	2,4
Japan	2,4	2,7	2,9	2,7	2,4	2,4
Switzerland	2,4	1,9	2,1	1,8	1,6	1,5
AV1	1,8	1,5	1,6	1,3	1,1	0,07
AV2	1,9	1,6	1,7	1,5	1,2	0,08
AV3	2,4	2,2	2,4	2,2	1,7	0,09
AV4	2,1	2,0	2,1	2,0	1,6	0,13

Note: AV1 = Weighted average of ERM currencies, ecu weights.
AV2 = Weighted average of EC currencies, ecu weights.
AV3 = Weighted average of EC non-ERM currencies, ecu weights.
AV4 = Unweighted average of non-ERM currencies.

a much higher level of variability, they can expect a reduction in (intra-Community) variability of about 1,9 % .

Table 3.6 can be used to indicate the benefits participation in Stage I might bring to those countries that have not until recently participated in the narrow margins of the ERM. A comparison with Table 3.5 suggests that for a country like the UK the absolute reduction in exchange rate variability through Stage I is equal to about 1,2 % (i.e. from the value of 1,6 in Table 3.5 to 0,4 in Table 3.6), i.e. three times larger than the additional reduction that is obtained by going from Stage I to EMU.

While it is clear that EMU reduces nominal exchange rate variability to zero it is not as clear what level of real exchange rate variability will remain. The evidence from Canada discussed in Chapter 2 above suggests that the real exchange rate variability that exists at present between narrow band ERM members might actually constitute the level to be expected under EMU. This implies that Member States that at present do not participate in the narrow band ERM will experience some reduction in real exchange rate variability as well.

Assuming that the variability of the other major currencies against the ecu remains unchanged the last column of Table 3.4 shows the average variability in nominal exchange rates member countries can expect once intra-Community exchange rates have been irrevocably fixed. This table suggests that the countries that will gain most from EMU under this aspect are countries like Spain, Portugal and the UK which trade relatively more with the rest of the world and where exchange rates are at present more variable.

3.2.2. Exchange rate variability and trade

The preceding subsection has measured the reduction in exchange rate variability from EMU. But what economic benefits will result from this reduction in exchange rate variability? This subsection discusses the impact which more stable exchange rates might have on trade starting with the theoretical arguments.

Table 3.5

Bilateral nominal exchange rates against EUR 12 currencies

Variability as weighted sum of standard deviation of monthly percentage changes

	1974-78	1979-89	1979-83	1984-86	1987-89	EMU
B/L	1,3	1,0	1,3	0,7	0,5	0
DK	1,5	1,1	1,3	0,8	0,7	0
D	1,7	1,1	1,3	0,9	0,7	0
GR	1,8	2,2	2,4	2,6	0,7	0
E	2,9	1,7	2,0	1,1	1,2	0
F	2,0	1,1	1,3	1,0	0,7	0
IRL	1,5	1,3	1,3	1,4	0,8	0
I	2,2	1,1	1,2	1,1	0,8	0
NL	1,3	0,9	1,0	0,7	0,5	0
P	2,8	1,7	2,2	1,1	0,8	0
UK	2,0	2,2	2,4	2,2	1,6	0
USA	2,2	2,8	2,6	3,0	2,8	
Japan	2,3	2,4	2,8	2,3	1,8	
Switzerland	2,2	1,5	1,7	1,3	1,1	
AV1	1,7	1,1	1,3	0,9	0,7	0
AV2	1,9	1,3	1,4	1,1	0,8	0
AV3	2,3	2,0	2,3	1,9	1,9	0
AV4	2,2	2,0	2,1	1,9	1,5	1,4

Note: AV1 = Weighted average of ERM currencies, ecu weights.
AV2 = Weighted average of EC currencies, ecu weights.
AV3 = Weighted average of EC non-ERM currencies, ecu weights.
AV4 = Unweighted average of non-ERM currencies.

Table 3.6

Bilateral nominal exchange rates against ERM currencies

Variability as weighted sum of standard deviation of monthly percentage changes

	1974-78	1979-89	1979-83	1984-86	1987-89	EMU
B/L	1,1	0,8	1,1	0,5	0,3	0
DK	1,2	0,7	0,9	0,5	0,4	0
D	1,5	0,7	0,9	0,5	0,4	0
GR	1,8	2,2	2,4	2,5	0,6	0
E	2,9	1,6	2,0	0,9	1,2	0
F	1,8	0,8	1,0	0,7	0,4	0
IRL	2,0	0,9	0,8	1,3	0,4	0
I	2,2	0,8	1,0	.0,8	0,6	0
NL	1,1	0,6	0,7	0,4	0,3	0
P	2,7	1,6	2,1	0,9	0,6	0
UK	2,0	2,2	2,4	2,2	1,7	0
USA	2,2	2,9	2,6	3,0	2,8	
Japan	2,3	2,3	2,7	2,1	1,9	
Switzerland	2,1	1,3	1,5	1,1	1,0	
AV1	1,6	0,7	0,9	0,6	0,4	0
AV2	1,7	1,0	1,2	0,8	0,6	0
AV3	2,2	2,0	2,3	1,8	1,4	0
AV4	2,1	1,9	2,1	1,8	1,5	1,4

Note: AV1 = Weighted average of ERM currencies, ecu weights.
　　　AV2 = Weighted average of EC currencies, ecu weights.
　　　AV3 = Weighted average of EC non-ERM currencies, ecu weights.
　　　AV4 = Unweighted average of non-ERM currencies.
ERM currencies as selected here do not include the Spanish peseta or the pound sterling.

Theoretical considerations

The main theoretical argument as to why exchange rate variability should adversely affect trade is that risk-adverse agents will reduce their activity in an area, such as trade or investment for export, if the risk, i.e. the variability of the return they can obtain from this activity, increases. The theoretical literature on the effects of exchange rate variability usually refers implicitly to floating exchange rates and does not always distinguish clearly between real and nominal exchange rate variability because, as mentioned above, for free floating exchange rates nominal and real exchange rate variability are equivalent. This subsection discusses therefore how both nominal and real exchange rate variability can increase the riskiness of international trade.

The most direct channel for nominal exchange rate variability to affect international trade arises because most international trade contracts involve a time lag between the time the contract is made, and when the exporter obtains his payment. All exporting therefore involves an exchange rate risk from the point of view of the exporting firm which has

its accounting and most of its costs in the domestic currency. The exporter can eliminate this risk for himself by agreeing only to contracts in his own domestic currency. This might be the reason why most trade among the major industrialized countries is invoiced in the exporters' currency. However, this practice only shifts the risk from the exporter to the importer who will then face the uncertainty that the price in his domestic currency can change between the time he places the order and when he receives the merchandise (or service). The only way the risk can be eliminated for both partners is through the use of forward or future markets.

The forward and future markets for foreign exchange have indeed expanded considerably since the advent of floating exchange rates and it is now possible to hedge exchange rate risk among the major currencies. For the simplest operations, for example a simple forward contract, the direct costs involved are of the same order of magnitude as the spreads on spot transactions. However, in many cases a simple forward contract is not sufficient to cover all exchange rate risk. For example, a firm that submits an international bid, say for a large investment project, does not know in advance whether it will obtain the contract. In order to be able to submit a bid in foreign currency it will have to buy a foreign exchange option, which involves much higher transaction costs.

A further limitation of the usefulness of forward and future markets for foreign exchange is that they are not complete in terms of maturity and currency. Forward cover on maturities of up to one year are readily available in most major currencies, but no developed markets exist for longer maturities. For long-term delivery contracts, for example for aeroplanes for which delivery lags of several years are common, this is a potentially important limitation. It is possible to construct forward cover indirectly by issuing debt in foreign currency,[12] but this technique involves more costs and can be used only by large firms which have access to foreign capital markets or the market for foreign currency swaps. For firms located in small countries it is generally more difficult to obtain forward cover since the range of forward contracts available in the less important currencies is usually much more limited.[13]

---

[12]　An exporter expecting a foreign currency payment in the future can be certain about the domestic currency equivalent if he sells the corresponding amount of foreign currency forward. He can obtain the same result by contracting a loan in foreign currency (that matures at the time of the expected payment) and converting the foreign currency he obtains against the loan on the spot market into domestic currency.

[13]　At present currency options exist against the US dollar.

Exchange rate variability is, therefore, a more important factor in countries with less developed financial markets because of the higher cost and limited availability of forward cover. However, the 1992 internal market programme, which will open all national financial markets to competition should mitigate considerably this particular problem. Once the internal market programme has led to an integrated European financial market all enterprises in the Community will have access to the common financial market which should be as efficient and complete in terms of coverage as any of the existing national financial markets.

The time lag between contract and payment represents the most direct way in which exchange rate variability, through unexpected changes in the nominal rate, can make trade riskier. However, even if exporters and/or importers perfectly hedge against this risk exchange rate variability will still increase the risk of foreign trade because it introduces an additional source of uncertainty regarding the real ex change rate that will prevail in the future. Movements of the real exchange rate, i.e. the nominal rate adjusted for domestic costs and the costs of the competition, will determine future profits, which thus can become highly uncertain. [14] This risk can, of course, not be hedged with simple forward contracts. However, it is possible to hedge against this risk, also called economic exposure, by a suitable choice of the currency in which to denominate the assets and liabilities of the firm. Sophisticated techniques to hedge against this economic exposure are, however, followed mostly by large firms, for which exchange rate changes have a more complicated impact on profits since both costs and revenues are often in several different currencies.

The risk of unpredictable large swings in real exchange rates would, however, not exist in EMU (nor in the EMS) since in EMU real exchange rates would move only through the slow and relatively predictable movements of overall price levels. EMU (and the EMS) provide therefore also a hedge against the risk of economic exposure.

Financial markets offer therefore a variety of ways to obtain insurance against exchange rate risk in international trade, but this insurance is not costless and not always available. The price of this insurance diminishes and its availability increases with the degree of sophistication of financial markets and the size of the firm.

---

[14] For a small competitive firm costs and the market price are given and changes in the nominal exchange rate will directly determine the real price it can obtain for its output. For the often more realistic case of a firm which can influence the market price the nominal exchange rate will not directly determine the price, but will shift the entire demand schedule expressed in domestic currency.

Empirical evidence on exchange rate variability and trade

There exists a large body of empirical studies on the effect of exchange rate variability on trade. However, this literature has not been conclusive. A number of studies have found no convincing effect and a major survey undertaken by the IMF (see IMF (1984)) concluded that it had not been able to find a systematic link between short term exchange rate volatility and the volume of international trade.

Some individual studies (De Grauwe (1987) and Perée and Steinherr (1989)) have found a significant effect of exchange rate variability on international trade. However, these studies generally refer to the major floating currencies. It is therefore difficult to decide whether a similar effect operates also at the much lower level of exchange rate variability among EMS currencies. The only two studies that concentrate specifically on European currencies and intra-EC trade appear to be Bini-Smaghi (1987) and Sapir and Sekkat (1989). However, even these studies find only very small effects. Bini-Smaghi finds a significant, but very small, effect of exchange rate variability on bilateral trade for France and Italy and no effect for Germany; Sapir and Sekkat find no significant effect at all.

Since the empirical research has not found any robust relationship between exchange rate variability and trade it is not possible to estimate the increase in intra-EC trade that might derive from the irrevocable fixing of exchange rates. However, this does not imply that no such link exists. The theoretical discussion suggests that exchange rate variability should have no impact, if exchange risk is either hedged or irrelevant to the firm because it is diversified. Neither of these two conditions is satisfied in reality as only a fraction of total trade is hedged through forward operations and the available data on international portfolio diversification suggests that exchange rate risk is not diversified by shareholders.

One way to reconcile the lack of empirical results with these considerations might be that the effect might be just too small to be detected in the available samples. This is suggested by Gagnon (1989) who simulates a theoretical model in which exchange rate variability should have an impact on trade. He finds that the impact is numerically very small. In his model the switch from the Bretton Woods to the floating exchange rates regime in the 1970s, which was followed by a very large increase in exchange rate variability, would have reduced global international trade only by about 1 %.

The same model also predicts that, despite the small quantitative impact of exchange rate variability on trade, the switch to floating exchange rates might have had a considerable impact on the welfare of traders. [15] This result would be able to reconcile the scientific economic literature with regular opinion surveys of business leaders, which repeatedly indicate that exchange rate uncertainty has adverse effects on trade and investment. For example surveys conducted by the Confederation of British Industry found that over half of all the companies questioned, and all firms with less than 1 000 employees, considered that exchange rate stability was important to their operations. [16] Similar results were obtained in a European-wide survey conducted on behalf of the Association for the Monetary Union of Europe which found that among the advantages from a single currency 'reduction in monetary fluctuations' ranked first among eight other reasons.

3.2.3. Exchange rate variability and capital movements

Exchange rate variability affects not only international trade in goods and services, but also international capital movements. Since the determinants of short- and long-term capital movements differ considerably they will be discussed separately.

For long-term capital movements, and direct foreign investment, which is usually based on a long-term horizon, the short-term variability of nominal and real exchange rates discussed here should not be important as long as movements up and down average out over time. [17] So-called misalignments that persist over several years would, of course, be more important, but such misalignments are not typically observed among Community currencies.

The evidence of a direct impact of exchange rate variability on foreign direct investment is somewhat stronger than the

one relating to trade, as reported in Molle and Morsink (1990) which analyses exchange rate variability and intra-EC direct foreign investment. The estimates reported there imply that EMU might increase intra-EC direct foreign investment considerably by reducing an important 'friction' factor.

Short-term capital movements may be more strongly affected by exchange rate variability. However, it is difficult to say what the impact of the elimination of exchange rate variability will be on short-term capital movements. On the one hand many capital movements may actually be caused by exchange rate variability, for example if they serve to hedge against exchange rate risk in trade. Moreover, if exchange rate variability reduces the correlation in the returns from investments in otherwise similar assets, to the extent that this also reduces the correlation with the market portfolio this makes international investment more attractive. On the other hand, exchange rate changes also increase the absolute risk of investing in foreign currency denominated securities and might therefore deter individuals from engaging in full international diversification. In practice, however, the extent of international portfolio diversification is much lower than one would expect given the gain in a reduction of risk that could be achieved through it by most investors. But it is difficult to say whether this fact is a result of the high transactions costs that arise often in international investment (i.e. a lack of economic union) or of exchange rate variability.

Given these conflicting theoretical arguments it is therefore difficult to decide whether a reduction in exchange rate variability would increase short-term capital movements and whether any induced increase in asset trade should be regarded as welfare enhancing. [18]

3.2.4. Efficiency gains from the elimination of exchange rate uncertainty

Given the difficulties in estimating empirically the impact of exchange rate variability on trade and investment it might be more convenient to characterize the direct [19] economic benefits that may be obtained from the elimination of exchange rate uncertainty by saying that the irrevocable fixing of exchange rates provides free unlimited hedging for all trade and capital movements. Since the cost of hedging varies with the size and type of transaction (trade versus

---

[15] A large effect of exchange rate variability on welfare is compatible with a small effect on trade if trading is very profitable. An increase in exchange rate variability might reduce the welfare of traders considerably (in technical terms it might reduce the consumer and producer surplus) but if there is no good alternative use for the resources used in foreign trade the effect on trade will be small.

[16] See CBI (1989).

[17] If fluctuations in the exchange rate do not average out over time to allow exchange rates to return to some long-run equilibrium level, it can be shown that in the presence of sunk costs even a very low level of exchange rate variability can induce firms not to react to sizeable changes in the exchange rate because there is still a small probability left that the investment might be lost, or that the conditions might be even better in the future. This idea implies that eliminating even a low level of residual exchange rate variability might considerably increase the elasticity with which trade reacts to the exchange rate. See Dixit (1989) for an analytical framework for this idea.

[18] See also Persson and Svenson (1987) which also comes to the result that the relationship could go either way.

[19] As mentioned above the indirect and dynamic effects of EMU are discussed separately in Section 3.4 below.

investment, contract already concluded versus tender offer, etc.) the implied benefit from this 'free' hedging is difficult to evaluate. The savings for firms from the elimination of the need for hedging in intra-EC trade have therefore to be estimated by combining an estimate of the total, direct plus indirect, costs of hedging standard international trade transactions with information about the frequency of the various transactions considered. Moreover, it appears that only a small part of intra-EC trade is hedged in reality. This estimate would therefore provide only a lower limit on the real savings from irrevocably fixing exchange rates to the extent that smaller firms do not hedge because it is too expensive or difficult for them. [20]

The irrevocable fixing of exchange rates might bring an additional benefit by leading to the complete equalization of interest rates. The experience in the EMS has shown that even if exchange rates are *de facto* fixed for some time interest rates do not converge completely as long as the possibility of exchange rate changes remains. The Dutch guilder/German mark rate provides a good example for this phenomenon given that since1983 the Dutch guilder has *ex-post* not depreciated against the DM and the exchange rate has never moved outside a corridor of about $+/- 0,5\%$ from the average. Despite all this, three months' Euro-interest rates on Dutch guilder deposits have on average been about 50 basis points higher than comparable DM deposits. The reason for this difference is usually taken to be the uncertainty that was created in financial markets, when in the 1983 realignment the Dutch guilder did not follow the DM. Only an irrevocable commitment of locking exchange rates could be expected to eliminate these residual interest rate differentials.

These unwarranted differences in interest rates which continue to exist in the present EMS can be considered equivalent to differences in the cost of capital which lead to welfare losses in the traditional sense (see Chapter 2). In Price Waterhouse (1988) it was estimated that the elimination of the residual differences in interest rates would lead to welfare gains of about 0,05 % of Community GDP. While the welfare gains that come from the elimination of interest rate differentials appear to be modest, the gains that can be reaped from a reduction in the overall level of interest rates, and therefore the cost of capital, can be very important as discussed more in detail in Section 3.4 below.

3.3. Building on 1992

The main pillar of economic union is the completed internal market within which persons, goods, services and capital move freely. The potential economic impact of the completion of the internal market was estimated in the so-called Cecchini Report. Using a microeconomic approach the Cecchini Report found welfare gains in the range of 2,5 to 6,5 % of Community GDP. Macroeconomic simulations indicated that these microeconomic welfare gains should translate into a medium-term increase in GDP of 4,5 %, a decrease in the price level of 6 % and an increase of employment of 1,5 %, i.e. almost 2 000 000 jobs. Following the Cecchini Report, the economic implications of the internal market have been the subject of considerable additional research efforts. These complement the original global assessment but they also begin to look into the regional and sectoral impact of the completion of the internal market. [21] On a global level,the additional research effort largely confirms the findings of the Cecchini Report, and goes further in analysing dynamic effects not encompassed in the above figures (see Section 3.4 below).

In some specific fields the Commission has taken or will take initiatives going clearly beyond the 1985 White Paper. This is particularly the case for energy and transport. Recent studies have found that the benefits from going beyond the measures contained in the White Paper can be substantial. In the field of energy it is estimated (Commission of the EC (1989)) that the long-term gains from a free internal energy market in electricity are ECU 11 billion as compared with the ECU 6 billion estimated in the Cecchini Report. Similarly, in the field of transport, the benefits of a greater degree of competition among airlines are now estimated (McGowan and Seabright (1989)) to be about twice those found in the Cecchini Report. Moreover, the cost of fragmentation of European airspace due to different air traffic control systems has been estimated by the Association of European Airlines and an independent group of economists at ECU 4-5 billion per annum.

The term 'economic union' as used in this study goes beyond the internal market. It also includes the assignment of certain economic policy functions to the Community level wherever this is necessary to achieve all the economic gains from market integration, i.e. wherever there are Community-wide external effects. The areas where this is the case are competition policy, commercial policy, R&D, human resource development, European-wide infrastructure and the environ-

---

[20]   If firms do not buy cover because exchange rate variability is irrelevant to them this estimate would not constitute a lower limit.

[21]   For a review of some of the additional literature see Italianer (1990).

ment. [22] In all these areas Community policies can be justified on the principle of subsidiarity, as explained in Chapter 2. The increasing degree of market integration has also underlined the need for Community programmes of transnational collaboration in areas such as higher education (e.g. Erasmus and Comett), vocational training and permanent education, in order to stimulate the development of human resource skills.

A Community involvement in these policy areas based on the principle of subsidiarity yields net economic benefits for the Community as a whole since the Community will intervene only in those cases where the efficiency gains due to the Community involvement outweigh the cost of administration. While these benefits can be appreciated in qualitative terms, a reliable quantification is often very difficult, if not impossible. First, there is sometimes no clear blueprint for the greater Community involvement, for example the political decisions on European-wide infrastructure networks have begun only recently. Thus the degree and intensity of future Community involvement is uncertain. But even where the Community has been involved in a policy area for some time, such as R&D, no global assessment of the economic cost and benefits has been made so far, even if, as part of the Monitor programme, specific research programmes such as Brite (concerning new industrial materials) have been evaluated and found to yield significant benefits.

In the field of commercial policy, the Community seeks to ensure that the removal of internal barriers is paralleled by progress towards a more liberal multilateral trading system. The potential economic benefits of such progress are considerable and have been repeatedly demonstrated by economic research. [23]

In the field of environmental policy a greater Community involvement can be expected to yield considerable net benefits. First, some global problems, such as the greenhouse effect, require a world-wide solution, the value of which could be crucial even if it is not only economic in nature and cannot yet be quantified with any precision. If the

Community makes a constructive contribution towards this, the probability of securing a satisfactory global outcome is likely to be considerably greater than the chances in the event of disparate individual contributions from the Member States. Secondly, a Community recognition that economic efficiency becomes more and more interrelated with ecological efficiency could provide an anchor for environmental concerns in the Member States, including those where such concerns have hitherto had a rather low priority. Thirdly, in the context of the internal market, national environmental policy could be misused as an instrument to create new segmentations of markets in Europe, this would be costly in economic terms and could be largely avoided through an active Community role in this field.

In the field of competition policy the need for a Community policy is apparent since only the Community is able to monitor the internal market and make sure that competition is not distorted by dominant market positions or State aids. The importance of surveillance over State aids can be seen by considering that, on average over the period 1986-88, aids to manufacturing in the Community amounted to about 4 % of value added. With EMU the need to restrict State subsidies is much increased since it will no longer be possible to compensate for differences in the overall level of aid through the exchange rate.

Major economic benefits can therefore be expected from an improved competition policy, in particular with respect to the surveillance of State aids.

Table 3.7 gives a breakdown of the average annual aid volume by principal objectives.

In the context of the completion of the internal market, the Commission is determined to make additional forceful efforts to restrict State subsidies. This should bring economic welfare gains by reducing a drain on public budgets and removing distortions of competition which are a source of economic inefficiency. For the Community as a whole these potential benefits have not been assessed quantitatively but country-specific and sectoral results suggest that they are likely to be substantial.

For example, a recent comprehensive study for Germany (Weiss et al. (1988)) estimated that the elimination of State aids would result in a gain of 0,9 % of GDP. The study uses a general equilibrium model and assumes that the budget savings from the dismantling of subsidies are used to reduce direct taxes. The gains estimated in this study may be considered a lower bound since the model does not allow for economies of scale nor for a reallocation of factors of production between Community Member States.

---

[22]   A case can also be made for Community functions in the area of macroeconomic policies (other than monetary policy), especially fiscal policy, but this is discussed in Chapter 5.

[23]   For example, the negative overall effect of protection on economic growth has been estimated by Donges (1986) who found that protection may have slowed down the rate of economic growth by approximately 2 % a year in the world economy as a whole, by 1,3 % for the group of industrial countries and by 2,3 % for the developing country group.
It has also been shown that the global gains from eliminating quotas and tariffs in 14 key textiles and clothing categories exceed USD 15 billion annually.

Table 3.7

State aids in the European Community, by main objective

Annual average 1986-88 in MECU

Horizontal objectives — Total	**12 581**
Innovation/R&D	3 330
SMEs	2 838
Trade/export	3 239
Environment/energy saving	630
General investment	1 508
Other objectives	1 036
Sectoral objectives — Total	**9 102**
Steel	1 365
Shipbuilding	1 563
Other sectors	6 174
Regional aids — Total	**12 037**
Least developed regions	5 252
Other regions	6 785
Manufacturing and services excluding transport — Grand total	**33 720**

Source: Commission of the European Communities (1990).

3.4. Indirect and dynamic gains from economic and monetary union

The previous sections of this chapter discussed the direct gains in terms of hedging and transaction costs from monetary union and additional gains from economic union. These direct gains can best be understood as increases in potential income with given endowments of factors of production, such as capital and labour. This section shows that these direct productivity gains should increase the capital stock over time and therefore lead to additional indirect gains which are called 'dynamic' because they arise over time as the capital stock responds to efficiency gains. [24] Moreover, this chapter also indicates how the reduction in uncertainty through EMU can have dynamic effects that are similar to the ones that derive from the direct efficiency gains.

Since the internal market programme and EMU form two parts of an interlinked system whose effects reinforce each other mutually, it will, however, not be possible to dis-

tinguish sharply between the effects of the internal market programme and the additional effects of EMU.

This section starts with a discussion of the economic effects of market integration and then turns to an estimate of the overall efficiency gains from EMU.

3.4.1. Integration and dynamic gains

Although most economists agree that integration of markets brings large benefits it is difficult to estimate them quantitatively within the context of the usual models of economic growth. In part this may be due to the large gap between the formal theoretical models explaining the gains from economic integration and the benefits as they are perceived by economic agents. Most of the difficulties arise from the fact that the standard theories of economic growth that incorporate constant returns to scale and perfect competition do not leave any room for integration to affect growth in the long run. This is explained briefly in Box 3.2. The evaluation of dynamic gains made here is, however, based on the standard and widely used models which do not incorporate economies of scale that lead to continuing growth. A class of newer models that does allow for continuing (endogenous) growth is briefly discussed at the end of this subsection.

Recent developments in the theory of international trade [25] have started to bridge the gap between theory and the way markets are perceived to work by recognizing that markets are not always characterized by constant returns to scale and perfect competition. Monopolistic competition and economies of scale are known to prevail in many markets, and theoretical and empirical models taking these properties into account have started to develop. Nevertheless, this approach does not lead to essentially different conclusions in terms of long-run growth and can therefore not be used to explain dynamic gains. [26]

---

[24] 'Dynamic gains' are defined here as the gains from integration taken over a period long enough for the capital stock to have adjusted to the new equilibrium. In most economic analysis the capital stock encompasses human as well as physical capital. This implies efficiency gains lead not only to increased investment in plant and equipment, but also education and training.

[25] See Helpman and Krugman (1985) for further references.
[26] As explained in Romer (1989) economies of scale lead to continuing (endogenous) growth only if they affect the accumulation of capital. This is not the case in the models referred to in this paragraph.

Box 3.2: The neoclassical growth model

The standard 'neoclassical' theory of growth is based on a model in which firms produce one (possibly composite) product with capital and labour under constant returns to scale and perfect competition. Given an exogenous labour supply the steady state or long-run equilibrium is reached when the marginal productivity of capital is equal to the discount rate of consumers. This can be illustrated using a diagram that relates the capital stock (per capita) on the horizontal axis to output (per capita) on the vertical axis.

The curve F(k) shows how much output can be produced given the per capita capital stock k. The long-run level of output is determined at the point of tangency between the straight line DD whose slope is given by the discount rate and the production function F(k). This point of tangency determines the steady state capital stock denoted by k_{ss}. It is apparent that this framework explains only the level of steady state income (per capita). Continuing growth is possible in this framework only if productivity grows. (Growth in the labour force leads only to growth in total output, but does not affect income per capita.) But the factors that cause growth in productivity are taken to be exogenous to the model. In this sense this framework cannot explain continuing growth.

The specific curve used in this graph was obtained by setting the elasticity of output with respect to capital equal to one half $(F(k) = B.k^{0,5})$. This corresponds to a multiplier of two as in Baldwin (1990) and as assumed widely in this chapter. For illustrative purposes it was assumed that the discount rate is equal to 10 %. The units of output can be freely chosen by the choice of the scale factor B and have no meaning; in this graph B was arbitrarily equal to 10. This yields a steady state level of output of 5 'units'.

The long run equilibrium in the neoclassical growth model

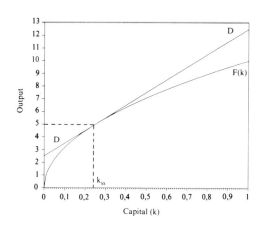

The Cecchini Report, while drawing on results incorporating economies of scale and monopolistic competition, did not give an estimate of the dynamic gains to be expected from the completion of the internal market, although these gains were presaged. [27] Part of these dynamic gains were ascribed to the effects on business strategies of the completion of the internal market. The buoyant investment climate in 1988 and 1989 and the currently much increased activity in terms of mergers and acquisitions [28] seem to indicate that firms are responding to the opportunities they expect from the internal market even before this programme is completed. This is an example of the adaptation of business strategies to 'news' about future economic integration.

The improved business climate could of course also be due to other factors, but a major business survey conducted in the spring of 1989 on behalf of the European Commission has shown that the internal market positively influences investment intentions for the period up to and after 1992.

This effect of the 1992 programme on investment intentions and growth expectations can be explained in terms of the neoclassical growth framework as a medium-run response of the capital stock to the static efficiency gains. This implies that there exist theoretical arguments for the existence of dynamic gains which are briefly explained in Box 3.3 (for a rigorous exposition see Baldwin (1989)). It is shown in this box that if the efficiency gains from the internal market are equivalent to shifting the production function upwards, the marginal productivity of capital will increase at any given capital stock. Starting from an initial equilibrium position where the opportunity cost of capital was equal to its marginal productivity this implies that firms will increase their capital stock until the marginal efficiency of capital has returned to the opportunity cost of capital (which did not change). This increase in the capital stock, until the new equilibrium level has been reached, leads, of course, to an increase in output.

This effect does not change the long-run or steady-state growth path, but there will be an increase in output over the medium run. It might therefore be called, as in Baldwin

27   See Emerson *et al.* (1988).
28   See *European Economy* No 40, May 1989.

Table 3.8

The influence of the internal market on the expectations of firms

Effect on	Up to 1992		From 1993 to 1996	
	Increase[1]	Neutral[2]	Increase	Neutral
Sales	26	12	27	20
Domestic	6	7	0	17
Other EC	33	10	37	17
Rest of the world	7	13	10	20
Investment	28	15	26	22
Domestic	28	8	23	17
Other EC	19	18	19	25
Rest of the world	5	20	7	27
Employment	13	17	13	25
Domestic	9	8	7	18
Other EC	13	20	15	27
Rest of the world	3	21	4	30
Productivity	38	10	38	17

Source: European Economy No 42, November 1989.
[1] Increase: Difference between the percentage of firms expecting an increase and those expecting a decrease.
[2] Neutral: Don't know/no answer.

(1990) the 'medium-run growth bonus'. On the basis of production function estimates for a number of European countries, Baldwin (1989) calculates that the medium-run bonus may range between 24 % and 136 % of the initial static gains (see Table 3.9). Since he also provides reasons to believe that his calculations could prove to be underestimates, he concludes that the point estimate of the medium-run growth bonus should be close to the upper bound and that the static efficiency gains should therefore be doubled.

Table 3.9

The medium-run growth bonus as a percentage of static efficiency gains

	B	D	F	NL	UK	Average
Low estimate	38	36	30	35	24	32,6
High estimate	136	129	80	124	93	112,4

Souce: Baldwin (1989).

It has to be emphasized, however, that the welfare implications of the medium-run growth bonus are quite different from those of the direct efficiency gains. The direct efficiency gains are equivalent to a gain in welfare since they just increase the output that can be produced with given factors

of production. The medium-run growth bonus, in contrast, works through an increase in the capital stock that has to be 'earned' by forgoing consumption. The welfare gains (in the sense explained in Chapter 2) from the medium-run growth bonus are therefore much smaller than the ones from the direct efficiency gains even if the medium-run growth bonus is as large as 100 %. Baldwin (1989) shows that the welfare gain (in present value terms) of the direct efficiency gain is almost 20 times higher than the welfare gain (again in present value terms) of the indirect dynamic effects.

The increase in income through the medium-run growth bonus comes through additional investment and therefore takes time to materialize until the capital stock has reached its new equilibrium level. The build-up of the capital stock and associated production capacity may well take several years. An example may illustrate this effect: with a linear depreciation scheme, Baldwin expects half of the growth bonus to take 10 years to be realized. If the static efficiency gains of the completion of the internal market in the run-up to 1992 and in the years thereafter take about the same time span, one may thus expect, all other things being equal, an increase in the Community growth rate of two-thirds of a percentage point during a period of 10 years and a quarter of a percentage point thereafter.[29] These would be average increases per annum. If firms anticipate correctly the gains to be expected in the future they might take their decisions in the earlier phase of the period, thereby frontloading the effects.

As argued in Section 3.1 of this chapter exchange rate stability can lead to additional gains because it reduces the riskiness of investment to the extent that firms cannot hedge or diversify exchange rate risk. Box 3.4 explains how a reduction in the riskiness of investment can be translated into an increase in output in the standard neoclassical framework.

It has long been recognized that the standard growth theory with constant returns to scale was not satisfactory since it could not explain continuing economic growth, except by invoking exogenous technological progress. Models incorporating increasing returns to scale have therefore been developed recently that explain endogenous economic growth.[30] These models are, however, not yet widely accepted and must therefore be considered somewhat more speculative.

---

[29] Calculated, for the first 10 years, by taking one-tenth of 6,75 %, being the sum of 4,5 % static efficiency gains plus half of 4,5 % dynamic gains. The other half of the dynamic gains, 2,25 %, divided by 10 represents the average growth over the remaining period.
[30] See in particular Romer (1986); Romer (1989) provides a survey of this approach.

Box 3.3: Medium-term growth effects of efficiency gains

The neoclassical framework explained in Box 3.2 can be used to explain the 'medium-term growth bonus' mentioned in the text. If EMU increases the overall level of productivity the production function F(k) shifts upwards, say to AF(k), where A is a number that exceeds one. At an unchanged capital stock the increase in production is exactly equal to the increase in productivity, i.e. the difference between $F(k_{ss})$ and $AF(k_{ss})$. However, the point of tangency with the discount rate line will now shift. The new long-run equilibrium has to be at the higher capital stock, k'_{ss} so that output increases by more than the amount of the gain in productivity.

It is apparent that the assumption that the production function is increased proportionally is crucial for this result. If the production function shifts up by a constant amount the point of tangency would remain unchanged at k_{ss} and no additional investment would occur.

Algebraically this can be seen most easily by considering a change in the productivity factor A. If the production function is AF(k) any increase in A increases also the marginal productivity of capital, which is AF'(k). However, if the production function is F(k) + A, the value of A does not affect the marginal productivity of capital which would be given by F'(k). In the text it is assumed that the former is the case, which seems reasonable since a doubling of production of income and trade inside the Community should also double the transactions costs of keeping different currencies.

This graph uses the same values as the preceding one. In order to obtain a convenient graphical representation the production function was assumed to shift upwards by 25 % (A goes from

10 to 12,5). Given the multiplier of two, this illustrative example implies that output increases by 50 %, i.e. from 5 to 7,5 'units'.

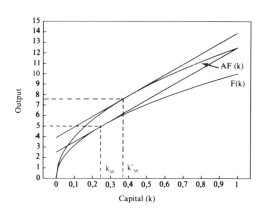

Two of these so-called 'new growth models' are analysed by Baldwin (1989) who comes to the conclusions that the static efficiency gains from the internal market could permanently increase the Community growth rate. The first of these models relies on a specific value for the elasticity of output with respect to capital. In a second model, any increase in the profitability of innovations permanently increases growth. Calibrating these models, Baldwin finds that the completion of the internal market could increase the Community's growth rate permanently by 0,3 to 0,9 percentage points. These results obviously rest on very specific assumptions, nevertheless they are important because they provide an analytical hinge for the relationship between integration and long-term growth conditions.

It has to be emphasized, however, that the standard framework with constant returns to scale and the new growth models are not compatible in the sense that the mechanisms that determine growth in the long run are radically different. It is therefore not possib e to add permanent growth effects (from the new models) to the level effects (from the standard framework).

3.4.2. Quantifiable dynamic gains from economic and monetary union

The preceding analysis can be applied in general to the case of economic and monetary integration. Whenever static efficiency gains occur which raise the marginal productivity of capital, it may be expected that, in the medium term, the capital stock and therefore output will increase to a level that exceeds the initial shift in output. Similarly, any reduction in the riskiness of investment would also increase capital accumulation, and, over time, output. In order to estimate these effects it is therefore necessary to first obtain estimates of the static efficiency gains and the reduction in the risk premium which form the basis to which the medium growth multiplier can be applied. [31] This is done separately for these two elements in the remainder of this subsection.

---

[31] If one accepts the more speculative new growth models these direct efficiency gains could also be translated into a permanent increase in long-term growth.

Box 3.4: Growth effects of a reduction in the risk premium

The medium-term growth effect of a reduction in the risk adjusted discount rate can be illustrated using the standard neo-classical growth framework already explained in Box 3.2. In this framework the steady state level of the stock of capital (per capita) and hence of the steady state level of income (per capita) is determined by the condition that the marginal productivity of capital equals the discount rate. Although the standard neo-classical growth model does not take into account uncertainty the discount rate which in that framework represents the pure rate of intertemporal time preference of consumers could be reinterpreted as the risk adjusted required rate of return firms face. A reduction of the risk premium would then be equivalent to a reduction in the slope of the discount rate line.

This implies that a reduction in the risk premium leads to an increase in the capital stock from k_{ss} to k'_{ss} and hence an increase in (per capita) income equal to the difference between $F(k_{ss})$ and $F(k'_{ss})$. Mathematically this can also be seen by using the steady state condition that the marginal product of capital $F'(k)$ equals the discount rate. If the discount rate declines $F'(k)$ has to decline as well and this can happen only if k increases.

Using once again the same production function it is assumed in this illustrative example that the discount rate goes from 10 % to 8 %, which is equivalent to a reduction of 20 %. Given that the multiplier for this type of change is equal to one this illustrative example implies an increase in output of 20 %, i.e. from 5 to 7 'units'.

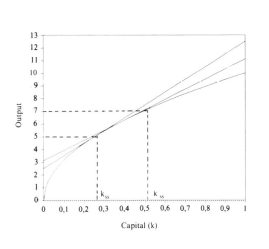

(i) Dynamic effects of static efficiency gains

For the static efficiency gains there are two sources since EMU comprises the internal market programme and the additional benefits from monetary union: (a) The Cecchini Report estimated the efficiency gains from the internal market programme to lie between 2,5 and 6,5 % of the GDP of the Community; (b) Sections 3.1 and 3.2 above estimated the direct efficiency gains from the elimination of transaction and hedging costs to be about 0,4 % of GDP.

Applying the range of parameters for the medium-term growth bonus discussed in the previous section this implies that the total direct static plus dynamic gains from EMU should be between 3,6 and 16,3 % of GDP with the central estimate equal to 9,8 % of GDP. [32]

By assuming the static gains to be spread out over a period of 10 years, and half of the dynamic gains to be realized in the first 10 years, [33] the impact on the medium-term growth rate of GDP could be in the order of 0,7 percentage points per annum in the first 10 years and 0,25 percentage points thereafter.

A point estimate for the long-term effect on growth of the efficiency gains would be in the order of an additional 0,7 % per annum, with a range varying between 0,4 % and 1,0 % per annum, but this estimate is surrounded with even more uncertainty.

As mentioned above the medium-term growth effect and the long-term growth effect cannot be added because they are based on two different underlying growth models. They should therefore be identified with two different scenarios, one where the increase in growth eventually dies out, [34]

---

[32] The lower bound is obtained by multiplying the lower bound of the total static efficiency gains (2,9 %) with the lower bound of the (medium term growth) multiplier (1,24); the upper bound is obtained by multiplying the upper bound of the total static efficiency gains (6,9 %) by the upper bound of the multiplier (2,4). The central estimate is based on total static efficiency gains of 4,9 % and a multiplier equal to 2.

[33] See Baldwin (1989).
[34] The increase in growth dies out in these models. But afterwards growth can continue at the same pace as before since the exogenous factors that are the underlying cause should continue to operate as before.

and another where it has a permanent effect. Despite their different implications for the long run the two models come approximately to the same conclusion for an initial period of 10 years for which they imply that growth increases by about 0,7 % points.

(ii) Dynamic gains from a reduction in risk

However, the potentially most important source of gains from EMU comes from the reduction in overall uncertainty EMU might provide. EMU should not only eliminate exchange rate fluctuations, which should have the direct effects that are discussed in Section 3.2 above, but it should also reduce the overall uncertainty that affects investment in the Community. The overall uncertainty affecting investment might be reduced not only through the elimination of exchange rate movements, but also through a reduction in the uncertainty about monetary policy when there are no longer distinct national central banks, and possibly through a more stable fiscal policy.

Baldwin (1990) analyses a number of reasons why uncertainty, especially exchange rate uncertainty should affect investment. Only the most important of these, risk aversion, is briefly discussed below. This is not to deny the other channels through which uncertainty may affect investment, but this particular one is the most widely known and it illustrates the general principle that the market imperfections that exist in the real world may make uncertainty much more important than theory would suggest.

It is generally accepted that if firms are risk averse they will reduce investment if profits become more uncertain. However, the theory of corporate finance also indicates that in a perfectly functioning financial market firms should not be averse to exchange rate risk because they could hedge against exchange rate exposure through a variety of financial instruments. Moreover, even if a firm cannot hedge against exchange rate variability its investors could diversify this risk by holding shares of different firms, perhaps located in different countries. [35]

The extent to which exchange rate risk will affect the risk adjusted discount rate which a firm applies to a particular investment project depends therefore on the degree to which financial markets allow managers and investors to hedge against exchange rate risk. This issue is discussed in more detail in the Baldwin study already referred to where it is found that in general financial markets do not seem to provide substantial hedging against exchange rate risk, since

investors are usually not diversified internationally and a significant proportion of trade is not hedged. This implies that risk, especially exchange rate risk should affect investment.

There also exists, however, a broader theoretical argument that exchange rate variability might not affect trade and investment adversely after all. This argument starts from the idea that trade always represents an option; and it is a well-known principle that the value of an option increases with its variability. This basic argument in less technical terms simply means that changes in the exchange rate represent not only a risk, but also an opportunity to make profits. A firm involved in trade can export, it does not have to, and it will do it only if it is profitable. If the exchange rate becomes more variable the probability of very favourable exchange rates and therefore high profits increases. The probability of very unfavourable exchange rates also increases, of course, but this does not have to lead to offsetting losses since the firm can always stop exporting. [36] A higher variability of the exchange rate leads therefore to a higher probability of making high profits, which is not matched by an equivalent probability of high losses, only somewhat lower profits. This implies that higher exchange rate variability offers on average the opportunity to make higher profits. [37]

The argument that exchange rate variability might increase the expected value of profits does not deny that it certainly makes profits more uncertain. But it does imply that the impact of exchange rate variability on investment is difficult to determine on theoretical grounds alone. Investment is usually taken to increase with the difference between the expected rate of return and the risk adjusted discount rate. Since exchange rate variability affects both the expected rate of return and the risk adjusted discount rate it follows that from a theoretical point of view it is not possible to decide a priori what effect a reduction of exchange rate variability

---

[35] For small investors this service can be provided cheaply by investment funds, the so-called Ucits, which can since October 1989 be sold freely throughout the Community.

[36] The classic reference is Oi (1961); see also Pindyck (1982) and Gros (1987).

[37] This argument is not invalidated by the existence of adjustment costs. It is sometimes argued that exchange rate uncertainty should have a negative impact on trade because it is costly for firms to adjust their production plans to changing market conditions. However, adjustment costs do not affect the nature of the argument that a firm will react to a change in the exchange rate only if it is profitable, taking into account all factors, i.e. also adjustment costs. Exchange rate variability can therefore have a positive effect on trade even in the presence of adjustment costs (see Gros (1987)). Adjustment costs may, however, reduce the speed with which the firm reacts to realized changes in the exchange rate, especially if they are asymmetric, i.e. if there are sunk costs. As discussed above, in the presence of sunk costs even a very small degree of exchange rate uncertainty could delay investment considerably. But this does not imply that there has to be necessarily less investment, it only implies that investment might react slowly to changes in the exchange rate.

(and other risk) will have on investment if financial markets can be used to hedge and diversify this risk.

Moreover, the empirical economics literature has not found any strong relationship between investment and exchange rate variability (or other sources of risk). One of the difficulties in doing this is that only a fraction of total investment is directly affected by the exchange rate. Moreover, it is in general difficult to isolate the factors that determine investment.

In contrast to this lack of decisive theoretical and empirical results business surveys indicate consistently that business leaders judge exchange rate variability as one of the factors that most inhibit investment. The results of business surveys are compatible with the available data on portfolio diversification which indicates that investors even in countries with sophisticated financial markets are generally not well diversified internationally. This can be taken to imply that in reality most exchange rate risk is not diversified. It is this non-diversified risk that should affect investment. However, it has not been possible to detect empirically a direct link between exchange rate variability and investment.

In spite of the weak empirical evidence concerning the impact of exchange rate variability on investment it is clear from a theoretical point of view that all exchange rate (and other) risk that is neither hedged nor diversified increases the riskiness of investment. [38] Empirical studies might not be able to measure this effect because it is in general difficult to account for the observed variability in investment, maybe because investment decisions have to be taken on the basis of expectations of the future course of a number of variables and these expectations are difficult to measure in empirical work. EMU should, however, as argued above, reduce the uncertainty about some important variables, for example the exchange rate, the price level and national fiscal policies. This reduction in overall uncertainty, which goes beyond the mere suppression of exchange rate variability, should increase investment by reducing its perceived riskiness.

The 'riskiness' of investment in real capital is usually measured by the so-called equity premium, i.e. the difference in the rate of return on (risky) equity and riskless securities, such as government paper. This risk premium has been found to be about 8 to 10 % in industrialized countries. It is therefore an important overall component of the cost of capital for firms. If EMU reduces the riskiness of investment in the Community the risk premium should fall; to estimate by how much is, however, very difficult since little is known about the determinants of the risk premium.

Baldwin (1990) shows that a reduction in the risk premium yields the same medium growth bonus in terms of a higher output in the long run as the static efficiency gains. The only difference is that in this case there is no direct effect on output so that the medium-term growth bonus is the only source of gains. The gains from a reduction in uncertainty are therefore equal to the proportional reduction in the risk adjusted rate of return times the estimated multipliers displayed in Table 3.9, which range from 0,24 to 1,4, with the central estimate equal to one.

The main difficulty of this approach lies in determining the potential reduction in the risk premium because little is known about its determinants. Baldwin (1990) argues that a reduction of the risk premium of up to one percentage point cannot be ruled out, and that a drop of 0,5 percentage points constitutes a reasonable central estimate. The available data suggest to him that the risk adjusted rate of return lies between 5 and 10 %; using the lower value this implies that a 0,5 percentage point reduction in the risk premium represents a drop of 10 % in proportional terms. [39] It follows that even a reduction in the risk premium of only 0,5 % could raise the GDP of the Community by 5-10 % in the long run if the central estimate for the medium-term multiplier is applied to a risk adjusted rate of return varying between 5 and 10 %. [40] EMU could therefore lead to important gains in output if it reduces the overall uncertainty affecting investment in the Community.

3.5. Business expectations and growth

Up to now the discussion of this chapter has been based on relatively well-established microeconomic principles. The purpose of this brief section is to discuss some recent research (see Baldwin and Lyons (1990)) of a more macroeconomic nature which suggests that if EMU affects the business climate favourably it could lead to a self-reinforcing cycle of stronger growth which would reduce unemployment considerably.

This research is based on the idea that due to economies of scale investment in manufacturing is subject to forces that drive it to either very high or very low values. According to this framework, a high rate of investment increases overall productivity over time and makes additional investment even more profitable; this can lead to a cycle of investment that

---

[38] Baldwin (1990) discusses a number of additional different 'market failures' that provide channels through which exchange rate variability can distort investment decisions.

[39] The same proportional drop could result from a reduction in the risk premium of 1 percentage point starting from an initial value of 10 %.

[40] These are gains in terms of increased production. As mentioned above the gain in terms of welfare that can be reaped from the medium-term growth effect is much smaller than the increase in output.

increases until the entire labour force is fully employed. (The converse case of ever-falling investment leads, of course, to high unemployment.) This framework also suggests that expectations can be decisive in determining whether the economy experiences high investment growth or the opposite since it is well known that expectations are an important determinant of investment.

If EMU raises the expectations of business leaders that future investment will become more profitable it could initiate a cycle of increasing investment and lower unemployment whatever the precise magnitude of the microeconomic gains discussed at some length in this chapter. Given the persistent high unemployment in the Community, which still stood at 9 % in 1989 it is clear that this effect could lead to economic gains that are of the same order of magnitude as the efficiency gains discussed so far. However, since this research is still tentative and of a qualitative nature it is not possible to give a precise estimate of the reduction in unemployment and the increase in investment which EMU could bring about through this channel.

Nevertheless, the interest of these newer analytical approaches is enhanced by the results of a business survey of European industrialists undertaken for the present study. A sample of industrialists was asked how the business climate would be affected (i) with completion of the single market by 1992; (ii) by supposing in addition that exchange rates were fixed; (iii) by introducing a single currency to add to the single market. The results, portrayed in Graph 1.1, show that somewhat over 80 % of industrialists view the single market as having a positive impact on the business climate, but only 10 % judge it to be very positive. Adding fixity of exchange rates changes the result only a little, perhaps because the industrialists may not perceive this to be very different to the existing EMS. On the other hand, the single currency is rated as a much more important development, and in this case there is a large number (45 %) judging the likely impact on the business climate to be very positive.

Taken together with the experience of the already more dynamic business environment in the run-up to 1992, it seems justifiable on grounds both of theory and of expectations of industrialists to consider a significant growth bonus from EMU, while unproven, to lie well within the bounds of plausibility.

References

Akerlof, G., Yelen, J. (1989), 'Rational models of irrational behaviour', *American Economic Review*, May, pp. 137-142.

Artis, M. (1989), 'The call of a common currency', in *Europe without currency parities*, Brittan, S., and Artis, M., Social Market Foundation, London, 1989.

Artis, M., Taylor U. (1988), *Exchange rate, interest rates, capital controls and the European Monetary System: assessing the track record*, Chapter 7: 'The European Monetary System', Giavazzi, F., Micossi, S., and Miller, M., etc., USA, 1988.

Baldwin, R. (1989), 'The growth effects of 1992', *Economic Policy*, October 1989, pp. 248-281.

Baldwin, R. (1990), 'On the microeconomics of the European monetary union', in *European Economy* — 'The economics of EMU', special issue, 1990.

Baldwin, R., Lyons, R. (1990), 'External economies and European integration: the potential for self-fulfilling expectations', in *European Economy* — 'The economics of EMU', special issue, 1990.

BEUC - Bureau européen des unions de consommateurs (1988a), 'Transferts d'argent à l'intérieur de la CEE', April.

BEUC - Bureau européen des unions de consommateurs (1988b), 'Holiday money', July.

Bini-Smaghi (1987), 'Exchange rate variability and trade flows', mimeo, University of Chicago and Banca d'Italia, 1987.

Black, S. (1989), 'Transaction costs and vehicle currencies', working paper, International Monetary Fund, November.

Boyd, C., Gielens, G., Gros, D. (1990), 'Bid/ask spreads in the foreign exchange markets', mimeo, Brussels, February.

Commission of the European Communities (1989), 'The benefits of integration in the European electricity system', DG XVII, December.

Commission of the European Communities (1990), 'Second survey on State aids in the European Community', Brussels.

Confederation of British Industry (1989), *European monetary union: a business perspective*, London, November.

Cukierman, A. (1990), 'Fixed parities versus a commonly managed currency and the case against "Stage II"', Ministry of Finance, Paris, 21 June.

De Grauwe, R. (1987), 'International trade and economic growth in the European Monetary System', *European Economic Review*, No 31, pp. 389-398.

De Jonquières, G. (1990), 'Counting the costs of dual pricing in the run-up to 1992', *Financial Times*.

Dixit, A. (1989), 'Entry and exit decisions under uncertainty', *Journal of Political Economy*, 1989, Vol. 97, pp. 620-630.

Donges, J. (1986), 'Whither international trade policies? Worries about continuing protectionism', Institut für Weltwirtschaft, Kiel.

Dornbusch, R. (1990), 'Problems of European monetary integration', Massachusetts Institute of Technology.

Emerson, M., *et al.* (1988), 'The economics of 1992', *European Economy*, No 35.

European Economy (1990) — 'The economics of EMU', special issue.

Gagnon, J. (1989), 'Exchange rate variability and the level of international trade', Board of Governors of the Federal Reserve System, International Finance, Discussion Paper No 369, December 1989.

Gros, D. (1987), 'Exchange rate variability and foreign trade in the presence of adjustment costs', Working Paper No 8704, Département des sciences économiques, Université Catholique de Louvain, Louvain-la-Neuve.

Gros, D. (1989), 'On the volatility of exchange rates — A test of monetary and portfolio models of exchange rate determination', *Weltwirtschaftliches Archiv*, June 1989, pp. 273 - 295.

Helpman, E., Krugman, P. (1985), *Market structure and foreign trade*, MIT Press, Cambridge, May.

International Monetary Fund (1984), 'Exchange rate variability and world trade', Occasional Paper No 28, IMF.

Italianer, A. (1990), '1992 hype or hope: a review', *Economic Papers*, No 77, Commission of the European Communities, February.

McGowan, F., Seabright, P. (1989), 'Deregulating European airlines', *Economic Policy*, No 9, Cambridge, October.

Meese, R., Rogoff, K. (1983), 'Empirical exchange rate models of the seventies: Do they fit out of sample', *Journal of International Economics*, 1983, pp. 3-24.

Molle, W., Morsink, R. (1990), 'Direct investments and monetary integration', *European Economy* — 'The economics of EMU', special issue.

Mussa, M. (1986), 'Nominal exchange rate regimes and the behaviour of real exchange rate: evidence and implications', *Carnegie Rochester Series on Public Policy* (1986), pp. 117 - 214.

Oi, W. Y. (1961), 'The desirability of price instability under perfect competition', *Econometrica*, Vol. 29, No 1, January, pp. 58-64.

Perée, E., Steinherr, A. (1989), 'Exchange rate uncertainty and foreign trade', *European Economic Review*, No 33, pp. 1241-1264.

Persson, M., Svenson, L. (1987), 'Exchange rate variability and asset trade', presented at the Conference on exchange rate variability, Toronto, September 1987.

Pindyck, R. S. (1982), 'Adjustment costs, uncertainty and the behavior of the firm', *American Economic Review*, No 72, June 1982, pp. 415-427.

Poloz, S. (1990), 'Real exchange rate adjustments between regions in a common currency area', mimeo, Bank of Canada, February.

Price Waterhouse (1988), *The cost of 'non-Europe' in financial services*, Commission of the European Communities.

Romer, P. (1986), 'Increasing returns and long-run growth', *Journal of Political Economy*, No 94, October, pp. 1002-1037.

Romer, P. (1989), 'Increasing returns and new developments in the theory of growth', NBER Working Paper No 3098, September.

Sapir, A., Sekkat, K. (1989), 'Exchange rate variability and international trade: the effects of the European Monetary System', mimeo, Université libre du Bruxelles.

Ungerer H., Evans, O., Mayer, T., Young, P. (1986), 'The European Monetary System: recent developments', Occasional Paper No 48, International Monetary Fund, Washington DC, December.

Weiss, F.D., *et al.* (1988), 'Trade policy in West Germany', *Kieler Studien*, No 217, Tübingen.

Chapter 4

Benefits of stable prices

It is generally agreed that the EuroFed which determines monetary policy in EMU should aim at price stability. The first section of this chapter argues that this choice is based on sound economic criteria because price stability brings economic benefits. The second section then briefly discusses the costs of reaching price stability, i.e. the cost of disinflation. Finally, the third section then discusses what kind of monetary regime is most likely to yield the benefits of stable prices.

The main findings of this chapter are:

(i) Inflation involves substantial costs that are, however, difficult to measure. The nature of these costs differs between anticipated and unanticipated inflation.

(ii) Standard microeconomic theory suggests that anticipated inflation of 10% leads to direct welfare losses that are of the same order of magnitude, about 0,3% of GDP, as the direct transaction costs savings through EMU.

(iii) The post-war macroeconomic experience of the industrialized world suggests that, on average, high inflation countries have a higher unemployment rate and a lower per capita income.

(iv) High inflation is usually associated with highly variable inflation rates and therefore also with unanticipated inflation. Since unanticipated inflation can affect output temporarily this explains why countries with higher inflation have also on average more unstable growth rates.

(v) The costs of disinflation are minimized if there is a credible commitment to stable prices and backward-looking wage indexation is abolished or reformed into a forward-looking scheme.

(vi) A stable and credible monetary regime requires an independent central bank with the statutory mandate to guarantee price stability. Otherwise the public might expect that the authorities might be tempted to use surprise inflation to temporarily increase output or temporarily reduce the real interest rate on public debt. These anticipations can lead to higher inflation and make it difficult to reduce inflation. This idea is supported by empirical experience which shows that there is a strong link between central bank independence and inflation in the long run.

4.1. The cost of inflation

The economic benefits from stable prices, or rather the economic costs of inflation, have been discussed extensively in the literature. This discussion has not come to any definite results concerning the overall analytical basis on which to measure the costs of inflation as summarized in a well known study on the costs of inflation: [1]

'It is well known that the costs of inflation depend on the sources of the inflation, on whether and when the inflation was anticipated, and on the institutional structure of the economy. There is, therefore, no short answer to the question of the costs of inflation. Further, since the inflation rate is not an exogenous variable to the economy, there is some logical difficulty in discussing the costs of inflation *per se* rather than the costs and benefits of alternative policy choices.'

Despite these difficulties in establishing an overall analytical basis on which to measure the costs of inflation there is wide agreement that inflation does cause considerable costs. This chapter discusses the main sources of economic costs of inflation and illustrates their likely magnitude with the help of some simple, but forceful, statistical indicators. It does not, however, try to present an overall evaluation of the costs of inflation because these costs come from many different sources and are therefore not comparable, as suggested in the above quotation. For the purpose of the discussion the term 'inflation' is taken to mean sustained increases in the general price level. A once-and-for-all jump in the price level should therefore not be regarded as inflation.

The quote above also suggests strongly that the economic effects of inflation are different if it is anticipated than if it comes as a surprise. The discussion in this chapter will therefore distinguish between anticipated and unanticipated inflation. The effects of anticipated inflation are discussed first, because they can be more precisely determined.

4.1.1. The effects of anticipated inflation

In discussing the effects of anticipated inflation it is convenient to distinguish between the effects that are based on generally accepted microeconomic theory and the macroeconomic effects that are not as well established.

At the microeconomic level the main effects are:

(i) inflation reduces the demand for money,

(ii) it forces economic agents to obtain additional balances from the central bank in order to keep the real value of their money holdings constant, and

(iii) it forces producers to change price lists continually.

---

[1] Fischer (1981), p. 5.

The first effect is an immediate implication of generally accepted microeconomic theory and the resulting economic welfare losses can in principle be estimated. The second effect is also called the inflation tax; it constitutes the only potential argument for a positive rate of inflation. The direct costs of changing prices, called 'menu costs', are also a clear consequence of inflation, but their importance is more debatable.

At the macroeconomic level it is less clear on theoretical grounds whether anticipated inflation should have any effects, and it is therefore also much more difficult to estimate empirically the macroeconomic costs of inflation.

The three abovementioned effects are now discussed in turn. Additional effects that come from non-indexed tax systems or non-indexed contracts, which lead to changes in income distribution, are discussed under the third heading since they are all related to the cost of changing contracts.

Suboptimal money holdings

The earlier contributions concerning the costs of inflation focused on the reduction in money holdings it causes. The main argument in this line of thought is that the social cost of producing money can be taken to be zero because the cost of printing additional bank notes is negligible. It follows that an economic optimum is attained only if the private cost of holding money is also equal to zero. However, if the alternative to holding money is to buy storable consumption goods, the private opportunity cost of holding money is not zero, but equal to the rate of inflation. If the alternative to holding money is holding bonds, or other 'near money' assets that yield interest, the private opportunity cost of holding money is equal to the rate of interest. Depending on what the alternative to holding money is taken to be, the optimal inflation rate would therefore be either zero or negative. [2]

The welfare losses from a rate of inflation that is different from the optimal rate can then be calculated, according to the standard 'triangle' methodology, as the area under the money demand curve. The general idea behind this approach is discussed in Chapter 2 of this volume. In the present application the source of the welfare loss lies in the lower balances households and firms hold if inflation goes up. With lower balances available to finance their regular flow of expenditures, households and firms have to incur more

often the cost of going to a bank to obtain additional money. These more frequent transactions with banks imply a loss of time and expense for households and firms and they also imply higher costs for banks which have to execute more transactions. These transaction costs determine the slope of the demand curve for money and the 'triangle' area below the curve therefore represents the additional transaction costs caused by inflation. The only input required to measure these costs are the two variables that determine the slope and position of the money demand curve, i.e. estimates of the elasticity of money demand and of the velocity of circulation. [3] These two variables can, however, not be estimated without first determining the proper definition of money in this theoretical context. This is done in Box 4.1, which shows that this theoretical framework leads to the conclusion that a 10 % rate of inflation would cause a welfare loss of 0,1 to 0,3 % of GDP depending on whether the appropriate definition of money is taken to be the monetary base (cash plus required reserves of commercial banks) or M1 (cash plus sight deposits). This effect alone is of the same order of magnitude as the transaction costs that can be saved by a common currency and indicates the importance of stable prices.

Inflation tax

The concept of economic welfare loss from inflation used so far is based on the assumption that inflation is the only distortion in the economy. It assumes in particular that the government can finance its expenditure through lump sum taxes. This is a crucial condition because a lower inflation rate implies also a lower [4] revenue from the inflation tax and in reality most taxes cause distortions since they are not lump sum. The literature on the optimal inflation tax therefore argues that inflation should just be viewed as any other tax that causes distortions and should therefore be used to some degree alongside other taxes. However, the existence of lump sum taxes represents only a sufficient condition that makes it possible to ignore public finance considerations. Even admitting that in reality no lump sum taxes exist does not necessarily lead to the result that the optimal inflation rate is positive. The large amount of literature on this issue [5] has not come to any definite results; the theoretical issue concerning the optimal inflation rate in the absence of lump sum taxes therefore remains open.

---

[2]   The latter result is based on the requirement that the nominal interest be zero; see Friedman (1969).

[3]   See, for example, Lucas (1981), p. 43.

[4]   This is true for low to medium rates of inflation. Most money demand research estimates that for inflation rates in excess of 100% p.a. further increases in inflation lead to lower seigniorage revenue because the tax base, i.e. money demand, becomes very sensitive to inflation.

[5]   See Spaventa (1989) for a recent survey.

It is usually assumed that money refers to a means of payment and that the main alternative to money is interest bearing assets. This implies that the proper definition of money in this context should be the sum of all non-interest bearing assets, or all assets on which interest payments are restricted to below-market rates. Cash and required reserves on deposits with commercial banks, i.e. the monetary base, would therefore certainly have to be included in this definition of money. Bank accounts would have to be included only if interest payments on them are restricted. Since the degree to which interest is paid on bank accounts varies at present considerably from country to country it is difficult to measure exactly this definition of money for the entire Community. However, by using the monetary base it is still possible to obtain a lower limit for the welfare loss.

Following Lucas (1981) the welfare loss as a percentage of GDP can be based on a standard money demand function and is approximately equal to $0,5*(b/v)p^2$ where b is the semi-elasticity of money demand and v is velocity at the optimal inflation rate. If money is taken to be the monetary base the average velocity

of circulation in the Community would be about 10. Recent estimates of money demand for the EC (see Bekx and Tullio (1989) and Kremers and Lane (1990)) give an interest rate elasticity of about 2. A conservative estimate of the welfare loss from a 10 % rate of inflation in the Community would therefore be $0,5*(2/10)*0,01$, or about 0,1 % of Community GDP. An upper limit for the welfare loss can be obtained by using M1, i.e. cash plus sight deposits, as the definition of money. Since the average velocity of circulation of M1 in the Community is about one third of that of the monetary base the upper limit for the welfare loss would be about 0,3 % of Community GDP.

These two estimates rely on the present average velocity in the Community, which hides large differences among member countries. It can be expected, however, that with EMU these differences will to a large extent disappear. National reserve requirements will be abolished and it is not clear whether the EuroFed will impose a uniform Community wide reserve coefficient. This alone would imply that the average velocity of the monetary base should increase. A further reason to expect velocity to increase in EMU is that modern payment instruments will be adopted also in countries which at present have an inefficient banking system. This suggests that the lower estimate might be closer to the true value under EMU.

It has been suggested, [6] however, that as a practical matter the inflation tax is important in a number of Community countries so that convergence to a low inflation rate in EMU would at least imply a certain loss of revenue for these countries. The revenue loss some member countries would experience if their inflation rates go to the level experienced by the more stable countries is calculated in Chapter 5. It is found there that the loss would be minor for most countries, except possibly Portugal and Greece, where it might be about 1 % of GDP. It should be apparent, however, that this loss of revenue is not a welfare loss. The revenue loss can be made up through lower expenditures and higher taxes. Only to the extent that this is impossible would there be any welfare loss. Chapter 5 on fiscal policy issues discusses this in more detail.

Menu costs

Even a completely anticipated inflation forces all economic agents to revise their prices frequently. Just to change price lists, i.e. 'menus', should not be very costly in itself. These direct costs of inflation, called menu costs, are therefore usually taken to be negligible. However, some recent theoretical contributions suggest that even if the direct costs are very small they can still have sizeable indirect effects on

production and prices. [7] The reason for this result is that small direct costs can be magnified if they interact with other important distortions that exist somewhere else in the economy. For example, if the marginal productivity of labour is far above the wage rate (maybe because of income taxes), even a small fall in employment due to the menu costs can have a large cost for the economy. However, at the present stage of knowledge it appears that it is not possible to quantify these indirect effects. [8]

The expression 'menu costs' refers to the cost of changing price lists. This cost might be considered negligible in general, not only for the private sector, but also for the public sector since the cost of changing for example the income tax schedule should also be trivial. In reality, it seems, however, that these costs are substantial in the area of taxation. In most countries, income tax rates are progressive and not indexed; moreover, in the computation of the income of capital all nominal interest earnings are considered income although a part of them constitutes a reimbursement of the principal in real terms. This implies that any positive inflation rate increases the effective rate of taxation of labour

[6] See notably Dornbusch (1988).

[7] See Akerlof and Yeelen (1989).
[8] Bénabou (1989) contains an attempt to quantify the welfare costs of anticipated inflation based on a framework in which discrete price adjustments lead to speculation in storable goods.

and capital over time. It is difficult to say a priori whether this increase in tax revenue constitutes a cost or a benefit. To the extent that it increases a distortion it should be classified as a cost. However, to the extent that the government can use the revenue productively it should be classified as a benefit.

Macroeconomic effects

The macroeconomic effects of anticipated inflation have been thoroughly discussed in the literature. Macroeconomic theory of the 1960s held that there was a stable relationship between inflation and unemployment (the so-called Phillips curve) so that the authorities could attain and maintain any desired level of unemployment by choosing the appropriate inflation rate. This view of the world is no longer accepted on theoretical and empirical grounds. On theoretical grounds the main objection is that it assumes that economic agents never learn about inflation. On empirical grounds the 1970s, which had on average higher inflation and higher unemployment, showed that there was no stable trade-off between inflation and unemployment.

This observation has been confirmed by a large body of empirical literature. Graph 4.1 visualizes the same result by displaying a scatter diagram of average inflation and unemployment rates for OECD countries over the 15-year period 1970-85. It is apparent that higher inflation is not associated with lower unemployment in the long run. On the contrary, the regression between the two variables yields even a statistically significant positive coefficient which implies that, at least over the 15-year period considered here, countries with higher inflation had also, on average, higher unemployment. The point estimate of the inflation coefficient suggests that a one percentage point higher inflation rate was associated with a 0,3 percentage points higher unemployment rate. [9]

This does not imply that the Phillips curve necessarily has a positive slope, but it does show that in the long run higher inflation is certainly not associated with lower unemployment.

Further evidence that inflation does not have positive effects is provided by Graph 4.2 which depicts the relationship between inflation and per capita GDP. It is apparent that there is a strong negative relationship between income

GRAPH 4.1 : **Unemployment and inflation in OECD countries, 1970-85**

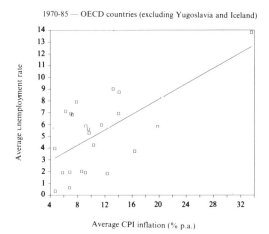

1970-85 — OECD countries (excluding Yugoslavia and Iceland)

Source : OECD, data available from 1970.
Regression result: Unemployment rate = 1,6 + 0,33 inflation
                                                          (3,82)
T-statistic in parentheses R squared = 0,41; 23 D.o.F.

and inflation. This is what one would expect if inflation reduces the overall efficiency of the economy. Although the relationship is very strong, it cannot be regarded as proof that inflation reduces the efficiency of the economy so strongly that differences in inflation can account for the observed differences in per capita income. Nevertheless, this stage suggests that countries with higher inflation on average do not perform better than countries with low inflation.

Other economic theories of the 1960s held that inflation was necessary to achieve growth in actual output. This might be true even if there is no relationship between the unemployment rate (which represents only the gap between potential and actual output) and inflation, as suggested above. However, there is now wide agreement even at the theoretical level that inflation does not increase growth. This is also suggested by Graph 4.3 which displays average growth rates (of real per capita GDP) and inflation rates (of the consumer price index (CPI)) for all OECD countries for the period 1955-85. Inspection of this scatter diagram suggests that there is no systematic relationship between the two variables. A regression confirms this impression since it shows that there is no statistically significant relationship between growth and inflation.

---

[9]   It is apparent from Graph 4.1 that the outlier in the upper right-hand corner strongly influences the regression result. The equation was therefore re-estimated without this outlier (Turkey). The coefficient was still positive, but the t-statistic fell to 1,63.

GRAPH 4.2: **Real GDP per capita and inflation in OECD countries, 1975-85**

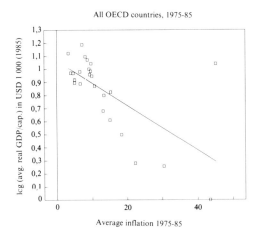

Source: IFS.

GRAPH 4.3: **Inflation and growth of real GDP per capita**

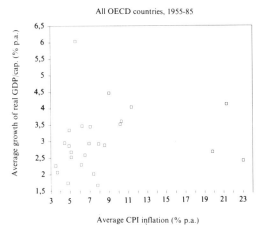

Source: IFS.
Note: except for the Netherlands, Austria, Italy and Yugoslavia, the period of observation is 1955-85.
Regression result: Growth = 2,8 + 0,025 inflation
                                              (0,67)
T-statistic in parentheses R squared = 0,02; 23 D.o.F.

Theoretical considerations therefore suggest that in the long run, i.e. when expectations have had time to adjust and correctly anticipate inflation, inflation does not yield any macroeconomic benefits in terms of unemployment or growth. On the contrary, some evidence suggests that higher inflation is associated with higher unemployment and low levels of real per capita income and that there is no significant correlation with growth.

4.1.2. The effects of unanticipated inflation

Up to this point the discussion has focused on the effects of a steady rate of inflation that is entirely predictable. However, in reality inflation is never constant and therefore never entirely predictable. Moreover, economic theory suggests that surprise inflation has much stronger adverse economic effects than anticipated inflation. This is true in particular for the macroeconomic effects and the effect on government revenues. The potential welfare losses from a highly variable inflation rate are therefore much larger than the losses that could result from a high, but stable, inflation rate. Moreover, unanticipated inflation also tends to create variability in relative prices which should have similar effects to variability

in exchange rates. A detailed discussion of the various channels that link inflation, the variability of inflation and the variability in relative prices is set out by Cukierman (1983).

This subsection therefore first presents some evidence about the link between inflation and its variability. This evidence suggests that in reality high inflation is usually linked to highly variable — and hence also highly unpredictable — inflation. Having established this link it then discusses the main channels through which unanticipated inflation causes economic costs.

The available evidence suggests that high but stable inflation rates are very rare because there is a strong link between the level of inflation and its variability. One reason for this might lie in the stop-and-go policies that are discussed briefly below. This link has been well documented in the economics literature [10] and is visually apparent in Graph 4.4 which shows the average and the standard deviation of inflation for all OECD countries between 1955 and 1985. The existence of a strong link between the average and variability, as expressed by the standard deviation, of inflation is also

---

10   See, for example, Cukierman (1981).

GRAPH 4.4: **Inflation and its variability in OECD countries**

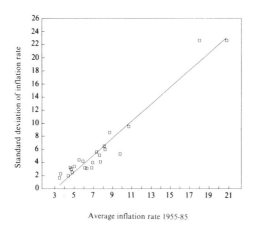

Average inflation rate 1955-85

Source: IFS.
Regression result: Standard deviation of inflation = 3,8 + 1,29* average inflation
       rate (18,2)
T-statistic in parentheses, 21 D.o.F.

confirmed more formally by the regression result reported below Graph 4.4. The estimated coefficient suggests that a one percentage point increase in the average inflation leads on average to a 1,3 percentage point increase in the standard deviation of inflation. [11] These results suggest that if inflation is high on average it also becomes largely unpredictable.

The remainder of this subsection discusses the main channels through which surprise inflation causes welfare losses.

Surprise inflation tax

Unanticipated inflation has much stronger effects on government finances than anticipated inflation which works through the inflation tax. The base for the inflation tax is the monetary base, i.e. cash and required reserves which are often remunerated at below-market rates. However, the base for the surprise inflation tax is the entire stock of government debt that carries a fixed nominal interest rate because the

real value of that debt is reduced by a surprise inflation. Since the total debt in almost all countries of the Community exceeds the monetary base by a large multiple, a 1 % surprise inflation yields a much higher government revenue than a 1 % inflation that is anticipated (see Chapter 5 for a discussion of the public finance effects of inflation).

However, the large potential revenue effect of surprise inflation cannot be considered beneficial. To begin with, it cannot, of course, be reaped in the long run since financial markets anticipate the incentive for the government to use it and interest rates will then contain an inflation risk premium. This implies that the mere possibility that the government may use the surprise inflation tax leads to higher interest rates even if the government does not intend to create any surprise inflation. The higher interest rates that result from this situation might be considered the cost of weak credibility. This cost should be most important for countries that have a high public debt and a poor inflation record.

Menu costs

In principle the menu costs from unanticipated inflation should be similar to the ones from anticipated inflation. This implies that they should correspond to the costs of printing new price lists (i.e. 'menus') or new income tax schedules. However, there might still be substantial indirect effects, especially through a non-indexed tax system which can lead to considerable distortions in the price system. However, these indirect consequences cannot be measured quantitatively.

Macroeconomic effects

Modern macroeconomic theory holds that unanticipated inflation can temporarily increase output and employment above the equilibrium level (i.e. a short-run Phillips curve does exist). However, since the reverse holds when inflation is lower than anticipated it follows immediately that a highly variable inflation rate keeps output continuously away from the equilibrium level and thus leads to losses.

The discussion of the effects of surprise inflation on public finance and output suggests that the authorities may perceive an incentive to use surprise inflation to reduce the real value of their public debt and to increase output and employment. Modern economic theory assumes, however, that the public anticipates this so that the government cannot obtain any advantage from an inflationary policy. However, even if the authorities realize that the public anticipates their actions they will still create inflation because otherwise inflation would be much lower than expected, and temporary unem-

---

[11]   It is clear that on a theoretical level variability and predictability are two separate concepts. However, as shown for example in Cukierman (1981), an increase in the variability of inflation is usually equivalent to a reduction in its predictability.

ployment might result. To reach a situation in which prices are stable and expected to remain so therefore requires that the public can trust that the authorities will not give in to the temptation to use surprise inflation. [12] In other words, this raises again the issue of 'credibility', which is taken up in Subsection 4.3 which discusses the requirements for a credible anti-inflationary monetary regime.

A further reason to believe that inflation involves macro-economic costs is that in most countries with high inflation the authorities periodically try to suppress it with tight monetary and fiscal policies. However, as these policies are often not maintained, but reversed when they cause unemployment, a cycle of 'stop-and-go' policies can develop. Since this cycle can never be predicted with accuracy it implies that on average high inflation rates may be associated with periods of disinflation and (re)accelerating inflation. This involves considerable macroeconomic costs because demand and output are destabilized.

This idea is borne out to some extent in the evidence presented in Graph 4.5 which relates average inflation to the variability of output growth.

---

[12] See Barro and Gordon (1983) for an analytical description of how an inflationary equilibrium can arise even if only unanticipated inflation affects output.

GRAPH 4.5: **Inflation and variability of output growth for OECD countries, 1955-85**

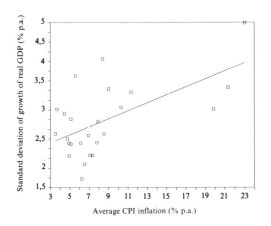

Source: IFS.
Note: the observed period is 1956-85 for the Netherlands and 1960-85 for Austria and Yugoslavia (earlier years unavailable).
Regression result: Standard deviation of growth = 2,1 + 0,08 inflation
(3,52)
T-statistic in parentheses R-squared = 0,35; 23 D.o.F.

This graph suggests that higher inflation indeed tends to be associated with a higher variability of real growth. Given the high correlation between average inflation and its variability it is difficult to decide whether this relationship comes from the level of inflation or its variability. Several of the effects discussed in this subsection, as well as the previous one on anticipated inflation, could be the cause for this result.

Relative price variability

Higher inflation and therefore also higher variability of inflation has been shown to lead to higher variability in relative prices as well. [13] This higher variability of relative prices, which is not justified by changes in demand and supply conditions, causes welfare losses in much the same way as excessive variability of exchange rates. Estimates for Germany suggest that a 1 % increase in the variability of relative prices lowers potential output by about 0,3 %. [14]

The arguments of this subsection indicate that inflation is also costly because high inflation rates are associated with highly variable inflation and a higher variability of output growth. Moreover, an unpredictable inflation rate is undesirable because it makes real interest payments on government debt unpredictable.

4.2. The cost of disinflation

While it is widely accepted that inflation is costly it is often argued that inflation should not be reduced because disinflation also involves costs. [15] Modern macroeconomic theory argues that these costs arise for two reasons: (i) wage rigidity; and (ii) lack of credibility in the adjustment process. Box 4.2 visualizes the adjustment path during disinflation that might be caused by either of these two reasons.

---

[13] See Cukierman (1983).
[14] See Neumann and von Hagen (1989).
[15] This consideration does not really apply to EMU, because convergence to price stability should already be substantially complete in Stage I. However, as discussed further in Chapter 8 of this volume, the cost of disinflation might be an important consideration for some countries during Stage I.

Box 4.2: Disinflation and the short-run Phillips curve

The adjustment path from a high to a low inflation rate can be visualized as in the adjacent diagram. The two negatively sloped lines denote two short-run Phillips curves that may be thought of as being the result of either a different initial nominal wage rate (effect (i) or different inflationary expectations of the public (effect (ii)).

Starting from the initial high inflation rate p (associated with the natural rate of unemployment because it is assumed to have persisted for some time) any reduction in inflation leads to an increase in unemployment because it involves a movement along the short-run Philips curve PP. However, as time passes, the rate of growth of nominal wages (and/or inflationary expectations) adjusts downward, implying that the short run Phillips curve shifts downwards, say to PP'. In the long run the economy eventually will settle down again at the natural rate of unemployment, but with the lower inflation rate.

Since the position of the short-run Phillips curve depends on the inflation rate wage earners expect to prevail in the future this picture can also be used to illustrate the effect of income policies which can be thought of as lowering inflationary expectations 'by decree'. A successful income policy would reduce increases in wages and other income to the rate that is compatible with the lower inflation, thus allowing the economy to move directly to a lower inflation rate without transitional unemployment. In terms of the picture this means that income policy

would shift the short-run Phillips curve downwards at the same time as actual inflation falls, thus leading to a vertical drop in inflation from p to p'.

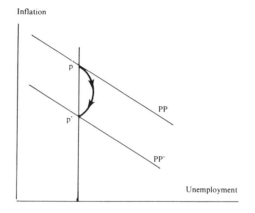

(i) It is widely accepted in the economics literature that rigidities in the wage-setting process can create a short run trade-off between inflation and output. This implies that disinflation can be associated with temporary losses of output. One example of wage rigidity is backward-looking wage indexation schemes which lead to a rise in real wages if inflation diminishes. The rise in real wages reduces demand for labour and hence causes unemployment (and losses of output). Lack of credibility in the adjustment process can also lead to output losses because if the decline in inflation is not anticipated nominal interest rates remain high. With actual inflation low this implies that realized real interest rates are high. This in turn increases the debt service burden on the public debt and might depress investment.

Although the precise reasons for wage rigidity vary from country to country, experience shows that most episodes of disinflation coincide with considerable, but temporary, unemployment. However, the precise value of the 'sacrifice ratio', i.e. the output loss per percentage point reduction in inflation, is not a constant. It changes over time and it is different across countries. For this reason alone it would be

extremely difficult to estimate quantitatively the output cost of disinflation.[16]

(ii) An even more important reason why it is impossible to estimate the cost of disinflation is that economic theory suggests that it depends decisively on the policy regime, especially the exchange rate regime, under which it occurs. In the absence of an exchange rate commitment the mere announcement of a disinflation programme might not be credible and therefore lead to large losses if it is actually implemented. In contrast, a credible commitment to a zone of monetary stability, such as the EMS, should reduce output losses, because it should reduce nominal interest rates and should also lead to a faster adjustment in wage setting.[17] It

---

[16]   The seigniorage loss from disinflation is discussed in detail in Chapter 5.
[17]   Under the assumption that institutional rigidities, such as backward-looking wage indexation, are remedied during the disinflation period.

is often argued that an exchange rate target in the EMS is superior to other forms of domestic commitments (such as a commitment to a low rate of monetary expansion) because in the EMS no country can change its exchange rate without the consent of its partners and because the cost of deviating from price stability comes immediately in the form of a real exchange rate appreciation that reduces output and demand.

It has been argued that this effect has allowed some EMS member countries to minimize the losses from disinflation during the 1980s. However, the statistical evidence on this point is weak, basically because it is impossible to determine exactly the degree to which the EMS commitment was 'credible' given that realignments did always provide some leeway for more inflation.[18]

The two arguments discussed so far suggest that disinflation should involve a cost in terms of unemployment unless the commitment of the authorities is completely credible and there is no wage rigidity. It has been suggested, however, that disinflation through a credible exchange rate commitment might not involve any unemployment, but on the contrary an increase in demand and economic activity.[19] This line of argument does not imply that disinflation imposes no costs, but it does suggest that with a credible exchange rate commitment the disinflation process might follow a quite different path than the one sketched out above.

The possibility that a credibly fixed exchange rate may lead to a different disinflation process depends on the degree of capital mobility and therefore the adjustment of nominal interest rates. With a high degree of capital mobility, a credibly fixed exchange rate leads to an equalization of interest rates, but if inflation has a certain inertia, real interest rates (the nominal rate minus inflation) will *not* be equalized.[20] A country that starts out with some inflation and fixes its exchange rate to a low-inflation (and therefore low-interest-rate) currency would therefore immediately have a low nominal domestic interest rate, and, until inflation has also been reduced, also a very low real interest rate.

In the beginning of the disinflation process real interest rates could therefore be low. This should stimulate investment demand. According to this model of disinflation there might therefore initially be an expansion of output. The cost of

disinflation in this case arises through the current account deficit that is needed to finance the increase in investment.[21]

The problems arising from external current account deficits that may occur from the fixing of exchange rates before inflation rates have converged should only be of a transitional nature. After the initial adjustment period the expectations that underlie the process of wage and price formation should adjust and inflation rates should converge. However, the countries with initially high inflation might have accumulated in the mean time a considerable stock of external debt because they will have had a current account deficit in the mean time. In EMU an external debt should not create any particular problems by itself since the intra-Community balance of payments constraint will disappear. But the debt service will, of course, reduce the standard of living of the population, unless the debt has been used to finance productive investment.

4.3. Requirements of a stable and credible monetary regime

The benefits from price stability outlined in the preceding sections can be assured only if the institution that is responsible for the aggregate monetary policy of EMU follows, and is seen to follow, the appropriate anti-inflationary policy. Moreover, as was also argued, a credible strict monetary policy would also reduce the costs of disinflation. However, this condition cannot be taken for granted. The extent to which the EuroFed will (be able to) conduct a credible policy geared towards assuring price stability for the Community depends on a number of factors, the most important of which are its constitution and the budget policy followed by Member States. Other important features are the aversion against inflation of the public and the behaviour of the representatives of employees and employers. However, as these are, partly at least, dependent on the behaviour of the central bank this section concentrates on the role of the constitution of the central bank in EMU, called EuroFed, in assuring a credible anti-inflationary policy. The role of budget policy is analysed separately in Chapter 5 below.

---

[18] See the evidence in Giavazzi and Giovannini (1989), de Grauwe and Vansanten (1989) and Begg (1990).

[19] See Giavazzi and Spaventa (1990).

[20] *Idem.*

[21] It has even been suggested that the increase in demand through higher investment would tend to put pressure on prices and that capital inflows would make it impossible for the national monetary authorities to restrict liquidity. In this case the fixed exchange rate commitment might initially slow down the disinflation process. An imperfect degree of capital market integration could also lead to a process of 'overfinancing' of current account deficits. The still imperfect degree of capital market integration of some Community countries gives the authorities the possibility to keep national interest rates high to restrict liquidity. But given that capital markets are highly, even if not perfectly integrated, such a policy leads to large capital inflows which would exceed the current account deficit.

It is widely recognized that two constitutional features of a central bank are of great importance in determining to what extent it pursues a monetary policy geared towards price stability: its statutory duty to assure price stability and its political independence. These two elements are now discussed in turn.

4.3.1. A statutory mandate for price stability

A statutory mandate to aim at price stability will give Euro-Fed a clear direction for its policy. It is therefore, without any doubt, a necessary element of the constitution of the EuroFed. The issues that remain open in this context are the definition of the price index which EuroFed should stabilize and whether the mandate should also contain other provisions.

The concept of price stability

The discussion of the costs of unanticipated inflation in the previous section implies that price stability should not be taken to mean only an average inflation rate close to zero, but also that prices should remain predictable, i.e. inflation should not vary around the average value of zero. The task of EuroFed should therefore be not only to keep inflation at or close to zero in the medium term, but also to make sure that it does not fluctuate in the short term.

In order to make the concept of price stability operational it is necessary to specify what price index is to be stabilized.[22] This choice is rarely made explicit even in countries where price stability is the main mandate for the central bank, probably because at the national level most prices move closely together. However, since prices can diverge much more at the European level than inside any member country it might be preferable to give some indication to EuroFed what price index it should look at. From a theoretical point of view the appropriate target index is the one that is most closely related to the source of the cost of inflation. For example, if one considers the main cost of inflation to be suboptimal money holdings the appropriate index would be the consumer price index (CPI). But if the main cost of inflation is taken to derive from the variability in relative prices which leads to lower investment and production the appropriate price index to stabilize might be the producer price index. It is therefore difficult to decide on purely

theoretical grounds what price index should be stabilized by EuroFed.

The main factor in this choice might therefore be availability and comparability across countries. The CPI has the advantage that it is published monthly everywhere, in contrast to wholesale and producer prices which are not always available with this frequency. A further advantage of the CPI is that it is widely understood and used in wage negotiations.

Price stability as the overriding mandate

A statutory duty for price stability is, of course, effective only to the extent that the central bank does not have other policy goals that can make this goal impossible to achieve. The provisions that are most likely to make price stability impossible to achieve concern the exchange rate and the management of government debt.

It is apparent that if the central bank has to support the exchange rate[23] it may not always be able to combat the imported inflation that results if the exchange rate is pegged to an inflationary currency. However, since the decision about the exchange rate regime (i.e. whether the exchange rate of the ecu should be fixed, be kept inside a target zone, or be floating vis-à-vis the other major currencies) could be considered of wider political importance, it should therefore be taken by the appropriate democratically legitimated Community institution. To be able to pursue the goal of price stability EuroFed would, however, have to be independent in its management of the exchange rate within the limits implied by the exchange rate regime that has been decided at the political level.

Similarly, if the central bank has to finance government deficits, or if it can be required to buy certain amounts of government debt, it may be forced to follow a more expansionary policy than would be compatible with stable prices.

A provision that might be compatible with the goal of price stability is the requirement to support the general economic policy of the government.[24] If given a subordinate rank, i.e. if price stability remains the overriding goal, such a requirement would effectively be suspended if it conflicts with the need to pursue restrictive policies. Moreover, since it does not provide a direct channel through which it could affect monetary policy it would seem to pose less of a danger

---

[22] It is assumed here that EuroFed should not be concerned with the variability of prices inside the union because these relative prices will just represent the effects of regional shifts in demand, supply or other non-monetary factors. EuroFed should therefore not be concerned with the lowest or highest regional inflation rate, but only with the average.

[23] At present the government decides on the exchange rate in all member countries.
[24] This is the case at present in the Federal Republic of Germany.

to a consistent anti-inflationary policy than the other two provisions discussed so far. In the Community such a requirement would, however, be difficult to interpret since the policy stance of different Member States can be expected to diverge considerably at times even in EMU and the Community itself would not be able to establish an overall fiscal policy stance because its budget would remain small relative to national budgets.

For the case of the Community this implies that EuroFed would have the means to pursue price stability only if monetary financing of public deficits (at the national or the Community level) is excluded and if it does not have to stabilize the exchange rate of the Community currencies (or the single currency at the end of Stage III) against the rest of the world (i.e. effectively the US dollar).

4.3.2. Central bank independence and price stability[25]

Even if a central bank has a formal statutory duty of price stability and the means to pursue this goal, it may not always be able to do so if it is not politically independent. There are strong theoretical reasons to believe that independence is a necessary condition for price stability.

The main reason is that, as shown above, unanticipated inflation has the potential to stimulate, even if only temporarily, economic activity (especially when facing short electoral timetables) and reduce the real value of public debt. Even well-intentioned policy-makers would therefore always face the issue of how to convince the public that they will never succumb to the temptation to create surprise inflation. Since in democratic societies elected officials are in general free to determine economic policy at their discretion it is very difficult for political bodies to acquire enough credibility to convince the public that inflation will always stay low. An independent central bank, however, does not face this temptation to create surprise inflation because, if its statutory duty is to safeguard price stability, it has no interest in temporarily increasing economic activity or lowering the value of public debt through surprise inflation. Central bank independence can therefore solve, at least to some extent, the credibility problem.[26]

The relationship between central bank independence and price stability has been investigated empirically. The degree of political independence of any given central bank is, of course, difficult to measure in practice. However, it is possible to find some objective indicators of independence, such as the formal institutional relationship between the central bank and the government, the extent of formal contacts between the two and the existence of rules forcing the central bank to automatically accommodate fiscal policy. These indicators have been used in empirical research to establish a measure of independence, which was then compared with the price stability record.[27] This research shows that there is a strong link between political independence and performance in terms of low inflation. In particular the two most independent central banks (in Germany and Switzerland) had also the two lowest inflation rates.

As explained in Box 4.3 the elements of the statutes of a central bank that determine the degree to which it is politically independent are the following:

(i)   Independence of instructions from government bodies (in the EC this means *vis-à-vis* the Community and the national level);

(ii) Personal independence of Board and Council members;

(iii) Legal rank of its statutes.

(i) The first element is indispensable. If the central bank had to accept instructions from political institutions it would not be able to fulfil its mandate to maintain price stability since these political institutions will often have different objectives.

(ii) The second element ensures that individual members of the policy-making bodies of the central bank cannot face personal conflicts of interest, because, for example, their reappointment might be subject to political pressures. Personal independence could be achieved if the term to which members of the Board and the Council are appointed is sufficiently long and if the appointment process cannot be subject to political pressures. It has also been argued that the degree of personal independence would be strengthened if a reappointment is not possible.

(iii) The last element determines the conditions under which the statutes of the central bank can be changed; the more difficult this is, the more secure the central bank — and hence the public — could be that its independence is permanent. In the case of the Community the structure of the constitution of EuroFed would be laid down in an amend

---

25   Much of the following draws on Neumann (1990).
26   The theoretical and empirical contributions concerning the issue of credibility always take as their point of departure countries where there is a political cycle with well-defined dates at which national elections take place. This will not be the case in the Community and one could therefore argue that the issue of credibility and the political business cycle is less important for the Community than for countries that also represent a political union.

---

27   See Alesina (1989).

98 Main benefits and costs

Box 4.3: Inflation and central bank independence

GRAPH 4.6: **Central bank independence and inflation**

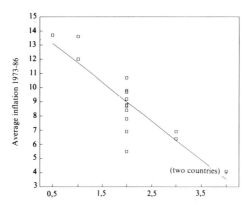

Index of central bank independence

Source: based on Alesina (1989).
Regression result: Independence = 4,6 − 0,29 inflation
(−7,50)
T-statistic in parentheses R squared = 0,79; 15 D.o.F.

Alesina (1989) classifies central banks on a scale going from the least independent, associated with a value of 0,5, to the most independent, with a value of 4. This classification, based in turn on Bade and Parkin (1985) and Masciandaro and Tabellini (1988), takes into account several institutional characteristics of different central banks, such as the the formal institutional relationship between the central bank and the Executive (for instance who appoints the head of the central bank, and how often, the presence of government officials on the executive boards of the central bank, and so on); the extent of informal contacts between the Executive and the central bank, and the existence of rules forcing the central bank to automatically accommodate fiscal policy.[28]

---

[28] The ranking in this graph is based on the situation in the early 1980s (corresponding roughly to the end point of the period given for average inflation). It therefore does not reflect the current degree of independence of these central banks. For example, in the case of Italy the graph does not take into account the so-called divorce (between the Treasury and the Banca d'Italia) that in 1985 relieved the Italian central bank from the requirement to automatically accommodate fiscal policy, which is one of the parameters mentioned above.

---

ment to the Treaty of Rome which can be changed only if all Member States agree. In the case of the Community the statutes of the central bank would therefore certainly have a special legal rank.

This section has argued that an effective statutory duty for price stability and political independence appear to be necessary conditions for a consistent and credible anti-inflationary policy. However, these two elements would not be sufficient to guarantee that the central bank responsible for the common monetary policy in EMU, i.e. EuroFed, will always pursue stable prices. Its task may become difficult if[29]

tensions on the labour market result in excessive increases in nominal wages because this would leave EuroFed only the choice of accommodating the inflationary pressure or pursuing a restrictive policy with adverse consequences for employment. Such a conflict is less likely to arise to the extent that the value of stable prices is generally recognized. The environment in which EuroFed operates is therefore an important element in determining to what extent EuroFed will be able to attain the goal of price stability.

It has therefore been suggested that regular contacts between EuroFed and democratically elected institutions could increase public support for the policy of EuroFed and make it easier for it to achieve its target of price stability. Some degree of democratic accountability, for example in the form of regular reports from EuroFed to the European Parliament, might therefore actually facilitate the task of EuroFed.

---

[29] Or if budget policy puts pressure on financial markets which is possible even in the absence of direct monetary financing of the deficit as discussed in Chapter 5 below.

References

Akerlof, G. and Yeelen, J. (1989), 'Rational models of irrational behaviour', *American Economic Review,* May, pp. 137-142.

Alesina, A. (1989), 'Politics and business cycles in industrial democracies', *Economic Policy* 8, pp. 57-89.

Bade, R. and Parkin, M. (1985), 'Central bank laws and monetary policy', unpublished.

Barro, P. and Gordon, D. (1983), 'A critical theory of monetary policy in a national rate model', *Journal of Political Economy*, 91, August, pp. 589-610.

Begg, D. (1990), 'Alternative exchange rate regimes: The role of the exchange rate and the implications for wage-price adjustment', in *European Economy* (1990).

Bekx, P. and Tullio, G. (1989), 'A note on the European Monetary System and the determination of the DM-dollar exchange rate', *Cahiers économiques de Bruxelles,* No 123, pp. 329-343.

Bénabou, R. (1989), 'Optimal price dynamics and speculation with a storable good', *Econometrica,* Vol. 57, No 1 (January 1989), pp. 41-80.

Cukierman, A. (1981), 'Interest rates during the cycle, inventories and monetary policy — A theoretical analysis', *Carnegie-Rochester Conference Series on Public Policy* 15, pp. 87-144.

Cukierman, A. (1983), 'Relative price variability and inflation: A survey and further results', *Carnegie-Rochester Conference Series on Public Policy* 19, pp. 103-158.

Cukierman, A. (1990), 'Central bank behaviour, credibility, accommodation and stabilization', draft, May 1990.

de Grauwe, P. and Vansanten, K. (1989), 'Deterministic chaos in the foreign exchange market', University of Leuven.

Dornbusch, R. (1988), 'The EMS, the dollar and the yen', in Giavazzi, F., Micossi, S. and Miller M. (eds), *The European Monetary System,* Banca d'Italia, CEPR.

European Economy (1990) — 'The economics of EMU', special issue.

Fischer, S. (1981), 'Towards an understanding of the costs of inflation: II', *Carnegie-Rochester Conference Series on Public Policy* 15, 5-42, p. 5.

Friedman, M. (1969), 'Nobel lecture: Inflation and unemployment', *Journal of Political Economy,* 1977, Vol. 85, No 3.

Giavazzi, F. and Giovannini A. (1989), *Limiting exchange rate flexibility,* MIT Press, Cambridge, Mass.

Giavazzi, F. and Spaventa, L. (1989), 'The new EMS', CEPR, paper No 363, January 1989.

Giavazzi, F. and Spaventa, L. (1990), 'The new EMS', forthcoming in *The European Monetary System in the 1990s,* Paul de Grauwe and Lucas Papademos (eds), Longman 1990.

Kremers, J. J. M. and Lane, T. (1990), 'Economic and monetary integration and the aggregate demand for money in the EMS', IMF Working Paper 90/23, March.

Lucas, R. E. (1981), *Studies in business cycle theory,* MIT Press, Cambridge.

Masciandaro, D. and Tabellini, G. (1988), 'Fiscal deficits and monetary institutions: a comparative analysis', in Cheng H. (ed.), *Challenges to monetary policy in the Pacific-Basin countries,* Kluwer Publishers.

Neumann, M. (1990), 'Central bank independence as a prerequisite of price stability', in *European Economy* (1990).

Neumann, M. and von Hagen, J. (1989), 'Conditional relative price variance and its determinants: Open economy evidence from Germany', forthcoming *International Economic Review* (February 1991).

Spaventa, L. (1989), 'Seigniorage: old and new policy issues', *European Economic Review* 33, pp. 557-563.

Chapter 5

Implications for public finance

EMU will have strong implications for economic policy at large, including policies for product and factor markets. These policies will be regulatory and financial in character. Aspects of these policies, for example in the structural and income domains, are discussed elsewhere in this study (Chapters 3 and 6). The aim of this chapter is to discuss two major issues raised by EMU in the public finance domain and to assess the associated costs and benefits:

(i)   What are the logical implications and requirements arising from EMU for budgetary policy? (Section 5.1.)

(ii) How will EMU affect the income and expenditures of governments, and their ability to take autonomous taxing and spending decisions? (Section 5.2.)

Although these two questions are closely linked in practice, they are analytically distinct since the first mainly refers to demand policy and debt/deficit issues, whereas the second primarily regards the level and structure of taxes and public spending, which are more in the domain of supply policy. Table 5.1 summarizes these two types of effects while emphasizing the distinction between those of economic union and monetary union.

The main conclusions of this chapter are the following:

(i)   The challenge that has to be faced in the design of the fiscal regime of EMU is to provide an adequate mix of autonomy, discipline and coordination, for those are the logical requirements of a well-functioning economic and monetary union.

(ii)   The need for fiscal autonomy and flexibility arises from the loss of the monetary and exchange rate instrument for individual countries. Indeed, EMU will place new demands on fiscal policy at the national level for short-term stabilization and medium-term adjustment purposes in the case of country-specific disturbances.

(iii) The mere creation of a monetary union requires, however, long-term consistency between the common monetary policy and the fiscal policies of the Member States. Unsustainable budgetary positions in a Member State, ultimately leading to either default or debt monetization, would be a major threat to the overall monetary stability. High and growing public debt ratios would lead to pressures on EuroFed to soften its policy stance and more generally on the Community as a whole to provide financial relief. Fiscal discipline is therefore a vital component of EMU. Since the present fiscal position of some Member States cannot be considered as sustainable, this is a serious matter of concern.

(iv) An important issue is whether EMU could weaken the incentives towards fiscal discipline. Effects in opposite directions can be expected. On the one hand, participation in EMU is indeed disciplinary since it implies the acceptance of monetary discipline and therefore the renunciation of debt monetization. Financial integration should also lead to a better market assessment of national fiscal positions, although the effectiveness of market discipline cannot be taken for granted. On the other hand, markets cannot be expected to behave as if solidarity across Community Member States were completely ruled out, since concerns for solidarity are integral to the philosophy of the Community. Other, frequently discussed arguments regarding interest rate costs or current account constraints do not lead to clear-cut conclusions either. Uncoordinated policies might also lead to inappropriate deficits in the medium term, but only to the extent that coordination and surveillance procedures are not effective. On balance, there is no compelling evidence that EMU would have strong adverse effects on fiscal discipline, but there is a case for addressing the risk of failures of market discipline.

(v)   Although macroeconomic interdependence between Member States will be affected by EMU, there is no evidence that short-term spill-over effects of fiscal policies would be so strong that fiscal policies should be tightly coordinated on a day-to-day basis. However, coordination would be required if the common exchange rate and current account needed correction, and more generally in the context of policy coordination at the G7 level. In the medium term, surveillance will have to correct possible tendencies for budget deficits to become too large as their interest rate cost is spread throughout the Union.

(vi) As inflation rates converge to a low level, four southern Member States where the 'inflation tax' is presently above average due to higher inflation, wider use of cash, and higher bank reserves, will suffer seigniorage revenue losses. However, taking present inflation rates as a reference, this revenue loss of monetary union amounts to about 1 % of GDP in two Member States, and is below 0,5 % of GDP in the two others. Moreover, since seigniorage revenues can be replaced by explicit taxes, the welfare cost of this revenue loss can be considered to be much lower.

(vii) On the spending side, a timely move towards EMU would substantially reduce the ex-post cost of public borrowing during the transition to price convergence since present interest rates carry inflation expectations *and risk premiums. Some countries would also experience a more permanent decline in the cost of public borrowing. However, this gain should not be regarded as general.*

(viii) As the Community progresses towards EMU, the general issues of efficient taxation and provision of public goods arise. Even with a high degree of integration, *there is no case for an overall harmonization of the tax systems and Member States would remain free to choose their spending and taxing levels. However, care should be taken with respect to spill-over effects in the cross-frontier incidence of taxing and spending, and to problems of migration of tax bases. In the absence of cooperation these can lead to undertaxation and an insufficient provision of public goods. Therefore, minimal standards and common rules should be set when necessary.*

Table 5.1

Summary presentation of the fiscal policy and public finance effects of EMU

	Monetary union (I)	Economic union (II)	Aggregate effect in the medium term (I + II)
1. Fiscal policy			
(a) Need for autonomy	increases	decreases	increases
(b) Need for discipline	increases	neutral	increases
(c) Incentives to discipline[1]	+ / −	+ / −	+ / −
(d) Need for coordination	increases	increases	increases
2. Government income and expenditure			
(a) Seigniorage revenues	decrease	decrease	decrease
(b) Debt service	decreases	+ / −	decreases
(c) Tax revenues[2]	neutral	decrease	decrease
(d) Provision of public goods[2]	neutral	decreases	decreases
Government balance (a + c − b − d)[3]	increases	+ / −	+ / −

[1] Without specific Community budgetary rules.
[2] Without coordination.
[3] Increase means increased budget surplus.

5.1. Budgetary policy in a monetary union

The optimal design of the fiscal system for the Community is only partially a matter of economic efficiency. Analysis can help to identify those public goods and services which should be supplied at the Community level in order to maximize the overall welfare, and those which, according to the principle of subsidiarity, should be provided by national or regional governments. This approach, known as the theory of fiscal federalism, can provide insights regarding the desirable allocation of different functions among different levels of government.[1] However, the design of a fiscal

model is more fundamentally a matter of political choice, and it remains for the governments and citizens of Europe to decide whether or not to transfer new fiscal functions at the Community level. Indeed, the diversity of the budgetary systems in existing political federations confirms the viability of alternative models.

The purpose of the present analysis is therefore not to discuss what should be *in abstracto* the fiscal regime of the Community. Throughout this section, it is assumed without discussion that the Community budget remains too limited to have any significant macroeconomic role for the Community as a whole, and therefore that any fiscal policy measure belongs to the autonomous or coordinated action of the Member States. Taking as given this institutional framework, the main focus is rather on the logical impli-

---

[1] See Van Rompuy *et al.* (1990) and, for an early attempt to define the adequate fiscal regime for the Community, the MacDougall Report (1977). See also Section 5.2.3 below.

cations and requirements for national fiscal policies of the next developments of the Community: the completion of the internal market and monetary union.

An appropriate starting point is to analyse the demands EMU will place on national fiscal policy. This is the purpose of Section 5.1.1, from which the conclusion emerges that there is indeed a case for national fiscal autonomy in a monetary union. Then the key point is whether and to what extent EMU makes the fiscal position and policy of a Member State also a matter of concern for the Community as a whole. In dealing with this question, a distinction is be made between those aspects which relate to fiscal discipline (Section 5.1.2) and those which relate to fiscal policy coordination (Section 5.1.3). The root of this distinction, which is fully spelled out in the text, is that discipline mainly refers to the risks that unsustainable debt/deficit paths of national budgets would present for the monetary stability of the union, i.e. to the externalities associated with a violation of the government's intertemporal constraint, whereas coordination refers to the appropriateness of the fiscal policy stance in the Member States and the Community as a whole, i.e. to the standard demand and interest rate externalities.[2] In other words, fiscal deficits are envisaged as problems in the first case, while they are treated as instruments in the second.

To supply the adequate mix of autonomy, discipline and coordination is the challenge the fiscal regime of the Community has to meet. It is not an easy task since these objectives are not spontaneously assured. Nor are they antinomic, either. Autonomy and discipline refer to different time horizons. Indeed, it is inherent to a monetary union that it relaxes the constraints to fiscal policy in the short run (because of an easier and wider access to external financing), but simultaneously makes the long-term budget constraint more strict (because the possibility of monetizing the public debt is eliminated). In other words, EMU replaces short-term constraints by an intertemporal constraint.[3] However, even if the budgetary policy of a Member State conforms to the discipline conditions, changes can be necessary in order to achieve the right policy stance for the Community as a whole. This is what coordination and surveillance of fiscal policies are about.

Basically, fiscal policy will be considered here as demand policy, and one whose impact is primarily measured by the evolution of the budget deficit. Autonomy, discipline and coordination mainly concern those deficits. The implications of EMU for taxation and spending are discussed in Section 5.2.3.

5.1.1. The need for autonomy

One of the most obvious consequences of monetary union is that monetary policy is lost as an instrument of national macroeconomic policy. This is the primary basis for the presumption that monetary union leads national fiscal policy to assume a larger function. However, this argument needs to be further elaborated in order to specify what fiscal policy should aim at and to assess the degree of fiscal flexibility which is required. A good starting point is to examine how the relative macroeconomic positions of economies participating in EMU (relativities) could be affected, knowing that monetary policy would only be directed towards the aggregate management of the Community economy. This is an important issue because the need for a modification of relativities would arise from any kind of asymmetry, whatever its precise origin, namely different initial positions, shocks, structures, behaviours or preferences.[4]

Obviously, not all asymmetrical reactions or differences in economic performance would need to be corrected, and even less through fiscal demand policy only. Chapter 6 deals at length with the cost of losing the exchange rate as an adjustment instrument and discusses the effectiveness and assignment of alternative adjustment mechanisms, including fiscal policy. Without entering this discussion, it is worth mentioning here that wage-price flexibility remains the basic adjustment channel as a substitute for the nominal exchange rate. Neither economic theory nor the practice of economic policy recommend replacing the loss of such a nominal instrument by fiscal policy. However, in so far as nominal rigidities hamper market adjustments, fiscal policy measures can alleviate temporary country-specific disequilibria. This is indeed the traditional role of fiscal policy as a tool for stabilization. Budgetary adjustments can also be a necessary medium-term component of the path towards a new equilibrium in the case of permanent shocks, although this adjustment role is not specific to EMU. Both roles can best be illustrated with the help of an example. Corresponding model simulations are given in Box 5.1.

Budgetary policy as a tool for stabilization

Suppose that a national economy which is initially in internal and external equilibrium is hit by a demand shock, e.g. a temporary increase in households' propensity to consume (a fall in the saving ratio) lasting for a few periods. Due to imperfect goods market integration, most of the increase in demand falls on home goods, with the associated conse-

---

[2]   This distinction, which was not made in the Delors Report (1989), has been stressed *inter alia* by Bredenkamp and Deppler (1989) and Padoa-Schioppa (1990).
[3]   See Artus (1988).

[4]   The nature of asymmetries in EMU is discussed in Chapter 6.

quences for inflation. In a floating rate regime, monetary policy would respond to these developments by a rise in interest rates which would reduce domestic demand and appreciate the exchange rate. Both effects, would contribute to reducing the inflationary impact of the shock. In so far as the shock is temporary, this would in addition reduce the need for further wage-price adjustments when the saving ratio returns to the baseline level.

In EMU, EuroFed monetary policy would only very partially respond to the shock affecting a specific country since its primary task is to aim at stability in the union as a whole. But since goods markets would still not be perfectly integrated, equilibrium in the goods markets would still require a real exchange rate appreciation.[5] Most of the burden of stabilization would fall on spontaneous price and wage adjustments. The main channel would in that case be the real demand impact of the loss of price competitiveness induced by higher domestic prices, which would offset the effect of the rise in household demand. However, with imperfectly integrated markets, this adjustment could well take time. This is why fiscal policy could be used in order to offset directly the impact of the increase in domestic demand. Assuming a timely fiscal tightening, prices would therefore rise less and the subsequent adjustment when saving resumes would be less costly in terms of lost output and unemployment. This illustrates the stabilization role of autonomous budgetary policy in EMU.

This role has to be qualified. Although both exchange rate fixity and free capital movements would increase the effectiveness of fiscal policy in EMU,[6] most of the reasons which have led governments to opt for medium-term oriented budgetary policies instead of short-term fine-tuning remain valid: the lack of budgetary flexibility will still be a major obstacle, and, as argued below, concern about excessive deficits should only grow with monetary union. Moreover, fiscal policy should not be used to delay market adjustments (e.g. real wage adjustments) when those adjustments are required. Therefore, a reason for not using fiscal stabilization policy systematically in EMU is that it could well amount to trading-off short-term stabilization for a more sluggish adjustment in the longer term.[7]

EMU would therefore not require a reversion to fiscal fine-tuning management. Indeed, no such tendency has been observed in the ERM which to a large extent raises the same kind of issue. Only in the case of well-identified and severe country-specific shocks would the case for fiscal demand management be compelling (an example of this in practice is described in Annex B, in the case of hydrocarbon price shocks and the Netherlands). In addition, the need for national stabilization in the short-term would be reduced by the development of 'shock-absorber' assistance mechanisms at the Community level as discussed in Chapter 6.

[5] On the role of imperfect goods market integration, see Krugman (1989) and Aglietta, Coudert and Delessy (1990).

[6] In a standard Mundell-Fleming framework, the conditions for fiscal policy to be the most effective are (i) fixed exchange rate, and (ii) free capital movements, since in that case the interest rate cost of fiscal policy is minimum.
[7] See Chapter 6 and Begg (1990).

Box 5.1: Macroeconomic effects of a fall in the saving rate under alternative policy regimes

The Multimod model developed by the IMF (see Box 2.5) has been used in order to evaluate the effects of a shock to the household saving rate under different exchange rate regimes. Multimod, a small-scale multinational model with model-consistent expectations, is adequately tailored for this task. It includes separate models for the four largest Member States (Germany, France, Italy and the United Kingdom).

Three exchange rate regimes are considered:[8] a pure float, the EMS in Stage I (with the UK participating in the ERM) which is modelled according to the German anchor hypothesis, and EMU. Monetary policy is set according to the same rule for all countries in the float regime, for Germany in the EMS regime, and for EuroFed in the EMU regime; this rule gives priority to the maintenance of price stability. Only its scope changes, i.e. national monetary policies respond to deviations in national variables whilst EuroFed considers the performance of the Community as a whole. For non-German ERM members, a high

priority is given to Deutschmark exchange rate stability; however, bands allow for some flexibility in the short term.

Dollar exchange rates are in each case determined by a forward-looking uncovered interest rate parity condition under the assumptions of perfect capital mobility, asset substitutability and perfect foresight. In other terms, the evolution of exchange rates equalizes the expected return on short-term assets denominated in different currencies. With such a determination of the exchange rate and such a monetary rule, a rise in domestic demand both deteriorates the current account and appreciates the exchange rate because of the rise in domestic interest rates. This result might be contrary to European conventional wisdom. However, it holds once full capital mobility and asset substitutability are assumed.[9] The model is used to simulate the macroeconomic consequences of a permanent fall in the British saving rate by two percentage points under three alternative exchange rate regimes:

(i) Under a float regime, a fall in private saving provokes an immediate 2 % exchange rate appreciation since monetary policy is expected to be tight in the years ahead. Domestic

[8] Details on Multimod, the exchange rate regimes and simulation results are given Annex E.

[9] The US experience of the early 1980s shows that this is not only theoretical.

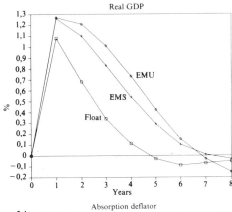

GRAPH 5.1: **Effects of a fall in UK household saving under three exchange rate regimes**

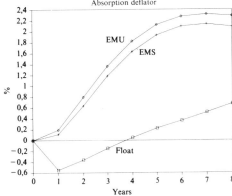

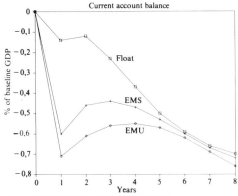

Source: **Multimod simulations by the Commission services.**

demand therefore crowds out external demand, the expansion is short-lived and inflation remains low, as shown in Graph 5.1.

(ii) In the EMS, monetary policy can no longer be directed towards demand management although bands allow for a limited interest rate rise.[10] The exchange rate appreciates only by 0,4 % in the first year. Domestic demand is higher, and translates more into output growth. However, the rise in inflation induces a real appreciation, which deteriorates the trade balance.

(iii) The behaviour of the economy under EMU does not differ much from the experience under the EMS. Interest-rate and nominal exchange-rate effects of the fall in saving are smaller, with the consequence that growth and inflation are slightly higher (Graph 5.1).

In order to illustrate the potential role of fiscal policy in EMU, Table 5.2 gives the effects of the shock to the saving rate under the three regimes and its effect under the EMU regime assuming an (unanticipated) reduction in government expenditures in year 1 calibrated in order to minimize the deviation of inflation from the baseline over eight years. It is apparent that fiscal policy, by offsetting most of the effects of the decline in the saving rate, could help to reduce the adverse effects of such shocks. Obviously, this could also be the case in the EMS. Alternatively, the country could settle for a realignment.

---

[10] The shock is not large enough to trigger a realignment, which is supposed to happen only when the inflation differential with respect to Germany reaches 8 %.

Table 5.2

Medium-term effects of the saving decline

(Present value of deviation from baseline over eight years)

	Float	EMS	EMU	EMU with fiscal policy
GDP	1,89	3,66	4,21	− 0,13
Private consumption	21,07	19,95	22,59	23,70
Inflation (absolute deviation)	1,47	1,87	2,05	0,45
Current account	− 1,81	− 2,84	− 3,28	0,03
Real effective exchange rate[1]	1,9	1,4	1,7	0,2

[1] Present value of average appreciation.
Source: Multimod simulations by the Commission services.

Budgetary policy as a tool for adjustment

Suppose now that instead of being temporary, the fall in the saving rate is permanent.[11] The medium-term impact is the same whatever the exchange rate regime. In all regimes, the fall in the saving rate leads to a permanent real exchange rate appreciation (in order to achieve internal equilibrium) and to an external deficit. In EMU, real appreciation takes place through a rise in domestic prices, whereas in a floating regime the main channel is a rise in the nominal exchange rate. The difference lies in the possible reactions to the external deficit.

Ultimately, external balance must be achieved in all exchange rate regimes. Among possible adjustment mechanisms are (i) a build-up of the external debt, which erodes wealth and disposable income, and leads agents to reduce their consumption, (ii) inflation, which also reduces wealth by wiping out the real value of monetary balances, and (iii) a permanent reduction in the budget deficit, which raises the aggregate national saving rate.[12] The first mechanism is independent from the exchange rate regime; however, it only acts in the very long run; relying on it implies one is ready to accept the build-up of net foreign debt or assets in so far as it arises from private sector behaviour. The second rests on the possibility of adjusting the nominal exchange rate to offset the effects of higher inflation. It is not available in EMU where inflation differentials would entirely translate into real exchange rate changes. Thus, except for the Com-

munity as a whole in relation to the rest of the world, an adjustment mechanism is lost in EMU. This is the basic rationale for expecting more reliance on the third mechanism, namely fiscal policy.

The above example is only a specific case for what could be called the adjustment role of fiscal policy in EMU. The general point is that if there is a need to change the real exchange rate within EMU because of the build-up of undesirable external imbalances, the only available macroeconomic instrument is fiscal policy.[13] Whether the need for using fiscal policy as a tool of adjustment will increase or decrease in EMU depends on the balance between two opposite effects: on one hand, as developed in Chapter 6, current account surpluses and deficits should be less of a problem within the Community once capital moves freely and exchange rate risk is eliminated; on the other hand, in so far as changes will be required in the real exchange rate or the external account, fiscal policy will be the main available adjustment mechanism. However, the instrument which is lost, i.e. adjustment through inflation, is neither a very powerful nor a desirable one, since it is at odds with the objective of price stability. The loss of inflation and associated real wealth effects as an adjustment mechanism cannot be considered of real significance in the Community context.[14] On balance, it can therefore be assumed that the need for fiscal policy adjustments will decrease.

---

[11] This permanent fall in the saving rate could arise, for example, from changes in the rate of time preference.

[12] Provided Ricardian equivalence does not hold. For a discussion of some of these mechanisms and the consequences for fiscal policy in EMU, see Begg (1990), and Masson and Melitz (1990).

[13] Masson and Melitz (1990) exhibit another case for fiscal differentiation: assuming the common EMU exchange rate has to appreciate in the medium run in order to contribute to the correction of US current account imbalances, they show that only fiscal policy could be used to achieve the desired sharing of this adjustment between Member States presently in surplus (Germany) and in deficit.

[14] Begg (1990), which bases the role of fiscal policy as an adjustment mechanism on the loss of the real balance effect, reaches therefore a different conclusion.

A related issue is whether fiscal convergence is desirable over the cycle, i.e. whether cyclically-adjusted deficits should be at the same level (presumably zero) across the Community. In such a context, and assuming the fiscal position is sustainable, the deficit can best be viewed as an intergenerational transfer mechanism since it must be repaid by the following generations in the form of higher taxes. The issue therefore is whether such transfers are warranted and whether there are good reasons for socially desirable deficits to differ from one Member State to another.

The need for sustained surpluses or deficits mainly arises from either long-term social security equilibrium, public investment financing or intertemporal market failures. The first case can be expected to imply wide variations across countries since both the features of the pension regimes and the demographic perspectives differ within the EC. In some Member States which mostly rely on pay-as-you-go systems and face the perspective of rapid ageing, it could be desirable for the general government to run substantial surpluses in the years ahead, allowing these to accumulate in a trust fund in order to be able to meet the commitments to future pensioners, while no such need exists in other Member States. [15] The second, which generally arises from the search for an optimal financing of public investment yielding social benefits in the long run, can be significant in catching-up Member States, and especially relevant in the case of the infrastructure effort required by the modernization of East Germany. The last argument concerns, for example, the adequate size of the capital stock. It can be desirable that the government runs a deficit if the capital stock is too low and the current generation unwilling to reduce its own consumption for the benefit of future generations. [16] Therefore, there is no need for fiscal surpluses or deficits to converge in the medium term at any particular level within the Community under any of the three arguments presented.

Summing up, the stabilization role of fiscal policy at the national level is bound to remain important in EMU as long as asymmetries persist, at least in the period before the full effects of economic integration are felt, but only in the case of severe country-specific disturbances. As to the role of fiscal policy as an adjustment instrument, it mainly arises from the need to achieve external equilibrium. It would only remain important in so far as governments still have external targets in the medium run. But legitimate domestic targets could also imply that fiscal deficits remain different in one Member State from another in the medium run. Fiscal autonomy is therefore warranted. However, this does not mean that all fiscal deficits are acceptable. This issue is taken up in the next two sections.

5.1.2. The need for discipline

Since the publication of the Delors Report, budgetary discipline has been a matter of discussion in both academic and policy circles. Among the most debated issues are the extent of need for discipline, and whether it should be achieved through market discipline or through rules governing deficits. In order to clarify this question, three points are successively addressed below:

(i) what fiscal discipline is about and why it is a major concern in a monetary union;

(ii) why fiscal discipline is empirically a serious issue in the Community; and

(iii) whether the incentives to discipline will be stronger or weaker in EMU.

The whys and wherefores of discipline

Discipline is an intuitive notion, but not an easy concept to define and quantify. Its most straightforward and only indisputable definition relates to the fact the government has to ensure that it does not become insolvent. This definition, which is both referred to as the intertemporal budget constraint and as the condition of sustainability of the debt/deficit path, is admittedly narrow (see Box 5.2). Whether or not a budget policy which does not put the sustainability of the debt/deficit path at stake can be deemed undisciplined is also a matter of discussion. However, a first step is to assess the consequences of a lack of discipline in the narrow sense.

Budgetary sustainability is always a concern for monetary policy because monetary and budgetary policy are interdependent in the long run: protracted deficits leading to unsustainable budget positions end up either in debt monetization or government default. In the first case, monetary authorities give up their autonomy in order to rescue the government; in the second, they stick to their own objective but force the government to repudiate part of its debt. [17] These are surely

---

[15] As an illustration, the immediate rise in the budget surplus needed to maintain the real value of retirement benefits in a 30-year perspective may exceed 10 % of GDP in some Member States. Actually, the existence of implicit liabilities arising from contractual commitments to future pensioners raises also sustainability issues. For an analysis of the budget positions along these lines, see Hagemann and Nicoletti (1989) and OECD (1990).

[16] This argument, first raised by Diamond, is discussed by Wyplosz (1990) together with other rationales for differences in the level of public deficits.

---

[17] This has been shown by Sargent and Wallace (1981).

extreme cases. But they are still a legitimate matter of concern in the context of EMU since the consequences of such a situation would be very serious: EuroFed would have to deal with the risk of a financial crisis and, theoretically at least, central bank independence could be endangered.

More precisely, lack of discipline in one or more Member States could jeopardize the policy stance of an independent EuroFed and affect the other Member States through three channels.

(a) The first and most obvious would be a pressure on EuroFed to soften its overall monetary stance. It is well known that in highly indebted countries, the room for manoeuvre of monetary authorities tends to be restricted because monetary tightening aggravates the budgetary problem: both the reduction in tax income brought by a temporary slow-down and the increase in the interest burden on the public debt worsen the deficit. [18] Even if monetary policy is formally insulated from Treasury pressures, the very fact that a monetary tightening could turn a difficult budgetary situation into a genuine financial crisis acts as a *de facto* constraint to the central bank. [19] This risk could be aggravated in the case of a short maturity of public debt or the use of floating-rate debt instruments since in such cases even a temporary tightening can have very severe consequences on the debt burden and precipitate at least a liquidity crisis, as the experience of the city of New York in 1975 demonstrated. Moreover, markets may expect the central bank to be tempted to resort to inflation to alleviate the budgetary problem. This immediately affects its credibility and therefore interest rates. [20] These considerations could well be relevant for the Community if due to a lack of discipline, the budgets of some Member States remain on the edge of sustainability.

(b) Even if EuroFed sticks to its predetermined stance without consideration for public borrowing costs or government default risks, violation of the budget constraint in one Member State could affect the others. This is because this country would either have to declare default or to withdraw from the EMU in order to be free to resort to debt monetization. To the extent that its debt would still be denominated in the home currency (instead of ecus), this second option could alleviate its public finance crisis. However, such a withdrawal could have an impact on the other members of EMU since it would signal that adhesion to the union was not irrevocable after all, and therefore reduce the market assessment of the substitutability of assets issued by agents of different countries.

(c) The third channel is of a distributive character. [21] Financial difficulties in one Member State would raise the issue of financial solidarity across the Community. At the extreme, this would take the form of pressures to bail out an insolvent government. But milder forms of solidarity can exist, e.g. through the purchase by EuroFed of a disproportionate share of public bonds from a specific country (which would be equivalent to a Community loan) or in the form of explicit transfers. In each case, the ultimate result would be felt in the overall market for government paper instead of being bottled up in the country of origin.

In all three instances, it is apparent that externalities are at work, which make unsustainable deficits and debts a matter of concern for the Community as a whole.

Fiscal discipline defined as the avoidance of an unsustainable build-up of public debt is therefore a vital condition for the success of EMU. Has this definition to be extended, i.e. is there a legitimate concern that sustainable deficits could be deemed excessive because they would have damaging effects on the Community? Although there are obvious instances where a sustainable budget deficit in a Member State could unambiguously be considered inappropriate from a Community point of view, it is also apparent that as the problems arising from such a deficit would be of a different nature from those arising from an unsustainable fiscal situation, they would call for a different type of solution.

Such a situation could arise for example if due to a lack of domestic (private and public) savings, a Member State runs a large current account deficit. Without accommodation by EuroFed, this could provoke a rise in the common interest rate, an external deficit for the Community as a whole, and therefore affect the common dollar exchange rate. Therefore the interest of the Community as a whole would call for a reduction of this deficit even if it would not be appropriate from the domestic point of view of that Member State. However, symmetric instances could also happen where fiscal policy in a Member State could be considered too tight

---

[18] With a 100 % debt to GDP ratio, any significant monetary tightening would cost an indebted government several times more than the country's contribution to the Community budget.

[19] It can be recalled in this context that in 1982, the US Federal Reserve is widely reported to have softened its monetary stance in order to contribute to a solution of the emerging Latin-American debt crisis. Although it can be argued that domestic considerations were pointing in the same direction, this can be taken as an example of *de facto* pressure towards monetary softening without any restriction of formal monetary independence.

[20] For a discussion along these lines, see Van der Ploeg (1990), and Bovenberg, Kremers and Masson (1990).

[21] The distinction between global and distributive issues in this context has been made by Padoa-Schioppa (1990).

Box 5.2: The arithmetic of budget constraints

The standard expression of the intertemporal budget constraint is a straightforward application of the accounting equation describing the dynamics of debt and deficits:[22]

(1) $dB/dt = -S + i B$

where B is the public debt, S is the primary surplus (i.e. the government balance less interest payments), i is the nominal interest rate, and d is the usual derivation operator. Seigniorage revenues are neglected for the sake of simplicity (this issue is taken up in Section 5.2.1 below).

(1) can be rewritten in terms of ratio to GDP. Simple calculations lead to:

(2) $db/dt = -s + (r-y) b$

where b and s are respectively the ratios of debt and primary surplus to GDP, r is the real interest rate and y is the growth rate of real GDP. This condition states that when the debt ratio multiplied by the difference between the real interest rate and

the growth rate exceeds the primary surplus, the debt to GDP ratio grows.

Integrating (2) yields the expression of the intertemporal budget constraint :

(3) $b \leqslant \int_{o}^{\infty} s\, e^{-(r-y)t}\, dt$

i.e. the initial debt must at most equal the present value of future primary surpluses, the discount factor being the excess of the real interest rate over the growth rate. This condition only holds if the real interest rate exceeds the growth rate. If not, growth wipes out any debt which can be issued.

Equation (3) shows that the sustainability criterion is clearly of a forward-looking nature. Its empirical implementation has to rely either on forecasts or on assumptions regarding the maximum future primary surplus.[23] Without resorting to such norms, equation (2) can be used to assess the gap between the present primary surplus and that which would stabilize the debt ratio under normal long-term conditions. This is done in Table 5.3. Graphs 5.2 and 5.3 are based on the same approach.

---

[22]   This derivation follows Blanchard (1990). See also Wyplosz (1990).

[23]   The first approach is followed by the OECD (1990), the second by Blanchard (1985) and Wyplosz (1990).

---

from a Community point of view, because it would lead to national and Community current account surpluses, and to undesirable exchange rate effects. Whether or not a sustainable deficit is inappropriate should therefore primarily remain a matter of judgment. When there is a problem of this kind, regular policy coordination and surveillance procedures should address the problem and pave the way for a policy correction.

Assessing fiscal discipline in the Community

Were fiscal positions in all Member States basically sound, then the above considerations could be dismissed as excessively theoretical. However, this is not the case, since in spite of favourable economic conditions several countries are still characterized by high and rapidly growing public debt ratios. Thus, an assessment of these fiscal positions is required.

The empirical assessment of sustainability is not straightforward because it is inherently a forward-looking condition: at any point in time, whether or not a budgetary policy meets the substainability criterion depends on the the future course of taxes, spending, and macroeconomic variables like the growth rate and the real interest rate. Technically, this condition states that if the real interest rate exceeds the growth rate, the present value of future primary surpluses must exceed the debt level, the discount factor being the difference between the real interest rate and the growth rate (Box 5.2).

A sustainability criterion of frequent use in policy discussions is the evolution of the public debt. The fiscal position is considered sustainable if the debt to GDP ratio is stable or decreasing. This kind of criterion approximates the formal budget constraint condition and is useful, with qualifications however.[24] Table 5.3 and Graphs 5.2 and 5.3 are based on a related approach, but instead of using the current values of the growth rate and the real interest rate, the sustainability condition is computed with normal values of these two factors which presumably reflect more adequately long-term growth conditions.[25] Table 5.3 gives for all Community Member States the gap between the primary budget surplus and the one that would stabilize the debt ratio in the medium term.

In order to synthesize this material, Graph 5.2 presents actual debt levels together with the gap between the primary surplus and that which would be consistent with a stabilization of the debt ratio assuming a 5 % real interest rate.

---

[24]   Major limitations of this indicator are the following: (i) it does not take the level of debt into account, although stabilization of the debt ratio is more an issue when this ratio reaches 100 % than when it amounts to 20 %; (ii) it depends on short-term conditions regarding growth rate and real interest rates rather than on long-term conditions; and (iii) it ignores future implicit or contractual liabilities arising from social security commitments.

[25]   A specific reason for that choice is that real *ex-post* interest rates are probably above their long-term levels in ERM Member States whose disinflation and exchange rate commitment are not yet fully credible. See 5.2.2 below.

Table 5.3

Debt sustainability conditions in the Community

	Debt ratio[1] (1989)	Current surplus[1] (1989)	Primary surplus[1] (1989)	Growth rate (assumed)	Required primary surplus		Sustainability gap	
					r = 4 %	r = 5 %	r = 4 %	r = 5 %
Belgium	128,4	−6,3	2,4	3	1,3	2,6	−1,1	0,2
Denmark	63,5	−0,7	4,7	3	0,6	1,3	−4,1	−3,4
Germany	43,0	0,2	1,6	3	0,4	0,9	−1,2	−0,7
Greece	86,2	−17,6	−10,1	3,5	0,4	1,3	10,5	11,4
Spain	43,8	−2,1	−0,9	3,5	0,2	0,7	1,1	1,6
France	35,5	−1,3	0,8	3	0,3	0,7	−0,4	−0,1
Ireland	104,9	−3,1	7,7	3,5	0,5	1,6	−7,2	−6,1
Italy	98,9	−10,2	−2,3	3	1	2	3,3	4,3
Luxembourg	9,0	3,3	1,2	3	0,1	0,2	−1,1	−1
Netherlands	78,4	−5,1	1,1	3	0,8	1,6	−0,3	0,5
Portugal	73,1	−5,0	−3,2	3,5	0,4	1,1	3,6	4,3
United Kingdom	44,3	1,6	4,3	3	0,4	0,9	−3,9	−3,4
EC	58,4	−2,8	1,2	3,2	0,5	1,1	−0,7	−0,1

[1] As a percentage of GDP.

Source: Commission services. Data refer to general government. Debt ratios are gross public debt as a percentage of GDP at market prices. Primary surpluses (government surpluses net of interest payments) for 1989 include stock-flow adjustments in order to be made consistent with the evolution of public debt.

Real interest rates are supposed uniform across Member States. The same applies to the growth rates, except for Member States whose GDP per head is more than 25 % below average, for which growth is 0,5 percentage points higher. The required primary surplus is computed using equation (2) in Box 5.2, i.e. s = (r − y) b. Thus, for example, at a 5 % real interest rate Italy needs to improve its primary budget balance by 4,3 % of GDP to achieve sustainability, whereas the UK's primary surplus is 3,4 % higher than necessary for this purpose.

GRAPH 5.2: **Debt ratios and sustainability gaps in the Community, 1989**

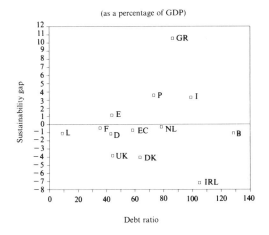

Source: Commission services.
Note: the sustainability gap is defined as in Table 5.3. Countries above the horizontal axis are characterized by growing debt to GDP ratios under normal long-term conditions.

Critical situations, i.e. large and growing debt ratios, are represented by points in the north-east region of the graph.

The above material shows that the higher the debt ratio, the higher the primary balance compatible with a stability of this ratio. Therefore the limit to the debt ratio effectively becomes the ability of the government to devote a large amount of taxes to the primary surplus and the service of public debt, i.e. to tax heavily the present generation in order to pay for previous expenditures. Although no confident assessment of the maximum debt/GDP ratio can be made, it is fair to assume that debt ratios above 100 % of GDP should imperatively be stabilized since at that level, taxes devoted to debt stabilization already amount to about 9 % of GDP. [26] Moreover, closer integration within EMU puts further limits to the possibility of increasing future taxes in order to service high debt ratios. A Member State which was compelled to raise taxes without supplying a proportionate level of public goods, because tax revenues were devoted to the sole purpose of servicing the debt, could face the risk of large-scale migration of mobile factors of production. Large intergenerational transfers are indeed only possible to the extent that factors are of a limited mobility. Taking this

[26] With 3 % growth, 2 % inflation and 5 % real interest rate, this corresponds to 2 % primary surplus plus 7 % debt service. Wyplosz (1990) considers the maximum debt ratio is about 150 to 250 % of GDP.

element into account leads to a lower upper bound for sustainable debt ratios.[27]

Table 5.3 and Graph 5.2 highlight the wide dispersion of fiscal positions within the Community. Although most Member States can be considered to be in a sustainable position, the debt ratio is both high and increasing in Greece, Italy, and Portugal, and the present fiscal position of these Member States can be considered as violating the discipline which would be required in EMU. Fiscal action is needed also in the case of very high debt ratios, even if these ratios are stable. This concerns Belgium, Ireland and to a lesser extent the Netherlands.

In order to illustrate possible stabilization paths, Graph 5.3 depicts for two heavily indebted Member States the path of the actual effective primary deficit and debt burden, together with the equilibrium condition which gives the primary deficit required in order to stabilize the debt ratio at any particular level. This highlights the contrast between the Belgian situation, where debt sustainability has been approximately achieved in spite of a very unfavourable initial situation and that of Italy where the situation has not improved much in recent years. The graph also shows how the Italian debt ratio began to increase in the 1980s, after remaining stable for a long time because of a very low real effective cost of borrowing.

Are the incentives to discipline weaker in EMU ?

Fiscal discipline ought to be primarily a matter of concern for national governments and parliaments, not the Community. However, it has been demonstrated that a lack of fiscal discipline by a Member State would affect the union as a whole. This is a classic case of externality, which a priori calls for Community rules and procedures aiming at the enforcement of discipline. Yet the nature of the rules and procedures that could be most effective is a difficult question, since it immediately raises issues of incentives, and of market versus government failures. Before turning to these issues in detail, it can be useful to describe briefly why and how the problem arises and what is the relation between the present topic and the revenue issues which are the topic of the next section.

A useful benchmark case is the one where all necessary conditions for effective market discipline hold. These conditions are as follows. First, there would be a precise distribution of roles between different types and levels of fully independent government institutions (EuroFed, EC budget

GRAPH 5.3 : **Evolution of public debt and primary deficit in selected Member States**

(as a percentage of GDP)

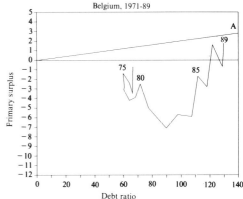

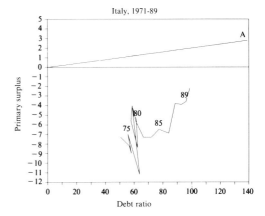

Source : Commission services.
For each of the above figures, the evolution of the debt to GDP ratio is reported along the horizontal axis and that of the primary deficit along the vertical axis. The upward-sloping OA schedule describes the equilibrium condition for a 2 % discount factor (e.g. 5 % real interest rate and 3 % growth).

authorities, national governments) without any financial solidarity between them. Second, the design of the system ensures the independence and credibility of EuroFed. Statutory clauses guarantee that it is fully sheltered from government pressures.[28] It would also be committed to follow

---

[27]   This point is made by Bovenberg, Kremers and Masson (1990). See also Section 5.2.3 below.

[28]   Examples of provisions of the first type, i.e. regarding the prudential treatment of government paper in bank portfolios are given by Bishop (1990). Regarding the provisions aiming at isolating EuroFed from government pressures, specific proposals are given in Neuman (1990) and Padoa-Schioppa (1990). All three authors suggest EuroFed could be forbidden to hold public sector debt.

certain rules in order to avoid time inconsistency.[29] Third, prudential rules have to be modified in order to make sure (i) that markets have full information on the state of public finance, (ii) that the maturity of government debt is not too short, and (iii) that regulations neither force private agents to hold government securities nor lead them to consider the securities as free of risk.

Assuming these conditions hold, market discipline would operate through increases in the marginal cost of borrowing according to the assessment of default risk by market participants. If the sustainability of the debt-deficit path of a given government were put into question, markets would react by changing the credit rating of the undisciplined government and by increasing the marginal cost of borrowing it faces, presumably triggering a timely fiscal adjustment programme. Neither quantitative norms regarding the amount of borrowing by governments nor procedures regarding the monitoring of their behaviour would therefore be needed. Moreover, any change in the cost of public borrowing consistent with an exact assessment of default risks would be welcomed, whether a rise or fall.

The above image helps to clarify the discussion but relies on simplifying assumptions. First, whether financial solidarity among Member States can be effectively ruled out is disputable. As the default of a single Member State would affect the Community as a whole, there would be a rationale for providing support to an insolvent government. Only an absolute 'no bail-out' clause, prohibiting financial support not only from EuroFed, but also from the Community as a whole, could persuade the markets that no solidarity measures can be expected. Moreover, the Community has already chosen to set up a regional policy and to organize a system of cross-country transfers on solidarity grounds. This does not imply automatic solidarity, and a 'no guaranteed bail-out' clause could feature in the rules of EMU, but it nevertheless means that markets cannot be expected to behave as if financial solidarity were completely ruled out in such an environment. Second, the record of markets in assessing the degree of government default risk is disputed. Although some evidence points in the direction of a true assessment of default risks, the experience of the Latin American debt crisis is the most recent case that exemplifies the weaknesses of pure market discipline. Third, there is no guarantee that governments would effectively react to a worsening of their

credit rating as private borrowers would. As high public debts frequently result from political polarization or distributional conflicts over the allocation of the fiscal burden rather than from intertemporal maximization, one can doubt that a rise in the cost of borrowing would necessarily trigger the required fiscal adjustment.[30] Furthermore, the size of the public debt of large countries with respect to the Community GDP could limit the effectiveness of market discipline.

Once these elements are taken into account, it is no longer clear whether constraints which are suboptimal in a first-best situation because they tend to limit fiscal flexibility remain so, or whether the removal of such constraints *per se* would have perverse incentive effects.

On the basis of the above discussion, incentive effects of EMU can be classified under three different headings:

(i) those which arise from the rules governing the behaviour of EuroFed and other Community institutions;

(ii) those which arise from the effectiveness of market discipline in the context created by capital market liberalization;

(iii) those which arise from the macroeconomic role and stance of fiscal policies in the EMU context since in an imperfect context it could happen that a loosening of the macroeconomic incentives to sound fiscal policies would ultimately raise sustainability problems.

(i) The first issue is whether the behaviour of EuroFed or other Community institutions will enhance or weaken discipline. Concerning EuroFed, as argued in Chapter 3, both its independence and its commitment to price stability will contribute to a high standard of monetary discipline. One should therefore expect governments to be aware that by adhering to EMU they would *ipso facto* accept a strict intertemporal budget constraint, and renounce future debt monetization. Moreover, as demonstrated by Wyplosz (1990), even assuming that without EMU monetary authorities would already rule out debt monetization, the budget constraint in EMU should become tighter.[31] For some Member States where the government still has access to privileged central bank financing, this could significantly

---

[29] In monetary policy, time-inconsistency refers to the dilemma of policies which aim at price stability, but face an incentive to attempt a surprise inflation, for instance in order to reduce the real value of public debt. In so far as the public is aware of this incentive, it expects monetary policy to depart from price stability. The result is that inflation is too high, but without any gain regarding the public debt. See Kydland and Prescott (1977), Barro and Gordon (1983).

[30] See Alesina and Tabellini (1990).

[31] This is because in the case of government default the reduction in the wealth of private agents does not have as much impact on goods market equilibrium as in a non-EMU. The argument runs as follows: in a non-EMU, the fall in private wealth due to partial government default reduces the demand for goods, and therefore the real interest rate falls to restore goods market equilibrium, therefore reducing the debt service burden. In the EMU, interest rate equalization leads to a much smaller fall in the real interest rate. See Wyplosz (1990) for the demonstration.

change the framework of incentives faced by policy-makers. This would come with costs, namely that of fiscal adjustment in the medium term and the reduction in seigniorage revenues which would result from lower inflation, but as shown in Section 5.2 below these costs should not be overestimated. Concerning the other Community institutions, a strengthening of Community integration inevitably leads to an expectation of more solidarity between its members, and could therefore weaken discipline. A specific issue is whether Community assistance in the case of severe country-specific shocks could have such discipline weakening effects. This issue is taken up in Chapter 6 where it is argued that an appropriate design of such a transfer scheme, including conditionality provisions, could reduce the risk of moral hazard.

(ii) The second issue relates to the effectiveness of market discipline, i.e. the ability of markets to evaluate correctly default risk premiums and to trigger the appropriate response in the case of government borrowing. Empirical evidence confirms that markets do differentiate among sovereign borrowers, but that spreads are usually small once tax factors are taken into account. Market differentiation across provinces or states exists in Canada, where borrowing costs differ by about 50 basis points, for example, and in the US, where the spread is about 40 basis points.[32] In the US case, there is only weak evidence that higher debt burdens increase the cost of borrowing, and no evidence at all that at some point high-debt states get rationed out of the market.[33] Evidence from Eurobonds markets does not show any strong relation either between the yield to maturity of public bonds of the same currency denomination and characteristics, and the budgetary situation of the borrower.[34]

Although both the developing countries' debt crisis of the 1980s and that of New York City in 1975 exemplify the risks of imprudent behaviour of sovereign borrowers, there is no agreement on the causes of this poor record. Some authors analyse it as illustrating the inherently limited capacity of markets in assessing system risks (i.e. risks which involve not only standard random shocks, but also uncertainty regarding events for which there is no relevant prior experience, e.g. because they depend heavily on outside macroeconomic

factors).[35] Others point to violations of the conditions which are required for market discipline to work properly (e.g. regarding the access to full information or the exclusion of any possibility of bail-out) or to the inadequate reactions of the borrowers as the major explanations of that record.[36]

In the Community context, capital market integration should contribute to a better evaluation of risks; therefore markets can be expected to exert disciplinary effects. However, even assuming an appropriate degree of risk assessment by the markets, it cannot be taken for granted that market discipline would be sufficient, due to expectations of Community assistance and/or inadequate response of governments to market signals.

(iii) Although a tendency for fiscal policies to be too lax would not necessarily imply a failure to achieve sustainability, it has to be discussed whether EMU would give rise to such a tendency by relaxing the constraints which presently press in favour of fiscal tightness. This could in principle happen even if the relaxation of these constraints could from a different angle be considered as a benefit from EMU.

A first issue is whether the removal of constraints which presently act as incentives to fiscal restraint would weaken discipline. Major constraints are at present high real *ex-post* interest rates in non-German ERM Member States, and the 'external constraint' which acts as a barrier to fiscal expansion when the country experiences a current account deficit or when a currency devaluation is at risk. Both will to a large extent disappear or be transferred to the Community level with the creation of EMU. Therefore, discipline could be weakened.

However, the relevance of this argument can be disputed, since none of these constraints directly addresses fiscal discipline. High *ex-post* real interest rates primarily reflect sluggish adaptation of exchange rate expectations rather than default risks: for example, *ex-post* real interest rates have been almost at the same level in France and Italy over the 1985-89 period in spite of very different budget situations.[37]

---

[32]   Figures are taken from Bishop, Damrau and Miller (1989).
[33]   See Eichengreen (1990).
[34]   Alesina, Prati and Tabellini (1989) report that risk premiums are apparent on Italian Government bonds. They find evidence in interest rate differentials between Treasury bills and private certificates of deposit, and between public and private medium-term bonds. However, as mentioned by the authors themselves, differences in the degree of liquidity could also be an explanation. Fiscal bias could also intervene.

[35]   More precisely, this failure can be related to the inherent uncertainty of an evaluation of the creditworthiness of public agents who can always rely on taxation to service their debt.
[36]   The first line of reasoning is illustrated by Aglietta, Brender and Coudert (1990), the second by Bishop, Damrau and Miller (1989).
[37]   Bredenkamp and Deppler (1989) remark in addition that the reduction in interest rates brought by EMU would only arise because of the acceptance of monetary discipline by Member States. Hence, one should not consider as anti-disciplinary what in reality arises from a stronger discipline.

The Italian case also exemplifies the fact that a public debt build-up is perfectly compatible with external equilibrium provided the private saving rate is high. More generally, Graph 5.4 shows that there is no apparent correlation between the budget balance and the current account balance within the EC. To the extent that these constraints act as disciplinary devices, it is only as a kind of surrogate discipline whose optimality and efficiency are both highly questionable [38]. Their replacement by an explicit commitment to fiscal discipline would clearly be beneficial.

GRAPH 5.4: **Budget and current account balances, 1989**

(as a percentage of GDP)

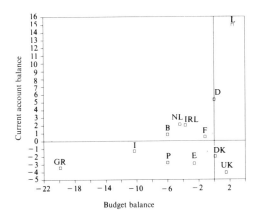

Source: Commission services.

A second point is whether coordination failures in EMU would lead governments to pursue excessively loose fiscal policies. Standard coordination models show that in a non-cooperative equilibrium, fiscal policies are too loose in the presence of cross-border welfare-reducing effects because in that case each country would only care about its own welfare without taking into account adverse spill-over effects on other EMU members. This issue is taken up in Section 5.1.3

below, where it is argued that no compelling evidence indicates that EMU would give rise to a bias in favour of excessively expansionary fiscal policies. There is however a risk that without coordination, budget deficits would not be corrected in time and remain too large in the medium run because their interest rate cost would be spread across the Community. This problem should be addressed through coordination and surveillance procedures.

Summing up, there is no compelling evidence that EMU would have strong adverse effects on fiscal discipline, but there is no reason either to rely exclusively on markets to enforce discipline, since the conditions for this discipline to be effective cannot be assumed to hold fully. Thus, there is a case for addressing the risk of failures of market discipline through Community rules and procedures.

5.1.3. The need for coordination

Policy coordination is, after autonomy and discipline, the third component of the budgetary regime of EMU. The purpose of this section is to analyse the rationale for strengthening fiscal policy coordination and surveillance.

Much of the policy debate about coordination has so far focused on global issues at the G7 level, and much less on intra-EC coordination. [39] This could be interpreted as a sign of success since the EMS has been set up partly in order to trigger monetary and exchange rate coordination. However, there is another explanation: intra-EC and especially intra-ERM policy discussions in the 1980s have been dominated by the search for a convergence of inflation rates at a low level. To a large extent, fiscal policy discussions have been dominated, and still are, by the need for an adjustment in high-deficit and high-debt countries. Due to this priority for convergence, genuine coordination issues have so far been left in the shade. However, it remains an important topic that could come to the forefront in the years ahead.

Coordination has in reality two different meanings. In the policy debate, it often refers to all kinds of discussions among governments and central banks. Coordination may then be implicit and not formalized. Recent developments of economic theory have emphasized coordination in the narrow sense of a formal and negotiated coordination in policy-making whose need arises from the game-theoretic aspects of interdependence, and specifically from the risks of collective welfare losses if governments and/or monetary

---

[38]   If one assumes Ricardian equivalence, i.e. that public dissaving is fully compensated by private saving, the disciplinary effect of the current account constraint disappears entirely. Interestingly, a recent OECD study by Nicoletti (1988) rejects Ricardian equivalence for most countries, but with the exception of Belgium and Italy.

[39]   Exceptions are, for example, Oudiz (1985), Coudert (1987), Amalric and Sterdyniak (1989), Cohen and Wyplosz (1989, 1990).

authorities independently aim to achieve contradictory results. [40] In what follows, coordination will be used in this narrow sense.

Coordination of economic policies is called for in all instances where spill-over effects of domestic policies on partner countries are not taken into account by the policy-maker. When such externalities arise, independent policy-making is bound to be sub-optimal, but this sub-optimality can generally be corrected by coordinated policy changes, with the result that the welfare of all participants improves. A prerequisite to the analysis of coordination is therefore to review how EMU will affect cross-country budgetary policy spillovers. This provides the basis for discussing whether EMU calls for a strengthening of coordination procedures. A final point comments on possible costs or benefits of EMU in this respect.

Are spill-over effects of budgetary policy stronger in EMU?

EMU will affect cross-country spill-overs through three different channels:

(i)   economic union will foster goods and capital market integration, thereby affecting the intensity of cross-country spill-overs;

(ii) the adoption of a common monetary policy handled by EuroFed will remove the possibility of beggar-thy-neighbour monetary and exchange rate policies, but at the same time increase spill-over effects of policies that affect the interest rate since all EC countries will share the same interest rate;

(iii) the common exchange rate *vis-à-vis* the rest of the world will be turned into a major spill-over channel, since budgetary policy in any country will affect this EC-wide variable. In the absence of coordination, the current account of the Community becomes for Member States a kind of 'public good' whose determination is beyond the reach of any single policy body. [41]

Thus on the one hand, EMU will remove the risk of non-cooperative monetary policies, but on the other hand it could increase externalities of fiscal policies and therefore call for stronger fiscal coordination. For assessing fiscal policy spill-overs, different approaches may be followed. A first approach relates to the conventional cross-country effects of fiscal policies in the short to medium term, i.e. to those effects which arise while adjustments to goods and labour markets are still under way (this can be related to what have been called the 'stabilization' aspects of fiscal policy in Section 5.1.1 above). A second approach focuses on the specific, but important, type of externalities arising from the sharing of a common current account and a common exchange rate. A third approach relates to longer-term channels of externalities which can arise from long-lasting changes in fiscal position after adjustments in relative prices have been completed (i.e. to the 'adjustment' role of fiscal policy).

(i) In the short to medium term, i.e. in a period up to five years, fiscal policy primarily impacts on aggregate demand, and the main concern of policy-makers is with respect to growth and inflation. Spill-overs arise, first from income and price transmission through trade flows, and second, from interest rate effects on demand. Interest rate changes also influence trade volumes and prices via the exchange rate. The standard framework of analysis for these effects is the Mundell-Fleming model in which economies characterized by sticky prices and unemployment are linked by goods and capital markets. Although some of the simplifying assumptions of the original Mundell-Fleming model have to be relaxed, it remains a very useful framework from which clear conclusions can be drawn. [42] Major results are the following:

(a) Goods market integration increases spill-overs through both demand and relative price effects.

(b) In a fixed exchange rate regime, capital market liberalization, which increases capital mobility and asset substitutability, increases the effectiveness of fiscal policy at home because access to world capital markets reduces (or, for a small country, eliminates altogether) crowding-out effects. It also reduces the 'locomotive' character of fiscal policy, i.e. its impact abroad, possibly leading to negative spill-overs of expansionary policies.

(c) With free capital markets and therefore high capital mobility, the domestic impact of fiscal policies on output is minimal with fully flexible exchange rates, and maximal with fixed exchange rates.

---

[40] A classic example in the monetary field drawn from the experience of the 1970s is the attempt to export the inflationary consequences of a supply shock (e.g. oil) by appreciating the currency: when all countries simultaneously (but in vain) try to achieve this result, monetary policy is too tight, such that policy coordination, alternatively, would achieve a Pareto-superior outcome which provides welfare gains to all participating countries.

[41] Both of the last two effects arise from the same cause, namely monetary union. However, analytically they are of a different nature because the former arises in a two-country world whereas the latter depends on the relations with third countries. See Cohen and Wyplosz (1989).

[42] Major modifications of the Mundell-Fleming model relate to price determination and the exchange rate. For a recent and comprehensive presentation, see Frenkel and Razin (1987). For a discussion of the effects of EMU in a Mundell-Fleming framework, see Van der Ploeg (1989, 1990), from which this presentation draws.

The move towards EMU therefore amplifies the domestic effectiveness of national fiscal policy for stabilization purposes. The assessment of spill-overs is less straightforward because they depend both on the relative magnitude of income and interest rate effects, and on the asymmetries of the exchange rate regime. In a pure float, fiscal policy tends to be expansionary abroad due to both demand and competitiveness effects (Table 5.4). Indeed, under perfect capital mobility a fiscal expansion appreciates the exchange rate, and hence increases the competitiveness of the partner countries. Within an asymmetric EMS, fiscal expansion in the anchor country might be beggar-thy-neighbour because interest rate and exchange rate effects could dominate income effects. This is because Germany determines interest rates and dollar exchange rates for the whole EMS, whilst exports to Germany do not exceed 3 % of GDP in France, Italy or the UK; hence, the 'monetary' weight of Germany exceeds its 'economic' weight within the system. Although the sign of the aggregate spill-over effect of a fiscal expansion in Germany is an empirical issue, there is a presumption that it could be negative. In contrast, a fiscal expansion in a non-anchor country has a 'locomotive' effect because it has no direct interest rate effect.

In a symmetric regime like the EMU, under the assumption of common, stability-oriented monetary policy, the sign of these spill-over effects is theoretically ambiguous: fiscal pol-

icy in one Member State can either increase or decrease output abroad since the 'monetary' weight of each Member State, which depends on its share in the aggregate indicators (prices, money demand, etc.) upon which EuroFed bases its policy, is close to its 'economic' weight. Thus, the sign of the spill-over effect depends on the relative magnitude of the income effects with respect to interest rate and exchange rate effects. However, the direction of change when one moves from the EMS towards EMU is clear since fiscal policy in the anchor country tends to become less 'beggar-thy-neighbour' while it tends to become less 'locomotive' in the other countries.

Model simulations with Multimod and Quest broadly confirm the above qualitative conclusions (Box 5.3). Concentrating on the effects of the move from the EMS towards EMU, simulation results show that in EMU the impact of a bond-financed expansion in the EMS anchor country (Germany) becomes more expansionary at home and less contractionary abroad since monetary policy reacts to the EC's economic performance rather to that of Germany. The opposite is true for France, for which the major change concerns the interest rate/exchange rate nexus. Generally speaking, short-term spill-over effects of fiscal policies appear to be small in EMU due to the offsetting effects of import growth and interest rate/exchange rate increases.

These results tend to show that under normal circumstances, national budgetary autonomy in EMU should not lead governments to opt for suboptimal policy stances because of a failure to take spill-over effects properly into account. In other words, there does not seem to be an a priori case for a major strengthening of coordination in day-to-day policy-making. However, these results depend both on the assumption of no monetary accommodation and on the characteristics of the model. Furthermore, they crucially hinge on the assumption that under a float, a fiscal expansion appreciates the exchange rate.

Although this normally holds once capital mobility is effective, exchange rate determination is admittedly not precise enough to rule out the possibility of opposite effects. In that case, positive spill-over effects of fiscal policy would be much stronger.

Table 5.4

Short-term spill-over effects of a bond-financed fiscal expansion under alternative exchange rate regimes

Exchange rate regime	Country originating the policy move	
	EMS anchor country	Other countries
Float	+	+
EMS	+/− to −	+ +
EMU	+/−	+/−

Note: Signs in this table refer to those of spill-over effects on the GDP of other Member States. In all regimes, full capital mobility is assumed and European currencies are supposed to float with respect to non-European currencies. Monetary policy is assumed to be directed towards price stability.

Box 5.3: Shorter-run spill-over effects of fiscal policies

Model simulations can help to assess the sensitivity of spill-over effects to different exchange rate regimes. However, only some of the linkages are sensitive to the exchange rate regime. Demand impacts on goods markets due to a bond-financed fiscal expansion are quite independent of the exchange rate regime. On the other hand interest rate and exchange rate linkages are, in contrast, a function of the exchange rate regime. Four regimes are considered in Table 5.5 below.

Table 5.5

Spill-over effects of a rise in government expenditures by 2 % of GDP, Multimod simulation

| | Country originating the policy move: | | | | | | | |
| | Germany | | | | France | | | |
	Float	EMS	AEMU	EMU	Float	EMS	AEMU	EMU
GDP (first year effect)								
Germany	1,1	1,06	1,04	1,6	0,12	0,14	0,18	− 0,16
France	0,06	− 0,24	0,34	0	1,18	1,62	1,74	1,6
Italy	0,12	− 0,24	− 0,36	0	0,1	0,10	0,1	− 0,08
United Kingdom	− 0,02	− 0,26	− 0,32	− 0,02	0,04	0,06	0,06	− 0,1
Short-term interest rate (first year effect)								
Germany	0,2	0,26	0,26	0,18	0,12	0,12	0,1	0,14
France	0,18	0,4	0,26	0,18	0,28	− 0,12	0,1	0,14
Italy	0,26	0,42	0,26	0,18	0,18	0,18	0,1	0,14
United Kingdom	0,26	0,42	0,26	0,18	0,14	0,14	0,1	0,14
Dollar exchange rate (first year effect)								
Germany	− 2,2	− 2,26	− 2,28	− 0,9	− 0,44	− 0,42	− 0,3	− 1,22
France	− 0,48	− 1,9	− 2,28	− 0,9	− 3,26	− 1,30	− 0,3	− 1,22
Italy	− 0,38	− 1,88	− 2,28	− 0,9	− 0,28	− 0,46	− 0,3	− 1,22
United Kingdom	− 0,44	− 1,84	− 2,28	− 0,9	− 0,28	− 0,42	− 0,3	− 1,22
Absorption deflator (fifth year effect)								
Germany	1,3	1,24	1,2	2,0	0,26	0,34	0,26	0
France	0,4	− 0,34	− 0,62	0,16	2,06	3,48	3,4	3,66
Italy	0,52	− 0,44	− 0,76	0,1	0,34	0,24	0,18	− 0,34
United Kingdom	0,4	− 0,22	− 0,36	0,1	0,28	0,24	0,16	− 0,14

Source: Multimod simulations by the Commission services. Standard monetary policy. A decrease in the dollar exchange rate means appreciation. AEMU: asymmetric EMU.

Since the EMS is asymmetric, it is necessary to consider both the effects of a fiscal expansion in Germany and another ERM member, here France (the results would be similar with another large country). The asymmetry between these two countries is apparent for both the EMS and the asymmetric EMU, since a fiscal expansion in France has much smaller effects on the interest rate and the exchange rate than a fiscal expansion in Germany.

In a pure float regime, most of the effects of the expansion are bottled up in the originating country, which experiences a rise in interest rates and an appreciation of the currency. Spill-over effects are mainly positive, but small.

In the EMS, a fiscal expansion in Germany is 'beggar-thy-neighbour' in character and provokes disinflation abroad because interest rates and exchange rates increase for all members of the ERM (although the fluctuation bands of the EMS allow for some offsetting of this effect); in contrast, fiscal policy in France is 'locomotive' in character (and inflationary for ERM members) because trade linkage effects dominate.[43]

The hypothetical 'asymmetric EMU' is intermediate between EMS and EMU. Since monetary policy is entirely set by Germany (without the flexibility that bands allow for), the fiscal policy multiplier is higher than in any other regime in France;[44] in contrast, the beggar-thy-neighbour effects of the German fiscal expansion are amplified. Price effects are also amplified with respect to the EMS case.

In EMU, the effects of a fiscal policy are qualitatively the same for Germany and France, since in both cases the reaction of monetary authorities is supposed to be identical. For the German expansion, trade and interest rate linkages turn out to offset each other almost completely. In the French case, beggar-thy-neighbour effects dominate slightly.[45] Inflation spill-overs are small.

---

[43] The small decline in the French interest rate is due to the reaction of the French authorities to the appreciation of the currency within EMS bands.

[44] It is, however, still low in comparison with the results of standard macro models. This is due, first, to the remaining interest rate and exchange rate effects (because France is not a smaller economy within the EC), and second to the forward-looking nature of the model, which reduces the effectiveness of fiscal policy.

[45] Different sizes, degrees of openness, and wage-price behaviour in Germany and France account for a large part of the difference between the simulation results for the two countries. Another factor is a technical hypothesis made for these simulations, namely that the weighting of country variables for the computation of EC aggregates which enter the reaction function is equal for France and Germany. A more realistic assumption would be to weight countries according to their GDP. This would reduce the contrast between France and Germany in the EMU regime.

The spill-over effects broadly conform to the qualitative results which can be derived from a standard Mundell-Fleming model. However, the results could be model-specific since the sign of the spill-over effects depends on the relative intensity of trade and financial linkages. Therefore, a Quest linked simulation has also been carried out to test for the size of spill-over effects of a German fiscal expansion under an EMU regime, setting the exogenous value of interest rates and exchange rates at levels consistent with the monetary policy reactions function and the open interest rate parity condition (Table 5.6). Under the same kind of assumptions regarding monetary policy and exchange rates, these results broadly confirm the small size of spill-over effects of fiscal policy in EMU.

Table 5.6

Spill-over effects of a rise in German government expenditures by 2% of GDP under an EMU regime, Quest simulation

	GDP	Interest rate	Dollar exchange rate	Absorption deflator[1]
Germany	2,1	1,5	−2,7	4,5
France	0,14	1,5	−2,7	−1,5
Italy	0,18	1,5	−2,7	−0,9
United Kingdom	0,34	1,5	−2,7	−1,7

[1] First-year effect for GDP, interest rates and exchange rate. Fifth-year effect for absorption deflator. Interest rate and exchange rate effects are exogenous.
Source: Quest simulation by the Commission services.

(ii) The sharing of a common exchange rate *vis-à-vis* third currencies and of a common external balance will be direct consequences of EMU. As no individual Member State will be able to target those variables, the fact that these objectives will be shared will appear to policy-makers as the most visible sign of the increased interdependence across the Community.

To what extent will this channel of externalities be important in practice? The current account and the exchange rate of the Community will probably remain two among many policy objectives, as long as their level and evolution do not depart from normal limits. However, since the variability of both variables is high, circumstances will presumably arise where their evolution will be regarded as of paramount importance by European policy-makers. For instance, if the external deficit of the Community reaches certain limits, it will become the key policy target. Since monetary policy has an ambiguous action on the external account (because of the opposite effects on foreign trade of a slower domestic demand and of exchange rate appreciation), correction of this deficit will presumably need a fiscal policy move. However the benefits of a fiscal correction by a national government would accrue to the Community as a whole (through a reduction in the external deficit), whereas the home economy would bear almost all the costs. This is a textbook example of strong externality.

(iii) In the long run, the main focus shifts from growth, unemployment and inflation spill-overs to externalities through real interest rates and terms of trade effects.[46]

---

[46] The following draws on Wyplosz (1990).

Assuming that in the long run price flexibility ensures market clearing, and that all economies are at full employment, the issue is whether and how a protracted deficit in a Member State affects its neighbours through higher real interest rates and a deterioration of the terms of trade.[47] This can be related to the ongoing discussion regarding what has been called the risk of 'undue appropriation of EMU savings' (Lamfalussy, 1989).

Since EMU removes the possibility of adjusting the nominal exchange rate, the rise in real interest rates can no longer be limited to the country running a budget deficit and is felt in the union as a whole. As the deficit country experiences a real exchange rate appreciation, this also affects its neighbours. These terms of trade effects are not specific to EMU, but EMU makes two differences: first, some of the change in the terms of trade would be common to all EMU members, because it would arise from changes in the value of the ecu with respect to third currencies; second, intra-EC terms of trade changes would have to be achieved through changes in the price system instead of the exchange rate, with associated adjustment and menu costs.

Budgetary policy coordination in EMU

The above analysis provides the basis for a discussion of the need for budgetary coordination in EMU. What matters is (i) whether in EMU coordination is likely to be a major requirement in policy-making and (ii) whether uncoordinated policies would tend to be too lax or too tight.

Turning first to coordination of short and medium-term policies, the evidence presented above does not call for a tight coordination of day-to-day national demand policies, since within the EC cross-country spill-over effects on growth and inflation are not likely to be much greater than at present. As long as no special circumstance calls for joint action, existing coordination and surveillance procedures, which provide channels for information exchange and consultation, would be adequate. However, this conclusion immediately has to be qualified because of the externalities through the common exchange rate and current account. As exemplified by the experience of the industrialized countries in the 1980s, conflicts over shared targets like the exchange rate and the current account are in practice much stronger incentives to coordination than an inadequate overall policy

stance.[48] Although simulations (see Box 5.3) confirm that spill-over effects of fiscal policies through the exchange rate are already present in the EMS, non-anchor Member States theoretically retain the possibility to settle for a realignment. This possibility would no longer exist in EMU.

When needed, coordination with respect to the common exchange rate and the common external account would have to be tight since failure to take joint action would severely impact on these important variables. In the absence of coordination, no national government would be willing to deflate for the benefit of the Community as a whole. Even if a number of Member States were tempted to take action, other Member States could be willing to free-ride, i.e. to reap part of the benefits of this action without taking part in it. Thus, in such a situation a prima facie case for coordination and surveillance would arise. A related motive for greater fiscal coordination within EMU would stem from the need to define a policy for the Community in the larger context of the world economy.[49] Even if intra-EC spill-overs did not call at all for fiscal coordination, as argued in Chapter 7, there would still be a need for coordination in the search for a good policy mix because the Community budget would remain too small to have a significant macroeconomic impact. Without fiscal coordination, only EuroFed would be able to engage in policy coordination at the world level and, in the absence of a fiscal policy actor, could be subject to pressures to adopt an inadequate stance. In this respect, the preservation of EuroFed's independence could well call for fiscal coordination.

As the need for coordinated policies would presumably not be a day-to-day feature of fiscal policy in the Community, but could become the priority in some circumstances, special coordination procedures could be designed in order to guarantee an efficient handling of these external aspects of interdependence. These procedures would have to ensure that commonly agreed decisions would be enforced and to address the risk of free-rider behaviour.

These needs for coordination would not conflict with the need for autonomy since what would be called for is a change in the budgetary policy of the Community as a whole.

---

[47] The discussion here focuses on 'protracted' deficits and not on permanent deficits since as discussed by Wyplosz (1990), in an intertemporal setting the budget constraint has to be fulfilled and a budget deficit has ultimately to be financed through higher taxes. Therefore, a 'permanent' deficit is in reality a rise in the size of the government. These EMU effects are discussed in Section 5.2.3 below.

[48] In other words, although the economic literature emphasizes the gains from absolute coordination, real coordination tends to be relative, and to focus on the settlement of possible disputes over these shared targets (Currie, Holtham and Hughes Hallett, 1989). To some extent, the experience with the ERM confirms the prevalence of relative coordination since discussions over the right level of the exchange rates were much more frequent than discussions about the overall policy stance of the Community.

[49] See Lamfalussy (1989), Padoa-Schioppa (1990), Cohen and Wyplosz (1989).

This would be perfectly compatible with differentiated national positions. In other words, coordination would have to ensure that the overall policy mix of the Community is adequate, whereas differentiated national policies would address relativities, i.e. national macroeconomic performances with respect to the rest of the Community.

A related issue is whether coordination failures would induce excessively lax short-term fiscal policies. According to standard coordination models, this would be the case if fiscal expansions were systematically beggar-thy-neighbour in character in EMU, since governments would tend to overlook the adverse consequences of their actions on partner countries. As discussed above, the evidence derived from empirical models does not unambiguously point in that direction. Although fiscal policies in non-anchor countries would become less expansionary in their external impact than in the present EMS, this would mainly be a correction for an existing bias since the interest rate and exchange rate crowding-out effects would roughly compensate for the income effect. Indeed, an opposite bias could arise if individual Member States were seeking employment and output gains through real depreciation.[50]

As to coordination in the medium to long term, more clearcut conclusions can be drawn from analysis. Assuming full employment, spill-over effects of a protracted deficit would be felt by partner countries through higher real interest rates and a worsening of the terms of trade. Since these adverse consequences of domestic policy would be overlooked without coordination, a tendency for budget deficits to be too large could appear.[51] In this instance, coordination and surveillance would be needed in order to avoid too lax a policy.

Summing up, there is no compelling evidence that EMU would call for close coordination in day-to-day fiscal policy. However, coordination would be required in two instances:

(i) in order to ensure an appropriate policy mix of the Community in the context of the world economy, particularly with respect to the common exchange rate and current account;

(ii) in order to correct possible medium-term tendencies for budget deficits to be too large.

In both cases, mutual surveillance procedures should explicitly address the risk of free-rider behaviour.

Does EMU yield coordination gains?

International macroeconomic policy coordination is generally considered as yielding welfare gains to the participating countries.[52] Therefore, the question arises whether such effects should be considered in the cost-benefit analysis of EMU.

Since EMU would remove an instrument (the nominal exchange rate) whose cooperative setting would be welfare-improving, there is no doubt that it would entail a loss in comparison to full coordination in the management of the exchange rates.[53] This is just another way to present the cost of losing the exchange rate instrument which is discussed in Chapter 6. However, this is not fully relevant, because the reference situation to which EMU is to be compared is not one where coordination can be assumed to be perfect. With respect to a floating rates regime, EMU would remove the inefficiencies associated with non-cooperative monetary policies. It could therefore be considered a form of 'surrogate coordination' but at the cost of nominal exchange rate rigidity.[54] With respect to a '1992 + EMS' baseline, EMU would not yield the same kind of gains. Indeed, the EMS is already a form of surrogate coordination which practically rules out non-cooperative exchange rate management, the associated cost being the suboptimality of an asymmetric system when non-anchor countries are hit by shocks (plus, at least in Stage I, part of the cost resulting from nominal exchange rate rigidity). Thus, EMU would substitute the rigidity cost for the asymmetry cost.

The relevant comparison therefore has to be made between two second bests whose relative performance would have to be assessed (i) with respect to a given distribution of shocks, and (ii) taking into account the degree of policy coordination that could be expected in each case. A quantitative comparison is clearly out of reach.

[50] See Cohen and Wyplosz (1990), Wyplosz (1990).
[51] This assumes that each government determines the size of its budget deficit according to domestic considerations, i.e. by maximizing a welfare function which takes into account the impact of higher interest rates at home but not abroad. Whether this could be called 'undue appropriation of Community saving' is not so clear. As pointed out by Bredenkamp and Deppler (1989), this appropriation cannot be qualified as undue if the return on government investment equals or exceeds the market real interest rate.

[52] See, for example, Oudiz and Sachs (1984). Gains from coordination are however disputed. For a recent survey, see Currie, Holtham and Hughes Hallet (1989).
[53] This is demonstrated by Giavazzi and Giovannini (1987) and discussed by Van der Ploeg (1989, 1990).
[54] See Hughes Hallet, Holtham and Huston (1989).

5.2. Impact on income and expenditure of governments

This section focuses on the effects of EMU on the resources and expenditure of governments.

Three types of effects have to be considered. First, as inflation rates converge, governments lose the possibility of deriving resources from a higher inflation rate, either through seigniorage revenues or, in the short run, because of the non-indexation of tax brackets and rates. This issue of seigniorage losses has been much discussed in the recent academic literature. However, as shown in Section 5.2.1, its empirical relevance appears to be relatively minor in the Community context.

A second effect concerns government expenditure. As the nominal interest rate is reduced in the most inflationary Member States, the public debt service and therefore also the recorded deficit shrink. This nominal effect also goes with a real, but mostly transitional one since real interest rates are presently significantly higher in the most inflation-prone countries. This is the topic of Section 5.2.2.

These two effects are direct consequences of monetary union. However the broader issue of tax and spending convergence in the Community has also to be raised in relation to EMU. To what degree, and through which mechanisms, should this convergence be achieved? This theme is briefly addressed in Section 5.2.3.

5.2.1. Seigniorage revenue losses

Seigniorage is the ability of the government to finance its expenditure by issuing money. Governments extract seigniorage revenues (also called the inflation tax) through the issuance of non- or low-interest bearing debt which is held by the public in the form of currency or by the commercial banks in the form of reserves at the central bank. [55] For this reason, even fully anticipated steady-state inflation is not neutral with respect to public finance.

The possibility of financing government expenditure by issuing money was for long a seigniorial privilege, later accruing to the State. Such a financing of large budget deficits has in the past been at the origin of major inflationary crises. But seigniorage can also accrue to governments without large scale debt monetization, and constitute a steady-state channel of government revenue. It is therefore a legitimate matter of concern in the design of a monetary union. There are, in addition, other reasons for inflation to affect public finance. As a rule, tax systems are not neutral with respect to inflation since many taxes are based on nominal instead of real incomes. This could be called another form of seigniorage (or inflation tax) and will be briefly discussed at the end of the present section.

Seigniorage is a major source of government revenues only for economies suffering high inflation. However, it has also been significant in recent years for some Member States due to above average inflation, the wide use of cash for day-to-day transactions and high bank reserve ratios (Graph 5.5). EMU will not lead seigniorage to disappear, but as argued below both the likely convergence of compulsory bank reserve ratios on a low level and the low inflation performance of the Community will reduce this resource to a modest level. [56] For those countries which still significantly rely on the inflation tax to finance their budget, EMU will entail permanent *ex-ante* government revenue losses, which will have to be compensated by a rise in taxes or a cut in expenditure. Therefore, two questions arise:

(i) What is the gross public finance cost of reducing inflation, taking into account that independently of monetary union, changes in the banking legislation brought by the single market will induce convergence in the levels of required reserves?

(ii) Is there a net economic welfare cost of permanently replacing the inflation tax by explicit taxes? [57]

Obviously, the issue of seigniorage revenues only arises in comparison to a situation where Member States are free to choose independently their inflation rates. As argued in Chapter 2, this would already not be the case in Stage I. Therefore, this section implicitly refers to another baseline,

---

[55] Bank reserves yield zero interest rate in most EC countries. However, reserves are remunerated, but below market rates, in countries characterized by high reserve requirements. Hence, seigniorage revenues are not proportional to the size of the monetary base. These revenues do not only appear as central bank profits, but also as lower interest payments in the government's accounts since in some countries the Treasury borrows from the Central Bank on subsidized terms. For an examination along these lines of the case of Italy, see Mohlo (1989).

[56] We do not discuss how seigniorage revenues will be redistributed among Member States. This issue is related to the distribution of the capital of EuroFed.

[57] For high-debt countries, the reduction in seigniorage revenues can impact on the dynamic of the public debt as shown in Section 5.1. Whether this could be an argument for giving priority to fiscal consolidation over disinflation is discussed in Section 5.2.2 below.

which is either a floating regime or a soft exchange rate arrangement (like a crawling peg) which allows for permanent inflation differentials.

(as a percentage of GDP)

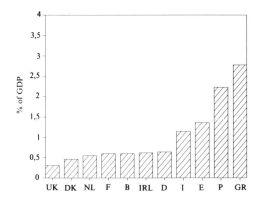

Note: Seigniorage revenues have been computed using the opportunity cost definition of seigniorage, i.e.: $s = i*c + (i-i_r)*r$ where i is the market short-term interest rate, i_r is the interest rate on (compulsory) bank reserves, and c and r are respectively the ratios of currency and bank reserves to GDP. It is implicitly assumed that the same interest rate applies on free reserves. See Gros (1989) for details.

Gross public finance cost of seigniorage losses

Seigniorage can be measured either as a flow of cash or as an implicit revenue. The first measure, which is the most commonly used in the literature, is given by the ratio of the change in monetary base outstanding to nominal GDP. However, it can exhibit wide variations over time and is not appropriate if bank reserves, which are part of the monetary base, are remunerated. The second measure is based on the difference between the effective interest rate on the monetary base (which is zero for cash, but can be positive for required bank reserves) and the market interest rate. It is much more stable over time, and is therefore used in what follows. However, it should be kept in mind that the corresponding revenues result from an accounting imputation.

Graph 5.5 shows that seigniorage revenues, which are close to 0,5 % of GDP or even below in most Member States, are nevertheless significant in the southern countries (Portugal

and Greece and, to a lesser extent, Spain and Italy). Closer examination shows that as the four countries are characterized by both a wider use of cash (except for Italy) and higher reserve requirements than in the rest of the Community, this difference is rooted in both technological and regulatory factors. For these countries, an evaluation of the public finance cost of EMU is therefore warranted.

However, this cost cannot be assessed readily on the basis of present seigniorage revenues, since, following the full implementation of the Second Banking Directive by 1993, bank competition in the internal market will already impose convergence in reserve requirement ratios. Although this directive does not address monetary regulation *per se*, higher reserve requirements act like a tax on home banks which would be a disadvantage in international competition. Market pressures can therefore be expected to lead to convergence in the reserve ratios. In the same period, the use of cash is also expected to decline due to the modernization of the payment system. In order to evaluate the specific effect of monetary union, one has to make hypotheses regarding the convergence of reserve ratios and ratios of currency to GDP brought by technological change and the completion of the internal market. [58]

Table 5.7 gives, for the four Member States whose seigniorage revenues were above 1 % of GDP in 1988, an assessment of the gross public finance cost of EMU. This evaluation is based on the comparison of two scenarios. Scenario 1 incorporates in '1993' the full effects of the internal market programme: convergence in the reserve ratios at a 2 % level, elimination of interest payments on reserves, further reductions in the use of cash due to technological changes; but while real interest rates are assumed to converge, no convergence in inflation rates is assumed. Scenario 2 or 'EMU' assumes in addition convergence in inflation rates at a 2 % per annum level. [59]

---

[58]   Interestingly, Spain has already in 1990 legislated a progressive reduction in the required reserve ratio from 17 % to 5 %.

[59]   The 2 % reserve ratio hypothesis in scenario 1 ('1993') corresponds to the average level of the other EUR 8 countries. Giovannini (1990) assumes 1,5 % reserve ratios after the liberalization of the banking industry. Currency to GDP ratios have been projected using the 1979-88 time trends. Real interest rates are supposed to converge at the 5 % level. Inflation is supposed to remain at the level forecast for 1991. In both scenarios, seigniorage revenues are distributed among Member States according to their monetary base.

Table 5.7

Gross seigniorage revenue effects of monetary union

(Seigniorage revenues as a percentage of GDP)

	1982-84 (1)	1985-87 (2)	1988 (3)	'1993' (4)	'EMU' (5)	Single market effect (6) = (4) − (3)	EMU effect (7) = (5) − (4)
Greece	2,46	2,34	2,75	1,84	0,71	0,91	1,13
Portugal	4,39	2,85	2,23	1,62	0,71	0,61	0,91
Spain	1,93	1,03	1,36	1,20	0,86	0,16	0,34
Italy	2,23	1,21	1,13	0,72	0,51	0,41	0,21

Source: Commission services.

As shown in Table 5.7, except for Greece seigniorage revenues are already well below their levels of the early 1980s. Even assuming that without EMU governments would not choose to reduce inflation, the gross public finance cost of seigniorage revenue losses implied by monetary union only exceeds 1 % of GDP in Greece, because inflation in this country would still be at a high 15 % level in the '1993' scenario. However, this is clearly an upper bound since even without participation in EMU, Greece would be very likely to disinflate. The same is true to a lesser extent for Portugal whose inflation is still above 10 % in the first scenario. For Spain and Italy, however, the EMU effect is below 0,5 % of GDP.

Welfare effects of seigniorage losses

To the extent that a reduction of seigniorage revenues eliminates a perverse incentive towards inflation and fiscal laxity, it should be seen as a source of welfare gains whatever its gross public finance cost. However, the question has to be raised whether there are good economic reasons to prefer seigniorage finance over tax finance. The optimal taxation theory has pointed out that since taxes are distortionary, a welfare-maximizing government would not choose zero inflation, but rather combine explicit taxes and the inflation tax in order to minimize distortions. [60] Hence, countries characterized by distortionary taxes, less efficient tax collection, or a larger underground economy should accept a higher inflation rate. In this respect, it has been argued that

participation in a low-inflation EMU could be suboptimal for southern and/or catching-up Member States because it would lead them either to raise taxes or to lower public spending excessively. [61]

Although this argument has its logic, its pertinence is questionable since it relies on the assumption that economic policy can choose — and does choose — a 'socially optimal inflation rate' and, moreover, can stick permanently to this inflation rate without incurring credibility losses. There is no evidence, however, that past or present inflation rates would be optimal. [62] Moreover, the possibility of achieving that optimal mix of taxation and inflation is theoretically disputed: since the governments of the four Member States under consideration are all heavily indebted — Spain being in a better situation than the other three — they face a strong incentive to reduce the *ex-post* real cost of servicing the public debt through one-shot surprise monetization, i.e. inflation. This motive interferes with the choice of an optimal steady-state inflation rate and, to the extent that it is aware of this temptation, leads the public to expect inflation to be high. If this happens, the country reaches an inefficient equilibrium: inflation is permanently above the optimal level and the country therefore endures welfare losses but, since

---

[60] In technical terms, the marginal social cost of raising revenue through direct taxation and the marginal cost of raising revenue through seigniorage should be equalized. See Phelps (1973) and, for a recent presentation, Mankiw (1987).

[61] This issue has first been raised by Dornbusch (1988). Subsequent analyses include, for example, Drazen (1989), Giavazzi (1989), Grilli (1989) and Gros(1989a, 1989b).

[62] Poterba and Rotemberg (1990) find no evidence of correlation between inflation rates and tax rates in a sample of OECD countries. Cukierman, Edwards and Tabellini (1989), working on a sample of developed as well as developing countries, find no correlation between inflation and structural economic variables and argue that inefficiencies in the tax system leading to resort to seigniorage should not be regarded as exogenous, but rather as linked to features of the political system, e.g. polarization and instability.

the price rise has been anticipated, without any gain regarding the debt-service burden of the government. In these conditions, participation in a low-inflation EMU is welfare-improving even if it forces the choice of an inflation rate below the optimal level. [63]

These objections notwithstanding, simple computations have been be made in order to assess the maximum welfare cost of the seigniorage loss. Computations with a numerical example (Appendix 1 to this chapter) show that the welfare cost of EMU is in any case much smaller than the gross public finance cost for two reasons: first, the optimal inflation rate is not independent from the reserve ratio, but decreases with it; second, the welfare cost of higher taxes has to be weighed against the welfare gain of lower inflation. Therefore, calculations with this simple model indicate that even assuming for illustration that the 'optimal' inflation rate is presently 10 % (which is a quite pessimistic assumption), and that seigniorage revenues amount to 1,5 % of GDP, the welfare cost of seigniorage losses due to monetary union would not exceed that of a *ceteris paribus* rise in taxes by a third of a percentage point. [64]

Taken together, the above developments show that the welfare cost of EMU for countries facing seigniorage losses can be considered minor to negligible.

Inflation and the tax system

As mentioned above, seigniorage is not the only channel for inflation to affect real government revenues. Tax systems are rarely neutral with respect to inflation. Among the most important factors are delays in the collection of taxes (e.g. for VAT or income tax); lags in the indexation (even non-indexation) of the income tax brackets and/or the social security benefits; non-discrimination between nominal and real interest income (also nominal and real capital gains); non-discrimination between nominal and real capital con-

sumption allowances and interest charges in the computation of taxable profits of the firms.

As apparent in the above list, inflation can either increase or decrease government revenues. However, there is a fundamental difference between the effects of seigniorage and those of the non-neutrality of inflation with respect to the tax system. Although the latter can be significant in the short term, there is no welfare motive for taxes not to discriminate between nominal and real income. Actually, taxation of nominal interest income, or deductions of nominal interest charges and capital allowances are highly distortionary because they lead individuals and firms to suboptimal investment choices. A standard consequence of non-indexation in the tax system is therefore that a rise in the rate of inflation increases distortions and therefore reduces welfare. For this reason, even if a low-inflation EMU would lead to an increase in tax rates in order to compensate for revenue losses, there is no a priori evidence that this would be welfare-reducing.

5.2.2. Interest rates and public debt service

Interest payments on the public debt amount approximately to 5 % of GDP in the Community as a whole. In the most indebted countries like Belgium, Greece, Ireland, and Italy, interest payments are close to 10 % of GDP or even above, and represent more than 20 % of total government expenditure. Hence, any effect of EMU on the interest rate on public debt would be a major issue for public finance.

Graph 5.6 depicts the relation between long-term nominal interest rates and inflation in the Community. Obviously, most of the variance in interest rates is accounted for by inflation differentials. Member States experiencing higher inflation also experience higher interest rates and therefore higher interest burden on the public debt. However, this is basically a nominal phenomenon: increased interest payments on the public debt only compensate for the real depreciation of the principal. In so far as participation in EMU would reduce both inflation and the nominal interest rate, leaving the real interest rate unchanged, this would cut the budget deficit, but simultaneously reduce real depreciation on existing public debt.

Some real consequences would nevertheless arise because of the tax treatment of nominal interest income and capital losses. In addition, the public perception of the deficit issue would surely be affected since the policy debate frequently focuses on the observed deficit, without consideration for debt depreciation effects.

---

[63] The problem arises because the optimal public finance policy of choosing the right mix of taxation and inflation is time-inconsistent. The argument summarized in the text is fully spelled out in Gros (1989a) and Van der Ploeg (1990), where it is shown that the higher the public debt, the higher the incentive to engineer surprise inflation and the more a country gains from participation in EMU. Although tax distortions reduce this benefit, back-of-the-envelope calculations show that under the assumptions, of the model (i.e. welfare maximization by the authorities and rational expectations by the public), the present level of the debt to GDP ratio is above its critical value in the four Member States.

[64] In a recent paper, Canzioneri and Rogers (1989) use a different approach: they consider the trade-off between seigniorage and the reduction in transaction costs involved in the choice of forming a monetary union. Even assuming that the black economy is about 20 % of GDP in Italy, they conclude that even very small conversion costs outweigh the welfare losses arising from seigniorage revenue losses.

GRAPH 5.6: **Long-term nominal interest rates and inflation, average 1985-89**

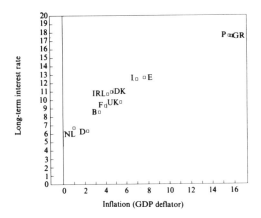

However EMU will also affect real interest charges on the public debt, at least in a transitory way, because for inflation-prone Member States it will enhance the credibility of the commitment to exchange rate and price stability. As shown in Graph 5.7, in the second half of the 1980s *ex-post* real long-term interest rates were far from being equalized across the Community. They were high by historical standards and above the German level for ERM countries, quite independently of the inflation differential. For Greece and Portugal, *ex-post* real rates were lower because of the maintenance of capital controls.

EMU and real interest rate differentials

A decomposition of the factors behind interest rate differentials helps to clarify the potential effects of EMU on real interest rates.

Cross-country differences in real *ex-post* (or realized) interest rate on assets of the same category and specific risk can be analytically decomposed into four components:

(i)   country premiums resulting from capital controls and other limitations to capital mobility;

(ii) exchange risk premiums resulting from exchange rate variability;

(iii) real exchange rate depreciation;

(iv) expectational errors regarding the evolution of the exchange rate.

Each of these factors is considered separately below. The decomposition is carried out analytically in Appendix 2 to this chapter.

GRAPH 5.7: *Ex-post* real long-term interest rates and inflation, average 1985-89

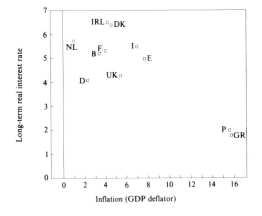

(i) Capital market liberalization has the effect of reducing the country premium component of interest rate differentials to zero. Hence, after-tax domestic nominal interest rates only differ from one country to another by the amount of the forward discount, i.e. the difference between current and forward exchange rates. A practical consequence is that for any agent within the Community, it becomes equivalent to borrow in currency x or to borrow in currency y and to hedge against exchange rate variations (assuming capital markets provide hedging for the adequate maturity).[65]

---

[65]   This is known as the covered interest rate parity condition. Transaction and hedging costs are neglected. See Chapter 6, Section 6.5 for a quantification.

(ii) A second factor is the existence of currency risk premiums, i.e. of spreads between the forward discount on the exchange markets and the depreciation expected by market participants. This term cannot be observed, but is analytically important to isolate: even if investors do not expect exchange rates to be changed in the foreseeable future, assets denominated in a foreign currency remain more risky than home assets of the same category. Hence, exchange rate risk acts as a barrier to capital mobility even without any capital control. Moreover, as long as exchange rates can be changed at low cost, investors are aware of the possibility of depreciating the weak-reputation currencies. Therefore, currency risk premiums can persist for previously weak currencies even if exchange rates are kept fixed for a long period of time.

Since EMU would eliminate exchange rate risk altogether, it would also eliminate exchange risk premiums. This would be for weak-reputation countries a gain of a permanent nature, but presumably a relatively small one. Although these premiums cannot be observed directly, they cannot be expected to account permanently for a large fraction of interest rate differentials.

(iii) A third factor of divergence is that purchasing power parity does not hold. As long as exchange rate realignments do not compensate fully for inflation differentials, real interest rates are bound to differ. This factor could lead to a permanent effect only if EMU were in the long run to affect real exchange rate changes within the Community. As argued in Chapter 6, this should not be the case. Regarding the transition, as documented in Chapter 2, realignments within the ERM have since 1985 systematically been of a smaller magnitude than cumulated inflation differentials. Therefore, this factor should actually reduce *ex-post* real rates in the more inflationary countries.

(iv) However a fourth factor, which probably accounts for the largest part of differences in real rates, results from expectational errors regarding exchange rates. Markets appear to judge the ERM commitment as not fully credible and to expect the weak-reputation currencies to devalue. In that respect, exchange rate expectations appear to adjust very sluggishly.

EMU would presumably remove all expectations of exchange rate changes within the Community. Since it cannot be assumed that without EMU market expectations would permanently remain wrong, this cannot be considered a permanent gain with respect to the Stage I baseline. However, this is an important topic for the transition because a rapid move towards EMU could alleviate the costs associated with a protracted period of high *ex-post* real rates.

Permanent effects of EMU

From the above discussion, it is apparent that permanent effects of EMU on real interest rate differentials with respect to a stable Stage I baseline are bound to be limited. The first and only undisputable permanent effect would be the disappearance of exchange risk premiums, which have been assessed as relatively small. Moreover, in a stable Stage I exchange rate risk could limit capital mobility, but as exchange rates should be stable (except in the presence of shocks), there is no reason to expect that risk premiums would still be biased in any significant way.

In EMU, nominal interest rates on assets of the same maturity and risk would be fully equalized across the Community. After this equalization becomes effective, the only remaining issue concerns the general level of market interest rates. A straightforward assumption, which is made here, is that it would be the baseline level in the previous anchor country. This assumption is warranted because as capital market liberalization would already be effective in the baseline, the effect of EMU should only be to eliminate the monetary 'noise' that affects real interest rates. There is no reason to expect real interest rates to average out within the Community as is the case when capital controls are removed between two countries.[66] Moreover, as EuroFed should broadly maintain the same stance as the most stability-oriented central banks of the Community, there are no reasons from the monetary side why interest rates in Germany should change to some Community average. The validity of this assumption is however obviously conditional on policy assumptions: if the policy stance of EuroFed were not judged by markets as convincing as that of the Bundesbank, inflation risk premiums and therefore interest rates would rise.

Summing up, EMU should not have important permanent effects on interest rates. This, however, only holds for identical assets. A separate issue, which relates to the identity of the borrower, is whether specific effects can be expected regarding the yield of government bonds. Since bond rates on the public debt may differ for two reasons, namely either because of different degrees of credit-worthiness of the governments, or because of portfolio effects, EMU effects regarding these two aspects will be examined separately.

As discussed in Section 5.1.2, evidence indicates that default risk premiums are at present low, which can be interpreted as reflecting the market judgment that public debt unsustain-

66 Since capital market liberalization is *erga omnes*, real interest rates within the Community would only differ from interest rates abroad for one of the reasons spelled out above.

ability would actually lead to debt monetization (and therefore a depreciation of the currency), rather than to default. In so far as EMU would rule out monetization, this could only lead borrower's risk premiums to increase for high-debt countries. In other terms, an increase in the specific risk premium on public debt would (at least partially) offset the disappearance of the currency premium. In EMU, governments whose debt cannot be regarded as sustainable could for this reason face a higher cost of borrowing than other public borrowers.

Portfolio effects do not arise from default risk, but rather because public bonds and other financial assets (e.g. liquid assets and stocks) differ as regards their yield and its variability. When choosing the structure of their portfolio, risk-adverse agents take both the yields and their variability into account, thus determining the desired shares of each category of asset. Therefore, as long as financial markets are segmented and the public debt is mainly held domestically, a high debt ratio is likely to lead to an increase in public bond rates because private agents are reluctant to increase the share of that asset in their financial portfolios. [67]

Following this approach, the effects of EMU would depend on both domestic and foreign portfolio diversification effects. Since exchange rate risks would be eliminated, capital market segmentation would disappear altogether. As bonds of the same maturity and risk issued by different EC governments would become perfect substitutes, their yields would be equalized. High-debt countries should therefore benefit from EMU as access to a wider capital market would lower the risk-adjusted cost of government borrowing. [68] Whether or not this could offset the increase in risk premiums is an open issue, but it should be noted that capital market integration, by permitting a better diversification of risk, would *ceteris paribus* reduce the size of the risk premiums. It can therefore be presumed that, at least, the net effect would be a gain for countries whose debt is high but stable. However, possible regulatory bias favouring the holding of government paper should also be taken into account. If

specific regulations allow the government to borrow at preferential rates, a cost-increasing effect could dominate.

Transitional effects of EMU

Examination of the behaviour of bond rates in the course of disinflation shows that uncertainty regarding the commitment to exchange rate stability in the non-German ERM countries has probably significantly contributed to their high real interest rates record. The specific contribution of weak credibility can be assessed by comparing both long-term rates and inflation in ERM countries with those of Germany, the anchor country. Starting in the early 1980s from a situation characterized both by higher inflation and higher nominal rates (but frequently lower real interest rates because of widespread capital controls), most countries have gone through a protracted phase of significantly higher *ex-post* real rates than in Germany. The typical movement of inflation and interest rate differentials, shown in the top panel of Graph 5.8 below, is a counter-clockwise move: a disinflation programme is characterized by a simultaneous decrease in nominal interest rates and inflation towards the origin of the diagram (complete convergence), but as the nominal rate decrease lags behind disinflation, the path remains above the *(ex-post)* real interest rate parity locus represented by the diagonal. [69]

This is best illustrated by the case of the Netherlands, which has gone all the way down to the German inflation rate level (and even below), but as depicted in Graph 5.8 at the cost of several years of high real rates. Interestingly, the interest rate differential between the Netherlands and Germany lasted a long time in spite of (i) a strong commitment to exchange rate stability, illustrated by the history of ERM realignments (the guilder has been devalued with respect to the Deutschmark only twice, in 1979 and 1983 by 2 % each time), and (ii) an early achievement of price convergence (actually better performance than in Germany since 1983). This high interest rate cost of disinflation is the effect of the risk premium and the persistence of expectations of realignments. [70] By contrast, disinflation in Italy is still not complete and the *ex-post* real interest rate differential remains significant.

---

[67] This result holds in standard empirical portfolio models. However, as documented by Wyplosz (1990), investigations on cross-country interest rate differentials do not yield clear results in that respect. The same holds for time-series analysis.

[68] This assumes, first, that in the reference situation agents only hold domestic financial assets, and second that agents across the EMU would have the same preferred portfolio. Both assumptions are simplifying. However inspection of the Italian case shows that the budget deficit is primarily financed by domestic agents, mainly households (53 % of the debt in 1986) and secondly banks (30 %). Borrowing in foreign currencies is a tiny fraction (3 %) of the total debt outstanding. As a consequence, access to a wider market could have significant effects.

---

[69] A precise discussion of the typical bond rates behaviour during a disinflation in a fixed-but-adjustable exchange rate regime can be found in Andersen and Risager (1988).

[70] The better inflation performance of the Dutch economy is somewhat exaggerated by the choice of the GDP deflator as a measure of inflation. This is because the share of energy in the Dutch GDP is much higher than in Germany. See Annex B.

GRAPH 5.8: **Long-term interest rate and inflation differentials with respect to Germany**

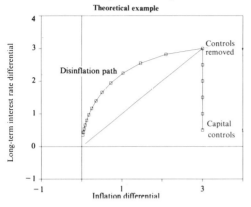

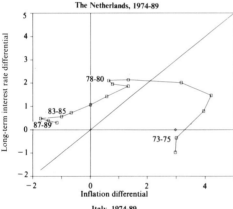

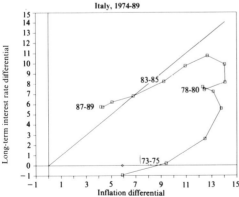

Note: moving average over three years. The diagonal locus corresponds to *ex-post* real interest rate parity. Points above the diagonal are characterized by positive real rate differentials. Note that scales differ.

A timely move towards EMU could substantially reduce the *ex-post* cost of State borrowing during the transition towards price convergence. Referring to Graph 5.8, for the Member States whose disinflation would not be completely achieved at the outset of Stage III, EMU would imply immediate nominal interest rate convergence instead of a slow downward move.[71]

This could be a sizeable benefit for high-debt countries whose disinflation programmes are difficult to achieve because of their public finance cost. Indeed, this public finance cost has frequently been considered the major obstacle to full price convergence for high-debt countries: because disinflation would reduce seigniorage revenues and initially increase real interest rates, at least in the first year it could make the situation of public finance worse. Thus, it has been argued that priority should be given to debt stabilization over price convergence, and even suggested that disinflation could be contradictory itself because it would make the public debt path unsustainable and therefore ultimately force the authorities to monetize the public debt.[72] By reducing significantly the public finance cost of disinflation, EMU could remove this possible contradiction.

A precise evaluation of the quantitative gain would require detailed country-by-country assumptions. Only a very rough measure of the potential gains can be given here for illustrative purposes. The Dutch case provides a useful benchmark case since it is the only one for which complete convergence of both inflation and interest rates with Germany has already been achieved, and because, as documented in Annex B, the two countries exhibit at least since 1983 a textbook case of *de facto* monetary union; this is presumably what some other Member States could individually achieve within the framework of Stage I by unilaterally committing themselves to a fixed Deutschmark exchange rate.

From the beginning of the EMS in 1979 until 1989, the cumulative nominal interest rate differential between the Netherlands and Germany amounted to 11 percentage points, and the *ex-post* real differential to 15 percentage points, if measured using the GDP deflator because of better inflation performance on average in the Netherlands.[73] Tak-

---

[71] This is indeed the strategy already followed by several Member States, the most recent example being the Belgian announcement of a Deutschmark peg policy. However as this type of commitment remains unilateral, it cannot have the same credibility as EMU. Moreover, it presumably benefits already from market expectations of the next moves towards EMU.

[72] This is known as the Sargent-Wallace (1981) argument. For an application to the European case, see Dornbusch (1989, 1990).

[73] This differential is somewhat lower — 12,8 percentage points — if the consumption deflator is used because of the effect of energy prices.

ing the nominal differential, which is the lowest of these figures, the (gross) public finance cost of disinflation can be approximated by 0,11 times the average value of the debt to GDP ratio over the period (60 %), i.e. 6,6 % of GDP.[74]

This is not a measure of EMU savings, since disinflation is already under way in most Member States and some ERM members are already close to the Dutch situation. However, these figures indicate that in the medium term potential budgetary savings could offset the consequences of seigniorage losses for high-inflation and high-debt countries. For Italy, Spain, Portugal and Greece the inflation differential with respect to Germany was above 4 % in 1989, i.e. higher than the Dutch-German differential at the beginning of the 1980s. EMU is not an immediate prospect of course, and these countries should first achieve a better convergence. But starting from a reduced inflation differential (about 2 to 3 %), EMU could help complete disinflation at a lower cost than otherwise. As a benchmark, it can be assumed that this strategy would cut the interest rate cost by half of the Dutch figure (i.e. 5,5 cumulated percentage points). The associated public finance benefit would range between 2,3 % of GDP for Spain, whose debt is relatively low, to 5,4 % for Italy. These would be once and for all gains; but in the medium term, their budgetary impact could offset the seigniorage costs given in Table 5.7.

Admittedly, disinflation could also raise temporary difficulties for governments whose debt is of a long maturity because it would increase the *ex-post* real yield of existing bonds. This effect, which also holds for private borrowers, arises in any disinflation programme. It would only be significant for countries whose government has mostly issued long-term fixed-interest bonds, and for which EMU can be expected to bring a significantly speedier disinflation.

Macroeconomic implications

These interest rate effects would have a macroeconomic impact on the economy as a whole, going beyond public finance issues. A sharp distinction has however to be made between the effects of EMU on *ex-post* (or realized) real interest rates discussed above and its effects on *ex-ante* real rates which determine the investment and saving decisions of economic agents. Genuine *ex-ante* real rate reductions in the transition would boost investment and growth in the medium run. In the long run, lower risk premiums would stimulate investment as discussed in Chapter 3. In contrast,

lower *ex-post* real rates do not change investment decisions, but provoke transfers between borrowers and creditors and only impact on the real economy to the extent that agents react to these wealth effects.

The potential for a drop in *ex-ante* real interest rates appears to be smaller than for *ex-post* rates, as discussed in Appendix 2. In addition to the exchange risk premium effect, the only motive for a decrease would arise either from present expectations of real depreciation of the non-anchor countries or conversely from expectations of real appreciation during the first period of EMU. Both are possible, but to a lesser extent than for *ex-post* rates. Regarding this second possibility, it should be mentioned that an early EMU commitment could have negative side-effects precisely because of an excessive drop in real interest rates in the more inflation-prone countries. Since irrevocably fixed exchange rates imply nominal interest rate parity, they also imply that real rates are the lowest in the more inflationary countries. A too early commitment to exchange rate stability could therefore make disinflation slower and more painful. Indeed, it has been argued that this is already the case in countries like Italy since firms can borrow abroad at a lower real rate.[75] As further discussed in Chapter 8, the right strategy should follow a middle route between the two extremes of 'coronation theory' and immediate commitment to exchange rate fixity.

5.2.3. Taxation and the provision of public goods in EMU

Throughout the foregoing discussion, it has been assumed that Member States would retain their full autonomy in taxing and spending decisions, i.e. that neither the level of non-interest spending nor the structures of taxes and expenditures would be affected. The aim of this section is to discuss briefly whether and to what extent EMU would in addition impose convergence in taxing and spending. Since it is a broad and complex issue, only the main arguments directly related to EMU will be given here.

The issue of tax convergence has already been the focus of numerous policy discussions within the Community, but mostly in the specific fields of indirect taxation (following the Commission's harmonization proposals of 1987) and capital income taxation (in the context of capital market liberalization). A more general discussion of taxation and of the parallel issue of provision of public goods and services in the context of EMU is warranted. As argued below,

---

[74]   The true public finance cost of disinflation is probably lower because a higher (even constant) inflation rate in the Netherlands would have raised risk premiums.

[75]   This point is made by Giavazzi and Spaventa (1990).

for taxation and spending in general EMU should not be expected to introduce major qualitative changes with respect to the '1992 + EMS' reference situation. It will, however, have an impact in specific fields, especially capital income taxation.

Fiscal federalism and EMU

The theory of fiscal federalism[76] provides an appropriate point of departure as it envisages issues of optimum assignment in a system characterized by the existence of a large number of local jurisdictions which independently levy taxes on their citizens (supposedly mobile) and provide them with public goods.[77] The purpose of this theory is to delimit the respective domains of competition and cooperation among lower jurisdictions, and to determine which resources and functions should be assigned to higher or lower levels of government.

The basic model is one in which goods, capital and citizens can and do move freely across jurisdictions, where citizens have full information and where private as well as non-private goods and services are produced under competitive conditions. In such a highly simplified model, individual citizens could choose the level of public goods provision (and related taxation) which they prefer by 'voting with their feet', i.e. by moving from one jurisdiction to another in order to find the package of goods and services that suits them best. Jurisdictions would not be bound to uniformity; on the contrary, some would be characterized by a higher level of public goods provision. (e.g. in the domain of public education), but also by higher taxes. Nevertheless, all jurisdictions would be concerned for efficiency in public services since a higher cost of production financed by higher taxes, but not matched by better public services, would lead citizens to migrate.

These conclusions are important in the Community context as they emphasize the irrelevance of any overall requirement for convergence in the fields of taxation and public services: for example, following this model Member States could retain significant differences in the level of old-age social security contributions, provided they would be matched by differences in real wage levels. They could also still choose to levy taxes through a variety of different systems, subject to a general requirement of efficiency in the management of

the public sector arising from mobility. Although as already argued labour mobility is bound to remain relatively low within the Community, at least across language frontiers, large differences in public sector efficiency could be a motive for enterprises and certain categories of labour to migrate.

However, the above model has immediately to be extended to cover the issue of externalities. Benefits and costs derived from public goods can spill over from one jurisdiction to another: for example, better transportation infrastructures or cultural facilities benefit residents from other jurisdictions, whereas pollution is not restricted to the area in which it originates. With neither coordination nor assignment of those functions to a higher level of jurisdiction, the non-cooperative equilibrium would be characterized by an insufficient provision of public goods, but an excessive provision of public 'bads' like pollution.[78] Externalities also arise in the tax field. Problems of tax competition originate in the migration of tax bases, for example in the case of capital income taxation, corporate taxation or expenditure taxation.[79] With neither coordination nor harmonization, such externalities would lead jurisdictions to choose too low tax rates on mobile tax bases. A similar problem arises also as regards interpersonal redistribution through taxation, since if households (at least some categories of them) are mobile, redistributive policies spill over from one jurisdiction to another. This limits the possibility for any single jurisdiction to engage in redistributive policies which depart from that of its neighbours, and can generally lead to reducing the scope for redistributive fiscal policies in comparison to each jurisdiction's preferences.[80] Negative revenue spill-overs can also exist, since an increase in taxes in a jurisdiction reduces the income being spent on private goods produced in the neighbouring region.[81] Coordination and bargaining among lower levels of jurisdiction, the fixing of minimum standards in the field of taxation, revenue-sharing provisions, commonly agreed norms (regarding, for example, the environment) and assignment of certain resources and functions to the higher federal levels are all, therefore, relevant techniques in order to improve the overall welfare compared to the non-cooperative equilibrium.

---

[76] For a survey of the theory of fiscal federalism and its implications for EMU, see Van Rompuy, Abraham and Heremans (1990).

[77] Public goods are those whose consumption by an individual does not reduce the availability for other individuals. Classic examples are TV broadcasting and clean air.

---

[78] This risk is underlined by Van der Ploeg (1990).

[79] This should not be mixed with the mobility of citizens from one jurisdiction to another. Whereas this mobility is a condition for competition among jurisdictions to hold, mobile tax bases can give rise to problems of tax avoidance. Examples can be found in the taxation of capital income (Giovannini, 1989) and of corporate income.

[80] See Van Rompuy *et al.* (1990), and Wildason (1990).

[81] See Eichengreen (1990), and Wyplosz (1990).

Implications for EMU

The above approach offers some basic insights on the issues of taxation and public spending in the Community. Additions to the model, allowing for the imperfect mobility of citizens, information costs and economies of scale in the provision of public goods do not alter the basic results. However, they strengthen the case for harmonization and an assignment of resources and functions to the upper, federal level: imperfect information increases the costs of decentralized bargaining among jurisdictions and of the enforcement of agreements; economies of scale call for centralization. Furthermore, restrictions in the mobility of some factors (e.g. semi-skilled workers and employees) while others (e.g. skilled labour and capital) are mobile raises issues of distortions and vertical equity.

In addition, the need for tax convergence can also result from purely administrative requirements, frequently related to the enforcement of tax compliance. This arose in two recent cases of tax harmonization within the Community in the context of the single market. In the case of indirect taxation, a certain degree of convergence in VAT rates is required as border controls are eliminated, since wide differences in rates would give rise to tax evasion. The same issue of tax evasion arises also in the case of capital income taxation where the case for minimum rates, or a common withholding tax, specifically results from differences in national reporting systems. However on purely economic grounds, neither of these taxes would in principle need to be harmonized.[82]

A number of studies have already discussed tax convergence constraints which arise from the internal market and capital market liberalization.[83] A general conclusion of these studies is that the need for harmonization or centralization is limited to certain categories of taxes which account for a relatively small part of government revenues: in particular, neither income taxes nor social security contributions need to be harmonized, while for VAT rates, only a reduction in cross-country differences is warranted. Corporate and capital income taxation, however, are exceptional cases.

In the field of corporate income tax, a case can be made for harmonization of the tax base and for fixing a minimum rate as economic union draws nearer. Minimum conditions to be fulfilled are tax neutrality with respect to foreign

investment, cross-border cooperation, and the prevention of tax avoidance. In the long term, some studies suggest that as the internal market becomes the natural habitat for Community companies, the corporate income tax could become one of the Community's own resources.[84] An alternative could be to retain different tax rates but to establish a fixed apportionment scheme (based, for example, on the share of the country in the total EC turnover of the firm) as in certain federal States. However, it remains to be clarified how far existing differences in marginal effective tax rates result in inefficient distortions in corporate resource allocation between countries.

In the field of capital income taxation, the introduction of a single currency would introduce a qualitative change, since there would no longer be any currency discrimination in the financial assets held in different Community countries. The potential for a migration of this tax base would therefore encompass the totality of financial assets. This would further increase the need for a Community solution, either through the adoption of common reporting rules or through the establishment of a minimum withholding tax.

In other fields, the specific effects of EMU can be considered incremental. The largest part of the effects of economic union already result from the completion of the internal market. As to monetary union, apart from the fact that it would strengthen integration, additional effects would result from (i) inflation convergence, (ii) tighter sustainability constraints on fiscal deficits and (iii) the loss of the exchange rate instrument. None of these effects would impose a closer convergence of the tax systems. The effects of inflation convergence relate to the seigniorage issue discussed in Section 5.2.1 above and would only lead to a minor increase in taxes. Tighter constraints on fiscal deficits could lead to tax increases in some countries, but without clear implications for convergence. The loss of the nominal exchange rate could lead governments to rely on tax instruments to influence the real exchange rate, thereby leading to tax competition, but this problem should be dealt with through coordination.

Empirical evidence derived from the experience of federal States confirms that inter-state tax differentials are lower within, for example, the United States than in Europe. Nevertheless, provided specific problems arising from tax competition are dealt with in an appropriate way, there is still considerable room for tax autonomy.[85] However, it should be recalled that within EMU differences in the level

[82]   Regarding capital income taxation, it should be added that since capital market liberalization is *erga omnes*, enforcement of tax compliance requires cooperation with non-Community governments.

[83]   See, for example, Artus (1988), Giovannini (1989), Gros (1989c), Isard (1989), CEPII-OFCE (1990a, 1990b), and the references therein.

[84]   See Padoa-Schioppa (1987), Devereux and Pearson (1989), CEPII-OFCE (1990a, 1990b).

[85]   See, for example, Van Rompuy et al. (1990), and Eichengreen (1990).

of taxation will be matched by differences in the real after-tax income of individuals. One can therefore expect a certain degree of pressure towards public sector efficiency to result from a higher mobility of persons and increased competition in the product markets.

As cross-border mobility increases, the issue of externalities in the provision of public goods is bound to gain in importance. Specific fields of Community competence like energy, transport and the environment have been discussed in Chapter 3. In other fields like for instance higher education, risks of undersupply of public goods should as much as possible be prevented through cooperation among Member States.

Problems might also arise in high-debt countries, since, as a large proportion of public resources is devoted to servicing the public debt, public goods tend to be in short supply with respect to the level of taxes (or taxes to be too high with respect to the provision of public goods). This creates an incentive for agents to migrate, i.e. to repudiate the liabilities of the previous generations. The same kind of intertemporal problems could arise in the future due to contractual liabilities embodied in social security arrangements. Generally speaking, mobility in EMU would limit the possibility to organize large-scale intergenerational transfers within national budgets.[86] More precisely, tax convergence (resulting either from harmonization or market pressures) could lead high-debt countries which devote a significant part of their resources to the interest cost of the public debt to reduce the provision of public goods to a suboptimal level. These problems are not severe in the short term, but deserve attention in a long-term perspective. At present they only really call for a sound management of public finance, rather than specific Community initiatives.

Appendix 1: The welfare cost of a seigniorage loss: an illustration

The welfare cost of a reduction in seigniorage can be illustrated by using a very simple numerical example.

Assume the welfare loss function can be represented in a simplified fashion by:

(1) $L = ap^2 + t^2$

where p is the inflation rate, t is the tax rate, and a characterizes the relative distortionary effect of taxes and inflation (a lower a means taxes are more distortionary).

---
[86] This relates to the discussion of sustainability in Section 5.1.2 above.

The problem of the government is to minimize L subject to the budget constraint:

(2) $mp + t = e$

where m is the monetary base and e is the level of public expenditure, both measured as ratios to GDP (the deficit is assumed to be zero).

Minimization of L subject to (2) yields the optimal inflation rate:

(3) $p^* = em/(a + m^2)$

If a is not too small, and m is not too large, (3) can be approximated by:

(3) $p^* = em/a$

Inflation depends positively on the level of public expenditure and on the distortionary effect of taxes. It also depends positively on the size of the monetary base (except for very small values of a).

In order to assess the welfare cost of a seigniorage loss, suppose the monetary base is 15 % of GDP, a typical value for southern Member States, and suppose the optimal inflation p^* is 10 %, which is high and means taxes are quite distortionary. Seigniorage revenues amount therefore to 1,5 % of GDP. With e = 0,4, i.e. government spending represents 40 % of GDP, this gives the value of coefficient a = 0,5775.

Suppose now that due to the completion of the single market the monetary base is reduced to 10 % of GDP (e.g. 2 % reserves + 8 % currency). This already reduces the optimal inflation rate to 6,8 %. According to (2), taxes have to be raised by 0,8 percentage point of GDP.

Assume now that due to EMU inflation is reduced to zero. Seigniorage disappears. Taxes have to be raised by an additional 0,7 percentage point. The associated welfare loss of the combined decrease in inflation and increase in taxes can be computed by using (1). It comes out to be about the welfare loss implied *ceteris paribus* by a rise in taxes by one third of a percentage point.

The above model can be modified in order to take into account the welfare cost of excess reserve holdings. Suppose the loss function is:

(1') $L = ap^2 + b(m - m_0)^2 + t^2$

where $m_0 = 10 %$ is a technically efficient ratio of monetary base to GDP. Coefficients a and b can be identified assuming that $p = 10\%$ and $m = 15\%$ correspond to an optimum. Assuming that m is reduced to m_0 with the single market, reoptimization with respect to p yields the same result as above.

Appendix 2: EMU and real interest rates

This appendix discusses the effects of EMU on real interest rate differences between Member States. The emphasis is on the difference between the present situation, which has some transitory elements in it, and the steady-state EMU. Both ex-ante real rates (R), which determine investment decisions, and ex-post (or realized) rates (r), which are important for the interest cost on public debt, are considered.

Perfect capital mobility and asset substitutability are supposed to hold, whatever the exchange rate regime. It is also assumed that the overall monetary policy is set by an anchor country in the baseline situation and by EuroFed in EMU, but that both policies are identical, implying that the short-term nominal interest rate for the union will be the same as for the anchor country in the baseline.

For assets of the same category, maturity and risk, the ex-post real interest rate differential between the home country and the anchor country is:

(1) $r - r^* = (i - p) - (i^* - p^*)$

where i, i^* are nominal interest rates and p, p^* are the rates of inflation (starred variables denote the anchor country). However, ex-ante real interest rates depend on expected inflation, not on realized inflation:

(2) $R - R^* = (i - i^* - f^d) + (f^d - Ee) + (Ee - Ep + Ep^*)$

Where R, R^* are ex-ante real interest rates, and Ep, Ep^* are expected rates of inflation, Ee is expected depreciation and is f^d the forward discount. The first term in (2), usually referred to as the country premium, is an effect of capital controls. It is therefore assumed to be equal to zero, which is equivalent to say that covered interest rate parity holds. The second term, i.e. the difference between the forward discount and expected depreciation, is the exchange risk premium; it represents the part of the interest rate differential which is not explained by expected depreciation. The third term, the expected real depreciation, is non-zero if ex-ante PPP does not hold.[87]

Hence, real ex-ante interest rate differentials can be decomposed in the following way:

(3a) $R - R^* = (f^d - Ee) + (Ee - Ep + Ep^*)$

and for ex-post differentials:

(3b) $r - r^* = ((Ep - p) - (Ep^* - p^*)) + R - R^*$

Assuming that real ex-ante and ex-post interest rates in the anchor country are not affected by EMU, if subscript 0 refers to the present situation, the effect of EMU on interest rates in the non-anchor countries is:

(4a) $R_{EMU} - R_0 = - (f^d - Ee)_0 + [(Ep - Ep^*)_{EMU} - (Ee - Ep + Ep^*)_0]$

(4b) $r_{EMU} - r_0 = - (f^d - Ee)_0 + [(-p + p^*)_{EMU} - (e - p + p^*)_0] - (Ee - e)_0$

The first term in both expressions is due to the disappearance of the exchange risk premium. This effect, which is due to the suppression of exchange-rate variability in EMU, should contribute to lower rates in peripheral countries in so far as in general the forward discount overpredicts exchange rate depreciations.

The second term in (4a) represents the extent to which EMU changes expectations regarding the real exchange rate. Assuming that real exchange rates can be expected to evolve on average in the same way in a permanent Stage I as in EMU, this effect would be zero. However it could be important in the transition, either because of present expectations of real depreciation of the non-anchor currencies or, assuming to the contrary that nominal exchange rates are already credible, because of remaining price divergence.[88]

In a similar way, the second term for ex-post real rates corresponds to ex-post real exchange-rate change. This term will on average be important only if there are significant real exchange rate adjustments in the transition. It can lead either to interest rate decreases or increases depending upon whether the non-anchor currencies experience real depreciation or appreciation in the transition.

However the last term in (4b), which represents expectational errors, is specific to ex-post rates. The associated effect, which could be termed the 'peso problem', offers the possibility of significant reductions in ex-post real interest rates in the transition if exchange-rate expectations are sluggish and/or if the commitment to a hard-currency option is not judged credible. The experience of the last couple of years indicates that this effect might be important.

---

[87]   This decomposition follows Frankel (1989).

[88]   In this case real rates in peripheral countries could even become lower than in the anchor country at some stage during the transition.

References

Aglietta, M., Brender, A. and Coudert, V. (1990), *Globalisation financière: l'aventure obligée*, Economica — CEPII, Paris.

Aglietta, M., Coudert, V. and Delessy, H. (1990), 'Politiques budgétaires et ajustements macro-économiques dans la perspective de l'intégration monétaire européenne', in *Lectures critiques du rapport Delors*, De Pecunia Vol. II, No 2-3, Brussels, September.

Alesina, A. and Tabellini, G. (1990). 'Voting on the budget deficit', *American Economic Review*.

Alesina, A., Prati, A. and Tabellini, G. (1989), 'Public confidence and debt management: a model and a case study of Italy', CEPR Discussion Paper No 351, October.

Amalric, F. and Sterdyniak, H. (1989), 'Interdépendance et coopération: les leçons d'une maquette', *Observations et diagnostics économiques* No 26, January.

Andersen, T. and Risager, O. (1988), 'Stabilization policies, credibility, and interest rate determination in a small open economy', *European Economic Review* 32, pp. 669-679.

Artus, P. (1988), 'Integration européenne et degrés de liberté de la politique économique', Document de travail No 1988-03, Service des Études Économiques et Financières, Caisse de Dépôts et Consignations, Paris, November.

Baldwin, R. (1990), 'On the microeconomics of EMU', in *European Economy* (1990).

Barro, R. J. and Gordon, D. (1983), 'A critical theory of monetary policy in a natural rate model', *Journal of Political Economy*, 91, pp. 589-610, August.

Begg, D. (1990), 'Alternative exchange rate regimes: the role of the exchange rate and the implications for wage-price adjustment', in *European Economy* (1990).

Bishop, G. (1990), *Creating an EC monetary union with binding market rules*, Solomon Brothers Inc, February.

Bishop, G., Damrau, D. and Miller, M. (1989), *Market discipline CAN work in the EC monetary union*, Solomon Brothers Inc, November.

Blanchard, O. J. (1985), 'Debt, deficits, and finite horizons', *Journal of Political Economy*, April.

Blanchard, O. J. (1990), 'Suggestions for a new set of fiscal indicators', OECD/DES Working Paper No 79.

Bovenberg, L., Kremers, J. and Masson, P. (1990), 'Economic and monetary union in Europe and constraints on national budgetary policies', paper prepared for a conference on 'The political economy of government debt', University of Amsterdam, June.

Bredenkamp, H. and Deppler, M. (1989), 'Fiscal constraints of a hard currency regime', in *Choosing an exchange rate regime: the challenge for smaller industrial countries*, edited by V. Argy and P. De Grauwe, CEPS/IMF.

Canzoneri, M. and Rogers, C. A. (1989), 'Is the European Community an optimal currency area? Optimal taxation versus the cost of multiple currencies', *American Economic Review*, November.

CEPII-OFCE (1990a), 'Vers une fiscalité européenne?', report to the French Senate, in *Rapport d'information fait au nom de la Commission des Finances*, No 211, Sénat, Paris, April.

CEPII-OFCE (1990b), 'Vers une fiscalité européenne?' *Observations et diagnostics économiques*, No 31, April.

Chouraqui, J.-Cl., Hageman, R. P. and Sartor, N. (1990), 'Indicators of fiscal policy: a reassessment', OECD/DES Working Paper No 78, April.

Cohen, D. and Wyplosz, Ch. (1989), 'The European monetary union: an agnostic evaluation', CEPR Discussion Paper No 306, April.

Cohen, D. and Wyplosz, Ch. (1990), 'Price and trade effects of exchange rate fluctuation and the design of policy coordination', CEPR Discussion Paper, April.

Coudert, V. (1987), 'Asymétries et coopération économique européenne: le cas France - Allemagne', *Économie Prospective Internationale*, 4° trimestre, No 32.

Cukierman, A., Edwards, S. and Tabellini, G. (1989) 'Seigniorage and political instability', paper presented at the National Bureau of Economic Research Conference on Political Economy, Cambridge, Mass., May.

Currie, A., Holtham, G. and Hallet, A. H. (1989), 'The theory and practice of international policy coordination: Does coordination pay?', in *Macroeconomic policies in an interdependent world*, edited by R. Bryant, D. Currie, and R. Portes, CEPR/The Brookings Institution/IMF.

Devereux, M. and Pearson, M. (1989) 'Corporate tax harmonization and economic efficiency', *Institute for Fiscal Studies Report Series* No 35, London.

Dornbusch, R. (1988), 'The EMS, the dollar and the yen', in *The European Monetary System*, edited by F. Giavazzi, S. Micossi and M. Miller., Banca d'Italia, CEPR.

Dornbusch, R. (1989), 'Ireland's disinflation', *Economic Policy*, April.

Dornbusch, R. (1990), *Problems of European monetary integration*, mimeo, Massachusetts Institute of Technology.

Drazen, A.(1989), 'Monetary policy, capital controls and seigniorage in an open economy', in *A European Central Bank?*, edited by M. De Cecco and A. Giovannini, Cambridge University Press.

Eichengreen, B. (1990), 'One money for Europe? Lessons from the US currency union', *Economic Policy* No 8, pp. 173-209.

European Economy (1990) — 'The economics of EMU', special issue.

Frankel, J. (1989), 'Quantifying international capital mobility in the 1980s', NBER Working Paper No 2856, National Bureau of Economic Research, Cambridge, Mass., February.

Frankel, J. and Razin, A. (1987), 'The Mundell-Fleming model: a quarter of a century later', *IMF Staff Papers*, Volume 34, No 4, December.

Froot, K. and Frankel, J. (1989), 'Forward discount bias: is it an exchange risk premium?', *Quarterly Journal of Economics*.

Giavazzi, F. (1989), 'The exchange rate question in Europe', EC Economic Paper No 74, January.

Giavazzi, F. and Giovannini, A. (1987) 'Exchange rate and prices in Europe', *Weltwirtschaftliches Archiv* 124, No 4, pp. 592-604.

Giavazzi, F. and Spaventa, L. (1990), 'The new EMS', CEPR Discussion Paper No 369, January.

Giavazzi, F. and Pagano, M. (1989), 'Confidence crises and public debt management', CEPR Discussion Paper No 318.

Giovannini, A. (1989), 'National tax systems versus the European capital market', *Economic Policy* No 9, October.

Giovannini, A. (1990), 'Money demand and monetary control in an integrated European economy', in *European Economy* (1990).

Grilli, V.(1989), 'Seigniorage in Europe', in *A European Central Bank?*, edited by M. De Cecco and A. Giovannini, Cambridge University Press.

Gros, D. (1989a), 'Seigniorage and EMS discipline', Centre for European Policy Studies Working Document No 38, Brussels.

Gros, D. (1989b), 'Seigniorage in the EC: the implications of the EMS and financial market integration', IMF Working Paper No 89/7.

Gros, D. (1989c), 'Capital-market liberalization and the taxation of savings', Centre for European Policy Studies, Working Party Report No 2, Brussels.

Hagemann, R. and Nicoletti, G. (1989), 'Ageing populations: economic effects and implications for public finance', OECD/DES Working Papers, No 61, January.

Hughes Hallet, A., Holtham, G. and Hutson, G. (1989), 'Exchange rate targeting as surrogate international cooperation', in *Blueprints for exchange-rate management*, edited by M. Miller, B. Eichengreen and R. Portes, Academic Press.

Isard, P. (1989), 'Corporate tax harmonization and European monetary integration', CEPS Working Document No 41, Brussels.

Krugman, P. (1989), *Exchange-rate instability*, MIT Press.

Kydland, F. E. and Prescott, E. C. (1977), 'Rules rather than discretion: the inconsistency of optimal plans', *Journal of Political Economy*, Vol. 85, No 3.

Lamfalussy, A. (1989), 'Macro-coordination of fiscal policies in an economic and monetary union in Europe', in *Collection of papers, Report on economic and monetary union in the European Community* (Delors Report), Commission of the EC.

Mankiw, G. (1987), 'The optimal collection of seigniorage, theory and evidence', *Journal of Monetary Economics*, 20, pp. 327-341.

Masson, P. and Melitz, J. (1990), 'Fiscal policy independence in a European monetary union', CEPR Discussion Paper, No 414.

Masson, P., Symansky, S., Haas, R. and Dooley, M. (1988), 'Multimod: a multi-region econometric model', Staff studies for the world economic outlook, International Monetary Fund, Washington, July.

McDougall, Sir D. (1977), *The role of public finances in European integration*, Commission of the EC.

Mohlo, L. (1989), 'European financial integration and revenue from seigniorage: the case of Italy', IMF Working Paper, No 89/41, Washington.

Neuman, M. J. M. (1990), 'Central bank independence as a prerequisite of price stability', in *European Economy* (1990).

Nicoletti, G. (1988), 'A cross-country analysis of private consumption, inflation and the debt neutrality hypothesis', *OECD Economic Studies*, No 11, autumn, pp. 43-87.

OECD (1990), *OECD Economic Outlook*, No 47, Paris, June.

Oudiz, G. (1985), 'European policy coordination: an evaluation', *Recherches économiques de Louvain*, Volume 51, No 3-4.

Oudiz, G. and Sachs, J. (1984), 'Macroeconomic policy coordination among the industrial economies', *Brookings Papers on Economic Activity*, No 1.

Padoa-Schioppa, T. (1987), *Efficiency, stability and equity*, Oxford University Press, Oxford.

Padoa-Schioppa, T. (1990), 'Fiscal prerequisites of a European monetary union', Conference on Aspects of Central Bank Policymaking, organized by the Bank of Israel and the David Horowitz Institute, Tel Aviv, January.

Phelps, E. S. (1973), 'Inflation in the theory of public finance', *Swedish Journal of Economics*, No 75, pp. 67-82.

Poterba, J. M. and Rotemberg, J. J. (1990), 'Inflation and taxation with optimizing governments', *Journal of Money, Credit and Banking*, February.

Sargent, T. and Wallace, N. (1981), 'Some unpleasant monetarist arithmetic', *Federal Reserve Bank of Minneapolis Quarterly Review*.

Van der Ploeg, F. (1989), 'Monetary interdependence under alternative exchange rate regimes: a European perspective', CEPR Discussion Paper, No 358.

Van der Ploeg, F. (1990), 'Macroeconomic policy coordination during the various phases of economic and monetary integration in Europe', in *European Economy* (1990).

Van Rompuy et al. (1990), 'Economic federalism and the EMU', in *European Economy* (1990).

Wyplosz, Ch. (1990), 'Monetary union and fiscal policy discipline', in *European Economy* (1990).

Wildason, David E. (1990), 'Budgetary pressures in the EEC: a fiscal federalism perspective', *American Economic Review*, May.

Chapter 6

Adjusting without the nominal exchange rate

The loss of the exchange rate as a policy instrument has important implications for macroeconomic stability. In a world in which countries are faced by unexpected shocks of either domestic or foreign origin, real and nominal macroeconomic variables will tend to fluctuate. A large variability of variables such as output or inflation is generally considered to be welfare-reducing. The disappearance of the nominal exchange rate, assuming it is instrumental in affecting macroeconomic variability, could therefore have implications in terms of welfare.

How serious is this loss likely to be for EC Member States? Are there alternative means of handling country-specific economic shocks? These are the questions addressed in this chapter.

Graph 6.1 gives an overview of the chapter. If shocks are symmetric, intra-Community exchange rates are not needed. If shocks are asymmetric (Section 6.2), intra-EC exchange rates could be used (Section 6.1). This possibility is no longer present in EMU, and so either factor adjustment (Section 6.3) or financing must take its place. The combination of asymmetric shocks and factor adjustment is a major determinant of the impact of EMU on macroeconomic stability (Section 6.4). Financing may either be private, through capital flows (Section 6.5), or public. In the latter case, both national borrowing (Section 6.6) or Community transfers (Section 6.7) could be used. The choice between adjustment instruments depends on collective welfare considerations. The first choice between factor adjustment or financing concerns the trade-off between the real wage and employment. Secondly, within the financing instrument, equity considerations determine the choice between national or Community financing, subject to the requirements of fiscal discipline.

The conclusions can be summarized as follows:

The fixing of exchange rates within the Community represents, at worst, only a very limited loss:

(i) Fixing intra-Community exchange rates in EMU still leaves the possibility for the Community to change its exchange rate with respect to the rest of the world.

(ii) For the original members of the exchange rate mechanism of the EMS, nominal exchange rates have hardly changed at all for several years. The 'costs' associated with this nominal fixity have been borne or adjusted to

already, although the benefits of EMU are still to be obtained.

(iii) Since wages and prices are rigid in the short run, nominal exchange rate changes may affect real exchange rates for a while. This may dampen output fluctuations, but may increase inflation fluctuations. Over a longer period, nominal exchange rates tend at best to accommodate inflation differentials without having a lasting impact on real exchange rates.

(iv) Real exchange rate changes are still possible through relative price movements within EMU, as the examples of existing federations and the experience of the EMS clearly show.

(v) Taking long-run trends, real exchange rates do not seem to contribute much in sustaining growth differentials between Community countries, since there are many other factors involved.

(vi) Economic integration will make the occurrence of country-specific shocks less likely since product differentiation tends to dominate product specialization.

(vii) Enhanced competition in the internal market will ensure that profit margins carry part of the price adjustment burden.

(viii) Wage discipline will also be more effective in a credible EMU, as witnessed already in the EMS, but this will need encouragement. To a minor extent, greater regional and occupational mobility may also contribute to labour market flexibility.

Additional financing will facilitate adjustment and help cushion shocks:

(ix) EMU removes the external constraint inside the Community, facilitating external financing of temporary external imbalances for individual countries.

(x) Budgetary policy, at central and national level, will also help adjustment or cushion it, provided a certain trade-off between national budgetary autonomy and central public finance is respected.

Overall, EMU will probably improve macroeconomic stability:

(xi) The disappearance of exogenous asymmetric intra-Community exchange rate shocks, the absence of non-cooperative exchange rate policies and the disciplinary effect on wages and prices tend to offset the negative impact of asymmetric shocks.

(xii) Compared to a floating exchange rate regime inside the Community, EMU will reduce the variability of output and notably inflation; compared to the EMS, variability also decreases, since asymmetric monetary policy is replaced by a common monetary policy which is con-

GRAPH 6.1: **Schematic overview of the chapter**

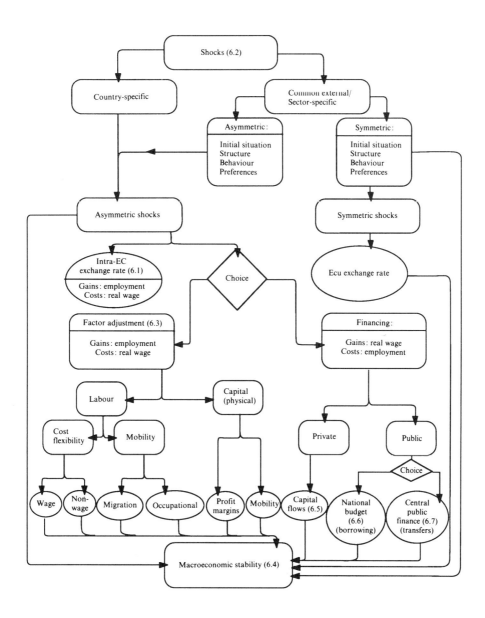

Note: Figures between brackets represent sections of the chapter.

cerned with macroeconomic stabilization of the Community as a whole.

(XIII) *The decrease in output and inflation variability may be experienced by all EMU members, but is also dependent on national economic policies and the behaviour of economic agents, notably for output stabilization.*

6.1. Do nominal exchange rate changes have real effects?

In discussing the real effects of exchange rates, it is usually assumed that there is a shock to external demand or international competitiveness which brings the current account out of equilibrium. A change in the real exchange rate may then ensure the return to equilibrium. The usefulness of the nominal exchange rate instrument should therefore be judged in the context of changes in real exchange rates. In the case of an adverse shock, a lasting real exchange rate depreciation requires a decrease in the real wage. [1] With nominal wages highly responsive to unemployment, this would happen immediately and the nominal exchange rate instrument would not be needed. The potential usefulness of the nominal exchange rate therefore derives from the fact that nominal wages are not fully flexible downward. [2]

In such a case, a devaluation has the benefit of 'front-loading' the required real exchange rate adjustment. Under normal conditions, [3] the improved real exchange rate and the higher level of import prices will start to improve the trade balance rather fast. After a while, however, import prices work through into consumption prices. These price increases will sooner or later feed through in nominal wages and therefore in domestic output prices, undoing the initial real depreciation brought about by the nominal depreciation. Consequently, unless the real wage decreases some time after the nominal exchange rate adjustment, there is no lasting real depreciation. Thus, the slower wages are indexed to prices, the higher is the benefit derived from the nominal exchange rate. As a drawback, however, the increase in domestic inflation may increase inflationary expectations, implying an inflationary cost for the devaluation instrument.

These arguments may be illustrated empirically in several ways.

Firstly, the relationship between nominal and real effective exchange rates at the intra-EC level may be examined. Empirical evidence shows that the quarterly growth rates of nominal exchange rates are highly correlated with those of real exchange rates for the same quarter. For the period 1979-89, using effective real exchange rates with respect to Community partners with unit labour losts in manufacturing as deflator, these correlations range from 0,75 to nearly 1,0 depending upon the country. [4] This does not necessarily imply that the levels of nominal and real exchange rates are also correlated in the long run.

A formal test of such a correlation, which is also called co-integration, is presented using quarterly data for 1980-89 in Appendix 6.1. It shows that the levels of nominal effective intra-EC exchange rates of all Community countries are non-stationary, i.e. they have no tendency to return to a given mean. The same result is found for the corresponding real exchange rates, except for Belgium/Luxembourg, the Netherlands and Portugal. Since for these three countries the real exchange rate returns to a mean but the nominal exchange rate does not, their levels are by definition not 'co-integrated'. For the remaining eight countries, which could still be co-integrated, a further test reveals that this is not the case. Although the levels of nominal and real X-rates are therefore not correlated in the long run for all Community countries, a change in the nominal X-rate may go hand in hand with a change in the real X-rate for quite some time. Using some plausible parameters for a wage-price block, Annex D gives an example showing that 50 % of the effect still remains after two years, and that it only disappears completely after five years.

A second illustration of the theoretical argument concerning the impact of a devaluation compared to a situation where it is not available may be obtained from model simulations (see Box 6.1). In a first simulation, a permanent negative shock to exports was simulated, keeping nominal exchange rates fixed. In a second simulation, the same shock was imposed, but in addition a devaluation was assumed to take place at the same time as the export shock. [5] With respect to real exchange rates, output and inflation, this exercise illustrates the following points:

---

[1] See Dornbusch (1980).
[2] This discussion does not treat explicitly the use of the exchange rate to neutralize imported inflation through nominal appreciation. However, this aspect is present implicitly through the real effects of inflation.
[3] Well-known is the so-called Marshall-Lerner condition for price elasticities, but this is a special case of a more general condition on elasticities, (see Gandolfo (1987)).

[4] This is a property generally observed among floating exchange rates (see Mussa (1986)).
[5] In both simulations, the nominal exchange rate was kept constant at baseline values, or baseline values after the devaluation. Government expenditure was assumed to be unchanged in real terms, while nominal interest rates were also kept at their baseline values. The devaluation was chosen so as to bring nominal GDP back to its baseline value in year 7 after the shock.

Box 6.1: Model simulation of an export shock with and without devaluation

The impact of a devaluation in the face of negative export shocks was simulated with the Commission's Quest model.[6] In a first simulation, the Quest submodel for France was simulated with a permanent negative shock to exports of 5 %. In a second simulation, the same shock was imposed, but in addition a devaluation of 7,25 % was assumed to take place at the same time as the export shock.

Graph 6.2.(a) displays the trajectory of deviations with respect to baseline (assumed to be the equilibrium value) for real GDP and the real effective exchange rate over a period of seven years. The initial equilibrium is at point A. The negative export shock shifts the demand curve D inward to D'. Without adjustment of the real wage, a new equilibrium with output below potential would be established at a point like B. However, in order to restore the equilibrium for output equal to potential, at point A', the real wage would have to decrease to move to the long-run supply curve AA'. With short-run price stickiness, however, the short-run supply curve will be completely inelastic (horizontal), and there will be underutilization of production capacity at point B before the economy moves upwards along the new demand curve D', passing through E and further upwards to the extent that real wages decrease sufficiently to reach the long-run supply curve.

The trajectory of the simulation without devaluation (solid curve) follows this path, and comes close to a new equilibrium at point A' after seven years. The effect of the devaluation is to shift the short-run horizontal supply curve AB upwards to a point such as C, which is still characterized by output below potential. If real wages do not change, the economy will stay at point C with output below equilibrium. To return to equilibrium output, a decrease in real wages is still needed. The conclusion is thus that the devaluation diminishes the output loss in the short run, but that real wage adjustment is delayed as well as the return to equilibrium output.

Moreover, as illustrated in Graph 6.2.(b), the delayed adjustment has its price in terms of inflation. Without devaluation, the negative demand shock shifts the equilibrium output level to a point such as B. The real wage decrease shifts the equilibrium back to its original level, but at a lower rate of equilibrium inflation, at point A'. The effect of the devaluation is, instead of moving to a point like B, to use inflation to move upward a short-run Phillips curve and have higher output, at E, in exchange for more inflation. The result is that there will be less output loss but for a longer period, and that given the upward shift in the short-run Phillips curve to a point as high as D, relatively more inflation is incurred than without devaluation.

A further discussion of these issues, including the role of the Phillips curve, is given in Annex D.

[6]   See Bekx *et al.* (1989).

GRAPH 6.2: Adjustment with and without devaluation
(percentage deviation from baseline)

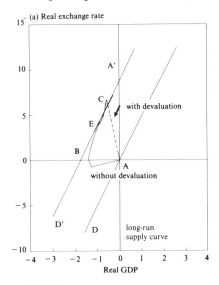

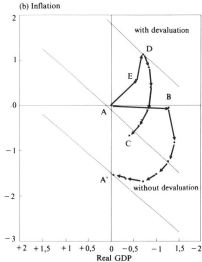

This graph presents the time-paths for combinations of the real exchange rate or inflation (on the y-axes) and real GDP (on the x-axis), both measured as percentage deviations from baseline values. If the baseline values are interpreted as the equilibrium values, these graphs show how fast the real exchange rate, inflation and real GDP adjust to their equilibrium values after a negative export shock to the French model of 5 %, with and without devaluation.

(i)   The degree of initial output loss without devaluation is higher than with devaluation. [7] This is the advantage of using the exchange rate instrument: it cushions the size of the immediate output shock in the first few years through its direct effect on real exchange rates.

(ii) Without devaluation, the return to equilibrium output is faster than with devaluation, where there is a delay in real-wage adjustment. This is the disadvantage of the devaluation: the output gap will take longer to disappear. This is due to the fact that the output gains from a devaluation cause tensions on the labour market which increase the real wage above its equilibrium level (see Annex D).

(iii) The 'soft landing' in the case of a devaluation has its counterpart in the fact that the devaluation results in a higher inflation rate than in the situation without devaluation.

A devaluation, therefore, has the benefit of not causing as much initial output loss as without devaluation, but the return to equilibrium takes more time and is accompanied by higher inflation.

Overall, therefore, nominal exchange rates may have an impact on real exchange rates for, say, two to five years, but this does not persist in the long run. The main advantage derived from the nominal exchange rate instrument resides in 'front-loading' the real exchange rate adjustment needed when a country is faced with an adverse shock. This reduces the initial output loss, but does not substitute for real wage adjustment. Delayed adjustment of the latter may even prolong the situation of underemployment of productive capacity. Moreover, a devaluation may shift inflationary expectations upward, thus also delaying the disinflation process needed to restore equilibrium.

This analysis is based on the role of nominal exchange rate changes in adjusting to shocks, starting from a situation of equilibrium. As is obvious from events in Eastern Europe or many developing countries, moving exchange rates to an appropriate level can play a useful role in a situation where economic reform or structural adjustment is required starting from a situation of clear disequilibrium. This, however, is not so relevant for Community countries in EMU.

6.2. Will asymmetric shocks diminish in EMU?

In a perfectly symmetrical world with countries identical in size, structure, behaviour and preferences, which all undergo the same shocks (unanticipated events), real exchange rates would not have to change. Only if the economic system displays asymmetries, may real exchange rate adjustments be needed. In the context of EMU, the question therefore arises whether asymmetries will have a tendency to decrease or to increase relative to the present situation. The cost of losing the nominal exchange rate (assuming it to be a valid instrument in at least some degree) will be diminished if asymmetries tend to disappear.

A useful way of analysing asymmetries is to look at different kinds of shocks and see how they may turn into asymmetries. Shocks may be classified (see Box 6.2) according to whether they are:

(i)   common or country-specific;

(ii) temporary or permanent.

Obviously, shocks are asymmetric if they are country-specific, such as policy shocks, resource shocks or changes in behaviour. Common shocks such as external shocks or sector-specific shocks, even when they are initially symmetric in nature, may however be asymmetric in their consequences, depending on differences among countries in initial situations, economic structures (e.g. production structures), economic behaviour or preferences. Each of these cases has to be analysed separately, therefore.

6.2.1. Country-specific shocks

Country-specific shocks are by definition asymmetric.

A first but simple approach to identifying the existence of country-specific shocks is to compare the behaviour of the same variable, e.g. real GDP, among two countries. If the variance of such a variable, when aggregated for these two countries, is greater than the variance of their difference, one may conclude that the variables are behaving symmetrically rather than asymmetrically. [8] A disadvantage of this approach is that it does not tell where the asymmetries come from. They may in fact be a combination of unknown country-specific and common shocks, the latter perhaps in combination with an asymmetric system.

Applying this approach to German and French data for real GDP, the GDP deflator, real wages and current account balances, Cohen and Wyplosz (1989) find symmetric behav-

---

[7]   Output is assumed to be measured by GDP.

[8]   In mathematical terms: if the correlation between x and y is positive (symmetry), the variance of $x + y$ will be larger than the variance of $x - y$, and vice versa when the correlation is negative.

Box 6.2: A taxonomy of shocks

In discussing the nature of shocks, it seems useful to search for an operational definition of what a shock really is. In order to do so, some sort of economic system has to be taken as reference. In the context of EMU, the reference economic system is taken to be a member country of EMU.

Secondly, a set of variables has to be defined which are considered to be determined endogenously and simultaneously inside the system. These can be taken to be the usual macroeconomic and sectoral variables such as output, inflation and employment. Given these definitions, a shock may be defined as any unanticipated event which has a direct or indirect impact on the endogenous variables of the reference system without, however, being part of them. Given this definition, a country-specific or local shock may be defined as a shock having a direct impact on only one country. Similarly, a common shock may be defined as a shock having a direct impact on all member countries of the union. A second distinction arises from the duration of the shock. A temporary shock is an event that disappears after a period of time, while a permanent shock is an event that remains present over the time period considered (this does not preclude that it eventually disappears).

Evidently, common shocks may have diverging effects in different countries if these countries do not react to these shocks in the same way, for example because they are in different initial situations, have different economic structures, display different behaviour of economic agents or have different policy preferences. Therefore, a distinction within common shocks has to be made on the basis of whether their impact is comparable or dissimilar among countries. If the impact of a shock (mostly a common shock) is comparable among countries, this will be referred to as a symmetric shock, if it is a country-specific shock or a common shock with an asymmetric impact, it will be called an asymmetric shock.

Common shocks versus country-specific shocks

In the EMU framework of reference, the two common shocks having had the largest impact over the last two decades have undoubtedly been the oil price hikes of 1973/74 and 1979 (typically sector-specific shocks) and the increase in interest rates in the United States which provoked the 1981-82 recession (i.e. a common external shock for the Community).

Country-specific or local shocks may be subdivided in a number of categories. A first source of local shocks arises from domestic policy instruments, to be broadly distinguished between monetary and budgetary policy. It might be argued that these instruments in fact react to changes in domestic economic performance, are therefore endogenously determined and not to be considered as shocks. This is certainly true for some elements of budgetary policy, but other elements, however, are of a more discretionary nature. Unless it is assumed that fiscal fine-tuning is still possible, changes in these elements will therefore act as random shocks to the national economy.

A second important set of country-specific shocks relates to changes in domestic natural, human or capital resources. Since resource shocks, notably concerning human resources, are evolving gradually over time, they tend to be of a permanent nature. The same can be said of capital resources to the extent that it concerns technical progress.

A third set of country-specific shocks resides in changes in behaviour of economic agents (households, firms). These changes may arise from changes in taste, business climate or any other form of news that has a random pattern in influencing economic behaviour. In econometric terms, these shocks are contained in the residuals of the behavioural equations.

Finally, if the concept of a shock is defined rather broadly, a fourth category of shocks is formed by inertia. This can be explained as follows. A broad definition of a shock would define it as all events without which the endogenous variables of the economic system would not change. Under this definition, past values of endogenous variables of the system, or inertia, which influence the present endogenous variables are also to be considered as a shock. They are the consequence of the existence of permanent shocks.

There is no unique measurement system available for shocks, be they common or country-specific. The main issue involved here is that shocks have different dimensions. How to compare an oil price increase to an earthquake, for instance? In order to circumvent this problem, the impact of a shock on one of the endogenous variables could be taken as a yardstick. Since the endogenous variables of the system are all determined simultaneously, a representation of the system which determines them is needed in order to be able to assess the final impact of a shock on any particular endogenous variable. A natural candidate for such a representation is an econometric model. See Annex D for an example.

iour to dominate for these two countries. Using data for the original members of the exchange rate mechanism (ERM) of the EMS before and after the start of the EMS, Weber (1990) has applied the same approach to all possible combinations between these countries. He finds that rates of inflation, as well as domestic demand and supply shocks, tend to be dominated by symmetric behaviour.[9] Real wages, on the other hand, tend to be dominated by asymmetric shocks, and similarly for unemployment rates during the EMS period. This shows precisely the weakness of this approach: asymmetric unemployment shocks may both have been the cause or the result of the real wage asymmetries. If they were the cause, the real wage asymmetries may be seen as a way of adjusting to these shocks. On the other hand, if real wage asymmetries caused the unemployment asymmetries, this would be perceived as less optimal.

A second approach is to use a complete model to analyse the origin of country-specific shocks. Fair (1988), for instance, has decomposed the variance of US real GNP and the GNP deflator into components due to the residuals of estimated equations for demand, supply, fiscal and monetary variables. While equation residuals represent shocks in economic behaviour, shocks may also come from other sources (see Box 6.2). Annex C therefore presents an exhaustive analysis of sources of short-term macroeconomic fluctuations based on model simulations. The results, even though they focus on the very short run,[10] suggest that shocks in the four big Community countries are permanent rather than temporary. About 50 % of the temporary shocks is due to equation residuals, i.e. shocks in the behaviour of economic agents. In addition, government policies, such as shocks in monetary policy, tax rates or government expenditure, also act as a source of fluctuations, albeit to a minor extent. In EMU, the latter factor as a source of country-specific shocks may be attenuated through the impact of multilateral surveillance.

6.2.2. When are common shocks asymmetric?

While country-specific shocks are by definition asymmetric, there are several circumstances under which a common shock may also have an asymmetric impact. This depends on the integration of product markets, differences in economic structures, differences in economic behaviour, divergences of initial situations or asymmetric preferences of govern-

ments. The last two sources of asymmetries will not be discussed here, since they are more related to the issues of transition and policy coordination.[11]

Product market integration

If product market integration is characterized by inter-industry specialization, this implies that a common shock to a specific sector (e.g. a general drop in demand for a certain product) will asymmetrically affect the country in which the industry concerned is located. On the other hand, if intra-industry specialization is taking place, the shock will be more symmetric, affecting all industries in different countries involved in the production of the product concerned.

Within the Community, product market integration tends to be of the intra-industry type, notably in the manufacturing sector.[12] A recent study by the Commission of the EC (1990), for instance, finds that except for Portugal and Greece the share of intra-industry trade in intra-Community trade varied between 57 % and 83 % in 1987. Since intra-industry integration is characterized by the occurrence of economies of scale and product differentiation, the removal of barriers obstructing the exploitation of these advantages will increase intra-industry integration.[13] Consequently, the completion of the internal market is likely to render the effects of sector-specific shocks more symmetric. This relationship is confirmed empirically if an index for symmetry is compared to an index of trade barriers which may be expected to disappear with the internal market (see Box 6.3 and Graph 6.4). Relatively speaking, this also holds for the lagging Community countries, whose specialization is presently more of the inter-industry type, from which they tend to switch to intra-industry specialization.

---

[9] The main exception is Germany for demand shocks.
[10] This is due to the fact that only the impact of shocks in the first quarter was calculated.

[11] For a discussion of the coordination problems in the case of different starting positions for the current account, see Masson and Melitz (1990). Begg (1990) also analyses the coordination problems in attaining an equilibrium from different starting positions. For an analysis of asymmetric government preferences, see Tootell (1990).
[12] See Greenaway and Milner (1986) for an overview.
[13] Jacquemin and Sapir (1988), for instance, find a negative effect of economies of scale on the Community share in total imports of Germany, France, Italy, and the United Kingdom for 1983. They interpret this as being the result of fragmented markets in the Community which have not allowed full exploitation of economies of scale.

Box 6.3: How asymmetric are sector-specific shocks?

If a common sector-specific shock occurs, the output of the sector concerned in a particular country would tend to move more in conjunction with the output of the same sector in other countries than with the output of other sectors in the same country. The more this phenomenon can be observed empirically, the more there is a general tendency for (a) the occurrence of common sector-specific shocks and (b) symmetric effects of the common shocks.

This has been tested on indices of industrial production for 31 sectors for all 12 Community countries. On the basis of statistical tests, an indicator has been developed which is able to say whether, at Community-wide level, a sector has undergone symmetric or asymmetric shocks. The indicator was constructed as follows. For each of the 31 sectors s in each of the 12 Community countries j for which data on the volume of industrial production are available, the annual growth rate of industrial production y_{sjt} was regressed on a sector-specific variable x_{sjt} and a country-specific variable z_{sjt}:

$$y_{sjt} = a_{sj} + b_{sj}*x_{sjt} + c_{sj}*z_{sjt}.$$

The percentages of variance explained by the sector-specific variable or the country-specific variable alone were aggregated over countries using production weights. The difference between the aggregated explained variances constructs the indicator, which therefore ranges between -100 and 100. For each regression, the sector-specific variable x_{sjt} was defined as the first principal component of the growth rates of industrial production in the same sector in all other (i.e. excluding country j) Community countries. Similarly, the country-specific variable z_{sjt} was defined as the first principal component of the growth rates of industrial production in all other (i.e. excluding sector s) sectors in the same country. The indicator is presented in Graph 6.3.

Inevitably, the indicator is surrounded with uncertainty. Nevertheless, several broad trends may be distinguished.

In the first place, natural circumstances cause several sectors to undergo asymmetric shocks because they produce products which are mainly destined for their local market. This concerns sectors such as the coke-oven industry, the printing industry, the construction sector and the production of timber and wooden products.

Secondly, there are sectors which produce relatively homogeneous goods with few trade barriers and which therefore are subject to symmetric shocks. This applies to petroleum extraction, the tobacco industry, the drinks industry and the metal industry as a whole.

Thirdly, for the remaining sectors the existence of trade barriers inside the Community seems to determine whether they are subject to symmetric or asymmetric shocks. This hypothesis is tested by looking at the correlation of the symmetry indicator with an indicator for trade barriers inside the Community. [14] The scatter plot in Graph 6.4 and the corresponding regression line show a significant negative relationship between the existence of trade barriers and the symmetry of shocks. Consequently, it can be expected that the completion of the internal market will tend to reduce the occurrence of asymmetric sector-specific shocks.

[14] The indicator for trade barriers is defined, per sector, as the percentage increase in intra-Community trade of products produced by this sector as a consequence of completing the internal market. This is the Stage I integration effect of the removal of trade barriers, see *European Economy* 'The economics of 1992', Commission of the European Communities (1988, Table A.5, column (i)). Graph 6.4 incorporates all the sectors of Graph 6.3 for which these data were available. The regression line has the following characteristics:

I = 36,7 − 12,6*TB R^2 = 0,435
   (33,7)   (3,3)

with I the asymmetry index and TB the trade barrier index (standard errors in brackets).

Economic structures

Differences in economic structures may cause a national economy to react differently to a common shock than other members of the union. Consequently, common shocks may result in asymmetric effects on economic objective variables such as output, employment and inflation.

An often cited example of an asymmetric structure is the presence of oil and natural gas production. Nevertheless, such differences in the availability of primary energy production may not necessarily show up in comparable differences in all economic variables. Table 6.1, for instance, illustrates the effects of differences in economic structure after a 10% in oil prices using 1980 input-output tables. Taking into account international price linkages, domestic prices in the two oil/gas-producing countries the Netherlands and the

United Kingdom increase by 1,7-1,9%, whereas domestic prices in the other countries increase by 1,3-1,4%. Given the particularities of this example (an industry for which production endowments are very different, and which has generated very large shocks in the past), the figures may serve as an upper bound.

The effects of economic structure are not confined to the structure of production, but may also concern the structure of consumption, the labour market or international trade. Nevertheless, the production structure is an important source of asymmetries. In fact, production structures tend to become more similar in the case of intra-industry specialization. Given the tendency already noted towards intra-industry specialization, this again suggests that the effects of common shocks become less asymmetric as integration proceeds.

Table 6.1

Effects of economic structure on domestic prices after an increase of 10% in oil prices, using 1980 input-output tables

(%)

	With price linkages[1]	Without price linkages
Germany	1,3	1,2
France	1,4	1,3
Italy	1,3	1,2
Netherlands	1,9	1,7
United Kingdom	1,7	1,6

[1]   Price linkages among the five countries.
Source: Giavazzi and Giovannini (1987).

Behaviour of economic agents

Differences in behaviour of economic agents in the face of similar shocks may be an important source of asymmetric effects of common shocks. This is particularly true for wage behaviour due to its central role in the determination of inflation, real exchange rates and unemployment. Different degrees of real wage rigidity will imply different effects on unemployment. An analysis of differences in real wage rigidity may therefore reveal an important source of asymmetric shocks.

From a macroeconomic point of view the flexibility of real labour costs depends on two factors:

GRAPH 6.3 : **The symmetry and asymmetry of sector-specific shocks in the EC: 1979-88**

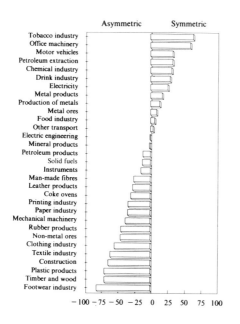

Community average, index − 100 to 100

This graph compares the symmetry/asymmetry index described in Box 6.3 among a number of sectors for the Community average. The index ranges between − 100 and 100 and is defined as the difference between the variance of the growth rate of sectoral production in a country explained by production growth in the same sector in other countries (symmetry) compared to production growth in other sectors in the same country (asymmetry). A positive index for a sector means that the variation of growth rates of industrial production in that particular sector is, per country, more correlated with that of the same sector in other countries than with that of other sectors in the same country. The interpretation is that sector-specific shocks in that case are symmetric. A negative index implies the converse, and is an indication of the predominance of asymmetric shocks.

GRAPH 6.4 : **The symmetry of shocks and trade barriers in the EC**

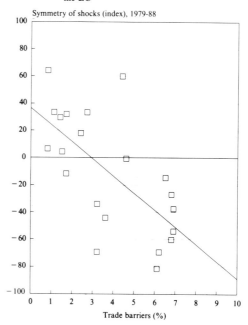

This graph plots the symmetry/asymmetry index of Graph 6.3 (y-axis) against a measure of trade barriers. A negative correlation between the two means that the existence of trade barriers may be a factor causing asymmetric shocks. Consequently, the removal of trade barriers in the context of the completion of the internal market may be expected to make shocks more symmetric. The trade barrier indicator has been taken from *European Economy* No 35, Table A.5. column (i). It corresponds to the Stage I integration effect of the removal of trade barriers.

(i)   The price elasticity of nominal wages. The smaller the degree of indexation of nominal wages, the smaller will be the inflationary effect of the wage-price spiral. This, in turn, implies lower costs in terms of unemployment of a disinflationary policy after an inflationary shock.

(ii) The elasticity of nominal wages with respect to excess supply or demand in the labour market. The higher the sensitivity of nominal wage growth to the level of unemployment, the lower will be the cost in unemployment of a local wage push that initially sets the real wage level out of line.

Taken together, these two elasticities may be combined to form a measure of real wage rigidity. [15] There appears to be evidence (see Appendix 6.2 and Graph 6.5) that this measure of real wage rigidity is more similar among Community countries than compared to countries such as the United States or Japan, but they remain divergent to a significant extent. Even although they are imperfect and model-dependent measures of wage behaviour, this points to the possibility that on the basis of these data wage behaviour may have been a component of asymmetric shocks, and will remain so in the future unless wage responses in the Community to identical shocks become more similar, for instance through pan-European sectoral wage negotiations.

More comprehensive evidence concerning asymmetries in economic behaviour may be obtained by comparing complete models. This confirms however the uncertainty surrounding conclusions on asymmetric behaviour. In practice, asymmetries among models may be of the same size as, or larger than, asymmetries among countries. A comparison of the slopes of aggregate supply curves, [16] which are a concise measure of the elasticity of supply, for four countries in four different international linkage models (see Appendix 6.3) shows that the disparity across models is almost double that across countries, on average. This indicates that the models are convergent in their assessment of the degree of disparity of supply reactions among countries but not in respect of the average size of supply reactions in each country.

GRAPH 6.5: **Real wage rigidity**

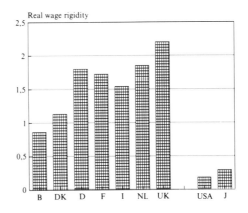

This graph plots an indicator of real wage rigidity from OECD (1989a). Let W be the growth rate of nominal wages, P the growth rate of (expected) prices, U the unemployment rate, and let the wage equation have the following form:
$$W = a_1 P + a_2 P_{-1} - b_1 U - b_2 U_{-1} + ...$$
Then real wage rigidity is defined as a_1/b_1, see Coe (1985).

The effect of EMU on the asymmetries of behaviour of economic agents falls into two parts: (1) wage behaviour and (2) other behaviour. Concerning wage behaviour, the disinflationary period of the 1980s has seen the demise of many automatic indexation schemes which were one of the causes of real wage rigidity. A credible EMU regime may generate low inflation expectations and therefore contain this factor of asymmetric behaviour. [17] Asymmetric forms of other behaviour could be the subject of multilateral surveillance procedures and expected to be reduced in that way. This, however, is not obtained automatically and is conditional on adequate surveillance procedures.

6.2.3. Trend real exchange rates

A different possible rationale for changes in real exchange rates is related to permanent shocks, and concerns such effects as secular movements in productivity, changing trends in tastes or demographic factors. An allegedly important type of permanent shock arises when countries want to

---

[15] Let W be the growth rate of nominal wages, P the growth rate of (expected) prices, U the unemployment rate, and let the wage equation have the following form:
$$W = a_1 P + a_2 P_{-1} - b_1 U - b_2 U_{-1} + ...$$
Then the short-run real wage rigidity may be defined as a_1/b_1, and the long-run real wage rigidity as $(a_1 + a_2)/(b_1 + b_2)$, (see Coe (1985)).

[16] The slope of the aggregate supply curve is calculated by dividing the three-year effect of a government expenditure shock on the level of the GDP deflator by the three-year effect on real GDP, both measured as percentage deviations from baseline values.

---

[17] This issue is discussed in more detail in the next section.

maintain differences in output growth over a sustained period of time (10-20 years). The faster growing country would import more than the slowly growing country, and therefore its bilateral real exchange rate should depreciate with a trend in order to maintain an external equilibrium between them. This case warrants particular attention in EMU given the catching-up process of the poorer countries which could be hampered in this way.

This section analyses, therefore, to which extent fixing nominal exchange rates in EMU really implies costs as described above.

In the first place, there is the evidence presented before that nominal exchange rates do not determine real exchange rates in the long run. Trend changes in real exchange rates would therefore have to be brought about by prices rather than nominal exchange rates. As discussed earlier, for countries undergoing structural adjustment or economic reform, the exchange rate may have to be changed to reach a correct level, but this is less relevant for Community countries.

Secondly, historical evidence for the Community (see Graph 6.6 and Appendix 6.4) suggests that there is only a very weak positive relationship between growth differentials with respect to the Community average and a trend depreciation of the real effective exchange rate.[18] Trends in real exchange rates have indeed appeared over the period 1973-88, but the direction of these trends is not stable over the two subperiods considered. Furthermore, the correlation between positive growth differentials and trend real depreciation, as expected on the basis of the theoretical conditions discussed above, is rather weak. Regressions between these two variables show a positive, but insignificant relationship between them with a slope which is so flat that real depreciation cannot plausibly have been of use. The evidence is even weaker for a country such as Japan, which coupled faster growth than its trade partners with a real exchange rate appreciation in the 1960s-70s. Apparently, the

reason for the weak link between trend real exchange rates and faster growth lies in the existence of other factors influencing growth.

A third argument relates to the effects of stronger growth on the current account. There is an empirical regularity to be observed between growth differentials and income elasticities (see Appendix 6.5). This tends to move the trade balance towards equilibrium without needing real exchange rate changes. An explanation for this phenomenon may lie in supply factors. Krugman (1989), for instance, developed a model with monopolistic competition and economies of scale where trade arises from product differentiation, in which a fast-growing country will be able through supply effects to increase the apparent foreign income elasticity for its exports and to lower the domestic-income elasticity of its imports. As a consequence, the trade balance would not be affected. This model fits in with the effects expected from the internal market completion as enhanced by EMU, and will therefore in any case not work against the empirical regularity observed between the ratios of income elasticities of exports and imports and domestic and foreign growth rates. Moreover, the external constraint as such is considerably weakened in EMU, as discussed below.

The conclusion from the above theoretical and empirical evidence seems to be that there is only a weak link between faster growth in the Community and trend nominal exchange rate changes or even trend real exchange rate changes. Faster growth seems mainly attributable to other, possibly supply-related, factors. To the extent that the external constraint inhibits faster growth, it will be considerably relieved in EMU.

6.2.4. Conclusion on shocks

The nature of shocks in EMU is crucial, since it presents the origin of the potential cost. In a simplified framework, for instance, Cohen and Wyplosz (1989) have shown that temporary, asymmetric shocks have the most negative impact in terms of deviations from a social optimum.[19] Thus,

---

[18]   This is illustrated by the results for the regression line in Graph 6.6:
GDP = 0,363 + 0,095*REER   Corrected $R^2 = -0,018$
(0,296) (0,105)
with GDP = growth rate of GDP minus growth rate of EC GDP, annual average 1973-88, REER = estimated linear trend growth rate of unit labour costs in manufacturing industry relative to Community partners, annual rate 1973-88. (Standard errors between brackets.) The coefficient for the real exchange rate is not significant; abstracting from this, it would indicate that an annual difference in GDP growth rates of one percentage point would be accompanied by a real exchange rate vis-à-vis Community partners which would have to depreciate annually by more than 10 %.

[19]   A negative implication for fiscal policy is that it goes against the objective of tax smoothing.

GRAPH 6.6: **Real depreciation and growth, 1973-88**

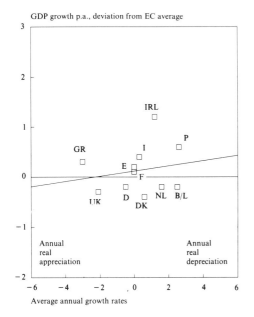

GDP growth p.a., deviation from EC average

This graph plots the average annual deviation of GDP growth from the EC average (on the y-axis) against an estimated trend real depreciation of the real exchange rate *vis-à-vis* Community partners (estimated as linear trend). The average growth rates have been calculated over the period 1973-88. As real exchange rate, the real effective exchange rate against Community partners was used, with unit labour cost in manufacturing as deflator. The regression line shows that there is a very weak positive relationship between trend real depreciation relative to Community partners and higher growth relative to the Community average.

the temporary nature of an adverse shock may induce one country to run a trade deficit (while it would have to adjust spending in the case of a permanent shock); whereas the asymmetric nature of the shock will create an incentive to do so through a real appreciation, which is not in the interest of the other country. The results from this section indicate that asymmetric shocks in the Community, even though they exist, are likely to diminish with the disappearance of trade barriers through the completion of internal market. Furthermore, shocks apparently are permanent rather than temporary, which reduces their cost. On the supply side, and notably on labour markets, there are divergencies among Community countries which may cause asymmetric reactions to common shocks. This therefore points to the importance of a common behaviour of the social partners when faced with

identical shocks. From the point of view of catching-up, finally, trend real exchange rates (and therefore certainly nominal exchange rates) have not contributed significantly in the past, and so there is little reason to expect that they would be needed in the future.

6.3. Factor adjustment

In the absence of exchange rate changes, an adverse asymmetric shock can be countered in two other market-clearing ways, and the question is how these adjustment mechanisms can substitute for the exchange rate in EMU.

The first is through lower labour costs as a contribution to the relative price decrease needed to restore the competitive position of the country and to bring output and employment back to equilibrium. This solution, price flexibility, is the one which is most closely related to the nominal exchange rate since both prices and the nominal exchange rate influence the real exchange rate. Secondly, factor mobility, and more in particular labour mobility,[20] may solve the problem through migration towards another region or country, notably if the shock is region-specific or country-specific. Obviously, the stronger factor adjustment capacities are, the lower the costs of EMU are in terms of transitory unemployment.

This section will not discuss the adjustment capacity of the factor capital, since the competitive pressure on X-inefficiencies and on profit margins, notably monopoly profits, was already extensively discussed in the context of the internal market.[21] As part of EMU, the flexibility of profit margins may be assumed to be further enhanced. In what follows, the present state of labour market flexibility in the Community is briefly examined, with reference to wage flexibility and labour mobility, and the effects of EMU on both are analysed.[22] It is concluded that EMU will bring

[20] In practice, if the shock is sector-specific, occupational mobility may also be of help if the unemployed find employment in another sector. This argument, and other elements of structural labour market policies, are, however, less related to the loss of the exchange rate in EMU, even though the Commission programme for the implementation of the Social Charter (see Commission of the European Communities (1989)) may be expected to improve occupational mobility, vocational training, etc.

[21] Commission of the European Communities (1988).

[22] Concerning labour mobility, only regional mobility will be treated, since other aspects of labour mobility such as occupational mobility and flexible working-time are less directly related to the loss of the exchange rate instrument.

GRAPH 6.7: **Relative unit labour cost and relative unemployment rates inside Germany and the Community**

(a) *Länder* of the FRG

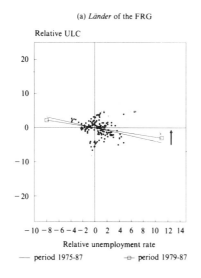

(b) Initial ERM countries

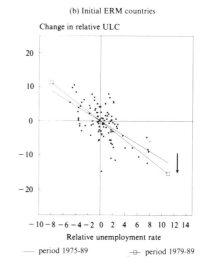

(c) Non-ERM countries

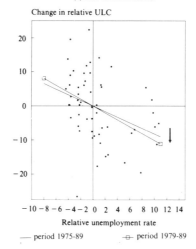

This graph plots the relationship between relative unit labour cost (on the y-axis) and relative unemployment rates (on the x-axis) in (a) the German federation, (b) the initial ERM countries and (c) the non-ERM countries (Greece and Portugal which remain outside the ERM, and Spain and the United Kingdom which joined in 1989 and 1990, respectively). A steep relationship between relative unit labour costs and relative unemployment implies that unit labour cost is relatively flexible in response to unemployment. The regression lines for Germany and the ERM members are significant, and much steeper for the ERM than for Germany, indicating that unit labour cost flexibility among the ERM countries is stronger than between the German *Länder*. Moreover, the steepness is increasing over time for the ERM members, but decreasing inside Germany. It is clear that the non-ERM members have less discipline, signified by a non-significant regression line. There are however signs that it is becoming steeper and more significant.

For the Community countries, the y-axis gives first differences of relative unit labour costs, centred around zero. For Germany, the levels are given, also centred around zero (for comparable estimates, see Appendix 6.6). For Germany, the unit labour costs and the unemployment rate are measured relative to the average for Germany; for the ERM and non-ERM this is relative to the Community average.

some automatic improvement in labour market flexibility, but that much depends on changes in behaviour of economic agents. It is argued that additional policies may be conducive to these required changes in behaviour.

6.3.1. The impact of EMU on real wage flexibility

Real wage flexibility does not apply only to the effects on the labour market situation of the loss of the exchange rate instrument, but is important for the situation on the labour market in general. This implies that real wages have not only to adjust to shocks in international competitiveness or foreign demand, but also to domestic shocks such as productivity changes or movements of other factor prices.

A comparison of existing measures of real wage flexibility was presented in Section 6.2. While this is important in relation to the asymmetric effects of shocks, the role of wage flexibility in relation to the exchange rate instrument in EMU should rather focus on the response of relative labour costs to differences in unemployment performance. The role of wages as a substitute for the nominal exchange rate will then appear more clearly, since the effects of absolute wage levels on the functioning of domestic labour markets are thereby disregarded. [23]

A comparison of the relative performance of the Community countries with that of the *Länder* of the Federal Republic of Germany (see Appendix 6.6 and Graph 6.7) shows that relative unit labour costs tend to decrease in response to a positive unemployment differential inside the German Federation, but that this response is weaker than that of initial ERM countries inside the Community. Non-ERM countries have a response which lies in between these two cases, but it is not statistically significant. Moreover, the flexibility of relative unit labour costs inside Germany is weakening over time, while that of Community countries improves.

The preceding results provide an illustration of two more general arguments likely to create a higher degree of wage flexibility in EMU.

(i) The discipline of the exchange rate regime appears when comparing the results for ERM and non-ERM countries. EMU with a single currency may be seen as the most credible commitment to a system of fixed exchange rates. In a less credible setting, the temptation for the government to pursue a devaluation policy may tend to induce inflationary wage

increases. [24] In a situation of disequilibrium, this may slow down the adjustment process of the economy to equilibrium. It may therefore be expected that EMU will return faster to equilibrium than, say, the early EMS. [25] This argument may be illustrated with the results of a simulation with the IMF Multimod model (Graph 6.8), which shows the response of French inflation to a domestic price shock in regimes of pure float, the EMS with a realignment rule, and EMU. In the pure float regime, depreciation of the currency generates a devaluation-price spiral which only dies out slowly. In the EMU regime, the absence of depreciation against other currencies of the union ensures that inflation quickly dies out. In the EMS regime, the inflation differential with Germany triggers off a devaluation in year 3, which prolongs the inflationary effects somewhat compared to the EMU regime (see also Annex E).

(ii) A second argument concerns the impact of fiscal discipline on the speed of adjustment to equilibrium in the case of temporary shocks. If fiscal policy is perceived to be less likely to 'bail out' a region lacking wage adjustment, wage adjustments are likely to come faster than otherwise. This is demonstrated by the German results compared to those for the Community countries. As seen in Section 6.7, Germany has a high degree of fiscal equalization.

(iii) A third argument why real wage flexibility is likely to be enhanced in EMU relates to the effects of the completion of the internal market. In a more highly integrated product market the degree of monopoly of individual suppliers decreases and product demand is more price elastic, and so is the derived demand for labour. If labour unions take into account the derived demand for labour in setting their wage demands and the unemployment/real wage trade-off becomes steeper, wage setting will become more responsive to labour market conditions: increased competition in product markets may result in an increased responsiveness of wages to unemployment. [26]

There are also factors, however, whose impact on wage flexibility in EMU is less certain a priori.

(iv) Considerations concerning social cohesion in EMU might put a limit on too large deviations in income levels. To the extent that this translates into 'wage norms' of any kind, it has been demonstrated by Abraham (1989), that an

---

[23] If relative unit labour costs are used, this has as additional advantage that differences in labour productivity are taken into account.

[24] See Horn and Persson (1988).
[25] See Begg (1990). For a rather pessimistic account of the Irish experience in the EMS, see Dornbusch (1989).
[26] See Marsden (1989).

GRAPH 6.8: **The disciplinary effect of EMU on inflation after a price shock**

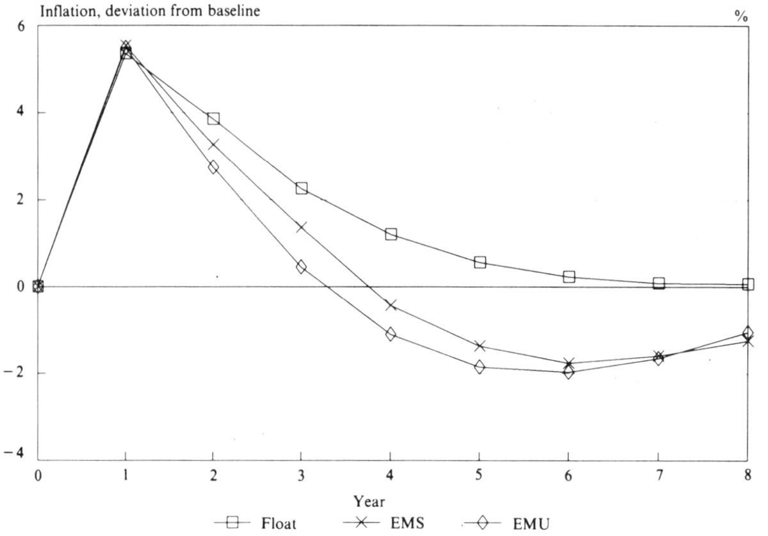

Inflation, deviation from baseline   %

Source: Multimod simulations.

This graph displays the effect on inflation of a 5% price shock in France, simulated with the Multimod model under three regimes: 'free float', 'EMS' and 'EMU'. Inflation is measured relative to the baseline, which is assumed to be the equilibrium value. The disinflation process is fastest under the EMU regime due to the fact that the pure float and the EMS allow competitiveness to be restored through depreciations or devaluations. The negative inflation deviation from baseline after year 3 for the 'EMS' and 'EMU' regimes are due to technical assumptions for the simulations on the desirable long-run price level, the speed of adjustment of the regimes being independent of these assumptions (see also Annex E).

'absolute norm' aggravates unemployment problems in the poorer regions. This might, for instance, explain the weak response of German unit labour costs to unemployment differences. As proposed by Van Rompuy et al. (1990), a 'relative norm' would be more desirable in this case, e.g. an unemployment benefit defined as a percentage of the wage rather than an absolute amount.

(v) An important factor influencing the flexibility of wages may be the wage determination process itself. A view which seems to emerge holds that real wage rigidity may be relatively low when there is either highly centralized wage bargaining (allowing macroeconomic externalities to be taken into account) or very decentralized wage bargaining (giving leeway to market forces and therefore resulting in socially efficient outcomes). In this view, rigidity would be the highest under intermediate forms of centralization, since the organizations bargaining at that level would be large enough to cause disruptions, but not sufficiently large to bear the costs of these disruptions. [27] Although this hump-shaped

relationship between the degree of centralization of wage bargaining and real wage rigidity is not a uniformly accepted view, [28] it appears that the Community countries presently are often characterized by an intermediate degree of centralization, thus pointing to room for improvement in the wage bargaining process in EMU. This does not impose any particular wage bargaining model such as extreme centralization or decentralization, as long as there is a system or procedure which guarantees that the externalities implied by the bargaining result are taken into account. [29]

Taken together, these arguments indicate that the effects of EMU on wage flexibility are largely dependent, either di-

---

[27]   See Calmfors and Driffill (1988).

[28]   An alternative view posits that there exists a monotonic relationship between the degree of 'corporatism' and real wage flexibility. As pointed out by Calmfors and Driffill (1988), the definition of corporatism is not very well described, but is generally taken to denote the extent to which 'broader interests' enter into wage bargaining, e.g. through government involvement.

[29]   At the Community level, information and consultation procedures regarding the externalities of wage bargaining results could take place in the context of the multilateral surveillance and through a dialogue between the social partners at Community level.

rectly or indirectly, on changes in the behaviour of economic agents determining and influencing wage behaviour. For governments this concerns their reactions to temporary shocks, whereas the participants in the wage bargaining process would have to take account of the implications of EMU in the field of inflation expectations and its effects on real exchange rates. Conditional on such considerations, wage flexibility may be able to substitute for the cushioning effect of the nominal exchange rate instrument.

6.3.2. Regional mobility

In theory, regional mobility could substitute for real wage adjustment to absorb a regional shock. Unemployed workers could migrate to another region, add to its labour force, increase its income and demand, and would therefore undo the effects of the shock. However, it has been recognized that large-scale labour mobility in the Community is neither feasible, at least not across language barriers, nor perhaps desirable.

A comparison with existing federal States may serve as an upper ceiling for the extent to which migration may contribute to the absorption of regional shocks. Table 6.2 shows that regional net migration in the Community as a percentage of that in the United States declined to 25 % in the first half of the 1980s down from 50 % in the preceding decade.

Table 6.2

Regional net migration in the EC, the USA and Sweden

		(average rates p.a., % population)
	1970-79	1980-85
EC (64 regions)	0,4	0,2 (1980-85)
USA (50 states + DC)	0,8	0,7 (1980-85)
Sweden (24 counties)	—	0,4 (1985)

Note: Numbers represent total net migration movements across regional boundaries, and thus include movements to or from regions from other Member States and third countries as well as movements between regions within a country. The figure shown for each country is the average of the absolute values of the net migration balance for its regions.

Sources: EC: Commission of the EC (1987), 'Third periodic report on the social and economic situation and development of the regions of the Community', Tab. 2.2.2-B-2, p. 74; USA: U.S. Dept. of Commerce and Bureau of the Census, 'Statistical Abstract of the United States 1987', Tab. 27 p. 24; Sweden: Statistika Centralbyran, 'Statistical Abstract of Sweden 1990', Tab. 37, p. 43.

In addition, since migration would tend to equalize regional unemployment rates, a comparison of dispersion measures for unemployment rates inside federations would be another useful indicator. Eichengreen (1990), for instance, compared the dispersion of unemployment rates of nine regions in the

GRAPH 6.9: **The dispersion of regional unemployment rates**

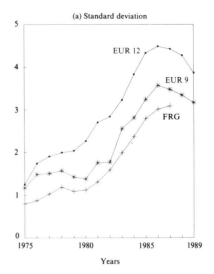

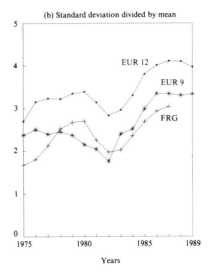

The graph compares the dispersion of unemployment rates among Community countries to that among the 11 *Länder* in Germany. Two measures are used, the standard deviation and the standard deviation divided by the mean (coefficient of variation). According to the latter criterion, the dispersion of unemployment rates among EUR 9 countries (i.e. excluding Greece, Portugal and Spain) is close to that inside Germany.

United States to those of the Community (excluding Greece, Portugal and Spain). He concludes that the measures of dispersion for the Community are 50 to 100 % higher in the Community than in the United States. [30] A similar comparison between the German *Länder* and the Community (see Graph 6.9) shows that for the same nine Community members the degrees of dispersion are only slightly above those for Germany. This result is mainly determined by a combination of cultural barriers and levels of social security. If the contribution of migration to the decrease in dispersion of unemployment rates would have to increase substantially in the Community, this would either require a strong decrease in cultural barriers or a strong decrease in the level of social security in the Community.

Concerning the cultural barriers, the completion of the internal market will assure the complete freedom of movement of persons in the Community. In practice, Community residents are already allowed to stay in another Community country for a period of three months in order to find a job. The main effect of the internal market resides in the mutual recognition of professional qualifications, which will therefore primarily benefit the mobility of qualified workers. Since this is a relatively small layer of the labour force, [31] the additional effect on labour mobility will be commensurate. In any case, the evidence on regional mobility in existing federations and even inside Member States does not suggest that it would be large enough to bear a significant proportion of the adjustment to a regional-specific shock. In the Community, cultural barriers and language differences seem to exclude that the degree of regional mobility of existing federations will ever be achieved. [32] Similarly, it is unlikely that the level of social security would decrease substantially. On the whole, and quite apart from its desirability, the role of regional mobility in EMU as an adjustment instrument will therefore remain small, except in higher income brackets and certain border regions. [33]

---

[30] Using regressions Eichengreen (1990) also finds, however, that the speed of adjustment to the (US or Community) average unemployment rate is only 25 % higher in the USA than in Europe. Furthermore, he finds that regional unemployment rates are weakly related to each other not only in the Community but also in the USA. This suggests that the theoretical role for migration to smooth differences in unemployment rates, even in a country which is renowned for its regional labour mobility, is fairly limited.

[31] As an illustration, 6,8 % of the population between 5 and 24 years was enrolled in full-time tertiary education in the Community in 1985/86, see Eurostat (1989).

[32] Molle and van Mourik (1988) found that the responsiveness of migration in the Community with respect to wage differentials is strong but that, on the other hand, cultural differences are a strong impediment.

[33] For example between Ireland and the United Kingdom, where the language problem does not play a role. In addition, there is the theoretical argument that if exchange rate stability increases real income variability, the option value of not migrating is high, which should reduce migrations, see Bertola (1988).

Conclusion

In addition to the effect on profit margins, labour market flexibility, and more in particular wage flexibility, is the single most important adjustment instrument in the absence of the nominal exchange rate instrument. Since nominal exchange rates do not determine real exchange rates in the long run, an adjustment in the latter would have to come from labour costs, with the nominal exchange rate delaying the adjustment. There is theoretical and empirical evidence suggesting that wage flexibility in the Community under a regime of increasingly fixed exchange rates is improving. Conditional on the behaviour of governments (in their stabilization efforts) and the social partners (in their wage bargaining processes), this improvement is likely to be strengthened in EMU. Regional mobility may add to labour flexibility to a minor extent. Labour cost-increasing aspects of social cohesion, on the other hand, may exert a dampening influence on labour cost flexibility, but may be desirable on equity grounds. In such a case, relative rather than absolute norms should be introduced to enhance the effect of automatic stabilization.

6.4. Shocks, adjustment and macroeconomic stability

The macroeconomic effects of EMU discussed so far in this chapter concerned not so much the levels of variables such as output and inflation, as their variability. Random shocks due to temporary changes in the behaviour of economic agents or originating abroad generally frustrate the attempts of the authorities to stabilize the economy around desired levels for macroeconomic variables. As argued in Chapter 2, an increase in the variability of these variables is therefore welfare-reducing. Since fixed exchange rates imply that national monetary policy can no longer be used to stabilize the consequences of asymmetric shocks, the variability of national macroeconomic variables might increase in EMU. In this sense, the loss of the exchange rate instrument might be considered to have a welfare cost.

This cost is conditional on the presence of asymmetric shocks and on the absence of instantaneous adjustments of wages and prices to disequilibria on the labour and goods markets. Some attenuation of the cost may take place due to the fact that EMU could reduce these asymmetries and enhance wage and price discipline (as argued in the previous sections). There are two additional factors, however, which independently will tend to reduce macroeconomic variability in EMU and may therefore offset at least part of the cost.

(i) The first factor relates to the fact that flexible exchange rates tend to change unexpectedly on exchange markets even if policies or underlying economic factors ('fundamentals') do not change. These unpredictable disturbances in exchange rates increase real and nominal macroeconomic variability through their effects on real exchange rates and prices of imported goods. By fixing intra-Community exchange rates, this source of exogenous asymmetric exchange rate shocks will disappear as a source of instability, representing a gross gain from EMU.

(ii) Secondly, there are gains related to the disappearance of suboptimal or non-cooperative exchange rate or monetary policies. For instance, when faced with a common inflationary shock, individual countries might try to export inflation through competitive appreciations, whereas they could do better in terms of macroeconomic stability to coordinate their exchange rate policies. [34]

Giving up the exchange rate instrument therefore does not only entail costs for macroeconomic stabilization, but also some gains. Whether the net effect of all these factors is positive or negative depends on the precise alternative (the 'baseline') with which to compare EMU, and on the empirical magnitudes which are involved.

As discussed in Chapter 2, the baseline will not be the same for all Community countries, not only because they presently do not all share the same exchange rate regime, but also because, even if they all participate in the EMS in Stage I, this would not necessarily be a stable regime. Instead of trying to work with one single baseline, therefore, EMU could also be compared to different regimes. For instance, EMU would represent a larger gain from the disappearance of asymmetric exchange rate shocks compared to the hypothetical situation of a free float inside the Community rather than with respect to the EMS; and similarly, also with respect to the effects on wage and price discipline. The EMS also removes non-cooperative exchange rate policies as they might exist in a floating exchange rate regime, since realignments are usually negotiated. On the other hand, the EMS introduces an additional cost due to the asymmetry of monetary policy in the system. Since monetary policy is mainly determined by German domestic policy objectives, monetary policy in other EMS members can hardly react to domestic asymmetric shocks. This will reduce macroeconomic stability

for the EMS as a whole since German macroeconomic variables represent less than half of the EMS total. [35]

In order to obtain a global idea of the size and the direction of the net effects on macroeconomic stability, a simulation exercise (see Box 6.4) was performed to compare a model representation of EMU, defined to consist of Germany, France, Italy and the United Kingdom, with three hypothetical baseline regimes. These regimes, chosen not so much for their degree of realism, as to clarify analytically specific properties of EMU, [36] were:

(i) 'Free float': inside the Community, each country pursues the same monetary policy (interest rate reaction function) with respect to its domestic objectives for output and inflation; all countries freely float with respect to the dollar on the basis of uncovered interest rate parity, i.e. with expected exchange rate changes equal to interest rate differentials.

(ii) 'EMS': this stylized regime resembles most the EMS of the mid-1980s. It is assumed that Germany independently sets its monetary policy and is floating against the dollar and that the other countries pursue their own monetary policy only to the extent that their exchange rate remains inside a band with respect to the DM. It differs from the observed EMS since there is an automatic realignment rule based on price differentials relative to Germany which offsets a price differential of 8 % with a devaluation of 4 %.

(iii) 'Asymmetric EMU': this is the same regime as the 'EMS', but without realignment rule and zero band width. All countries therefore follow German monetary policy. This regime might be interpreted as an intermediate stage of EMU with fixed exchange rates but no common monetary policy.

(iv) The EMU regime itself ('Symmetric EMU') is defined as a system of fixed exchange rates with the same monetary policy (interest rate reaction function) as before, but with average Community output and inflation as macroeconomic policy objectives. This could be interpreted as the final stage of EMU with a single currency.

___

[34] See Van der Ploeg (1990).

[35] This analysis is not in contradiction with the credibility other EMS members may derive from German monetary policy in the face of a common inflationary shock. Recent developments in the EMS have shown, moreover, that there is a tendency for monetary policy to become more symmetric. This points once more to the difficulty of choosing an evolutionary system such as the EMS as a baseline.

[36] For this reason, the United Kingdom was assumed to participate in the EMS regime, ahead of its entry in the ERM on 8 October 1990, but assuming narrow margins rather than wide margins.

Naturally, the results of this analysis are surrounded with uncertainty due to the technique used and factors which could cause underestimation or overestimation of the reductions or increases in variability which are obtained. Subject to this important caveat, the following results emerge (see also Graph 6.10).

GRAPH 6.10: **Macroeconomic stability of EMU**

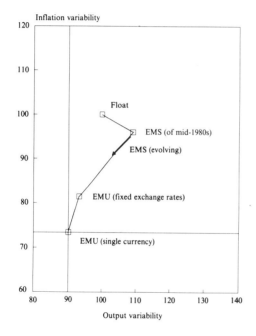

Indices EC average, free float = 100

This graph plots the combinations of variability of output (GDP) and inflation for the Community average in index form as resulting from the stochastic simulations. The position of each of the four regimes ('free float', 'EMS', 'asymmetric EMU', and EMU) corresponds to an intersection between a regime-dependent output-inflation trade-off curve and a shifting preference curve.
Source: Stochastic simulations with the Multimod model of the IMF under the responsibility of the Commission services. GDP is measured as a percentage deviation from its baseline value, inflation is measured in percentage point differences with respect to baseline inflation rates. The indices used in the graph are obtained by averaging, first, the squares of the deviations for 43 simulations over the period 1990-99 and by taking the square root. Dividing by the root mean-squared deviations for the free float regime and multiplication by 100 then gives the indices.

Comparing the 'EMS' regime to the 'free float' regime, the Community reduces its inflation variability but increases its output variability:

(i) The reduction in inflation variability is the consequence of the reduction in asymmetric intra-Community exchange rate shocks and wage and price discipline effects. Only for Italy inflation variability increases rather strongly. This may be due to the nature of the historical shocks and backward-looking wage behaviour in Italy.

(ii) The increase in output variability is due to the constraint on monetary policy from the peg to the DM for the countries other than Germany. The wage and price discipline effects on factor adjustment and reduction in asymmetric exchange rate shocks are present, but apparently not large enough to compensate for the reduced room for manoeuvre in monetary policy, except in Germany which retains its independent monetary policy.

The move from 'EMS' to 'asymmetric EMU' brings strong reductions to both output and inflation variability in the Community:

(i) The output effect is due, firstly, to the disciplinary effects on factor adjustment in returning output to equilibrium which are now much stronger in all countries pegging to the DM due to the complete elimination of the remaining band width for exchange rates and the absence of realignments. In addition, there is the effect of the disappearance of intra-Community exchange rate shocks. The effect on output in Germany remains virtually the same due to its monetary leadership.

(ii) The decrease in inflation variability is stronger in France and Italy, followed by the United Kingdom and Germany. This order is partly determined by the fact that the former three countries lose the possibility for realignment relative to the DM.

For the Community, the regime change from 'asymmetric EMU' to 'symmetric EMU' would bring a further large gain for inflation and a small further gain in reducing output variability:

(i) The inflation gain outside Germany is considerable, and may be ascribed to the fact that all countries' inflation objectives are now taken into account in the Community monetary stance, removing suboptimal asymmetric monetary policies. Consequently, German inflation experiences a slight increase in variability which does not exceed that of 'EMS', however.

(ii) The small effect on output is the net result of sizeable improvements for France, Italy and to a minor extent the United Kingdom, and a loss for Germany. Again this is due to the disappearance of suboptimal asymmetric policies.

Although there are some arguments which give grounds for uncertainty about these results (see Box 6.4), these results provide an indication that for the Community as a whole the EMU regime contains features which could to an important extent offset the costs in terms of macroeconomic stability incurred from the loss of the exchange rate instrument. The disappearance of asymmetric exogenous exchange rate shocks and asymmetric suboptimal monetary policies could reduce inflation and output variability considerably. Also effects of exchange rate discipline on wage and price behaviour are present.

Due to differences in behaviour and the asymmetric functioning of the 'EMS', the effects are not completely uniform across countries. Compared to the 'EMS' as defined here, i.e. a semi-crawling peg system with German monetary leadership, the effects are different for Germany than for the other Community countries. The latter could be expected to gain considerably relative to the 'EMS', both in terms of output and inflation, whereas Germany's inflation variability would remain unchanged and its output variability could increase. With a high preference for inflation stability and relatively low historical output variability, the loss from giving up monetary policy sovereignty by Germany has therefore to be judged small, certainly since no account was taken of the role of fiscal policy and the reduction of asymmetric shocks.

A final issue is whether the expected improvements in macroeconomic stability in EMU will lead to higher levels of output or lower levels of inflation. The empirical results obtained here might add to those of Chapter 4, which showed the existence of positive correlations between the level of inflation and the standard deviations of both inflation and GDP growth. Combined with the empirical results, this would suggest that EMU could contribute to a decrease in inflation via an improvement in macroeconomic stability. Since there is no conclusive evidence on a possible negative link between GDP variability and GDP growth [37] a similar case is more difficult to make for output. As suggested in Chapter 4, there is, however, an indirect positive effect on real income per capita via lower inflation.

---

[37] The relationship may be positive or negative depending on the measure of variability used:

$$\text{Growth} = 0.023 + 0.607 * \text{SDEV} \qquad R^2 = 0.187 \text{ 24 observations}$$
$$\qquad\qquad (0.009) \quad (0.270)$$
$$\text{Growth} = 0.054 - 0.022 * \text{CFVAR} \qquad R^2 = 0.244 \text{ 24 observations}$$
$$\qquad\qquad (0.009) \quad (0.008)$$

where growth is the average GDP growth for 24 OECD countries over 1960-88, SDEV the corresponding standard deviation and CFVAR the corresponding coefficient of variation.

Box 6.4: Empirical evaluation of macroeconomic stability in EMU

This box presents an empirical illustration of the effects of fixed intra-Community exchange rates in EMU on the variability of output and inflation using the technique of stochastic simulations. In other words, it is not the impact of EMU on levels of output and inflation which is analysed, but the impact on the variation around these levels. The technique used, which involves the repeated use of random shocks to the economy, gives an opportunity to obtain an average idea of how the variation will change in EMU.

Expected effects

A priori, the absence of intra-Community exchange rates exerts both positive and negative effects on the variability of output and inflation:

(i) There will be a positive disciplinary effect on wage and price formation, since economic agents will incorporate in their price expectations that inflationary intra-Community devaluations are excluded; this will dampen wage-price spirals and increase the speed of adjustment of output to equilibrium through the adjustment of factor prices.

(ii) When a common adverse supply shock occurs (e.g. an oil price shock), EMU members can no longer try to export inflation through futile competitive intra-Community ap-

preciations; the elimination of such non-cooperative policies removes a source of inflation variability.

(iii) Asymmetric exchange rate shocks on exchange markets which are not policy-induced will also disappear, removing another source of instability of inflation and output.

(iv) With respect to the EMS, asymmetric policies which mainly take the German output and inflation variability as objectives disappear, since the common monetary policy focuses on average EMU output and inflation; since Germany represents less than half of the Community, this should improve the average stabilization record.

(v) Asymmetric shocks other than exchange rate shocks are likely to increase output variability due to the absence of the monetary policy instrument at national level to stabilize output, although, as discussed in Section 6.2, the occurrence of asymmetric shocks is likely to diminish (this possible reduction was not taken into account).

(vi) Fiscal policy could play an important role in stabilization, but this effect was left out of consideration in order to isolate the effects of factor adjustment.

Given that there are both positive and negative factors at work, the net impact of EMU on output and inflation variability is ultimately an empirical matter. Broadly speaking, it may be said to depend on the effects of the EMU regime change on shocks, as well as on economic behaviour in reaction to these shocks. This could be analysed by regarding the effects of individual shocks. But in order to obtain a global idea of the order of magnitude of the net impact, stochastic simulations were undertaken whereby shocks were given to all residuals from the behavioural equations simultaneously.

Methodology

The stochastic simulations were performed with the Multimod model of the IMF, slightly adapted for the purposes of the present study.[38] Multimod is a small-sized annual model incorporating both backward-looking and forward-looking features, linking country models for all G7 countries and the rest of the world, which therefore contains models for four Community countries. The method consists of making repeated draws from the observed statistical distribution of shocks, the latter being based on the historical residuals of the behavioural equations of the model, as measured over the past 15 years. The draws for the shocks are introduced as a disturbance in the corresponding equations. This implies that the shocks are unexpected when they occur, but that their effects are known afterwards due to the forward-looking nature of the model. In reacting to these disturbances (keeping fiscal policy unchanged), the authorities are assumed to use the short-term interest rate to stabilize, around their equilibrium values, a certain combination of output, inflation and possibly the exchange rate. The equilibrium values are taken to be the baseline values of the model. An effective policy is therefore one which is able to obtain output and inflation values close to the baseline values.

Due to the problems with the identification of a proper baseline with which to compare the EMU regime (see Chapter 2), this exercise is repeated for four different intra-Community exchange rate regimes. These regimes are not so much modelled for their realism, but rather to clarify analytically certain specific issues:

'Free float': All Community currencies are assumed to float freely against the dollar, and therefore against each other. It is assumed that there is perfect capital mobility, perfect asset substitutability and perfect foresight. Exchange rates therefore follow uncovered interest rate parity (UIP); each country has the same interest rate reaction function focusing on deviations of domestic output and inflation from equilibrium.[39] This function is in accordance with observed behaviour of monetary targeting.

'EMS': Germany freely floats against the dollar on the basis of UIP and the same interest rate reaction function as above; the other Community countries use their interest rates to peg their exchange rate to the DM within a band, allowing them only

very partially to stabilize their domestic output and inflation. Moreover, there is a stylized realignment rule derived from the EMS experience over the period 1985-87, saying that when an accumulated price differential with Germany of 8 % is reached, the DM parity is devalued by 4 %.

'Asymmetric EMU': Germany freely floats against the dollar on the basis of UIP and has the same interest rate reaction function as above. The other Community countries follow German interest rate movements completely; this pegs their exchange rates fully to the DM, and does not take account of their domestic output and inflation objectives.

'EMU': All Community countries float together against the dollar on the basis of UIP. The Community interest rate follows the same reaction function as before, but the output and inflation objectives now concern deviations from equilibrium for the average Community output level and inflation rate. This symmetric system is taken to be the final stage of EMU.

As between the four regimes, the only equations which change are the interest rate reaction function and, directly or indirectly, the determination of the exchange rate. All other equations are left unchanged. Disciplinary effects of EMU therefore come about entirely through the forward-looking features of the model, not through changes in model coefficients. This holds notably for future inflation, which determines real interest rates and appears in the wage-price block.

A second aspect which changes between the four regimes is the nature of shocks. In order to avoid arbitrary assumptions, exchange rate shocks and shocks to other variables are assumed to be independent from each other in all four regimes. The size of, and dependence between, the non-exchange rate shocks is also kept the same between the regimes. The exchange rate shocks themselves have to be modified, however. On the basis of observed shocks over the 1979-88 period, this involves increasing the average correlation among shocks to Community dollar exchange rates from 0,7 in the free float regime, via 0,9 in the EMS regime, to 1 in the EMU regimes. Furthermore, the size of the exchange rate shocks is allowed to differ, in the light of historical data (see Annex E), between Germany (standard deviation of shocks of 10,9%) and the other Community countries (standard deviation of 9,6%) in the free float regime, whereas it is assumed to be equal in the three other regimes (standard deviation of 10,9 %).

Assessment

Analysing the effect of EMU on output and inflation variability with stochastic simulations in the way it was done for the purpose of this study has its strong, but also its weak points. Consequently, the results have to be interpreted with caution.

(i) Economic issues

The exercise only covers Germany, France, Italy and the United Kingdom. If all Community countries had been included, shocks might have been more asymmetric on the whole and the reduction in variability smaller. This would have introduced the

---

[38]   See Masson *et al.* (1988, 1990) for a description of the Multimod model and Annex E for the modifications.

[39]   It is assumed that a one-percentage point increase of inflation increases the short-term interest rate by two percentage points and vice versa. A 1 % increase of output relative to baseline increases the short-term interest rate by 0,4 percentage points and vice versa. This reaction function was derived from the money demand equation of the model. Half of the interest rate effect is assumed to take place in the current year, and half in the next year.

problem of how to deal with the effects of the transition on the nature of the shocks, however, notably for the peripheral countries. After the transition, price shocks could decrease, for instance.

The EMS was modelled in a stylized way as a semi-crawling peg much like the situation in 1985-87, but assuming free capital mobility, completely anticipated realignments and participation of the United Kingdom. Since the EMS is an evolutionary system, any way of modelling it is bound to be *ad-hoc*. With the participation of the United Kingdom as of 8 October 1990, the present EMS presumably lies in between this semi-crawling peg and the asymmetric EMU regime. This should be taken into account when evaluating EMU relative to the EMS baseline.

Another issue related to the question of baseline is the use of the same monetary reaction functions in the free float regime for all countries. The variability in the free float regime would presumably be reduced if there were asymmetric interest rate reactions to common shocks

Similarly, the results depend on the assumption that fiscal policy was kept unchanged. As argued in Section 6.6, the use of fiscal policy with temporary asymmetric shocks may delay adjustment and increase output variability.

Another issue concerns the size of the exchange rate shocks. *Ceteris paribus,* the higher the shocks, the stronger will be the reduction of output and inflation variability due to the disappearance of asymmetric exchange rate shocks. Although shocks in dollar exchange rates of some 10 % on an annual basis seem not unreasonable for the 1980s, these could change depending on future international monetary arrangements.

(ii) Technical issues

An argument frequently used against policy evaluation with econometric models (the so-called Lucas critique) is that they would not be able to deal with the effects of changes in policy regimes. The forward-looking aspects of the model go a long way in meeting this objection since once a regime (free float, EMS, EMU) is in place, the model behaves as if all agents knew its macroeconomic features. At the same time, this also implies that the results are conditional on changes in actual behaviour, notably concerning wage and price discipline.

The reduction of asymmetries in shocks was only introduced for exchange rate shocks and not for shocks to other variables, even though it was argued elsewhere in this chapter that for the latter also such a decrease could be expected. This could be a source of underestimation of the possible reduction in variability. Moreover, the shocks were drawn on the basis of residuals from equations which, with some exceptions, were imposed to have the same coefficients among countries. On the one hand, this may have introduced additional asymmetries in the residuals which would not have been observed otherwise, but on the other hand it may have reduced behavioural asymmetries.

Although the policy reaction function used for interest rates is consistent with the estimated money demand equation of the model, it was not derived from full optimization. This raises the issue of possible suboptimality of monetary policy. Since observed behaviour may not be optimal either, this avoids making arbitrary assumptions.

From the methodological point of view, finally, the technique of stochastic simulations in evaluating policy regimes is still under development.[40] Some technical aspects are discussed in Annex E. Compared to the evaluation of regimes using single shocks whose effects may go in opposite directions, stochastic simulations have the merit that they provide an overall evaluation of stability, even though the shocks on which this is based are historical. But this problem is not much different for single shocks.

---

[40] See Frenkel *et al.* (1989) or the Brookings conference 'Empirical evaluation of alternative policy regimes', 8 and 9 March, 1990.

Results of stochastic simulations

Root mean-squared deviations, free float = 100

		Free float	EMS	Asymmetric EMU	Symmetric EMU	Historical variability[1] 1973-88 (PM)
EC[2]	GDP[3]	100	109	93	90	1,4 - 3,5
	Inflation[4]	100	96	81	73	2,2 - 6,0
Germany	GDP	100	94	96	108	1,9
	Inflation	100	86	83	86	2,2
France	GDP	100	135	104	93	1,4
	Inflation	100	98	72	60	3,7
Italy	GDP	100	131	114	103	2,4
	Inflation	100	125	104	90	5,2
United Kingdom	GDP	100	98	81	80	2,5
	Inflation	100	86	75	68	5,6

[1] Standard deviation of inflation and growth rate of GDP at annual rates.
[2] Variables measured as unweighted average of Germany, France, Italy and the United Kingdom; for variability: minimum and maximum of all Community countries.
[3] Measured as percentage difference with respect to baseline.
[4] Measured as difference with respect to baseline in percentage points.
Source: Simulations with the IMF Multimod model under the responsibility of the Commission services. The numbers in the table are root mean-squared deviations for annual data with respect to baseline (= equilibrium) for 43 simulations over the period 1990-99, thus representing a draw of 430 shocks for all 95 behavioural variables.

6.5. Adjustment through external financing

With a single currency, the current account constraint *vis-à-vis* the other members of the union disappears. In a Tinbergen-type target-instrument framework with external balance as one of the objectives and the exchange rate one of the instruments, the disappearance of the exchange rate instrument would be exactly compensated by the elimination of the external balance target. In that context, there would be no loss from the exchange rate instrument. There are, however, several reasons to pay separate attention to the external constraint. Firstly, since there are usually more targets than instruments, the exchange rate loss can never be completely compensated by the disappearance of the external constraint. Secondly, the extent of attenuation of the exchange rate loss through this mechanism can only be assessed by analysing the current state of the external constraint ('baseline'). Thirdly, the external balance can keep a signalling function in EMU. Fourthly, as argued below, in a world of free capital mobility, there is still the constraint of long-run solvency. Sustainability conditions require that the trade balance cannot stay in deficit forever. An external equilibrium over the medium run may be interpreted as

a sufficient, though not necessary, condition for long-run equilibrium, in this context.[41]

There are two important ways in which the absence of constraints on the balance of the current account in EMU may (partially) substitute for the exchange rate instrument. Both cases rest upon the interpretation of the current account surplus as the excess of national saving over investment.

The first case is when there is a temporary adverse shock, e.g. a decrease in external demand, causing a decrease in income and therefore in consumption. If there is no possibility of modifying the real exchange rate, the same level of consumption can be maintained by temporarily decreasing the savings ratio, which will then deteriorate the current account balance further. In a financially integrated area with free capital mobility, the shock is therefore absorbed through temporary borrowing abroad.

---

[41]   See also Oliveira-Martins and Plihon (1990).

A second case arises when a country for some reason expects a future increase in productivity but has insufficient savings to bring about the international equalization of real rates of return implied by this productivity differential, as may be the case with the poorer countries of the Community. A real depreciation could generate a surplus on the current account which could be used to finance the investment. Alternatively, with free capital mobility the investment could be financed by incurring a deficit on the current account through increased borrowing from abroad. When the borrowing has been transformed into productive capital, the faster growth allows the foreign debt to be repaid.[42]

These two cases provide clear examples of how the current account may take over the role of the nominal exchange rate. Nevertheless, they hinge crucially on assumptions about the free mobility of capital, or, more generally, on the constraints on the current account or 'external constraint'. It is therefore important to analyse the role of the external constraint in order to assess to what extent its removal compensates for the loss of the exchange rate instrument. Major issues in this respect are:

(i) the operation of the external constraint;

(ii) the implications of EMU for the external constraint.

6.5.1. The external constraint

The external constraint may be defined as the extent to which, for a particular country or economic region, there exist limitations on the net acquisition of foreign financial assets and liabilities. These limitations may be described under several headings:

(a) Barriers to capital market integration: these may consist of capital controls, transaction costs, information costs, discriminating tax laws or the risk of future capital controls. These barriers may be measured by the so-called country premium,[43] i.e. the deviation from covered interest rate parity.

(b) Real exchange rate uncertainty: even in the absence of barriers to capital market integration (zero country premium), real exchange rate uncertainty may prevent the equalization of real rates of return and therefore the optimal international allocation of capital. A country with good investment opportunities but high exchange risk may thus be deprived of the flow of capital needed to exploit the existing opportunities.[44] With zero country premium, the deviation from real interest rate parity may be due to (i) a nominal exchange risk premium, measured by the deviation from uncovered interest parity, i.e. the difference between the forward discount and expected nominal depreciation; and (ii) the deviation from relative purchasing power parity (PPP).

(c) Correlated savings and investment: if there is a common determinant for the savings rate and the investment rate other than the internationally equalized real interest rate, changes in the domestic savings rate may crowd out the investment rate and therefore interfere with the optimal international allocation of capital. In practice, this may therefore operate as a limitation to capital mobility. If there are no limitations of this sort and if there is real interest rate parity, the savings rate and the investment rate should be uncorrelated. This would typically be expected in countries small enough not to influence the world real interest rate. This is the definition of perfect capital mobility first presented by Feldstein and Horioka (1980). Government intervention and limited substitutability between bonds, equity and physical capital (e.g. due to sunk costs) may be the basic reason why the Feldstein-Horioka definition is violated.

---

[42] The difference between the two approaches lies in intertemporal welfare considerations. The trend real depreciation implies a substitution of current consumption by saving, and is therefore inferior from the point of view of consumption smoothing. See Blanchard and Fischer (1989) or Frenkel and Razin (1987).

[43] This terminology was developed by Frankel (1989). See also Box 6.5.

[44] See Baldwin (1990).

Box 6.5: Measuring capital mobility in the Community

The table, calculated on the basis of Frankel (1989), decomposes the mean deviation from *(ex-post)* real interest rate parity into a country premium, exchange risk premium and deviation from *(ex-post)* relative purchasing power parity for the Community countries relative to Germany over the period September 1982 to April 1988.[45] Ideally, each of these factors should be zero for perfect capital mobility to hold.

The table allows the following conclusions to be drawn:

(i) The least stringent condition by which to judge the absence of the external constraint is the country premium, i.e. the deviation from covered interest rate parity, which should be zero. If it is negative, it means that domestic interest rates are artificially low compared to the DM interest rate. This may be due to capital controls, as is clearly the case with Greece and Portugal (but also the other countries having maintained capital controls over the period), or due to transaction costs. For the three countries with the least capital controls over the period, the United Kingdom, the Netherlands and Belgium, the country

Measures of capital mobility relative to Germany, 1982-88

	Country premium (1)	Exchange risk premium (2)	Relative PPP deviation (3)	Currency premium (4) = (2) + (3)	Real interest parity (5) = (1) + (4)
Belgium	− 0,23	3,40	− 1,34	2,08	1,82
Denmark	− 3,88	3,39	− 1,59	1,80	− 2,13
Greece	− 9,74	− 0,47	4,53	2,49	− 7,93
Spain	− 2,75	4,87	0,34	4,78	1,82
France	− 2,09	3,35	0,11	3,01	0,81
Ireland	− 1,14	3,16	0,50	4,80	2,82
Italy	− 0,75	4,66	− 1,66	3,08	2,30
Netherlands	− 0,14	0,26	0,26	0,74	0,58
Portugal	− 8,28	7,16	− 1,77	6,60	− 2,61
United Kingdom	− 0,49	− 0,34	3,51	2,27	1,75

(1): $i - i^* - fd$
(2): $fd - E$
(3): $E - (P - P^*)$
(4): $fd - (P - P^*)$
(5): $i - P - (i^* - P^*)$
with fd = three-month forward discount with respect to the DM.
with E = observed depreciation with respect to DM (proxy for expected value), three-month percentage change at annual rate.
with P = observed inflation (proxy for expected value) over three-month period at annual rate.
with i = money market interest rate over three-month period.
with $*$ = refers to German variables.
Note. The identities (5) = (1) + (4) and (4) = (2) + (3) are not always respected due to inconsistencies in the original data material.
Source. Calculated from Frankel (1989), averages of monthly observations over the period September 1982 to April 1988.

premium is not more than minus 50 basis points, reflecting probably only transaction costs.

(ii) Due to the proxies used in its measurement, the exchange risk premium (deviation from uncovered interest rate parity) is linked to the variability of observed rather than expected local currency/ DM exchange rates. Of the countries participating in the exchange rate mechanism (ERM) of the EMS in the measurement period, the premium for the Netherlands is the smallest, followed at some distance by the other narrow-band countries and finally Italy. Outside the ERM, the premiums for Spain and Portugal are both larger than for Italy.[46]

(iii) The *ex-post* real depreciation, i.e. deviation from relative PPP, is surrounded with even more measurement errors than the previous criterion, since not only expected depreciation but also expected relative price changes are approximated by observed values. Nevertheless, on the basis of this criterion, it seems that this source of limitation to capital mobility does not play a significant role.[47]

How may the Feldstein-Horioka hypothesis for the Community countries be analysed? Feldstein and Horioka (1980) had to

---

[45]   Price expectations and exchange rate expectations have been proxied by their observed values.
[46]   The results for Greece and the United Kingdom may seem anomalous at first sight, implying negative risk premiums. This may be due, however, to the fact that *ex-post* instead of *ex-ante* depreciation has been used. If there is *ex-post* more depreciation than expected, which does not seem an unreasonable assumption in these two cases, this reduces the observed risk premium.

[47]   The exceptions being, as for the previous criterion, Greece and the United Kingdom. The stronger depreciation than presumably expected shows up with a mirror image. As a consequence, this measurement error cancels out if the exchange risk premium and the *ex-post* deviation from relative PPP are added to form the so-called currency premium; see Frenkel (1989).

reject the hypothesis of uncorrelated savings and investment using data for most OECD countries over the period 1960-74. In so far as Community countries were included in the sample, the implied hypothesis that financial markets would not be integrated was jointly rejected for them as well. Various authors have advanced arguments which could explain the particular rejection of the hypothesis on the basis of cross-section estimates.[48] The two most important aspects from the point of view of EMU in this respect are the influence on the Feldstein-Horioka result of capital controls and exchange rate risk.

One way to proceed is to analyse periods and/or areas for which it is known that there were no capital controls and exchange risk. If savings and investment are uncorrelated for such regimes, it may be inferred that capital controls and exchange rate uncertainty play an important role in impeding perfect capital mo-

bility. In this vein, Bayoumi (1989) ran several cross-section regressions among savings and investment rates over the Gold Standard period 1880-1913, finding them to be uncorrelated. Given that the Gold Standard was a period with fixed exchange rates, no capital controls and limited government intervention, this suggests evidence in favour of the Feldstein-Horioka hypothesis. Bayoumi and Rose (1989) obtained a comparable result using regional data for the United Kingdom over the period 1971-85.

A second possibility, more focused on the EMU perspective, would be to single out the ERM countries in regressions covering the EMS period and to test whether the ERM countries display correlation between savings and investment. This line of research was pursued by Bhandari and Mayer (1990). Their cross-section estimates indicate that the ERM countries (plus Austria) show no significant correlation between savings and investment for the periods 1979-82 or 1983-87, thus suggesting that the ERM has contributed positively to the mobility of capital. The present current account imbalances inside the Community remain, however, much lower than those observed in federal States or monetary unions. Among Community members current account positions ranged from a surplus of 5,8 % of GDP for Germany to deficits of 4,1 % and 3,4 % for the UK and Greece, respectively. In contrast, Luxembourg, which forms a monetary union with Belgium, had a current account surplus of 14,9 % of GDP and the estimates of regional accounts in the MacDougall report[49] also contain a number of examples of current account imbalances of over 10 % of GDP.

---

[48] Feldstein and Horioka themselves already took account of the fact that savings and investment could both behave pro-cyclically by averaging data over the cycle. They also took account that both could be influenced simultaneously by demographic factors. Similarly, they also analysed whether a breakdown of savings by economic agent and investment by component influenced the results. Finally, they tested for spurious correlation by taking the changes in the savings and investment rates between 1970-74 and 1960-69. In all cases, their basic conclusion was not affected. Feldstein and Bacchetta (1989) found that the correlation had decreased, but was still significantly different from zero, over the period 1980-86 compared to earlier periods, a result confirmed by Frankel (1989) using time-series regressions for the USA. Artis and Bayoumi (1989) estimated policy reaction functions showing that current-account targeting played a role in government behaviour in the 1970s which diminished in the 1980s, thus highlighting the role of endogenous government behaviour interfering with movements of savings and investment.

[49] See Commission of the European Communities (1977).

Data on these criteria for the 1980s (see Box 6.5) seem to indicate for the measures related to real interest rate parity (country premium, exchange risk premium and deviation from relative PPP) that in the last decade the necessary conditions for perfect capital mobility were met inside the Community to a limited extent. This was more the case for the narrow-band ERM countries which have liberalized capital flows than for other Community countries. But even there, the most simple criterion, i.e. almost zero country premium relative to Germany, was only met for Belgium and the Netherlands. Outside the ERM in the measurement period, the only exception concerns the country premium in the United Kingdom which is low, as could be expected due to its lack of capital controls over the period concerned. The currency premium (sum of risk premium and deviation from relative PPP) is only below 1 % for the Netherlands, and varies between 2 and 7 % for the other countries. Looking at the real interest parity deviation, which is an aggregate of the three measures used, perfect capital mobility could only be said to exist between Germany and the Netherlands. Naturally, this is based on imperfect measures. Furthermore, the present situation is likely to have improved with ongoing capital liberalization and low inflation differentials.

Concerning the correlation between savings and investment, there is strong historical evidence of the absence of such a correlation in regimes with fixed exchange rates, no capital controls and limited government intervention. This is corroborated by regression results reported in Box 6.5 for ERM members relative to other Community countries, demonstrating the positive impact of fixed exchange rates for capital mobility.

6.5.2. Effects of EMU on the external constraint

The previous evidence indicates that the absence of capital controls and exchange rate risk are important factors in enhancing the international mobility of capital. These two cornerstones of EMU may therefore be expected to stimulate positively the optimal allocation of capital inside the Community. For instance, it may be expected that the complete liberalization of capital flows as agreed for eight Community countries by 1 July 1990 and the other countries by the end of 1992,[50] will reduce the country premium to figures

---

[50] Portugal and Greece may delay the liberalization until the end of 1995.

comparable to those for Belgium, the Netherlands and the United Kingdom.

In principle, the only remaining limitation in EMU consists in a long-run solvency constraint of companies, households and governments. The current account may for a long time be in disequilibrium as long as there is the expectation that in the end the foreign debt will be repaid without issuing new liabilities.[51] Since there is one single currency, the constraint is not much different from that facing domestic borrowers *vis-à-vis* domestic lenders, and becomes less binding in the short run.

This conclusion needs to be qualified, however, since it does not mean that the current account completely loses its meaning. For one thing, there is the problem that agents are not able to observe the intertemporal solvency constraint. They may therefore still want to analyse the origins of current account imbalances. An imbalance due to net imports of capital goods might be viewed differently from an imbalance due to net imports of consumption goods. For another, governments might still want to use the current account as an indicator of possibly inflationary policies. Moreover, as argued by Artis and Bayoumi (1989), the government might still want to target the current account for several reasons, such as the fear for the influence of foreign capital on the domestic economy, or the difference between social and private benefit, e.g. due to the fact that taxes paid in the home country or abroad may have the same welfare implications for an individual, but not for the home country.

The conclusion is, therefore, that the complete liberalization of capital flows and the irrevocable fixing of exchange rates or a single currency would imply that the disappearance of the intra-Community external constraint would be at least partially a substitute for nominal exchange rate adjustment in EMU.

6.6. Budgetary policy as an alternative to the exchange rate instrument

In relation to the loss of the exchange rate instrument in EMU, budgetary policy may have a role as one form of financing to compensate temporarily for the loss of the exchange rate instrument, next to other forms of financing such as private borrowing abroad or a transfer or loan from other members of the union. The importance of budgetary policy in this context derives from the assumption that the government cares about both internal and external equilibrium, although the role of the latter changes in EMU, as discussed in the previous section. These two policy objectives will in general require two instruments, and the loss of the exchange rate instrument could imply the need to rely more on an alternative instrument such as budgetary policy.

The two main issues in this respect are:

(i) when to assign budgetary policy rather than other instruments;

(ii) the effectiveness of budgetary policy relative to the exchange rate instrument through monetary policy.

Throughout the discussion, it will be assumed that shocks which occur disturb external equilibrium, such as a shock to external demand or competitiveness (real exchange rate). In other words, the shocks are such that the optimal policy assignment in a system of flexible exchange rates and nominal rigidity would have been the exchange rate. Chapter 5 has shown the need for budgetary policy in the case of shocks of domestic origin.

6.6.1. The need for budgetary policy

The assignment of budgetary policy as an alternative to the exchange rate instrument in the face of a shock depends basically on three elements:

(i) policy objectives,

(ii) adjustment mechanisms in relation to objectives,

(iii) the nature of the shocks.

Starting from a shock which disturbs equilibrium, it is assumed for the discussion here[52] that the policy objectives are internal equilibrium (output equal to production capacity) and external equilibrium (equilibrium on the current account).

The adjustment mechanisms which may return the economy to equilibrium are usually not the same in the short run as in the medium run. Moreover, their effects on the policy objectives depend on the view taken regarding the working of the economy.

---

[51]   As indicated above, this can only happen under certain circumstances, such as a temporary adverse output shock or an expected future increase in productivity. On the other hand, and in line with the theory of intertemporal optimization, a permanent adverse shock to output should decrease the permanent income level and therefore not lead to increased borrowing from abroad as with a temporary shock.

[52]   This abstracts from other policy objectives such as inflation stabilization.

In the short run budgetary policy may have a direct impact on demand. Monetary policy influences domestic demand indirectly via interest rates, and the current account via the exchange rate, given that exchange rates are flexible. Assuming wage and price rigidity in the short run, this implies that budgetary policy and monetary policy — via the exchange rate — are the two instruments to be assigned to the two policy objectives in the short run.[53]

In the medium run, monetary policy loses much of its impact because the effect of the nominal exchange rate on the real exchange rate disappears through its effect on domestic prices. Budgetary policy may also lose some impact, for instance because future tax changes to offset the budgetary policy are expected. Wage and price adjustments therefore inevitably have to supplement government policies, notably in order to maintain the effect on real exchange rates. There are still two objectives, but more than two mechanisms to establish equilibrium since the mechanisms may lose part of their effect.

How do policy objectives and instruments change in EMU? As discussed in the previous section, external equilibrium disappears as a constraint in the short run, although it remains a valid objective for the long run. This lengthens the period over which the current account can stay in disequilibrium before it needs to be returned to balance. This implies a significant compensation for the loss of the nominal exchange rate and independent monetary policy.

The assignment of alternative instruments is less needed due to the short-run loosening of the external equilibrium objective. To the extent that it still has to take place, the impact on domestic demand which is lost with monetary policy can be taken over by budgetary policy. Wage and price adjustments should mainly be geared to influence the real exchange rate.[54] In the medium run, budgetary policy, wages and prices are therefore the remaining instruments.

The precise assignment of these instruments is related to the nature of the shocks which cause the disequilibria in the first place.

A temporary shock to domestic (relative to foreign) demand or the real exchange rate could usually be corrected by

wage and price adjustments. But with nominal rigidity, the correction of internal disequilibrium which such a shock implies may be temporarily taken over by budgetary policy, although this risks delaying the medium-run adjustment to external equilibrium since economic agents know that the government will try to dampen fluctuations.[55]

A permanent shock to either relative demand or competitiveness requires inevitably that factor markets adjust through changes in wages and prices, since budgetary policy cannot be changed permanently without affecting government debt. So again, budgetary policy may help temporarily, but could cause the factor adjustment to be sluggish.

Summing up, the assignment of budgetary policy as an alternative to the exchange rate instrument is only partially needed due to the virtual disappearance of the objective of external equilibrium. If needed, it may be of some use in the case of temporary shocks when there are nominal rigidities. Permanent shocks require the adjustment of factor markets, but should not be delayed by relying on budgetary policy.

6.6.2. The effectiveness of budgetary policy

The effectiveness of budgetary policy in general is the subject of a long-standing debate among different schools of thought, which will not be discussed here.[56] What is important, however, is the time framework to which these discussions apply. With nominal wage rigidity, a severe adverse shock causing unemployment may be countered effectively in the short run through an increase in government spending. In the medium run, there should be an adjustment of the nominal wage to restore equilibrium on the labour market. Once this has happened, the government does not have to maintain its deficit and can start repaying its debt long before the intertemporal budget constraint starts influencing private saving behaviour.

In addition to these general arguments, there are a number of arguments that may have a particular influence on the effectiveness of the instrument of budgetary policy in EMU.

---

[53] The short run is assumed to cover several years, so that the feasibility or desirability of fiscal fine-tuning is not an issue. Alternatively, the asymmetric shock may be assumed to be severe enough to warrant active policy action.

[54] Alternatively, Begg (1990) assigns a more important role to wages and prices in obtaining internal equilibrium. This approach rests strongly on the rather theoretical assumption that real balance effects are important.

[55] See Begg (1990).

[56] The 'classical' and 'Keynesian' visions are opposed in their assumptions on the flexibility of money wages. For an analysis, see Sargent (1987). This analysis is essentially comparative-static. In an intertemporal framework, another controversy concerns the impact of the deficit incurred by the government on its intertemporal budget constraint. People may see through the action of the government and anticipate future taxes by increasing private saving, thus rendering budgetary policy completely ineffective. This is called Ricardian equivalence, see Frenkel and Razin (1987).

In the first place, there is the familiar Mundell-Fleming proposition that in a world of free capital mobility budgetary policy is more effective in a regime of fixed exchange rates than in a regime of flexible exchange rates. The reason is that a fiscal expansion in a flexible regime will, through an increase in interest rates, appreciate the currency and therefore exert a negative effect on competitiveness which is absent in a system of fixed exchange rates such as EMU. The counterpart in EMU is that the increase in interest rates will spill over to other member countries and reduce their output, which raises coordination problems (see Chapter 5).

The differences in impact on GDP of a fiscal expansion are illustrated, in this case for France, on the basis of simulations with the IMF Multimod model[57] in Graph 6.11. As expected on theoretical grounds, the effect is stronger in EMU than in the case of a free float, with the EMS as intermediate case.

---

[57]   For a description of the treatment of the float, EMS and EMU exchange rate regimes, see Annex E.

GRAPH 6.11: **The effectiveness of budgetary policy in EMU**

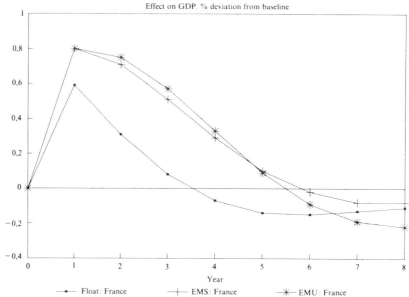

Source: Multimod simulation.

This graph shows the impact on GDP relative to a baseline of a simulation of an increase in government expenditure. The results were obtained from a simulation for France with the Multimod model under three regimes: 'free float', 'EMS' and 'EMU'. The traditional Mundell-Fleming result that fiscal policy is most effective in a system of fixed exchange rates appears for the first five years after the shock.

Secondly, in addition to the requirements on budgetary policy following from spill-over considerations, budgetary policy will be confronted, in EMU, with more constraints than would otherwise be the case:

(i) the need for fiscal discipline;

(ii) a possible contribution to the Community policy mix.

These constraints, discussed in Chapter 5, may restrict the leeway for an independent budgetary policy, although the particular country situation might of course be taken into consideration in the coordination procedure or as part of the Community policy mix.

Thirdly, as shown by Begg (1990), there is the point that in EMU (but also in alternative regimes) fiscal stabilization policy in the case of supply shocks may be counterproductive to real wage adjustment. [58] In a model with perfect foresight, households will adjust their wages less quickly to restore equilibrium on the labour market if they know that they are — at least temporarily — bailed out by the government. This reduces the speed of adjustment of the economy towards equilibrium. On the other hand, given that there is a gain in the speed of adjustment to equilibrium in EMU compared to more flexible exchange rate regimes such as the EMS (see Section 6.3), this creates some room for fiscal stabilization, assuming the government is prepared to trade off the latter against the former. The trade-off between real wage adjustment and budgetary policy is illustrated, on the basis of simulations with the Commission's Quest model for France, in Graph 6.12. The graph plots different combinations of present values of the real wage and the government budget deficit in the case of a negative export shock, each combination representing a different policy alternative to a devaluation. [59] The loss of the exchange rate instrument is represented by the distance between the devaluation point and the trade-off curve. Obviously, wage moderation causes the largest real wage loss, whereas an increase in government investment is the most desirable from this point of view.

Conclusion

In EMU, the objective of external equilibrium becomes less important. This reduces the need to replace the exchange rate instrument by an alternative policy such as budgetary policy. Nevertheless, free capital mobility renders budgetary policy more efficient in a system of fixed exchange rates such as EMU than in more flexible exchange rate regimes such as the early EMS. If external equilibrium is of concern, budgetary policy can therefore play a useful role. This holds more in the case of temporary shocks than in the case of permanent shocks, where factor adjustment inevitably has to take place. More generally, there is a trade-off between the use of budgetary policy and the speed of factor adjustment.

GRAPH 6.12: **The trade-off between budgetary policy and wage adjustment**

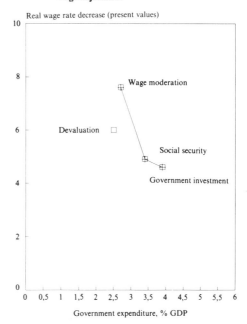

Source: Quest simulations.

This graph displays different adjustment policies in the wake of a negative export shock, in this case simulated for France with the Quest model. The y-axis shows the present value over a seven-year period of the real wage rate decrease which follows from the shock. The x-axis gives the present value over the same period of the effect on government expenditure. The seven-year period corresponds to the period which is needed to bring real GDP back to baseline (equilibrium) if the negative export shock is followed immediately by an offsetting devaluation. Next, three other instruments are used as an alternative to the devaluation, which result in exactly the same present value of the output loss as the devaluation (there is an output loss due to the initial negative effect on output before it returns to equilibrium). Wage moderation has the most negative impact on the real income loss, as could be expected. A decrease in employers social security contributions reduces the real income loss strongly, but has a budgetary cost. An increase in government expenditure results in even slightly less real income loss, but comes at a greater budgetary cost. The cost of the loss of the exchange rate instrument in terms of real wage decrease or government expenditure increase is measured by the vertical or horizontal distance from the devaluation point to the trade-off curve for the other instruments.

[58] Historically, an extreme case is that of the Mezzogiorno in Italy, discussed in Chapter 9. See also OECD (1990).

[59] The size of the policy instruments were chosen so as to obtain the same present value for the loss of real GDP over a seven-year period as for the devaluation. The size of the devaluation was chosen so as to return to baseline real GDP after seven years. For a complete description, see Annex D.

Moreover, budgetary policy should take account of the implications for spill-over effects on other EMU members and the constraints arising from fiscal discipline.

6.7. The role of central public finance in assisting regional adjustment

There are several ways in which central public finance in a federal system can contribute to the cushioning of country-specific shocks. The two most important areas are those of interregional and interpersonal redistribution. By taking the role of central public finance in the case of existing federations as a baseline, this section tries to draw inferences for the role of public finance in EMU. It is argued that EMU is a unique case, but that the trade-off between fiscal autonomy and interregional fiscal equalization, which is a characteristic of existing federations, nevertheless applies.

6.7.1. Central public finance in existing federations

Central public finance has an important place in existing federations (see Table 6.3). This importance may be judged from several indicators.

Federal expenditure as a percentage of total government spending is a composite indicator since it comprises several functions of public finance. Even in the more decentralized federations like Switzerland, federal expenditure represents at least 30 % of total spending. Excluding social expenditure, this figure attains a maximum of 54 % in the United States. Federal expenditure in existing federations includes major expenditure functions in the provision of public goods, but may also cover part of the interpersonal grants reducing personal income losses due to economic shocks.

On the revenue side, federations usually have a considerable degree of tax harmonization, and the highest level of government is normally the dominant tax authority in the sense that few federations (e.g. USA and Switzerland) attribute exclusive tax competences to regional governments.

Federal grants, which give an indication of the size of interregional distribution, constitute between 15 and 30 % of regional revenue.[60] In terms of GDP, this amounts to figures between 3 % (USA) and 7 % (Australia) of GDP.

As a consequence, primary income differentials between regions in existing federations are reduced by 30 to 40 % through the workings of central public finance.[61] Roughly half of this is automatic through taxation and direct government expenditure, the other half is discretionary and intentional in the form of specific and general purpose grants. Central public finance also provides for automatic stabilization of regional income in the case of economic shocks. It has been estimated in the MacDougall report[62] that for unitary States such as France and the United Kingdom, one

---

[60]   See Lamfalussy (1989).
[61]   See the MacDougall report, Commission of the European Communities (1977).
[62]   See Commission of the European Communities (1977).

Table 6.3

Central public finance in five major federations

	Expenditure (net federal spending as % of total consolidated spending[1])		Revenue (degree of State autonomy[2])	Grants (% of GDP[3])
	(a)	(b)		
Switzerland	28	56	79	3,6
USA	54	63	78	2,7
Canada	37	45	56	4,2
Germany	31	67	16	3,4
Australia	40	56	36	7,0

[1]   Data for 1987. *Source:* calculated from OECD (1989b). Measured as (a) total current disbursements of central government minus transfers to other sectors of government, social security benefits, social assistance grants and unfunded employee pension and welfare benefits, as a percentage of general government total current disbursements minus the same social expenditures; (b) total current disbursements of central government plus social security funds minus transfers from central government to other sectors of government, as a percentage of total disbursements of general government. General government includes social security funds.
[2]   Data for 1980-81. Measured as the percentage of exclusive and competing taxes and non-fiscal income in total State revenue.
[3]   Data for 1987. *Source:* calculated from OECD (1989b).

Source: Van Rompuy and Heylen (1986) and Commission services.

Box 6.6: Fiscal autonomy and interregional equalization

This box examines the relationship between fiscal autonomy and interregional equalization in five major federations, Switzerland, USA, Canada, Germany and Australia. In order to determine the degree of fiscal autonomy of a region (state) in a federation, three aspects are considered: revenue sources, policy competences, and the associated volume of expenditure and the degree of independence with respect to borrowing and levels of budget deficits. For interregional equalization the results of the MacDougall report[63] are referred to in view of the lack of more recent comparable empirical evidence.

Fiscal autonomy

The degree of autonomy in terms of revenue sources is evaluated by looking at the percentage of exclusive and competing taxes and non-fiscal income in total regional revenue (Table 6.3, third column). For Switzerland and the USA the percentage is between 75 and 80 %, for Canada it is in the order of 50 % whereas for Germany and Australia the figures are much lower; in Australia this is due to the fact that a region's revenue is determined for about one-third by shared taxes and about one-third by federal grants, while in Germany shared taxes represent 70 % of the *Länder* revenue.

The degree of expenditure competence is evaluated by looking at the share of state and local spending in total government spending, excluding social security for reasons of comparability (Table 6.3, column (a)). In Germany and Switzerland, the sub-federal level has a dominant expenditure competence of around 70 %; in Canada and Australia this is around 60 %, while it is lowest in the USA with about 45 %.

As regards the degree of independence with respect to borrowing and budget deficit levels, the only example of permanent federal controls over state borrowing or debt is found in Australia. In the USA, the state constitutions impose their own constraints, usually in some form of balanced budget rules. The German *Länder* are constitutionally bound to the golden rule of limiting borrowing to the financing of investment expenditure; under exceptional circumstances, this rule can be deviated from. In

Ranking of fiscal autonomy

	Revenue	Expenditure	Independence	Total
Switzerland	1	1	1/2/3	1
USA	2	5	1/2/3	3
Canada	3	3	1/2/3	2
Germany	5	2	4	4
Australia	4	4	5	5

addition the government can temporarily limit recourse of the *Länder* to loans. Deficit spending and borrowing by Canadian provinces and Swiss cantons are not subject to any legal constraints.

On the basis of these three criteria, a rather clear ranking of fiscal autonomy emerges. In Switzerland the regions have the highest degree of fiscal autonomy; they are followed closely by Canadian provinces. On the other hand, Australian states have very little fiscal autonomy. In Germany and the USA, the states have a similar degree of fiscal autonomy with perhaps a somewhat greater autonomy in the USA: whereas in the USA states have limited spending responsibilities but considerable revenue autonomy, the German situation is the other way around, i.e. the *Länder* have a considerable degree of spending responsibilities but very limited taxation powers.

Interregional equalization

The MacDougall report[64] provides two measures of interregional income equalization through federal public finances. On average, Australia is clearly leading with a reduction of interregional income disparities due to public finance of more than 50 %, followed by Germany with about 35 %, Canada with about 30 %, the USA with about 25 % and Switzerland with a somewhat incomplete figure of 15 %.

63 Commission of the European Communities (1977).

64 Commission of the European Communities (1977, p. 30).

half to two thirds of the short-term loss in primary income, due to a shock, may be offset through central public finance. More recently, it has been estimated for the United States that about 35 % of the loss is compensated for through the federal budget.[65]

In addition, a typical characteristic of existing federations is the trade-off between fiscal autonomy and interregional transfers through central public finance. This is illustrated in Table 6.4, which ranks existing federations according to the two criteria. The ranking of Australia, Germany, Canada, the United States and Switzerland in terms of the overall budgetary autonomy of States/regions is clearly inversely related to the degree with which interregional transfers reduce income differences and thus exert a dampening effect on the adverse consequences of economic shocks.

Table 6.4

Fiscal autonomy and fiscal equalization in existing federations

	Ranking of fiscal autonomy	Ranking of interregional income equalization
Switzerland	1	5
USA	3	4
Canada	2	3
Germany	4	2
Australia	5	1

Source: see Box 6.6.

6.7.2. Central public finance in EMU

According to any indicator, whether it is expenditure, revenue or the size of its interregional grants, the Community in its present state is characterized by a very high degree of national fiscal autonomy.

This is combined with a very low degree of interregional fiscal equalization. Concerning the latter, the Community provides some degree of cushioning of regional shocks through the Community's grant and loan instruments, in particular the structural Funds and balance-of-payments loans, but this is incomparably smaller than what can be observed in federal States. For the whole of the Community budget, Eichengreen (1990), for instance, estimates that not more than 1 % of an income loss in a member country would be compensated by lower taxes paid to the Community.

From the point of view of public finance, the Community is therefore a unique case compared to existing federations, combining high fiscal autonomy with low fiscal equalization. There are three arguments which plead in favour of some recalibration of the present role of central public finance in EMU.

The first argument arises from equity considerations, and concerns the impact of EMU on regional disparities.[66] This impact will result from the combined effect of the shocks with which national economies are faced and the adjustment capacities with which they are able to respond to these shocks. If this impact is negative, collective welfare considerations in EMU could lead to the decision to reduce it by enhancing the role of central public finance.

If the latter does not take place, regional disparities might become such that countries may have an incentive to withdraw from EMU. This does not only concern these countries, but may also weaken the credibility of EMU as a whole for those who stay in. Enhanced central public finance may therefore serve as an insurance for credibility of the system.

The third argument derives from the role of public finance itself in the provision of public goods. It says that in order to maintain the same level of public goods, a reduction in fiscal autonomy has to be compensated by an increase in the role of central public finance. In other words, there is a trade-off between the two. Van der Ploeg (1990), for instance, enumerates five reasons why the size of the public sector could be reduced in EMU:[67]

(i) the decrease in seigniorage revenue;

(ii) the possibility that national government spending becomes more and more like a European public good, whose supply will be sub-optimal;

(iii) the downward effect on government revenue from tax competition;

(iv) fiscal policies pursued to obtain a real exchange rate appreciation in order to boost real income will be tighter than in a cooperative situation due to spill-over effects on other EMU members;

(v) as markets become more integrated, a budgetary expansion is likely to be a locomotive policy, which will discourage a fiscal expansion in the face of common adverse supply shocks.

---

[65]   See Sachs and Sala-i-Martin (1989).

[66]   This issue is taken up in more detail in Chapter 9.
[67]   See also Chapter 5.

There are several ways in which the role of central public finance could be enhanced. The structural Funds in general support the adjustment capacity of regions. The negative consequences of shocks could be countered through Community shock-absorption mechanisms. Van Rompuy *et al.* (1990) emphasize the need for interregional distribution by the Community in support of vital public functions in the poorer regions, such as education, transportation and housing. This would therefore imply a widening of the eligibility criteria of the structural Funds. If horizontal transfers are established in the case of adverse shocks, they suggest linking it to close surveillance of economic performance, which introduces an element of conditionality in the shock absorption mechanism. Both Van der Ploeg (1990) and Wyplosz (1990) suggest interpersonal redistribution schemes to cope with the unemployment effects in depressed regions of adverse shocks. Van der Ploeg proposes to set up a budget-neutral European Federal Transfer Scheme (EFTS) which would distribute transfers on the basis of regional differences in unemployment. To avoid problems of moral hazard, the transfers should be conditional, for instance in the form of matching grants for training and schooling. Wyplosz goes further by proposing an explicit insurance scheme, also consisting of conditional matching grants. Participation should be compulsory to avoid the problem of 'adverse selection'.

Conclusion: a trade-off between fiscal autonomy and fiscal equalization

The adjustment to adverse shocks in EMU can to some extent be borne through labour market flexibility. Political considerations (in the case of regional migration) or welfare considerations (in the case of wage flexibility) may however put a certain limit on this adjustment instrument. The remaining adjustment will have to come from national or central public finance. Existing federations each have their own mixture between federal and sub-federal spending, but in any case there is a trade-off between fiscal autonomy and interregional fiscal equalization.

This line of argument leads to the conclusion that in order to minimize the costs of EMU, either the role of central public finance in EMU has to be strengthened or Member States/regions need to be left with a very high degree of fiscal autonomy. Subject to the required amount of fiscal discipline, the Community should strike a balance between the two. If the role of central public finance is enhanced, the structural Funds may improve the adjustment capacity of regions, while — possibly conditional — shock-absorption

mechanisms could provide insurance against the remaining burden of shocks.

Appendix 6.1: Do nominal exchange rates determine real exchange rates in the long run?

If nominal exchange rates are able to determine real exchange rates in the long run, this implies that their levels should move together in the long run. This is the hypothesis of so-called 'co-integration' of nominal and real exchange rates. For testing, the null hypothesis is usually that of no co-integration. A co-integration test between two variables is performed in two stages (see also Engle and Granger (1987)). In the first stage, it is tested whether the levels of the two variables are each non-stationary, i.e. that they have no tendency to revert to a given mean (this property is also called random walk or unit root). If they revert to given means, further testing makes no sense since they are then co-integrated by definition. Similarly, if one of the variables is non-stationary and the other is stationary, they are non-co-integrated, also by definition. When the variables are each non-stationary in levels but stationary in first differences, the second step of the test consists of testing whether the residual of the regression of the level of one of the two variables on a constant and the level of the other variable is itself non-stationary. If this hypothesis is rejected, the two variables are said to be co-integrated. Intuitively this is clear: if one variable is linearly related to another variable in the long run, the residual of that relationship should have a tendency to revert to zero.

The table overleaf presents the co-integration tests for the logarithms of quarterly nominal and real effective exchange rates with respect to Community partners over the period 1980 Q3 to 1989 Q4. From columns 1 and 2 it appears that for Belgium, the Netherlands and Portugal the hypothesis of non-stationarity has to be rejected for the real exchange rate but not for the nominal exchange rate, so that they are not co-integrated by definition. For the remaining countries, the co-integration tests in columns 3 and 4 never reject the hypothesis of no co-integration at a significance level of 5 %. The overall conclusion is therefore that since nominal exchange rates and real exchange rates are not co-integrated in the long run, the nominal exchange rate cannot *a fortiori* be considered as determining real exchange rates in the long run.

Co-integration tests for nominal and real effective exchange rates, 1980 Q3 - 1989 Q4

	Step 1: Non-stationarity?		Step 2: Co-integration?	
	Nominal exchange rate	Real exchange rate	Nominal on real exchange rate	Real on nominal exchange rate
Belgium/Luxembourg	2,076 yes	3,217** no		
Denmark	1,706 yes	0,925 yes	1,769 no	2,490 no
Germany	1,171 yes	0,933 yes	2,279 no	2,330 no
Greece	0,002 yes	2,597 yes	2,967 no	0,145 no
Spain	1,891 yes	1,545 yes	0,450 no	0,484 no
France	2,508 yes	0,654 yes	1,107 no	2,563 no
Ireland	2,059 yes	0,698 yes	0,406 no	2,401 no
Italy	2,424 yes	1,425 yes	2,227 no	2,175 no
Netherlands	1,074 yes	2,792** no		
Portugal	1,486 yes	4,173*** no		
United Kingdom	1,180 yes	1,433 yes	2,146 no	1,739 no

*,**,***: significance at 10%, 5% and 1%.

The values shown in the table are T-statistics of the coefficient b in the regression

$$\ln(u_t/u_{t-1}) = a + b \ln(u_{t-1}) + c_1\ln(u_{t-1}/u_{t-2}) + c_2\ln(u_{t-2}/u_{t-3}) + c_3\ln(u_{t-3}/u_{t-4}) + c_4\ln(u_{t-4}/u_{t-5}).$$

If e is the quarterly nominal effective exchange rate with respect to Community partners and r the corresponding real exchange rate, the variable u is defined per column as:

Column 1: u = e
Column 2: u = r
Column 3: u = residual from regression ln(r) = const + f ln(e).
Column 4: u = residual from regression ln(e) = const + g ln(r).

The tests are augmented Dickey-Fuller tests. The critical values for columns 1 and 2 are from Fuller (1976), and have the values 2,60 for a 10% significance level, 2,93 for 5% and 3,58 for 1% with 50 observations. The critical values for columns 3 and 4 are from Engle and Granger (1987) and have the values 3,17 for 5% and 3,71 for 1% with 100 observations. The regressions for columns 3 and 4 excluded a constant. The real exchange rate was calculated using unit labour costs in manufacturing.

Appendix 6.2: Real wage rigidity

On the basis of recent econometric estimates the OECD combined the short-run elasticity of nominal wages with respect to consumer prices and the elasticity of nominal wages with respect to unemployment to a measure of real wage rigidity. Those Member States for which estimates exist appear clustered together at high degrees of rigidity (very high for the United Kingdom, the Netherlands, Germany and France, lower for Denmark and Belgium, with Italy in between) far above the rigidity observed in the USA or Japan (see Graph 6.5). While quite intriguing at first glance, closer examination reveals a high degree of uncertainty about these measures.

The first element, the short-run elasticity of nominal wage growth with regard to inflation, indicates very different degrees of temporary absorption of price shocks by moderation in nominal wage claims between the Member States (see Table 6.5).

The estimates for single Member States vary widely due to different estimation periods, equation specifications, choice of variables, etc. According to the most recent estimates by the OECD (1989a), the immediate (i.e. first half-year) pass

through of inflation to nominal wages is highest for Germany and rather low for Belgium, Denmark, Spain and the United Kingdom. For Belgium the respite is only brief, however, due to full *ex-post* indexation (shown by the Snessens estimate based on annual data). In comparison with the OECD estimates of Coe (1985), the drop in Italian price elasticity of wages corresponds well with the reduced coverage of the 'scala mobile'; the reasons for the sharp increase in indexation in Germany are less obvious. But in Germany, and to a lesser extent in Belgium, Denmark and Spain, money wages are found to react accommodatingly to short-term productivity changes which provides for additional shock absorption.

The other major macroeconomic component of labour market flexibility is the impact of labour market tensions on wage claims (the slope of the short-term Phillips curve). Again estimates (see Table 6.6) are not robust to changes in specification, etc. The OECD (1989a) estimates imply that — *ceteris paribus* — increases in unemployment between 2,5% points (Italy) and 10% points (Denmark) would be required to slow money wage growth by one percentage point — as compared to 1,3 percentage points in the USA and 0,5 percentage points in Japan. In addition several estimates for the United Kingdom find unemployment hysteresis, i.e. the dampening effects of labour market slack on wage growth are diminishing over time.

Table 6.5

Short-term price elasticity of money wages

	OECD (1989a)	OECD[1]	Schultze (1985)	Others[2]
Belgium	0,25			1,31/0,91
Denmark	0,25			
Germany	0,75	0,44	0,53/0,61	
Spain	0,25			
France	0,50	0,47	0,65/0,79	
Italy	0,60	0,96	0,3/0,57	0,41
Netherlands	0,50	0,47		
United Kingdom	0,33	0,04/0,12		
For comparison:				
United States	0,14	0,22	0,60/0,66	
Japan	0,66	0,93		

Sources:
[1] Coe (1985).
[2] For Belgium: Sneessens and Drèze (1986); for Italy: Zenezini (1989).

Table 6.6

Elasticity of money wages with regard to unemployment

	OECD (1989a)	OECD[1]	Others[2]	Quest' 88	Quest' 90
Belgium	− 0,25		− 0,11/− 0,43		
Denmark	− 0,10				
Germany	− 0,11	− 0,25		− 0,12	− 0,10
Spain	− 0,20				
France	− 0,29	− 0,31		− 0,10	− 0,13
Italy	− 0,39	− 0,65		− 0,09	
Netherlands	− 0,27	− 0,44			
United Kingdom	− 0,15	− 0,17		− 0,09	− 0,01
For comparison:					
United States	− 0,61	− 0,33		− 0,30	− 0,19
Japan	− 1,87	− 3,31			

Sources:
[1] Coe (1985).
[2] For Belgium: Sneessens and Drèze (1986); for Quest: Bekx *et al.* (1989) and Commission services.

Appendix 6.3: Country asymmetries versus model asymmetries: the aggregate supply curve

The results in the table are calculated from non-linked simulations of an increase in real government expenditure. The slope of the aggregate supply curve is calculated by dividing the three-year effect on the GDP deflator by the three-year effect on real GDP, both expressed as percentage deviations from baseline values. Averages are arithmetic.

	Germany	France	Italy	United Kingdom	Average	Mean absolute deviation
Hermes	0,00	0,48	1,09	0,28	0,46	0,32
Quest	2,28	1,26	2,18	2,82	2,14	0,44
Interlink	0,73	0,38	0,30	1,50	0,73	0,39
Mimosa	0,90	0,06	0,52	0,69	0,54	0,25
Average	0,98	0,55	1,02	1,32	0,97	0,35
Mean absolute deviation	0,65	0,36	0,61	0,84	0,62	

Source: For Interlink: Richardson (1987); Quest and Hermes: Commission services; Mimosa: CEPII and OFCE (1990).

Appendix 6.4: GDP growth rates relative to Community average and trend real effective exchange rate changes

The differences in GDP growth rates are at annual rates; the trend real effective exchange rate (REER) is at annual rates and based on a trend regression (*, **, *** = significant at 10 %, 5 % or 1 %) with as dependent variable the REER with respect to Community countries using unit labour costs in manufacturing industry, a plus-sign denoting a depreciation.

Countries	GDP 1981-73	Trend REER 1981-73	GDP 1988-81	Trend REER 1988-81	GDP 1988-73	Trend REER 1988-73
Belgium/Luxembourg	0,1	1,4	− 0,5	0,3	− 0,2	2,5***
Denmark	− 0,7	2,4**	− 0,1	− 3,9**	− 0,4	0,6
Germany	0,0	1,0	− 0,4	− 2,9**	− 0,2	− 0,5
Greece	1,1	− 3,8***	− 0,7	2,6	0,3	− 3,0***
Spain	− 0,1	− 2,9***	0,6	1,2	0,2	− 0,0
France	0,6	− 0,2	− 0,4	0,6	0,1	0,0
Ireland	2,4	0,6	− 0,2	3,8***	1,2	1,2***
Italy	0,7	2,2***	0,1	− 0,7	0,4	0,3
Netherlands	0,1	2,0**	− 0,6	0,2	− 0,2	1,6***
Portugal	1,1	4,0*	0,0	1,5***	0,6	2,6***
United Kingdom	− 1,2	− 5,6**	0,7	5,4***	− 0,3	− 2,1***

Source: Commission services.

Appendix 6.5: Elasticities and equilibrium on the trade balance

If exports are a function of foreign real income and the real exchange rate, and if imports are a function of domestic real income and also the real exchange rate, the equilibrium condition for the trade balance is equal to (see Krugman (1989)):

$R = a.(X_y.Y^* − M_y.Y),$
where R = growth rate of the real exchange rate

X_y = elasticity of exports with respect to foreign real income

Y^* = growth rate of foreign real income

M_y = elasticity of imports with respect to domestic real income

Y = growth rate of domestic real income

a = constant with negative sign if the Marshall-Lerner condition holds.

If $X_y = M_y$ and the constant a satisfies the Marshall-Lerner condition, stronger domestic growth $(Y > Y^*)$ implies that R should increase (i.e. depreciate) at a constant rate to maintain equilibrium.

The Marshall-Lerner condition for the elasticities with respect to the real exchange rate is usually assumed to be valid. This is less so for the condition on elasticities with respect to real income. In a two-country world, the elasticity of imports with respect to domestic real income for one country is the same as the elasticity of exports of the other country with respect to foreign real income. In a world with more than two countries, such a condition is only globally valid, i.e. the weighted sum of income elasticities of imports should be equal to the weighted sum of foreign income elasticities of exports. Moreover, as observed by Krugman (1989), the ratio of the foreign income elasticity for a country's exports compared to the domestic income elasticity for its imports tends to be positively correlated with the ratio of long-term domestic growth compared to long-term foreign growth. In terms of the formula, this implies that X_y/M_y is proportional to Y/Y^*. This empirical regularity has considerable impli-cations for the role of the real exchange rate in equalizing the trade balance. It implies that part or all of a long-term growth differential is absorbed by differences in elasticities with respect to real income. This explains why countries may experience strong growth while at the same time appreciating in real terms, as happened to Japan over the last decades. As a consequence, the real exchange rate is deprived of its role as adjustment instrument.

Appendix 6.6: Wage flexibility in the Community compared to the German federation

This appendix presents regression results which compare the responsiveness of relative unit labour costs to relative unemployment rates in the Community to that inside the German federation. For the Community, estimates are pre-sented for the initial ERM members, the non-ERM members and the Community as a whole (see table below).

Time series cross-section regression results for relative unit labour costs on relative unemployment rates, 1975-89

$$ULC_{it} = a_i + b*[UR_{it} - UR]$$

Period		Germany	ERM	Non-ERM	EUR 12
1975-89[1]	b	− 0,394	− 1,767	1,017	− 0,148
		(0,108)	(0,537)	(0,831)	(0,438)
	sdev/mean	1,4%	9,1%	14,3%	11,9%
1979-89[1]	b	− 0,276	− 2,533	0,090	− 1,420
		(0,121)	(0,490)	(0,974)	(0,497)
	sdev/mean	1,2%	7,2%	10,2%	9,0%

$$ULC_{it} - ULC_{it-1} = a_i + b*[UR_{it} - UR_t]$$

Period		Germany	ERM	Non-ERM	EUR 12
1976-89[1]	b	− 0,020	− 1,110	− 0,823	− 0,947
		(0,078)	(0,274)	(0,548)	(0,286)
	sdev/mean	1,0%	4,2%	9,7%	6,7%
1980-89[1]	b	− 0,002	− 1,401	− 1,013	− 1,236
		(0,095)	(0,301)	(0,876)	(0,387)
	sdev/mean	1,0%	4,1%	10,1%	6,9%

[1]   For Germany, the period ends in 1987.

Legend:
i = Germany: 11 *Länder*; ERM: BLEU, D, DK, F, I, IRL, NL; Non-ERM: GR, E, P, UK.
ULC: Unit labour cost in manufacturing in country i in year t/average unit labour cost (Germany or EUR 12).
UR_{it}: Unemployment rate in country i in year t — average unemployment rate (Germany or EUR 12).
a_i: Country-specific constant, not reported.
b: Semi-elasticity of relative ULC with respect to relative unemployment (standard error between brackets)
sdev: Estimated standard error of the regression.
mean: Sample mean of the dependent variable.

The results are presented for two models, one with the level of the relative unit labour cost as dependent variable and another with the first difference of the relative unit labour cost. Each estimation was performed for two periods, one including the pre-EMS period and a second on the EMS period alone. The model in levels shows that the response of unit labour costs to differences in unemployment is significant both in Germany and the ERM, but that it has decreased in Germany and increased in the ERM during the EMS period. For the non-ERM countries the response has a positive sign and is not significant, although it has decreased in the EMS period. As a result, the responsiveness of the Community as a whole has become significant for the EMS period compared to the period before. The model in first differences provides the same conclusions concerning the direction of changes in coefficients, but gives non-significant coefficients in the cases of Germany and the non-ERM members, and significant coefficients for the Community as a whole.

These results suggest that: (i) wage flexibility is highest in the initial ERM countries, somewhat weaker in Germany and still low in the non-ERM countries; (ii) wage flexibility has improved in the EMS period for all Community countries, but has deteriorated inside Germany.

References

Abraham, F. (1989), 'Wage norms and Europe's single market', International Economics Research Paper 63, Centrum voor Economische Studiën, Katholieke Universiteit Leuven.

Artis, M., Bayoumi, T. (1989), 'Saving, investment, financial integration and the balance of payments', IMF Working Paper 89/102, International Monetary Fund, Washington DC, 14 December.

Baldwin, R. (1990), 'On the microeconomics of the European monetary union', in *European Economy* (1990).

Bayoumi, T. (1989), 'Saving-investment correlations: immobile capital, government policy or endogenous behaviour?', IMF Working Paper 89/66, International Monetary Fund, Washington DC, 22 August.

Bayoumi, T. A., and Rose, A.K. (1989), 'Domestic savings and intra-national capital flows', mimeo, December.

Begg, D. (1990), 'Alternative exchange rate regimes: the role of the exchange rate and the implications for wage-price adjustment', in *European Economy* — 'The economics of EMU', special issue, 1990.

Bekx, P., Bucher, A. Italianer, A. and Mors, M. (1989), 'The Quest model (version 1988)', *Economic Papers*, No 75, Commission of the European Communities, Directorate-General for Economic and Financial Affairs, March.

Bertola, G., (1988), 'Factor flexibility, uncertainty and exchange rate regimes', in De Ceccho, M., Giovannini, A. *A European Central Bank?*, Cambridge University Press, Cambridge, pp. 95-119.

Bhandari, J., Mayer, T. (1990), 'Saving-investment correlation in the EMS', mimeo, January.

Blanchard, O. J., Fischer, S. (1989), *Lectures on macroeconomics*, MIT Press, Cambridge Massachusetts/London.

Calmfors, L., Driffill, J. (1988), 'Centralization of wage bargaining', *Economic Policy* No 6, April, pp. 13-61.

CEPII and OFCE (1990), 'Mimosa, une modélisation de l'économie mondiale', *Observations et diagnostics économiques* No 30, Observatoire français des conjonctures économiques, Paris, January, pp. 137-197.

Coe, D. T. (1985), 'Nominal wages, the NAIRU and wage flexibility', *OECD Economic Studies* No 5, autumn, pp. 87-126.

Cohen, D., Wyplosz, C. (1989), 'The European monetary union: an agnostic evaluation', in Bryant, R. C., Currie, D.A., Frenkel, J.A., Masson, P.R., Portes, R. (eds), *Macroeconomic policies in an interdependent world*, International Monetary Fund, Washington DC, pp. 311-337.

Commission of the European Communities (1977), Report of the study group on the role of public finance in European integration, collection of studies, Economic and financial series Nos A13/B13, Commission of the European Communities, Brussels/Luxembourg, April.

Commission of the European Communities (1987), *Third periodic report on the social and economic situation and development of the regions of the Community*, Commission of the European Communities, Luxembourg.

Commission of the European Communities (1988), 'The economics of 1992', *European Economy* No 35, Commission of the European Communities, Luxembourg, March.

Commission of the European Communities (1989), Communication from the Commission concerning its action programme relating to the implementation of the Community Charter of basic social rights for workers, COM(89) 568 final, Brussels, 29 November.

Commission of the European Communities (1990), 'The impact of the internal market by industrial sector: the challenge for the Member States', *European Economy/Social Europe*, special issue, forthcoming.

Dornbusch, R. (1980), *Open economy macroeconomics*, Basic Books, New York.

Dornbusch, R. (1989), 'Credibility, debt and unemployment: Ireland's failed stabilization', *Economic Policy* No 8, pp. 173-209.

Eichengreen, B. (1990), 'One money for Europe? Lessons from the US currency union', *Economic Policy* No 10, April, pp. 117-187.

Engle, R. F., Granger, C.W.J. (1987), 'Co-integration and error-correction: representation, estimation and testing', *Econometrica* Vol. 55, No 2, March, pp. 251-276.

European Economy (1990) — 'The Economics of EMU', special issue.

Eurostat (1989), *Basic statistics of the Community*, Commission of the European Communities, Luxembourg.

Fair, R. C. (1988), 'Sources of economic fluctuations in the United States', *Quarterly Journal of Economics*, May, pp. 313-332.

Feldstein, M., Horioka, C. (1980), 'Domestic saving and international capital flows', *Economic Journal* No 90, June, pp. 314-329.

Feldstein, M., Bacchetta, P. (1989), 'National saving and international investment', National Bureau of Economic Research paper presented at conference on savings.

Frankel, J. A. (1989), 'Quantifying international capital mobility in the 1980s', NBER Working Paper No 2856, National Bureau of Economic Research, Cambridge, Massachusetts, February.

Frenkel, J. A., Razin, A. (1987), *Fiscal policies and the world economy*, MIT Press, Cambridge Massachusetts/London.

Frenkel, J. A., Goldstein, M., Masson, P. R. (1989), 'Simulating the effects of some simple coordinated versus uncoordinated policy rules', in Bryant, R. C., Currie, D.A., Frenkel, J.A., Masson, P.R., Portes, R. (eds) *Macroeconomic policies in an interdependent world*, International Monetary Fund, Washington DC, pp. 203-239.

Fuller, W. A. (1976), *Introduction to statistical time series*, John Wiley, New York.

Gandolfo, G. (1987), *International economics*, Springer Verlag, Berlin/Heidelberg.

Giavazzi, F., Giovannini, A. (1987), 'Exchange rates and prices in Europe', *Welwirtschaftliches Archiv*, 124, No. 4, pp. 592-604.

Greenaway, D., Milner, C. (1986), *The economics of intra-industry trade*, Basil Blackwell, Oxford/New York.

Horn, H., Persson, T. (1988), 'Exchange rate policy, wage formation and credibility', *European Economic Review*, 32, No 8, October, pp. 1621-1636.

Jacquemin, A., Sapir, A. (1988), 'International trade and integration of the European Community: An econometric analysis', *European Economic Review*, 32, No 7, September, pp. 1439-1449.

Krugman, P. (1989), 'Differences in income elasticities and trends in real exchange rates', *European Economic Review*, 33, pp. 1031-1054.

Lamfalussy, A. (1989), 'Macro-coordination of fiscal policies in an economic and monetary union in Europe', in *Report on economic and monetary union in the European Community*, Committee for the study of economic and monetary union, Commission of the European Communities, Luxembourg, pp. 91-125.

Marsden, D. (1989), 'Occupations: The influence of the unemployment situation', in Molle, W. T. M., van Mourik, A. (eds), *Wage differentials in the European Community*, Avebury/Gower, Aldershot, pp. 105-139.

Masson, P., Melitz, J. (1990),'Fiscal policy independence in a European monetary union', paper prepared for a conference on 'Exchange rate regimes and currency unions', Deutsche Bundesbank, 21 to 23 February.

Masson, P., Symansky, S., Haas, R., Dooley, M. (1988), 'Multimod — A multiregional econometric model', World economic and financial surveys, International Monetary Fund, Washington DC., April, pp. 50-104.

Masson P., Symansky, S., Meredity G. (1990), 'Multimod Mark II: a revised and extended model', Occasional Paper No 71, International Monetary Fund, Washington DC, July.

Molle, W. T. M., van Mourik, A. (1988), 'International migration of labour under conditions of economic integration: the case of Western Europe', *Journal of Common Market Studies* 26, pp. 369-394.

Mussa, M. (1986), 'Nominal exchange rate regimes and the behaviour of real exchange rates: evidence and implications', *Carnegie-Rochester Conference Series on Public Policy*, 25, pp. 117-224.

OECD (1989a), *Economies in transition*, OECD, Paris.

OECD (1989b), *National accounts*, Volume II, 1975-87, OECD, Department of Economics and Statistics, Paris.

OECD (1990), Italy, OECD economic surveys, Paris.

Oliveira-Martins, J., Plihon, D. (1990), 'Transferts inter nationaux d'épargne et intégration financière', *Economie et Statistique*, forthcoming.

Richardson, P. (1987), 'A review of the simulation properties of OECD's Interlink model', OECD Working Paper No 47, OECD, Economics and Statistics Department.

Sachs, J., Sala-i-Martin, X. (1989), 'Federal fiscal policy and optimum currency areas', mimeo, Harvard University.

Sargent, T. J. (1987), *Macroeconomic theory* (2nd edition), Academic Press, London.

Schultze, C. L. (1985), 'Real wages, real wage aspirations, and unemployment in Europe', in Lawrence, R. Z., Schultze, C. L. (eds), *Barriers to European growth*, The Brookings Institution, Washington DC, pp. 230-291.

Sneessens, H. R., Drèze, J. H. (1986), 'A discussion of Belgian unemployment', *Economica*, 53, pp. S89-S119.

Tootell, G. M. B. (1990), 'Central bank flexibility and the drawbacks to currency unification', *New England Economic Review*, Federal Reserve Bank of Boston, May/June, pp. 3-18.

Van der Ploeg, F. (1990), 'Macroeconomic policy coordination during the various phases of economic and monetary integration in Europe', in *European Economy* (1990).

Van Rompuy, P., Abraham, F., Heremans, D. (1990), 'Economic federalism and the EMU', in *European Economy* (1990).

Van Rompuy, V., Heylen, E. (1986), *Openbare financiën in de deelgebieden van federale landen* (Public finance in the regions of federal countries), Acco, Leuven.

Weber, A. A. (1990), 'Asymmetries and adjustment problems: some empirical evidence', in *European Economy* (1990).

Wyplosz, C. (1990), 'Monetary union and fiscal policy discipline', in *European Economy* (1990).

Zenezini, M. (1989), 'Wages and unemployment in Italy', *Labour* 3, No 2, pp. 57-99.

Chapter 7

External dimensions

The primary economic aim of EMU is to strengthen the integration of the Community and to improve its economic performance. However, due to the Community's weight EMU will also have far-reaching implications for the world economy.

Two types of effects are considered in this chapter. First, EMU will tend to redistribute responsibilities within the international monetary system in line with the relative weights of the main regions, increasing the Community's influence. Changes would mainly arise in the international role of different currencies (Section 7.1) and in the field of macroeconomic policy coordination (Section 7.2). Secondly, it could foster a more fundamental change of monetary regime, from a still asymmetric system to a multi-polar one (Section 7.3).

Most of the benefits and costs discussed in this chapter will only arise with the adoption of the ecu as the single European currency. Throughout this chapter, it will be assumed that Stage III of EMU implies a single currency.

The main conclusions are the following:

(i)   The ecu will emerge as a competitor to the dollar as an international currency. However, neither dramatic nor instant changes should be expected since for some functions (trade invoicing, asset holdings) the role of the dollar has already been significantly diminished, while for others (use in exchange markets), technical reasons favour a single standard, giving the dollar an initial advantage.

(ii)   Expansion of the ecu as a vehicle currency will yield some small microeconomic efficiency gains for the EC economy, by reducing transaction costs on the exchange market for trade with non-EC countries (up to 0,05 % of Community GDP), by reducing exchange rate risks due to the development of ecu invoicing (which might increase by about 10 % of EC trade), and also by giving to European banks enlarged opportunities to work in their own currency.

(iii) Regarding the official sector, EMU would allow a saving on the exchange reserves of Community Member States, amounting perhaps to USD 200 billion. It would also be beneficial to partner countries, especially in Eastern Europe, who could choose to peg their currency to the ecu. Additional gains would come from revenues of public seigniorage arising from foreign cash holdings of ecus, the importance of which (0,045 % of Community GDP annually, corresponding to about USD 35 billion

of foreign holding) is however likely to be much more modest than sometimes argued.

(iv)   As the European currency will become a vehicle for trade, an increase in the demand for ecu assets can also be expected in financial markets. This effect is likely to be of a relatively small size (about 5 % of total international markets) since international portfolios are already well diversified. This would increase the exposure of the European monetary policy to external shifts in preferences or in the amount of ecu borrowing by non-residents, but this exposure would remain more limited than it would be for Germany if the DM were to develop further as an international currency. Whether or not this would also lead to a temporary appreciation of the ecu cannot be assessed with certainty. However, the exchange rate policy of the Community should be ready to react to an exchange rate shock.

(v)   EMU will strengthen the Community as an economic policy pole within the world economy because adoption of a common monetary policy under the responsibility of EuroFed will enhance the Community's identity and weight in international policy cooperation. This will be felt in macroeconomic policy coordination within the G7. Monetary coordination at this level can be expected to become easier, provided the sharing of responsibilities for exchange rate policy between EuroFed and the Council ensures an efficient handling of this policy. To some extent, fiscal policy coordination could also improve, although there is a risk that coordination might be restricted to monetary policy.

(vi)   As the Community becomes a policy pole, spill-over effects of domestic policies and therefore the need for coordination at the global level increase. Since the reduction in the number of policy actors would also make it easier to reap coordination gains, EMU could act as an incentive to tighter policy coordination at the global level.

(vii) EMU could finally be a decisive building block for a more stable multi-polar monetary regime. Monetary cooperation among the G7 countries still falls short of an adequate monetary system. The establishment of such a system, that would remove all remaining asymmetries and provide the public good of monetary and exchange rate stability, would be a major benefit for all countries participating in world trade and finance.

7.1. Recasting of international currencies

Although the present monetary system is characterized by the predominant role of the US dollar, a trend towards a more symmetric multi-currency regime is already present.

The emergence of a genuine European currency would accelerate these changes. Absorbing the already internationalized European currencies, the ecu would become a major international currency alongside the dollar and the yen. However, both the magnitude and the effects of these changes have to be qualified:

(i) Assuming that in a multi-polar monetary regime the distribution of roles among the three major currencies would become roughly proportional to the economic weight of each region, many of the changes to be considered would be incremental since the dominance of the US dollar has already been significantly reduced, and since the United States would in any case remain a major player on the world economic scene. In addition, since the quality of a currency as a vehicle basically depends on its use by other agents, former dominant currencies tend to retain a large part of their role for a significant period of time. [1]

(ii) Being the issuer of an international currency is frequently considered as a privilege yielding significant economic benefits. However, a large part of these benefits do not hold. The issue of an official reserve currency does not provide additional room for manoeuvre in a world of open capital markets, and it does not yield any significant direct revenue either. The gains a country can draw from the issue of an international currency arise either from borrowing and trading in its own currency, which means lower transaction costs and the possibility of shifting part of the burden of exchange rate risks to the rest of the world, or from seigniorage revenues derived from private holding of its banknotes, which even for the United States are small. These benefits, however, come with a cost due to a relaxation of the control a country has over the use of its currency by third countries in trade and finance. As the experience of the United Kingdom and the United States has shown, this implies a greater exposure of monetary policy and the exchange rate to shocks unrelated to any domestic development. Since the exchange rate and interest rates of each international currency are set on the world market, demand and supply for assets denominated in this currency can change independently of the balance of payments of its issuer, and even independently of any macroeconomic developments among the issuers of the international currencies. [2]

In order to assess the extent of changes that could be brought about by the emergence of the ecu and their possible economic effects, the different kinds of shifts in the use of international currencies that might result from the completion of EMU will be considered in turn, assuming that no changes occur in the international monetary system itself. The effects to be considered are those corresponding to the standard functions of an international currency as unit of account, means of payment and store of value. Table 7.1 presents the major uses of international currencies with respect to these categories.

Table 7.1

Functions of international currencies

Function	Private sector	Official sector
Unit of account	Vehicle for trade invoicing and quotation of merchandise	Definition of parities, or target zones
Means of payment	Vehicle currency in foreign exchange markets	Intervention on exchange markets, balance of payments financing
Store of value	Assets and liabilities	Reserve holdings

Source: adapted from Kenen (1983).

While the above presentation draws clear distinctions between different functions of money, there are in practice close relationships between, for example, the use of a given currency as vehicle in foreign exchange markets and for trade invoicing. The sections below are therefore based on a slightly different categorization: Section 7.1.1 presents the use of the ecu as a vehicle for trade and payments in exchange markets; Section 7.1.2 discusses the role of the ecu as an official currency and Section 7.1.3 international seigniorage effects; finally, Section 7.1.4 is devoted to the portfolio and exchange rate effects of EMU.

7.1.1. The ecu as a vehicle currency

The functions of vehicle for trade invoicing, quotation of merchandise like oil and raw materials, and foreign exchange transactions are analytically distinct. [3] In each case, however, the same issues arise in the choice of a currency as a vehicle: for a currency to be chosen it has to be widely used, competitive in terms of transaction and hedging costs, and backed by a financial market which is substantially free of controls

[1] This point is underlined by Alogoskoufis and Portes, (1990).
[2] For example, an increase in the dollar debt of LDCs increases the supply of US dollars independently of US macroeconomic policy.
[3] For example, as mentioned by Krugman (1984), until 1974 smaller Persian Gulf nations used to require payment in sterling although the price of their oil was set in dollars.

and of sufficient breadth (i.e. large assortment of instruments) and depth (i.e. existence of well-developed secondary markets). Also the use of a currency as a unit of account determines to a large extent its use as a means of payment.[4]

The present situation

In spite of the move to flexible exchange rates, the US dollar remains by far the dominant vehicle currency for trade invoicing and, overwhelmingly, for foreign exchange transactions.

The first panel of Table 7.2 gives an aggregate picture of the role of different currencies in trade invoicing. As a rule, large industrialized exporters invoice their exports in their own currency, because this saves the cost of acquiring information about and techniques of foreign exchange.[5] It also

saves transaction and hedging costs if the buyer is indifferent to the currency denomination of its imports. Smaller exporters, however, generally invoice in a vehicle currency or in the currency of the importer. Hence, the picture of Table 7.2 partly reflects relative weights in world trade. However, about 15 % of the exports of European countries and as much as 60 % of Japanese exports are invoiced in dollars.[6] Therefore, the share of currencies in trade invoicing still differs significantly from trade shares (given in the second panel of Table 7.2). Only for Germany is the share of the currency in line with the trade share.

For the major industrial countries, the weight of the dollar is greater in imports, due to the fact that trade in oil and other primary commodities is mostly invoiced in this currency as is natural for goods whose prices are set on a world market. This implies also more variability since trade in fuels

---

[4] See, for example, Tavlas (1990)
[5] Figures in Table 7.2 should be considered as indicative only since statistical information regarding the use of different currencies is incomplete. The same applies to the other tables of this section.

[6] Exports of manufactures by the LDCs, which are also mostly invoiced in dollars, do not appear in Table 7.2. Therefore, the share of the US dollar is somewhat underestimated. According to Chevassus (1989), for a set of countries representing some 72 % of world exports, the dollar share was 55 % in 1980 and 44 % in 1986; for imports, shares were respectively 53 % and 49 %.

Table 7.2

Trade invoicing currencies of the six major industrialized countries

A. Currency breakdown of foreign trade invoicing[1]

(%)

	Dollar	Yen	Mark	FF, UKL, LIT	Total
Exports: 1980	44,6	4,6	25,5	25,3	100
1987	41,7	7,5	26,7	24,1	100
Imports: 1980	63,6	1,2	16,7	18,5	100
1987	49,5	2,9	18,3	22,9	100

B. Shares in total trade of the six countries

(%)

	USA	Japan	Germany	France, UK, Italy	Total
Exports: 1980	26,0	15,3	22,8	35,9	100
1987	21,6	19,9	25,3	33,2	100
Imports: 1980	26,1	15,3	20,4	38,2	100
1987	33,2	12,3	18,7	35,8	100

Sources: A. Calculated from Black (1989), B. Eurostat.
[1] Merchandise trade calculated on 95,5 % and 93,4 % respectively of exports in 1980 and 1987, and on 91,5 % of imports in 1980 and 1987, the rest being invoiced in other currencies.

fell from 23 % of world merchandise trade in 1980 to 11 % in 1987. Thus, the oil price fall could explain most of the decrease in the dollar share for import invoicing in the late 1980s. [7]

Graph 7.1 gives an aggregate picture of the role of the major currencies in foreign exchange markets. The first diagram gives the role of each currency in local trading, i.e. transactions involving the home currency on one side. The second concerns non-local trading, i.e. for market transactions between third currencies. Both types of transactions amount approximately to the same volume. The role of the dollar is emphasized in both cases, but overwhelmingly in the second. This predominance can be explained by lower transaction costs related to the size of the market, and almost independent from the variability of exchange rates. [8] In fact, transactions via the dollar between two other currencies are often less costly than a direct bilateral exchange. Since it is used as a vehicle currency in the interbank market for foreign exchange, most interbank transactions involve the dollar on one side. [9]

---

[7]   See Chevassus (1989).
[8]   See Boyd, Gielens, and Gros (1990).
[9]   See Black (1985) for a survey, and Alogoskoufis and Portes (1990).

Possible changes

For an assessment of the consequences of EMU, a distinction has to be made between those functions of the vehicle currency which can be shared (between the dollar, the ecu and possibly the yen) and those which are linked to the use of a standard and can only shift entirely from a currency to another.

(i) Regarding trade invoicing, effects of the first type can be expected, since the ecu would be the single money of the largest world exporter and of the biggest monetary and financial markets, with monetary policy oriented towards stability. But these changes would be incremental. Assuming as a benchmark that the share of the ecu in total trade invoicing of the six major industrial countries of Table 7.2 were to reach the level of the trade share of the Community as is presently the case for Germany (i.e. that the figures in the top and bottom panel of Table 7.2 were equalized), some 13 % of EC exports and 24 % of imports would shift from invoicing in US dollars to ecu invoicing. [10] These figures,

---

[10]   According to Tavlas (1990), 7,4 % of German exports were denominated in dollars in 1987, but the proportion was 12,3 % for France, 16,6 % for the UK and 23,8 % for Italy. The share of dollar denominated exports tends to be higher for smaller countries.

GRAPH 7.1 : **Currency breakdown of transactions in foreign exchange markets, 1989**

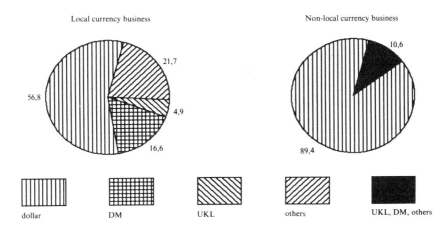

Local currency business refers to all exchange transactions involving the home currency. Non-local currency business refers to transactions among third currencies. In both cases, each transaction is only counted once. For example, the 89,4 % share of the dollar in the diagram on the right-hand side means that 89,4% of total transactions involve the dollar on one side. Note that the share of the DM is underestimated due to the non-participation of Germany in the survey, so that the German transactions are only captured to the extent that institutions in these countries conduct operations with parties participating in the survey.
Source : BIS, Survey of foreign exchange market activity, February 1990.

however, should be taken as an upper bound which would probably not be reached in the medium term due to conservatism in invoicing practices, and the likely persistence of dollar invoicing for oil and raw materials which represented about 15 % of EC imports in 1987.[11] A reasonable assumption is therefore that some 10 % of EC foreign trade (including intra-Community trade) could shift from dollar to ecu invoicing. Furthermore, the use of the ecu could also extend to trade between countries linked to the Community, especially those of EFTA and Eastern Europe.

(ii) Regarding quotation of oil and other raw materials, only a shift from one standard to another can be envisaged. This would happen only if the ecu were to replace the dollar as the predominant world currency. Such a hypothesis would be inherently speculative since the weight of the present EC in the world economy is similar to that of the United States of America.

[11] However, bilateral ecu contracts could be arranged for oil and raw material imports from African, Middle Eastern or East European countries.

(iii) Regarding the function of vehicle in the exchange market, EMU would eliminate intra-European transactions, the majority of which involve the dollar. It would also lead to direct dealing in exchange markets between the ecu and third currencies, instead of going through the dollar because of lower transaction costs. These changes, combined with the unification of the European money market, which will become the largest in the world, could make the ecu a more serious competitor to the dollar in exchange markets. However, hysteresis is strong in this field.[12]

[12] Krugman (1980) shows that even if fundamental trade and investment patterns do not exhibit a strong dominance of a particular country, economies of scale can lead to making all foreign exchange transactions with a single vehicle. A schematic example may help to understand the consequences: suppose currencies A, B and C have equal weight, but day-to-day operations in the interbank market are conducted with A as a vehicle. Then, every transaction involves A on one side. This obviously is only valid for the interbank market. But this market represents about three quarters of the total exchange rate market turnover.

Box 7.1: EMU and transaction costs in trade with third countries or in third currencies

The gains from eliminating transaction costs evaluated in Chapter 3 only relate for each country to intra-EC payments which involve a foreign Community currency. Similar gains arise in intra-EC transactions in third currencies (mainly the dollar) and in transactions with the rest of the world.

The gains brought by EMU in that respect can be best illustrated by an example. Consider the case of a Portuguese trader (i.e. exporter or importer) facing a given payment (receipt or expenditure). Four different cases arise.

(i)   The payment is denominated in escudo; with EMU, as the ecu replaces the escudo as the domestic currency, no change occurs from the point of view of the trader.

(ii) The payment is denominated in another Community currency, say UKL; then, if it is an intra-Community payment, transaction costs are eliminated as evaluated in Chapter 3; the same is true for a payment with third countries, but the corresponding volume is very small, so no evaluation is warranted.

(iii) The payment is denominated in a third currency, say the USD, and remains so. Then, EMU yields a saving because USD/ecu transaction costs are bound to be significantly lower than USD/escudo costs due to the breadth of the ecu market.

(iv) The payment is presently denominated in USD, but shifts to the ecu. This could happen because for most partners, except the USA, the choice of the ecu instead of the dollar would be neutral since both would be major vehicles.

Therefore, the saving would amount to the USD/escudo transaction cost. If the partner is not indifferent to the replacement of the USD by the ecu, which would be obviously the case for the USA, part of the gain would be offset by price decreases, possibly reducing the saving to the level of that of (iii).

The above classification can be used as a basis for a rough evaluation of transaction costs savings.

Assuming dollar invoicing remains unaffected, savings of type (iii) provide a lower bound of the EMU effects. According to Annex A, total transaction costs for current payments amount on average to about 0,4 % of the flow, with a range from 0,3 % to 0,8 %. Since dollar invoicing is much more frequent for smaller EC countries whose financial markets are less efficient, associated transaction costs can be supposed to be in the upper range of that bracket, say 0,6 %. Since USD/ecu transaction costs would be minimal, say 0,3 %, the saving would amount to (0,6 % − 0,3 %) times the share of the dollar in EC current transactions, which is about one fifth. With trade in goods and non-factor services amounting to about 26,5 % of EC GDP, this would give savings of the order of 0,03 % of EC GDP.

Assuming alternatively that one half of EC dollar trade, i.e. 10 % of Community trade, were to shift from dollar to ecu invoicing, this would eliminate transaction costs altogether for this fraction of trade. Total savings would then amount to 0,05 % of EC GDP.[13]

Thus, overall savings on transaction costs in trade with third countries or in third currencies should amount to 0,03 % to 0,05 % of Community GDP.

[13] Under the assumption that dollar invoicing presently concerns only trade with third countries. The figure would be slightly lower, due to double counting, for dollar trade within the EC.

Associated costs and benefits

What would be the consequences of changes of that nature? Three types of effects could be (i) a reduction in transaction costs; (ii) a reduction in short-term exchange-rate variability and risk; (iii) wider opportunities for Community banks.

(i) The emergence of the ecu would, in addition to eliminating intra-Community transaction costs, reduce the costs arising from transactions between European and non-European currencies. This would be a gain of microeconomic efficiency of the same nature as those analysed in Chapter 3. Rough calculations show however this gain would only amount to 0,03 % to 0,05 % of Community GDP (Box 7.1).

(ii) As a larger share of EC trade would be denominated in ecus instead of dollars, the exposure of the Community to short-term exchange rate variability would be reduced. Invoicing in ecus by producers or manufactures from third countries (like NICs and more generally LDCs) would eliminate the effects of dollar exchange rate variability, and the associated risk. This would be to the benefit of both partners since both would gain in stability (although obviously the bilateral exchange-rate risk would remain, and be supported by the non-European trader). Effects of the same kind would arise if the price of oil and other raw materials were denominated in ecus. The elimination of exchange rate risk would be an unqualified benefit for the EC, and also a benefit for the oil exporters whose trade is more oriented to the EC than to the dollar zone. In addition, the ecu price of oil would become more stable because it would not reflect ecu/dollar exchange-rate movements any more. Although in the medium to long term the currency denomination of prices does not affect the real price of oil, this could have lasting effects due to the short-run rigidity of nominal oil prices. However, such a hypothesis remains speculative.

(iii) European banks will benefit from the enlarged opportunities to work in their own currency (less risk exposures to hedge, better access to their lender of last resort) and to see an increase in the transaction balances held in ecus. The development of international ecu markets would provide to these banks a significant opportunity to compete in world financial markets.

Due to the increased role of the ecu in trade invoicing, an additional effect would be that economic agents engaged in foreign trade would increase their demand for ecus for transaction purposes. Although it is not known with precision, estimates suggest that the size of transaction balances may be about 20 % of all current account transactions.[14]

On this basis, an increase in the use of the ecu for trade invoicing of 10 % of the EC's current transactions would imply an additional demand of USD 60 billion of ecu-denominated assets (1988 figures), which would add to the portfolio effects discussed in 7.1.4.

7.1.2. EMU and the official monetary sector

EMU will substantially change the official monetary landscape. For Member States, the elimination of intra-Community exchange rates will reduce the need for reserve holdings. To third countries, EMU will offer the opportunity of an alternative anchor and the ecu will become a major reserve asset.

The rationale for holding reserves lies in the need to intervene on exchange markets in order to stabilize the exchange rate and to counter runs on the currency. A generally accepted assumption is that for a given exchange rate system the optimal amount of reserves depends on the volume of foreign exchange transactions. On this basis, it can be assumed that EMU would reduce Community reserve holdings by the same percentage as the share of intra-Community transactions in total foreign transactions. This would free about USD 230 billion in reserves[15] of a total of about USD 400 billion. An alternative hypothesis would be to assume for the Community the same ratio of total reserves/imports as in other industrial countries. Savings would then amount to USD 200 billion. One can therefore consider that savings on reserves could amount to approximately 4 % of GDP.

However, these savings should not be taken directly as economic benefits since reserves already yield revenues. They should be considered as capital that could be redirected to other uses by the Community or the Member States, which would give them more room for manoeuvre. Monetary authorities would also have to take care of undesirable exchange rate effects of a reduction of their dollar reserves. Indeed, they would probably have to retain these reserves in the initial period of EMU, since a tendency towards the appreciation of the ecu would already exist.

The above considerations only hold on a *ceteris paribus* basis. Further savings could arise from the move towards a tri-polar monetary system, as discussed in Section 7.3, since in such a system foreign exchange reserves could technically be replaced by swap agreements among the major monetary policy centres.[16]

---

[14] This figure is taken from Brender, Gaye and Kessler (1986), which use data for a sample of LDCs to estimate the size of transaction balances, since indebted LDCs presumably only hold hard currency balances for payment purposes.

[15] Including USD 85 billion of gold reserves, evaluated at market price.

[16] This only concerns the use of reserves as an instrument for exchange rate stabilization, not their disciplinary function in an asymmetric monetary system.

The ecu would also be used as an official currency by third countries. Since the collapse of the Bretton Woods system, a progressive diversification of currencies used internationally as the numeraire for exchange rate policies can be observed. Table 7.3 shows this decrease in the unit of account function of the dollar. However this fall is somewhat exaggerated because of the remaining role of the dollar in some of the basket peg practices and flexible arrangements. Nevertheless, a clear trend of diversification appears, exemplified by the EMS, the creation of baskets adapted to the specific interests of individual countries, and the DM peg option chosen by Austria.

Table 7.3

Shares of different types of exchange rate regimes in 1975, 1981 and 1989

(by number of countries, %)

	1975	1981	1989
I. Pegging			
Dollar peg	50,8	29,5	25,5
Sterling peg	7,8	0,7	—
French franc peg	10,2	10,1	9,2
Other currency peg	3,1	2,2	2,6
SDR peg	—	10,8	5,2
Own basket peg	10,2	16,5	20,3
II. Limited flexibility			
Snake/EMS	4,7	5,0	5,2
SDR peg with margins	—	—	2,6
Other more flexible	—	2,9	3,3
III. Other including float	13,2	22,3	26,1
(Number of countries)	(128)	(139)	(153)

Source: 'Exchange arrangements and exchange restrictions' IMF Annual Reports 1975, 1981, 1989.

The role of means of payment and store of value of international currencies can be assessed by the distribution of foreign exchange interventions, when available, and by the distribution of reserve stocks. The trend towards a tri-polar monetary world is confirmed by the currency breakdown of official reserves. Holdings of reserve assets denominated in a particular currency are related to transaction needs and to the ease of liquidating assets to make payments, as some empirical studies have shown.[17] The three main determinants of these needs are the kind of exchange rate arrange-

ments of a country, the share of its trade with a particular reserve-currency country and the currency denomination of its debt service.[18] Since the trade structure has an impact on the two other determinants, the importance of a reserve centre as a trading partner is the basic long-term determinant of the official use of a reserve currency.

Table 7.4 gives the evolution in currency composition of foreign exchange reserves, by group of countries.

For all countries combined, the share of reserves denominated in dollars has significantly declined. This fall has been matched by a rise in the shares held as DM and yen. For the industrial countries, the fall of the dollar share has been more pronounced since 1976. Paradoxically, countries participating in exchange rate cooperative arrangements not based on the dollar, like the EMS, tend to hold relatively higher shares of dollar reserves, since the dollar has been for long the main intervention currency. For developing countries, the lower share of the dollar, despite the importance of their dollar indebtness, is explained by the more exclusive transaction role of their reserves. Thus, the actual and optimal portfolios are more similar for developing countries.[19]

EMU can be expected to accelerate the trend towards diversification, since it will offer to third countries the opportunity to link their currency to that of a major economic pole whose monetary policy would be oriented towards stability.

A first, almost mechanical, effect would be the substitution by official sectors in some non-EC countries of European national currencies for the ecu to peg or to target the external value of their currencies, to intervene on exchange markets, and to hold foreign reserves. This would especially apply to some EFTA countries like Austria and the Nordic countries, but also to African or Mediterranean developing countries, some of which already link their currency to that of a Community Member State.

As the role of the ecu as a vehicle increases, EMU will attract more countries to link with the EC for commercial or financial reasons. This trend will be reinforced by the de-

---

17 Heller and Knight (1978) explain variations in the proportions of a country's foreign exchange reserves held as assets denominated in the international currencies.

18 Dooley, Lizondo and Mathieson (1989).

19 See Braga de Macedo, Goldstein and Meerschwan (1984). The difference in behaviour between LDCs and industrial countries is due to the different needs to pursue an active exchange rate policy (increasing with convertibility, with financial role of a currency, with managed float and the EMS), and to the financial surplus aspect most pronounced for the reserves of the industrialized countries. The result is for this group an excess of reserves denominated in dollars in comparison with the optimal portfolio structure.

Table 7.4

Currency composition of official reserves

(%)

Currency	1973	1976	1981	1986	1988
A. All countries					
US dollar	78,4	79,6	71,5	66,0	63,3
Major European currencies	13,2	10,4	17,3	20,0	22,1
(of which DM)	(5,5)	(7,0)	(12,8)	(14,9)	(16,2)
Yen	—	0,7	4,0	7,6	7,2
B. Industrial countries					
US dollar	87,3	86,9	78,7	68,4	67,4
Major European currencies	6,7	4,9	14,7	20,8	22,9
(of which DM)	(2,6)	(3,8)	(12,8)	(7,5)	(18,3)
Yen	—	0,4	3,7	8,2	6,4
C. Developing countries					
US dollar	55,2	72,7	64,1	62,1	53,9
Major European currencies	30,3	15,7	19,9	18,8	20,5
(of which DM)	(13,2)	(10,1)	(12,8)	(10,8)	(11,9)
Yen	0,2	1,1	4,4	6,8	9,0

Source: 'Exchange arrangements and exchange restrictions', IMF Annual Reports 1975, 1981, 1989.

Note: Major European currencies are DM, UKL, FF, HFL. Shares of national currencies in total identified official holdings of foreign exchange, at current exchange rates. Identified holdings amount to about 85 % of total holdings.

crease in transaction costs due to the development of an integrated money market in Europe and to the increase in the transaction needs for third countries to make payments in ecus. However, this does not necessarily imply a return to fixed exchange rates, since countries might choose more flexible arrangements. It means in any case the use of the ecu to target, to intervene and to accumulate reserves.

The importance of the opportunity EMU would provide to Eastern European countries must be underlined. The ecu would be a natural choice as an international vehicular currency for countries engaged in a redefinition of their external economic relations in the direction of stronger links with the Community. It would also be a natural choice as an anchor for exchange rate policy.[20] Without the EMU, an alternative choice would be the DM. However, the creation of a DM-zone in Eastern Europe might increase the degree of asymmetry among the currencies of the Community and place an excessive burden on German monetary policy.

7.1.3. Seigniorage effects

It is often argued that the current role of the US dollar as the major vehicle currency carries significant, if not exorbitant, privileges for the United States in the form of involuntary and interest-free lending by the rest of the world. This relates to what is usually called international seigniorage (implicit income received by the authorities from home currency assets held internationally but which bear no interest, or yield interest income below market rates) and is of the same nature as the domestic seigniorage discussed in Chapter 5.[21]

International seigniorage revenues may be derived by monetary authorities from three types of central bank liabilities: official reserves of foreign central banks, required deposits of commercial banks with the central bank, and cash held by private non-residents.

---

[20]   Bofinger (1990) discusses the exchange rate policy options of Eastern European countries and the possibility of using the ecu as an anchor.

[21]   We do not consider private seigniorage revenues such as those derived by banks from issuing traveller's cheques or demand deposits since they correspond to bank intermediation margins in open competitive markets.

Since official reserves are mainly held in the form of interest-bearing assets like Treasury bills, their holding cannot give rise to direct seigniorage revenues. Holdings of government securities by foreign central banks indirectly lower the interest rate on public debt because they reduce the supply of bonds to the public, but although theoretically correct, this argument is empirically unimportant. For example, the 'above-normal' holdings of dollars in foreign central bank reserves (assuming the 'normal share' of the dollar corresponded to the weight of the US in the total G7 GNP) was about USD 300 billion in 1988. This has to be compared to a total US federal debt outstanding of about USD 2 700 billion or, alternatively, to a total dollar portfolio of non-residents of about USD 2 500 billion. Hence, official holdings do not represent more than 12 % of either aggregate. For some years, purchases of US Treasury securities by foreign central banks have been much higher, but this relates to exchange rate interventions, not to seigniorage revenues.

Since neither Eurodollar deposits nor deposits by non-residents through the New York International Banking Facili-

ties (IBF) are subject to compulsory reserves, the second category of holdings is also empirically irrelevant for the US. Thus, only seigniorage revenues arising from cash holdings outside the territory have to be considered. Except for a few marginal cases of official use of a foreign currency (e.g. the dollar in Panama and Liberia), the use of cash by non-residents is a phenomenon mostly related to economic and political disorders such as the 'dollarization' of economies experiencing very high inflation, political turmoils, and part of illegal transactions in drugs, arms, etc. Anecdotal evidence indicates wide use of US dollars for hoarding and transaction purposes in Latin America, Eastern Europe and the Middle East.

Although estimates of both present dollar holdings outside the US and the potential shift towards ecus are extremely weak, computations based on reasonable assumptions suggest that the potential stock of international cash holdings of ecus should not exceed some USD 35 billion. The associated permanent revenue would then be limited to about 0,045 % of Community GDP (Box 7.2).

Box 7.2: Estimating potential shifts in international cash holdings and associated seigniorage revenues

Most international cash seigniorage accrues today from dollar holdings outside the US, since international holdings of Swiss francs, Deutschmarks, Pounds sterling and French francs are relatively minor.

According to surveys conducted by the US Federal Reserve, only some 15 % of the dollar stock outstanding is explained by standard domestic household behaviour. Research in progress at the US Federal Reserve indicates that holdings by the business sector, including estimated holdings for illegal and underground activities, do not explain more than 50 % of total dollar holdings, even when statistical problems are taken into account. Thus, holdings of dollars outside the US might represent as much as half of the outstanding total. Further evidence is provided by the fact that per capita cash outstanding of Canadian dollars

(which are not held outside Canada) is only about half of that of the US. Hence, a reasonable estimate of the stock of international dollar holdings is 50 % of the total outstanding in circulation, i.e. USD 100 billion in 1988.

Assessment of the share of these USD 100 billion that could shift to ecus should be based on the geographical breakdown of present dollar holdings, since Latin American holders would surely not react to the emergence of the ecu in the same way as Middle Eastern or Eastern European holders. Due to the lack of reliable information, crude methods have to be used. Since the weight of the EC in OECD GDP is around one-third, this share can be used as a benchmark. Thus, maximum potential shifts in currency use might lead to a once and for all stock adjustment of USD 35 billion (0,6 % of Community GDP) in favour of the ecu. Assuming a 7 % nominal interest rate, the associated annual seigniorage revenue in the steady state would (using the same definition as in Chapter 5) amount to a maximum of USD 2,5 billion, i.e. 0,045 % of Community GDP.

7.1.4. Portfolio adjustments and exchange rate effects

It has been argued above that EMU should lead to a shift of private transaction balances and official reserves from dollar to ecu holdings. Both effects would mean a portfolio adjustment in favour of the ecu or, equivalently, an upward

drift in the demand for ecu assets since they would arise independently of any change in expected returns.

This relates to the more general issue of the private portfolio adjustments that could occur as a consequence of EMU. Due to the segmentation and the relative thinness of European and Japanese financial markets, private financial portfolios are biased in favour of the US dollar. In the present context of rapid financial globalization and deregulation, the emergence of the ecu would offer to private asset holders a better alternative to the dollar than national European currencies, leading therefore also to an upward drift of the demand for ecu assets.

Such a drift could theoretically be accommodated either through price changes, i.e. exchange rate and interest rate changes, or through a parallel shift in supply. Empirically, price adjustments are likely to occur in the short term due to the inelasticity of supply, whereas in the long term the supply of ecu denominated assets can be expected to adjust, mainly through EC balance of payments deficits and development of ecu borrowing by the non-EC private sector. Whether EMU would have significant exchange rate effects in the medium term depends basically on the degree of substitutability between assets denominated in different currencies and on the relative speed of those demand and supply drifts.

A shift in the demand for ecus

Due to both methodological and statistical problems, no precise assessment can be given of the currency composition of private financial portfolios. Only rough figures can be obtained, which rest on a number of a priori assumptions. Table 7.5, which presents the result of an attempt to draw an overall picture, is based on assumptions detailed in the appendix to this Chapter. It is important to keep in mind that it aims at representing the currency composition of

gross financial wealth denominated in foreign currencies, not that of total financial wealth. Data on the currency denomination of assets are only available for international bonds and bank deposits (either at foreign banks or at home banks, but in foreign currencies). For 'other financial securities', i.e. stocks and bonds held by non-residents, the average currency composition of the three other categories has been used.

Two major conclusions emerge from these data. First, taking as a rough benchmark shares in world GNP, the financial role of the dollar still exceeds the economic weight of the US, the reverse being true for Europe and especially Japan. For Europe, the remaining gap is significant, but not as large as frequently believed if the share of the EC in OECD GDP is taken as a ceiling for the share of the ecu. This result, which is based on currency breakdown data covering more than two-thirds of the total portfolio, can be considered relatively robust. The second conclusion is more tentative: although no comparable global picture can be given for previous years due to a lack of data, a trend towards diversification is already apparent[22] in the data for international bonds and deposits at foreign banks: the share of the dollar has decreased to the benefit of European currencies and the yen. This result has however to be taken with caution because of the insufficient coverage of the 1981 data. Currency breakdown is only available for about 60% of the total portfolio. In so far as it can be relied upon, this

---

[22] As explained in the appendix, the figure for 1981 is based on incomplete data. However, partial figures for bonds also suggest a decline of the dollar.

Table 7.5

Size and currency composition of world financial wealth, 1988 and 1981

(billion US dollars and %)

	Billion USD	1988 of which in %:				Billion USD	1981 of which in %:			
		USD	ECU	Yen	Others		USD	ECU	Yen	Others
World reference portofolio	4 086	50,3	26,6	7,9	15,2	1 652	n.a.	n.a.	n.a.	n.a.
International bonds	1 086	43,3	25,1	12,2	19,4	194	52,6	20,2	6,9	20,3
Other financial securities	1 063	n.a.	n.a.	n.a.	n.a.	641	n.a.	n.a.	n.a.	n.a.
Deposits at foreign banks	964	56,5	28,7	3,6	11,2	572	71,7	16,4	1,6	10,3
Foreign currency deposits of residents	973	65,8	18,7	4,9	10,6	245	68,9	n.a.	n.a.	n.a.
Benchmark data										
OECD GNP (current prices)	14 084	34,41	33,79	20,20	11,58	7 804	34,39	39,30	13,62	12,66
Ratio: share in portfolio/share in GNP		1,59	0,71	0,34	1,2		1,94	0,44	0,21	1,01

Source: Evaluation by Commission services on the basis of BIS data. See appendix to this chapter.

result is illuminating because it shows that diversification has been under way for several years in spite of an important supply of dollar assets due to the US current account deficit.[23]

The creation of EMU would give rise to a specific effect: it would lead private agents to increase their demand for ecu-denominated assets in order to reweight their transaction balances and to achieve a more balanced distribution of their portfolios between the major currencies of the three major economic zones. It is often argued by financial market participants that no real alternative to the dollar exists at present since the size, liquidity and depth of European and Japanese markets are still very inferior to those of the US market. As this would no longer hold as EMU with a single currency triggers the unification of European markets, a move towards the ecu can be expected. The anti-inflationary stance of EuroFed can only reinforce this effect.

An opposite effect has nevertheless to be taken into account which stems from risk-aversion considerations. The behaviour of European and non-European residents towards the ecu would not be identical. For third-country holders outside the US, the emergence of the ecu will make European assets more attractive as compared to assets in the US. But for an Italian resident, for example, ecu assets will be at the same time substitutes for lira, DM and assets denominated in other European currencies. Hence, EMU will mechanically reduce this exposure to exchange rate risk. He might therefore be led to increase his demand for dollar or yen assets in order to keep the same balance as before between risk and yield. However, as exchange rate variability is already low inside the Community, this diversification effect would only partly offset the pressures towards higher demand for ecus.

On the basis of the above considerations, room for a specific EMU effect appears to be rather limited. Economic weight considerations lead to a shift in a range of 5 to 10 percentage points. Taking into account the trend that already exists and the European diversification effect, a shift of 5 percentage points in favour of the ecu appears to be a reasonable conjecture for the EMU effect.

Macroeconomic consequences

What would be the effects of such a shift? A necessary condition for *ex-ante* changes in relative asset supplies or demands to impact on the exchange rate is that investors do not regard assets denominated in different currencies as perfect substitutes. This hypothesis has been tested by a large number of researchers under the assumption of rational expectations, and it has been consistently rejected by the data.[24] Therefore, it is legitimate to assume that a shift in the demand for ecu assets would impact on the exchange rate. However, there is no consensus on the degree of asset substitutability, i.e. on the magnitude of the associated exchange rate. A number of studies find quantitatively small effects, while others suggest larger effects.[25] Therefore, the discussion below will remain qualitative.

In the long run, the required adjustment to the upward drift of the demand curve is bound to be a corresponding increase in the supply of ecu-denominated assets. This would be of the nature of a stock adjustment, resulting in a new equilibrium after a temporarily higher flow of ecu assets. In this new equilibrium, agents would hold a larger share of their portfolio in ecu-denominated assets, but neither the exchange rate nor the interest rate would be affected.[26] Real exchange rates would also be stable in the steady state, and real interest rates would be equalized across countries, so assets denominated in different currencies would yield the same rate of return.

The main consequence of this shift would therefore arise from a greater use of the ecu by non-European residents, which implies that external shifts in preferences for assets of different currency denomination or changes in the amount of ecu borrowing by non-Europeans would have a greater impact on the market for foreign exchange. In so far as monetary authorities care about the exchange rate, this also implies a greater exposure of monetary policy to external influences. As mentioned, this is the kind of exposure already experienced to a high degree first by the United Kingdom, and later by the United States, and it has been until recently a major reason for German reservations against the internationalization of the DM. However, this exposure would be much smaller for a major zone like the Community than for a medium-sized economy. Internationalization is

---

23 Barenco (1990), which presents data on the net dollar position of the non-US private sector, seems to reach an opposite conclusion. However, he focuses on net dollar positions while the present study focuses on gross portfolios. The increase in the gross dollar position of the non-US private sector, as computed from Table 7.5, amounts to USD 1 275 billion between 1981 and 1988, which estimated by Barenco is more than twice the increase of the net dollar position of the non-US private sector.

24 See Edison (1990), who surveys the recent literature, and the references therein. It should be noted that the assumption of perfect asset substitutability has not been tested in isolation, but rather jointly with the hypothesis that current market prices perfectly reflect future prices as suggested by rational expectations.

25 See e.g. Blundell-Wignall and Masson (1985), Brender, Gaye and Kessler (1986), Frankel (1982, 1986).

26 Except for effects resulting from the higher interest payments by the Community to the rest of the world or from hysteresis after a temporary appreciation. These are, however, second-order effects.

problematic when it gives to a currency a role out of pro-portion with the economic weight of the issuing country, as for the UK in the interwar period. In that respect, EMU would indeed be beneficial for Germany as it would reduce the risks of destabilizing shocks arising from the inter-nationalization of the DM. For an economic zone like the EC in a multi-polar world economy, this risk would be much reduced as there is no a priori reason to see the ecu taking the role of a monetary hegemon.[27]

Turning now to short- and medium-run effects, the basic issues are through which channels the increase in supply of ecu-denominated assets would arise, and whether and to what extent it could take place without exchange rate and interest rate changes.

Since changes in reserve holdings by the official sector would not offset the private portfolio effects, but rather add to the portfolio shift, the standard channel through which the increase in demand for ecus could be matched would be the accumulation of current account deficits for the Community as a whole. *Per se,* this should not be seen as negative since in this case, the deficit would not signal any weakening of the competitive position of the Community, but rather be the consequence of capital account developments. A temporary current deficit arising, for example, from a lasting increase in productive investment in the context of faster growth as a response to EMU, combined with the need for East German reconstruction, should therefore not be taken as risky but rather as a welcome development which would limit the need for exchange rate appreciation. Indeed, some adverse effects could appear if those deficits were to result from a real appreciation of the ecu, for this could have undesirable effects on the traded goods sector, whose competitiveness would be temporarily reduced.

Two important additional channels of supply of ecu assets are however also worth considering. These are capital ac-count deficits arising for example from a higher flow of Community direct investment abroad, and ecu borrowing by official and non-official agents from the rest of the world. Both would have exactly the same direct effect on the market for ecu assets as a current deficit of the Community. Both could also be relevant in the context of the 1990s since the capital needs for reconstructing Eastern European econom-ies as well as of developing countries could be financed either through Community direct investment or through ecu loans and bonds.

To the extent that the drift of the demand for ecu assets remained smooth, it could therefore probably be accommo-dated by parallel changes in supply of one of the above types, without significant exchange rate effects. This could happen if agents were willing to adjust progressively the structure of their portfolios. However, a more sudden shift cannot be ruled out because the creation of EMU and the establishment of a credible EuroFed would represent a major signal to the markets. In the present context of protracted US deficits, and given that the safe haven argument in favour of the dollar has weakened in recent years, a strong tendency towards appreciation of the ecu could appear. Recent monet-ary history indeed provides examples of large exchange rate swings.

From a policy viewpoint, an *ex-ante* ecu shock cannot be a priori unambiguously qualified as either a cost or a benefit. Monetary authorities would face a modified choice between appreciation of the currency and reduction in interest rates. Whether this would be an advantage or a loss depends on the baseline situation. However, if this shock were to lead to a persistent real exchange rate misalignment it should be considered as a cost. Therefore, the practical consequence that can be derived from this discussion is that since such shocks could already arise by anticipatory behaviour in private markets as soon as the EMU perspective was judged to be credible, provisions for common exchange rate policy in the transitional stages may be of some importance.

7.2. The Community's part in international cooperation

The developments envisaged so far are primarily direct consequences of the emergence of the ecu as a major inter-national currency. This section is devoted to another type of international effects of EMU, which would arise from the strengthening of the Community as an economic policy pole with a single monetary policy and a close coordination of fiscal policies.

These effects cannot be described as yielding direct economic benefits of the same nature as those analysed in the previous chapters. Gains could arise, however, from a change in the conditions of international economic cooperation with the United States and Japan. This means that the discussion of these gains has to be based on a prior assessment of the changes in the cooperation practices that could be brought about by EMU. This is the purpose of subsection 7.2.1 below, whereas subsection 7.2.2 discusses possible coordi-nation gains. Throughout this section, it is assumed that no major change in the international monetary regime occurs. More fundamental effects of EMU are discussed in Section 7.3.

---

[27] A 5 percentage-points increase in bank liabilities to non-residents de-nominated in home currency would imply for the EC a rise in the ratio of these liabilities to the monetary base from 59 % to 71 %. This would still be substantially lower than present ratios for the US (185 %) or Japan (85 %).

7.2.1. EMU and international cooperation

The G7 is presently the key institution for macroeconomic and especially exchange rate policy coordination, in its two related forms of summits of Heads of State and more economic policy-oriented meetings of finance ministers and central bank governors.[28] EMU would have a major impact on this policy forum since the unification of monetary and exchange rate policies of the EC would *de facto* reduce the number of players in this field from seven to four (US, Japan, EC—whatever its representation—and Canada). This could presumably facilitate exchanges of information among policy-makers and also, when necessary, make coordinated policy changes easier to negotiate and to enforce.

This characterization obviously goes with important qualifications. First, as fiscal policy would not be centralized at Community level, the fiscal side of policy coordination would spontaneously be less changed than the monetary side. Secondly, as the responsibility for exchange rate policy would be shared between the Council and EuroFed, the institutional setting of exchange rate policy coordination within the G7 would depend on the relative role of the two Community bodies.

(i) Fiscal policy would remain the responsibility of national governments. Hence, one should not expect a representative of the Community to replace the ministers of finance in G7 meetings.[29] Cooperation will probably have to deal with four monetary and seven fiscal authorities. This could reinforce the already existent tendency to restrict the formal coordination exercise to the monetary side, with fiscal policy lagging behind. Such an outcome would not be desirable, since an excessive emphasis on monetary coordination at the expense of fiscal coordination might be suboptimal, if not counterproductive.

However, as discussed in Chapter 5, EMU would also foster greater intra-EC coordination of fiscal policy with a view to external variables like the current account and the exchange rate, since a large part of the spill-overs across Member States would precisely be felt through these variables. One can therefore expect fiscal coordination procedures within the EMU to be tailored in order to ensure an adequate aggregate policy mix of the EC in the world economy.[30] In

this respect, EMU could well foster fiscal policy coordination within the G7.

(ii) Regarding the exchange rate policy, the responsibility for it would belong to the Community, but would be shared as in all major countries between the institution in charge of general economic policy, which would be responsible for the definition of the policy, and the central bank, which would be in charge of its management. The frontier between these two fields, however, is not clear-cut in the present context of managed floating among the major currencies, and, indeed, differs from one country to another.[31]

For international policy coordination at global level to become more efficient, it is of paramount importance that the definition of responsibilities ensures an efficient handling of this policy. The two major requirements for the Community in that respect are to be able to speak with one voice in exchange rate policy discussion at G7 level, and to ensure consistency between its exchange rate and monetary policy objectives. In what follows, it is assumed that both conditions are fulfilled.

Bearing those qualifications in mind, EMU could have strong effects on the practice of policy cooperation. Obviously, some coordination of EC positions within the G7 already exists. However, according to political scientists Community members are far from speaking with one single voice in G7 meetings.[32]

7.2.2. Global coordination gains from EMU

Economic policy coordination has been for several years a topic of extensive research, at both the theoretical and the empirical levels. The purpose of this section is to draw on this literature (actually, on the most basic models) to examine how EMU would affect the gains from coordination and their distribution. This issue should neither be neglected nor overestimated: empirical evaluations tend to show that potential welfare gains from coordination for the G7 countries as a whole should be in a range of 0,5 % to 1,5 % of their GDP.[33]

---

[28] A more detailed discussion of the impact of EMU on the major economic policy forums can be found in Alogoskoufis and Portes (1990).

[29] Representatives of the Council and the Commission might however participate in the meetings.

[30] The new convergence decision already includes a provision for fiscal coordination in the presence of external shocks. See Council of Ministers (1990).

[31] At one extreme, exchange rate policy definition is limited to the choice of a legal regime (i.e. fix versus floating). At the other end of the spectrum, the management of interventions by the central bank is done under specific instructions of the Treasury (although the central bank is free to decide whether or not to sterilize the intervention). Germany and the United States are approximately at the two ends of that spectrum.

[32] See Putnam and Baynes (1987), Funabashi (1988).

[33] Gains measured in terms of GDP by using a macroeconomic welfare function, with respect to a full information non-cooperative case. See, for a recent survey, Currie, Holtham and Hughes Hallett (1989).

EMU can be expected to bring three types of effects:

(i) As the spill-over effects of Community policies on the rest of the world would be larger than those of individual Member States, the need for, and the benefits of policy coordination would increase.

(ii) As the number of actors would be reduced, some of the usual obstacles to coordination would be alleviated.

(iii) A greater bargaining power for the EC, which would have a single voice, might also affect the distribution of gains between the Community and the rest of the world.

The economic consequences of these changes will be examined in turn.

(i) The basic rationale for explicit policy coordination is that coordination through the market is inefficient when one country's policy decisions significantly affect its neighbours. This is because by making economic policy decisions separately, governments do not take into account the welfare of their economic partners, and can therefore make suboptimal choices while reacting to shocks. Coordination allows governments to take full account of these externalities and to maximize the collective welfare of the participating countries.[34] Coordination gains therefore increase with the degree of cross-country spill-overs: they can be weighty for large interdependent economies.

As long as Community governments and central banks set their policy in a non-coordinated way, Europe appears as a collection of medium-sized policy centres facing two major poles, the US and Japan. Spill-over effects of individual European policy decisions on non-European countries are small, while those of the US on Europe are several times larger. This asymmetry, which arises from relative sizes and degrees of openness, implies that *ceteris paribus* the United States has presently less to gain than Europe in transatlantic coordination. Since coordination always involves risks, because of imperfect information, and costs, at least those which arise from domestic political considerations, the incentive for the US to engage in such an exercise is weak. To some extent, the United States can exploit this asymmetry by making its policy choices in a non-coordinated fashion without suffering much from a similar behaviour of European nations.[35]

The effect of EMU would be to aggregate 12 economies into a single major block whose degree of interdependence with the US, Japan and the rest of the world would be meaningful. Therefore, a lack of coordination among the three major policy centres would cause more welfare losses than at present, and the benefits from global or at least transatlantic coordination would be increased accordingly. This would especially affect the Community's partner countries since as coordination improves within the Community, some gains could be reaped for the Member States whilst the cost of a lack of global coordination would be increased for the US and Japan. Roughly speaking, as the sizes and degrees of openness of the EC and the US would become close to each other, the welfare costs of uncoordinated policies would become less unevenly distributed. This is illustrated in Graph 7.2 in Box 7.3 below.[36]

(ii) The above considerations relate to the gains from full coordination. However, it has been frequently argued that practical obstacles make full coordination very difficult to achieve. In practice, coordination is often restricted to information exchange and partial bargains over specific targets. Another, different impact of EMU would be to change the conditions of information exchange and partial coordination.

A first result, which directly derives from the previous considerations, is that as coordination gains would be larger and more evenly distributed, all partners could become more willing to cooperate in order to reap these benefits. Increased spill-overs might in particular make the United States more concious of the limits of independent policy-making, and this would be a benefit to its partners. This illustrates the more general point that EMU could not only result in absolute gains from coordination, but also in relative gains arising from a better distribution of policy changes among countries.

Moreover, according to recent research, information problems (regarding either the economic situation, the economic mechanisms or the policy preferences of the partner countries) are a key obstacle to coordination.[37] Disagree-

---

[34] In technical terms, the first outcome is labelled non-cooperative equilibrium and the second one cooperative equilibrium. It can be shown that coordination leads to a Pareto-superior outcome, i.e. that it can increase the welfare of all partners.

[35] Size and degree of openness are obviously not the only factors affecting coordination gains. Differences in size and behaviour, e.g. wage and price behaviour, also impact on the magnitude and the distribution of coordination gains. See Oudiz and Sachs (1984), Hughes Hallett (1986) and, for a recent survey, Currie, Holtham and Hughes Hallett (1989).

[36] This only holds in so far as the economies of the Member States are not characterized by strong asymmetries. Were the national economies of the Community very different in structure and behaviour, one could imagine that their aggregation in a single EMU would have mixed effects on the intensity of spill-overs on the US because opposite effects of national policies would offset each other. Here, we suppose that the economies of the Community are to a large extent symmetric (see Chapter 6 for a discussion), and we focus on the pure aggregation effect, leaving aside the issue of differences in behaviour between the US and Europe as a group.

[37] See, for example, Feldstein (1988), Frankel and Rockett (1988).

ments often arise more from differences in the perception of reality than from genuine distributional issues. Indeed, recent research has come to the conclusion that significant gains can be reaped through information exchange without entering a costly formal bargaining over the whole range of policy instruments. This is called partial coordination and is in fact to some degree permanent among policy-makers.

The reduction in the number of actors could make an important difference in that field as information problems grow rapidly with the number of players. In particular, EMU could force European countries to reveal their collective preferences more clearly. Hence, partial coordination through information exchange would allow to secure a larger part of the potential benefits, and monitoring of the compliance of more ambitious agreements would be facilitated. Bargaining over specific policy targets would also become

easier and the risks arising from free-rider behaviour or from unsustainability of the agreement would be less critical.

This would obviously not remove the most frequent objections to coordination but probably make it more feasible. Although no precise estimation of the associated gains can be confidently made, indications arising from coordination models suggest that this could be a significant improvement (see Box 7.3).[38] This gain would not especially accrue to the Community, but to all nations taking part in coordination.

---

[38] One could object that coordination is already highly centralized with the G7 being the key institution and in some instances the US, Japan and Germany acting as a *de facto* G3. However, this structure also carries costs since participating authorities cannot confidently act on behalf of non-participating ones, and because information problems arise regarding the policies of the smaller countries.

Box 7.3: EMU and macroeconomic policy coordination

The purpose of this box is to illustrate how the aggregation of Community countries within a single EMU would affect the size and distribution of coordination gains. For the sake of simplicity, it is assumed that prior to EMU, there is no intra-EC coordination whatsoever (but possibly global coordination, in which all EC countries take part), and that after EMU there is only one macroeconomic policy for the Community as a whole, with a single Community authority taking part in global coordination. This policy is supposed to be optimal in the sense that no EC country suffers welfare losses arising from intra-Community coordination failures. As developed in the main text, these are obviously simplifying assumptions whose only purpose is to help to clarify the mechanisms at work.

Only two 'countries' are therefore considered, which are represented in Graph 7.2: the Community and the US, which are assumed to be similar in size, structure, degree of openness and policy preferences. The criteria for evaluating coordination gains are the welfare losses of both partners, which measure the deviation from target of a few macroeconomic variables.

1. Full versus partial coordination

These gains can be discussed by using the following benchmark cases:[39]

(i) Degree zero (not depicted on Graph 7.2): small country case. Each government acts independently taking all its external environment as given.

(ii) Degree one (D1 on Graph 7.2): non-cooperative isolationist policies. Each government knows the structure of its neighbours' economies, but not the preferences of the other governments. It can take cross-country spill-overs into account, but not the policy reactions of its partners.

(iii) Degree two (D2): optimal non-cooperative policies with full information exchange. By exchanging information, governments can know the reactions of their partners to their own policies; however, they do not engage in bargaining as each country maximizes its welfare separately, taking as given the actions of the other countries.

(iv) Degree three (D3): full coordination. Governments jointly set their instruments in order to maximize welfare. The locus of possible outcomes is represented by the FF curve. The choice of an optimal point on this curve depends on the weights attached to the respective welfares of Europe and the US, which in turn depend on their respective bargaining powers.

Like that of Oudiz and Sachs (1984), most empirical studies focus on a full coordination involving a bargain over the whole range of target variables (real GDP, inflation, the current account, etc.), i.e. on the FF schedule. For this purpose, national welfare losses (with respect to the objective function) are weighted with coefficients reflecting the weight of each country in the bargaining. No universally accepted procedure exists to estimate these weights, which are often chosen by judgment.

However, evaluations with several models tend to show that larger gains arise while moving from degree zero to degree one and from degree one to degree two. In comparison, gains provided by the move from degree two to degree three are much smaller.[40] This is because important gains can be achieved

---

[39] This classification is adapted from Brandsma and Pijpers (1985).

[40] See Brandsma and Pijpers (1985), Hughes Hallett (1986), Brandsma and Hughes Hallett (1989).

through better information. Full coordination remains a theoretical case, which is only approximated in rare circumstances (the Bonn Summit of 1978 being the classic example). Coordination in the real world is a mix of incomplete information exchange and partial bargaining, which can be represented by a point like A between D1 and D2.

2. The EMU effect

Prior to EMU, the small size of spill-over effects of individual European policies leads the welfare cost of uncoordinated policies to be larger for Europe than for the US. This is represented by D1. As EMU brings more symmetry, the non-cooperative solution moves to D1 (EMU), a gain for the EC and a loss for the US. The same holds for the Nash full-information case D2, but associated gains or losses are smaller.[41]

As to full coordination, the same outcome can be achieved with or without EMU,[42] but the distribution of gains depends on the bargaining weights of the players. Here it is assumed that the weight of the EC also increases with EMU (illustrated by the move from D3 to D3 (EMU)). However this appears to be a relatively minor issue: since large gains can be achieved through information exchange and without formal bargaining, it immediately follows that the distribution of weights is not crucial. The range of possible outcomes is also bounded because no country would agree to engage in coordination without the perspective of a gain as compared to the full-information case D2.

Important gains can reasonably be supposed to be achieved through information exchange. As the number of actors is reduced, the outcome from real coordination comes closer to the full information case, as illustrated by A (EMU). As the US becomes more willing to engage in coordination, some further effects can also arise. What the figure illustrates is that depending on the relative magnitude of spill-over effects and information problems, the global effect of EMU, which is unambiguously a gain for Europe, can be either harmful or beneficial to the US.

GRAPH 7.2: **EMU and global coordination: an illustration**

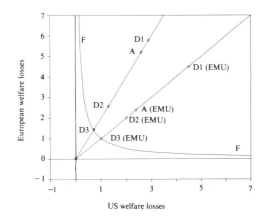

US welfare losses

---

[41]   This illustrates a well-known result of game theory: that a coalition among a subgroup of players is welfare-reducing for the other players. See Van der Ploeg (1990).
[42]   This neglects the fact that EMU would reduce the number of available policy instruments.

A caveat should however be added: partial coordination frequently tends to focus on specific targets or instruments; in some instances this can be very suboptimal. A further focusing of international coordination on exchange rate and monetary matters would not depart from recent trends, but could well be counterproductive if fiscal policies were left entirely uhcoordinated. For example, exchange rate targeting with monetary policy being used as the corresponding instrument can become counterproductive if exchange rate targets are inconsistent with fiscal policies.[43] Although this is clearly a risk, EMU could facilitate fiscal coordination if intra-EC procedures are adequately tailored.

---

[43]   This point has been made by Feldstein (1988).

(iii) A third, purely distributional effect of EMU on policy coordination has to be discussed: would a more united expression of the Community change the distribution of the coordination gains between the US, Japan and Europe?

The issue might be of a less importance than appears at first sight. First, the distribution of coordination gains is influenced both by economic determinants like size international linkages, and behaviour, and by the bargaining power of the players. Formal models indicate that it is more linked to the former than to the latter (see Box 7.3). As to genuine bargaining issues, economic theory has little to say on the factors determining the weighting of each country's welfare in cooperative bargaining. On the one hand, one could argue that a united EC would represent all Member States (instead of four) and could discuss on an equal footing with the USA and Japan, and hence that its weight would be increased. On the other hand, four EC countries participate in G7 meetings, and although there is no formal voting, scholars of coordination indicate this has given them some weight in discussions.[44] There is no strong evidence that Europe's interests are presently underweighted in coordination when European governments agree on the policy prescription.

Summing up, the most important effects of EMU would be to increase the need for global coordination, especially from the point of view of partner countries, and to make the corresponding gains easier to achieve. As both would be beneficial to the Community, this could be a significant gain, but the net effect for the rest of the world could be also positive.

7.3. Towards a better international monetary regime

A common feature of the changes discussed in the previous sections is that EMU would bring more symmetry in international economic and monetary relations. This holds both for the international role of currencies and for policy coordination. Such an evolution would not be a consequence of EMU *per se*, but EMU would amplify a trend arising from changes in the world economy towards a more balanced distribution of wealth and power. As these changes take place, genuine systemic effects can be expected to appear, as opposed to the mere incremental effects within a given system which have been analysed so far. The present section is devoted to these systemic issues, i.e. to the international regime that could emerge at the beginning of the next century.

Although most of this chapter has to rely on a priori assumptions, economic analysis can provide assessments of the possible impacts of EMU. This is not true for systemic effects since (i) there is no experience of genuine multi-polar monetary regimes, (ii) opportunities for the creation of a more balanced and more stable world economic system will appear, but there are also risks of instability; and (iii) the final outcome will depend on the ability of the major economic powers to profit from these opportunities. Hence the discussion in this field necessarily has a somewhat speculative character.

Therefore, only general issues will be debated here, since it would not be relevant for the present study to enter specific discussions regarding the design of the future international regime. For similar reasons, the discussion will also remain entirely qualitative. Section 7.3.1 briefly presents the limits of the present monetary regime, while Section 7.3.2 discusses whether a more symmetric regime is indeed desirable.

7.3.1. The limits of the present regime

The international monetary regime is presently of a hybrid nature. Since 1973, both floating and various degrees of managed floating have been experienced. The experience with floating rates is widely considered disappointing.[45] As already discussed in Chapter 2, floating rates have led to high exchange rate variability and, what is more, long-lasting real misalignments. Consequences have been both a degradation of the quality of price signals, and disruptive real effects on manufacturing and other traded goods sectors, with the associated welfare losses. By aggravating trade frictions, exchange rate misalignments have in some instances posed threats to the maintenance of an open multilateral trading system. The record of floating rates has not been better regarding policy discipline since pressure from the exchange markets to make policy adjustments has frequently been insufficient, delayed or even misleading. Finally, permanent asymmetries regarding the burden of adjustment have persisted in spite of the formally symmetric character of the regime because of the special international significance of the dollar exchange rate and of the US interest rate.

Since the Plaza-Louvre agreements of 1985-87, the regime has *de facto* evolved in the direction of a target zone system: central bank intervention on the exchange markets, target rates set by G7 ministers and (limited) domestic policy adjustments in the context of multilateral surveillance have been used with a view to influencing the evolution of exchange rates. However, cooperation remains extremely pragmatic and short of the more precisely defined systems proposed by various economists or officials. This *ad hoc* character has a number of disadvantages, since the permanence of the system rests on the persistence of a political consensus instead of being rooted in commonly agreed rules. As long as monetary cooperation is not based upon firmer grounds, it is bound to lack the robustness that is required to ensure credibility. The lack of rules also means lack of clarity as regards the responsibility for overall monetary stability (N-1 problem) and the distribution of adjustment across

[44]   See Putman and Bayne (1987), and Funabashi (1988).

[45]   See, for example, Williamson (1985), Krugman (1989a).

countries. Finally, excessive reliance on announcements of exchange rate targets and on monetary instruments (interventions, frequently sterilized, and domestic policy changes) does not do enough to foster fiscal policy changes.

Nevertheless, the cooperative experience of the last five years provides a basis upon which a more structured regime might be designed. A number of proposals have been made whose technical features are beyond the scope of the present study.[46] However, a distinctive effect of EMU would be to give a decisive boost to the search for a genuine multi-polar regime. By leading to the emergence of a unified European monetary pole, EMU would be an important building block for a tri-polar structure in which Japan, the USA and Europe would have equal weight and responsibility.

However, these considerations might be challenged on two grounds: first one can argue that a multi-polar monetary system is prone to instability; second and more generally, regional arrangements can be challenged because it is not clear whether they increase the aggregate welfare of the world.

7.3.2. Is a multi-polar system desirable?

It has been argued for long by some scholars that for a regime to be stable it has to be hegemonic.[47] Examination of the arguments for the hegemonic stability thesis leads to distinguish between three different aspects of a monetary system: genesis, operation and dynamic evolution.[48]

(i) Regarding genesis, history gives some support to the hegemony thesis since a single country has frequently played a leading role in the establishment of a new regime. However, this is of limited relevance for the present discussion, for no country is in the situation of taking over the role of hegemon. Moreover, the Community experience shows that hegemony is not a precondition for the design of a new system.

(ii) Regarding operation, the very purpose of a regime is to set rules which apply to all participating countries and which can be maintained without hegemony. The most forceful case for a hegemonic regime, made by

Kindelberger (1973) focuses on the lender-of-last-resort function in crisis situations. However, Eichengreen (1989) points out that for this function to be effective, the market power of the hegemon has to exceed by a considerable margin that of the other countries. Since economic weight is now more evenly distributed, the case for hegemony appears to be weakened. This does not mean that the monetary regime could not exhibit a *de facto* asymmetry in the conduct of monetary policy, as is presently the case within the EMS. Indeed, the leadership issue arises in any monetary regime, because the overall stance of monetary policy has to be set by a policy centre. However, this kind of *de facto* asymmetry within a formally symmetric regime, which does not determine a priori which country should be the anchor of the system, is very different from the structural asymmetry of for example the Bretton Woods system whose rules gave the leadership to a particular country independently of the quality of its policy. Moreover, it can be considered desirable that the operation of the system rewards performance by linking effective leadership to reputation.

(iii) As far as dynamic evolution is concerned, the built-in problem of a hegemonic system is precisely that it cannot evolve over time with economic fundamentals and can even accelerate the relative decline of the hegemon. Although the presence of a hegemon may be beneficial as long as it remains the anchor of the system, it is no longer so when it ceases to provide stability.

Concerns for stability have also been raised in a more narrow sense:[49] it has been argued that asymmetry is indeed desirable because if one economy is much larger and more closed than the others, it may act as a leader, while smaller countries devote their monetary policy to exchange rate targeting *vis-à-vis* the large country, and that this kind of arrangement might be more stable than a symmetric system. However, the present situation is already very far from this kind of asymmetry. Moreover, the advantages of such an asymmetric system can also be challenged on systemic grounds. First, a multi-polar system does not have to rely permanently on the policy of a single, specific country to provide the nominal anchor of the system. This should be considered a benefit since, if the international monetary responsibilities of a country are out of proportion with its economic capacity, a conflict of objectives is bound to arise. Second, it does not raise the kind of free-rider issues which are frequent in structurally asymmetric systems, where countries face the temptation to benefit from the public goods (e.g. stability,

---

[46] See e.g. Lebègue (1985), Williamson and Miller (1987), McKinnon (1988).

[47] The theory of hegemonic stability is rooted in the analysis by Kindelberger (1973) of the modern monetary systems. It has been developed by Keohane (1984) and other political scientists. For a recent discussion and empirical examination, see Eichengreen (1989).

[48] The following paragraphs draw on Eichengreen (1989) and Keohane (1984).

[49] This paragraph follows the discussion of Giavazzi and Giovannini (1989) by Alogoskoufis and Portes (1990).

liquidity) provided by the anchor country without participating in the required disciplines.

The hegemonic stability argument does not therefore appear very convincing in the present context. The optimality of a system consisting of three major monetary zones may however also be challenged on welfare grounds. Indeed, it is not self-evident whether this particular arrangement is superior to for example a genuine multilateral arrangement in which European countries would participate individually, or a system with a single world currency as proposed by some scholars.[50] While this issue may appear highly theoretical, it deserves a short discussion because it is sometimes argued that among all possible systems the worst is that which consists of a few blocks.

Although precise results only apply to specific policy fields (e.g. trade) and are model-dependent, the more general reasoning behind this argument is that a trade-off is involved in the choice of regional arrangements within the world economy: on the one hand, such arrangements could be welfare-improving for their members but on the other hand, they could be welfare-reducing for the rest of the world. This reasoning can be applied to the creation of a free-trade area,[51] but also to monetary arrangements. In both cases, it can be argued that the first-best solution would be a single zone, i.e. free trade or one money, and the second best an atomistic world. Therefore, an arrangement consisting of a few large blocks might be undesirable.

However, such arguments are based upon two conditions which do not hold. First, the world has to be homogeneous, i.e. there should be no natural trading or currency zone, which in practice is a highly questionable hypothesis. Second, the suboptimality of regional trade or exchange rate arrangements always rests on the assumption that the zone pursues non-cooperative policies *vis-à-vis* the rest of the world, through, for example, beggar-thy-neighbour tariffs or monetary policies. Once this assumption is relaxed, the suboptimality of a tri-polar arrangement does not arise anymore.[52] Indeed, one of the major purposes of a tri-polar system would be to foster cooperative behaviour among the three blocks.

The costs and benefits of a tri-polar monetary system have to be assessed with respect to realistic alternatives. A first alternative would be returning to the floating regime, with the associated efficiency and stability losses. A second could be the maintenance of the present *ad hoc* arrangements, whose robustness remains subject to the persistence of a political consensus. A third could be a US-Japanese duopoly, which is not a very desirable perspective from a European point of view. A fourth would be a tri-polar system with the Deutschmark being the third pole. As argued above, this could be harmful for Germany itself, because it would carry a monetary role out of proportion with its economic weight.

A tri-polar monetary regime offers therefore better perspectives. In so far as EMU would be a building block for such a regime, this could be a major benefit accruing not only to the Community, but to all countries participating in world trade and finance.

Appendix to Chapter 7: Estimating a reference portfolio for the evaluation of potential shifts in the private demand for ecu assets

Potential shifts in the demand for assets denominated in different currencies may concern a wide range of assets: mainly bonds denominated in home or foreign currency, shares, bank deposits. A first step is therefore to establish the size and the structure of the reference portfolio. This raises both methodological and statistical questions.

Since one is interested in assessing potential shifts in the currency composition of private wealth, the aim is to evaluate a gross world portfolio. This distinguishes the present approach from that of for example Barenco (1990), whose aim is to assess the net dollar position of the non-US private sector.

Theoretically any type of financial (and to a certain extent real) wealth of private agents may be subject to shifts in preferences for assets denominated in other currencies. In practice, simplifying hypotheses have to be made regarding both the holders of the portfolio and the nature of the assets. Table 7.5 is based on the following:

(i) Separability hypothesis: due to aversion towards risk and preferred habitat behaviour, the choice by private agents among assets denominated in different currencies can be split between two separate choices between, first, home and foreign currencies, and second, different foreign currencies. Thus, the reference portfolio is restricted for each country of residence to assets denominated in foreign currencies.

---

[50] See, for example, Cooper (1984). The McKinnon proposal also comes near to such an arrangement.

[51] This point is explicitly made by Krugman (1989b).

[52] This can be linked to the above discussion on coordination gains.

(ii) Liquidity hypothesis: only financial wealth is considered, as real wealth and notably direct investment is more subject to other determinants like real exchange-rate level, access to market, industrial strategy, etc. Hence, main categories in the reference portfolio are international bonds, national bonds and shares (other financial securities) held by non-residents, deposits at foreign banks (net of some interbank positions), and foreign currency deposits of residents.

Both hypotheses may be questioned: diversifiable wealth obviously encompasses both assets denominated in the home currency and part of non-financial wealth. In addition, there can be no specific supply for this kind of portfolio since securities are not primarily issued for non-residents only. However, this portfolio is valid as long as it is used for descriptive purposes. Alternative hypotheses are even more questionable. [53]

Table 7.5 presents an estimated world reference financial portfolio compounded of assets denominated in foreign currencies. As detailed below, the construction of this portfolio for 1988 is mainly based on data published by the BIS.

Aggregate portfolio

1. The point of departure is the recently published BIS estimate for the world external liabilities (USD 8 505 billion at the end of 1988), estimated through the addition of total private and public foreign liabilities of each country. [54]

2. Total deposits from residents denominated in foreign currencies as currently published by the BIS [55] have to be added (USD 798 billion). This gives the world international portfolio (USD 9 303 billion) which is a gross total including double counting due to some interbank positions. Therefore, interbank assets corresponding to such double counting (USD 3 115 billion) are eliminated, following the method of the BIS to estimate a total net of the international banking market. [56]

3. The next adjustment is to subtract from this portfolio the worldwide stock of direct investment (USD 1 077 billion at year-end 1987, [57] liability side, plus an estimated USD 150 billion corresponding to 1988 balance of payment flows [58] = USD 1 227 billion at year-end 1988).

4. Finally, world official reserves (USD 875 billion [59]) are subtracted since their purpose is quite different from private portfolios. This gives an estimate of the size of the world international financial portfolio (USD 4 086 billion at year-end 1988).

Decomposition by category of asset

5. This global amount can be split into four main categories, using mainly BIS statistics for three of them, the last one (other financial securities) being estimated by difference. However, only international bonds issued and corrected for redemptions and repurchases are known with precision (USD 1 086 billion). [60] Corrections for the other categories are as follows.

6. Deposits at foreign banks are obtained by addition of bank liabilities to the non-bank sector (USD 817 billion [61]) and liabilities resulting from placement of trustee funds channelled via banks in Switzerland (USD 146,5 billion [62]) since the placements were deducted as interbank assets by the reporting banks. This adjustment leads to an amount of USD 963,5 billion for the net deposits at foreign banks.

7. For the deposits of residents in foreign currencies, the BIS statistics are less exhaustive than for cross-border business; in particular, domestic interbank assets in foreign currency between different branches of the same banks are excluded. Identified non-bank sector deposits of residents [63]

---

[53] Frequently used alternatives are gross or net financial wealth of private agents. Gross wealth is obviously biased by dominant monetary habitat behaviour. Net wealth is a too restrictive definition of the diversifiable portfolio.

[54] Appendix Table 2, p. 36 in M. Delatry and J. Van 't dack (1989).

[55] *International Banking and Financial Developments Quarterly*, Table 3 d.

[56] *Guide to the BIS statistics on international banking*, Basle, February 1988, pp. 54-56. *International Banking and Financial Market Developments*, May 1989, p. 1.

[57] *US industrial outlook 1990*, Department of Commerce.

[58] *Balance of payments statistics*, Yearbook 1989, IMF.

[59] Delatry and Van 't dack, (1989).

[60] Table 7, *International Banking and Financial Market Developments*, May 1989.

[61] Table 3b *International Banking and Financial Market Developments*, May 1989, revised series.

[62] Swiss National Bank.

[63] Tables 3d, 5b and 7 of *International Banking and Financial Market Developments*. The total recorded deposits amount to USD 137.5 billion. The USD 190 billion figure includes an estimate of foreign currency deposits of US and Japanese residents, which are not recorded in BIS data.

only amount to USD 190 billion, while total loans to residents made in foreign currencies amount to USD 1 020 billion. This means that the banks themselves provide foreign currency loans with money taken from national markets. From these liabilities, following this methodology, only USD 47 billion (USD 3 115 − USD 3 068 billion) are considered as double counting in bank activities with residents. Although there is some risk that part of these liabilities could have a counterpart in other items already registered, Table 7.5 considers that these liabilities behave as non-bank deposits from the point of view of currency management of foreign banks. So, this item reaches USD 973 billion (USD 1 020 − USD 47).

8. Other financial securities, estimated by difference, amounted to USD 1 063 billion at the end of 1988.

Decomposition by currency

9. The currency breakdown is available for bonds. For deposits, BIS data exist but have to be taken with caution

since the coverage is incomplete: the breakdown for deposits of non-residents in domestic currencies is not published for the non-dollar currencies, and the breakdown for the deposits of banks in off-shore centres does not exist. This partial subset of data has to be extrapolated for the other (unidentified) financial assets, for which no statistics exist.

Table 7.6

Construction of the world reference portfolio

	(billion US dollars)	
	1988	1981
World external liabilities (= assets)	8 505	3 745
+ Deposits of residents in foreign currency	798	312
= World international portfolio	9 303	4 057
— Interbank assets	3 115	1 190
— Direct investment	1 227	700
— Official reserves	875	515
= World reference portfolio	4 086	1 652

References

Alogoskoufis, G., Portes, R. (1990), 'International costs and benefits from EMU', in *European Economy* (1990).

Bank for International Settlements (1990), 'Survey of foreign exchange market activity', Basle, February.

Barenco, B. (1990), 'The dollar position of the non-US private sector, portfolio effects, and the exchange rate of the dollar', OECD Working Paper No 76, February.

Black, S. (1985), 'International money and international monetary arrangements', in *Handbook of International Economics*, Volume II, edited by R.W. Jones and P.B. Kenen, Elsevier Science Publishers BV.

Black, S. (1989), 'Transaction costs and vehicle currencies', IMF Working Paper No 89/96, November.

Blundell-Wignall A., Masson, P. (1985), 'Exchange rate dynamics and intervention rules', *IMF Staff Papers*, Vol. 32, pp 132-159, March.

Bofinger, P. (1990) 'Economic reform in Eastern Europe: Implications for the ecu, the EMS, and European monetary union', paper for the Conference 'Vers L'Union Economique et Monétaire', organized by the Ministère de l'Economie, des Finances et du Budget, Paris, June.

Boyd, C., Gielens, G., Gros, D. (1990), 'Bid/ask spreads in the foreign exchange markets', unpublished.

Braga de Macedo, J., Goldstein, M. and Meerschwan (1984), 'International portfolio diversification', in *Exchange rate theory and practice*, edited by Bilson and Marston.

Brandsma, A., Hughes Hallett, A. (1989), 'The design of interdependent policies with incomplete information', *Economic Modelling*, July.

Brandsma, A., Pijpers, J. R. (1985), 'Coordinated strategies for economic cooperation between Europe and the United States', *Weltwirtschaftliches Archiv*, Heft 2.

Brender, A., Gaye P., Kessler, V. (1986), 'L'après-dollar', *Economica*, Paris.

Canzoneri, M., Gray, J. A. (1985), 'Monetary policy games and the consequences of non-cooperative behaviour', *International Economic Review*, Vol. 26, No 3, October.

Chevassus, E. (1989), 'Le choix de la monnaie de facturation', Ph.D. thesis, Université de Paris X Nanterre.

Cooper, R. (1984), 'A monetary system for the future', *Foreign Affairs,* autumn.

Council of Ministers (1990), 'Décision du Conseil relative à la réalisation d'une convergence progressive des politiques et des performances économiques pendant la première étape de l'Union économique et monétaire', in *European Economy,* Supplement A, No 3, March.

Currie, D., Holtham, G., Hughes Hallett, A. (1989), 'The theory and practice of international policy coordination: Does coordination pay?', in *Macroeconomic policies in an interdependent world*, CEPR/IMF and Brookings Institution.

Delatry, M., Van 't dack, J. (1989), 'The US external deficit and associated shifts in international portfolios', *BIS Economic Papers*, No 25, September.

Dooley, M., Lizondo, Mathieson, D.J. (1989), 'The currency composition of foreign exchange reserves', *IMF Staff Papers*, Vol. 36, No 2, June.

Edison, H. J. (1990), 'Foreign currency operations: an annotated bibliography', International Finance Discussion Paper, No 380, Board of Governors of the Federal Reserve System, May.

Eichengreen, B. (1989), 'Hegemonic stability theories of the international monetary system', in *Can nations agree? Issues in International Economic Cooperation*, edited by R. Cooper, B. Eichengreen, C. Randall, G. Holtham and R. Putnam, The Brookings Institution, Washington.

European Economy (1990) — 'The economics of EMU', special issue.

Feldstein, M. (1988), 'Distinguished lecture on economics in government: Thinking about international economic coordination', *Journal of Economic Perspectives*, Vol. 12, No 2, spring.

Frankel, J. (1982), 'In search of the exchange rate premium: a six currency test assuming mean variance optimization'. *Journal of International Money and Finance*, Vol. 1, pp. 255-274, December.

Frankel, J. (1986), 'The implications of mean-variance optimization for four questions in international macroeconomics'. *Journal of International Money and Finance*, Vol. 5, March.

Frankel, J. (1988), 'Obstacles to international macro-economic policy coordination', *Princeton Studies in International Finance*, University of Princeton.

Frankel, J., Rockett, K. (1988), 'International macro-economic policy coordination when policymakers do not agree on the true model', *American Economic Review*, Vol. 78, June.

Funabashi, Y. (1988), 'Managing the dollar: From the Plaza to the Lonne', Institute for International Economics, Washington.

Giavazzi F., Giovannini, A. (1989), 'Monetary policy interactions under managed exchange rates', *Economica* 56, pp. 199-213.

Heller and Knight (1978), 'Reserve-currency preferences of central banks', essay in *International Finance*, No 131, Princeton University.

Heller and Knight (1986), 'An analysis of the management of the currency composition of reserve assets'.

Hughes Hallet, A. (1986), 'Autonomy and the choice of policy in asymmetrically dependent economics', *Oxford Economic Papers*, Vol. 38.

Kenen, P. (1983), 'The role of the dollar as an international currency', The Group of Thirty, Occasional Papers 13, New York.

Keohane, R. O. (1984), *After hegemony*, Princeton University Press.

Kindelberger, Ch., (1973), *The world in depression, 1929-39,* University of California Press, Berkeley.

Kiyotaki, N., Wright, R. (1989), 'On money as a medium of exchange', *Journal of Political Economy*, Volume 97, No 4, August.

Krugman, P. (1980), 'Vehicle currencies and the structure of international exchange', *Journal of Money, Credit and Banking*, August.

Krugman, P. (1984), 'The international role of the dollar: theory and prospect', in J. F. O. Bilsen and R. C. Marston (editors), *Exchange rate theory and practice*, University of Chicago Press/NBER.

Krugman, P. (1989a), *Exchange rate instability*, The MIT Press.

Krugman, P. (1989b), 'Is bilateralism bad?', NBER Working Paper No 2972, May.

Lebègue, D. (1985), 'Pour une réforme du système monétaire international', *Economie Prospective Internationale*, No 24, fourth quarter 1985.

McKinnon, R. (1988), 'Monetary and exchange rate policies for international financial stability: a proposal', *Journal of Economic Perspectives*, Volume 2, No 1, winter 1988.

Oudiz, G., Sachs, J. (1984), 'Macroeconomic policy coordination among the industrial economies', Brookings Papers on economic activity, No 1.

Putnam, R., Bayne, N. (1987), *Hanging together: cooperation and conflict in the seven power summits*, Harvard University Press.

Tavlas, G.S. (1990), 'On the international use of currencies: the case of the Deutschmark', IMF Working Paper WP/90/3, January.

Van der Ploeg, F. (1990), 'Macroeconomic policy coordination during the various phases of economic and monetary integration in Europe', in *European Economy* (1990).

Williamson, J. (1985), *The exchange rate system*, Institute for International Economics, Washington.

Williamson, J., Miller, M. (1987), 'Targets and indicators: a blueprint for the international coordination of economic policy', Institute for International Economics, Washington.

Part C

The impact through time and space

Chapter 8

Transitional issues

This chapter discusses the economic mechanisms that operate during the transition towards EMU and thus determine the desirable speed of transition. The main consideration concerning the speed is the extent to which different costs and benefits arise already at different intermediate stages and whether these intermediate stages are stable. These two issues are discussed in the following two sections. The third section then deals with the issue of convergence, i.e. to what extent convergence has to be achieved before exchange rates are fixed and how to minimize the cost of reducing inflation.

The main findings of this chapter are:

(i)   Stage I yields already substantial benefits in terms of exchange rate and price stability and also implies the main cost of EMU, i.e. the loss of the exchange rate as an adjustment instrument.

(ii) However, the full benefits from the elimination of exchange transaction costs and from the greater role of the Community in the global monetary system arise only in the final stage of EMU. Since going beyond Stage I would not involve any costs this implies that beyond Stage I there are only benefits.

(iii) The preceding considerations imply that the transition should be fast. The main factor limiting the desirable speed for the transition might be the cost of too rapid or insufficient convergence.

(iv) Under certain circumstances the transitional Stages I and II may not be stable because of the potential for speculative attacks. It would therefore seem prudent to prepare for a rapid passage to Stage III so that this step could be taken without further delay if instability manifests itself.

(v)   The need for convergence in other areas, especially external current account and public deficits is more difficult to assess. A stable and credibly anti-inflationary EMU requires, however, that the explosive growth of public debt of some countries be stopped.

(vi) Convergence towards low inflation would be made easier through a credible exchange rate commitment, as shown by the experience with the EMS. The extreme form of an exchange rate commitment would be the adoption of the single currency. For some of the high inflation countries the cost of disinflation might therefore be substantially reduced and the transition period much shorter if they adhered to the single currency once the low inflation countries decide to take this step.

8.1. Benefits and costs by stage

The economic benefits and costs identified in Part B of this volume do not only arise in the final stage of full EMU. This section therefore discusses to what extent different costs and benefits arise already during the intermediate stages of the transition. In doing so it is convenient to discuss separately the different costs and benefits described in Chapters 3 to 7 of Part B.

The different stages that are compared here are Stages I and III of the Delors report since Stage II does not introduce significant economic effects. It is, however, difficult to assess the costs and benefits that arise in Stage I because Stage I is defined in the Delors report mainly by the elimination of capital controls which has already happened. However, for the purpose of this chapter it is assumed that Stage I comprises not only full capital mobility, but also infrequent realignments that are limited in size to the overlapping bands. The benchmark to which this Stage I is compared has to be assumed arbitrarily since it is impossible to say what would happen if capital controls are not liberalized. For the purpose of evaluating the benefits of Stage I the benchmark and starting point is therefore taken to be the years preceding the formation of the EMS.

The only officially proposed alternative to the stages advanced in the Delors report is that of the British Government, which in July 1990 proposed an alternative Stage II. This would be based on a revision of the definition of the ecu such that it would never be devalued in relation to any EMS currency, thus becoming a 'hard ecu'. Executive functions related to the 'hard ecu' would be entrusted to a European Monetary Fund. As in the case of the Stage II of the Delors report, this proposal is intended to be transitional, and its overall economic implications are hard to evaluate as distinct from a fully developed Stage I (see Chapter 2).

8.1.1. Price stability

The original narrow band ERM members have already achieved a considerable degree of convergence and price stability. This suggests that by the end of Stage I, when realignments would no longer be available to offset differences in inflation, the goal of price stability will have been realized to a large extent.

As underlined in Chapter 4 the benefits of price stability are conditional since they depend on the policy of EuroFed. The full benefits will therefore be available only if EuroFed has established its credibility for a consistent anti-inflationary policy. However, this can occur only in Stage III, when Eurofed obtains exclusive responsibility for the common monetary policy. Stage III would therefore yield additional benefits in terms of price stability, as well as in terms of minimizing the cost of price stability.

8.1.2. Efficiency gains

Chapter 3 identified four main sources of efficiency gains which arise at different stages of the transition and are therefore discussed separately.

Exchange rate variability

Exchange rate variability has already been reduced considerably by the EMS as shown in Chapter 3 above.[1] For example, among the three major EMS countries intra-ERM exchange rate variability has already been reduced to one quarter of its pre-EMS level. Taking the present exchange rate variability as a good approximation of Stage I this implies that the elimination of exchange variability is three quarters achieved in Stage I so that Stages II and III add only one quarter.

Moreover, it was argued in Chapter 3 that the marginal cost of exchange rate variability is an increasing function of the degree of variability. This implies that even more than three quarters of the benefits from reduced exchange rate variability should arise already in Stage I.

Although Stage I should reduce actual exchange rate variability it might not reduce uncertainty about exchange rate adjustments to the same extent. As argued in Chapter 3 the interest rate differential between the Dutch guilder and the Deutschmark shows that financial markets can perceive exchange rate uncertainty even if actual exchange rates do not move for quite some time. This residual uncertainty might persist in Stage II and even in the beginning of Stage III, when exchange rates are supposed to be irrevocably fixed. In this sense only, Stage III and in particular the introduction of a single currency would completely eliminate exchange rate uncertainty.

Transaction costs

Exchange rate related transaction costs, such as bid-ask spreads and other commissions, are not eliminated by fixing exchange rates. Indeed, no significant reduction of these

transaction costs can be expected in Stages I and II (and possibly Stage III as long as national currencies continue to exist) since they do not appear to depend strongly on exchange rate variability, but rather on the economy of scale properties of dominant international currencies. The savings in transaction costs would therefore arise only very late in the transition towards monetary union, probably only with the introduction of a single currency which constitutes the only certain way to eliminate all transaction costs.

Foreign exchange transactions could, conceivably, also be almost completely eliminated even before the introduction of a single currency by a system of 'par clearing', i.e. a system in which all foreign exchange transactions (among Community currencies) that go through financial intermediaries are executed at one central rate, without a bid-ask spread and without any allowance for foreign exchange commissions. However, such a system would be acceptable to financial intermediaries only if exchange rates are irrevocably fixed.

While transaction costs would therefore be eliminated only late in the transition towards monetary union, i.e. in Stage III, it is apparent that these costs should be significantly reduced through the internal market programme that will increase the efficiency of the financial sector.[2] Part of the savings in transaction costs should therefore arise already during the transition towards economic union.

Building on 1992 and dynamic effects

The gains from building on 1992 and the dynamic effects might arise in a more continuous way throughout the transition towards EMU.

The dynamic effects are caused in principle mainly by the complete integration of financial markets that comes from a single currency. However, as can be observed at present with the 1992 internal market programme, they could already be triggered by the anticipation that EMU will be completed soon. It is therefore probable that they will not arise only at the end of Stage III. Through the anticipation effect they might therefore come about in a continuous way, but only if there is no doubt that the transition would lead to full EMU, and notably within a fixed time horizon that is sufficiently short to be relevant to entrepreneurial decision-making.

[1]   See Chapter 3 for a discussion of the related concepts of variability and uncertainty.

[2]   The potential importance of the internal market programme in this area is demonstrated by the study on the cost of non-Europe, which shows that the cost of certain types of foreign exchange transactions should fall by as much as 10 to 15 % in some countries through the effect of greater competition in the banking industry (see Commission of the European Communities (1988) and Price Waterhouse (1988) for further details).

A credible commitment to the definitive EMU is therefore important to achieving dynamic gains at an early stage, and thus offsetting in some degree the transitional costs of adjustment. The example of 1992 in fact suggests that this offset may be more than complete. In its study on the economics of 1992 the Commission hypothesized a 'J curve' pattern in the evolution of the employment effect, with some net employment losses early in the process. In fact there has been continuous and substantial employment expansion in the Community since the late 1980s when the credibility of the 1992 programme was established.

8.1.3. Public finance effects

The main benefits of sounder public finances can be harvested only once the disinflation process has established its credibility because only at that point can interest payments on public debt diminish in those countries that at present still have higher than average inflation rates and where the interest rate on public debt therefore incorporates an additional risk premium. It is difficult to establish at what point this risk premium would be eliminated. Experience suggests that it declines gradually over time if inflation remains low. This suggests that to some extent the risk premium on public debt should decrease significantly already in the course of Stage I. The experience of the Netherlands shows, however, that even after a long period of stable exchange rates and low inflation a small risk premium can persist. This benefit would therefore be fully available only in Stage III.

The reduction in seigniorage revenue for some countries would also occur to a large extent already in Stage I since during that period inflation rates would already converge considerably and the increasing degree of financial market integration would lead to pressures to lower required reserves on commercial banks.

8.1.4. Adjusting without the nominal exchange rate

The nominal exchange rate is, of course, no longer an adjustment instrument once exchange rates are irrevocably fixed. As discussed in Chapters 2 and 6 this can be considered the main cost of a monetary union because an adjustment of the nominal exchange rate might at times constitute a more efficient response to a country-specific shock than an adjustment in wages and prices, which are often not very responsive to economic conditions in the short run. However, as argued in Begg (1990) this cost arises to a significant extent already in Stage I since at this point realignments should be infrequent and are limited in size to the overlapping bands.

Moreover, Begg (1990) also finds that the nature of the adjustment should change with the approach towards EMU. With exchange rates totally fixed the adjustment of wages and prices is considerably faster than in the EMS because economic agents realize that they have to react faster to a given shock if they cannot rely on the authorities to adjust the exchange rate.

It is a matter for political choice how far the mechanisms of the EC budget are developed in each stage, in order to compensate in some degree for the loss of the nominal exchange rate instrument. It is likely that such mechanisms would be more amply developed in Stage III, and in particular under the single currency, given the definitive loss of the national exchange rate and enhancement of the union's responsibilities.

8.1.5. External effects

As argued in more detail in Chapter 7 EMU will have an impact on the international monetary system mainly through the single currency which has the potential to become an international vehicle currency as important as the dollar. The seigniorage benefits and the portfolio shifts that can be expected from EMU should therefore arise only when the single currency has been introduced. In addition gains from a more effective role by the Community in international coordination are likely to be easier to harvest when the Community's representation is completely unified on the monetary side.

8.2. Stability in the transition

The previous section discussed what costs and benefits arise in the different stages of the transition towards EMU. However, this assumes that the intermediate stages are not inherently unstable. If they did prove to be unstable it would mean that these stages were harbouring serious problems (and therefore in some sense costs). Indeed, it has been argued that the transitional Stages I and II are likely to be inherently unstable.[3] It would follow from this view that EMU would be the only alternative to fluctuating exchange rates. This section therefore discusses the systemic stability of the transitional Stages I and II.

Stages I and II of the Delors plan are essentially a 'fixed but adjustable' exchange rate system without capital controls. The main danger for the stability of such a system comes

---

[3]   See Padoa-Schioppa (1987) and (1990).

from the absence of capital controls which creates the potential for (i) speculative attacks, and, (ii) currency substitution.

8.2.1. Speculative attacks

It has been argued that any fixed exchange rate system is inherently unstable because the authorities always have only limited reserves whereas speculators in the foreign exchange markets can demand to convert unlimited amounts of assets into foreign currency, thus forcing the authorities to abandon the fixed exchange rate commitment. If the authorities follow a policy of full (or more than full) accommodation, that is if they ratify any increase in prices by a devaluation or if they link the money supply to the exchange rate a potential for self-fulfilling attacks arises. Such a self-fulfilling attack might then arise if agents in financial markets have doubts about the exchange rate. If enough speculators demand foreign exchange for their assets they can exhaust the foreign exchange reserves thus forcing the authorities to abandon the fixed exchange rate and let the currency float. According to this line of argument the assumed policy of full (or more than full) accommodation then implies that the monetary authorities would increase the money supply after the speculative attack so that the floating exchange rate will be at a lower level than the previously fixed rate and the doubts of the speculators would have been confirmed.[4]

It is apparent that a policy of at least full accommodation is essential for this to happen. If the authorities react to the speculative attack by lowering the money supply, the floating exchange rate that results after the speculative attack would be above the pre-attack level. In this case the initial expectations of a devaluation would not be confirmed and speculators would lose money in participating in the attack. Since this would be anticipated in the markets no speculative attacks of this sort could therefore arise if the authorities are known not to accommodate them.

A potential for speculative attacks might also arise in the absence of an accommodating monetary policy stance if the authorities of a country with a very large public debt are perceived as not being willing to raise interest rates to defend their currency because this would have undesirable consequences for their public finances via higher interest payments.[5] The mere perception of this reluctance in financial markets might induce many speculators to exchange their domestic currency assets into foreign currency and this capi-

tal flight would require the domestic central bank to intervene to support its own currency. However, in doing so it would lose reserves and this loss of reserves might worsen the confidence crisis. Without capital controls the capital flight could then rapidly increase and become so large (if the loss of confidence is strong enough) that the amounts converted by speculators exceed the foreign exchange reserves the domestic authorities have at hand. The latter would then no longer be able to maintain the exchange rates at the intervention margin and the entire system might collapse.

It is important to note that this process can be set in motion only if a large proportion of the public debt needs to be refinanced at the time the doubts arise about the authorities' willingness to pay higher interest rates. It is apparent that if most of the public debt is in foreign currency the problem does not arise because in this case a devaluation does not lower the value of the debt. Nor can it arise if public debt has, on average, a long maturity because in this case turbulences in financial markets could affect only the interest rate on a small proportion of the total debt.

The Basle/Nyborg agreement which increases the availability of the 'very short-term facility' may be viewed as an attempt to lower the probability that a speculative attack could not be contained by increasing the amount central banks can mobilize immediately for the defence of their exchange rate.

A factor that could further reduce the danger of speculative attacks in the intermediate stages is the binding procedures for budgetary policy that may be established in Stage II. These may require or induce member governments to take corrective action well before their financial situation becomes unreasonable in the eyes of the markets. In this sense one could argue that constraints to prevent excessive debts/deficits might be more useful in the intermediate stages than in the final stage, for which they are foreseen in the Delors report.

The basis for the argument that a fixed exchange rate system is inherently unstable, because in the absence of capital controls there exists a potential for these self-fulfilling speculative attacks, is, however, that financial markets have some reason to doubt the commitment of the authorities to defend the exchange rates. If no such doubts exist a fixed exchange rate system might be stable even without capital controls as suggested by the Dutch experience.

The Dutch guilder has since 1983 been pegged much more closely to the German mark than required by the EMS rules, which allow for margins of ± 2,25%. Indeed it has never moved outside a corridor of about 1%, i.e. it has behaved

---

[4]   See Obstfeld (1988)
[5]   See Giavazzi and Pagano (1989).

as if the allowed margins were ± 0,5 %. Despite full capital mobility, continuing large public deficits, and a growing public debt that is now close to 80 % of GDP, there have never been any speculative attacks on the Dutch guilder/German mark exchange rate nor has the potential for such an attack been noted by the Dutch authorities.

The Dutch-German experience (as also the linkage of the Austrian schilling to the German mark outside the EMS) represents, of course, a special case since these two countries are even more highly integrated in terms of trade and financial flows than the members of the Community in general. The differences in their approaches to economic policy making are also smaller than among Community members in general. Moreover, the Dutch-German monetary union represents an 'asymmetric' union to a degree that would not be the case for the entire Community in Stages II and III. Other cases have been similarly 'asymmetric', for example the pegging of the Irish pound to that of the UK until the creation of the EMS, and currently the pegging of the Hong Kong dollar on that of the USA. Indeed some observers[6] have argued that historically symmetric monetary unions have never been stable. In many instances countries have preferred to reimpose capital controls or to devalue, rather than accept the discipline coming from a fixed exchange rate and open capital markets.

A related argument why the system of fixed exchange rates in Stages I and II might not be stable relates to the observation that most fixed exchange rate systems contain a country that provides effective leadership either because of its economic weight, or because of its superior price stability record.[7] Up to now Germany has provided this leadership because it had a superior price stability record and the mark was the only major international reserve currency in the system. However, as the price stability record of some other currencies gets close to that of the mark and as capital market liberalization gives the other currencies a potentially bigger international role the predominant position of the Bundesbank in the system may indeed be weakened.

Tighter voluntary cooperation in Stage I and the establishment of EuroFed in Stage II might overcome this potential leadership vacuum. However, it remains to be seen how well these arrangements can provide for an effective leadership, as opposed to the mere resolution of conflicts about the thrust of national monetary policies.

Recent events in Eastern Europe, in particular the unification of Germany, have further complicated the issue of the leadership within the EMS. It is not possible to say at this point what the overall effects of these developments will be, but the reaction of financial markets suggests that the outlook for price stability in Germany has become more uncertain. One indicator of this is that in the spring of 1990 France and other EMS countries were able to reduce their interest rate differentials vis-à-vis Germany to a historically very low level.

The danger of speculative attacks is generally assumed to arise mainly in the intermediate Stages I and II, when realignments are still possible. In Stage III exchange rates are supposed to be irrevocably fixed and there should therefore be no danger of a lack of credibility of the exchange rate commitment. However, it is not clear how this 'irrevocable' commitment never to change exchange rates can be made credible. Economic theory has little to say about this except that the market will implicitly judge the strength of the political will to maintain parities unchanged.

Adoption of a single currency is the only sure way to overcome this credibility issue. This can be illustrated with the experience of the monetary union between Belgium and Luxembourg. Although this union, at the rate of one Belgian franc to one Luxembourg franc, has existed now for over 50 years, the mere rumours that Luxembourg was considering not to follow Belgium during the last EMS realignments were enough to induce financial markets to differentiate between these two currencies. At present forward cover against changes in the Belgian franc/Luxembourg franc parity costs about 25 basis points, which indicates only a low probability of a change actually occurring, but it does indicate that the market does not accept even the BLEU as an 'irrevocable' commitment. This suggests that at the European level it will be difficult to convince markets that exchange rates are 'irrevocably' fixed as long as national moneys continue to exist.

8.2.2. Currency substitution

This represents another potential source of instability for the intermediate stages. Even if exchange rates are expected not to change (and therefore interest rates have converged) certain currencies might become more attractive than others because they are more widely used in intra-Community trade.[8] The possibility therefore arises that especially large firms may concentrate their holdings of monetary balances on the larger EMS currencies and choose to use less the smaller, less important currencies. Although one would not

---

6 For example Carli (1989) and Giovannini (1990a).
7 See Matthes (1988).

8 See Giovannini (1990b) and HM Treasury (1989).

expect such a movement to be sudden it might still provoke large shifts in money demand over the short to medium run. Such shifts would make it more difficult for national central banks to interpret their own national aggregates. As long as national currencies continue to exist and national central banks retain some margins of manoeuvre, these shifts in demand across currencies constitute a potential factor of instability. However, since these shifts should net out for the system as a whole they should not jeopardize the capacity of EuroFed to maintain an anti-inflationary overall stance.

It is not clear, however, whether the fixing of exchange rates would increase or diminish the potential for currency substitution. The main reason why it is feared that currency substitution might become widespread is not the fixing of exchange rates, but the increasing integration of European markets in general and the financial markets in particular. The reduction or elimination of the residual exchange rate variability might therefore not be a decisive factor and the danger of currency substitution might therefore be viewed a side effect of the internal market programme or the economic union aspect rather than a specific consequence of the transition towards monetary union in Stages I and II.

The argument that the transitional Stages I and II could be unstable implies that it might be preferable to keep them as short as possible and to take the final step of irrevocably locking parities even before full convergence has been achieved. However, if exchange rates are irrevocably locked before inflation rates have converged a different type of transitional problem might arise which is discussed in the next section.[9]

8.3. How much convergence remains to be achieved?

How much convergence needs to be established before undertaking the step of irrevocably fixing parities is an unresolved question. This section therefore describes what problems might arise when parities are locked before these conditions are met.

The degree of convergence that needs to be achieved varies from country to country. The country-specific issues are discussed in more detail in Chapter 10. This section discusses only the broad orders of magnitude of the adjustment that would be necessary in certain countries to enable them to participate in the transitional stages.

Regarding inflation, three broad groups of countries might be distinguished:

(i)   The original narrow band members are already characterized by a high degree of convergence towards low inflation since inside this group inflation differentials are only about 1 %, not far from what is required by EMU as suggested by the examples examined above.

(ii) More adjustment in terms of inflation is needed in Italy, Spain and the UK where inflation has now stabilized at a level that is about 3 to 5 percentage points above the best performance in the EC. However, for this group participation in Stage I should be feasible provided the adjustment is seen to continue.

(iii) In Portugal and Greece inflation is still above 10 % so that even participation in Stage I clearly needs more time.

As discussed in Chapter 2, there are, however, reasons to expect that non-negligible inflation differentials can arise if productivity growth differs across countries. Full convergence in inflation can therefore be expected only once all member countries have reached a similar productivity level.

Regarding the need to establish sound public finances, it is again possible to identify three groups of countries (see Chapter 5 for a further analysis of the concept of a sustainable fiscal position):

(i)   In Denmark, Ireland and the United Kingdom the level of the public debt/GDP ratio is declining and France and Germany are very close to this situation so that in this group of countries budget policy should be under control.

(ii) In Belgium, Spain and Portugal, the public debt/GDP ratio has not yet been stabilized, but this objective seems to be in reach within the near future since it requires only an adjustment in the primary balance of about one percentage point of GDP.

(iii) In Greece, Italy and the Netherlands present trends in budgetary policy would lead to a rapid deterioration in the public debt/GDP ratio and must therefore be urgently rectified.

The examples of Italy and Belgium show, however, that these imbalances do not necessarily need to be an obstacle to participation in Stage I. However, they would need to be addressed during that stage to achieve the necessary convergence for the following stages.

Convergence to sound public finances is necessary for a stable EMU in the long run. However, lack of convergence

---

[9]   See Giavazzi and Spaventa (1989).

in short run fiscal policy can also create problems even if the debt to GDP ratio does not explode because large differences in the stance of fiscal policy can create tensions in the exchange market and slow down convergence in other areas. For example, a combination of a tight monetary policy (to keep the nominal exchange rate within the EMS margins) with an expansionary fiscal policy can create a situation in which, temporarily, inflation convergence is stopped and a large current account deficit arises. Since such a policy cannot be sustained forever, it will lead to a need for faster convergence later. To avoid the adjustment problems that arise when the policy has to be reversed some convergence in the stance of fiscal policy is therefore desirable even during the transition towards EMU. It is apparent that, to the extent that exchange rates become more and more fixed, no individual member country will be able to determine its own monetary policy and therefore a mix of a tight monetary and a lax fiscal policy should be avoided.

The need for convergence towards a sustainable external equilibrium is less apparent since the external current account disequilibria that exist at present might be financed without difficulty once capital markets are completely integrated. As discussed above, further convergence in external current accounts is desirable from a policy point of view only if the current disequilibria reflect excessive public dissavings. It is therefore not evident that further policy action would be necessary to correct current account imbalances once sound public finances have been achieved in all member countries.

8.3.1. How to achieve convergence

While it is clear that a stable EMU needs a considerable degree of convergence the important question might be how best to achieve this degree of convergence to minimize the macroeconomic costs of disinflation. As discussed in Chapter 3, modern macroeconomic theory argues that these costs arise for two reasons: wage rigidity and lack of credibility in the adjustment process. Both of them affect the desirable mode and speed of the transition.

One extreme position concerning the debate about convergence is the so-called 'coronation theory' according to which the passage to a higher stage of monetary integration should only ratify or 'crown' the convergence that has already been achieved. At the other extreme the so-called 'monetarist' school holds that convergence could always be achieved through exchange rate commitments, which could therefore be taken without any prior convergence.[10]

The experience of the EMS so far suggests that neither of the two extremes should be followed. On the one hand it is widely acknowledged that the EMS has been a useful 'disciplinary device' for more inflation-prone countries.[11] In this view the EMS was established to enforce convergence through the ERM. When the ERM was established the convergence which some observers regarded as a necessary precondition did not exist. Instead it was brought about by the ERM only later and this convergence to low inflation is considered the main achievement of the EMS. On the other hand, the strains the EMS experienced in the first years of its existence also illustrate the difficulties that can arise when convergence is insufficient.

The influence of the EMS in reducing the cost of disinflation in the 1980s has been analysed quite extensively in the economics literature.[12] This analysis suggests that the EMS did not have a strong impact on the credibility of disinflationary policies in the years up to 1983 because there were frequent realignments that were used to validate ex-post inflationary tendencies in order to keep real exchange rates approximately constant. However, there is a clear break after 1983 which suggests that after that date the EMS has been influential in reducing the cost of disinflation. This date coincides with a change in emphasis inside the EMS since after 1983 realignments were less frequent and did not compensate fully for past inflation differentials.

The experience of the EMS suggests therefore an intermediate position: without any exchange rate commitment or policy coordination full convergence might never come about and the goal of monetary union might not be achieved. It might therefore be useful to proceed with Stages II and III even without full convergence in terms of price stability. Convergence would then be achieved through market forces provided there is a credible commitment of the authorities not to slide back. Such a credible commitment requires, of course, that the initial situation is not such as to imply an unrealistically fast convergence.

The rigidities in the wage-setting process that create a short-run trade-off between inflation and output are, of course, not directly affected by the exchange rate regime. However, even in the case of the most important type of wage rigidity, namely backward-looking wage indexation schemes, a credible commitment to a fixed exchange rate with a stable currency could provide the necessary degree of confidence

---

[10] This debate concerns especially convergence of inflation rates; the issues raised by the adjustment in fiscal policy are discussed in Chapter 5.

[11] Of the large literature on this subject, see for instance Giavazzi and Pagano (1988).

[12] See De Grauwe (1989), Giavazzi and Giovannini (1988) for further references.

that inflation will remain low to induce the social partners to abandon this instrument, or reform it on a forward-looking basis during the transitional period.

The experience with the EMS has shown that the credibility of the exchange rate commitment can be an important factor in reducing the cost of disinflation. At its extreme this idea implies that by exchanging the national currency for another one, in this case the single European currency, the macroeconomic cost[13] of disinflation could be eliminated altogether. One could therefore argue that less than full convergence by all members is needed before the single currency is introduced. As long as there is a stable core of countries with a reputation for price stability which ensures a credible anti-inflationary policy for the single currency some peripheral countries could therefore join in the final stage of EMU even if convergence in inflation is not complete. This radical step would ensure immediate convergence, provided, of course, that the initial level of real wages is appropriate and that all links with the past in the form of backwards-looking wage indexation are eliminated.

8.4. Speed of transition

The foregoing analysis has implications for the question of the speed with which the transition should be effected.

The discussion of the costs and benefits by stages suggests that the main costs in terms of achieving price and exchange rate stability arise early in the transition towards EMU. The

---

[13]   The need for a fiscal adjustment would not be affected by this strategy.

move to the final stage of EMU, i.e. the introduction of the single currency, should therefore imply no significant economic cost and it would yield the benefits in terms of eliminating transaction costs and induced dynamic effects. This suggests that the transition should not be too long.

The danger of instability of the transitional Stages I and II provides another argument for proceeding with the subsequent steps towards Stage III as soon as possible. Even if the probability of speculative attacks and large scale currency substitution is only minor, it would still be prudent to prepare for this potential instability by making the necessary preparations for the passage to Stages II and III. These additional steps could then be taken without further delay should the instability become a real danger for the system.

The cost-benefit analysis therefore suggests that the transition should be kept relatively short. However, it is more difficult to describe how this could be achieved. On the one hand irrevocably fixing exchange rates before full convergence is achieved involves costs; but, on the other hand, waiting for full convergence before taking this step might lengthen the transition because in the absence of an exchange rate constraint convergence might slow down.

The main factor limiting the speed in the transition might therefore be the costs that arise during the process of disinflation and fiscal adjustment. These costs are of a strictly transitory nature (as opposed to the benefits of EMU which would be permanent), but they might increase if the adjustment is too fast. They should be reduced by a credible framework that clearly establishes the path for convergence. The transition should therefore not only be fast, but also provide clear signals about the need for convergence.

References

Alesina, A. (1989), 'Politics and business cycles in industrial democracies', *Economic Policy*, April, pp. 57-89.

Begg, D. (1990), 'Alternative exchange rate regimes: The role of the exchange rate and the implications for wage-price adjustment', in *European Economy* — 'The economics of EMU', special issue.

Bhandari, J., Mayer, T. (1990), 'Saving-investment correlations in the EMS', mimeo, International Monetary Fund, Washington DC.

Carli, G. (1989), 'The evolution towards economic and monetary union: a response to HM Treasury paper', mimeo, Italian Ministry of Treasury, December 1989.

Commission of the European Communities (1988), 'The economics of 1992', *European Economy* No 35, Commission of the European Communities, March.

Commission of the European Communities (1977), *Public finance in European integration* (the 'MacDougall report'), Office for Official Publications of the European Communities, Luxembourg.

Committee for the Study of Economic and Monetary Union (1989), 'Report on economic and monetary union in the European Community' (the 'Delors report'), Office for Official Publications of the European Communities, Luxembourg.

De Grauwe, P. (1989), 'The cost of disinflation and the European Monetary System', International Economics Research Paper No 60, Katholische Universiteit Leuven.

European Economy (1990) — 'The economics of EMU', special issue.

Giavazzi, F., Giovannini, A. (1988), 'The role of the exchange rate regime in disinflation: empirical evidence on the European Monetary System', in Giavazzi, Micossi and Miller (eds), *The European Monetary System*, Cambridge University Press.

Giavazzi, F., Pagano, M. (1988), 'The advantage of tying one's hands', *European Economic Review* 32, pp. 1055-82.

Giavazzi, F., Pagano M. (1989), 'Confidence crises and public debt management', CEPR discussion paper No 318.

Giavazzi, F., Spaventa L. (1989), 'The new EMS', CEPR paper No 369, January.

Giovannini, A. (1990a), 'Currency substitution and monetary policy', paper prepared for the conference on 'Financial regulation and monetary arrangements after 1992', Mantana and Gothenberg, 20 to 24 May 1990.

Giovannini, A. (1990b), 'Money demand and monetary control in an integrated European economy', in *European Economy* (1990).

HM Treasury (1989), 'An evolutionary approach to economic and monetary union', London, November.

Matthes, H. (1988), 'Entwicklung des EWS mit Blick auf 1992', in Duwendag, Professor D. (ed.), *Europa Banking*, Baden-Baden.

Obstfeld, M. (1988), 'Competitiveness, realignment and speculation. The role of financial markets', in Giavazzi, F., Micossi S., Miller M. (eds), *The European Monetary System*, Cambridge University Press, pp. 232-246.

Padoa-Schioppa, T. (1990), 'Towards a European central bank: fiscal compatibility and monetary constitution', paper presented at the Bank of Israel and David Horrowitz Institute, conference on aspects of central bank policy making, Tel Aviv, January 1990.

Padoa-Schioppa, T. (1987), *Efficiency, stability and equity*, Oxford University Press, Oxford.

Poloz, S. (1990), 'Real exchange rate adjustments between regions in a common currency area', mimeo, Bank of Canada, February.

Price Waterhouse (1988), *The cost of non-Europe in financial services*, Commission of the European Communities.

Chapter 9

Spatial aspects

The purpose of this chapter is to complement the previous discussion of the overall costs and benefits of economic and monetary union by examining in the light of economic theory and empirical evidence its regional impact, especially on the Community's peripheral regions. The following main conclusions are possible:

(i)   Concern with the distribution of benefits (and losses) from economic integration has been expressed at every stage of development of the EC: its creation in the 1950s, the northern enlargement in the 1970s, the southern enlargements in the 1980s and more recently the 1992 single market. After an initial reduction in the 1960s, there has been no clear long-term trend in regional disparities. In the period up to the first oil crisis, there was an overall convergence of living standards. However, this was followed by a slight increase of disparities in the second half of the 1970s and early 1980s. Since then, regional disparities have remained at roughly at the same level.

(ii) Economic literature has been dominated by a debate between the presumption that economic integration, per se, aggravates the problems of peripheral regions and the view that convergence is a more likely outcome. Earlier attempts to model the effects of economic integration upon regional imbalances were based almost exclusively on the consideration of transport costs and scale and agglomeration economies. Recently attention has shifted towards the importance of structural disadvantages which limit the competitive strengths of firms in lagging regions. Business surveys are viewed as a useful tool for providing a detailed assessment of factors shaping the competitiveness of regions.

(iii) Empirical evidence from Commission studies suggest that reduction of regional disparities coincides with periods of rapid growth whereas the problems of poorer and disadvantaged regions are accentuated in periods of recession. Also, convergence occurs more spontaneously among countries and regions that have already reached a relatively mature stage of economic development.

(iv) The adjustment of less favoured regions to the 1992 single market is being assisted by the Community structural Funds which were significantly enhanced for that purpose. The financial envelopes for these Community policies are settled up to 1993. Monetary union adds to the regional consequences of the single market and economic union in that the nominal exchange rate instru-

ment can be more important to economies undergoing deep structural change. The transition to monetary union calls therefore for adequate support from Community policies.

(v)   The key to the catching-up of the less favoured regions lies in obtaining synergies between Community and national policies. Together with policies geared at reducing locational disadvantages and enhancing market efficiency, the fixing of clear and credible policy objectives such as for the single market and EMU are also highly relevant. Indeed, given the ambitious nature of the catching-up process, the appropriate concept seeems to be that of a credible and comprehensive regime change for the countries and regions concerned.

9.1. Principles

9.1.1. Concepts: regions and regional problems

Although the principal tools of economic analysis ignore the spatial dimension, this becomes important once it is realized that:

(a) the impact of economic measures and policies is in fact variable throughout a continuum of regions that differ in terms of natural characteristics and economic structures; and

(b) such measures and policies interact with the specific objectives of policies designed to tackle localized regional problems or overall imbalances in the spatial structure of the economy.

Therefore, the consideration of the spatial dimension or the implications for regional problems has become an important part of economic policy analysis.

The concept of 'region' may vary according to the purpose: it can be defined in geographical, political or economic terms. In the latter case, regions can be delimited on a homogeneity criterion, or by trying to capture the highest degree of interdependence within each region. In our case, the most important level is that of political regions: the Member States of the Community. Their importance comes from the fact that the centre of political power is concentrated at that level, and that they play the main role in the bargaining process inside the Community. The various stages of economic integration concern mainly the relinquishing of national policy instruments — not regional ones — and thus its effects are felt in all regions of a country. As shown below, regional disparities in the enlarged EC are increasingly determined by inter-country differences. The intra-country regional level nevertheless continues to be quite relevant for the purposes of this analysis.

There is no simple definition of what constitutes a regional problem. The following goals, which are not equivalent, might be considered in alternative or complementary ways:

(i) a spatially balanced distribution of population and economic activities — in order to avoid negative externalities and long-run social and environmental problems;

(ii) an adequate level of provision and accessibility of public goods and local services to all the populations;

(iii) equalization of levels of GDP per capita;

(iv) equalization of levels of personal disposable income, or per capita consumption, or welfare — not the same as the previous due, *inter alia*, to taxes, transfers and price changes affecting the consumer surplus.

As examples, relocation of industry towards more peripheral regions has coexisted historically with the migration of workers towards more central regions, where job creation in the services sector is faster; economic decline of some regions in terms of relative GDP can also coexist with an increase in per capita consumption and better provision of basic services by the welfare state in the region. The first objective — spatial balance of population — is in a sense more demanding than the fourth, since welfare equalization may be achieved through emigration and large-scale subsidization of a region. GDP per capita as an indicator combines several elements: to satisfy this criterion the region must have an economic basis to provide its inhabitants with a high standard of living, assuming certain distributional conditions are fulfilled.

It is not the purpose of this chapter to select one or another criterion, but one should remember that all of them may be implicit in the discussion. In particular regional GDP per capita is a criterion used in Community structural intervention.

9.1.2. Geographical effects of economic integration

One traditional view of the effects of economic integration, known as the 'convergence school', derives from the neoclassical theory of international trade, and holds that the free movement of goods and services will, under strong assumptions, equalize factor returns and living standards. At regional level, under somewhat different assumptions,

mobility of the factors of production is emphasized as the force equalizing income levels among regions (see Borts, 1960). According to neo-classical theory, the subsistence of regional disparities would be mainly due to the time-lags inherent to the process of integration and to imperfect factor mobility.

Another school of authors preferred to stress the mechanisms that work towards greater divergence instead of convergence. This is in the tradition of Myrdal (1957) but it can also be found in the early works of Giersch (1949), Byé (1958) and Scitovski (1958). Regional problems might arise in a customs union, as the abolition of restrictions on trade and factor movement increase the attractiveness of highly industrialized centres for the location of new activities. This conclusion was based on the role of agglomeration economies of scale in the observed patterns of regional development within industrialized countries. A similar conclusion is reached by Perroux (1959), whose views on development are based on the concept of a growth pole, offering a good infrastructure as well as external economies. To the extent that some countries or regions do not possess such poles, they will lose from integration, at least in relative terms. The emphasis of this literature was on the real side of the economy, and the centripetal effects of a monetary union, as opposed to a customs union, were generally considered to be rather small (see Stahl, 1974, p. 220).

Balassa (1961) defends the convergence school by claiming that these arguments put too much emphasis on agglomeration economies of scale, and disregard the increased opportunities for taking advantage of lower costs in backward regions. Frontier regions in particular are prone to benefit from greater integration. Other positive spread effects could also benefit the relatively poor regions, given the tendency of industries to become less bound by natural resources, local external economies and transport costs, as a result of technological developments. That view prevailed during the conception and earlier years of the Community (see Section 9.2).

An instrument of the divergence school is the concept of 'economic potential' of C. Clark (see Clark *et al.*, 1969) representing the availability of inputs and, especially, the proximity of markets to the region. The economic potential of a region is defined as the summation of its income and those of the surrounding regions, divided by the transport costs between them. Depending on the measure of income and cost, economic potential will no doubt vary, but almost by definition economic integration will increase the economic potential of the central — and already developed — areas while increasing the disadvantage of peripheral areas.

The traditional arguments about convergence or divergence in an integrated area thus try to balance two types of effects:

(i) the allocative benefits of interregional trade and better exploitation of comparative cost advantages, and

(ii) the centripetal forces resulting from agglomeration economies of scale, externalities and transport costs

The basic insight is correct but its loose analytical underpinning makes it difficult to reach a consensus on the basis of this type of consideration. Without a proper model, the sign and nature of externalities, and the way they extend through space, are not a priori clear. Similarly, the temptation to find the determinants of comparative advantage and specialization among regions is often frustrated as these cannot be identified by an economic model. In the case of developing regions or countries it is hazardous to attempt to distinguish theoretically or empirically where *ex ante* comparative advantages lie and to predict what pattern of specialization might evolve. Who is poised to benefit most from integration is therefore impossible to ascertain with any degree of precision. Policies which will hinder the realization of these gains are, however, easier to identify.

This may be why the geographical aspects of economic activity have not played a very prominent role in economic theory. Stressing the issue of method, Krugman (1989) observes that the traditional model of competitive general equilibrium does not provide answers to the more pertinent issues raised by economic geography. In particular, that model cannot take into consideration facts such as economies of scale and externalities which currently are accepted to play an important role in the location of production factors and, *a fortiori*, of economic activity. The analysis of the spatial effects of economic integration is no exception to this. In a nutshell, economic theory does not currently provide definite and well-established results on the issue. Naturally, the empirical analysis of economic geography is affected by this situation.

In order to provide new approaches to the theory of economic geography and in the line of recent contributions to the theory of international trade, Krugman (1989) presents a model of specialization among regions, with factor mobility, which does not depend on resource-based comparative advantage, nor on vaguely defined externalities (technology, etc.). Instead, he uses a model of imperfect competition, with economies of scale and transport costs in the manufacturing sector. There are two regions, with labour mobility between them, and two sectors, agriculture (immobile) and manufacturing (mobile). The question is whether manufacturing activities, and the corresponding workers, will tend to concentrate themselves in one of the regions, or whether from arbitrary initial conditions, an equilibrium will be reached where manufacturing is distributed between the two regions.

The answer depends on three key parameters of the model, which bring greater precision to the centripetal forces mentioned in the traditional discussion. The forces working towards and against regional convergence in a union are then:

(i) *Economies of scale.* The more important they are, the greater the tendency to concentrate manufacturing in one region — even though they may be purely internal to each firm.

(ii) *Transport costs.* The higher those costs, the more unlikely concentration becomes. This suggests that the opening of trade, by lowering the costs on the movement of goods, works towards divergence.

(iii) *The size of the (footloose) manufacturing sector.* Since only in this sector can circular causation set in, the larger it is, the more likely divergence becomes.

The second point can be further qualified by the following reasoning due to Krugman and Venables (1990): the common assumption is that the elimination of barriers (which can be assimilated to a reduction of transport costs between countries) will bring about a concentration of production in the central location, in order to take advantage of economies of scale and easy access to markets. If, however, one takes this reduction of barriers to the extreme and they become insignificant, economies of scale may instead be achieved by location on the periphery, where variable costs are generally lower. In other words, the usual argument that the reduction of barriers benefits the centre assumes that some kind of barriers or costs (transport) remain so that the advantage of geographical proximity to the markets (the centre) supersedes the lower production costs at the periphery. This implies a U-shaped curve in the relocation of certain industries when trade barriers are progressively reduced. Even when totally free trade would foster economic activity in the periphery, partial liberalization might be the worst option from the point of view of those economies. The pattern applies also to the relative wages of the periphery, with implications for the welfare situation mentioned earlier.

Another element typically absent from the traditional models of circular causation of regional disparities is the existence of multiple economic centres among, and even within, countries. If a small country integrates with a larger one and both have an established centre, it may happen that the centre of the smaller country benefits at the expense of the larger country's by recapturing a part of its natural hinterland — see Krugman (1989). Even when integration does result into a net relocation of industries in favour of the centre (larger market) it remains true that a smaller country is likely to reap more important welfare benefits from integration. With barriers to trade, a small country is unable to achieve economies of scale and, furthermore, is characterized by a low level of domestic competition. These two effects, which add to the more conventional gains from comparative advantage, are highlighted by recent models of international trade with economies of scale and oligopoly (see Krugman and Venables, 1990) and constitute an important asymmetry favouring, this time, small countries.

To summarize, the traditional view of the spatial effects of economic integration, which emphasizes external economies of agglomerations, overlooks a number of elements that have recently been focused on:

(i)   the interaction between economies of scale and transport or transaction costs;

(ii) imperfectly competitive market structures;

(iii) the larger welfare (static) benefits for small countries;

(iv) the multipolar structure of the real world.

The addition of these aspects will result in a more complex pattern of locational changes and implies that the overall effect of market integration will differ from one lagging region to another.

9.2. Basic facts and trends

9.2.1. Empirical evidence

Overall, the existence of the European Community has marked the period of strongest convergence of national wealth levels of its members in the last 150 years or so (see Molle, 1989). But the convergence trend was interrupted in the 1970s. As Table 9.1 shows, it is too early to judge whether the more favourable growth environment of the late 1980s has resulted in a sustained resumption of the catching-up process.

Global measures of the intensity of regional problems, like that of Table 9.1, are plagued by many problems: the definition of 'regions', which are more determined by statistical, administrative and political convenience than by economic criteria;[1] the lack of reliable regional data; and the sensitivity of the results to the measure of dispersion used (like the Theil coefficient in the table). Even if it was possible to have a clear picture of the evolution of regional disparities within the Community of 6, 9 or 12, this does not amount to passing a judgment on the regional impact of economic integration. For that, one would have to be able to observe the *anti-monde* where the relevant countries would stay outside the Community and find out whether there would be more or less convergence of economic performances.

International comparisons (also suffering from the problems mentioned above) show, however, that regional disparities within the Community, with respect to a variety of socio-economic indicators, are important. For example, regional income dispersion is about twice as great as in the United States. As far as structural backwardness is concerned there is within the Community of 12 a clear centre-to-periphery pattern, as well as a northeast-southwest gradient. A study sponsored by the Commission (see Keeble *et al.*, 1988) computed an index of peripherality for EC regions,[2] and grouped them accordingly into central, intermediate and peripheral regions. Box 9.1 contains a map from that study, together with a comparison between the characteristics of peripheral, intermediate and central regions, using regional data relating to demographic trends, economic activity and the labour market. These indicators give a clear illustration of the economic dimension of peripherality: in the outermost ring

---

[1] In the Eurostat NUTS II list of regions — the one most often used by analysts — the smallest region has 404 km^2 and the largest 94 200 km^2.

[2] The study used 1983 data for 166 Community regions of NUTS level II. See Box 9.1. for details.

Table 9.1

Disparities in per capita GDP in EUR 12, 1950-87 (Theil coefficient)

	1980	1981	1982	1983	1984	1985	1986	1987	1988
Average 10 weakest regions	47	46	46	45	45	45	45	45	45
Average 10 strongest regions	145	146	147	149	149	150	151	151	151
Weighted coefficient of variation	26,1	26,5	26,8	27	27,2	27,5	27,9	27,5	27,5

Source: Commission services.

of peripheral areas of the Community, representing 40 % of its surface, live about 20 % of its population and only 13 % of GDP is produced.[3] Those areas also represent more than half of the agricultural population of the Community and have significantly higher rates of unemployment than the average.

A glance at the map also shows that the degree of peripherality is broadly in line with the boundaries of what has been called, in the reform of the structural Funds, the Objective 1 regions (see Section 9.4.1), i.e. Ireland, Portugal, Greece and parts of Italy and Spain. That is not surprising, given the correlation between peripherality and regional GDP per head, the criterion used in the definition of Objective 1. The German Democratic Republic, although not covered by the abovementioned study nor (yet) by the reform of the Funds, would also qualify as a major problem region of the Community.

In a broader context, Williamson (1965) examined the long-run evolution of interregional income disparities in a number of countries and proposed a two-stage model of regional development. In the first stage, economic development seems to take root in some sectors and regions of a country; above a certain threshold, it begins spilling to the rest of the economy. Thus, in the first stage of growth there is regional divergence, in the second, regional convergence. However, many questions remain unanswered, namely when and how the divergent trend is reversed.

Many studies have tried to relate integration-specific variables such as trade flows, migration and foreign investment to the convergence performance of the national economies. In general, no clear relationship emerges which is valid for all countries at all times. However, one conclusion at least can be drawn from the EC experience and all the related empirical studies: convergence tends to dominate in periods of strong growth, and to recede in periods of stagnation. This may be explained by two reasons:

(i) Weaker regions tend to contain a higher proportion of sensitive sectors and small and marginally efficient firms (see Vanhove and Klaassen, 1980). These are the first to be affected by a recession, leading to a relative decline of the whole region;

(ii) Those regions also receive a relatively higher proportion of public investment and new — as opposed to replacement investment — from the private sector. Empirical evidence and past experience show those categories are the most responsive to the economic climate.

Historically, the reduction of regional disparities in some federations, like the United States, has been ascribed to two main factors:

(i) financial transfers through the central government budget, and

(ii) mobility of the factors of production.

This may explain the higher degree of regional differences in income — as well as in rates of unemployment — in the Community compared to the United States despite the much greater geographic extension and natural diversity of the latter (see Box 9.2). Whereas the income differences may point to different stages of economic development, the disparities in unemployment rates may be a sign of weaker adjustment capacities to shocks than in existing federal States. The weaker adjustment capacity may in turn be linked to the stage of economic development, underlining the balance between convergence and divergence that emerges from the recent theoretical literature.

9.2.2. The response in EC policies

In the late 1950s and early 1960s, there was considerable anxiety about the impact of the integration process and increased competition upon the Community's problem regions. In the original EC, these regions consisted predominantly of localized problems of industrial decline (like in the coal and steel and a number of other traditional sectors). The creation of the EC seemed somewhat in conflict with the tendency at the time in European countries to answer those sectoral problems, as well as promote the industrialization of backward regions, through the use of strong and interventionist regional policy tools. Within the fast growth of the EC's early years, however, those regions performed in general quite well, being able to attract modern investment and share in the overall rising prosperity of the Community.

There were also some regional safeguards in the articles of the EEC Treaty covering the agriculture, transport and competition policies. It was considered that the dynamic effects of the creation of the Community would spread strongly enough to the problem regions so as to promote convergence and that any further measures should be left to national governments. Nevertheless, a Community institution was created, the European Investment Bank, whose main task was promoting regional development. Special regional protocols concerning southern Italy and the intra-German border regions were also agreed. Thirty years later, the Mezzogiorno and East Germany remain special cases of the regional problem in the Community.

---

[3]   Since the figure is in PPS, it probably underestimates the imbalances in the location of economic activities among the regions.

In 1970 the Werner report on economic and monetary union brought to the discussion the need for accompanying structural measures in the integration process. The first enlargement brought in a number of new problem regions, and the 1973 oil shock, to which Member States reacted in very different ways, made regional problems worse: the decline of manufacturing accelerated and spread to new sectors and regions. Unemployment also increased sharply, stemming the traditional migration flows among regions and countries. Profitability and investment also experienced a strong decline, with a more marked effect on lagging regions, for the reasons mentioned above (9.2.1).

All these events marked a turning point in the acceptance by the Community of a larger responsibility for structural and regional problems. The justification for this has been two-fold:

(i) on economic grounds, closer forms of integration are inhibited by an excessive disparity of structures and income levels;

(ii) on political grounds, the pursuit of internal cohesion and equity which is characteristic of national States should gradually be extended to the Community level as integration progresses.

Within the envisaged EMU, also, the transfer of an increasing number of policies to the Community level and the suppression of important national policy instruments should be counterbalanced by more active Community structural policies. This is more so if one believes that the natural consequence of integrating the national economies is to increase regional problems, as was the prevailing view.

The first movement towards a regional policy at Community level was the adoption in 1971 of the principles of coordination of regional aid regimes, which aimed at minimizing the distortions in competition within the Community while protecting national regional development objectives and avoiding an overbidding in the level of aid. 1975 saw the creation of the European Regional Development Fund. The ERDF was thereafter reinforced, especially after the EC's southern enlargements, and an effort was made to include a regional dimension in the most important Community policies. That is the case of the Guidance Section of the European Agricultural Guidance and Guarantee Fund, introduced in the early 1970s in the aftermath of the Mansholt Plan, and the European Social Fund which, although present since the founding of the Community, was significantly reformed in 1972 and 1977 and had the regional objective explicitly included. Finally, the importance of regional and inter-country disparities and the prospects of a deepening of the integration process after the Single European Act prompted a major overhaul of the Community's structural policies in 1988, as will be described more in detail in Section 9.4.1. Table 9.2 gives an idea of the increasing importance assumed by the structural Funds in the EC budget since the 1970s.

9.3. Businesses' perceptions of regional handicaps and competitiveness

One important source of empirical information in assessing the effects of policy measures is provided by the surveys conducted for the EC Commission among industrial and

Table 9.2

The structural Funds and the EC budget, 1970-90

	1970		1975		1980		1985		1990	
	MECU	%	MECU	%	MECU	%	MECU	%	MECU	%
Regional			75,3	1,2	1 126,4	7,0	2 495,3	8,8	4 704,5	10,1
Social			157,9	2,5	1 014,2	6,3	2 188,5	7,8	3 321,9	3,1
Agriculture			158,8	2,6	624,7	3,9	852,9	3,0	1 449,0	3,1
Total funds	64,0	1,2	392,0	6,3	2 765,3	17,2	5 536,6	19,6	9 475,4	20,2
Total EC budget	5 448,4	100,0	6 213,6	100,0	16 057,5	100,0	28 223,0	100,0	46 808,7	100,0

Source: European Economy No 42; Court of Auditors' Annual Report, several issues.

business services firms. Those surveys show that positive expectations as to the effects of the European single market and EMU are widespread in the countries of the Community. But the positive expected effects are not evenly spread over the regions. Graph 9.1 shows the results of a 1989 survey (IFO, 1989) where businessmen were asked to assess the likely impact of the completion of the internal market upon their companies and the regions they are located in. This survey covered about 9 000 companies situated in three types of regions: lagging, declining industrial regions and prosperous (control) regions (see Box 9.3).

The companies located in the control (central and prosperous) regions see their own prospects as well as those of their region, after the completion of the internal market, more positively than the companies in problem regions. The prospects for declining regions are seen, moreover, as less favourable than those for lagging ones, although there is a considerable degree of subjectivism in this assessment.

Similarly, prospects for the declining areas are viewed as less favourable than for the control regions in Belgium and Germany.[4] However, for the Netherlands and the UK one cannot say the same, since in declining regions the firms evaluate the impact upon both region and company more positively than in control regions. In Spain, on the other hand, firms have more optimistic views for the impact upon lagging regions than for the control regions. These results confirm the suggestion of Section 9.1.2 that no uniform conclusions are likely to be valid for the spatial distribution of the economic benefits of EMU.

Further disaggregation of the survey data shows that the expected benefits increase nearly always with firm size, particularly in the lagging regions; the orientation of the firm towards foreign markets — measured by the percentage of turnover from exports — unsurprisingly produces a similar effect; and firms producing investment goods and, especially, business services, have better expectations than those producing intermediate and consumer goods. The latter result has strong regional implications and probably accounts for most of the differentiated expectations between lagging, declining and prosperous regions: the most dynamic sectors tend to be concentrated on the latter.

Behind the attitudes of enterprises towards the effects of economic integration lies their assessment of a number of

factors that influence their ability to compete in a more open international environment. The IFO survey also provides a detailed insight on the relative importance of factors affecting firm and regional competitiveness, as evaluated by firm managers. Both factors which are country-specific and those which are region-specific were listed, with the results summarized in Box 9.3.

Graph 9.1 represents the difference between the evaluation of those factors in lagging and declining regions and their evaluation in the control regions. The exchange rate as a factor of competitiveness does not seem to affect firms situated in problem regions more critically than those situated in the control regions. This suggests a relatively neutral regional impact of monetary union, at intra-country level. The cost of credit and availability of risk capital, on the other hand, work to the disadvantage of the lagging regions whereas the cost of labour works to their advantage, but not so much to that of the declining regions. The impact of EMU will be to improve the efficiency of financial markets, especially in the lagging countries. However, in Section 9.4.2 it is also shown that financial integration may bring about some disruption of the local credit markets, where small entrepreneurs are totally dependent on the banking system and that this effect may be a disadvantage to set off against the gain of greater overall monetary stability and efficiency in the financial sector.

Among the regional factors, it is interesting to note that the physical distance to markets (consumers and suppliers) is not perceived as a serious disadvantage in the lagging, and generally peripheral, regions. Instead, the lack of certain types of infrastructure (transport, communications, social facilities, education and training centres) are seen as making a more important difference. In short, geographical disadvantage is less important than 'economic' — and amendable — backwardness.

In this respect, the main difference between lagging regions and the industrial declining ones is the availability of economic and social infrastructure. These are at the head of the regional factors negatively affecting the lagging regions. Problem industrial regions, however, have inherited a much more developed infrastructure even if it is often outdated and badly maintained. The absence of such established facilities, as mentioned in Section 9.1.2, is an obstacle to the catching-up of lagging regions.

Finally, services to enterprises (legal, consulting, etc.) also figure highly among the relative factors of disadvantage in lagging regions and also to some extent in declining regions.

---

4   Note that in Belgium, Germany and the Netherlands there are no lagging (Objective 1) regions.

GRAPH 9.1 : **Enterprise assessment of factors of regional competitiveness**

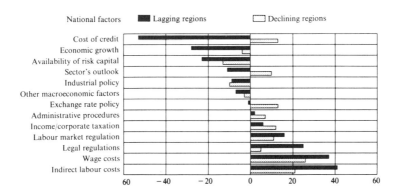

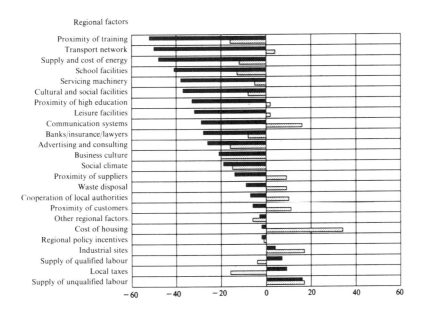

Note: Figures represent the net balance of respondents, in percentages, making negative or positive assessments for the lagging or declining regions.

9.4. Wider strategic considerations

9.4.1. The less favoured regions and economic union

As the previous sections showed, there are no unambiguous results for the EC less favoured regions as regards the deepening of the European integration process and EMU in particular. The outcome will very likely depend on the combination of the policies implemented with the 'initial conditions' of each region. Policies should be geared to the enhancement of the economic and social cohesion within the Community which means, for the EC lagging regions, to promote their catching-up to the EC levels. Both the Community and the Member States are committed to follow policies aiming at economic and social cohesion: Member States gear domestic economic policy towards cohesion and the Community supports its implementation through the intervention of the structural Funds, the EIB and other financial instruments. This arrangement of goals, policies and levels of decision was defined at the outset of the single market programme, and is effectively aiming at a successful construction of economic union within the Community. Indeed, this is the message of Article 130 (a) to (e) of the EEC Treaty.

The 'initial conditions' embrace a wide spectrum of factors, ranging from endowments to political attitudes. As regards endowments, the initial conditions of the EC lagging regions may be synthetically described by a few quantifiable factors, the first of which is the simple indicator of GDP per head already mentioned. Second, as the survey results suggest, come infrastructure and human capital. A third dimension is industrial structure, including for some purposes financial structure as well.

Less favoured regions have lower levels of GDP per head than the core. Within the EC, GDP per head (in purchasing power standards) in Greece, Ireland, Portugal and the GDR, as well as in most of the Spanish regions and the south of Italy, lies under 70 % of the Community average. Among these regions there are — and will remain for a while — two distinct groups: the first constituted by Ireland and the lagging regions of Italy and Spain, which are not far from that threshold, and the second by Portugal and Greece, who are well below and not much above one half of the Community average.[5]

---

[5]   Recent studies of these countries and regions can be found in Bliss and Braga de Macedo (1990), chapters by Viñals, Katseli and Braga de Macedo on Spain, Greece and Portugal. On Italy see Faini (1990).

Although having in common lower levels of income per head, the EC lagging regions have not displayed identical growth performances. Taking the year of adhesion to the EC as a benchmark, the evolution of GDP per head varies widely among Ireland, Greece, Spain and Portugal, the four poorer Member States. Convergence has not occurred uniformly, neither through time nor space, suggesting that the adequacy of domestic economic policies play a crucial role.

The Italian Mezzogiorno was experiencing a catching-up process towards northern Italy's level of income when the Treaty of Rome was signed. The promotion of development in the Mezzogiorno had been made an explicit policy objective for the Italian authorities at the end of World War II and significant resources (both institutional and financial) had been allocated to it. This effort was continued and reinforced in the new framework brought about with the creation of the EC. However, the catching-up process came to a halt in the aftermath of the first oil shock and up to 1987 the income gap relative to northern Italy actually widened. Explanations for the break in the convergence process generally point to a slackening of the investment effort targeted at southern Italy. This was related to the deterioration of profitability conditions due, *inter alia*, to the reduction in wage cost differentials with the north. The Mezzogiorno was in risk of becoming a declining rather than a lagging region, without ever in recent times having been prosperous. This reversal shows the narrow limits of structural interventions which are not supported by a viable microeconomic environment.

In Ireland, a sound catching-up process has been evident only since 1985, after the successful implementation of a fiscal adjustment programme. Until then, the growth performance of the Irish economy was very disappointing with GDP per capita relative to the Community average fluctuating around 65 %. The contrast between the recent period and the first 12 years of membership is thus clearly apparent. Given the marked progress in nominal convergence which occurred in recent years and the growth momentum currently experienced, the Irish economy seems quite favourably positioned to face the challenges of the EMU process.

Accession to the EC did not yet prompt any durable catching-up process in Greece. In the course of the 1980s the income gap between Greece and the EC widened: GDP per capita (in purchasing power standards) declined from 58 % of the Community average in 1980 to 54 % in 1989. In the most recent years the economic situation in Greece deteriorated sharply, with the imbalances in the fields of public finance, inflation and external accounts reaching unsustainable levels. The 'initial conditions' of Greece *vis-a-vis* EMU thus seem weak, calling for a period of rigorous domestic stabilization in order to create the basis for a sound catching-up process.

As regards the new members, both Spain and Portugal seem to have well exploited the opportunities offered by full membership of the EC. In the first four years after accession (1986-89) both countries experienced steady growth well above the Community average. The prospects are for the continuation of the catching-up process. Nevertheless, unemployment in Spain and inflation in Portugal continue to be abnormally high. In Spain there is room for a more effective regional policy, especially in making the labour market less rigid. In Portugal, virtual full employment has been preserved, but structural adjustment away from widespread State intervention has only begun in the last few years. In both countries, and in Portugal in particular, domestic economic policies have to secure effective progress in nominal convergence so that the real convergence process not be put in jeopardy.

As seen above, the less favoured regions of the EC lie mainly in its periphery. The concept of peripherality is first of all a notion of distance. In economic terms, this means that for those EC regions both transport and communication costs do matter. An extra time-distance penalty is suffered by the less favoured regions because of factors such as border crossings (intra and extra-Community), lack of direct motorway links, sea crossings, etc. This may be calculated as a factor of proportionality between travel time and geographical distance, with respect to the centre. The penalty varies by a factor ranging from 1.9 for Athens to 1.8 for Dublin, 1.6 for Rome and Lisbon and 1.4 for Madrid. (Thus Athens' time-distance from the centre is 1.9 times its kilometre distance). In addition there are the problems of peripherality within countries; the figures given are for capital cities and take no account of time taken to travel from, say, Galway to Dublin, or Seville to Madrid which will add considerably to the above penalties.

Transport and communication costs can be reduced (in some cases very significantly, namely in the field of telecommunications) through the establishment of adequate infrastructural facilities. As mentioned, poor countries and regions are inadequately endowed with basic infrastructure. The number of kilometres of motorway per square kilometre in Greece and Portugal is below one tenth and one fifth, respectively, of the EC average. As another example, the number of telephone lines per thousand inhabitants in the less favoured regions of Spain is less then half of the EC figure while in the GDR it stands below one fourth. The enhancement of the infrastructural capital stock helps attenuate geographical disadvantage, both directly and by increasing the competitiveness of the countries and regions.

The less favoured regions also have a low qualified human capital stock largely reflecting the poor performance of the countries' education systems. In Greece, total public expenditure in education amounted to 2,9 % of GDP in 1986 while for the EC as a whole the figure is 4,8 %. Spending per pupil in Greece is only 28 % of the EC average while in Portugal and Spain it amounts to 40 % and 51 % respectively. Compulsory education in the five EC less developed countries ends earlier than in the core countries where the range is from the age of $15\frac{1}{2}$ in France to 18 in Belgium. The possibilities for increasing skills in these countries are therefore very large. The upgrading of manpower means not only an increase in the stock of knowledge (which will increase the marginal efficiency of labour) but also making people more open to innovation and to modern technologies. Labour productivity can thus increase significantly in the lagging countries.

The lagging countries and regions of the EC have a long tradition of migration from the south, west and east towards the central Member States. However, the situation has changed significantly in the last two decades and the process of European integration has not been accompanied by any large-scale movement of labour, despite the wide regional disparities. Ireland is the only less developed country of the EC where net emigration is still taking place, mostly towards the UK. As regards the new members, Spain and Portugal, freedom of circulation and establishment for people will only take place from 1993 onwards. Whether substantial migration to the EC will materialize after 1993 is not clear. If the experience with Italy and Greece is followed, no significant outflows of labour from Portugal and Spain are to be expected. Moreover, there is no tradition of migration from Portugal to Spain, unlike the relation between the Irish and the UK labour markets.

The determinants of migration are several. While traditional views emphasized the role of wage differentials as a cause for migration, current views stress that the absolute wage level of the potential migrant is decisive. Even in the presence of an important wage differential an adequate level of the local wage would discourage emigration. Moreover, the socio-economic situation of rural areas in Europe, which were the main source of emigration, has improved significantly, not least as a consequence of the implementation of Community policies, the CAP in particular. Therefore, the reasons that were behind the rural exodus of the 1950s and 1960s no longer prevail.

The situation of the GDR, as regards emigration, is a particular one. The large outflows to the FRG which occurred in the final part of 1989 and beginning of 1990 reflected both the exploitation of the breach opened in the repressed economy of the GDR and the uncertainties then prevailing regarding its future. Outflows began to decline when the prospects of German unification became clear. The eventual continuation of emigration from the GDR to the FRG will to a large extent depend on the success of the adjustment of its economy which, in turn, will be shaped by the terms of the State Treaty. Given that a single currency now applies in the German monetary union, the evolution of nominal wage differentials between the GDR and the FRG will be critical to the prospects for employment in the GDR.

Being small and open economies, the increase in welfare in the EC lagging regions has to come from external trade. The industrial structure of those regions will be decisive for their trade pattern *vis-a-vis* the EC. A recent study carried out by the Commission services[6] analysed the different sectoral positioning of each country *vis-a-vis* the completion of the 1992 single market. As theory would predict, it is observed that intra-industry trade is less developed in the European countries with a lower level of income per head. In fact, intra-industry trade is less important in Portugal, and especially in Greece, than in other member countries. Spain and Ireland, and in some respect Italy as well, stand in an intermediate situation.[7]

Greece clearly displays an inter-industry foreign trade pattern and relies on exploiting the comparative advantage stemming from low wage costs. As far as Portugal is concerned, inter-industry trade is concentrated on the stronger sectors, but some degree of intra-industry trade is already taking place in sectors which have a high technological content, and which host the export-oriented branches of foreign enterprises. Spain differs from the other southern countries in that the strong points of its external trade do not belong exclusively to the traditional industries but also include highly capital-intensive sectors utilizing highly qualified manpower. Considered as a whole, Spanish industry is much more engaged in intra-industry trade with the other European countries than Portugal or Greece.

The trade pattern of Ireland is clearly different and better positioned as far as modern sectors are concerned. In fact, this country is in a relatively favourable position in high-technology sectors such as informatics, telecommunications equipment, precision material and pharmaceuticals. However, these sectors are largely dominated by foreign firms,

which renders Irish industry rather dualistic and thus more vulnerable to the changes in the strategies of foreign investors.

It is possible to identify two scenarios for the dynamic adjustment of these countries' industrial structure to the single market. A first scenario would consist in the specialization in inter-industry trade in those sectors where the less developed regions currently have comparative advantages; in the second scenario the development of industry in those regions would follow the pattern of the more advanced EC countries with specialization in intra-industry trade. Naturally, a combination of these two scenarios is also possible. There are no grounds to conclude that the intra-industry scenario is uniformly better than the inter-industry one, or vice versa. Nevertheless, specialization in traditional industrial sectors (e.g. textiles) must be accompanied by an 'upgrading' in quality to avoid increased exposure to the competition of newly industrializing countries from outside the Community. Moreover intra-industry specialization is more compatible with EMU (see Chapter 6) since it decreases the likelihood of asymmetric shocks and adjustment problems. Foreign investment will be called to play a crucial role in both scenarios. In order to secure inflows of foreign capital, peripheral regions have to provide conditions for the economic efficiency of investment. In this respect, the perform-

GRAPH 9.2: **Spain and Portugal—trade and investment flows with EUR 10**

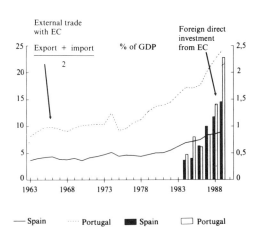

—— Spain   ······ Portugal   ■ Spain   ☐ Portugal

---

6   'Les États membres face aux enjeux sectoriels du marché intérieur', in *European Economy* No 44 and *Social Europe*.

7   A similar conclusion is presented by Neven (1990) and by the country studies on Spain, Greece and Portugal contained in Bliss and Braga de Macedo (1990).

ance of the newest EC members — Spain and Portugal — is quite striking. Since 1986 one has observed not only an acceleration and diversification of the trade flows between the EC and Spain and Portugal but, especially, a boom of foreign direct investment in the two countries (see Graph 9.2).

These initial conditions relative to GDP per head, infrastructure, human capital and industrial structure are the factors through which the economic impact of the completion of the single market will be channelled. Not surprisingly, the Community policies addressed to the adjustment of the lagging regions to the single market, notably the structural Funds, are directed to these factors. Indeed, the existing Community structural policies were designed in the context of the single market programme, and so are largely geared to the achievement of economic union. The Community structural policies were significantly enhanced with the adoption of the Single European Act and the 1992 single market programme. The structural Funds were reformed in 1988 and their financial allocations doubled in real terms from 1987 up to 1993. The interventions of the structural Funds were concentrated on five objectives, of which three have a regional dimension: Objective 1, promoting the catching-up of the regions whose development is lagging behind, Objective 2, for the reconversion of industrial zones in decline, and Objective 5b, promoting rural development. The less developed regions of the EC, excepting (for the time being) the GDR, are fully covered by these objectives, and are therefore the largest beneficiaries. Objective 1 regions — principally Greece, Ireland, Portugal, 70 % of Spain, the Italian Mezzogiorno and Northern Ireland — account for about 60 % of the total financial amount allocated to the structural Funds for the period 1989-93 (ECU 60,3 billion, 1989 prices). The reform of the Funds began to be implemented in 1989 with the adoption of the Community support frameworks within which the interventions of the structural Funds for the period 1989-93 were largely allocated (see Box 9.4). According to the 1988 reform of the Funds, decisions about the post-1993 period are to be based on a global evaluation of the reform to be carried out in 1991.

The Community structural policies are thus already set for the period up to 1993 which overlaps with Stage I of EMU. The rationale for these policies, as reflected in the Community support frameworks, was primarily to allow the enhancement in the adjustment of the less favoured regions to the new economic environment that the 1992 single market will bring about. As a consequence, these policies should be continued along with the completion of full economic union within the EC.

9.4.2. The less favoured regions and monetary union

The preceding section dealt, in a concise way, with the issue of the Community's less favoured countries and regions in relation to the construction of economic union. The economies of these countries may be hurt before they are helped according to the U-shaped curve mentioned in Section 9.1. To contribute to leading those regions to the upward sloping part of the curve may involve a significant lowering of trade barriers. It may also require Community accompanying policies

The question now arises whether the superimposition of monetary union will add any spatial effects to those of economic union. Are there any particular effects on lagging countries and regions which directly derive from monetary union? Even if the answer were clear-cut for the case where effects of currency areas take for granted that an economic union is already performing smoothly, that is not the relevant situation. As far as the EC is concerned, the construction of economic union and monetary union will be parallel processes. Will monetary unification amplify the impact on the less favoured regions of the real shocks stemming from the internal market? Will they be attenuated? Will there be any specific monetary shocks? Two domains where this issue is relevant have been analysed in Chapters 5 and 6, namely the abandoning of the nominal exchange rate and the elimination of hidden forms of taxation for the financing of public deficits.

Both domains are not particular to lagging regions but they may be felt there with more intensity. In fact, besides a higher possibility of being hit by an asymmetrical external shock, those regions have to adjust to the real shocks stemming from the completion of economic union; this adjustment may call for the utilization of the nominal exchange-rate instrument. Such a viewpoint relies on the acceptance that nominal instruments are adequate to cope with real shocks which is not accepted without dispute. Besides, the active management of the exchange rate as a policy instrument has been, *de facto,* relinquished by most of the EC peripheral countries. It is perhaps the perception of this situation that lies behind the fact that firms do not view the exchange rate as a major constraint for the development of lagging regions, as the survey quoted in Section 9.3 above displays.

However, as argued in Chapter 6, abandoning the nominal exchange rate is least costly for countries that are initially in equilibrium (including the exchange rate) conditions and only have random shocks to absorb. The situation of countries whose economies are initially very distorted is quite different and these may need structural adjustments to the exchange rate as part of their general policy strategy. Greece may be now in this latter category whereas the rest of the EC is in the former group. Portugal may find itself in an ambiguous position in between.

The issue of abandoning the nominal exchange rate effectively concerns mainly three countries which are eligible for structural interventions, namely Greece, Ireland and Portugal. The less-favoured regions of Spain and the Italian Mezzogiorno are already deprived of an autonomous exchange rate policy given that they belong to a (national) currency area. In an identical situation is now the GDR, given its monetary union with the FRG (see Annex B).

The adoption of a hard-currency policy with eventually fixing the exchange rate requires sound conditions of domestic monetary stability which, in turn, are associated with the public finance situation. Ireland is a member of the exchange-rate mechanism (ERM) of the EMS since its creation and a successful adjustment programme of its public finances has helped make it possible to avoid any unilateral devaluation of the Irish punt since 1986. Recent developments as well as the forecast of Ireland's external accounts do not warrant any departure from the existing exchange-rate policy. Spain joined the EMS in mid-1989; although benefiting from the wider band of fluctuation, the peseta has been close to the upper band due to capital inflows reflecting the fact that domestic policies continue to be geared to monetary and financial stability. Ireland and Spain are therefore at least half-way to locking their exchange rates, with the adjustments in relative prices having to rely, more and more, on wage developments. With the German monetary union, the economy of the GDR is covered by the Deutschmark exchange rate policy; as regards the adjustment of the GDR within an united Germany, the role of the exchange rate was confined to the bilateral parity adopted for monetary unification (see Annex B).

Portugal and Greece still follow autonomous exchange-rate policies. Portugal has adhered, for more than a decade, to a pre-announced crawling-peg regime reinforced by infrequent discrete devaluations, the last one dating from mid-1983. This policy, given the low degree of indexation of the economy, especially wages, has aimed at the maintenance of competitivity and allowed adjustment to domestic and external shocks. The balance of payments situation is now comfortable, and the country is faced with a similar dilemma to Spain's in the setting of the appropriate long-term level of the exchange rate in the prospect of ERM or EMU membership. The current account deficit is financed by strong capital inflows that respond to the tight internal monetary conditions as well as to the investment opportunit-

ies brought about by Portugal's integration in the EC. Meanwhile, the persistence of domestic inflation leads to a real appreciation of the escudo. It is hard to assess the sustainability of these trends, but the adoption of a firm pluri-annual fiscal adjustment programme would provide the necessary credibility for an early exchange-rate commitment.

Greece has been following a policy of managed floating, and is the peripheral country that has experienced the strongest overall devaluation since 1979. It is also the country with the highest level of inflation and public deficit, though the public debt to GDP ratio is not as high as Italy's, for example. Some arguments have been put forward against an early entry into the EMS: for example, strong disparities between Greece's economic and trade structure and those of its EC partners increase the possibility of asymmetric shocks that would require the exchange-rate instrument. Like Ireland, Portugal and Spain, Greece is committed to eliminating restrictions on capital movements by 1992.

Just like abandoning of the exchange-rate instrument, the issue of renouncing hidden or implicit forms of taxation is not limited to the less favoured countries and regions, as was stressed in Chapters 5 and 6. Nevertheless, the southern States of the Community are those where this phenomenon takes higher proportions (see Graph 5.5). On the other hand, the lagging countries are more expansionary-prone given the challenges of the catching-up. Budgetary policy is less flexible in the less developed regions with the consequence that the temptation for surprise inflation as well as for other forms of implicit taxation is higher. Finally, it should be borne in mind that, in their present form, the transfers of the Community's structural Funds have a direct impact on the national budgets, given that they co-finance public expenditure, and capital expenditure in particular. Having the nature of 'matching-grants' and having to respect the additionality principle, the transfers from the structural Funds are a constraint for the national (including regional) budgets' management. Such a constraint may have significant proportions in the national (and regional) budgets of the lagging countries given that they are the largest recipients of financial support from the Community and given the relative magnitude of the received transfers (in the order of 3 % of GDP, see Box 9.4). The importance of this constraint for the management of national public expenditure would be amplified in a framework of an enhanced role of central public finance in the Community (see Section 6.7). This fact gives a certain specificity to the lagging regions as far as the renouncement of implicit taxes is concerned, calling for the implementation of flexible mechanisms to encourage the national effort to reduce public deficits, e.g. through the widening of the eligibility criteria for structural Fund support.

Aside from abandoning nominal exchange rate changes and eliminating hidden forms of taxation, a specific effect of monetary union on less favoured regions and countries may be stressed. This is related to the underdevelopment of the financial market that often accompanies excessive public deficits and the resort to hidden taxes. One may refer to it as the crowding-out of weaker local borrowers. What is at stake, again, is the domestic financial sector and the ways of financing public-sector deficits. Very often, the monetary authorities of countries with less performing financial systems have to resort to direct methods of monetary control (credit rationing, administrative setting of interest rates, etc.) as the sole alternative for the management of domestic liquidity growth. Such direct controls impinge upon the private sector which is crowded out from the credit market. Recent theories and empirical studies (see Branson, 1990) have shown that local financial intermediaries are able to enjoy some monopoly power due to information asymmetries and sunken costs (e.g. lasting credit relationships with borrowers). In such a hierarchical structure of the financial system, local banks stand between international credit markets and domestic borrowers, impeding direct contact between them. Local lenders have an advantage over foreign banks because they trade instruments with costly local knowledge (e.g. the monitoring of clients), which can be considered non-traded internationally. With full monetary union local banks will loose this monopoly power assuming that borrowers will have direct access to foreign banks, either locally established or not, after the opening of the domestic financial market. Beside this credit availability effect, the borrowers of peripheral countries will also benefit from the level of interest rates which very likely will stay below those prevailing in the region before monetary unification. These two effects — availability and lower price — will represent a clear benefit for the borrowers of lagging regions.

However, local banks may be disrupted because foreign banks will rapidly seize the best segment of the market leaving the local banks with the less performing borrowers. Besides, the new and open financial market will develop in a context of tighter financial discipline and stricter rules for credit granting which may crowd out the (marginal) borrowers of the lagging regions. The net effect is ambiguous. For instance, it is not clear that a small enterprise in, say, the north of Portugal, which currently can only deal with its local bank to obtain credit, will be better off when it will have access to, say, a large British bank as well. With the local bank the small enterprise would eventually get some credit, but with the large foreign bank it may not because it does not meet the 'eligibility' standards of the bank. Naturally, the situation will disappear once the local bank has recovered and adapted to the new conditions. The effect of monetary union for the credit market of a lagging region could well be as ambiguous as was the case with

economic union. The possible crowding out of weaker local borrowers calls for the setting of adequate Community policies addressed to the adjustment of the local financial sector. Such policies would aim, *inter alia,* at securing credit availability for the 'marginalized' borrowers of lagging regions (e.g. funding of regional development societies, risk capital societies, etc). In the absence of such policies, the national authorities of the lagging countries would be tempted to oppose the opening of the financial markets through the maintenance of domestic regulatory practices. Such practices would go counter to the process of monetary union, not allowing the benefits of EMU to be fully reaped.

9.4.3. Regime change and regime structure

The bottom-line issue for the lagging countries and regions is how to overcome their development bottlenecks and catch up as fast as possible with the more prosperous parts of the Community. This objective translates into a need to sustain, for a long period, higher-than-average rates of real GDP growth. This in turn calls for a stable, though dynamic, economic environment, and the avoidance of unrealistic goals and stop-and-go policies.

Regime change. Given the ambitious nature of the catching-up objective, the appropriate concept seems to be that of a credible and comprehensive regime change.

A comprehensive regime change is a dynamic process where multiple synergies are at work between expectations and real economic variables, and which may radically alter the feasible dynamic path of the economy. For example, the insertion of a country into an economic space as the European single market can have such an effect upon the expectations and strategies of domestic and international investors that investment levels are achieved which otherwise might have required the maintenance of relatively much lower real wages. This effect is in fact currently observed in Spain and Portugal.

If a comprehensive and credible regime change is the key for the convergence of lagging countries and regions to EC standards, how far can one characterize the strategic aspects of that change, in terms of policies at the EC and national levels?

There is a widespread consensus on some elements, such as a unified and open European single market; national policies of enterprise reform, aimed at the introduction of market discipline mechanisms in all sectors of the economy; labour market regulatory reform, aimed at more flexibility, efficiency and employment; modernization of tax systems; and stability-oriented and transparent monetary and budgetary policies. As far as the latter are concerned, an important question is of course the distribution of responsibilities between the EC and national level but, more generally, all these aspects must be considered within the perspective of EMU.

In the previous section the abandoning of the nominal exchange rate as a policy instrument as well as the elimination of hidden forms of taxation for the financing of public deficits were already stressed. The peculiarity of underdeveloped local financial markets was also mentioned. In all cases, it was apparent that the prescription of regime change would not differ greatly between the countries and regions in question.

The most clear-cut and extreme examples of regime change are currently observed in Central and Eastern European countries. By comparison, the scale of the changes still to be made by Spain, Portugal or Greece is, of course, much smaller. These Community countries have already substantially changed their political and economic systems in the last 15 years or so. But credibility is an important element of any regime change, which is why a binding integration into an international structure like the EC can play a vital role. This was certainly appreciated by those three countries when they decided, in the 1970s, to apply for membership. Without the influence of this 'external liberalization constraint' upon expectations, desirable reforms might not have been feasible and the policy-maker's room for manoeuvre might in fact have been reduced by a lack of domestic credibility.

Regime structure. Important as these common desirable elements of regime change may be, there are also some key features of regime structure that separate the different lagging countries and regions of the Community. Since these involve Community policies, it is necessary to understand the patterns underlying these differences in regime structure.

The three issues in question, in fact interdependent, are:

(i)   labour migration: how much should be expected and considered desirable?

(ii) budgetary redistribution: how much interregional redistribution is appropriate?

(iii) the exchange rate: at what point should flexibility be reduced and, eventually, abandoned in EMU?

The initial conditions of the lagging regions of the Community differ most clearly according to whether they are sub-regions of nations (like parts of Italy and Spain, and now also East Germany) or nation-regions like Greece, Portugal or Ireland. The former group experience high internal migration and fiscal redistribution and zero exchange rate flexibility between regions; the latter group experience relatively little external migration and (EC) redistribution, while retaining at least some exchange rate flexibility.

With the progressive integration of the Community, these initial conditions gradually change, and the dynamic aspects of regime structure should also be taken into account. This is portrayed schematically in Table 9.3, with identification of four successive regimes: international relations, the EC of the 1980s, representing a transitional stage of integration, the EC under EMU conditions, and a mature federal State (notably one with considerable unity of language, culture and history).

From the standpoint of the public authorities a key difference between the three variables is that labour migration is a behavioural factor, assuming that the legal freedom to migrate is granted. The budgetary and exchange rate variables are policy instruments that may be adjusted, in reaction to the behaviour of the economy, or addressed to specific policy objectives.

Normatively all three variables have to be viewed with circumspection. None can be considered simply desirable or undesirable; each have their value or utility but also their hazards.

Table 9.3

Evolution of aspects of regime structure with the degree of integration

Variables affecting interregional relations	Type of regime			
	International relations	EC of the 1980s	EC with EMU	Mature federal State
Labour migration	little	some	more	much
Budget redistribution	none	some	more	much
Exchange-rate flexibility	considerable	some	none	none

As regards migration, its value for enhancing economic efficiency and welfare and as an adjustment variable for attaining economic equilibrium is widely acknowledged. However, at some point it can become socially disruptive and inefficient, notably where local regimes perform so poorly that mass emigration is a feature of its collapse (as East Germany has just illustrated). The propensity to migrate clearly is greater when there are no language frontiers. Within language communities migration can quite easily be triggered by differences in local fiscal capacities, which is an important reason for the budgetary redistribution and equalization mechanisms in mature federations. These considerations are in fact observed in the reunification of Germany, with the need to combat 'catastrophic migration' emerging with the extension of the normal mechanisms of fiscal federalism. They are also observed in the interregional redistribution mechanisms of Spain and Italy, which, less dramatically of course than in Germany today, have long been related to concern over migration and demographic trends as between regions.

The absence of these factors in the migration propensity of the nation-regions of the Community is an important reason why even in EMU it would not be expected that the Community's redistribution function replicate that observed in mature federations. That is at least the case at present, although the categories in question are by no means absolute or fixed. Thus Irish emigration is quite significant, facilitated by language. It is also not so many years ago that Portugal and Greece experienced structural emigration of considerable proportions. These three small nation-regions in fact benefit from redistribution from the Community on a scale that is qualitatively greater than for any other Member State.

While budgetary redistribution can thus serve efficiency as well as equity objectives, there are also hazards to be avoided. These are not in principle different from the hazards of any redistribution policy, and concern the risks of weakening incentives for production activity and creating a State welfare dependency. At the level of the region such hazards can operate either at the level of the wage bargaining system, which may be inclined to neglect regional productivity differentials, or at the level of local government, where the availability of ample external finance may fail to combine with efficient resource allocation. Community structural policy has recognized the existence of such hazards, and assistance is therefore directed towards promoting productive investment, human capital formation and infrastructures directly linked to economic development.

The exchange rate instrument, similarly, has its uses and hazards. For relatively underdeveloped economies, and areas in the course of eliminating major market distortions, a degree of exchange rate flexibility may be particularly important. The development process must not be blocked by a structurally overvalued exchange rate. On the other hand, repeated recourse to devaluation becomes itself no more than an illusion in relation to economic realities, and usually just a means of accommodating a high rate of inflation. In particular, as Chapter 6 has warned, persistent real exchange rate depreciation does not appear, in the EC at least, to buy faster longer-term growth.

Box 9.1: Peripherality in the Community of 12

Peripherality is related to both geographic distance and the volume of economic activity in different regions. The latter is meant to be a proxy for market opportunities, the availability of inputs and the various types of external economies.

A study published by the EC Commission in 1988 used the following formula:

$$P_i = \sum_{\substack{j-1 \\ j \neq i}}^{n} \frac{M_j}{D_{ij}} + \frac{M_i}{D_{ii}}$$

where M_j is the level of economic activity in region i, and is measured by regional GDP in ecus.

D_{ij} is the distance between regions i and j, and is represented by the shortest road link between the largest cities or towns in each region. Special treatment is given to islands, taking into consideration ferry and shipping costs

D_{ii} is defined as $\quad \frac{1}{3} \sqrt{\dfrac{\text{area of region (sq km)}}{\pi}}$

This index has been calculated with 1983 data for 166 NUTS II regions of the Community of 12, and its distribution is shown in the annexed map, with regions classified into central, intermediate and peripheral. The adjacent countries which are not members of the Community were also taken into account, after allowing for customs barriers.

Shares of central, intermediate and peripheral regions,[1] 1983

(EUR 12 = 100)

	Number of regions	Area	Popul.	GDP (PPS)	Employment				Unemployment		
					Total	Agric.	Manuf.	Serv.	Total	Young	Wom.
Central	44	10,0	31,0	37,9	35,6	11,6	37,9	38,8	31,5	25,8	29,5
inner	25	5,0	21,7	28,2	25,4	6,3	24,7	28,6	21,0	16,6	20,3
outer	19	5,0	9,3	9,7	10,2	5,3	13,2	10,2	10,5	9,2	9,3
Intermediate	62	33,9	35,7	37,0	37,0	31,6	40,0	36,5	29,3	29,4	31,2
Peripheral	60	56,1	33,3	24,5	27,4	56,8	22,1	24,7	39,3	44,8	39,3
inner	19	15,1	13,0	11,6	10,4	12,2	9,2	10,6	16,0	17,7	16,1
outer	41	40,2	20,3	12,9	17,0	44,6	12,9	14,1	23,3	27,2	23,2
EUR 12	166	100,0	100,0	100,0	100,0	100,0	100,0	100,0	100,0	100,0	100,0

[1] See map.

Source: Keeble *et al.* (1988).

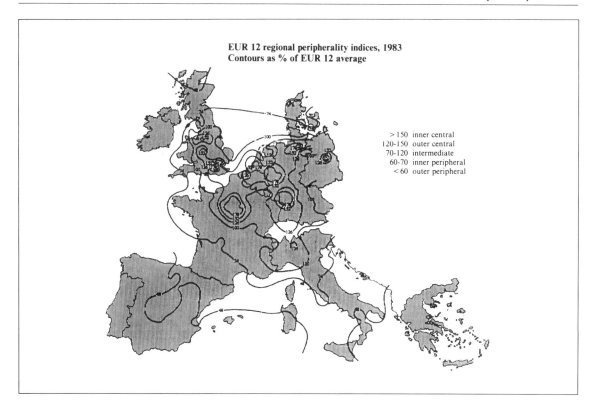

EUR 12 regional peripherality indices, 1983
Contours as % of EUR 12 average

> 150   inner central
120-150   outer central
70-120   intermediate
60-70   inner peripheral
< 60   outer peripheral

Box 9.2: Regional disparities in per capita GDP and unemployment rates: comparisons between the EC, the USA and Canada

General remarks

Indicators of regional disparities are strongly influenced by the degree of regional disaggregation: the greater the degree of disaggregation, the more pronounced are the regional disparities. Comparisons between the EC and Canada should be treated with particular caution, because of the latter's much smaller population and the small number of regions into which it is divided.

Regional disaggregation

The regional disaggregation used for this exercise is set out below. EC: 60 regions, Denmark, Greece, Ireland, Luxembourg and Portugal each being considered as one region. The other Member States are divided into NUTS I regions: 11 each for Germany, Italy and UK, 3 for Belgium, 7 for Spain, 8 for France and 4 for the Netherlands. USA: 51 regions — 50 states plus the District of Columbia. Canada: 11 regions — 10 provinces plus one region comprising the Yukon and North-West Territories. Because of lack of data, the latter region is excluded from the comparison of unemployment rates.

GDP per capita

	Ratio of top to bottom deciles[1]	Coefficient of variation[2]	Theil coefficient
EC (60 regions, 1986 data in PPS[3])	2,6	25,2%	0,0135
EC (12 Member States)	2,0	17,6%	0,0071
Germany (11 *Länder*)	1,6	13,7%	0,0037
USA (50 states + D. of Columbia, 1986)[4]	1,7	16,1%	0,0051
Canada (10 provinces + 1 region, 1984)[5]	2,2	20,1%	0,0086

[1] Deciles defined in terms of population. Averages for top and bottom deciles obtained by linear interpolation. In the EC the regions covering the top decile are: Nord-Ouest, Emilia-Romagna and Lombardia (Italy), Bremen and Hamburg (Germany), Noord-Nederland, Bruxelles and Ile de France. The regions covering the bottom decile are: Portugal, Greece, Sur and Centro (Spain) and Ireland.
[2] Weighted.
[3] *Source:* Eurostat, *Statistical indicators for the reform of the structural Funds*, November 1988.
[4] *Source:* US Department of Commerce, *Survey of current business*, May 1988.
[5] *Source:* Ministry of Supply and Services, *Canada Year Book 1988*

Unemployment rates

	Ratio of top to bottom deciles[1]	Coefficient of variation[2]	Theil coefficient
EC (60 regions, averages 1986-88)[3]	5,1	46,9%	0,0428
EC (12 Member States, averages 1986-88)	4,0	37,4%	0,0276
Germany (11 *Länder*, averages 1986-88)	12,9	33,0%	0,0224
USA (50 states + D. of Columbia, averages 1984-86)[4]	2,3	22,8%	0,0111
Canada (10 provinces only, averages 1984-86)[5]	2,1	25,6%	0,0135

[1] Deciles defined in terms of labour force. Averages for deciles obtained by linear interpolation. In the EC the regions covering the bottom (best) decile are: Rheinland-Pfalz, Hessen, Bayern and Baden-Württemberg (Germany) and Luxembourg (Grand Duchy). The regions covering the top (worst) decile are: Sur, Canarias, Este, Noreste, Centro and Madrid (Spain), Campania and Sardegna (Italy) and Norhern Ireland (UK).
[2] Weighted.
[3] *Source:* Eurostat, *Statistical indicators for the reform of the structural Funds*, November 1988.
[4] *Source:* US Department of Commerce and Census Bureau, *Statistical Abstract of the United States 1988*.
[5] *Source:* Ministry of Supply and Services, *Canada Year Book 1988*.

Box 9.3: Company view on the effects of the internal market

The Directorate-General XVI of the Commission of the European Communities commissioned a study whose main purpose was to identify the factors that either limit or promote expansion in terms of employment and production, by firms in lagging regions and in industrial regions in decline. To carry out this task, the IFO institute of Munich organized a large-scale survey covering about 9 000 companies in industry and business services in 45 problem regions, and for the purpose of comparison also in 10 prosperous regions (control regions).

The questionnaire asked firms to assess the incidence of different factors of competitiveness (regional or national) upon their firms as positive, negative or neutral. The same was asked about the impact of the completion of the European internal market. Tables A, B and C are based on their replies, where an index of 100 would correspond to a positive assessment by all firms, and − 100 a unanimous negative assessment.

Table A

Company assessment of the effect of the completion of the European internal market on company[1]

| | Types of region | | |
	Lagging	Declining	Control
Belgium	—	25,7	28,7
Germany	—	12,2	21,4
Greece	11,2	—	—
Spain	15,1	− 1,6	8,6
France	21,8	39,1	53,0
Ireland	37,8	—	—
Italy	27,9	—	36,5
Netherlands	—	22,0	10,9
Portugal	2,3	—	—
United Kingdom	21,1	24,1	− 23,4
EEC (sample)	17,4	17,9	25,1

Source: IFO (1989).

Table B

Company assessment of the effect of the completion of the European internal market on regions[1]

| | Types of region | | |
	Lagging	Declining	Control
Belgium	—	5,0	22,4
Germany	—	6,8	30,0
Greece	13,4	—	—
Spain	34,5	10,5	20,9
France	34,8	35,2	43,1
Ireland	14,2	—	—
Italy	7,1	—	19,3
Netherlands	—	22,0	11,9
Portugal	12,3	—	—
United Kingdom	4,4	8,1	− 19,2
EEC (sample)	14,2	9,4	23,4

Source: IFO (1989).

Table C

Company assessment of factors of regional competitiveness[1]

	Lagging	Declining	Control
National factors			
Exchange rate policy	− 21	− 7	− 20
Income/corporate taxation	− 70	− 64	− 76
Cost of credit	− 98	− 32	− 45
Availability of risk capital	− 18	− 8	5
General economic growth	44	68	72
Sector's outlook	34	55	46
Wage costs	− 42	− 53	− 79
Indirect labour costs	− 79	− 99	− 120
Labour market regulation	− 62	− 67	− 78
Industrial policy	1	0	10
Legal regulations	− 2	− 22	− 27
Administrative procedures	− 36	− 31	− 38
Other macro factors	− 9	− 5	− 2
Regional factors			
Proximity of customers	− 51	68	57
Proximity of suppliers	22	45	36
Business culture	10	11	31
Banks, insurance, lawyers	32	52	60
Advertising and consulting	14	24	40
Servicing machinery	9	42	47
Transport network	16	70	66
Supply and cost of energy	− 18	18	30
Communication systems	29	74	58
Waste disposal	− 21	− 3	− 12
Industrial sites	− 3	10	− 7
Cultural and social facilities	− 13	16	24
Leisure facilities	− 13	21	19
Social climate	17	21	36
Cost of housing	− 18	18	− 16
School facilities	− 3	25	38
Supply of qualified labour	− 18	− 29	− 25
Supply of unqualified labour	14	15	− 2
Proximity of training	− 15	21	37
Proximity of higher education	7	42	40
Regional policy incentives	1	2	3
Cooperation of local authorities	− 17	0	− 10
Local taxes	− 32	− 57	− 41
Other regional factors	3	0	6

Source: IFO (1989).

Box 9.4: Less favoured regions and Community structural policies for the period 1989-93

Public expenditure considered in the Community support frameworks (CSF)

Regions	Total (1) = (2) + (3)	Structural Funds (2)	National finance requirement (3)	Community loans (EIB, ECSC)
in MECU, 1989 prices				
Greece (entire country)	12 995	7 195	5 802	1 410
Ireland (entire country)	6 126	3 672	2 454	560
Portugal (entire country)	14 026	7 368	6 658	2 805
Spain (70% of the country)	16 507	9 779	6 728	2 206
Italy (Mezzogiorno)	14 062	7 583	6 479	1 475
in % of regional GDP				
Greece (entire country)	5,2	2,9	2,3	
Ireland (entire country)	3,8	2,3	1,5	
Portugal (entire country)	6,6	3,5	3,1	
Spain (70% of the country)	2,0	1,2	0,8	
Italy (Mezzogiorno)	1,5	0,8	0,7	

Note: Furthermore, these regions will benefit from the programmes adopted under Community initiatives which are not included in the CSFs. The GDR will benefit from a specific programme of structural Fund assistance for a period starting with the German political unification and ending in 1993. From this date on the GDR will be considered with the other EC countries.

CSF public expenditure — Breakdown by main categories in %

	Portugal	Spain	Italy	Ireland	Greece
Infrastructure	27,3	53,1	47,3	17,1	31,3
Aids to product. investment	17,0	9,9	29,0	26,5	7,0
Agriculture	11,9	14,0	8,3	24,5	13,0
Manpower	28,0	22,7	14,8	31,2	13,7
Regional programmes	15,6	1	1	1	34,5
Others	0,2	0,3	0,6	0,6	0,4
Total	100	100	100	100	100

[1] Included in the other categories.

References

Balassa, B. (1961), *The theory of economic integration*, Richard Irwin, New York.

Bliss, C. and Braga de Macedo, J. (1990), *Unity with diversity within the European economy: the Community's southern frontier*, Cambridge University Press.

Borts (1960), 'The equalization of returns and regional economic growth', *American Economic Review*, 50, pp. 319-347.

Braga de Macedo, J. (1990), 'External liberalization with ambiguous public response: the experience of Portugal', in Braga de Macedo and Bliss (eds), *Unity with diversity within the European economy: the Community's southern frontier*, Cambridge University Press.

Branson, W. (1990), 'Financial market integration, macroeconomic policy and the EMS', in Braga de Macedo and Bliss (eds), *Unity with diversity within the European economy: the Community's southern frontier*, Cambridge University Press.

Byé, M. (1958), 'Localisation de l'investissement et communauté économique européenne', *Revue économique*.

Buigues, P., Ilzkovitz, F. and Lebrun, J. F. (1990), 'Les États membres face aux enjeux sectoriels du marché intérieur', *European Economy* No 44 and *Social Europe*.

Clark, C., Wilson, F. and Bradley, J. (1969), 'Industrial location and economic potential in Western Europe', *Regional Studies*, 2.

Cohen, D. and Wyploz, C. (1989), 'The European monetary union: an agnostic evaluation', CEPR Discussion Paper No 306, London.

EC Commission (1990), 'The economic and financial situation in Germany', *Economic Papers*, forthcoming.

Faini, R. (1990), 'Regional development and economic integration: the case of southern Italy', paper presented at the conference 'Portugal and the internal market of the EC', Lisbon.

Giersch, H. (1949), 'Economic union between nations and the location of industries', *Review of Economic Studies*, 17, pp. 87-97.

IFO-Institut für Wirtschaftsforschung (1989), *An empirical assessment of factors shaping regional competitiveness in problem regions*, Munich.

Katseli, L. (1990), 'Economic integration in the enlarged European Community: structural adjustment of the Greek economy', in Braga de Macedo and Bliss (eds), *Unity with diversity within the European economy: the Community's southern frontier*, Cambridge University Press.

Keeble, D., Offord, J. and Walker, S. (1988), *Peripheral regions in a Community of 12 Member States*, Commission of the European Communities, Brussels.

Krugman, P. (1989), 'Increasing returns and economic geography', NBER Working Paper, Washington.

Krugman, P. and Venables, A. (1990), 'Integration and the competitiveness of peripheral industry', in Braga de Macedo and Bliss (eds), *Unity with diversity within the European economy: the Community's southern frontier*, Cambridge University Press.

Magnifico, G. (1973), *European monetary unification*, MacMillan, London.

Molle, W. (1989), 'Will the completion of the internal market lead to regional divergence?', paper presented at the conference 'The completion of the internal market', Kiel, June 1989.

Myrdal, G. (1957), *Economic theory and underdeveloped regions*, London.

Neven, D. (1990), 'EEC integration towards 1992: some distributional aspects', *Economic Policy*, April 1990

OECD (1989), *Regional policy developments in OECD countries*, Paris.

Perroux, F. (1959), 'Les formes de concurrence dans le marché commun', *Revue d'économie politique*, 1.

Stahl, H. M. (1974), *Regionalpolitische Implikationen einer EWG-Währungsunion*, Tübingen.

Scitovski, T. (1958), *Economic theory and and Western European integration*, Stanford University Press.

Vanhove, N. and Klaassen, L. H. (1980), *Regional policy: a European approach*, Saxon House.

Viñals, J. *et al.* (1990), 'Spain and the EC cum 1992 shock', in Macedo and Bliss (eds), *Unity with diversity within the European economy: the Community's southern frontier*, Cambridge University Press.

Williamson, J. (1965), 'Regional inequality and the process of national development: a description of the patterns', *Economic development and cultural change*, 13, pp. 3-45.

Chapter 10

National perspectives on the costs and benefits of EMU

It is understandable that the question is often put, for EMU as well as for the internal market, what the distribution of benefits and costs is likely to be by Member State.

The approach to answering this question taken in this study is to consider how the sources of benefits and costs (as listed above, in Box 1 or Table 1.1) relate to the initial situation of the different Member States. This is done in the first part of the short country sections that follow below, whereas the second part of each section gives a view of the present state of the national debate about EMU in political and opinion-forming circles. It will be evident, however, that these positions taken in political debates and negotiation may well evolve over time, and also become more precise when the Intergovernmental Conference gets under way. The information recorded in this chapter may thus be viewed as a photograph of positions at a certain point in time (October 1990). It has the none the less the important merit of recording the initial positions of the Member States, which, ultimately, will have to be adequately reconciled.

The potential economic impact of EMU is in the nature of a positive-sum game. It is not therefore, at least primarily, a matter of distribution of benefits and costs between countries, which would be the case if it were a zero-sum game. There are, certainly, inter-country distributional aspects which should not be neglected (some of these were discussed in Chapter 9). But those aspects should not divert attention from the fundamental point, which is this: the main sources of potential benefits from EMU are several in number and heterogeneous in character. Individual countries can identify the major sources of potential benefit, and risks of costs, that are most relevant to its specific economic structure. The cocktails of benefits and costs of individual countries will often be quite different.

The grouping of countries below, by the extent of their participation in the EMS, and by size, already indicates two important parameters for assessing the benefits and costs by country. As pointed out in Chapter 8, countries that are already highly convergent within the EMS will have already undergone the major adjustment costs of EMU, but have not yet reaped all the benefits. The less convergent countries have bigger gains on offer, but larger transitional costs to overcome as well. For small, very open economies the benefits of EMU are easiest to establish, especially those with currencies that are little used internationally and for which transaction costs are high.

Other important parameters include the extent to which the credibility of national institutions for stable and sound monetary and budgetary policies would be improved by EMU. This is a source of potential gain for most countries, and the mechanisms here lie in minimizing the transitional costs both of disinflation and the reduction of public sector deficits. On these accounts Germany is the notable exception given its anchor role in the EMS. The major potential benefits in this case are, therefore, of a different nature. As the largest exporter of goods and capital to other Community countries, Germany has an above-average interest in the stability and transparency of the price and monetary mechanisms of the whole of the union. Germany will be also most affected by the general reshaping of the international system.

10.1. Currencies in the narrow band of the exchange-rate mechanism

10.1.1. Germany

Benefits and costs

Germany would gain from the perfection of market mechanisms within the Community that would be achieved by EMU and, in particular, as a major exporter of capital, from the elimination of exchange-risk uncertainty for investors. By contrast, the reductions in transaction costs and uncertainty that would be generated by a single currency would not be so important for Germany, a sizeable proportion of whose trade is already invoiced in Deutschmarks.

For the past 40 years low inflation has been a key objective of German policy and has been achieved chiefly thanks to the monetary policy pursued by the Bundesbank. There is concern that EuroFed might have a weaker commitment to price stability and to discipline in public finances. However, to the extent that EMU would reinforce the commitment of others to price stability and to sound public finances, it would reduce the risk of imported inflation. In addition, Germany seeks to secure guarantees of price stability through the independence of EuroFed and the priority it would give to stability.

During the transition to EMU the risks of the Deutschmark being undervalued and, consequently, of some misallocation of resources to the export sector of the economy, might increase a little.

The replacement of the Deutschmark by the ecu as an international currency would relieve the German authorities of the inconveniences of having to cope with exchange-rate pressures that emanate from the role of the Deutschmark as a major reserve currency rather than as the national currency. This is also relevant in the context of the likely demand in Eastern Europe for parallel currencies in the years ahead: in the absence of the ecu as an adequate alternative, a strong demand for the Deutschmark would present a number of problems.

German economic and monetary unification will have repercussions on the German position in relation to EMU. It is likely to cause some increase in inflation and interest rates for a while and some reduction in the current-account surplus. This will make for closer convergence of economic performance, albeit as a result of changes in Germany rather than in other economies.

Perspectives

The Government has given strong support to the EMU objective and the broad approach proposed in the Delors Report.

In its September 1990 'Statement on the establishment of an economic and monetary union in Europe', the Bundesbank remains very much in favour of the 'coronation theory', i.e. there should at first be a convergence of economic key variables and institutional safeguards, before competences are transferred to EuroFed. In referring to 'substantial transitional problems as a result of the intra-German unification process, and when developments in Eastern Europe are still unclear in many respects' the Bundesbank prefers to postpone further steps to EMU 'until such time as the economic situation in Germany as a whole and in the European Community can be regarded as sufficiently consolidated'.

As regards the final stage of EMU, the Bundesbank enumerates several necessary pre-conditions related to the economic convergence in Europe and to the structure and conduct of monetary and fiscal policies in all member countries and at the European level which 'can be fulfilled only in the course of a lengthy transitional process. During this process, no institutional changes which result in any curtailment of the freedom of reaction of national monetary policy may be made'.[1]

Academics are less enthusiastic about EMU than other sectors of opinion in Germany. The Board of Academic Advisers, a group of 30 academics which advises the Economics Ministry, set out its reaction to the Delors Report in a letter sent to the Ministry in June 1989. This recognized that the Report was justified in rejecting the 'coronation theory', according to which monetary union can be introduced only when virtually perfect economic convergence has already been achieved, but criticized the approach to monetary union proposed in the Delors Report. The Board objected to the proposal that monetary union should be preceded by a two-stage transition period, because this involves the risk first, that the transitional arrangements would turn out to be permanent and second, that the Economic and Financial Affairs Council would in fact acquire a weight incompatible with the autonomy of national central banks. It also doubted the need for formal *ex-ante* coordination and binding rules for fiscal policy.

The Council of Economic Advisers in their Annual Report released in November 1989[2] commented that though the Delors Report provided a good basis for further discussion, serious objections could be raised to some of the positions it adopted. While acknowledging the advantages that a single currency would confer, the Council suggested that for the time being the Member States' economies were too heterogeneous for them to abandon the instrument of exchange rate adjustment without running grave risks. With the completion of the internal market, greater nominal and real convergence, and increasing integration, the conditions for monetary union would improve decisively, but for the time being it was necessary to retain the possibility of realigning exchange rates.

The Eurobarometer survey taken in autumn 1989 indicated that public opinion is mildly in favour of EMU. It is attracted by the advantages of a single currency for private transactions, but less keen than the EC average on economic integration.

10.1.2. France

Benefits and costs

EMU should consolidate the advances France has made in recent years towards much closer convergence with German economic performance in terms of price stability and sound public finance.

Pegging French monetary policy yet more firmly to the price stability standard of Germany should help ward off any remaining doubts as to the anti-inflation stance of the auth-

[1]   Deutsche Bundesbank (1990).

[2]   Sachverständigenrat zur Begutachtung der gesamtwirtschaftlichen Entwicklung (1989).

orities. As the continuation of low inflation becomes more credible and the residual degree of exchange risk perceived by the markets is eliminated, interest rates will decline. This progress is already in evidence, and will further assist public finances by alleviating the cost of servicing the public debt. Lower interest rates, together with savings in transactions costs, will also encourage an expansion of private investment.

France will thus strongly benefit from the effect of EMU on expectations about future inflation and monetary accommodation. The unambiguous signalling of a commitment to a stability-oriented EMU will help to persuade economic agents to adapt their behaviour, for example in wage bargaining strategies. This will be important for overcoming the persistent problem of relatively high unemployment.

The importance of the current-account constraint, a long-standing preoccupation for France, will diminish. Indeed, in an environment in which capital movements are already completely liberalized and the credibility of the commitment to a fixed exchange rate is becoming established, the financing constraint will be alleviated; without the exchange-rate risk only small interest rate differentials will be needed to produce the appropriate financial flows. With the advent of a single currency the financing constraint will be removed entirely.

Perspectives

The Government favours moving rapidly to EMU, for both political and economic reasons. Furthermore, it is widely accepted that devaluing the franc is not an efficient means of resolving current-account problems. The transfer of sovereignty is accepted, given that the French monetary authorities would exert influence on the common monetary policy. Some concern regarding budgetary policy has been voiced by the Minister of the Economy and Finance.[3] Too rigid a coordination of fiscal policies, and the consequent loss of sovereignty in this sphere, would create difficulties. These reservations apart, the strong support of the French authorities for EMU has been reiterated on several occasions. Furthermore, the French Government now supports the proposition of an independent central banking institution.

The Governor of the Banque de France in several speeches on EMU[4] stressed the importance of directing a common monetary policy towards price stability and of ensuring that fiscal policy is also consistent with that objective. He also supported the idea of an independent central banking institution.

Segments of the opposition political parties dissent from the proposal for a single currency in the third stage of the Delors Report. For them, a common currency existing in parallel with national currencies would suffice for the effective working of the single market and would avoid the loss of sovereignty of national governments in monetary policy-making.

In academic circles there is clear support for EMU. Surveys indicate that heads of large companies attach great importance to the setting up of EuroFed and the creation of a single currency, since transaction costs and uncertainty would be greatly reduced. Public opinion appears from Eurobarometer polls to be strongly in favour of a single currency.

10.1.3. Italy

Benefits and costs

Italy's currency was until recently in the wide band of the EMS exchange-rate mechanism. Consequently, proceeding to EMU represents a more important change than for many Member States. In recent years Italy's economic performance has been in many respects highly positive. With respect to inflation and public finances, however, it still lags significantly behind the best standards. This implies costs in the transition to EMU, but also potential gains if a credible commitment to EMU accelerates convergence. Not only would there be gain in terms of greater price stability and healthier public finances. Once economic agents adapted their expectations, there would be benefits too in the labour market and for employment.

The reduction in interest rates that will result from the elimination of exchange risk and inflation premiums will be a major gain for Italy because of its very high public debt (98 % of GDP in 1989) and the present wide margin between lira and Deutschmark rates. A decline of one percentage point in the treasury-bill rate is reckoned to save roughly LIT 3 000 billion in the first year and LIT 7 000 billion in the second.

None the less, though lower interest rates will significantly reduce the debt-service component of the budget deficit, this alone will not suffice to restore sound public finances. A concerted effort will still be necessary to bring the general government deficit (10,2 % of GDP in 1989) to a sustainable level. In addition, the establishment of a single financial

---

3   See, for example, Bérégovoy (1989).
4   See, for example, de Larosière (1989), and *Les Echos* (1990).

market will generate some losses in seigniorage revenue, resulting from the harmonization of marginal reserve requirements, and in fiscal revenue, resulting from the reduction in the withholding tax rate on bank deposits, which at present is 30 %. Although these losses will not be negligible, they will be smaller than the gains from lower interest rates and will be partly offset by the seigniorage gains of EuroFed.

The effect of losing the exchange rate as an adjustment instrument will depend importantly on how far economic agents are convinced that this option no longer exists and adjust their behaviour accordingly. Since the inception of the EMS significant changes in behaviour have occurred in the tradables sector (chiefly manufacturing industry) but far fewer in the non-tradables sector (chiefly services, public and private). With the removal of barriers to competition, market forces should bring about the desired change in sectors exposed to competition, e.g. financial services, but the Government will need to act directly on the public sector.

Perspectives

The Government is a forthright proponent of EMU, and stresses the need to bring the budget deficit under control as a Community discipline necessitated by EMU.

The Banca d'Italia supports both the principle of EMU and the three-stage process outlined in the Delors Report. It welcomes the prospect of a common monetary policy directed at price stability and would like independent status for EuroFed. It also favours binding budgetary rules.[5]

Academic opinion is strongly positive towards EMU, which it views as the culmination of the process of stabilizing exchange rates and reducing Italy's inflation to the lower levels of most of its EC partners. Some reservations are expressed regarding the premature loss of seigniorage tax while the public debt remains excessive. There are warnings too about the implications for the prospects of the less-developed regions of the country.

Public opinion broadly supports EMU. This includes the business sector, despite recurrent complaints from industrialists about deteriorating competitiveness. The public assesses EMU, beyond its economic merits, as part of the process of European integration. Eurobarometer surveys show that Italians favour the adoption of common policies, including a single currency, by a wider margin than any other nation.

Smaller economies

The smaller countries in the exchange-rate mechanism have already incurred, in the context of membership of the EMS, most of the costs of adjusting to EMU, in terms of reducing inflation to low levels and managing without an independent monetary policy. They retain, however, some drawbacks of monetary independence, such as transaction costs and exchange-risk premiums on their interest rates. In addition, in EMU they will have a full part in determining the policy of EuroFed.

The consequences of a single currency in lowering transaction costs and enabling the benefits of the single market to be reaped to the full will be particularly advantageous to small open economies.

10.1.4. Belgium

Benefits and costs

The principal benefits to Belgium will be the efficiency gains arising from the elimination of exchange-rate uncertainty and transaction costs, and the discipline that EMU will impose on public finances.

Commitment to EMU will reinforce the credibility of low inflation. The consequent reduction in interest rates will contribute significantly to lowering the budget deficit (6,3 % of GDP in 1989) because of the large sums that go to servicing Belgium's very high public debt (135 % of GDP in 1989). This will not, however, obviate the need for more stringent control of public finances. Indeed, progress towards EMU will entail both institutional and market pressure on Belgium to reduce both the budget deficit and the public debt faster than it is doing at present.

Perspectives

The Government has explicitly supported the Delors Report, including both the principle of EMU and the proposal to achieve it in three stages.[6] The transfer of powers to a supranational authority that EMU involves is not viewed as a diminution of national sovereignty, since Belgium retains little *de facto* autonomy in the relevant areas. Opposition parties accept the principle of EMU but question the Government's ability to deal satisfactorily with the problems posed by the state of public finances.

---

[5]   See Banca d'Italia (1990).

[6]   See Banque Nationale de Belgique (1990).

The governor of the central bank has stressed the implications of EMU for the financing of budget deficits, notably the abolition of monetary financing.[7] This was resorted to frequently in Belgium in the early 1980s but recently has been used much less.

10.1.5. Netherlands

Benefits and costs

For a very open economy, such as that of the Netherlands, the elimination of transaction costs and exchange rate uncertainty in relation to the EC as a whole will be a significant benefit.

A fixed parity has been maintained for several years between the guilder and the Deutschmark, which has contributed largely to achieving low inflation. Inflation is even slightly lower than in Germany, and the premium on Dutch interest rates over German rates is small and for long-term rates has almost been eliminated. As a result the main adjustments required for EMU have already been secured. (This experience is analysed in detail in Annex B, given its importance as a case study in gradual transition to effective monetary union.)

The Netherlands has a sizeable budget deficit (5,1 % of GDP in 1989), however, which partly reflects the interest rate burden of its high public debt (83 % of GDP in 1989). Both need to be reduced to ensure that the Netherlands has the freedom of manoeuvre in fiscal policy that will be necessary in EMU.

Perspectives

In his government statement of November 1989 the Prime Minister confirmed his government's support for EMU as reinforcing the benefits of the single market.[8] He also stressed the importance of Stage I of the Delors Report and the necessity to liberalize capital markets. There is a widespread view that it is in the interest of the Netherlands that monetary decisions should be taken by a Community body and not become in effect the preserve of the large countries. The Government shares this view and has also repeatedly emphasized the subsidiarity principle, insisting that to the extent compatible with the objectives that have been set, Member States should retain responsibility for policy.

The Social and Economic Council, in an opinion issued in June 1989,[9] favoured an independent central bank, along German lines, which it saw as offering a stronger guarantee of price stability.

Academic opinion supports the idea of a single currency as offering reduced transaction costs and a more useful unit of account while also eliminating speculation between Community currencies.

10.1.6. Luxembourg

Benefits and costs

In terms of its rate of inflation and financial situation the Luxembourg economy is already well adjusted to the prospect of EMU. Like other small open economies, it will benefit particularly from the disappearance of transaction costs and exchange rate uncertainty in relation to the country as a whole.

The importance of the financial sector to the Luxembourg economy, notably with regard to employment and fiscal revenue, has focused attention on the impact that EMU will have on it. The liberalization of capital movements could favour the development of Luxembourg as a financial centre, though closer monetary integration among EMS members could erode some of the advantages that Luxembourg currently enjoys. A fixed exchange rate or single currency and harmonization of banking legislation would tend to diminish the volume of banking activity generated by foreign exchange business, currency arbitrage and tax evasion.

Perspectives

The Government supports the three-stage process towards EMU outlined at the Madrid Council. None the less, it has some reservations. These concern not so much the loss of monetary independence, which has already been effectively relinquished, as the transfer of sovereignty in the context of economic and fiscal policy.

The Ministry of Finance expects that as the Community approaches the final stage of EMU, coordination, harmonization and convergence among the 12 Member States will intensify.[10] A specific fear is that revision of the Treaty of

---

7   Verplaatse (1989).
8   Regeringsverklaring, Tweede Kamer (1989).

9   Commissie voor Economische Deskundigen van de Sociaal Economische Raad (1989).
10 Bausch (1989).

Rome will entail abandoning unanimous decision-making in the realm of tax policy.[11]

In an interview in June 1989 the director-general of the monetary authority (Institut monétaire luxembourgeois) supported EMU but suggested that it should be achieved prudently and gradually in several stages.[12]

10.1.7. Denmark

Benefits and costs

Denmark might gain less than other small open economies from the removal of transaction costs and exchange rate uncertainty, because a relatively large proportion of its trade is with non-EC (Nordic) countries.

Through participation in the ERM the Danish economy has made substantial adjustment to the future disciplines of EMU, and the rate of inflation is now among the lowest in the ERM. The level of interest rates, however, still comprises exchange-risk premiums because of Denmark's previous record of inflation in excess of German rates. By bringing about lower interest rates, EMU will have a positive impact on public finances. (The internal market puts pressure on Denmark to reduce its very high indirect taxes, but EMU does not affect this.)

EMU will mean that the current-account constraint on Danish economic policy, which has frequently been a matter of great concern, will be substantially alleviated.

Perspectives

In a report on EMU published at the end of November 1989, the Economics Ministry supported full participation by Denmark in the process of EMU as set out in the Delors Report. It points up the macroeconomic advantages of EMU and of exchange rate stability for an economy in which small and medium-sized companies predominate and agriculture is a major export sector. Although irrevocably fixed exchange rates need not necessarily lead to a single currency, the Economics Ministry sees a number of advantages in this. It would like subsidiarity to be broadly applied, and suggests voluntary coordination of fiscal policy within guidelines aimed at avoiding destabilizing deficits.[13]

The Central Bank favours gradual movement towards EMU. Its 1989 annual report emphasized that the growing interdependence among economies has substantially reduced the room for manoeuvre of even medium-sized countries. In view of this, participation in EuroFed is seen to offer Denmark a better opportunity to exert influence on monetary policy in the Community.[14]

The Economic Council, a government-financed forum which is broadly representative of the academic community, assesses the EMS very positively. It has underscored the importance for Denmark of broadening European monetary cooperation to encompass other Nordic countries.

There has recently been a marked change in the views of the opposition Social Democrat Party, which previously had been critical of EMU. At the meeting of European Socialists in Dublin in May 1990 they evinced a more positive approach to the Community in general and to EMU.

10.1.8. Ireland

Benefits and costs

Ireland has made substantial progress towards economic convergence in terms of price and wage inflation, reduced budget deficits and a more favourable external balance. Hence much of the nominal adjustment required for passing successfully to economic and monetary union has been achieved. EMU, by reinforcing the credibility of these policies, will help to ensure that they are sustained.

In the real economy, significant weaknesses remain in terms of low income per head, high unemployment and emigration, continued heavy reliance on the primary sector and inefficiencies in the productive system. An EMU with adequate policies to promote cohesion, however, would represent a positive, if challenging, framework within which to overcome these. This implies, for example, an urgent need for changes in the structure of public finances and the economy in general.

In EMU, fiscal policy will, along with incomes policy, assume greater importance as an internal instrument of stabilization and adjustment. Although its effectiveness should, in principle, be enhanced, the need for overall budgetary discipline will be accentuated in an EMU committed to price stability. Further reduction of the high ratio of debt to GDP (104 % in 1989) is essential, both to permit the structural

[11] Hirsch (1989).
[12] *d'Letzeburger Land* (1989).
[13] Økonomiministeriet (1989).

[14] Danmarks Nationalbank (1990).

changes in the budget required for successful participation in EMU, and to create an adequate fiscal margin to respond to external shocks. Efforts in this regard would be facilitated by a reduction in interest rates within the completed EMU. A key requirement, nevertheless, is continued tight control on public expenditure.

Perspectives

The Government supports the principle of EMU, but it stresses the need for progress towards EMU to take full account of the Community's objective, as set out in Article 130(a) to (e) of the amended Treaty, to strengthen economic and social cohesion. This is also the position of the main opposition parties. The particular concerns in political circles are the problems likely to face a small, peripheral and less technologically-advanced economy in competing in an integrated Europe, and the budgetary consequences of the fiscal harmonization required for this to come about. There is a general consensus in Ireland in support of EMU. A report issued by the National Economic and Social Council in 1989 broadly represented the combined viewpoint of the administration, the trade unions, the employers, and agricultural interests. The NESC concluded that completion of the internal market should not be expected to narrow the income disparities between regions, let alone bring about convergence; serious concern was expressed at the difficulties likely to face the Irish economy, and industry in particular, in this regard. The NESC argued for a strategic objective of creating an advanced economic and monetary union, on the basis that a successful EMU required the formation of a substantial Community budgetary mechanism and extensive development of common Community policies, to ensure appropriate redistribution of the benefits of further integration.[15]

The Central Bank firmly supports monetary union in the belief that fixed exchange rates will provide the best environment for controlling inflation and promoting economic growth.[16] Monetary union must, however, be accompanied by greater coordination of other policies, particularly budgetary. The Governor of the Central Bank, in a paper submitted to the Delors Committee, argued that EMU will be feasible only if all regions of the Community have reached a 'broadly similar level of economic development', and recommended the mobilization of Community policies to that end and a greater degree of policy centralization as an element of the integration process.

10.2. Currencies in the broad band of the exchange-rate mechanism

10.2.1. Spain

Benefits and costs

Having recently joined the exchange-rate mechanism within the wider bands, Spain presently finds itself in a situation somewhat comparable to that of some other ERM participants a few years ago. The immediate priority is to use the ERM commitment as the framework within which to discipline economic agents and to reduce the main disequilibria: inflation and the external deficit. This also requires a redistribution of roles between monetary and fiscal policy. A fiscal policy adjustment to curb excess demand is required, given that monetary policy now has fewer degrees of freedom.

As has also been seen in Italy, this transition entails the risk of temporarily high nominal interest rates until inflation has been sufficiently reduced.

But a credible commitment to EMU will reinforce the effectiveness of an economic policy aimed at price and exchange-rate stability, bringing substantial gains from the reduction in uncertainty. Ultimately the decline in interest rates will assist efforts to eliminate the general government deficit (2 % of GDP in 1989, with a target of 0 % for 1992) as well as reduce the financing costs of the private sector. EMU, by providing an environment of free capital movements and fixed exchange rates, will make it easier to finance current-account imbalances with only small interest rate differentials. This could be a major benefit to a country such as Spain, which needs large capital inflows to boost investment and growth. The combination of 1992 and EMU will also have a radical impact on modernizing financial markets, which will result in major reductions in the costs to the Spanish economy of capital and financial transactions.

Perspectives

The Government favours closer economic and monetary integration but would like this to include measures to assist the less-developed regions of the Community. The Minister of Economy and Finance sees no reason why accepting the exchange rate discipline of the EMS should put a brake on medium-term economic growth, which would be better balanced if inflation slowed. Furthermore, long-term competitiveness could be improved.[17]

[15] National Economic and Social Council (1989).
[16] Central Bank of Ireland (1990).

[17] Solchaga (1989).

The Governor of the Central Bank, in a speech delivered in September 1989, voiced broad agreement with monetary union and its implications.[18]

Business leaders assess the EMU process very positively, since they reckon that the advantages of exchange-rate stability and economic discipline outweigh the disadvantages. They prefer some loss of national independence in economic policy-making to the fluctuations in the policy mix that have often occurred in the past. They also favour an independent central bank. Although in recent years the corporate sector has become more aware of the need to develop long-term competitiveness, there is concern that the Spanish economy will not adapt sufficiently rapidly to the new situation. To accelerate the process, most business leaders would like to see a firm commitment made to monetary union.

Academic opinion views Spain's participation in the EMS and subsequently in EMU as reinforcing the credibility of the counter-inflation policy. Most believe that EMU will have beneficial effects by obliging Spain to adopt a restrictive fiscal policy and to reintroduce an incomes policy, but add that it should be complemented by appropriate measures of regional policy. The independence of the central bank is regarded as important. Some academics are more pessimistic and believe that because of the gap that remains between Spain and the more developed EC economies, EMU could have negative effects, including impeding further catching up by the Spanish economy.

Public support for EMU is quite strong and increasing. Spanish public opinion, as measured by Eurobarometer, is second only to Italian in favouring a common monetary policy. Surveys also indicate that households' support for EMU is based on expecta- tions of lower financing and transaction costs.

10.2.2. United Kingdom

Benefits and costs

For the United Kingdom there are two specific issues in assessing the eventual benefits and costs of EMU: the extent

to which these would arise from sterling's participation in the ERM, which began on 8 October 1990; and the absence of a clear acceptance by the Government of further stages leading ultimately to the adoption of a single currency.

The serious aggravation of inflationary pressures during the past two years and the consequent decline in the credibility of the Government's own medium-term financial strategy for controlling inflation increased acceptance of the relative merits of participating in the ERM. The benefits of Stage I of EMU, through ERM participation, are thus potentially substantial for the UK. It should bring the disinflation advantages that original ERM members have largely already achieved through the discipline of maintaining an exchange rate objective. Significant reductions in nominal and real interest rates and a lessening of uncertainty will also be beneficial, particularly to the business environment.

The reduction in inflation expectations necessary for successful participation in the ERM, however, may entail substantial adjustment costs. Recent experience of UK labour markets suggests that any deterioration in competitiveness resulting from wage inflation is expected to be restored by depreciation of the nominal exchange rate. In the ERM this option will be severely limited. Wages and prices will have to adjust to maintain competitiveness, particularly in the more competitive environment that is likely to obtain after 1992. To ensure such adjustment during a 'learning phase' may entail output costs.

Full EMU, including a single currency and EuroFed, would lend additional credibility to the need for wage and price discipline. Other gains from a common currency include reductions in transaction and information costs and the elimination of concerns about financing external deficits. The UK could benefit too from an expansion of activity in financial services in a fully integrated economic and monetary union.

Perspectives

The British position in relation to public debate about EMU has developed rapidly since the Madrid European Council in June 1989. Then the Government committed itself to the objective of ultimate economic and monetary union and to Stage I of the Delors Report, during which sterling would participate in the ERM. The Prime Minister also clarified the conditions under which sterling would join the ERM, which included a reduction in UK inflation and the abolition of capital controls in the rest of the Community.

---

[18]   Rubio (1989).
[19]   See, for example, Instituto de España-Espasa-Calpe (1989).

Support for sterling joining the ERM was expressed by the Labour Party, the employers' organization (CBI) and the Trades Union Congress (TUC).[20] Academic opinion was also largely favourable. The principle of ERM membership is opposed chiefly by academic economists of the monetarist persuasion, who would prefer monetary policy to be free to pursue purely domestic objectives. Such reservations weakened as the UK met with increasing difficulty in controlling its own domestic monetary aggregates.

The Government published an alternative set of proposals to the Delors Report in November 1989.[21] Essentially this took Stage I to its limits by envisaging the removal of all restrictions on the use of the different national currencies and financial services throughout the Community, and competition among currencies to provide the non-inflationary anchor in the EMS. Eventually the system could evolve into one of fixed exchange rates, 'but that cannot and should not be decided now'. Binding rules on budget deficits were 'neither necessary nor desirable'. More recently, in June 1990, the Government published further proposals for Stage II, according to which a 'hard ecu' parallel currency would be managed by a European Monetary Fund.[22] This was followed, on 8 October 1990, by entry of the pound into the broader band of the ERM.

Regarding later stages of EMU, the Bank of England's view, as represented by its Governor, is that Stage I is likely to last until the efficient operation of the single market has been clearly demonstrated — probably the mid-1990s.[23]

The Labour Party and the TUC are chiefly concerned that EMU should be buttressed by more generous regional funding and that the democratic accountability of EuroFed should be ensured.

Business, in the form of the CBI, broadly supports EMU, including a single currency, but sees this only as the culmination of a successful process of economic convergence.[24]

Academic economists and independent commentators are critical not so much of the goal of a single currency as of the proposals for binding budget guidelines in the Delors Report, which is seen as unnecessarily centralized.[25]

[20] See House of Lords (1989).
[21] HM Treasury (1989).
[22] Bank of England (1990a and b).
[23] Leigh Pemberton (1989).
[24] Confederation of British Industry (1989).
[25] See, for example, National Institute of Economic and Social Research (1989).

10.3. Countries outside the exchange-rate mechanism

Greece and Portugal, the two least developed economies in the Community, both need to achieve substantial convergence with the rest of the Community, especially with respect to inflation and public finances, before joining the exchange-rate mechanism of the EMS. Portugal is considerably more convergent in these respects, however.

The example of the EMS and the prospect of EMU are of great importance to Greece and Portugal because they provide a clear framework and strong motivation for the modernization of their economies. While the 1992 process and the structural Funds strongly affect most of the productive sectors, the prospect of EMU emphasizes the need for stabilization and labour market reforms. EMU will be particularly important in reinforcing the institutional credibility of a modern, stability-oriented policy strategy. EMU also offers to both countries particularly large gains from the elimination of currency transaction costs, given their very high level and the importance of the tourist sector and emigrants' remittances.

10.3.1. Greece

Benefits and costs

Efforts to close the gap between the Greek economy and the rest of the Community have so far met with only limited success. Inflation was close to 14 % in 1989 and accelerated to over 20 % in the first half of 1990, so the already large differential with the EMS countries widened further. Large budget deficits (18 % of GDP in 1989) have caused a rapid increase in the public debt, which was 105 % of GDP in 1989.

The economic policy programme of the new government formed in April 1990 has opted against a fully accommodating exchange-rate policy. This, combined with the restrictive wage policy and, more importantly, the implementation of a medium-term fiscal consolidation plan aimed at halving the budget deficit by 1993, should ensure that the process of disinflation is set in train and so pave the way for participation in the exchange-rate mechanism.

Once inflation has slowed sufficiently to allow Greece to join the exchange-rate mechanism, its economic policy would be set to gain further in credibility.

During the disinflation transition real interest rates will necessarily be high to begin with. However, when convergence becomes highly credible these interest rate premiums will decline, and ultimately be eliminated in EMU. This interest rate effect could then offset the reduction in monetary seigniorage.

Most academic, business and political opinion favours progress towards EMU and Greece's eventual involvement.[26] The new government has repeatedly expressed its determination to implement its economic policy programme, which envisages Greece being able to join the ERM by 1993.

10.3.2. Portugal

Benefits and costs

Since Portugal joined the Community in 1986 the economy has made some progress towards convergence. Inflation has declined from 19 % in 1985 to 13 % in 1989. The state of its public finances remains weak, though it has improved slightly. In 1989 the budget deficit was 5 % of GDP, and the public debt stood at 70 % of GDP. Further improvement in public finances will be necessary before Portugal can participate successfully in the ERM and EMU.

Participation in the ERM and the EMU should reduce (and ultimately eliminate) both the exchange risk and the inflation premium elements of domestic interest rates, and so help to alleviate the burden of servicing the public debt.

The process of catching up with the rest of the Community will take some time, during which current-account deficits are likely to persist. With EMU, these would be less of a macroeconomic constraint and easier to finance.

---

[26] See, for example, Demopoulos (1990).

The Government supports the principle of EMU and the proposals of the Delors Report. But it has also argued that EMU risks widening again the gap between Portugal and the more developed Member States. To minimize the costs and risks that EMU entails for Portugal, it should be accompanied by a further increase in the Community's structural Funds.[27] The Portuguese authorities have recently stated that the escudo should join the ERM relatively soon, but that the present large inflation differential between Portugal and the core ERM countries (9 %) prevents this happening in the near future.

Among politicians there is broad but qualified support for joining the ERM and for EMU.[28] In business circles fears have been expressed about the possible deterioration of competitiveness, particularly by industrialists in traditional export sectors, such as textiles and footwear, and about the loss of control of domestic firms to foreign capital.

The academic community tends to support membership of the exchange-rate mechanism, mainly because of the greater price stability and fiscal discipline that would be implied. Most take the view that the escudo should join only when inflation draws closer to the EC average, but some believe that the escudo should join soon so that the effort to curb inflation can benefit from membership.

---

[27] See Ministerio las Finanças (1990).
[28] See Rodrigues (1990).

Table 10.1

Selected economic indicators for EC Member States, 1980-89

	B	DK	D	GR	E	F	IRL	I	L	NL	P	UK	EUR 12
GDP per capita (EUR = 100)													
1980	104,2	108,1	113,8	58,2	73,4	111,8	64,1	102,6	116,0	111,1	55,1	101,1	100
1989	102,3	106,5	112,7	54,2	75,8	108,8	67,1	103,7	125,8	103,0	55,0	106,3	100
Private consumption deflator (Annual percentage change)													
1980	6,4	10,7	5,8	21,9	16,5	13,3	18,6	20,4	7,6	6,9	21,6	16,2	13,5
1989	3,1	5,0	3,1	13,8	6,6	3,5	4,1	6,0	3,4	1,1	12,8	5,8	4,8
General government lending (+)/borrowing (−) (As % of GDP)													
1980	−9,2	−3,3	−2,9	:	−2,6	0,0	−12,7	−8,6	−0,4	−4,0	:	−3,4	:
1989	−6,3	−0,7	0,2	−17,6	−2,1	−1,3	−3,1	−10,2	3,3	−5,1	−5,0	1,6	−2,8
Intra-EC trade (as % of GDP)													
Imports													
1980	36,0	14,9	11,4	10,9	5,0	10,6	43,5	10,2	36,0	24,8	17,1	9,1	12,2
1989	45,4	14,1	11,9	15,2	10,2	13,8	36,6	10,1	45,4	30,0	27,0	12,2	14,2
Exports													
1980	38,5	13,2	12,1	6,4	5,1	9,3	33,5	8,9	38,5	32,1	10,8	9,6	12,3
1989	46,3	13,5	15,7	6,9	7,8	11,9	47,3	9,2	46,3	37,0	19,5	9,3	14,2

Table 10.2

Eurbarometer survey, autumn 1989

Unification of Western Europe[1]

	B	DK	D	GR	E	F	IRL	I	L	NL	P	UK	EUR 12
For very much	31	24	42	54	41	29	38	44	32	26	47	27	37
For to some extent	54	36	37	28	35	50	33	42	42	50	22	42	41
Against to some extent	6	19	8	3	4	7	4	4	14	11	4	12	7
Against very much	1	14	2	3	2	2	3	1	4	5	1	5	3
No reply	8	7	10	12	18	12	22	9	8	8	26	14	12
Total	100	100	100	100	100	100	100	100	100	100	100	100	100

Decision-making on currency[2]

	B	DK	D	GR	E	F	IRL	I	L	NL	P	UK	EUR 12
Community	67	54	59	44	46	72	57	68	56	53	28	42	57
National	28	38	35	39	39	23	35	24	33	38	49	51	35

Questions
[1] *Attitude towards the unification of Western Europe*
In general, are you for or against efforts being made to unify Western Europe? If FOR, are you very much for this, or only to some extent? If AGAINST, are you only to some extent against or very much against?
[2] *National or joint Community decision-making*
Some people believe that certain areas of policy should be decided by (national) government, while other areas of policy should be decided jointly within the European Community. Interviewees were given a range of policy areas (including currency) and asked to express a view as to the appropriate forum for decision-making.

GRAPH 10.1: **Variation of EC Member State currencies with respect to the Deutschmark**
(1980 = 100)

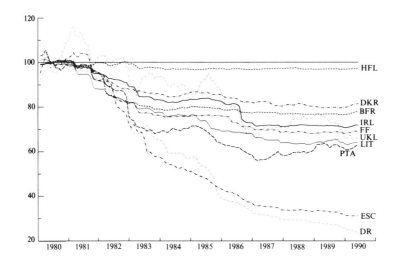

References

Banca d'Italia (1990), 'Considerazione finali' of the Governor of the Bank of Italy in *Relazione Annuale*.

Bank of England (1990a), 'EMU beyond Stage I: the hard ecu', paper published on 21 June.

Bank of England (1990b), 'The hard ecu in Stage II: operational requirements', paper published on 21 June.

Banque Nationale de Belgique (1989), *Revue de Presse*, various issues.

Bausch, R. (1989), 'La fiscalite de l'epargne', *d'Letzeburger Land*, 8 June, p. 36.

Beregovoy, P. (1989), 'Intervention de M. Pierre Beregovoy a la Chambre de Commerce et d'Industrie de Francfort, le 6 Novembre 1989', partially reprinted in Deutsche Bundesbank, *Auszüge aus Presseartikeln*, No 88, 8 November.

Central Bank of Ireland (1990), Annual Report, summer.

Commissie voor Economische Deskundigen van de Sociaal Economische Raad (1989), *Europese integratie en het sociaaleconomisch beleid*, 22 June.

Confederation of British Industry (1989), 'European monetary union: a business perspective', report of the CBI European Monetary Union Working Group, November.

Danmarks Nationalbank (1990), *Report and accounts for the year 1989*, Copenhagen.

de Larosière, J. (1989), 'National monetary policy and the construction of European monetary union', in Deutsche Bundesbank, *Auszüge aus Presseartikeln*, No 89, 10 November.

Demopoulos, G. D. (1990), 'Financial liberalization, the EMS and the consequences for macroeconomic policy in Greece', forthcoming in *The Greek economy: economic policy in the 1990s*, London, Macmillan.

Deutsche Bundesbank (1990), 'Statement on the establishment of an economic and monetary union in Europe', September.

d'Letzeburger Land (1989), 'Europäische Wirtschafts- und Währungsunion: Ein Optimum ist nicht garantiert', 8 June, p. 19.

Hirsch, M. (1989), 'Le Luxembourg et la Communauté européenne', *d'Letzeburger Land*, 8 June, p. 13.

HM Treasury (1989), *An evolutionary approach to economic and monetary union*, November.

Instituto de España-Espasa-Calpe (1989), *El Sistema monetario europeo y el futuro de la cooperacion en las CEE*.

House of Lords (1989), 'The Delors Committee Report', sound report of the Select Committee on the European Communities of the House of Lords, session 1989-90, HMSO, London.

Leigh Pemberton, R. (1989), 'The future of monetary arrangements in Europe', speech by the Governor to the Institute of Economic Affairs, 26 July, reprinted in *Bank of England Quarterly Bulletin*, August.

Les Echos (1990), 'de Larosière precise les contours de la future banque centrale européenne', 28 March.

Ministerio las Finanças (1990), *Quadro de ajustamento nacional para a transiçao para a união economica e monetario (versão premiminar)*, Lisboa.

National Economic and Social Council (1989), 'Ireland in the EC: performance, prospects and strategy', Report No 88, August.

National Institute of Economic and Social Research (1989), *National Institute Economic Review*, August.

Økonomiministeriet (1989), *Økonomisk og Monetar Union*, Copenhagen.

Regeringsverklaring, Tweede Kamer (1989), *Staatscourant*, 27 November, No 231, p. 4.

Rodrigues, F. (1990), 'O escudo no SME: potencialidades e exigencias', *Seminario Economica*, No 179, 16 June.

Rubio, M. (1989), 'La Economia española en la union monetaria Europea', *Boletin Economico*, Banco de España, September.

Sachverständigenrat zur Begutachtung der gesamtwirtschaftlichen Entwicklung (1989), *Jahresgutachten 1989/90*, Stuttgart and Mainz.

Solchaga, C. (1989), 'Comparecencia del Ministro de Economia y Hacienda ante el pleno del congreso de los Diputados para informar sobre la integracion de la peseta en el SME', Informacion Comercial Española, Ministerio de Economia y Hacienda, 3 to 9 July.

Verplaatse, A. (1989), interview in *De Standaard*, 3 July. Reprinted in *Revue de Presse* of the Banque Nationale de Belgique, No 126, and in *Annual Report 1989* of the National Bank of Belgium, p. xviii.

Annexes

Annex A

Exchange transaction costs

1. Introduction

Firms and individuals buying, selling, working or investing in another Member State incur currency conversion costs when their domestic money is not accepted as a medium of exchange.

Exchange transaction costs caused by the absence of a single currency in the Community can be split into two parts:

(i) on one hand, there are the 'financial' costs consisting of the bid-ask spreads and commission fees that households and non-bank enterprises pay to banks for foreign currency conversion. Under competitive circumstances these financial expenses mirror the cost of resources in the banking sector absorbed by the provision of foreign exchange;

(ii) on the other hand, there are the sometimes significant in-house costs companies operating internationally face in the form of resources tied up in departments like accounting and treasury to manage foreign exchange for intra-EC transaction needs, or in the form of payment delays or of poor return on cash management.

This annex is concerned with describing and quantifying the transaction gains EC firms and households will enjoy when payments or receipts in EC currency other than the domestic money related to intra-EC current or capital account transactions have been eliminated upon the introduction of a single currency. Other exchange transaction gains associated with a possible shift in payment denomination from dollars to ecus, or with a reduction of the cost of buying or selling dollars were dealt with in Chapter 7.

Apart from eliminating exchange transaction costs, a single currency is an indispensable instrument for cutting the relatively high expenses and long delays cross-border payments in the Community currently suffer from.

The quantifiable 'mechanical' savings a single currency will generate through the various channels identified in this annex can be put at between ECU 13 and 19 billion, or 0,3 to 0,4 % of the Community's GDP. The summary table at the end of this annex assembles the components leading to this overall estimate.

Annex A prepared by Marc Vaneukelen

2. Financial transaction costs

Financial transaction costs can best be approached by seeing them as resulting from two factors: the volume of foreign exchange transactions converting one EC currency into another, and the prices banks charge for these services.

2.1. The volume of foreign exchange transactions in the Community

Turnover on the Community's foreign exchange markets

In April 1989, central banks of some 20 countries carried out in collaboration with the Bank for International Settlements comprehensive surveys on the foreign exchange operations of banks and other dealers in their markets. The survey covered all EC Member States except Germany and Luxembourg.

The overall picture the survey provides is summarized in Tables A.1, A.2 and A.3 in which the original data have been converted into ecus and expressed on an annual basis.

The net turnover reported in Table A.1 indicates that the total volume of operations on 10 Community foreign exchange markets amounted to ECU 61 340 billion in 1989. According to the BIS staff[1] the net daily turnover in Germany and Luxembourg together may be put at USD 100 billion per day, bringing the EC's overall yearly total to ECU 84 067 billion. Half of this Community turnover is realized on the UK market, the world's largest. Apart from Germany, the other foreign exchange markets in the Community are rather small, with hedging and trading operations mainly conducted with banks in other countries rather than with local interbank counterparts.

The column 'business with customers' denotes the volume of direct foreign exchange transactions between banks and non-bank financial institutions, companies, or individual investors.[2] It represents a fairly small part (15 %) of total net turnover. However the indirect importance of business

---

[1] BIS (1990), p. 2.
[2] The distinction between interbank and customer business is not always easy to make; it becomes less and less so as large non-bank firms increasingly participate directly in the foreign exchange market, not only to meet the foreign currency needs arising from their main business, but also to engage in arbitrage or purely speculative operations.

Table A.1

Total foreign exchange market activity

(billion ECU, annual basis)

Country	Gross turnover	of which: Domestic interbank operations	Net turnover[2]	of which:[1] Cross-border interbank operations	Business customers	Net domestic interbank operations
UK	54 772	24 545[3]	42 500[3]	24 318[3]	5 909	12 273[3]
France (95%)[4]	7 272	2 500[3]	5 909[3]	3 409[3]	1 136	1 364[3]
Netherlands	3 636	1 386[3]	2 954[3]	1 932[3]	341	705[3]
Denmark (90%)[4]	3 409	795	2 954	2 272	295	409
Belgium (90%)[4]	2 727	727	2 272	1 727	295	364
Italy (75%)[4]	2 500	364	2 272	1 818	318	182
Spain	1 341	682	1 000	4 182	136	341
Ireland	1 250	159	1 182	1 045	23	68
Portugal	250	91	204	91	46	46
Greece	159	68[3]	91[3]	46[3]	23	23[4]
Total EUR 12 excluding Germany and Luxembourg	77 317	31 138	61 340	37 181	8 636	15 773
USA	39 545	20 454[3]	29 318[3]	16 136[3]	2 272	10 227[3]
Japan	32 954	13 863	26 136	10 682	7 727	7 045
Switzerland (85%)	15 454	5 000	12 954	8 182	2 045	2 500

[1]   Items do not always add up to total net turnover because the classification is not exhaustive.
[2]   Figures for individual countries indicate turnover net of double-counting arising from local interbank business.
[3]   Based on estimates of domestic and cross-border interbank business arranged through brokers.
[4]   No adjustment was made for less than full coverage. Figures in parentheses indicate the estimated market coverage.
Source: BIS.

Table A.2

Foreign exchange market activity, by type of transaction: gross turnover

(billion ECU, annual basis)

Country	Gross turnover	Spot	Forward Total	Swaps	Outright	Futures	Options Total	Bought	Written
UK	54 772	35 000	19 091	na	na	na	682	na	na
France	7 272	4 318	2 727	na	na	182	455	na	na
Netherlands	3 636	1 954	1 659	1 523	136	0	23	na	na
Denmark	3 409	1 636	1 772	1 432	341	—	45*	na	na
Belgium	2 727	1 386	1 341	1 250	91	0	23	na	na
Italy	2 500	2 091	409	na	na	10	0	0	0
Spain	1 341	818	523	477	45	—	—	—	—
Ireland	1 250	1 000	250	na	na	na	—	—	—
Portugal	250	227	23	na	na	na	—	—	—
Greece	159	136	23	0	23	0	—	—	—
Total EUR 12 excluding Germany and Luxembourg	77 317	48 568	27 818				1 205		
USA	39 545	25 000	12 045	9 545	1 956	636	2 500	1 227	1 205
Japan	32 954	13 181	18 863	16 818	1 956	—	955	na	na
Switzerland	15 454	8 409	6 818	5 909	773	0	277	na	na

na: not available.
—: (virtually) non-existent.
*: including futures.
Source: BIS.

Table A.3

Currency composition of foreign exchange market activity: gross turnover

(billion ECU, annual basis)

Country	Gross turnover in all currency	Domestic currency	USD	DM	Yen	UKL	ECU	Other[1]
UK	54 772	16 818	49 090	15 909	9 545	—	909	17 500
France	7 272	3 409	5 227	3 182	386	136	159	1 818
Netherlands	3 636	2 272	2 500	1 432	91	114	32	909
Denmark	3 409	1 068	2 727	1 068	68	91	23	1 659
Belgium	2 727	1 114	2 227	1 136	—	—	68	932
Italy	2 500	1 614	1 341	591	23	91	227	1 114
Spain	1 341	1 045	955	477	—	23	—	182
Ireland	1 250	136	750	705	23	227	250	68
Portugal	250	114	182	114	0	23	0	68
Greece	159	68	114	68	0	0	0	23
USA	39 545	37 954	37 954	13 182	10 909	5 682	114	11 136
Japan	32 954	26 363	31 363	3 182	26 363	1 227	—	3 864
Switzerland	15 454	9 318	11 591	5 000	1 205	1 182	114	2 500

[1]   Both currencies in individual transactions included.

Source: BIS.

with customers is much larger because it exerts a 'multiplier' effect, generating a sizeable portion of interbank activity. For instance, forward orders from non-bank enterprises are usually carried out by way of two deals: a swap and a corresponding spot transaction. When it involves two EC currencies, the forward contract is likely to give rise to at least four supplementary transactions in the interbank market: each of the two EC moneys will be swapped and exchanged spot for US dollars, the latter fulfilling the vehicle currency role discussed in Chapter 7.[3]

Table A.2 classifies foreign exchange activity according to the type of transaction. Spot transactions on EC markets still claim more than 60 % of turnover, compared to 36 % for forward contracts. No indication exists regarding the share of forward contracts arising from hedging needs for commercial purposes, the remainder being associated with purely financial operations like covered interest arbitrage. Currency options occupy as yet a marginal position on the Community's markets. Most of the options traded concern transactions relative to the dollar or yen. Given the low volatility of their bilateral exchange rates, options involving two ERM currencies hardly exist.

Table A.3. shows the currency composition of foreign exchange transactions when both sides of every deal are counted. It bears out the still overwhelming role of the dollar on European markets, with about 90 % of all transactions on the UK market involving the US currency (in 1986 it was even 96 %). On other Community markets, foreign exchange in and out of the dollar claims on average about 70 % of total turnover.[4]

As a corollary, direct transactions between EC currencies are relatively minor. Their precise volume is, however, unknown since the survey does not disclose systematically turnover per pair of currencies. The 'indirect' transactions may be equally if not more important but their magnitude cannot be measured accurately either for want of evidence on what part of EC currency/dollar exchange transactions constitutes one step of a foreign exchange transaction between two EC moneys, and what part concerns deals 'in their own right'. If foreign exchange deals on EC markets relating directly or indirectly to transactions between EC currencies are denoted by A and all other deals by B, and one assumes that half of the transactions between an EC currency and the dollar are intermediary exchanges linking one EC money to another, the way to measure properly the share of transactions between EC currencies in total foreign exchange market activity (i.e., A/(A + B)) is given in the first column of Table

---

[3]   More concretely, suppose a bank sells French francs forward to a customer against Dutch guilders. The bank will typically conduct this operation by two swaps (on the one hand, a forward purchase of French francs and spot sale of French francs against US dollars; on the other hand, a forward sale of guilders and spot purchase against US dollars) and two spot transactions (French franc purchase against dollars and guilder sale against dollars).

[4]   For the remainder of the analysis the hypothesis is adopted that half of the last column ('other') of Table A.3 is composed of EC currencies not accounted for explicitly in the table.

A.4. However, in the absence of information on turnover according to currency pairs, Table A.3 does not permit to apply this correct yardstick. Instead, two alternative computations using the data of Table A.3 are proposed, each exhibiting sources of over- and underestimation as signalled in the second and third column of Table A.4. The first computation leaves out the figures contained in Table A.3 for 'domestic currency' and half of 'other', whereas all figures are made use of in the second calculation. According to the first computation 34 % of all operations on the Community's foreign exchange markets concern transactions between EC currencies, whilst the second suggests it is 43 %. These figures would seem to provide a lower-bound estimate in view of the fact that the German foreign exchange market, where the position of the dollar and yen is probably much less predominant than in the UK, was excluded. More particularly, the EC currency component of foreign exchange operations on behalf of non-bank clients is very likely to exceed the indicated percentages since such operations are often driven by foreign exchange needs stemming from international trade and direct investment.[5]

Foreign exchange turnover and the balance of payments

As is well known, the turnover on foreign exchange markets is extremely high in comparison to the transactions recorded in countries' balance of payments, as shown in Tables A.5 and A.6 below. The net turnover on EC foreign exchange markets equals 65 times the sum of intra- and extra-EC goods trade. In fact, this disproportion is even larger since an important part of extra-EC trade is settled in an EC currency and therefore does not give rise to a foreign exchange transaction on the side of EC residents. Furthermore, not all foreign currency payments or receipts occasion exchange transactions as enterprises 'net' out their foreign exchange needs.

However, the foreign exchange market and balance of payments data become broadly reconcilable when looking only at the turnover in connection to business with non-bank customers and bearing in mind that the capital account figures of the balance of payments relate to stock changes, which may only be a fraction of the gross capital flows, the actual variable of interest.[6]

---

[5] P. Demarsin (1990), p. 9.
[6] This approximate compatibility shows up best in the case of countries where, on account of capital controls, gross capital flows by the non-bank sector are unlikely to have been considerable. For instance, the annual estimate derived from the BIS survey of Italy's foreign exchange turnover arising from business with non-bank customers amounts to ECU 318 billion. Given that about 70 % of Italy's current account related international payments and receipts is denominated in foreign currency and assuming this percentage to apply also to capital in- and outflows, the balance of payments data suggest Italy's (non-bank) international transactions in foreign currency equalled around ECU 260 billion.

Table A.4

Measurement of the share of transactions between EC currencies in total foreign exchange turnover

Possible foreign exchange transaction	Correct	Computation 1	Computation 2
Domestic currency — other EC currency	A	A	A, A[1]
Other EC currency — USD	A, B	A, B	A, B
Other EC currency — yen	B	A, B[1]	A, B[1]
Domestic currency — USD	A, B	B[2]	A, B
Domestic currency — yen	B	B	A, B[1]
USD — yen	B	B, B[2]	B, B[2]
Other EC currency — non-EC currency other than yen and USD	B	—[1]	A, B[1]
USD — non-EC currency	B	B	B, B[2]
Yen — non-EC currency	B	B	B, B[2]

[1] Source of overestimate.
[2] Source of underestimate.

Table A.5

Volume of EUR 12 goods trade, 1988

(billion ECU)

	Intra-EC	Extra-EC
Imports	530,3	389,8
Exports	530,3	367,0

Source: Eurostat.

Foreign currency transactions by households

Because the minimum values set in the foreign exchange market survey as lower thresholds for reporting were rather high, the figures contained in Table A.1 normally do not include the foreign currency payments by way of eurocheques, traveller's cheques, international credit cards, or banknotes. The latter are typically the international payment instruments of the individual cross-border shopper or tourist.

Table A.6

Member States' current and capital account transactions

(1988, billion ECU)

	Imports (M) Exports (X)	Goods trade	Current account transactions	Liabilities (L) Assets (A)	Capital account transactions by non-bank sector[1]
BLEU	M	72,9	118,3	L	27,3
	X	73,8	121,2	A	31,3
Denmark	M	21,7	37,2	L	8,4
	X	23,3	35,7	A	6,3
Germany	M	194,7	303,3	L	14,5
	X	260,1	344,4	A	62,3
Greece	M	10,1	13,5	L	1,9
	X	5,0	18,7	A	na
Spain	M	48,7	66,3	L	16,5
	X	33,5	63,2	A	3,8
France	M	142,5	237,4	L	48,1
	X	135,7	234,4	A	75,1
Ireland	M	12,9	19,9	L	3,1
	X	15,6	20,5	A	2,0
Italy	M	108,8	157,1	L	38,6
	X	108,3	152,6	A	22,1
Netherlands	M	76,4	116,4	L	19,9
	X	83,4	120,8	A	17,6
Portugal	M	13,4	17,2	L	5,2
	X	9,1	16,7	A	1,1
UK	M	152,8	275,4	L	32,0
	X	121,4	253,4	A	42,5

[1] Sum of stock changes with regard to direct investment, portfolio investment, other long-term capital, short-term capital other than by deposit banks.
Source: Eurostat.

Around 50 million eurocheques with an average value of ECU 125 are used annually for international settlements inside Europe. Since this figure also relates to EFTA countries like Austria and Switzerland where they form a common means of payment, eurocheques can be reasonably estimated to attain a yearly volume of ECU 5 billion as international payment instruments inside the Community.

The annual volume of traveller's cheques denominated in an EC currency and sold in the Community can also be set at about ECU 5 billion. Credit card payments by Community residents in foreign EC currency can be roughly estimated to total ECU 10 billion per annum.

Not all central banks of the Community keep a systematic record of the volume and currency breakdown of sales and purchases by the domestic bank sector of foreign banknotes.

The available information, covering five Member States that are jointly responsible for about two thirds of intra-EC trade, is presented in Table A.7.

The reported total for Germany needs to be revised upward because the Bundesbank data pertain to banknote trade arising from travel only. Data from other countries suggest tourism and travel generate just over 30 % of all foreign banknote sales and purchases. Accordingly, one can plausibly assume that the German bank sector turnover in foreign EC currency banknotes amounted to twice the reported volume, raising it to ECU 11 billion in 1988.[7] For Italy, the

[7] The added part was supposed to be exclusively in the money of EC Member States bordering on Germany (FF, BFR/LFR, HFL, DKR), the key for the distribution among these four currencies reflecting their relative importance in the travel-induced banknote transactions.

Table A.7

Currency breakdown of banknote transactions, 1988

(Purchase and sale of foreign banknotes in EC currency by domestic bank sector)

(million ECU)

	BLEU	(%)	Germany [1]	(%)	Italy [2]	(%)	France	(%)
BFR	—	—	201	(3,6)	74	(1,3)	240	(7,0)
DM	2 563	(41,5)	—	—	2 836	(49,0)	937	(27,3)
FF	670	(10,9)	1 339	(24,2)	1 512	(26,1)	471	(13,7)
UKL	193	(3,1)	384	(6,9)	671	(11,6)	471	(13,7)
LIT	170	(2,8)	1 127	(20,3)	—	—	648	(18,9)
PTA	123	(2,0)	—	—	448	(7,8)	798	(23,2)
HFL	2 270	(36,8)	1 357	(24,5)	153	(2,3)	154	(4,5)
ESC			674	(12,2)	9	(0,2)		
IRL	181	(2,9) [3]	13	(0,2)	—	—	157	(4,6) [3]
DR			43	(0,8)	47	(0,8)		
DKR			385	(6,9)	31	(0,5)	29	(0,9)
Total	6 170	(100)	5 541	(100)	5 787	(100)	3 434	(100)

[1] Banknote transactions associated with travel only.
[2] Banknote transactions by foreign exchange institutions other than banks are not included in these figures.
[3] Estimate.

total goes up to ECU 8 billion once the transactions by foreign exchange institutions other than banks are taken into account.

These revisions bring EC currency banknote trade in the five countries under consideration to ECU 28,5 billion in 1988. The latter figure can be used to arrive at an estimate for the Community in its entirety. An extrapolation based purely on countries' weight in intra-EC trade would not be appropriate, however, since it would suffer from a downward bias for two reasons. First, in countries like Greece, Spain and Portugal, cash is still a much more predominant payment instrument than elsewhere in the Community. Secondly, and partly because of this very prevalence of cash as a medium of exchange, converting foreign banknotes in the 'South' is clearly cheaper than in the 'North' , as is demonstrated in Table A.13 below. It follows that foreign banknotes are likely to be much more actively traded in a number of Member States outside the sample. For these reasons, the EUR 12 volume of banknote conversions involving two EC currencies is assumed to have lain in 1988 between twice and three times the ECU 28,5 billion turnover identified earlier, i.e. between ECU 57 and 85 billion.

Member State differences in foreign exchange exposure

The BIS data on foreign exchange turnover did not permit to determine accurately the part of foreign exchange transactions to vanish upon the establishment of a single Community currency. An alternative method of arriving at the transaction volume between EC currencies is to ascertain each individual Member State's gross current and capital account flows in foreign currency and to isolate the EC component.

Unfortunately, most countries lack the detailed statistical information necessary for such an exercise. This method is therefore unable to yield a meaningful assessment of the EC's aggregate amount of foreign exchange transactions. Additionally, it is liable to overestimation as it fails to distinguish between on one hand the volume of payments and receipts in foreign currency and on the other the volume of exchange transactions, the latter volume falling short of the former because firms net out their foreign exchange needs. Despite these problems and the limited sample, this approach yields interesting results as it illustrates clearly that the relative significance of intra-EC transactions settled in foreign currency, and hence the extent of foreign exchange exposure, differs considerably between Member States. This is borne out by Table A.8, which provides the current and capital account related receipts and payments in foreign EC currency arising from intra-EC transactions for the BLEU, Germany, Italy and France.

Table A.8

Balance of payments transactions with other EC countries in EC currencies (exclusive of the domestic currency) in 1988[1]

	BLEU		Germany		Italy		France[2]	
	Absolute value billion ECU	% of national GDP	billion ECU	% GDP	billion ECU	% GDP	billion ECU	% GDP
1. Through means of payment other than banknotes:								
Goods trade			51,4		64,3		59,7	
Services			13,5		} 17,1		} 40,4	
Transfers			5,1		}		}	
Investment income			9,2		5,6		}	
Current account	91,5	72,7	79,2	7,8	87,0	12,3	100,1	12,5
Direct investment	7,8	6,2	5,9	0,6	4,4	0,6	7,2	0,9
Other capital account transactions by non-bank sector	548,4	436	96,3[3]	9,5	na		283,8[4,5]	35,4
2. Purchases and sales of banknotes in EC currency by domestic bank sector	6,0	4,7	5,5[6]	1,1	8,1[7]	1,1	4,3	0,6
3. Total	653,7	519,6	186,9	19			295,4	49,4

[1]   Partly own calculations on working hypotheses.
[2]   Transactions in EC currency other than FF with rest of the world
[3]   Long-term capital account transactions only (securities, investment certificates and fixed-interest bearing assets). For short-term transactions only *net* stock changes on a monthly or yearly basis are available.
[4]   Figures for some important categories of short-term capital account transactions are not available in the form of gross flows. In that case, the stock changes on a monthly basis were included.
[5]   To derive the EC-currency component, the EC-currency share in worldwide investment income was taken (28,9%).
[6]   Banknote transactions related to travel only.
[7]   Banknote transactions by banks as well as other foreign exchange institutions.
na = not available.

Although a cross-country comparison should desirably refer to the balance of payments as a whole, the poor quality of the gross capital flow data for Germany and France as well as the fact that 1988 was still an unrepresentative year for France's and Italy's trade in financial assets due to remaining capital controls make it appropriate to focus on the current account and direct investment. Whereas foreign EC currency payments and receipts of the BLEU represented in 1988 79% of its GDP, the corresponding figure for Germany, Italy and France amounted respectively to 8,4%, 12,9% and 13,4%. Tables A.9 and A.10 show that the principal determinants of this striking disparity are the prominence of the domestic currency as an international means of payment and the degree of economic integration with other Member States.

As indicated in Table A.9, Germany pays for about 60% of its imports from other Member States with Deutschmarks; 77% of its exports are settled in Deutschmarks. France also enjoys the benefit of a national currency that is relatively well accepted as an international payments instrument. In contrast, 50 to 60% of payments and receipts by the BLEU or Italy are denominated in an EC currency other than domestic money.

The intensity of trade links is the chief factor explaining the difference between the BLEU and Italy as regards their exposure to other EC currencies. This is illustrated by Table A.10, where openness is measured as the sum of intra-EC imports and exports of goods relative to GDP. On this definition, the BLEU is more than five times more integrated with the rest of the Community than Italy and is therefore more vulnerable to the problems the multitude of EC currencies can give rise to.

Size distribution of payments and receipts in foreign currency

Foreign exchange transaction costs will be shown presently to decline in relative terms with the size of the transaction. An accurate evaluation of the transaction cost savings the introduction of a single currency will permit therefore requires information on the size distribution of settlements in foreign currency.

Table A.9

Currency distribution (%) of payments[1] by (or to) domestic residents to (or from) EC Member States (current account transactions and foreign direct investment)

	BLEU		Italy[2]		France[3, 4]		Germany[5]		Denmark[6]	
	Receipts	Payments	Receipts	Payments	Receipts	Payments	Receipts	Payments	Receipts	Payments
BFR	30,8	25,5	2,1	2,4	9,2	2,9	1,7	1,4	other	other
FF	12,5	11,8	17,6	15,6	59,1	51,9	6,3	7,5	other	other
UKL	5,9	5,0	1,1	4,3	5,5	4,6	4,7	5,1	7,0	4,0
HFL	8,0	8,6	2,6	4,9	1,7	1,8	1,6	2,9	2,0	3,0
DM	19,3	23,2	26,4	31,0	9,8	11,2	77,6	59,7	14,0	17,0
LIT	3,1	2,8	37,1	28,8	3,0	3,2	3,6	3,4	other	other
DKR	0,6	0,5	0,5	1,3	0,0	0,1	0,5	0,6	37,0	33,0
ESC	0,02	0,03	0,1	0,0	0,0	0,0	0,0	0,0	other	other
PTA	0,6	0,9	2,6	2,1	0,1	0,3	0,1	0,3	other	other
DR	0,01	0,1	0,0	0,1	0,0	0,0	0,0	0,0	other	other
IRL	0,1	0,2	0,1	0,2	0,0	0,1	0,1	0,2	other	other
USD	16,0	19,0	3,2	8,4	15,2	16,4	2,6	10,7	21,0	23,0
ECU	1,6	1,0	0,4	0,5	1,3	1,4	0,0	0,2	other	other
YEN	0,6	0,5	0,1	0,3	other[7]	other	0,1	0,2	other	other
Other	0,9	0,9	0,1	0,2	2,1	6,5	1,2	7,8	19,0	20,0

[1] Payments executed through the banking sector. Banknote payments are as a general rule not included.
[2] Payments arising from intra-EC trade account transactions and technology transfers.
[3] Payments arising from current account transactions only.
[4] Own computations on the basis of trade statistics according to the country of destination or origin and of the currency distribution of global current account transactions. Figures should therefore be seen as indicative, in particular as it proved hard to distinguish between the EC and the rest of OECD-Europe.
[5] Trade account transactions only.
[6] Global current account transaction.
[7] Subsumed under 'Other'

Table A.10

Sum of intra-EC imports and exports of goods, 1988

	(% of GDP)
BLEU	87,3
Denmark	25,9
Germany	25,6
Greece	27,3
Spain	17,1
France	23,8
Ireland	77,3
Italy	18,3
Netherlands	63,1
Portugal	44,8
UK	20,9
EUR 12	26,8

Source: European Economy, Statistical annex.

The limited evidence available to this effect is assembled in Table A.11. It suggests that more than 50 % of the volume of bank settlements connected with trade or current account operations within the EC takes the form of payments and receipts in excess of ECU 100 000. More than 90 % of the volume of cross-border capital flows appears to be generated by transactions worth ECU 1 million or more.

2.2. The cost of foreign exchange

The financial costs economic agents in the Community incur due to the multitude of currencies in the Community can vary greatly, depending on the currency of exchange, the nature of the foreign exchange 'product' (spot, forward, swaps, options, etc.), the size of the transaction and the importance of the bank customer. Typically, moving in and out of small-country or weak currencies proves more costly than buying or selling Deutschmarks or French francs; payments with foreign banknotes cost much more than by credit cards; exchange risk coverage is invariably more expensive

Table A.11

Size distribution of trade account settlements through means of payments other than banknotes

(%)

	BLEU		Germany	Italy	Weighted average of BLEU, Germany and Italy
	(a)	(b)	(c)	(d)	
ECU 1 to 1 0000	1,0	0,1	1,0	0,3	0,8
ECU 1 000 to 5 000	4,4	0,9	4,4	1,0	3,2
ECU 5 000 to 10 000	4,2	0,5	4,3	3,1	3,9
ECU 10 000 to 50 000	16,5	0,9	22,7	39,3	26,1
ECU 50 000 to 100 000	8,6	0,8	6,5	14,7	10,0
ECU 100 000 to 500 000	19,9	4,0		18,8	
ECU 500 000 to 1 mio	7,3 } 59,0	3,8 } 96,8	} 61,2	5,9 } 42,0	} 53,9
ECU 1 mio to 5 mio	17,6	26,0		11,0	
ECU 5 mio +	14,7	63,0		6,4	

(a)   Current account transactions and foreign direct investment with other EC Member States.
(b)   Gross capital flows (other than direct investment) to and from other Member States.
(c)   Trade account transactions with the rest of the world.
(d)   Trade account and technology transfer related transactions with the other EC Member States.

than transacting on the spot market; and due to the existence of overhead expenses, foreign exchange costs become relatively less important with the size of the transaction.

The bid-ask spread on the interbank market

At the lower end of the cost-range are foreign exchange operations in the interbank market. Table A.12 illustrates the size, expressed in percentage terms, of the bid-ask spread prevailing on this wholesale type of market. The underlying data relate to the purchase and sales rates displayed by a major British bank in London in November 1989.

Table A.12

Interbank bid-ask spreads expressed in percentage terms (data collected in November 1989)

	USD	UKL	DM	ECU	FF	HFL
USD	X					
UKL	0,06	X				
DM	0,04	0,11	X			
ECU	0,04	0,11	0,08	X		
FF	0,08	0,15	0,12	0,13	X	
HFL	0,05	0,10	0,09	0,10	0,13	X
YEN	0,06	0,14	0,13	—	0,20	0,13
BFR	0,10	0,18	0,16	0,14	0,33	0,16
LIT	0,07	0,13	0,12	0,13	0,20	0,20
DKR	0,10	0,17	0,14	0,13	—	—
DR	0,18	0,25	—	—	—	—
PTA	0,09	0,16	—	—	—	—
IRL	0,10	0,19	—	—	—	—
ESC	0,13	0,20	—	—	—	—

Source: Telerate.

The implicit cost for a bank of obtaining foreign currency on the spot market is half this spread. It averages around 0,05 to 0,10 % for deals between EC currencies. Differences in spreads across pairs of EC currencies appear primarily driven by market size. The economies of scale phenomenon explains why the spread on intensely traded European currencies like the Deutschmark or the pound is only about one third of the spread registered for moneys in which international transactions are very limited like the Greek drachma or the Portuguese escudo. The spread on the cross-rate between the latter two can easily exceed 0,30 %.

The figures in the table confirm the pivotal role of the US dollar on present foreign exchange markets: the bid-ask spread is always lowest when moving in and out of the dollar, with the spread relative to the cross-rate between two EC currencies equalling or exceeding the sum of the spreads on the exchange rate between each of the two and the dollar. For example, the spread on PTA/UKL was 0,16 %, which can be divided into PTA/USD (0,09 %) and USD/UKL (0,06 %). [8]

Bank transfers

Payments between firms of different countries are carried out by means of international bank transfers. The exchange cost of a transfer in foreign currency consists basically of

[8]   This should not be interpreted to mean that 0,16 % was the lowest PTA/UKL spread to be obtained on that day. One could do better through geographical arbitrage. For instance, the spread could be reduced by selling pesetas for dollars to a major bank in Madrid posting a spread of only 0,05 % and subsequently purchasing pounds for dollars in London.

two parts. Aside from an explicit conversion fee, which is largely fixed, a margin is added to the interbank rate at which the paying enterprise's bank has bought or sold the currency in question. This margin is inversely related to the amount, with the importance of the client and the currency of payment often playing a role as well. As a result of competitive bidding among banks and the fact that large enterprises increasingly have direct access to the foreign exchange markets, this margin is reduced to zero for very large amounts and top customers. For payments with a zero margin, the interbank spread dealt with earlier applies in effect.

As no published information exists on banks' charges for the foreign currency conversion of large amounts, the Commission services submitted a confidential questionnaire to this effect to a limited number of banks in each Member State. The replies received suggest that the spot purchase of another EC currency against the local money for an equivalent of ECU 10 000 costs about 0,5 %, with reported extremes ranging from 0,1 % to 2,5 %. The same foreign exchange transaction for an equivalent of ECU 100 000 would cost on average about 0,3 %. Although for amounts of the latter magnitude pricing differences are much smaller due to competitive pressure, costs can still rise above 1 % for purchases of weak currencies that are barely used in international transactions, like the drachma or the escudo.

Banks located in the less developed Member States appear to charge clearly higher prices than their counterparts elsewhere in the Community, a finding in keeping with the evidence on financial services' costs reported in Price Waterhouse (1988). [9]

Hedging by way of forward or similar contracts is bound to be more costly than transacting on the spot market because it always involves a spot transaction plus at least one other foreign exchange or loan operation. The replies to the questionnaire suggest that on average forward contracts cost about 0,2 to 0,3 percentage points more than corresponding spot deals for amounts equivalent to ECU 10 000. This cost difference narrows down with the value of the contract, diminishing to about 0,1 percentage points for transactions worth ECU 100 000. [10]

Eurocheques and credit cards

Eurocheques are a convenient international payments instrument when they are written in the currency of the foreign country and when the amount involved does not exceed the guaranteed disbursement limit (about ECU 160).

Domestic use of eurocheques is costless in most EC countries upon the payment of a fixed fee. For their international use the issuing bank charges a commission fee of about 1,6 % of the cheque's value (with a minimum amount), to which must be added the exchange margin when the cheque is written in a currency other than that of the account to be debited. The applied exchange margin is determined freely by the cheque issuing bank, but will typically lie around 1 %.

Exchange transaction costs with international credit cards are analogous to those incurred with eurocheques. Also free of charge for domestic use, the fixed fee for making payments in foreign currency equals 1 %, with the exchange margin approximating very closely the one charged by banks for eurocheques.

Traveller's cheques and foreign banknotes

The highest transaction costs are faced with the purchase or sale of traveller's cheques and cash.

Traveller's cheques are a form of quasi-cash in that they are directly and in principle costlessly convertible into local currency at banks. [11] They are also often accepted as direct payment at retail outlets in tourist areas. Traveller's cheques are guaranteed against loss or theft, for which a supplementary 1 % commission is charged. Price Waterhouse (1988) surveyed the cost of an ECU 100 traveller's cheque in seven EC countries. The lowest cost was observed in Luxembourg, Germany and the UK and amounted to ECU 5; France turned out most expensive at ECU 7,5.

An overview of the cost of foreign cash is provided in Table A.13 showing the differences expressed in percentage terms between banks' buying and selling prices of foreign banknotes. Columns indicate the place of currency conversion and all figures relate to exchange operations involving

---

[9] Price Waterhouse (1988), pp. 147-148.
[10] Prices of various hedging instruments like forward, future or option contracts can differ considerably due to their distinct insurance and expected return properties as well as to domestic tax- or regulation-induced distortions.

[11] Cashing-in a traveller's cheque costs nothing when it is denominated in the local currency. However, in the event of a different denomination — which is unavoidably the case in Belgium-Luxembourg, Denmark and Greece as traveller's cheques in the local currency do not exist — costs can rise steeply.

Table A.13

Buying-selling spreads in percentage terms for foreign banknotes

	B	DK[1]	D	GR[2]	E	F	IRL	I[3]	NL	P	UK
BFR	X	8,6	5,0	4,1	3,8	6,7	4,8	1,7	5,8	2,8	6,7
DKR	4,1	X	7,3	4,1	3,8	8,3	5,5	1,9	11,0	1,6	5,6
DM	4,6	1,9	X	4,1	3,8	6,4	5,5	1,8	3,6	1,3	6,2
DR	25,0	15,3	48,2	X	5,6	19,7	6,9	2,1	23,1	—	9,9
PTA	5,3	6,9	8,1	4,1	X	10,7	5,5	2,0	15,4	2,4	6,9
FF	5,3	4,7	6,4	4,1	3,8	X	5,4	1,9	9,5	1,6	6,4
IRL	4,4	4,5	6,6	4,1	3,8	—	X	1,9	10,7	1,6	6,7
LIT	5,0	11,1	7,7	4,1	3,8	11,4	6,1	X	14,0	6,2	6,4
HFL	4,9	2,4	2,6	4,1	3,8	6,5	5,5	1,9	X	1,4	6,5
ESC	22,8	14,5	30,0	4,1	5,7	19,2	6,8	1,9	21,7	X	6,7
UKL	5,0	3,3	6,3	4,1	3,8	8,3	3,0	1,7	10,0	1,6	X

[1] A fixed commission fee of about DKR 20 is charged.
[2] Regulated market; banks are free to charge additional fees.
[3] Banknote transactions are subject to a tax of 0,9%.
Columns denote the place of currency conversion. Figures concern exchange operations involving the local currency on one side of the deal.
Source: Data collected from newspapers and banks.

the local currency.[12] For example, the figure in the upper left-hand corner signifies that exchanging Belgian francs in Belgium for Danish kroner banknotes and back would entail a loss of 4,1 %.

The cost of obtaining foreign banknotes fluctuates widely, depending on the country and the currency, but the bid-ask spread will seldom fall short of 3 to 5 %. The banks in the poorer Mediterranean Member States display the smallest spread.[13] The biggest losses are incurred when buying and selling in the countries of the 'centre' banknotes of reputedly weak currencies like the drachma and escudo or, to a much

lesser extent, the peseta and lira. The worst case reported is that of moving in and out of the drachma in Germany, which would wipe out nearly half of the original amount.

2.3. The costs of cross-border payments

Individuals and enterprises making cross-border bank transfers in the Community not only have to put up with currency conversion costs, they are also subject to high payment execution fees and long delays compared to what it takes in terms of cost and time to carry out a domestic bank transfer.

This is borne out by a BEUC report, based on a sample of more than 100 international bank transfers or eurocheques executed criss-cross throughout the Community, each time for an equivalent of ECU 100 in the beneficiary's money. It observed that total costs associated with bank transfers were on average 12,1 % and that it took generally 5 working days for the recipient account to be credited. However, in a number of cases charges rose to twice the average and the time needed was much longer, sometimes lasting months.

Total costs of an international bank transfer from a Belgian franc to a sterling account, for an equivalent of ECU 80, amount to about 18,5 %. The foreign exchange margin and the explicit conversion fee equal 2,5 % or less than one-fifth of the total costs borne by the Belgian franc account holder.

---

[12] The data in Table A.13 should be seen as indicative because national markets for foreign banknotes are far from perfectly competitive. As the cost to foreign cash customers of gathering information rapidly surpasses the benefits, total expenses charged by different banks with respect to one and the same currency can vary by as much as 5 to 10 percentage points, in spite of the fact that banknotes form a classical example of a homogeneous service.

[13] In Greece (where pricing in the foreign banknote market is regulated) and, to a lesser degree, Portugal (where the lion's share of retail banking is still in public hands) this small spread stems from policy, inspired, *inter alia*, by a wish to secure a fair deal for the numerous banknote-purchasing foreign tourists. Two factors may go a long way towards explaining the low spread in Spain and Italy where there is no clear government involvement. First, holding strong-currency banknotes in a weak-currency country is a less unattractive proposition for a bank than the converse situation. Secondly, the possible existence of scale economies in the management of foreign banknotes may lower transaction costs in countries that still rely predominantly on cash as the means of payment.

This anecdotal evidence is consistent with information obtained on the costs for the German banking sector of treating bank transfers. Whereas the execution and processing of a domestic transfer costs German banks about ECU 0,5, the corresponding expenses for an international transfer amount to ECU 10, with approximately ECU 2 being directly attributable to currency conversion.

This contrasts with the minor costs charged in the USA, despite the fact that the American financial services market is still fragmented owing to the MacFadden Act. In the USA, a coast-to-coast cheque takes two working days and a fee ranging from 20 to 50 cents.

The relatively high expenses and long delays cross-border payments in the Community suffer from are in the first place due to the existence of several technical barriers that need to be removed in the internal market framework.[14] But a single currency would significantly facilitate further the treatment of cross-border payments since it would strongly simplify banks' treasury management and accounting. Banks' treasury management would become simpler as long and short positions could be summarized in one currency. So would bank accounting as the number of 'vostri' and 'nostri' accounts of correspondent banks will be halved. All such accounts vis-à-vis banks from other Member States could eventually disappear when every EC bank would hold an account with the European Central Bank.

2.4. The financial transaction cost savings from a single currency

The data on the volume of foreign exchange transactions between EC currencies laid out in Section 2.1. and the evidence reported in Section 2.2 on the cost of converting one currency into another can be combined to obtain some estimates of the exchange transaction gains a single currency would bring, be it for the Community as a whole, individual Member States, or specific payment instruments.

Financial transaction costs for the Community as a whole

Exchange transaction costs for the Community as a whole can be gauged from the turnover on the Community's foreign exchange markets when it is supposed that EC residents,

and only EC residents, purchase their foreign exchange services on EC markets (and those markets only). Two considerations suggest their correct measurement should be based on the foreign exchange transactions arising from business with non-bank customers only, thus leaving aside all interbank operations. First, the resources absorbed in the bank sector by interbank operations triggered by customer business are eventually remunerated by the non-bank sector through the foreign exchange margins and fees it pays to banks. As a corollary, the inclusion of interbank operations would give rise to double counting. Second, the bank resources currently employed in purely speculative or arbitrage operations involving two EC currencies are unlikely to be put to another use following the creation of a single currency, but may instead be shifted to ecu/dollar, ecu/yen, dollar/yen, etc. operations.

It was estimated in Section 2.1. on the basis of Tables A.3 and A.4 that between 34 and 43 % of foreign exchange turnover on the Community markets concerns direct or indirect transactions between two EC currencies. Relating this percentage range to the net turnover arising from business with non-bank customers, shown in Table A.1, an exchange transaction volume of between ECU 4 100 and 5 200 billion is arrived at for 1989.

The banking cost percentage to be applied to this aggregate volume can be derived fairly accurately from the data on the size distribution of current and capital settlements (Table A.11) and the confidential information on bankers' charges for spot and forward transactions.

For want of specific information, a working hypothesis needs to be adopted regarding the relative importance of the use of forward contracts for current account payments. The basic assumption made in this respect is that the portion of foreign currency transactions that is hedged goes up with the size of the amount. Thus, only 20 % of payments inside the ECU 1 000 to 5 000 bracket are supposed to be bought or sold forward, 30 % of the ECU 5 000 to 10 000 bracket, 40 % of ECU 10 000 to 50 000, 50 % of ECU 50 000 to 100 000. All transactions larger than ECU 100 000 are assumed to be covered. Hedging instruments other than ordinary forward contracts have been ignored since their use for commercial purposes is still very limited.

On the basis of this set of assumptions, the data in Table A.11 and information collected on bankers' charges, the average currency conversion cost associated with current account settlements can be assessed at 0,3 to 0,35 %. For capital account transactions by the non-bank sector, costs are clearly lower as the average size of transactions is much larger and as the latter have been supposed not to involve

---

[14] Handling costs would be diminished by measures that would allow transmitting electronically information on the payment of a eurocheque in lieu of physically; so would the elimination of licensing constraints on electronic value-added networks and the development of common technical standards. These issues are dealt with in somewhat greater depth in HM Treasury (1989).

forward contracts. Costs have therefore been set at 0,1 to 0,15 %. The data on the only country (BLEU) for which precise information is available to this effect, suggest that gross capital flows by the non-bank sector are at least five times as large as current account flows. A more conservative 4:1 ratio has been taken for the whole of the Community on account of the capital controls still operated in 1989 by several Member States, leading to an overall average transaction cost estimate of 0,15 to 0,2 %.

Applying this cost percentage to the ECU 4 100 to 5 200 billion transactions' volume identified earlier, the Community's financial transaction cost savings from a single currency as derived from data on the EC's foreign exchange market turnover can be estimated to have lain in 1989 between ECU 6,2 and 10,4 billion.

Obviously, if one were to include interbank operations, 'financial' savings from a single currency would grow much larger. Assuming that 40 % of such foreign exchange operations concern two EC currencies and that a quarter of the reported total take place with banks located outside the Community, the BIS survey data suggest that interbank operations involving two EC currencies equal about ECU 21 500 billion on an annual basis. Applying an average cost of 0,075 % in accordance with the findings of Table A.12, exchange transaction costs connected purely with interbank operations would amount to slightly more than ECU 16 billion.

The ECU 6,2 to 10,4 billion range just arrived at does not include the exchange transaction costs associated with smaller payment instruments like banknotes, traveller's cheques or eurocheques.

The gain from no longer having to obtain foreign banknotes upon the creation of a single currency can be gauged from the estimate of total foreign EC banknote sales and purchases based on Table A.7, and the bid-ask spreads on the banknote market reported in Table A.13. The weighted average of costs related to banknote transactions in the BLEU, Germany, Italy and France amounts respectively to 2,5 %, 2,5 %, 1,3 % and 3,8 %. The overall weighted average for these Member States together equals 2,3 %. Applying the latter percentage with the banknote turnover estimate of ECU 57 to 85 billion put forward in Section 2.1, banknote-related transaction cost savings can be thought to have varied in 1988 between ECU 1,3 and 2 billion. As regards eurocheques, potential savings can be set at around ECU 125 million (40 million cheques with an average value of ECU 125 and costs usually within the 2 to 3 % range). On the assumption that exchange transaction costs associated with traveller's cheques amount to 3 % on average, single

currency savings related to the latter payments instrument can be put at about ECU 150 million. The economies to be obtained with regard to the cross-border use of credit cards are likely to amount to between ECU 150 to 200 million, with average transaction costs somewhat smaller than 2 % and a total foreign EC currency payments volume of roughly ECU 10 billion.

Assembling the various cost components and expressing them in prices of 1990, the financial transaction costs incurred by the Community as a whole due to the absence of a single EC currency can be estimated to lie between ECU 8 and 13 billion or 0,17 and 0,27 % of the Community's GDP.

The validity of this cost range is confirmed by confidential evidence on the revenue the Community's banking sector derives from its foreign exchange related services.

This suggests that almost 5 % of the EC banking sector's income arises from intra-EC foreign exchange activities. The share of the banking sector in GDP standing at close to 6 %, it follows that this income is equivalent to about 0,25 % of Community GDP. It is noteworthy that almost half of the EC banks' intra-EC foreign exchange revenue turns out to accrue in the UK. This is largely due to the fact that as the UK hosts the world's biggest foreign exchange market, claiming 25 % of global net foreign exchange turnover, a large part of spot and hedging operations arising in other EC Member States also involve a financial institution located in the UK. Thereby, many non-financial EC companies outside Britain 'import' indirectly foreign exchange services from the UK.

Individual Member States' transaction costs

It was shown in Section 2.1 that the degree of exposure to foreign EC currencies varies strongly from country to country. The replies to the Commission's questionnaire provided evidence that there still exist strong differences between Member States regarding the prices banks charge for foreign exchange services. As a corollary, the transaction cost savings a single currency will generate will not be spread evenly across the Community. The small open economies and those characterized by a relatively inefficient banking sector will be the chief beneficiaries.

Combining the data of Table A.8, A.11 and the information contained in bankers' replies, it can be calculated that exchange transaction costs borne by the BLEU equalled close to ECU 1.2 billion in 1988 or 0,9 % of the BLEU's GDP. In contrast, even if one assumes, in conformity with the BLEU data, that Germany's capital imports and exports by non-bank enterprises and households to other Member

States in foreign EC currency are five times as large as its EC currency payment flows connected with current account operations, Germany's transaction costs would have amounted in 1988 to only ECU 2.23 billion or 0,11 % of its GDP. Calculations relying on the capital flow figure reported in Table A.8 put the exchange transaction costs for France in 1988 at ECU 920 million or 0,11 % of GDP.[15] Making the same relative assumption as for Germany with respect to the size of capital flows would raise the cost to 0,15 % of GDP. The same percentage would be obtained for Italy, where foreign exchange services appear cheaper than in the Community on average.

The available information thus suggests that in relative terms transaction costs can be 8 times more important for small open economies than for the largest Member State whose currency is a generally accepted means of payment inside the Community.

Although no precise figures can be put forward to this effect, all less developed Member States are also likely to reap higher than average transaction cost savings from the creation of a single currency. Ireland is strongly exposed to foreign EC currencies given the marginal international role of the Irish punt and the country's high degree of openness, particularly vis-à-vis the UK economy. The strong volatility of the pound has probably prompted systematic hedging on the part of Irish traders, aggravating the exchange transaction burden. The three most recent Member States stand to gain relatively much given the poor efficiency and degree of sophistication of the local banks' foreign exchange services. This holds especially for Portugal and Greece, whose intra-EC trade relative to GDP exceeds the Community average and whose currencies are virtually not accepted as means of international payment.

Cost reductions of cross-border payments

It can be estimated on the basis of BIS statistics that in 1988 around 4,4 billion so-called paper-based credit transfers were carried out in the 12 Member States.[16] Assuming that 5 % of these transactions concerned a cross-border transfer inside the Community and that, in conformity with the findings on the German banking sector, the difference in processing costs between a domestic and an international bank transfer equals ECU 6, the establishment of a single currency, along with internal market measures facilitating cross-border payments, would generate an additional transaction cost saving of the order of ECU 1,3 billion.

---

[15] For want of specific information on bank charges in Germany and France, average banking costs as derived in Section 2.2 were applied.
[16] BIS (1989).

3. In-house costs

As regards the costs borne inside non-financial companies from having to work in the Community with a variety of currencies, a distinction can be made between *direct* and *indirect* costs. Some of the direct effects to be identified presently are in principle quantifiable by means of a thorough internal audit of the company. The indirect effects relate primarily to the impact a single currency may have on a transnational corporation's business organization and strategy by removing a major factor of managerial complexity. They are likely to take more time to materialize and are impossible to quantify with any degree of precision. None the less, they may turn out to have a more pervasive impact on the business sector in the Community than the direct effects.

3.1. Direct and indirect effects

Four sources of direct costs — or of direct in-house gains from a single currency — can be identified.

First and most obvious, there are the people and equipment employed in treasury and accounting responsible for netting the company's foreign exchange exposure and overseeing the multitude of spot, forward, currency swap, etc. transactions. Yet, as these are primarily overhead expenses and business with non-EC countries will continue to require foreign exchange management, the scope for administrative savings from the establishment of a single currency is bound to be limited.

Second, multiple currencies lead to company cash being poorly remunerated or, conversely, to high interest costs on debit positions. This is due, on the one hand, to the dispersion of balances over an extensive number of accounts in various currencies held by the parent company or the foreign subsidiaries and, on the other, to the fact that banks offer cash pooling services only for accounts in one and the same currency. With a single currency it becomes much more convenient to finance the various units of a corporate group from a central source.

Third, the delay between the point in time of debiting an account and that of crediting the correspondent recipient account, the so-called 'float' is, as a general rule, much larger for transfers involving different currencies than for payments in one and the same money. Part of this difference in delays will be eliminated as a result of the measures in the framework of the 1992 programme towards the creation of a single EC financial market, but executing and clearing cross-border payments in the Community will remain inherently more complicated, hence costly, in the absence of a single currency.

Fourth, multiple currencies may cause firms to incur an opportunity cost arising from the search for natural hedges. Rather than managing it, many enterprises try to avoid as much as possible the foreign exchange problem by matching receipts and payments per currency or by pursuing a deliberate policy of diversifying foreign exchange risk.[17] To the extent that this strategy leads to business forgone, less favourable conditions at the purchase of inputs, or smaller profit margins, the company undergoes an implicit cost.

A single currency in the Community will induce indirect effects inside firms closely tied to the role of money as a unit of account. By virtue of the increased cost and price transparency it induces, a single currency will facilitate the monitoring of firms' internal transfer pricing practices as well as the reporting and analysis of foreign subsidiaries' performances. The resulting simplification of central management's task of control and evaluation should improve the decision-making process in transnational companies and render international business strategy in its various aspects more sound and easily adjustable.

Furthermore, a single currency is likely to exert a non-trivial influence on the cohesion between the various units of transnational firms. Along with the establishment of the four freedoms and the internationalization of share ownership and management, the use by business of a single currency will nurture the emergence of enterprises with thoroughly European business attitudes and strategies.

3.2. Size of in-house costs

Quantifying these in-house costs with a high degree of accuracy is very difficult. No relevant statistical material is available and none of the enterprises interviewed to this effect was able to come up with a precise comprehensive measure. This is not surprising, since obtaining a rigorous estimate would require a significant analytical effort on their side as the cost from not working in a single currency is widely

diffused over various central departments and foreign subsidiaries of a transnational group. Even multinational companies having imposed or thought of imposing a single currency for internal invoicing, payments and reporting purposes — often the currency of the headquarters, sometimes the ecu or dollar — based their analyses on primarily qualitative indications.

A small set of case-studies conducted by Ernst & Young on behalf of the Commission services (see Box) suggests that on average the cost of treasury and accounting personnel and equipment employed due to the existence of multiple currencies in the Community could amount to about 0,1 % of intra-EC exports. As those expenses are largely fixed, this figure is likely to be much higher for small and medium-sized enterprises and lower for multinational enterprises. For example, in a recent survey of Belgian small and medium-sized enterprises, internal foreign exchange management was estimated to occupy 1,2 % of personnel and cost around 0,3 % of total turnover.[18] The other quantifiable direct costs, primarily those related to the dispersion of balances over an extensive number of accounts in various currencies and to cross-border payment delays can be reckoned to be around 0,1 % of turnover in other Member States as well.

Given that a company's value-added amounts on average to about 55 % of its turnover, these direct sources of in-house costs would equal 0,36 % (i.e., 0,2/0,55) of the value-added generated through intra-EC exports. As intra-EC exports of goods and services represent close to 20 % of Community GDP, one can conclude that the costs borne inside companies from having to operate in the EC with 12 moneys are equivalent to 0,07 to 0,08 % (one fifth of 0,36 %) of Community GDP.

This figure is a lower bound estimate as it does not take into account the non-quantifiable direct and indirect sources of in-house costs related to avoidance of exchange risk exposure and managerial complexity. Evidence in support of this claim is that according to a large-scale business survey conducted by Ernst & Young (1990)[19] one internationally active EC firm out of three thinks a single currency will permit savings unrelated to banking costs exceeding 0,5 % of turnover in foreign EC markets.

[17] Foreign exchange risk is said to be diversified if the depreciation risk relative to one or more currencies is offset by an appreciation risk relative to other currencies.

[18] De Pecunia, (1990), p. 31.
[19] Ernst & Young, (1990), p. 54.

Box A.1: Evidence on in-house costs

A consultancy firm (Ernst and Young) was asked by the Commission services to undertake a small number of case studies with a view to obtaining an estimate of how large is the cost — as a percentage of turnover in other EC countries — to firms of having to deal with multiple currencies in the Community.

Two companies were examined in Germany, France, Spain and the United Kingdom. In order to enhance the representative character of the sample, the selection of enterprises was made so that one firm in each of the four countries produced only domestically, but with significant imported inputs and sales abroad, whereas the other company had a manufacturing base in more than one EC country.

The firms were requested to provide an estimate of total incremental costs due to the absence of a single currency and to isolate the administrative component of these expenses. Their replies are reported in the table below, the French enterprises having been omitted as they felt unable to advance specific cost figures.

Country	Company	Incremental costs – Administrative	Total costs (in-house + financial)
Germany	1	0,1%	0,1%
	2	0,05%	0,05%
United Kingdom	1	0,4%	1,0%
	2	0,1%	1,0%
Spain	1	0,5%	2,1%
	2	0,0%	0,3%

German firm No 1, active in shoe manufacturing and other leatherware, with a total turnover of more than ECU 300 million, thought that dealing in various EC currencies absorbed little administrative resources, since currency management is kept simple (all cash flows in foreign currency being covered forward), and invoicing and accounting largely automated. The currency denomination of bank transfers was not perceived as a source of payment delays. With netting of short and long positions in the same currency systematically pursued and an overwhelming share of international settlements either in Deutschmark or in dollars, financial exchange transaction costs in EC currencies were seen as insignificant relative to EC exports.

German firm No 2, a very large multinational company in electronics, with EC imports and exports amounting respectively to ECU 400 and 1 800 million, deems it incurs trivial exchange transaction costs as all exports are payable in Deutschmarks and only a small fraction of imports is in foreign EC currency. Areas where the absence of a single currency leads to very small incremental expenses are in marketing and the processing of foreign currency invoices.

UK firm No 1, a large company in garments and home furnishings, with a global turnover of nearly ECU 400 million, has production facilities and an extensive retail distribution network on the continent. It estimates the absence of a single currency causes significant administrative costs in the domains of sales, marketing, invoicing and accounting. Despite the complex international finance operations, it reckons the scope for savings in treasury are very limited because of the remaining need to manage foreign exchange with respect to non-EC currencies. Major sources of other than administrative costs are the delays in receiving funds as well as the maintenance of overdrafts in the UK, whilst EC subsidiaries have surplus cash balances that are uneconomic to remit to the parent company.

UK firm No 2, a small precision engineering firm with a turnover of around ECU 10 million has too little market power and therefore has to accept the importer's money as the currency of settlement. It only covers its foreign exchange exposure on contracts denominated in US dollars. Exchange risk in EC currencies is not hedged; instead, the normal contract price is increased by 0,5 % for sales in other EC markets. This uncovered position relative to EC currencies cost the firm dearly in 1988-89 when the company faced an exchange loss equal to 6 % of its exports to other Member States.

Spanish firm No 1, an important frozen seafood manufacturer, with exports to other EC markets of about ECU 20 million, thinks administrative costs could be reduced significantly by a single EC currency, although the figure mentioned in the table relates to the situation when *all* its foreign exchange operations, including those in non-EC currencies, would have been eliminated. The other costs would essentially be the payment of margins and fees to the banking sector. The 2,1 % reported in the table refers again to exchange transaction costs associated with all foreign currency operations.

Finally, Spanish firm No 2, an important manufacturer of petrochemicals, with sales in other EC countries of ECU 300 million, saw little scope for administrative cost reductions because its currency management is limited to simple forward contracts. Furthermore, in the petrochemical sector, the dollar occupies a predominant position. Financial costs were thought to amount to 0,3 % of EC turnover, although in this case as well the company was unable to distinguish between deals involving EC and non-EC currencies.

4. Once-and-for-all adjustment cost of introducing a single currency

Against the durable benefits arising from the elimination of transaction costs must be set the once-and-for-all adjustment costs in the transition to a single currency. National bank-notes and coins currently in circulation will have to be called in and reissued. Firms and banks will undergo some 'menu costs' as they have to convert prices, balances and wages into the new base. They will also need to modify their accounting and computing systems. Some equipment, in particular vending and teller machines, will have to be al-tered. Last but not least, the European public at large will have to adapt to the change, much in the same way as French economic agents had to do upon the introduction of the 'new' French franc at the end of the 1950s and the British following the decimalization of their currency some 20 years ago.

5. Cost summary

By way of conclusion, it is appropriate to sum up the various cost savings identified in the foregoing analysis. Table A.14 provides this summary picture.

Table A.14

Cost savings on intra-EC settlements by single EC currency

(billion ECU, 1990)

	Estimated range	
Financial transaction costs:		
Bank transfers	6,4	10,6
Banknotes, eurocheques, traveller's cheques, credit cards	1,8	2,5
Subtotal	*8,2*	*13,1*
In-house costs	3,6	4,8
Reduction of cross-border payments cost	1,3	1,3
Total	**13,1**	**19,2**

Note: Exchange transaction costs associated with several sources of in-house costs are not included in this table.

References

Bank for International Settlements (1989), *Statistics on payment systems in 11 developed countries*, Basle, December.

Bank for International Settlements (1990), *Survey of foreign exchange market activity*, February.

Black, S. (1989), 'Transaction costs and vehicle currencies', IMF Working Paper No 89/96, November.

Demarsin, P. (1990), 'Volume et structure des marchés des changes en Belgique et à l'étranger', *Cahiers de la Banque Nationale de Belgique*, No 6.

De Pecunia (1990), *PME, risque de change et écu*, February.

Ernst and Young (1990), *A strategy for the ecu*, London.

HM Treasury (1989), *An evolutionary approach to economic and monetary union*, London, November.

Price Waterhouse (1988), 'The cost of non-Europe in financial services', *Research on the cost of non-Europe, Basic findings*, Vol. 9, Commission of the EC, Luxembourg.

Annex B

Germany and the Netherlands: the case of a *de facto* monetary union

The Dutch-German quasi monetary union in the past decade, does not seem to have created major problems for the conduct of economic policy in the Netherlands. Monetary policy has followed closely the policy of the Bundesbank. The interest rate differential, both with respect to short and long-term rates, has narrowed gradually. This differential was significantly larger at the beginning of the decade, the narrowing process was interrupted after the 1983 depreciation but the differential has almost disappeared in the last two years. No speculation against the guilder seems to have occurred during the period under consideration, with short-term interest rates not experiencing greater short-term volatility in the Netherlands.

Fiscal policy, without triggering credibility problems for the exchange rate commitment, was more flexible in the Netherlands than in the Federal Republic, particularly in 1986-87 when it responded to the sharp fall of gas revenues. In the following years, despite a great need for fiscal consolidation, a certain degree of inflexibility frustrated the desire to reduce the deficit. As a result, the Netherlands experienced a different pattern of the public debt to GDP as compared with Germany, implying a huge consolidation effort for the future. However, monetary policy has never been damaged by fiscal developments.

Wage developments seem increasingly to reflect the external competitive position as an instrument of improving domestic employment. Such a flexible approach greatly facilitates the stabilization process.

As regards economic targets, it is highly doubtful if the Dutch economy would have performed better in a flexible exchange rate regime. The inflation performance would have been negatively affected by a depreciation of the guilder while the beneficial economic effects of a depreciation would have been offset by negative effects on confidence, i.e. higher long-term interest rates.

1. Introduction

In the EMS the exchange rate between the currencies of the Federal Republic of Germany and the Netherlands has been

Annex B prepared by Jürgen Kröger

most stable. Only two realignments in 1983 and 1979 respectively have seen the Deutschmark appreciate by two percentage points more than the Dutch guilder on each occasion. Since 1984, the bilateral nominal exchange rate of the Deutschmark and the guilder has actually been stable (Graph B.1). Therefore, the experience of the Netherlands provides an obvious example of a *de facto* monetary union between a small country and a large country. Indeed, the country which has the longest experience with fixed exchange rates in the EMS is also the country which has experienced the least variability and the smallest differentials in interest rates *vis-à-vis* the anchor country.

Several advantages to the Netherlands from the policy of a stable HFL/DM rate can been stressed:

(i) the Federal Republic of Germany is the most important trading partner of the Netherlands;

(ii) a stable relation between HFL/DM facilitates a high degree of price stability (low inflation) providing a nominal anchor for the smaller economy of the Netherlands;

(iii) the credibility incentive of this policy is reflected in the gradual decline in the interest rate differential *vis-à-vis* the Federal Republic; this might be advantageous to the process of budgetary consolidation;

(iv) the link of HFL/DM without conditions has given the financial markets confidence in the policy of the Dutch authorities.

As financial markets are at present very open and related between the two countries, any doubt about the exchange rate would now be translated in capital movements and pressures on interest rates. Integration of the financial markets makes it impossible for a small economy to control the growth of money supply, as only internal sources can be regulated by an independent monetary policy. This argues in favour of a small country pegging its exchange rate on the stable currency of a larger important economic partner.

On the other hand, the Dutch and German example facilitates the analysis of the potential costs of abandoning an economic policy instrument, i.e. the exchange rate. A larger burden will be placed on other instruments, particularly on fiscal policy. However, fiscal consolidation — which is one of the main objectives of economic policy in the Netherlands — might conflict with the greater stabilization role fiscal policy has to play.

The results of this analysis are tentative, however, because they are to a large extent judgmental. The difficulty is that a comparison cannot be drawn with possible economic policy development and performance in the alternative case where

GRAPH B.1: **The bilateral Deutschmark/guilder exchange rate: 1979-90 (HFl. per DM, annual average)**

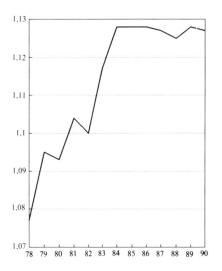

GRAPH B.2: **Growth of production potential in the manufacturing sector in the Federal Republic of Germany and the Netherlands**

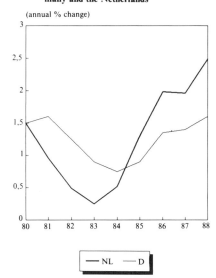

2. Comparison of economic performance

2.1. Macroeconomic performance

In terms of the supply side, the performance of the two economies shows a general similarity in the evolution. Graph B.2 shows that the growth in production potential of the manufacturing sector of both countries decreased to below 1 % during the first half of the 1980s but has accelerated since 1983-84. This acceleration has been more pronounced in the Netherlands. Until 1984 the growth of potential output in the Netherlands has been below growth in the Federal Republic and superior afterwards.

a flexible exchange rate would have been applied. The results should not be directly applied to other countries and particularly not to large countries. Thus the present paper is primarily devoted to analysing the adjustment mechanisms used in the Netherlands to cope with shocks which have asymmetrically affected both economies.

Graph B.3 compares the growth performance of the two countries. In the Netherlands real GDP growth was lower (between 0,5 and 1 % per year) in the period 1979-82. After the 1982 recession both countries recovered at a similar speed. After the oil price decline in 1986 real growth tended to be lower in the Netherlands than in the Federal Republic. Prospects for 1989 and 1990 indicate a renewed narrowing in the growth gap.

While output in the energy sector has followed a particular pattern of development and the public sector has expanded much less than the private economy, growth in private enterprises (excluding energy) has generally been (except in 1986) more favourable in the Netherlands than in the Federal Republic since 1984. During that period, following a deeper recession than in the rest of the Community at the beginning of the 1980s, the Netherlands experienced a rather sustained upturn in growth.

The comparison of the respective employment performances reflects the different economic growth patterns (see Graph B.4a). Graph B.4b shows that the unemployment rate (Euro-

GRAPH B.3: **Real growth in the Federal Republic of Germany and the Netherlands (1979-90) — Gross domestic product at constant market prices (annual % change)**

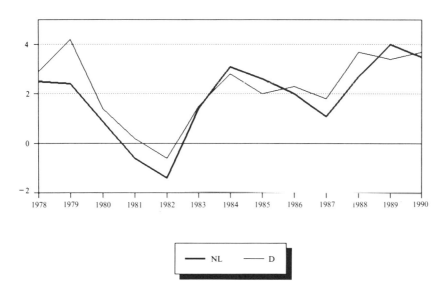

Table B.1

Growth in the value-added of enterprises in the Federal Republic of Germany and the Netherlands (excluding energy) (1980 prices)

	1981	1982	1983	1984	1985	1986	1987	1988	1989	1990
Germany	0,2	− 0,5	1,6	3,4	2,6	2,6	1,3	4,3	4,4	4,0
Netherlands	0,1	− 0,8	1,1	4,5	3,0	2,2	1,4	4,5	4,8	3,8

GRAPH B.4a: **Employment in the Federal Republic of Germany and the Netherlands (total economy) (changes in %)**

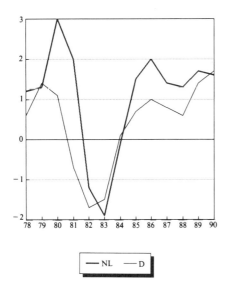

GRAPH B.4b: **Unemployment rate in the Federal Republic of Germany and the Netherlands (percentage of civilian labour force)**

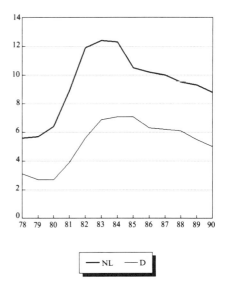

stat) is currently about 2,5 percentage points higher in the Netherlands than in the Federal Republic.

Between 1970 and 1979 inflation was very high in the Netherlands. The monetary authorities tried, by linking the guilder to the Deutschmark, to achieve an appreciation of the guilder in order to break the wage-price spiral and to obtain a lower inflation rate. After 1979, both countries experienced a period of gradual disinflation, during the first half of the 1980s, while having experienced inflation rates above 5 % immediately after the second oil price shock (Graph B.5).

The process of disinflation started in 1981 and in 1986 zero inflation was achieved in the Federal Republic. Since 1987, the inflation rate in the Netherlands has been lower than that of the Federal Republic. Most likely, underlying inflation was very similar during the period and, to a considerable extent, the relatively large gap evidenced in 1989 was the result of diverging tax policies. While VAT has been lowered in the Netherlands, excise duties were increased in the Federal Republic. In addition, the price dampening effect of the oil price drop in 1986 has materialized in the Netherlands with a certain time lag as natural gas consump-

tion is more important in the Netherlands than in Germany and the level of its prices is to a certain extent a discretional decision.

The overall increase in the price deflator of private consumption has actually been the same during the last decade, indicating that both countries pursue similar stability-oriented policies. This, indeed, is an important beneficial consequence of the strong currency option chosen by the Netherlands.

Graph B.6 indicates significant differences in the development of the current balance of payments. These differences can mostly be explained by different structural characteristics, since the dependence on energy imports differs. Whereas the Federal Republic is a net importer of energy, the Netherlands has become self-sufficient. Because of the time lag with which prices of natural gas follow oil prices, the current balance of the Netherlands improved significantly relative to that of Germany in 1981. On average, the current account surplus of the Netherlands was 2,5 % of GDP larger than that of the Federal Republic. After the fall in energy prices the relative position changed. In terms of GDP the

GRAPH B.5: **Inflation in the Federal Republic of Germany and the Netherlands — Price deflator of private consumption (changes in %)**

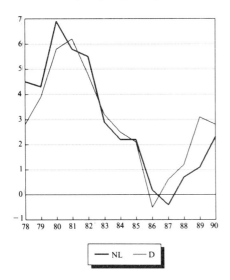

— NL   — D

GRAPH B.6: **Current balance in the Federal Republic of Germany and the Netherlands (% of GDP)**

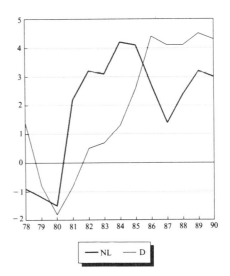

— NL   — D

German current account has exceeded the Netherlands current account by about 2,5 % since 1987.

2.2. Structural and sectoral characteristics

At the sectoral level, the two economies show a different structure (see Table B.2). In both countries, the service sector is the most important (42,5 to 44 %); the weight of the manufacturing sector is very high, although declining, and it shows a significant difference in the two countries (33 % in the Netherlands and 41 % in Germany); investment goods are more important in Germany, while for consumer goods the difference is less marked.

Both economies are strongly export oriented (see Table B.3). But the Netherlands, as a small open economy, has a

Table B.2

Production according to sector in the Federal Republic of Germany and the Netherlands (% of total)

	Federal Republic of Germany			Netherlands		
	1970	1980	1986	1970	1980	1986
Agriculture	3,3	2,4	2,0	6,2	4,5	5,3
Energy, water, mining	4,6	6,6	6,2	6,5	10,6	13,2
Manufacturing sector	48,5	41,6	41,4	34,3	30,7	32,7
basic materials	13,4	11,0	9,9	6,4	7,1	9,1
investment goods	17,8	16,5	17,9	9,8	8,5	8,7
consumer goods	17,4	14,0	13,0	18,1	15,1	14,9
Construction	7,5	6,8	5,6	9,6	9,0	6,3
Services	35,4	42,6	44,0	43,4	45,1	42,5

Source: BDS.

Table B.3

Export shares in the Federal Republic of Germany and the Netherlands (in % of total production)

	Federal Republic of Germany			Netherlands		
	1970	1980	1986	1970	1980	1986
Agriculture	4,4	5,9	8,7	30,2	42,0	39,1
Energy, water, mining	6,2	6,9	4,2	32,9	49,1	49,4
Manufacturing sector	18,8	27,0	33,0	46,3	53,7	60,4
basic materials	19,6	27,8	33,2	74,8	82,4	76,2
investment goods	29,4	37,5	19,1	49,0	58,0	68,9
consumer goods	7,5	14,0	19,1	34,6	37,8	45,7

Source: BDS.

significantly higher export ratio (almost 60 % of GDP) than the Federal Republic (33 %). This makes the Netherlands economy more dependent on developments in world trade. Export dependency is in general much higher in the Netherlands than in the Federal Republic in all branches.

In addition to the export share of total production, the degree of self-sufficiency is an important factor determining how susceptible a country is to fluctuations in world demand. From Table B.4 it is clear that the economy of the Federal Republic is more specialized than the Dutch economy. The self-sufficiency of the Dutch economy in energy production and consumption is also evident.

Table B.4

Export-import ratio in the Federal Republic of Germany and the Netherlands (in %)

	Federal Republic of Germany			Netherlands		
	1970	1980	1986	1970	1980	1986
Agriculture	12	14	19	86	96	107
Energy, water, mining	37	17	19	86	87	140
Manufacturing sector	133	112	138	89	100	102
basic materials	118	134	143	87	129	134
investment goods	277	231	220	67	82	76
consumer goods	59	69	86	109	96	112

Source: BDS.

3. Comparison of economic policies

3.1. Monetary policy and inflation

Graphs B.7 and B.8 show the development of interest rates in both countries. Short-term interest rates moved almost in parallel, although in the period 1985-87 rates in the Netherlands were above prevailing German rates. The narrowing of the differential was not primarily linked to the round of monetary tightening but can be considered as a return to a 'normal' situation after the reverse oil shock of 1986-87.

The movement of long-term interest rates shows a continuous narrowing of the interest rate differential between the two countries. In 1988, the interest rate gap actually disappeared. The disappearance of the long-term interest rate differential in 1988 might however be due to the introduction of the withholding tax which had an effect on German long-term interest rates in particular. The development of long-term interest rates indicates a progressive diminution of

GRAPH B.7: **Short-term interest rates in the Federal Republic of Germany and the Netherlands — 1978-90 (quarterly averages)**

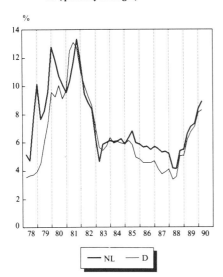

GRAPH B.8: **Long-term interest rates in the Federal Republic of Germany and the Netherlands — 1978-90 (quarterly averages)**

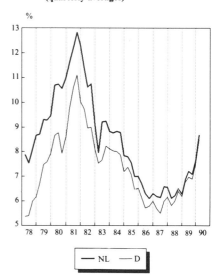

medium-term expectations of a guilder depreciation against the Deutschmark.

Graph B.7 shows that short-term interest rates have not been more volatile than would have been suggested by important changes in exchange rate expectations. Indeed, fluctuations have become much smaller than in the 1970s.

The fact that markets have actually attributed a large degree of credibility to the exchange rate commitment is illustrated by the fairly close movement of short-term interest rates and the progressive narrowing in the long-term interest rate differential.

The difference between long- and short-term interest rates can serve as an indicator of the stance of monetary policy. Developments in the two countries show that monetary policy was tighter in the Federal Republic in the early 1980s. Although since 1984 no major differences are detectable, monetary policy in the Netherlands seems to have become marginally more restrictive compared to the Federal Republic, since the yield curve is somewhat steeper.

3.2. Fiscal policy

In the period under review, net borrowing of the general government in the Netherlands was larger than in the Federal Republic. While net borrowing declined during a period of consolidation between 1982 and 1985 in the Federal Republic, the fiscal balance deteriorated significantly in the Netherlands (7,1 % of GDP) in 1982. The Government then introduced a stabilization programme and up to 1985 the deficit declined to about 5 % of GDP. The slight increase in the deficit in the Federal Republic after 1986 was a consequence of a fairly low growth of nominal domestic demand and reductions in income taxes. On the other hand, despite further attempts to cut back the public deficit in the Netherlands, it increased in 1986 and 1987 to more than 6 % of GDP, because of oil price-induced losses in revenues. In 1986-87 these losses represented some 4,1 % of net national income. The deficit in the Federal Republic has, over the whole period, been reduced from 3 % of GDP to 1 %. However, in the Netherlands the deficit, corrected for the gas revenue factor, passed from 6 to 5 % of GDP. The revenue from natural gas, which was 16 % of the total budget income, fell to 4 % in 1989.

GRAPH B.9: **The difference between long-term and short-term interest rates in the Federal Republic of Germany and the Netherlands (percentage point)**

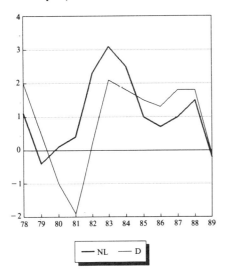

GRAPH B.10: **Net lending (+) or net borrowing (−) in the Federal Republic of Germany and the Netherlands — General government (% of GDP)**

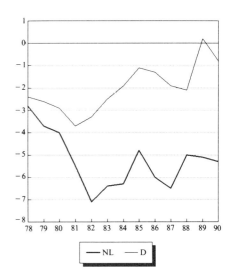

GRAPH B.11: **Compensation per employee in the Federal Republic of Germany and the Netherlands (annual % change)**

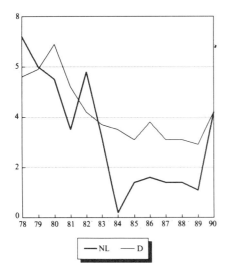

GRAPH B.12: **Real compensation per employee in the Federal Republic of Germany and the Netherlands (annual % change)**

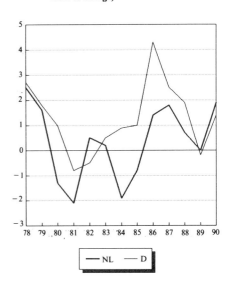

3.3. Wage developments

Between 1979 and 1982, wages in the Netherlands moved independently of wages in the Federal Republic. However, in the period 1983-89, wages in the Netherlands have increasingly responded to the need to preserve external competitiveness and to ensure a better employment performance. This development was merely a consequence of the agreement between the social partners in November 1982 to accept a period of wage moderation.

Since 1984, the increase in both nominal and real wages has been lower in the Netherlands than in the Federal Republic. The significant change in wage behaviour seems to have occurred after the last relative depreciation of the guilder on 21 March 1983. Nominal wages actually stagnated in 1984 and have risen by about half the German rate since then. Wages in the industry sector (in the Netherlands wages in the public sector were frozen) show a slightly different pattern; because of similar developments in prices, real wage moderation has been more significant in the Netherlands than in the Federal Republic (Graph B.12).

The exchange rate policy in the 1970s led to a sharp rise of relative prices in the Netherlands, an important factor of the deterioration of the competitive position in those years. To break the wage-price spiral with this policy a high price has been paid; the bad competitive position resulting from it could be reversed by the moderating effects of high unemployment figures on wages.

4. The asymmetric effects of shocks

4.1. Energy prices

Graph B.13 shows the development of the terms of trade in the Netherlands and the Federal Republic of Germany. Clearly the two oil price shocks have influenced the two economies asymmetrically. The increase in oil prices at the beginning of the 1980s led to a significant fall in the terms of trade of the Federal Republic relative to those of the Netherlands while the fall in oil prices in 1986 had the reverse effect. All in all, movements in the terms of trade have been more volatile in the Federal Republic than in the Netherlands, where the terms of trade have improved gradually over time.

The changes in the terms of trade are primarily reflected in the external current balances. In the Netherlands, the change in the terms of trade led to a significant increase in the current account surplus in 1981, while after the decline in oil prices the German current account rose significantly both in absolute terms and also relative to that of the Netherlands. In spite of the similar performance of almost all other economic target variables (with the exception of the public deficit) the current account moved independently. This, however, is consistent with the operation of a monetary union in which current accounts play a smaller role in adjustment.

The response of economic policy in the Netherlands to the fall in the terms of trade relative to Germany has been:

(i) monetary policy has become marginally tighter relative to Germany. Given the large asymmetry of the shock, the necessity for monetary policy response has been surprisingly small. This means that the exchange rate commitment has been allowed to become sufficiently credible;

(ii) the budget deficit became larger in 1986-87 when oil prices went down and the government receipts fell. The target of reducing the budget deficit at the end of the period has not been given up. However, as the budget deficit remained high (5 % of GDP in 1989) the public debt/GDP rate was still increasing.

(iii) in particular wage moderation and thus improved competitiveness protected the Dutch economy from employment losses in the aftermath of the fall in oil prices.

In order to assess the appropriateness of the economic policy response in the Netherlands, we should consider the alternative response, namely an exchange rate depreciation relative to the Deutschmark and/or an appropriate fiscal and structural policy. In the first case, because of an implied higher growth in nominal income, the effect on the fiscal deficit would have been reduced. However, it is by no means evident that interest rates would not have increased considerably because of the potentially significant shock to financial markets. In particular, long-term interest rates would probably have increased, triggering a detrimental effect on investment. The extent to which the strong exchange rate option was a precondition for wage moderation remains an open question. Furthermore, a decision to depreciate would imply competitive gains of much shorter duration, not to mention significant inflationary consequences.

In short, the response of the Dutch economic policy to the oil price fall has been a combination of wage moderation and a considerable short-term flexibility of fiscal policy, reducing the need for adjustment of monetary policy.

GRAPH B.13: **Terms of trade in the Federal Republic of Germany and the Netherlands (goods and services) (1980 = 100)**

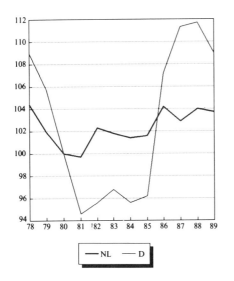

GRAPH B.14: **Competitiveness of the Federal Republic of Germany and the Netherlands — Unit labour costs (annual % change)**

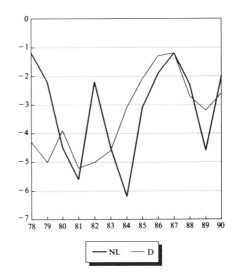

4.2. External trade cycle and the Dutch policy response

The Netherlands was hit harder than the Federal Republic of Germany by the slowing down of world economic activity in the early 1980s. This was due to less rapid growth in the export markets and even some loss in market shares. This led to a decline in the Dutch share in overall world trade in manufactures during the period 1980-82 while the German share increased by almost 1 percentage point during that period. Even the 1983 depreciation of the guilder relative to the Deutschmark improved the Dutch position in 1983 only. Therefore, the relatively weak growth performance of the Dutch economy at the beginning of the decade is mainly attributable to divergent external conditions.

As to the policy response, it seems that fiscal adjustment has been the main instrument to counterbalance the detrimental effects on economic targets and in particular on unemployment. It is interesting to note that the relative and absolute relaxation of fiscal policy in the Netherlands has not had detrimental effects on exchange rate expectations.

Wages were not supporting the adjustment needs of the Dutch economy during this period. Nominal wages grew

relatively fast in 1982. The implied deterioration in competitiveness contributed to the observed losses of export market share.

During the recovery of world trade in the second half of the decade, exports in the Netherlands grew faster than in the Federal Republic, explaining at least partly the change in overall growth performance. The faster increase in Dutch exports can be explained by more moderate wage increases and thus improved competitiveness. Although a quantitative assessment is difficult, it would appear that, without the export led growth, the deterioration in the fiscal deficit due to the fall in the terms of trade would have been more significant. But export performance would perhaps have been better with less deterioration of the fiscal deficit (making room for tax reductions).

4.3. Deutschmark weakness in 1988; German monetary union

In 1988, the introduction of the withholding tax in the Federal Republic led to an increase in long-term interest rates and to capital outflows, triggering a temporary weakness of the Deutschmark on foreign exchange markets.

The effect of this asymmetric shock on Dutch economic policies was not important. It led to a temporary narrowing of the short- and long-term interest rate differential. The position of the guilder in the EMS was hardly changed.

The German economic, monetary and social union will be a crucial test not only for the quasi monetary union between the Netherlands and the Federal Republic of Germany, but also with respect to the overall working of the EMS. Monetary policy in Germany will be confronted by greater uncertainties both as regards the appropriate stance and the interpretation of monetary indicators. The appropriate stance will crucially depend upon the extent to which fiscal policy in Germany will become more expansionary than before.

On the level of the interpretation of monetary policy, monetary targets will become less reliable indicators of monetary policy as money demand can become fairly volatile in Germany; other market-oriented indicators, including notably the exchange rates will have a greater role to play. Therefore, exchange rate policy in the EMS will become more an issue of common interest and the definition of the appropriate monetary policy stance will also depend upon economic policies in the EMS partner countries.

The crucial question will be whether the more expansionary stance of fiscal policy in Germany can be sustained without significantly changing the policy mix. A tighter monetary policy could prove necessary with implications for the stance of monetary policy in the whole EMS area.

Annex C

European and German economic and monetary union: a comparison

The purpose of this annex is to compare the economic effects that can be expected from the German economic, monetary and social union (henceforth GEMSU) with those of EMU (for the Community) that are analysed more thoroughly in this volume. This comparison has to take into account the obvious differences in terms of size, starting positions and speed of transition. It also has to take into account the act of political union, which took place on 3 October 1990 and which constitutes another important difference. In spite of these obvious differences it still appears reasonable to apply some of the same basic categories of economic effects that were used in the analysis of EMU in this volume to the analysis of GEMSU. The effects that seem most important in the case of GEMSU are (i) efficiency gains, (ii) benefits in terms of price stability, (iii) fiscal policy effects and, (iv) the loss of the exchange rate as an adjustment instrument during the transition. [1] These four effects are discussed below after a brief introduction which describes the way GEMSU was implemented and discusses the extent to which it has more of a Community than a purely German dimension. The annex concludes with some discussion of different speeds in the transition.

1. Introduction

Preparations for an economic, monetary and social union started after the first democratic elections in the German Democratic Republic on 18 March 1990 and the details were fixed in a treaty (Staatsvertrag) between the two German governments. That treaty took effect on 1 July 1990 and from that date the Deutschmark became the sole legal tender in the territory of the GDR. All current payments (wages, rents, etc.) formerly expressed in East German marks were converted at the rate of 1:1, whereas assets and liabilities were converted in general at the rate of two to one (except a lump sum of 4 000 per adult, 2 000 per child and 6 000 for persons over 59 years). At the same time the GDR also adopted laws and other legal dispositions, mostly identical to those in the FRG, that freed economic activity from the constraints imposed by the previous regime, thus creating the legal framework for a market economy. Starting on

2 July the free movement of goods, services and production factors was established, thus totally liberalizing trade between the former West and East Germanys with the exception of some quotas on agricultural products. On 3 October 1990 the former GDR legally became part of the Federal Republic of Germany, in accordance with Article 23 of the Grundgesetz.

An important aspect of this annex is that it is somewhat misleading to speak of an economic and monetary union between the two parts of Germany. The West German economy, like that of other member countries, is already integrated into the Community to such a considerable extent that the conditions inside the Community already come very close to the definition of an economic union (the free movement of goods and services and factors of production). It might therefore be more appropriate to speak of a participation of the GDR in the economic union that has already formed to a large extent in the Community. [2] The monetary union aspect, is, of course, more specifically German, but even here it is important to recognize that through the EMS the GDR participates immediately in a quasi-monetary union that already exists and incorporates part of the Community. [3]

For clarity of exposition and also to make the presentation comparable to the analysis of EMU this note distinguishes between the monetary union aspect (the introduction of the Deutschmark in the GDR) [4] and the economic union aspect (the freeing of economic activity and trade). The economic union aspect can be considered to consist of two elements: internal liberalization, i.e. the creation of a market economy (through the elimination of price controls, recognition of private property in capital, etc.) and external liberalization i.e. the suppression of trade barriers. The jump to a market economy is interesting in its own right, and might constitute a useful reference point for the more gradual transition process that is currently taking place in other central and eastern European countries. [5] However, given that all member countries already have market economies the second

---

[1] Because of the obvious difference in size GEMSU should not have important global implications.

Annex C prepared by Daniel Gros

[2] If another country, e.g. Hungary, had taken the same measures as the GDR in the economic field, one would have to speak of accession to the EC.

[3] It is clear that the social, and hence fiscal, aspects do not have this European component.

[4] The monetary union aspect can also be said to comprise the fact that the West German banking system was extended to the GDR and that all dispositions of the Bundesbank now apply to the territory of the GDR as well.

[5] This aspect is also relevant for those member countries that have State control over considerable parts of their productive sector.

aspect (external liberalization) is more relevant for the comparison with EMU.

2. Price stability

By adopting the Deutschmark, the GDR immediately gained all the advantages of a stable currency and of the credible anti-inflationary policy of the Bundesbank. Although overt inflation had not been high under the previous regime this can be considered an important economic benefit for the people in the GDR since experience has shown that periods of liberalization often bring high inflation. Moreover, it would have been impossible for the authorities in the GDR to establish quickly the reputation and hence credibility for price stability the Bundesbank has acquired over the last four decades. This gain must therefore be considered as even more important than that which some member countries can expect from EMU since most member countries have already reduced inflation considerably and can to some extent benefit from the reputation of the Bundesbank by participating in the EMS.

By simultaneously freeing trade, not only with the FRG, but in effect with the Community and the world, the GDR was also able to make sure that the elimination of price controls would not lead to inflation since prices, at least for tradable goods, stabilized quickly at the West German or world level. Thus the monetary reform means for the GDR also an instantaneous and radical reform of the price mechanism, with an enormous, indeed revolutionary, impact on the 'real' economy, which goes beyond its 'nominal' aspects. This price reform aspect of GEMSU represents a dimension that is only weakly present in the EMU case.

3. Efficiency gains

Notwithstanding the enormous initial adjustment losses being experienced in the GDR economy, it is appropriate to focus on the ultimate economic gains.

The most important long-term effect of GEMSU will be the gains from the complete integration of markets for goods, services and capital that was made possible by the introduction of the Deutschmark in the GDR.[6] The GDR did not

have a capital market prior to GEMSU; through this move, however, savers and investors in the GDR are put immediately into contact via an efficient capital market and financial system. The introduction of the Deutschmark has thus reduced the cost and increased the availability of credit and risk capital, which will allow surviving or new enterprises to finance the huge investment needed to modernize the capital stock of the East German economy and facilitate the creation of new enterprises, especially small to medium-sized ones. Without access to this capital market, investment and employment creation through new enterprises would be much more difficult and the catching-up process slower. Moreover, and more importantly, access to the world capital market via the Deutschmark will allow the private sector in the GDR to use foreign savings to finance the huge initial need for investment; i.e. the common currency has eliminated for the GDR the current account constraint. As discussed in Chapter 6 of this study the importance of the current account constraint may already be declining in the Community because of capital market liberalization. However, the GDR would certainly have been forced to maintain capital controls had a separate GDR currency been maintained. This benefit of a common currency should therefore be much more important for the GDR than in the context of EMU.

The economic benefits the GDR economy can derive from the creation of an efficient capital market and the elimination of the current account constraint depend on the extent to which an investment boom in the GDR does materialize. An efficient capital market and access to foreign savings are important only if investment is strong. The extent to which this will be the case is difficult to judge. On the one hand it has been argued that conversion of wages at 1 to 1 has led to wages that are above productivity and that very little investment might therefore take place in the GDR. On the other hand, it has also been argued that the GDR represents a market with a strong pent-up demand and productivity might increase rapidly with modern capital equipment, the right incentives for labour and given that the general level of education of the GDR work force is not too far from Western standards.

It is apparent that the liberalization of trade (the external economic aspect of GEMSU) also benefits the GDR economy immensely in the long run. In the case of EMU this aspect is not very important since the internal market programme will already eliminate all barriers to trade inside the Community. In the case of Germany, however, the starting point is totally different in that, before GEMSU, the GDR economy traded very little with market economies and the trade with the Comecon partners was conducted at artificial prices and distorted by political considerations. By opening the economy to international trade the GDR economy would

---

[6] By adopting the Deutschmark the GDR eliminated all transaction costs in intra-German trade and reduced the costs that arise in trade with the rest of the world to the low level enjoyed by exporters and importers from the GDR. For example, West German banking sources estimate that a transfer from East to West Germany cost about DM 100 before GEMSU. This would fall to the DM 1 a transfer is estimated to cost inside the German banking system. These direct savings far exceed what can be expected from EMU because the cost of international transactions inside the Community is estimated to be about DM 20, only about one fifth of the cost of an intra-German one before GEMSU.

reap all the well-known gains from trade through increased specialization and economies of scale.

The sudden introduction of free trade leads, however, to large adjustment costs for the GDR economy. As with all trade liberalization programmes these adjustment costs arise in the beginning. They are of a once and for all nature and ultimately much less important than the efficiency gains that will be reaped continuously once the GDR economy has adjusted and integrated itself in the global division of labour. None the less, the extremely large losses of industrial production in the first months of GEMSU show clearly that the future large gains cannot be rapidly secured without a corresponding rapid initial adjustment shock.

Because of the different starting points the efficiency gains, as well as initial adjustment costs, from both the economic and the monetary union aspects should therefore, here also, be several orders of magnitude higher in the case of GEMSU, than in EMU.

4. Fiscal effects

Here the qualitative differences between GEMSU and EMU are also very large. In the fiscal domain formal political unification, which took place on 3 October 1990, brought about important changes with respect to the situation prevailing immediately after 1 July 1990. For example, as long as the GDR State existed with its own government it was bound by the dispositions in the Staatsvertrag that stipulated that it could not finance any deficit without the approval of the FRG. Once the GDR ceased to exist this issue no longer arose. To respect the federal structure of the FRG, *Länder* have been recreated on the territory of the GDR, and these *Länder* will, after a transition period of 5 years, enjoy a degree of fiscal independence similar to the existing *Länder* in the FRG. The appropriate comparison in EMU is therefore the situation existing after political unification.[7]

The *Länder* on the territory of the GDR will receive considerable transfers directly from the federal government.[8] The economic rationale for the different size of these transfers

(as compared to what is planned inside the Community) can be found in the much higher degree of labour mobility that exists between these parts of Germany.[9] The mobility of labour between member countries of the EC is much lower so that much larger differences in income can persist without leading to unacceptable migration flows. Although common citizenship, i.e. political unification, is certainly also important, the fact that regional transfers between the two parts of Germany have a different dimension from those at the Community level can also be understood as a reaction to a different economic environment, i.e. a different degree of labour mobility.

With the disappearance of a 'central' government in the GDR the size of the federal budget relative to those of the *Länder* will be close to the present situation in the FRG; i.e. about 50 % of total expenditure, whereas the Community budget accounts only for 2 % of public expenditure in the Community. This implies that the issue of fiscal policy coordination has a different dimension than inside the Community where the central level accounts for a very small part of total public expenditure.

5. Adjusting without the exchange rate

The present study has argued that the main cost of a monetary union is the loss of the exchange rate as an adjustment instrument in the face of asymmetric regional shocks. This idea was also the main argument against the introduction of the Deutschmark in the GDR since the economy of the GDR will go through a period of profound adjustment whose success and speed cannot be predicted a priori. The changes in the product mix in the GDR and the rapid growth of income that can be expected during the catching-up process imply that the real exchange rate between the two parts of Germany has to change significantly in the near future. During a transition period the need for real exchange rate adjustments will therefore be much greater between the two parts of Germany than inside the Community. One could therefore argue that in this respect the potential cost of a monetary union could be higher in the German case.

As emphasized in Chapter 6 of this study the nominal exchange rate is a useful adjustment instrument only if nominal wages are somewhat rigid. Had the GDR maintained a separate currency, to be able to adjust the exchange rate during the transition period, exchange rate changes would have been effective only if wages could be relied upon not

---

[7]   This applies mainly to fiscal issues. Political unification does not alter the free trade and free movement of labour already established in July.

[8]   These *Länder* start with a much lower level of debt than their West German counterparts. They should therefore be able, at least initially, to run much larger deficits. The Finanzausgleich, which provides for horizontal transfers from richer to poorer *Länder* in the FRG, is not due to be revised until 1994, but it will probably have to be adjusted considerably after that date.

[9]   For a further discussion of the issue of fiscal federalism see the contribution by Van Rompuy *et al.* in *European Economy* (1990).

to react immediately. Given the high degree of integration of the German labour market (and of most other markets as well) it is, however, likely that workers would have been able to 'see through' the effects of exchange rate adjustments. It is therefore doubtful that the exchange rate would have been a more useful policy tool for the GDR than for other Community countries which have realized that exchange rate changes on their own cannot correct major external or internal imbalances. [10]

Another issue that arises more strongly in the case of GEMSU concerns the initial level of the exchange rate. In the case of EMU market exchange rates provide a reliable guide to the appropriate level at which to fix rates for the monetary union. Only for countries with large imbalances would it be appropriate not to fix exchange rates at the level at which they trade in the markets. However, in the case of GEMSU no such indicator existed and the conversion of wages at one to one, i.e. an exchange rate of one, had been chosen only on the basis of some rough calculations regarding productivity. At present there is still considerable uncertainty whether, or at what future point in time, this level might reflect the competitiveness of the GDR economy.

6. Transition

The German economic and monetary union went into effect literally almost overnight. In contrast, in the case of the Community it took over a decade to eliminate tariffs and the internal market programme will have taken a number of years to be completed since it was launched in 1985. In the monetary field it took several years of operation of the EMS to reduce exchange rate variability and achieve some convergence in inflation. The introduction of a common currency for the Community is also expected to take a number of years. Political factors certainly were the main reason for this difference in the speed of transition. However, there are also economic aspects to this choice.

In the economic field the standard argument for a slow liberalization of trade is that this reduces the social costs of adjustment. In the German case the financial costs of this social aspect are borne by the FRG and this makes an immediate trade liberalization possible.

In the monetary field the main economic reason for not going immediately to full EMU is that the institution that will manage the common monetary policy needs to establish its credibility and needs to learn how to operate on a Community-wide financial market. This consideration does not apply to GEMSU since in this case the Bundesbank, which is an experienced institution with a well-established reputation for price stability, will be in charge of the joint monetary policy.

Another reason for a gradual transition in the case of EMU is that convergence of inflation usually takes some time. However, as discussed in Chapter 8 this argument applies only if the introduction of a single currency is preceded by a period of fixed exchange rates. In the German case the jump to the single currency eliminated this consideration as well.

For the so-called 'coronation theory' monetary union can only be the crowning act of a long process of convergence in economic policy and performance. According to this theory the only way to verify that all the conditions for a stable monetary union are met is through this process of prior convergence. In the case of GEMSU, however, the GDR had signalled its willingness to fulfil all the conditions for a stable monetary union through the Staatsvertrag, which stipulates that all the dispositions of the Bundesbank apply to the territory of the GDR as well and establishes tight controls over the fiscal policy of the GDR.

In summary it is evident that the main arguments for a gradual transition towards EMU that can be made at the level of the Community did not apply in the case of Germany.

7. Concluding remarks

The economic, monetary and social union started between the FRG and the GDR in July 1990 and the political union which followed in October 1990 represent a dramatic example of a 'jump' to a different regime. This example will be of most relevance not so much for the Community's EMU process but rather for countries like Poland, Hungary and Czechoslovakia that plan to institute a market economy and have to decide how long the transition should be.

This study has argued that EMU can be considered a 'regime change'. In a certain sense GEMSU provides a special and particularly stark example of the profound effects a 'regime change' can have.

---

[10]   Chapter 6 shows that devaluations of the nominal exchange rate lead to a gain in competitiveness only in the very short run.

Annex D

Shocks and adjustment in EMU: simulations with the Quest model

1. Introduction and summary

Any assessment of the loss of the exchange rate instrument in EMU has to take account of the size of asymmetric shocks and the extent to which the exchange rate can be replaced by other instruments. The purpose of this annex is to identify the different shocks individual countries have faced in the recent past (Section 2), as well as to evaluate the costs of the loss of the exchange rate in terms of output and inflation in relation to alternative adjustment instruments (Section 3).

Both analyses are performed using the Quest model of the Commission.[1] Naturally, the results are influenced by the particular structure and properties of this model. Therefore, as far as possible, the arguments are supplemented by theoretical considerations justifying the results. The following conclusions emerge.

Concerning the different types of shocks:

(i) macroeconomic fluctuations in one quarter are only partially determined by shocks occurring in that same quarter, and more by the effects of previous shocks, i.e. permanent shocks are more important than temporary shocks;

(ii) of the temporary shocks to GDP (as measured by their impact in the first quarter), about one half are due to shocks in economic behaviour of private agents, one quarter are due to shocks in budgetary policy and about one-tenth are due to monetary policy shocks (the small size of the latter is due to the fact that monetary policy is only effective with some lags, in the model); governments may therefore be considered to be a non-negligible source of temporary shocks;

(iii) the importance of shocks in the behaviour of private agents is smaller in European countries than in the United States for the real side of the economy, but not as regards inflation, and therefore wages.

Concerning the loss of the exchange rate instrument:

(i) the exchange rate instrument serves to frontload real exchange rate changes needed to adjust to a shock; but

given that unemployment affects wages, this has the drawback that real adjustment to the new equilibrium level is delayed in time;

(ii) the cost of losing the exchange rate instrument in terms of output diminishes the higher the degree of indexation of wages to prices and the stronger the reaction of wages to unemployment;

(iii) alternatives to the exchange rate may be fiscal policy, wage policy, or a supply measure (e.g. social security contributions of employers); but relative to a devaluation, each of these instruments implies either a real wage loss or an increase in the government deficit;

(iv) the loss of the exchange rate instrument does not necessarily imply a cost in terms of inflation.

2. Sources of macroeconomic fluctuations in the Community

In the context of EMU, the loss of domestic monetary policy and the exchange rate instrument implies that national governments may lose some control over their economy in the face of country-specific shocks. This could increase macroeconomic fluctuations and therefore reduce welfare. Accordingly, it is particularly important to identify as far as possible the different categories of shocks that may influence an economy and the way in which they will evolve in EMU. The purpose of this section is therefore to describe different categories of shocks and give some empirical account of them. The latter is done using the Quest models for Germany, France, Italy, the United Kingdom, and the United States for comparison.

Emphasis is given to the short-term effects of shocks and the extent to which they are due to government policies. The former are captured by looking at the first-quarter instantaneous impact of different shocks. Even though shocks in reality often have an impact which lasts for a longer period, this makes it possible to focus on sources of short-term fluctuations, and therefore of uncertainty. As regards the influence of government policies, it is assumed that the stabilization function of the government implies that the monetary and fiscal authorities attempt to influence variables such as employment, income, price levels, rates of inflation, rates of investment and saving, and economic growth.[2] In doing so, the authorities have to take account of several factors influencing these variables, including the consequences of their own policies. Observed macroeconomic fluctuations are therefore the outcome of a combi-

---

[1] See Bekx *et al.* (1989).

[2] See Allen (1976).

Annex D prepared by Jean Pisani-Ferry, Alexander Italianer and Andries Brandsma

nation of the working of the economy and policy interventions. To the extent that the latter are unexpected, they also act as shocks and therefore as a source of macroeconomic fluctuations.

2.1. Categories of shocks

A shock cannot be defined without reference to a given economic system. In the context of EMU, the reference economic system is taken to be a Member State of EMU. Secondly, a set of variables has to be defined which are considered to be determined endogenously and simultaneously inside the system. These can be taken to be the usual macroeconomic variables such as output, inflation and employment. A shock may then be defined as any event which has a direct or indirect impact on the endogenous variables of the reference system without, however, being determined by it. Given this definition, a country-specific or local shock may be defined as a shock having a direct impact on only one country. Similarly, a common shock may be defined as a shock having a direct impact on all member countries of the union. A second distinction arises from the duration of the shock. A temporary shock is an event that disappears after a short period of time, while a permanent shock is an event that remains present over the whole time period analysed (this does not preclude that it eventually disappears).

There were two common shocks relevant to the EMU context which had a large impact over the last two decades: the oil price hikes of 1973-74 and 1979 (a typical sector-specific shock) and the increase in interest rates in the United States which provoked the 1981-82 recession (i.e. a common external shock for the Community). In addition, the reduced import demand in developing countries due to the debt crisis, wildly fluctuating commodity prices and the current-account deficit of the United States may also be considered to be in this category. This also holds for the dollar exchange rate movements of the 1980s, although after the Plaza/Louvre agreements these movements have become more or less the joint responsibility of the United States and its G7 partners. This is important as it implies for the Community the partial internalization of a foreign variable as a domestic policy instrument.

Country-specific or local shocks may be subdivided in a number of categories.

(i) An important source of local shocks arises from domestic policy instruments, which may be broadly divided between monetary and budgetary policy. It might be argued that these instruments in fact react to changes in domestic economic performance, are therefore endogenously determined and not to be considered as shocks. This is certainly true for some elements of budgetary policy, mainly those parts which act as automatic stabilizers (social benefits, progressive taxes) or which behave pro-cyclically (interest payments on debt). Other elements, however, are of a more discretionary nature. Unless it is assumed that fiscal fine-tuning is still possible, changes in these elements will therefore act as random shocks to the national economy. Moreover, it might be argued that domestic policies are exogenous for the private sector as a whole.

(ii) A second important set of country-specific shocks relates to changes in domestic natural, human or capital resources. Examples of the first are the oil extraction which started in the second half of the 1970s in the United Kingdom or the closing-down of coal mines in several Community countries. Changes in human resources arise as a consequence of demographic movements or modifications in the composition of the labour market (participation rates, workforce composition). Since resource shocks, notably concerning human resources, usually evolve gradually over time, they are classed as permanent. The same can be said of capital resources to the extent that technical progress is concerned.

(iii) A third set of country-specific shocks consists of changes in behaviour of economic agents (households, firms). These changes may arise from changes in taste, business climate or any other form of news that has a random pattern in influencing economic behaviour. In econometric terms, these shocks are contained in the residuals of the behavioural equations.

(iv) Finally, if the concept of a shock is defined rather broadly, a fourth category of shocks is formed by inertia. This can be explained as follows. A broad definition of a shock would define it as all events without which the endogenous variables of the economic system would not change. Under this definition, past values of endogenous variables of the system, or inertia, which influence the present endogenous variables are also to be considered as a shock. They are the consequence of the existence of permanent shocks. Empirically, not much is known about the causes of lags in economic behaviour. Usually they are assumed to be related to information costs, adjustment costs or the formation of expectations.

There is no unique measurement system available for shocks, be they common or country-specific. The main issue involved here is that shocks have different dimensions. How may an oil-price increase be compared to an earthquake, for instance? To circumvent this problem, the impact of a shock on one of the endogenous variables may be taken as a yardstick. Since the endogenous variables of the system are all determined simultaneously, a representation of the system which determines them is needed in order to be able to assess the final impact of a shock on any particular endogenous variable. A natural candidate for such a representation is an econometric model. Despite the fact that each econometric model has its unique features, any model that is a representation of the neo-Keynesian/classical synthesis will probably be a reliable guide.

2.2. Methodology

The methodology adopted may best be described by assuming that the model which is used is linear or linearized. In this form, a dynamic simultaneous model may then be written as

$$y_t = Ay_t + B + Ly_{t-1} + Dx_t + u_t,$$

with y an $n \times 1$ vector of endogenous variables, x a $k \times 1$ vector of exogenous variables and u an $n \times 1$ vector of disturbances. The reduced form of this model is

$$y_t = MB + MLy_{t-1} + MDx_t + Mu_t,$$

with $M = (I - A)^{-1}$. In first differences, this may be written as

$$y_t - y_{t-1} = y_{Lt} + y_{xt} + y_{ut},$$

with the three components on the right-hand side representing the contribution of the changes in lagged endogenous variables, exogenous variables and disturbances, respectively, to the change in the endogenous variables:

$$y_{Lt} = ML[y_{t-1} - y_{t-2}] = MB + MLy_{t-1} + MDx_{t-1} + Mu_{t-1} - y_{t-1},$$

$$y_{xt} = MD[x_t - x_{t-1}] = MB + MLy_{t-2} + MDx_t + Mu_{t-1} - y_{t-1},$$

$$y_{ut} = M[u_t - u_{t-1}] = MB + MLy_{t-2} + MDx_{t-1} + Mu_t - y_{t-1}.$$

This breakdown of contributions may be divided into more groups than the three presented here, down to the level of the individual variables. Furthermore, the results depend crucially on which variables in the model are endogenous and which variables are exogenous. For the results presented here, the existing division between exogenous/endogenous variables has been taken.

Technically, in order to calculate the contribution of each individual component to the change in period t, a static simulation is performed for period $t - 1$ in which the variables of the component concerned are set equal to their values in period t.[3] As may be seen from the above equations, the difference between the values of the endogenous variables calculated this way and the observed values in period $t - 1$ gives the contribution of the component considered. By running T static simulations for T periods $t = 1, ... T$, the changes in all endogenous variables due to one particular component may be calculated for a whole period. This may be repeated for each component. The relative importance of any component as a source of shocks may then be obtained by calculating the observed variance of each component and dividing it by the sum of the variances of all components. The latter has been taken as numerator instead of the variance of the endogenous variable in order to have the sum equal to 100 %, even though this has the disadvantage that the covariances between the different contributing factors (which are zero theoretically) are not taken into account. In practice, the variances are calculated after a stationary transformation of the variables in order to remove predictable elements: growth rates for GDP, first differences for unemployment rates, first differences relative to previous-period GDP for budget balances, etc. This implies, for instance, that the contribution to the variance of the growth rate of GDP of an exogenous variable which grows at a constant rate is zero.

Example:

Let y_{1xt} be the change in GDP (endogenous variable y_{1t}) in period t with respect to period $t - 1$ due to the changes in all exogenous variables. Furthermore, let V_{1x} be the calculated variance over the sample period of this component after the stationary transformation $[y_{1xt} - y_{1t-1}]/y_{1t-1}$. Similarly, V_{1L} and V_{1u} may be calculated. Then the relative variance of GDP due to changes in all exogenous variables is defined as:

$$V_{1x}/[V_{1L} + V_{1x} + V_{1u}]$$

The method described calculates the contributions of different components to the variance of the change in all endogenous variables between two consecutive periods. This implies that the effects of temporary shocks will be given relatively more importance than those of permanent shocks. In principle, this could be overcome by calculating contributions to changes over a longer time horizon, for instance eight

---

[3]   Indicated by italics in the equations. In practice, the contribution of the lagged endogenous variables is calculated by taking the difference between the observed change in the endogenous variables and the sum of the other contributions.

quarters.[4] Because of the technical complexity of such simulations, this was not done. Nevertheless, the extent to which permanent shocks play a role can be read off from the relative importance of the lagged variables, even though the origin of the permanent shocks is unknown.

2.3. Results

The method outlined above was applied to the Commission's Quest models for Germany, France, Italy, the United Kingdom and the United States.[5] The period covered was 1980.II to 1987.III, which is a period containing many of the shocks described above.

Each row in Table D.1 represents, for an endogenous variable (i.e. one element of the vector y), the variance of one explanatory component as a percentage of the sum of the variances of all explanatory components, as described above. The explanatory components have the following meaning:

Inertia: all lagged variables (calculated as residual on the basis of all other components);

Foreign: all foreign variables (foreign demand, foreign prices, autonomous components of the balance of payments);

Monetary: interest rates and dollar exchange rates;

Government expenditure: expenditure components on goods and services in constant prices, subsidies, autonomous transfer components, but not automatic stabilizers;

Government revenue: tax rates, rates of social security contributions and autonomous revenue components;

Resource: demographic factors, exogenous shocks to the labour force or productive capacity;

Behaviour: all disturbances of behavioural equations.

The first result is the importance of inertia, or permanent shocks, in explaining the variance of almost all the variables in the table. Only for inflation (Italy and the UK) and the government deficit (all except the UK) is the contribution of permanent shocks lower than 60 %. The exceptions for inflation are caused by the relative importance of behavioural shocks, and that of government revenue (for Italy). The latter could be due to shocks in social security contribution rates. Permanent shocks are less important for the

government deficit (except in the UK) due to the relative importance of shocks in government tax rates (revenue shocks) and, to a minor extent, in expenditure. Permanent shocks are especially important for the unemployment rate (due to demographic factors) and the current account (probably due to J-curve effects). This corresponds to a priori expectations, since these phenomena are known to be slow in practice and to take effect only with substantial lags.

Of the variance due to temporary shocks, the largest part is generally due to behavioural shocks. For GDP, for instance, this accounts on average for almost half of the variance due to temporary shocks. Of the remaining part, almost 25 % is due to government budgetary policy and some 10 % due to monetary policy. On the whole, the government therefore has a non-negligible role as a source of temporary shocks. The importance of the government also holds for variables other than GDP, and most notably for the government deficit for obvious reasons. Furthermore, the effect of tax rates (government revenue) on inflation is considerable, notably in the European countries.

Temporary shocks in monetary policy have a weak impact on inflation. This does not mean that monetary policy has no effect on inflation, but only that its short-term (first quarter) effects are rather weak. The strong impact of monetary policy on the Italian government deficit corresponds to the large Italian government debt.

For all behavioural shocks except for those to inflation, the European countries are more symmetric relative to each other than with respect to the United States, for which the share of behavioural shocks in the sum of variations is always the largest. For inflation, the performance is still rather asymmetric, which is mainly due to Italy and the United Kingdom.

2.4. Conclusion

The evidence presented in this section seems to indicate that permanent shocks are in general more predominant than temporary shocks. Speaking generally, this is among other things a sign that shocks, even after their origin has disappeared, may affect economic behaviour persistently through the lags that operate in the economy. While nothing specific can be said about the nature of the permanent shocks, it appeared that of the temporary shocks to GDP (as measured by their impact in the first quarter), about half is due to shocks in economic behaviour of private agents, a quarter is due to shocks in budgetary policy and about one-tenth is due to monetary policy shocks. Governments may therefore

[4] This was done in the study by Fair (1988), who used stochastic simulations to calculate the respective contributions of different equation residuals after one and eight quarters.
[5] See Bekx *et al.* (1989). Updated and re-estimated versions were used for all models, as well as a new model for Italy.

be considered to be a non-negligible source of temporary shocks. Furthermore, it appeared that shocks in the behaviour of private agents are of similar importance among European countries when compared to the United States for the real side of the economy, but not as regards inflation, and therefore wages.

Table D.1

Relative variances of shocks determining endogenous variables, 1980.II to 1987.III

(% of sum of variances)

| | | Inertia | Common | | Country-specific | | | |
| | | | Foreign | Monetary | Government | | Resource | Behaviour |
					Expenditure	Revenue		
Real GDP	D	66,6	3,7	3,8	4,7	4,2	2,7	14,3
	F	69,1	3,0	5,4	2,7	4,3	2,8	12,8
	I	73,8	2,3	3,2	3,5	4,6	2,9	9,7
	UK	69,3	3,0	3,6	2,8	3,2	3,0	15,1
	US	61,7	2,4	2,7	3,6	3,1	2,6	23,9
Inflation[1]	D	61,1	1,8	0,4	1,9	8,5	1,8	24,5
	F	71,1	1,1	1,1	1,1	10,1	1,1	14,5
	I	14,6	0,3	0,3	0,2	40,3	0,3	44,0
	UK	48,3	1,2	0,9	1,2	7,0	1,2	40,3
	US	70,3	0,7	0,7	0,8	3,4	0,7	23,4
Employment[1]	D	69,9	3,6	4,2	5,4	3,7	2,5	10,6
	F	72,2	1,8	2,0	6,4	1,9	1,7	14,1
	I	76,8	2,9	2,7	3,3	2,9	3,0	8,4
	UK	69,6	2,8	3,1	3,2	2,9	2,8	15,6
	US	66,9	1,8	1,8	2,3	2,2	1,8	23,1
Unemployment rate[2]	D	79,1	3,4	3,9	3,6	3,1	2,7	4,1
	F	81,6	3,1	3,1	3,5	3,1	3,1	2,5
	I	80,4	3,1	3,2	3,0	3,2	3,1	3,9
	UK	88,0	2,0	2,1	1,8	2,0	2,0	2,1
	US	79,4	2,7	2,7	2,5	2,9	2,7	7,0
Government deficit[3]	D	24,2	1,0	10,3	19,1	40,2	0,9	4,4
	F	45,8	1,5	2,5	3,4	40,2	1,5	5,0
	I	18,9	0,6	18,9	7,5	50,9	0,5	2,6
	UK	76,5	3,1	3,3	6,1	5,8	3,1	2,1
	US	45,0	1,4	3,0	17,7	22,5	1,5	8,9
Current account[3]	D	81,2	2,4	1,6	3,3	3,0	3,2	5,2
	F	81,2	3,1	0,9	3,1	3,1	3,1	5,4
	I	80,5	3,1	3,2	3,3	3,3	3,3	3,4
	UK	81,7	3,2	1,6	3,1	3,1	3,2	4,1
	US	77,7	2,9	3,0	3,6	2,9	2,9	7,1

[1] Growth rate.
[2] First difference.
[3] First difference as % of last period nominal GDP.
Source: Simulations with the Quest model of the Commission.

3. The loss of the nominal exchange rate as an adjustment instrument: an evaluation

As developed in Chapters 2 and 6, the main cost of EMU is that nominal exchange rates can no longer be used to bring about the adjustment to a new equilibrium after the economy has suffered an external or internal shock. The aim of this section is to propose an assessment of the associated cost with the help of Quest simulations. Alternative adjustment mechanisms are also discussed, and it is shown how their performance can be compared to that of exchange rate changes.

For the sake of simplicity, only two types of country-specific shocks are considered: a demand shock, consisting of a 5 % drop in the volume of demand for French exports, and a domestic supply shock, originating in a rise in employers' social security contributions by one percentage point of GDP in Germany. Most of the comments concentrate on the demand shock since this is the one for which an exchange rate policy can be most easily justified.

Although the quantitative results of these simulations are specific both because of the nature of the shock and because of the properties of the country model, fairly general conclusions can be drawn from this exercise. Indeed, results from the first simulation are representative of the effects of an external or internal demand shock for a generic Member State, while the results of the second simulation are characteristic of a wide class of supply shocks of domestic origin.

3.1. Nature of the cost

As discussed in Chapter 6, nominal exchange rate changes do not result in real exchange rate adjustments in the long run. This is also a property of most empirical macroeconomic models. Hence, the loss of the exchange rate instrument has no strong long-term implications. But short- and medium-term costs are incurred when prices are sticky since the exchange rate can no longer be used to smooth adjustments. The problem is to evaluate these costs.[6]

Suppose a given country experiences an unexpected drop in the foreign demand for its products. Let the working of

the model be represented in a simplified fashion within an aggregate supply/demand framework (Graph D.1). Aggregate demand depends positively on the real exchange rate, whereas aggregate supply is downward-sloping.[7] In the long run, the shift in the demand curve from AD to AD' implies a depreciation of the real exchange rate (equilibrium moves from A to A'). But in the short run, prices are sticky and the real exchange rate depends on the nominal exchange rate. Without nominal exchange rate adjustment, the economy moves to short-term equilibrium at B. Since B is below full employment, prices tend to fall and the economy moves towards A' along the demand schedule. Adjustment costs depend on the length of the move from B to A', which in turn depend on the degree of wage and price flexibility.

GRAPH D.1: **Effects of a demand shock with and without exchange rate change**

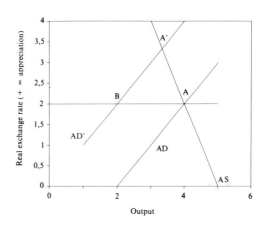

Nominal exchange rate depreciation can be used to reduce adjustment costs by 'frontloading' changes in the real exchange rate instead of having to wait for the completion

---

[6] Throughout this section, the exchange rate is considered as an instrument in the baseline regime. This corresponds to the EMS situation, where central parities rates can be modified in a discretionary way when a shock occurs. Shocks are assumed to be unanticipated, but when they occur, they are supposed to be fully observed by the authorities, who can then choose to modify the exchange rate. The exchange rate peg is always supposed credible, and therefore monetary policy is entirely determined by the foreign interest rate.

[7] This may come, for example, from the labour supply curve: by reducing real wage income, a real depreciation reduces the supply of labour.

of wage/price adjustments. Immediate depreciation limits underemployment in the short run and therefore the cost of adjusting to the new equilibrium real exchange rate.

Without nominal exchange rate changes, the adjustment cost can only be reduced by speeding up the move from B in the direction of A'. Candidate instruments are: (a) government borrowing (demand policy), (b) wage moderation (supply/demand mix), and (c) cost reduction (supply policy). The first would by, say, an increase in public spending reduce the effect of the export fall on GDP. The second would bring forward the shift from domestic to foreign demand, just as a nominal depreciation of the exchange rate would do. Ultimately, increased public expenditure would lead to real exchange rate appreciation, and thereby make adjustment more difficult, while nominal wage cuts would induce too much real depreciation. Such effects would have to be remedied, perhaps by a combination of both instruments. In the mean time, the adjustment in terms of real GDP could be favourably affected.

3.2. Evaluation with the Quest model

For simulation purposes, one has to choose the size of the initial devaluation. Empirically, it can be chosen so that it corresponds to the eventual real exchange rate adjustment. Alternatively, one could aim at minimizing the deviation from baseline of some target variable (i.e. nominal GDP) over the simulation period. In practice, both methods yield comparable results as long as the exchange rate change is a once and for all adjustment, similar to an EMS realignment.[8]

Graph D.2 presents the output and real exchange rate effects of the 5 % drop in the demand for exports with and without accompanying devaluation policy.

Without devaluation, price and wage rigidity precludes the necessary real exchange rate adjustment, and the initial effect of the shock is to dampen output. Real GDP drops by 1,3 % in the first year. By frontloading this adjustment, a 7 % devaluation significantly reduces the output cost of the shock during an initial period of three years.

However, in the medium run wages and prices react to the disequilibrium in goods and labour markets, and without devaluation the output loss is progressively reduced as the

real exchange rate depreciates. Devaluation is an obstacle to adjustment in the medium term, since the initial boost in output reduces real wage (and real exchange rate) adjustments. In this respect, devaluation leads to trading off a speedier adjustment in the short run against delays in the medium-term adjustment. As demonstrated in Box D.1, this is a fairly general result which holds in so far as wages are not completely insensitive to labour market developments.

GRAPH D.2: **Output and real exchange rate effects of an export demand shock with and without accompanying devaluation policy**

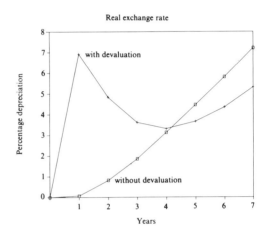

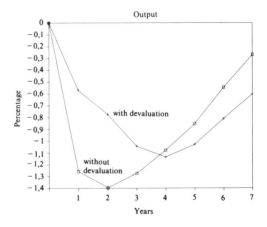

Source: Quest simulations with French submodel by the Commission services.

---

[8] The practice of realignments within the ERM can best be approximated by such a once and for all change. At a more abstract level, the possibility of an optimal exchange rate management could be taken into account: instead of 'frontloading' the depreciation, optimal control simulations could be used to determine the exchange rate path that would minimize the present value of a given macroeconomic welfare function.

Box D.1: Short-term and long-term effects of a devaluation policy

It is apparent in Graph D.2 that although devaluing the currency has the advantage of reducing the immediate output cost of the export demand shock, it also implies that further adjustment to the new equilibrium is delayed. Hence, devaluation seems to imply a trade-off between short-term gains and long-term costs.

A small reduced model of the wage-price block of a standard macroeconometric model helps to understand why. The model consists of four equations:

(1) $w = \delta p^c + (1-\delta) p^c_{-1} - \Theta v$

(2) $p = w$

(3) $p^c = \alpha e + (1-\alpha) p$

(4) $v = -\tau [E_{-1}/P_{-1} - 1]$

Upper case letters refer to variables in levels while lower-case letters refer to rates of change ($x = \text{Log } X - \text{Log } X_{-1}$). Equation (1) is a standard Phillips curve equation, with δ and Θ respectively characterizing the speed of indexation and the degree of wage responsiveness (flexibility); equation (2) gives GDP prices as a function of wage costs, equation (3) links consumption prices p^c to GDP prices and the exchange rate, with α being the imports to [GDP + imports] ratio, and finally equation (4) is a reduced form equation of the demand and employment blocks which gives the unemployment rate as a function of the lagged real exchange rate.

The solution of this model yields a first difference equation in P:

(5) $[1-\delta(1-\alpha)] p = (1-\delta)(1-\alpha)p_{-1} + \delta \alpha e + (1-\delta)\alpha e_{-1} + \Theta\tau [E_{-1}/P_{-1} - 1]$

Equation (5) can be either solved or simulated for different values of δ and Θ. Graph D.3 shows the time profile of the real exchange rate after a 10 % devaluation for $\delta = 0,5$, $\alpha = 0,2$ and $\tau = 0,07$, with $\Theta = 0$ (rigid wages) and $\Theta = 0,3$ (flexible wages). After the initial depreciation, the real exchange rate appreciates as domestic prices rise, however overshooting the new long-term equilibrium as is the case in the Quest simulations.

GRAPH D.3: Real exchange rate effects of a devaluation under alternative wage rigidity hypotheses

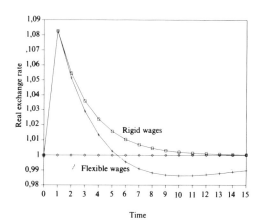

The reason behind this phenomenon can be understood by integrating (5):

(6) $[1-\delta(1-\alpha)] P_t = (1-\delta)(1-\alpha) P_{t-1} + \delta \alpha E_t + (1-\delta)\alpha E_{t-1} + \Theta\tau [\Sigma_u E_{u-1}/P_{u-1} - 1]$

The log-run equilibrium is characterized by $E_t = P_t = E_{t-1} = P_{t-1}$. However, this only holds if:

$\Theta\tau \Sigma_u E_{u-1}/P_{u-1} - 1 = 0$

As long as the Phillips curve coefficient Θ is not zero, long-run equilibrium implies that the integral of the real exchange rate has to be zero. This is because depreciation leads to output gains and therefore to tensions on the labour market which imply that the real wage is above its equilibrium level.

This shows that the output and employment gains initially procured by a devaluation not only disappear in the long run, but also have to be compensated by further output and employment losses.

3.3. Methodology of the simulations

The purpose of the simulations is to measure the cost of
losing the nominal exchange rate and to study the properties
of each alternative instrument individually. The results are
presented as deviations from a baseline, which is assumed
to be optimal. That is, it is assumed that the instruments of
economic policy have been set so that the targets for GDP
growth, inflation, unemployment and the balance of payments are tracked as closely (and with as little year-to-year
variation) as possible in the baseline, given the existing trade-
offs and the budget constraint of the government.

After the setting of the instruments, the economy is subject
to a shock in an uncontrollable variable (here the demand
for exports). Substantial shocks would have an impact on
the target variables and, since some of them will inevitably
be adversely affected, call for a reoptimization in the direction of the baseline values. As the exchange rate instrument
is lost, the question is whether it should be replaced by
another instrument. In a pure target-instrument framework
à la Tinbergen, it could be argued that, since balance of
payments equilibrium disappears as a target for each individual country in EMU, there remain just enough instruments
to reach the other targets. But if the use of the instruments,
and the frequency with which they can be changed, is restricted, it is interesting to see what the properties of alternative
candidates would be, compared to those of exchange rate
adjustments. Such restrictions are realistic as long as a precise 'fine-tuning' is ruled out.

The design of a comparative exercise in the case of an export
shock is therefore as follows:

(i) First run a simulation of a sustained drop in foreign
    demand with exchange rates and interest rates fixed in
    nominal terms.[9] This moves the economy away from
    the baseline, which is assumed to represent the optimal
    equilibrium path. The period of simulation should be
    long enough to reach the new equilibrium characterized
    by an x % real depreciation, although in practice it
    would be difficult to reach a steady state. (Let T be the
    required length of the period.)

(ii) Combine (i) with a once-and-for-all depreciation by x %
    which represents the policy that would be chosen in
    order to 'frontload' the real exchange rate adjustment.

(iii) Use an alternative instrument in order to achieve the
    same output loss as in simulation (ii) (measured by the
    present value of real GDP over T years).

The adjustment paths can be judged on different criteria:

(a) the result at the end of the period;

(b) the variability in growth rates along the way;

(c) the present value accumulated over the period (i.e. the
    equivalent change in period 1 of the total change over
    the [1,T] period).

All three criteria are employed in the presentation of the
results. The variability is measured as the root-mean-square-
error (RMS) of the variable itself, or of its growth rates, in
deviation from the baseline. The present value is presented
as a percentage difference from the corresponding starting
value in the baseline. The discount rate is the actual long-
term interest rate of the country in the 1980s, that is about
10 % for Germany and 15 % for France. Real variables are
discounted by the appropriate real interest rates of that time,
4 % for Germany and 6 % for France.

3.4. The exchange rate versus alternative instruments

To illustrate the cost of losing the exchange rate instrument,
a sudden permanent drop of 5 % in the demand for French
exports has been simulated.[10]

This shock is combined with either:

(a) fixed nominal exchange rates (EXP),

(b) a depreciation of 7 % (DEV),

(c) an increase in government investment (GVT),

(d) an ex-ante reduction of the wage rate in the first quarter
    of the simulation (WMOD),

(e) a reduction of social security premiums paid by em-
    ployers (SCC).

Without changes in nominal exchange rates (simulation (a)),
the 5 % export shock would be deflationary and ultimately
lead to a real depreciation of some 7 % in the 7th year of
the simulation (Table D.2, panel A).[11] Real GDP would

[9] Nominal interest rates are kept constant at baseline values throughout
the exercise. This is consistent with the following assumptions: (a) neither
the shock, nor the realignment are anticipated; (b) the country is small,
and therefore developments in the home economy do not affect the
interest rate of the monetary union.

[10] The nature and the size of the shock are only illustrative. However, an
export shock of that size is not unrealistic. In fact, for 1986 as a whole,
the residual of a conventional export equation for France was about
5 %.

[11] Examination of the simulation results shows that real depreciation
approximately reaches a plateau after seven years. However, this is still
not a steady state.

have almost returned to the baseline by then, but in the mean time the present value of the loss would amount to 6 percentage points, and the present value of real losses in income per wage earner would also be about 6 % (Table D.2, panel C).

According to the methodology detailed above, in simulation (b) the nominal exchange rate is depreciated by 7 % — roughly the same value as the real exchange rate change in year 7 of simulation (a) — at the beginning of the period. This depreciation reduces the present value of the output loss by 1,3 percentage points (Table D.2, panel C). The disinflationary impact of the demand shock is more than

wiped out and the price level is 1,6 % above the baseline in year 7. In spite of the output gains, the present value of the real wage (−6 %) is lower than for the pure export shock, because of the deterioration in the terms of trade.

The next three simulations are calibrated in order to achieve the same reduction in the present value of output loss as through the devaluation. Therefore, present values of real GDP deviations (Table D.2, panel C, column 2) all amount to 4,5 percentage points. For that purpose, an increase of government investment by 0,15 % of GDP would be sufficient. This would reduce the loss in real income to 4,6 % and leave GDP prices below the baseline. The deficit on the

Table D.2

Summary results for export demand shock: France

Standard Phillips curve

A — Results in year 7: differences from baseline

	Real GDP	GDP deflator	Real wage rate	Current balance[1]	Government deficit[1]	Unemployment rate	Real exchange rate
EXP	− 0,27	− 6,74	− 1,65	− 0,53	0,50	0,23	7,21
DEV	− 0,60	1,58	− 1,41	− 0,43	0,37	0,30	5,32
GVT	0,16	− 5,63	− 1,35	− 0,65	0,68	0,18	6,00
WMOD	0,03	− 8,60	− 1,88	− 0,46	0,45	0,09	9,40
SSC	− 0,03	− 7,03	− 1,37	− 0,57	0,57	0,12	7,55

B — Root mean square deviations in growth rates

	GDP growth	Inflation rate (PCP)	Real wage rate
EXP	0,53	0,96	0,24
DEV	0,29	1,03	0,35
GVT	0,45	0,79	0,20
WMOD	0,54	1,18	0,33
SSC	0,51	0,96	0,21

C — Present value in percentage of baseline

	Nominal GDP	Real GDP	Real wage rate	Current balance[2]	Government deficit[2]
EXP	− 24,0	− 5,8	− 5,6	− 4,0	3,0
DEV	8,8	− 4,5	− 6,0	− 3,3	2,5
GVT	− 20,1	− 4,5	− 4,6	− 4,6	3,9
WMOD	− 34,5	− 4,5	− 7,6	− 3,8	2,7
SSC	− 27,2	− 4,5	− 4,9	− 4,2	3,4

[1] % of nominal baseline GDP.
[2] % of nominal GDP.
EXP = export demand shock (− 5%); DEV = EXP + exchange rate devaluation (7%); GVT = EXP + government expenditure (0,15% of GDP); WMOD = EXP + wage moderation (0,45%); SSC = EXP + social security contributions (0,3% of wage bill).
Source: Quest simulation by the Commission services.

government's financial balance would, however, substantially increase: measured by its present value as a percentage of the present value of nominal GDP in the baseline, it would increase by 50 % compared to the case of depreciation.

An alternative adjustment mechanism is that of wage moderation exerted through income policy. Direct wage control is represented here by a downward shock in wage growth by 0,45 % in the first quarter of the simulation. The government may not have direct control over wage negotiations, but it could always use the instrument of changing the social security premiums to be paid by employers. The procedure set out above would imply a reduction in social security contributions by 0,3 % of the wage bill. That would be more of a supply-side shock, since wage costs are directly affected but the net wage income of employees is not. In the case of wage moderation, the downward adjustment of the wage rate per employee would leave the present value of real income below that of the nominal exchange rate adjustment and not improve the variability of GDP growth and inflation compared to the baseline. The supply-side shock would lead to more favourable results, at the cost of an increase in the government deficit.

Since the current balance loses its relevance as a target variable under an EMU system and since real GDP was selected as a benchmark, the costs and benefits of using the different instruments can be discussed by focusing on inflation on the one hand, and the trade-off between a larger government deficit and a smaller decline in real wage income per employee on the other hand.[12]

Regarding inflation, all simulations except devaluation exhibit a fall in the price level. However, since the baseline path is supposed to be optimal, there is no reason to consider this as a superior result. A better yardstick is provided by the variability of the inflation rate (Table D.2, panel B). The government expenditure instrument turns out to outperform the other instruments by this criterion, wage moderation being the worst because it increases the deflationary impact of the demand shock.

Comparing the present value effects on the government deficit and the real wage rate (Graph D.4) shows that:

(i) it is possible to improve upon the effect of the depreciation on real income, most by the government investment scenario and somewhat less by reducing social security contributions, both at the expense of a higher government deficit;

(ii) direct wage control would lead to approximately the same government deficit result as depreciation, at the cost of losses in real wages;

(iii) income policy as a whole (combination of wage moderation and social security contributions reduction) could approximate the efficiency of the exchange rate instrument rather well since for the same real income loss, the present value of the increase in government deficit would be about 0,6 percentage points of GDP.

The cost of losing the exchange rate instrument when other instruments are available can be assessed on Graph D.4. It is the implicit utility loss arising from the move from point 'devaluation' on to the wage moderation/social security/government investment schedule.[13]

GRAPH D.4: **Real wage loss/government deficit trade-offs with alternative instruments**

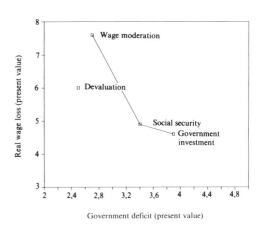

Source: Quest simulations by the Commission services.

---

[12] Another important variable is unemployment. The effects on unemployment go hand in hand with those on real GDP, except for substitution effects in the wage moderation and social security contribution simulations.

[13] As the loss of the exchange rate instrument implies either a higher government deficit or a real income loss, the associated cost can only be measured using a utility function.

Three conclusions emerge from this exercise:

(i)   The loss of the exchange rate instrument is unambiguously a cost for output, but not for inflation in the case of a demand shock.

(ii) If no other instrument is available to replace the exchange rate, the Quest model leads to the inference that this cost is equivalent to an immediate, once and for all 1,3 % loss in real GDP in the case of a negative 5 % shock to the demand for French exports.

(iii) If other instruments are available, the loss in real GDP can be eliminated at the cost of an increase in the government deficit. In the case of a negative 5 % shock to the demand for French exports, the budgetary cost is an increase in the deficit by 0,6 % of GDP lasting for one year.

3.5. Demand shocks under alternative wage behaviour

It is well known that the effectiveness of exchange rate policy strongly depends on the behaviour of wages. A higher flexibility, i.e. an increase in the responsiveness of wages to labour market conditions, and a speedier indexation both affect the reaction of the economy to a demand shock and also the impact of an exchange rate change. As shown in Chapter 6, Appendix 6.3, the aggregate supply curve of the French Quest model can be considered steep in comparison to other multinational models. This is because of both relatively rapid indexations and a strong responsiveness of wages to unemployment. Therefore, it is important to examine the sensitivity of the results to a change in wage behaviour.

Graph D.5 depicts the output and income effects of a demand shock with exchange rate 'frontloading' policy (lower case letters) and without changes in the exchange rate (upper case letters). In each case, three versions of the model are compared: the standard one, a model with a 100 % increase in wage responsiveness to the labour market conditions (high flexibility) and a model with slower indexation, doubling the mean lag (see Box D.2).

GRAPH D.5: **Effects of a demand shock upon real GDP and real wages with and without offsetting exchange rate policy**

(upper case letters refer to the fixed exchange rate case; lower case letters refer to devaluation)

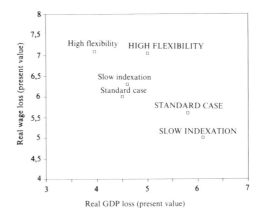

Source: Quest simulations by the Commission services.

Box D.2: Wage-price equations in the Quest model

The wage-price block in the country models for Germany, France, Italy, the UK and the USA have the common general specification:[14]

(1) $w = g_1(L) . p^c + c_1 . g_2(L).(1-\alpha). \text{upro} + c_2 . \text{LUR} + c_3 . (\text{LUR} - \text{LUR}_{-1})$

(2) $p^c = \alpha . pm + (1-\alpha) . p$

(3) $p = g_3(L) . w - c_1 . g_2(L) . \text{upro} + c_4 . \text{ucap}$

All variables are in rates of change, except for the unemployment rate, LUR, which is in levels. So, the Phillips curve equation (1) contains both the effect of the level of unemployment on the rate of change in the wage rate, and the effect of a change in that level (hysteresis). The speed of adjustment to a change in the price level is represented by the distributed lag function $g_1(L)$. In the long run there is therefore perfect indexation. Equation (2) defines consumption prices as a weighted average of import and value-added prices, where the weight α reflects the degree of openness of the country. A labour productivity (upro) term is present in both the wage equation and the value-added price equation. Its coefficient is constrained so that changes in labour productivity have no effect on nominal wages in the reduced forms. In addition, equation (3) contains a capacity utilization (ucap) effect.

The estimated coefficients are given in Table D.3. The distributed lag functions are characterized by their average lag in Table D.4.

Table D.3

Coefficients of the wage-price equations
in the Quest country models

	c_1	c_2	c_3	c_4
D	0,90	−0,09	−0,84	0,15
F	0,30	−0,13	−0,41	0,14
I	0,37	−0,22	−0,63	0,23
UK	0,31	−0,11	−1,36	0,09
USA	0,50	−0,22	−0,13	0,04

Table D.4

Average lag (longest lag)
of the distributed lag functions in quarters

	$g_1(L)$	$g_2(L)$	$g_3(L)$
D	0,67 (2)	0,67 (2)	1,33 (4)
F	0,67 (2)	0,67 (2)	0,67 (2)
I	1,00 (3)	1,00 (3)	1,33 (4)
UK	0,33 (1)	1,33 (4)	1,33 (4)
USA	1,00 (3)	1,00 (3)	5,5 (11)

High flexibility of wages to changes in labour market conditions (Graph D.5) is represented by doubling the coefficients c_2 and c_3 for France.

Slow indexation is imposed by replacing $g_1(L)$ in the French wage equation by a distributed lag over 4 quarters which doubles the average lag to 1,33 quarters.

[14] Some differentiations which only have a short-term effect have been left out of this presentation, as is the error-correction term which ensures a constant labour-income share in the long run.

It is apparent that at fixed exchange rates as well as with exchange rate policy, a higher wage flexibility reduces the impact of a demand shock on output because the shock translates faster into a real wage decline. Regarding indexation, a slower indexation increases the output loss both with fixed exchange rates and a frontloading exchange rate policy. This is because low indexation reduces the speed of adjustment in both cases. This is not a peculiarity of the model but rather a fairly general result, as demonstrated in Box D.3.

The output cost of losing the exchange rate can in each case be represented by the distance between upper case and lower case points. This cost is reduced by both a higher wage flexibility and a speedier indexation. Once again, this result appears to be fairly general, as demonstrated in Box D.3.

Box D.3: Exchange rate policy and wage behaviour

The purpose of this box is to evaluate how the cost of losing the exchange rate instrument is affected when wage behaviour changes. For that purpose, analytical results are derived from a simple illustrative model.

The model is a simplified linearized representation of the working of large-scale neo-Keynesian macro models like Quest. It consists of five equations:

(1) $y = d + \alpha x$

(2) $d = \tau [(p + y) - (\alpha e + (1 - \alpha) p)]$

(3) $x = \sigma (e - p) - m y + x_0$

(4) $p = w$

(5) $w = \delta (\alpha e + (1 - \alpha) p) + \Theta y$

where y is real GDP, d is real domestic demand, x is net exports, α the imports/[GDP + imports] ratio (equal to the exports/[GDP + imports] ratio), e the exchange rate, p the GDP deflator, w the wage rate. All variables are expressed as percentage deviations from the baseline, hence the model is linear.

Equation (1) is a linearized expression of goods market equilibrium, equation (2) links domestic demand to real domestic income, equation (3) gives net exports as a function of the real exchange rate, domestic demand and an exogenous term representing the demand shock, equation (4) gives GDP prices as a function of wage costs, and equation (5) is a Phillips-type equation with δ representing the indexation parameter and Θ representing the responsiveness of wages to labour market conditions (flexibility). It is assumed that wages are fully indexed in the long run, so $\delta_{LR} = 1$. However, indexation lags (e.g. due to overlapping contracts) lead to incomplete indexation in the short run. Only two periods are considered: the short run (first period result), and the long run.

Partial resolution of the model gives two equations for the aggregate demand and aggregate supply curves:

(AD) $y = A (e - p) + B x_0$

(AS) $p = [\Theta (1 - \delta (1 - \alpha))] y + [\delta \alpha / (1 - \delta (1 - \alpha))] e$

where A and B depend on the parameters in equations (1) to (4). Complete solution yields the following expression for y:

(6) $y = [B (1 - \delta (1 - \alpha)) / (1 - \delta (1 - \alpha) + A\Theta)] x_0$
$+ [A (1 - \delta) / (1 - \delta (1 - \alpha) + A\Theta)] e$

The above expression can be used to assess the effect on output of different shocks.

Demand shock with fixed exchange rates

This case corresponds to the effects of a demand shock in EMU. With e = 0, equation (6) yields:

(7) $y = L (\Theta, \delta) x_0$ $L'_\Theta < 0$ $L'_\delta < 0$

Simple calculations show that partial derivatives of L with respect to Θ and δ are both negative. This means that for an economy facing an adverse demand shock, a higher wage flexibility or a speedier indexation of wages on prices reduce the output loss. Referring to Graph D.1, both an increase in Θ and δ increase the slope of the aggregate supply curve, thereby reducing the output loss.

Exchange rate shock

Equation (6) can be used to assess the effects of a devaluation. With $x_0 = 0$, equation (6) yields:

(7') $y = M (\Theta, \delta) e$ $M'_\Theta < 0$ $M'_\delta < 0$

Thus, the output gain resulting from a devaluation is reduced by a higher flexibility or a higher indexation. A special case is that of instantaneous indexation ($\delta = 1$), where the output gain is reduced to zero. This is the familiar interdependence between wage behaviour and the effectiveness of exchange rate policy (see for example Marston, 1985).

Demand shock with offsetting exchange rate policy

The above model can be used to interpret the results of Quest simulations. Putting y equal to zero in equation (AD) gives the necessary long-run real depreciation,[15] i.e.:

(8) $e - p = - B x_0 / A$

Frontloading the long-run real exchange rate depreciation corresponds to an immediate nominal depreciation of the same magnitude. This yields:

(9) $y = [\delta \alpha / (1 - \delta (1 - \alpha) + A\Theta)] B x_0$, i.e.

(9') $y = N (\Theta, \delta) x_0$ $N'_\Theta < 0$ $N'_\delta > 0$

The effectiveness of such an exchange rate policy for reducing the output loss is therefore reduced if wages are flexible, but increased by a speedier indexation.

The cost of losing the exchange rate instrument

The output cost of losing the exchange rate instrument is given by the difference between the output effects of the demand shock with and without exchange rate devaluation:

(10) $C = - [(1 - \delta) / (1 - \delta (1 - \alpha) + A\Theta)] B x_0$

Since we are interested in the effect of negative demand shocks ($x_0 < 0$), (10) can be rewritten in terms of the elasticity of output with respect to the demand shock:

(11) $C = [(1 - \delta) / (1 - \delta (1 - \alpha) + A\Theta)] B$, i.e.

(11') $C = Q (\Theta, \delta)$ $Q'_\Theta < 0$ $Q'_\delta < 0$

Both partial derivatives are negative. Thus, the cost of losing the exchange rate instrument in terms of output is a decreasing function of the degree of wage flexibility and the speed of indexations. Equation (11) also shows that this cost is nil with instantaneous indexation.

---

[15] This assumes that the long-run aggregate supply curve is vertical.

3.6. A supply shock

An increase in social security contributions paid by the employers affects the real wage cost, the price level and the government deficit, but leaves *ex-ante* aggregate demand unchanged. Hence, it can be considered as a pure supply shock.

It is well known that the choice of an exchange rate reaction to a supply shock entails a trade-off between output and inflation. Since a supply shock is both inflationary and contractionary, the response can be either to appreciate (in order to counteract inflation) or to depreciate (in order to bring the real exchange rate back to the baseline value). Hence, the reaction depends on the preferences of the policy-maker.

In this context, the loss of the exchange rate instrument is not a cost of the same nature as in the case of the demand shock. However, the loss of this instrument reduces the possibilities of trading off growth against inflation.

This is illustrated by Graph D.6 which, in the case of the 1 % shock in German social security contributions, gives the present values of the GDP loss and the discounted change in inflation for different values of the exchange rate change. The resulting schedule depicts the trade-off between growth and inflation facing the policy-maker. Assuming the loss of the exchange rate would force him to stick at point A instead of choosing point B, the associated cost would be the corresponding utility loss.

This cost cannot be assessed without an explicit utility function. However, except for extremely strong preferences for either growth or price stability, it can confidently be assessed to be much smaller than in the case of a pure demand shock.

GRAPH D.6: **Exchange rate policy and output/inflation trade-off after a supply shock: Germany**

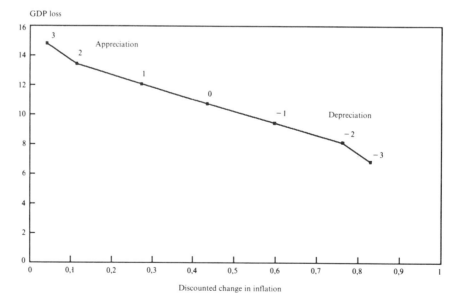

Appendix: Detailed simulation results

Table D.A1

Export demand shock: France, high wage flexibility

A — Results in year 7: differences from baseline

	Real GDP	GDP deflator	Real wage rate	Current balance[1]	Government deficit[1]	Unemployment rate	Real exchange rate
EXP	0,38	− 11,12	− 2,33	− 0,40	0,39	− 0,02	12,50
DEV	− 0,09	− 2,55	− 2,08	− 0,33	0,27	0,11	9,79
GVT	0,39	− 9,62	− 1,97	− 0,51	0,55	− 0,03	10,64
WMOD	0,51	− 11,67	− 2,32	− 0,36	0,37	− 0,10	13,21
SSC	0,46	− 10,57	− 1,97	− 0,44	0,46	− 0,07	11,81

B — Root mean square deviations in growth rates

	GDP growth	Inflation rate (PCP)	Real wage rate
EXP	0,58	1,63	0,37
DEV	0,32	1,11	0,40
GVT	0,50	1,40	0,32
WMOD	0,58	1,70	0,41
SSC	0,56	1,53	0,33

C — Present value in percentage of baseline

	Nominal GDP	Real GDP	Real wage rate	Current balance[2]	Government deficit[2]
EXP	− 37,6	− 4,2	− 8,5	− 3,8	2,6
DEV	− 1,8	− 3,4	− 8,2	− 3,1	2,1
GVT	− 32,6	− 3,4	− 7,3	− 4,3	3,4
WMOD	− 44,1	− 3,4	− 9,8	− 3,6	2,3
SSC	− 38,2	− 3,4	− 7,6	− 4,0	2,9

[1]   % of nominal baseline GDP.
[2]   % of nominal GDP.
EXP = export demand shock (− 5 %); DEV = EXP + exchange rate devaluation (7 %); GVT = EXP + government expenditure (0,15 % of GDP); WMOD = EXP + wage moderation (0,45 %); SSC = EXP + social security contributions (0,3 % of wage bill).
Source: Quest simulation by the Commission services.

Table D.A2

Export demand shock: France, slower indexation

A — Results in year 7: differences from baseline

	Real GDP	GDP deflator	Real wage rate	Current balance[1]	Government deficit[1]	Unemployment rate	Real exchange rate
EXP	−0,39	−5,88	−1,52	−0,56	0,52	0,28	6,24
DEV	−0,62	−1,98	−1,28	−0,43	0,38	0,29	4,92
GVT	−0,21	−4,60	−1,15	−0,70	0,76	0,19	4,81
WMOD	0,00	−8,50	−1,89	−0,47	0,45	0,11	9,28
SSC	−0,06	−6,47	−1,20	−0,61	0,61	0,13	6,91

B — Root mean square deviations in growth rates

	GDP growth	Inflation rate (PCP)	Real wage rate
EXP	0,52	0,84	0,23
DEV	0,26	0,79	0,39
GVT	0,42	0,65	0,17
WMOD	0,54	1,15	0,33
SSC	0,50	0,87	0,18

C — Present value in percentage of baseline

	Nominal GDP	Real GDP	Real wage rate	Current balance[2]	Government deficit[2]
EXP	−21,4	−6,1	−5,0	−4,0	3,1
DEV	6,4	−4,6	−6,3	−3,2	2,4
GVT	−16,8	−4,6	−3,9	−4,8	4,3
WMOD	−33,7	−4,6	−7,5	−3,8	2,7
SSC	−25,1	−4,6	−4,0	−4,4	3,7

[1] % of nominal baseline GDP.
[2] % of nominal GDP.
EXP = export demand shock (−5%); DEV = EXP + exchange rate devaluation (7%); GVT = EXP + government expenditure (0,2% of GDP); WMOD = EXP + wage moderation (0,6%);
SSC = EXP + social security contributions (0,4% of wage bill).

Source: Quest simulation by the Commission services.

Table D.A3

Increase in social security contributions (1 % of nominal GDP) paid by employers: Germany

A — Results in year 7: differences from baseline

Exchange rate change		Real GDP	GDP deflator	Real wage rate	Current balance[1]	Government deficit[1]	Unemployment rate	Real exchange rate
− 3%	depreciation	− 3,2	8,6	2,5	0,1	0,4	1,4	− 5,1
− 2%	depreciation	− 3,0	6,7	− 2,7	0,2	0,4	1,3	− 4,4
− 1%	depreciation	− 2,9	4,8	− 2,9	0,2	0,4	1,3	− 3,6
0%		− 2,6	3,0	− 3,1	0,2	0,4	1,2	− 2,9
1%	appreciation	− 2,4	1,2	− 3,3	0,2	0,5	1,1	− 2,2
2%	appreciation	− 2,3	− 0,5	− 3,5	0,1	0,5	1,0	− 1,5
3%	appreciation	− 2,1	− 2,2	− 3,7	0,1	0,6	1,0	− 0,8

B — Root mean square deviations in growth rates

Exchange rate change		GDP growth	Inflation rate (PCP)	Real wage rate
− 3%	depreciation	0,73	1,35	0,67
− 2%	depreciation	0,62	1,17	0,63
− 1%	depreciation	0,53	1,02	0,60
0%		0,50	0,91	0,58
1%	appreciation	0,53	0,86	0,57
2%	appreciation	0,60	0,87	0,59
3%	appreciation	0,72	0,95	0,61

C — Present value in percentage of baseline

Exchange rate change		Nominal GDP	Real GDP	Real wage rate	Current balance[2]	Government deficit[2]
− 3%	depreciation	29,6	− 6,8	− 4,6	− 0,3	− 2,1
− 2%	depreciation	23,5	− 8,1	− 5,9	− 0,3	− 1,4
− 1%	depreciation	17,6	− 9,4	− 7,3	− 0,4	− 0,8
0%		11,7	− 10,8	− 8,6	− 0,6	− 0,1
1%	appreciation	6,0	− 12,1	− 9,9	− 0,7	0,6
2%	appreciation	0,3	− 13,4	− 11,3	− 0,8	1,2
3%	appreciation	− 5,2	− 14,8	− 12,6	− 1,0	1,8

[1]   % of nominal baseline GDP.
[2]   % of nominal GDP.

References

Allen, P. R. (1976), 'Organization and administration of a monetary union', *Princeton Studies in International Finance* No 38, Princeton University.

Bekx, P., Bucher, A., Italianer, A. and Mors, M. (1989), 'The Quest model (version 1988)', *Economic Papers* 75, Commission of the EC, Directorate-General for Economic and Financial Affairs, March.

Fair, R. C. (1988), 'Sources of economic fluctuations in the United States', *Quarterly Journal of Economics,* May, pp. 313-332.

Marston, R. (1985), 'Stabilization policies in open economies', in Jones, R. W. and Kenen, P. B. (eds), *Handbook of International Economics* 2, Amsterdam, North-Holland.

Annex E

Exchange rate regimes in the EC: simulations with the Multimod model

1. Introduction and non-technical summary[1]

Standard model simulations (like those presented in Annex D) help to assess the effectiveness of alternative policy instruments when a given economy is hit by a specific shock, and more precisely to assess the cost of losing the exchange rate instrument in such circumstances. However, such simulations cannot provide a more thorough evaluation of the performance of alternative monetary policy and exchange rate regimes for two reasons: first, the quality of a policy regime cannot be judged with respect to a single perturbation affecting an identified variable, but rather when the economy faces disturbances affecting all variables simultaneously; therefore, model simulations should aim at assessing the performance of alternative regimes in an environment of repeated random shocks rather for a specific, single shock; secondly, the major consequences of the choice of an exchange rate regime, and especially of that of a precisely defined and highly disciplinary one like EMU, cannot be supposed to be simply ignored by agents, particularly with a single currency; for example, it cannot be assumed that agents would not be aware of the fact that participation in EMU implies that inflation in the domestic economy should not diverge from those of other EMU partners; in other words, if the so-called 'Lucas critique' of policy evaluation with standard econometric models (which states that estimated model parameters cannot be assumed to be invariant when the policy regime changes) has some relevance, it is certainly in the case of such a major and highly visible commitment resulting from an international treaty.[2]

The response to the first of these two limitations is to use the technique of stochastic simulations (see Box E.1). Basically, it consists in subjecting the model to repeated random shocks affecting a whole set of variables simultaneously.[3] With the policy regime represented by a rule linking policy instruments (in the present case the short-term interest rate) to observed deviations from target for key economic variables (like inflation and output), the result of such simulations represents for a given regime the behaviour of the economy in an environment of random disturbances. As for standard simulations, stochastic simulations are performed around a reference path (the baseline) where all available instruments are supposed to be used in an optimal way. Therefore, the aim of the authorities as described by the rule is to bring the economy back to the baseline. The economic criterion for judging the relative performance of different rules is their ability to minimize on average the deviation from baseline of key economic variables.

The second limitation raises deeper methodological issues. Basically, the response is to use a model whose representation of agents' behaviour is structural enough to remain invariant with respect to a change in the economic policy regime.

Unfortunately, there is no way to make sure that any particular model fulfils this condition. However, it is generally accepted that structural models are less subject to changes in parameters when the policy regime changes than small reduced form models whose equations represent a mix of genuine behaviour and policy reactions.[4] Another necessary characteristic of the model, at least for the comparison of exchange rate regimes, is that it includes forward-looking expectations. This is of paramount importance for the representation of financial and exchange markets, since the irrevocable fixing of the exchange rate, i.e. the expectation of no future exchange rate changes has to impact on current exchange rates and bond rates. This is also important for labour and goods markets, where expectations of future inflation impact on current wage claims and price setting.

By using a structural model incorporating forward-looking expectations, it can be expected that a large part of the objections to econometric policy evaluation with empirical models is removed. It is still possible that EMU could induce some genuine behavioural changes that would not be taken into account in the simulations, e.g. regarding wage/price

[1] The model simulations presented in this annex were performed under the responsibility of the Commission services with the Multimod model of the IMF. The support from the IMF staff, and in particular Messrs Paul Masson and Steven Symansky, is gratefully acknowledged.

[2] See Lucas (1976). This is not the place to discuss the relevance of the Lucas critique in the more general context of policy evaluation. However, it is worth mentioning that as EMU would be a regime change of an exceptional magnitude and clarity, a large part of the arguments put forward in the 'critique of the critique' (see for example Sims, 1982) do not hold in that context.

Annex E prepared by Jean Pisani-Ferry and Alexander Italianer

[3] Stochastic simulations can also refer to shocks affecting the parameters of the model. The aim of such simulations is not to assess the performance of a given economy (supposedly accurately represented by the model) in an environmernt of random shocks, but rather to assess whether the (forecasting or simulation) results are robust.

[4] A typical example of the latter is a two-equation reduced form determining output and inflation.

flexibility. However, in the absence of a methodology for evaluating possible changes of this kind, *ad hoc* changes in the parameters of the model can only be used for illustrative and normative purposes, but not for an *ex ante* evaluation. Conversely, it should be recalled that forward-looking models are frequently very reactive as expectations of future

changes trigger immediate adjustments, and that since expectations are by definition not observed, parameters of the model which describe the formation of expectations are not determined with precision. Therefore, it could also happen that the impact of EMU on for example wage and price formation is overestimated.

Box E.1: A schematic representation of the simulation techniques

Standard simulation techniques consist in subjecting the model to a shock to a particular variable (normally exogenous, but it can also apply to endogenous variables). The model then gives the impact of the shock on the macroeconomic variables, a subset of which are policy objectives. Assuming that the authorities have full information on the nature and the magnitude of the shock, a policy action can be taken to offset some of its undesirable effects. This setting is schematically represented in the top panel of Graph E.1.

The method of stochastic simulation can be described within the same framework. The core of the methods remains identical, but three major changes are introduced as represented in the middle panel of Graph E.1:

(i)   the model is now being subjected to repeated multiple shocks affecting at each period a whole range of variables; these shocks are not anticipated before they occur;

(ii) the policy action is no more supposed to be discretionary, but rather takes the form of systematic reactions to deviations from target in the policy objective variables; these reactions are given by a set of policy rules which characterize an economic policy regime.

(iii) agents are supposed to form forward-looking expectations of key economic variables; as expectations are based on the solution of the model for future periods, information regarding the policy regime is embedded in these future values.

In addition, shocks themselves can depend on the policy regime; this happens obviously in the case of the intra-EC exchange rate shocks in EMU, but could also arise from regime-induced behavioural changes.

The bottom panel of Graph E.1 explains the working of the simulations as regards the particular case of inflation.

The simulations presented in this annex have been run using a slightly modified version of the IMF Multimod model (see Box 2.5 in Chapter 2 and Appendix E.I for an overview of the model, and Appendix E.II for the modifications). This small model, which incorporates both Keynesian and classical features, has a forward-looking financial block which includes a determination of the exchange rate through an uncovered interest rate arbitrage condition. Wage-price, consumption and investment equations also incorporate forward-looking behaviour, although backward-looking indexation and liquidity constraints on consumers are also taken into account. Since Multimod has individual models for four EC Member States (D, F, I, UK), the impact of EMU has only been simulated for those four countries. However, the aim of the exercise is to provide an overall assessment of the consequences of EMU, not to discuss how specific countries would be affected.

A further reason to focus on general rather than individual country results is that due to the estimation technique used by the IMF, country models are very similar to each other. This is because only statistically significant differences in the

parameters of the equations were kept, while a common value was imposed in other cases. Therefore, country models exhibit fairly similar reactions in deterministic simulations. This does not mean, however, that results of stochastic simulations are biased towards the optimistic side. First, while the models are similar they are not identical because of asymmetries in structure (as regards for example the share and geographical pattern of foreign trade, the size of public debt, etc.) and in certain behavioural parameters (the degree of backward-looking wage indexation differs from one country to another). Second, as developed in Appendix E.I, to the extent that behaviour is more asymmetric in reality than represented in Multimod, this implies that residuals of the behavioural equations differ and are not correlated across countries. Since those residuals are used to generate the shocks in the simulations, any asymmetry which would be hidden in the estimated equation would reappear in the form of an asymmetry in shocks.

The first step in the design of the simulations is to represent adequately the different exchange rate and policy regimes. Four different regimes are simulated (see Table E.1):

GRAPH E.1: **Standard and stochastic simulations compared**

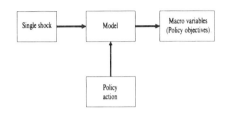

Standard simulations: overview

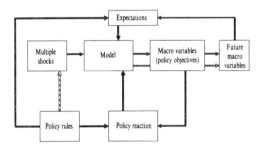

Stochastic simulations: overview

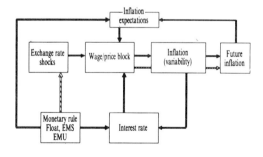

Stochastic simulations: example

(i)   a clean float, in which all countries use monetary policy to target domestic variables;

(ii) the EMS as it could presumably function in Stage I, which is modelled in accordance with the assumptions spelled out in Chapter 2; following the German anchor hypothesis, it is supposed to remain asymmetric; it is also supposed that all Member States, including the UK, would participate in the narrow band of the ERM;

(iii) a hypothetical asymmetric EMU (AEMU), which is not considered a realistic option but serves as a technical intermediate regime between the EMS and EMU, since it is characterized by both irrevocably fixed exchange rates and the maintenance of the German leadership hypothesis;

(iv) EMU, in which monetary policy is supposed to keep the same orientation as for Germany in AEMU, but whose scope is extended in order to cover the economy of the Community (in practice, the four aforementioned countries) instead of that of the FRG.

While the choice of these regimes is quite straightforward, their precise definition in terms of rules involves specific assumptions. First, the monetary policy rule followed by the authorities reflects a certain weighting of the policy objectives, notably output and inflation. It was chosen to mimic closely the practice of monetary targeting followed by central banks, and thus to give a high priority to the control of inflation in the definition of the policy rule. Also all countries are supposed to follow the same rule although differences in structure or policy preferences could imply that the optimal rule differs across countries. Second, modelling the EMS is especially difficult due to the existence of bands and the possibility of realignments. It was decided to try to capture the essential features of the ERM of the late 1980s, which has been much more disciplinary than the early EMS. However, the evolving nature of the system means that the simulated regime should be regarded as one among different possible representations of the system. Third, for the sake of clarity the monetary rule is kept unchanged in the EMU, although assuming no change in preferences it is no longer optimal. Fourth, no fiscal policy rules are introduced. The two latter assumptions imply the cost-benefit assessment of EMU could err on the pessimistic side.

The second major ingredient for stochastic simulation is the derivation of the shocks to the model. For non-policy shocks, the standard technique is to consider the residuals of the estimated equations as a sample of the shocks to endogenous variables. This means that departures from the behaviour represented by the equation are interpreted by the policy-maker as unanticipated shocks. An important issue is whether the size of and correlations between these shocks change between regimes, for instance because shocks could become more symmetric as argued in Chapter 6. For all variables save exchange rates, the size of and correlations between shocks have been kept unchanged among regimes. While this may introduce a bias against the EMU regime, it has the advantage that the regimes can be compared more easily. For exchange rate shocks, however, some assumptions have to be made since the correlation between exchange rate shocks is necessarily equal to one in the EMU regimes, close to one in the EMS regime but presumably lower in a free float. Here, the observed shocks for the three EMS members and the United Kingdom are used as being representative for the different regimes.

The adopted methodology implies that the results of the stochastic simulations are entirely driven by three factors. The first concerns the changes in exchange rate shocks between the regimes. As shown below, this implies that the disappearance of intra-Community exchange rate shocks is conducive to inflation stability and also output stability. Secondly, there is the impact on the monetary and exchange rate policy of the Member States, which is completely independent in the float regime, strongly geared towards the German monetary policy in the EMS and asymmetric EMU regimes and which becomes a common monetary and exchange rate policy in the symmetric EMU regime. The degree of monetary policy independence strongly influences the possibilities of accommodating real and inflationary shocks. Finally, there is the impact of the regimes on private behaviour through forward-looking expectations, notably concerning wage and price discipline. The absence of devaluation possibilities relative to other Community countries in the EMU regimes imposes more discipline on wage and price behaviour, as can also be demonstrated analytically. The combination of these three factors shows that the float, EMS, asymmetric EMU and symmetric EMU regimes, respectively, all improve upon each other in terms of reducing inflation variability. For the EMS, the reduction of intra-Community exchange rate shocks compared to the float regime is a decisive factor. This factor also plays a role for the asymmetric EMU regime relative to the EMS, helped by the stronger wage and price discipline imposed by the fixed exchange rates. The reduction in inflation variability in the symmetric EMU regime compared to the asymmetric EMU regime may largely be ascribed to the fact that monetary policy, while still as anti-inflationary, is now geared to the average Community inflation and output levels instead of focusing exclusively on the German situation. Taking the four regimes in the same order, there is no such uniform reduction in output variability. The relatively minor effect of the diminished exchange rate shocks on output variability in the EMS compared to the float regime does not compensate for the virtual loss of the monetary policy and exchange rate instrument used in the float regime for output stabiliza-

tion. In the asymmetric EMU regime output variability reduces compared to the EMS because of the strong effects of the absence of the devaluation instrument on wage and price discipline. The symmetric EMS improves on this because, while excluding the possibility of depreciation, the common monetary policy is concerned with average Community output rather than with that of Germany alone.

These results naturally depend on the assumptions made and methods used, which may all be subject to important caveats, notably concerning the impact of the EMU process on (forward-looking) expectations. Nevertheless there is at least a qualitative indication that there are elements which may compensate for the loss implied by the absence of the exchange rate instrument, presumably even to an extent that there is a net improvement in macroeconomic stability. Important conditions for this to become true are the monetary policy orientations of the future EuroFed, which should be geared to price stability, and the behaviour of private agents, which should take into account the constraints imposed by EMU.

2. Monetary policy and exchange rate regimes

2.1. General description

The simulations with the Multimod model are used to analyse the properties of four exchange rate regimes.

1. Free float: each G7 country pursues its own monetary policy to stabilize output (low priority) and inflation (high priority) under a system of floating exchange rates. Identical policy rules, which serve to mimic the practice of monetary targeting, apply to all countries of the model.[5]

2. EMS: the exchange rates of the four individual Community countries in the Multimod model are linked in a semi-crawling peg version of the European Monetary System (*NB:* it is therefore assumed that the United Kingdom takes part in the system). The overall monetary policy is determined by Germany, which is in a free float with respect to non-EMS currencies. The monetary policies of the three other EMS countries are such as to maintain the parity with respect to the DM, subject to margins of fluctuation corresponding to those observed in 1985-87 in the actual EMS. These margins are used to give a small weight to

---

[5]   In the Multimod model, the exchange rate of the block for smaller industrial countries is pegged to the DM. This assumption is maintained throughout.

considerations of domestic monetary policy. There is a re-alignment rule based on the price differential with Germany: each time the differential amounts to 8 %, a devaluation of 4 % takes place.

3. Asymmetric EMU: this is the same regime as the EMS, but with zero margins and no possibility for realignment. The asymmetry comes from the fact that monetary policy is determined exclusively by the German monetary policy objectives.

4. Symmetric EMU: this is the same regime as the asymmetric EMU, with the same monetary rule as for Germany, but with as monetary policy objectives the average performance of output and inflation for the four EMU members instead of that of Germany.

In each of these regimes, all countries are assumed to pursue monetary policy by means of a policy reaction function for the short-term interest rate. Due to the assumptions of free capital mobility, perfect asset substitutability and perfect foresight, exchange rates follow uncovered interest rate parity with respect to the dollar. The expected exchange rate is determined by the model (i.e. model-consistent expectations), given an exogenous long-term nominal steady state value of the exchange rate.

2.2. Free float regime

For countries in a floating rate regime, monetary policy is supposed to target a nominal aggregate. This implies that a monetary policy rule has to be devised. Standard monetary policy practices are money supply targeting and nominal GDP targeting. Since explicit introduction of a money supply target would introduce disturbances coming from money demand behaviour, the choice has been made for a rule targeting macroeconomic flow variables.

A first possibility, as for example chosen by Frenkel *et al.* (1989) for their simulations, is nominal GDP targeting specified in level terms:

$$(1)\ (i - i^b) = 100\ \alpha\ (y - y^b)$$

where i is the short-term nominal interest rate expressed in percentage points, y is the logarithm of nominal GDP, the superscript b indicates baseline values, and $\alpha = 0,25$ (1 % deviation of nominal GDP raises the interest rate by 0.25 percentage points).

This kind of specification has some undesirable medium-term properties: it implies that after an inflationary shock, monetary policy not only aims at reducing inflation, but

Table E.1

Monetary policy rules in the four simulated regimes

	Germany	Other Member States (F, I, UK)
Float	Policy aims at stability of domestic inflation (high priority) and real GDP (low priority) Same policy reaction function for all four Member States	
EMS	Same as float	High priority for DM exchange rate stability Limited domestic stabilization within narrow bands Realignment rule: devalue by 4 % when the price level differential reaches 8 %
AEMU	Same as float	Irrevocably fixed DM exchange rates Zero margins Zero policy autonomy
EMU	Same as float, but with Community variables replacing domestic variables in the monetary policy reaction function	

also at eliminating the deviation of prices from their baseline level. This does not correspond to standard behaviour of central banks, which are generally considered to be indifferent to price levels. Thus, an alternative rule is:

(1') $(i - i^b) = 100 [\alpha_1 (\pi - \pi^b) + \alpha_2 (q - q^b)]$

where q is the logarithm of real GDP, and π is the inflation rate $(p - p_{-1})$, with p the logarithm of the absorption price deflator.

It is easy to show that this kind of rule is consistent with the standard monetary policy practice of setting the money supply target for the year ahead in accordance with desired output and inflation. Moreover, values of α_1 and α_2 can be derived from the parameters of a money demand equation like that of Multimod (see Appendix E.III). After adding a partial adjustment mechanism for the interest rate this finally yields as monetary policy rule:

(1'') $(i - i^b) = 0,5 \{ 100 [2(\pi - \pi^b) + 0,4 (q - q^b)] \}$
$+ 0,5 \{i - i^b\}_{-1}$

This implies that the interest rate reaction to a 1 % deviation of real GDP is 20 % of that to a one percentage point deviation of inflation. This distribution of weights for the objectives puts a strong emphasis on inflation compared to other stochastic model exercises.[6]

2.3. The EMS regime

Any model representation of the EMS is bound to be *ad hoc* due to several factors. First, there is the exchange rate management inside the bands in the form of intra-marginal interventions. This problem has been solved by imposing a strong linearity in the interest rate reaction function when the bands are approached. Secondly, there is the debate on the asymmetric character of the EMS due to monetary leadership of Germany.[7] Since most empirical research confirms this hypothesis, it is retained for the simulations, implying that Germany conducts its monetary policy independently and the other EMS members are firmly constrained in their monetary policy because their parity with the DM has to be respected. Thirdly, there is the issue of realignments, which in the past were not subject to specific rules

but should be so in the model. Here a realignment rule based on the experience of the 1985-87 period has been adopted. There are thus several elements which make this representation of the EMS distinct from the past or from what can be expected in Stage I. Indeed, ever since its conception, the EMS has been an evolving system difficult to capture by the strict rules of econometric modelling. Consequently, the results for this regime are especially uncertain and should be regarded as emanating from a stylized EMS rather than a precise description of past, present or future forms of the system.

2.3.1. Monetary policy rule

In the EMS regime, the non-German ERM Member States are supposed to target their exchange-rate *vis-à-vis* the DM. Fluctuation bands, however, allow for short-term deviation from the central rates. These are a distinctive feature of the EMS as opposed to full monetary union. Exchange-rate fluctuations within the bands may act as absorbers for small shocks, and fluctuation bands are useful as long as realignments are not ruled out.

Monetary policy reaction functions for non-German ERM members therefore combine targeting of domestic variables and exchange-rate targeting. The rule has to be designed in order to allow for some limited flexibility, but to ensure that exchange rates are kept within the bands.

A straightforward solution is to specify a standard linear reaction function with inflation, output and exchange rates as arguments. Starting with a quadratic utility function:

(2) $U = (i - i^b)^2 + a_1 (\pi - \pi^b)^2 + a_2 (q - q^b)^2$
$+ a_3 (e - e^b)^2$

where e is the logarithm of the nominal exchange rate (local currency per DM), and an interest rate term is added in order to avoid instrument instability, a non-linear reaction function for the interest rate can be derived by differentiating (2).

(3) $(i - i^b) = 100 [\alpha_1 (\pi - \pi^b) + \alpha_2 (q - q^b) + \alpha_3 (e - e^b)]$

where $\alpha_1 = - (a_1/100) [\delta\pi/\delta i]$, $\alpha_2 = - (a_2/100) [\delta q/\delta i]$, $\alpha_3 = - (a_3/100) [\delta e/\delta i]$

Interpretation of the parameters α_i of the reaction function is thus straightforward. They are a combination of the parameters from the utility function and the elasticities of the model.

---

[6] For instance, the exercises presented at the Brookings conference 'Empirical evaluation of alternative policy regimes', 8-9 March 1990, which included an output-inflation rule, all gave at least the same weight to output as to inflation; see Bryant *et al.* (1990).
[7] See De Grauwe (1988) or Von Hagen and Fratianni (1989).

Even with a high priority for exchange rate stability, however, (3) does not ensure that the exchange rate is kept within the fluctuation bands. This may be obtained by adding a strongly non-linear term to (3), allowing to combine some flexibility with fixed fluctuation margins:

(3') $(i - i^b) = 100 [a_1 (\pi - \pi^b) + a_2 (q - q^b) +$
$$a_3 \{ (e - e^b) + \text{ß} (e - e^b)^\Theta\}]$$

Recent exchange rate behaviour within the ERM shows that observed exchange rate flexibility within fluctuation bands has been reduced to a large extent since 1987. The *de facto* band width is close to ± 1 %, or even below, for BFR, HFL and FF *vis-à-vis* the DM, instead of *de jure* ± 2,25 % for narrow-band currencies. Accordingly, the choice has been made to calibrate the ß and Θ parameters in order to exhibit strong non-linearity for exchange-rate deviations from the central rate above 1 % (see Appendix E.IV, which gives ß = 2.10^{18} and $\Theta = 11$).

In order to choose relative weights of the domestic and exchange rate targets, the working of the system in a simulation context has to be analysed. Since perfect capital mobility is assumed, exchange rate dynamics can be represented by a set of three equations:

(4) $i = i^o + a_3 (e - e^p)$

(5) $e^a_{+1} - e = i - i^*$

(6) $e^a_{+1} = e^p_{+1}$

Equation (4) follows from (3), with i^o representing the domestic terms (inflation and output) and e^b assumed to be equal to the ERM central rate e^p. Equation (5) is the open interest rate parity condition, with e^a being the (log of) expected DM exchange rate and i^* the foreign interest rate. Equation (6) gives the expected exchange rate, which is supposed to be the central rate for the next period. This is obviously a simplification, but it allows to restrict the analysis to a single-period set of equations. However, (6) would be replaced by a similar terminal condition in a dynamic multi-period system.

Without expected realignment, i.e. $e^p_{+1} = e^p$, (6) reduces to:

(6') $e^a_{+1} = e^p$

Equations (4) to (6) lead to the following equations for the interest rate and the exchange rate:

(7) $i = (1 - \mu) i^* + \mu i^o = i^* + \mu (i^o - i^*)$

(8) $e = e^p + \mu (i^* - i^o)$

where $\mu = [1/(1 + a_3)]$, with $0 \leqslant \mu \leqslant 1$.

As is clear from (7), μ measures the weight given to the domestic targets relative to that given to the exchange rate target.

The value of μ is of some importance for the properties of the system since this parameter determines the degree of freedom left to monetary policy for domestic targeting (as long as small interest rate variations are concerned, i.e. variations which only imply exchange rate movements within bands).

Since membership of the ERM implies that priority is given to exchange rate stability, it seems reasonable that the value of μ be below 0,5. For the simulations, it was assumed that $\mu = 0,33$ (i.e. $a_3 = 2$), which means that *ceteris paribus*, the interest rate response to domestic disturbances for ERM countries is one third of that of non-ERM countries.

Since ERM membership already dampens interest rate variability, no adjustment process has been taken into account like in (1'). Hence, the reaction function for ERM members is:

(3") $(i - i^b) = 100[2(\pi - \pi^b) + 0.4(q - q^b) + 2\{(e - e^b) +$
$$2.10^{18}(e - e^b)^{11}\}]$$

2.3.2. Realignment rule

Realignments are a distinctive feature of the EMS. Thus, a realignment rule has to be specified. Obviously, no such rule exists in practice, but for simulation purposes a prime candidate is a rule like: devalue the central rate by z % when the price differential reaches x %. This may include a constant real exchange rate rule as a special case (z = x), but encompasses a wide range of practices.

Derivation

Such a rule has to be chosen subject to the following requirements:

(a) the bands should be overlapping, since otherwise discrete exchange rate jumps offer a 'one way bet' for speculators; hence, z < 2L (where L is the band width, i.e. 2,25 %);

(b) incomplete offsetting of price differentials, since complete offsetting (i.e z = x) both lowers discipline and raises the possibility of self-fulfilling speculative attacks;[8] hence, z < x;

---

[8]   See Obstfeld (1989).

(c) consistency with the monetary policy rule; since agents know the rule, realignments are fully anticipated.[9] Hence, one has to examine the consequences of future realignments for current exchange rates and interest rates. This can be done on the basis of equations (4) to (6) above. Suppose a z % devaluation of the central rate is expected for the year ahead.[10] Hence, $e^a = e^p + z$. Equation (5) leads to:

(5') $e^p - e = i - (i^* + z)$

Hence, a z % expected devaluation is equivalent to a rise in the foreign interest rate of z percentage points. Thus,

(7') $i = (1 - \mu)(i^* + z) + \mu i^o$

(8') $e = e^p + \mu(i^* + z - i^o)$

A z % expected devaluation of the central rate for the year ahead triggers a μz % immediate depreciation and a $(1 - \mu)z$ % rise in the domestic interest rate. Condition (c) is therefore tantamount to $\mu \leq L/z$, since the immediate depreciation should be inside the band width L.

Empirical implementation

Since its creation, the EMS has experienced 12 realignments involving 39 bilateral DM central rate changes. Table E.2 gives some simple statistics based on this experience, which show that:

(i) the average size of the realignments, which was greater than the band width prior to 1985, has been reduced for all countries since 1985; during the 1985-87 period, the average size of the realignments has been 3,5 % for the narrow-band ERM countries;

(ii) the degree of offsetting of price differentials, which was close to 100 % in the first years of the system, has also been reduced for all members with the exception of Ireland; during the 1985-87 period, it has been close to 50 %.

The Delors report[11] states that in Stage I realignments will still be possible, but that efforts will have to be made to make the functioning of other adjustment mechanisms more effective. Already, no realignment has taken place from January 1987 until December 1989. The realignment rule for the simulations must therefore incorporate a strong disciplining effect for high inflation countries. As the latter was already the case in the 1985-87 period, a conservative choice is to derive the rule from this experience.

Thus, the simulations are run with z = 4 % and z/x = 50 %, i.e. x = 8: a 4 % devaluation occurs each time the price differential with Germany reaches 8 %. With $\mu = 0,33$, the immediate depreciation in the year before devaluation is $\mu z = 1,33$ %, which is consistent with the band width of 2,25 %. The rise in interest rates is $(1 - \mu)z = 2,66$ percentage points.

9 This is the case in the Multimod model.
10 Strictly speaking, expectations also take into account the possibility of fluctuation within the bands.

11 See Committee for the Study of Economic and Monetary Union in Europe (1989).

Table E.2

Realignments in the EMS, 1979-87

	B/L	DK	F	IRL	I	NL	Narrow band	ERM
1979-83								
Number of realignments	5	7	4	4	5	2	22	27
Average size	4,9	4,4	7,1	5,2	6,3	2	5,1	5,3
Offsetting of price differentials[1] (%)	296,6	139,8	105,4	43,5	64,4	203,2	101,2	89,7
1985-87								
Number of realignments	2	2	2	3	3	—	9	12
Average size	1,5	2,5	4,5	4,7	4,7	—	3,5	3,8
Offsetting of price differentials[1] (%)	28,5	36,5	54,5	77,2	50,7	—	52,7	52,1

All data refer to bilateral DM exchange rates.
1 Central rate variation over the period divided by the accumulated differential of consumer price indices relative to Germany since the last realignment, monthly data.
Source: Calculated using data from the Commission of the European Communities.

2.4. The EMU regimes

Asymmetric EMU

In the asymmetric EMU regime, Germany and the non-EMU countries follow the same monetary rule (1") as before. The non-German EMU countries follow German monetary policy completely:

$$(1''')\ (i - i^b) = (i_D - i^b_D),$$

with the subscript D indicating German variables.

Symmetric EMU

In the symmetric EMU regime, all EMU members follow the monetary rule (1"), but as it is assumed EuroFed would target Community variables, the output and inflation objectives are expressed as EMU averages:

$$(1'')\ (i - i^b) = 0{,}5\ [100\ (\ 2(\pi_{EMU} - \pi^b_{EMU})$$
$$+\ 0{,}4\ (q_{EMU} - q^b_{EMU}))]\ +\ 0{,}5\ [i - i^b]_{-1}$$

with the EMU averages defined as (given that only D, F, I and UK are represented in the model):

$$\pi_{EMU} = (\pi_D + \pi_F + \pi_I + \pi_{UK})/4$$

$$q_{EMU} = \log([y_D + y_F + y_I + y_{UK}]/4),$$

with y_i real GDP of country i.

This is obviously a simplification, since the size and therefore the economic weighting of the four countries in Community averages are not exactly identical.

3. Results from deterministic simulations

This section illustrates the effects of the EMU regime on the effectiveness of budgetary policies and on the behaviour of economic agents by means of some deterministic simulations. Two types of simulations are discussed: a government expenditure increase and a supply shock (autonomous price shock). In all cases the shocks were given to the French model since this allows to highlight the constraints imposed on monetary policy by the EMS or asymmetric EMU regime.

Generally speaking, the pattern of GDP reactions (Table E.3) illustrates both the properties of the model and the monetary and exchange rate policy assumptions. As a consequence of the Keynesian features of the model, an increase in government expenditure is expansionary in the short term, but as a consequence of the forward-looking character of the model the first-year multiplier is lower than

Table E.3

Effects of 1 % government expenditure increase in France

(% deviation from baseline)

Variable	Regime	Year 1	Year 2	Year 3	Year 4	Year 5
GDP	Float	0,59	0,31	0,08	−0,07	−0,14
	EMS	0,80	0,71	0,51	0,29	0,10
	AEMU	0,87	0,86	0,70	0,48	0,25
	EMU	0,80	0,75	0,57	0,33	0,09
Short-term interest rate[1]	Float	0,14	0,47	0,54	0,48	0,37
	EMS	−0,05	0,21	0,27	0,26	0,20
	AEMU	0,05	0,08	0,07	0,05	0,04
	EMU	0,07	0,16	0,17	0,18	0,15
Real effective exchange rate	Float	0,87	1,07	1,08	1,01	0,91
	EMS	0,43	0,79	1,04	1,18	1,24
	AEMU	0,22	0,53	0,82	1,04	1,16
	EMU	0,32	0,66	0,98	1,21	1,35
Inflation[1]	Float	0,02	0,34	0,30	0,23	0,17
	EMS	0,25	0,52	0,48	0,34	0,17
	AEMU	0,32	0,57	0,48	0,30	0,09
	EMU	0,30	0,56	0,50	0,36	0,17

[1] Difference with respect to baseline in percentage points.

AEMU = Asymmetric EMU.

Source: Multimod simulations.

for most empirical models of the French economy. It is also decreasing rapidly with time.

The simulations also illustrate the familiar Mundell-Fleming proposition that with capital mobility fiscal policy is more effective in a system of fixed exchange rates than in a system of flexible exchange rates. While the Mundell-Fleming result is derived in a system with fixed prices through differences in the crowding out of investment and foreign trade, the present simulations obtain the same effect through the impact of the government expenditure increase on output and inflation and the ensuing reaction of interest rates in accordance with the monetary policy reaction function. In the float regime, interest rates increase to choke off the higher levels of output and inflation, thus provoking a nominal and real appreciation which further reduces output. In the EMS and EMU regimes, the interest rate reacts less vehemently due to the exchange rate constraints in the EMS and the common (asymmetric or symmetric) monetary policy in the EMU regimes. The interest rate increase in the asymmetric EMU regime is equal to that in Germany and therefore represents the spill-over effect of the French expansion on German interest rates in the form of higher French export prices to Germany which increase inflation and of higher German exports to France which increase German economic activity, leading to an interest rate increase to dampen this price and output surge.

A second important aspect of the regimes is their impact on the behaviour of economic agents. More specifically, in setting wages and prices in the EMU regimes, households and firms have to take into account that unwarranted wage and price increases can no longer be compensated at intra-Community level in the form of currency depreciation relative to Community trade partners. A regime change basically impacts on wage and price discipline through an effect on price expectations. The extent to which price expectations affect actual wages and prices is however not known and can be modified by institutional changes in, for example, wage bargaining. Both types of effect can be illustrated by a supply shock, for instance by giving a one-period increase in the autonomous component of the price equation (thus keeping the price equation endogenous) and comparing the ensuing behaviour of inflation upon this price shock.

By affecting price expectations through the knowledge that a price shock will not be compensated through an intra-Community devaluation, the EMU regime should cause prices to return faster to equilibrium than the float or EMS regimes. This proposition is illustrated, using a small theoretical model in Box E.2, which shows that the first-year inflationary impact of a price shock under EMU is not necessarily lower than in a floating regime, but that the

return to equilibrium is faster afterwards. In fact, inflation (relative to baseline) eventually has to become negative under the EMU regimes due to the fact that the price level has to return to equilibrium, while this not the case in a float where the price level rise may be permanent.

This theoretical result is confirmed by the simulations presented in Table E.4, which shows the results of a single-period 5 % shock to French inflation under the four regimes analysed with Multimod. Under the float regime, the inflationary shock induces a strong increase in interest rates, causing a strong first year appreciation of the French franc relative to the Deutschmark (and other currencies). After this first year, however, the exchange rate starts to depreciate in order to compensate for the general increase in the price level. Since agents are forward-looking they incorporate this in their expectations so that inflation returns only gradually to equilibrium (assumed to be the baseline). In the EMS regime, this picture is followed for the first two years within the margins allowed by the exchange rate bands of the EMS. In the second year the price level differential with Germany surpasses 8 % so that, according to the EMS rules in the model, a 4 % devaluation is triggered off in year 3, which provides again some relief for the price level. Since the devaluation compensates only for 50 % of the price level difference, there is a nominal anchor implying that inflation eventually has to become negative to compensate for earlier increases (see also Graph E.2 and Box E.2). The EMS is therefore seen to have an impact on wage and price discipline which is however weakened by the possibility of devaluation. The devaluation possibility and intra-EC parity fluctuations being absent in the two EMU regimes, they show the fastest return to equilibrium for inflation, the asymmetric EMU regime being faster because it completely lacks an interest rate reaction.

While these simulations show the impact of the EMU regime on wage and price discipline through changes in expectations, the degree of forward-looking behaviour in EMU is an open issue. While it is impossible to estimate the effects of EMU on behaviour, some illustrative simulations may show the potential impact of behavioural changes. To that end, Table E.5 compares the results of a 2 % price shock in France under the EMU regime for two different speeds of indexation of prices to price expectations. Given the same forward-looking price expectations, this simulation therefore offers the possibility to analyse changes in behaviour. The simulation illustrates that from the second year onwards, inflation returns faster to equilibrium with normal than with slow indexation. Output, on the other hand, deteriorates less in the short run with slow indexation than with normal indexation, but in the medium run is slower to return to equilibrium, thus once more illustrating the trade-offs involved with wage and price behaviour.

Table E.4

Effects of 5 % shock to inflation in France

(% deviation from baseline)

	Regime	Year 1	Year 2	Year 3	Year 4	Year 5
GDP	Float	− 1,77	− 3,48	− 4,08	− 3,81	− 3,09
	EMS	− 1,26	− 3,01	− 3,95	− 4,09	− 3,83
	AEMU	− 1,06	− 2,71	− 4,07	− 4,75	− 4,68
	EMU	− 1,36	− 2,90	− 4,02	− 4,48	− 4,31
Inflation[1]	Float	5,36	3,86	2,26	1,20	0,56
	EMS	5,53	3,27	1,36	− 0,44	− 1,37
	AEMU	5,47	2,54	− 0,06	− 1,82	− 2,65
	EMU	5,49	2,75	0,45	− 1,10	− 1,85
FF/DM exchange rate	Float	− 4,06	0,30	5,58	9,82	12,51
	EMS	− 1,56	− 0,30	4,04	5,26	5,46
	AEMU	0	0	0	0	0
	EMU	0	0	0	0	0
Short-term interest rate[1]	Float	5,00	5,68	4,31	2,62	1,28
	EMS	1,49	4,76	1,27	0,23	0,05
	AEMU	0,08	0,09	0,06	0,03	− 0,00
	EMU	1,30	1,45	1,12	0,69	0,34
Real effective exchange rate[1]	Float	5,24	5,25	3,94	2,52	1,47
	EMS	3,85	5,22	3,94	3,24	2,49
	AEMU	2,93	4,54	4,86	4,20	2,94
	EMU	3,15	4,55	4,68	3,94	2,73

[1] Difference with respect to baseline in percentage points.
AEMU = Asymmetric EMU.
Source: Multimod simulations.

Table E.5

Effects of a 2 % price shock in France under EMU with normal and slow price indexation

(% deviation from baseline)

	Speed	Year 1	Year 2	Year 3	Year 4	Year 5
GDP	Normal	− 0,52	− 1,14	− 1,60	− 1,78	− 1,70
	Slow[1]	− 0,42	− 1,02	− 1,54	− 1,86	− 1,93
Inflation[2]	Normal	2,15	1,09	0,18	− 0,46	− 0,80
	Slow[1]	1,95	1,26	0,51	− 0,11	− 0,51
Real effective exchange rate	Normal	1,27	1,84	1,90	1,61	1,13
	Slow[1]	1,18	1,86	2,10	2,00	1,67

[1] Dividing the indexation coefficient by 2, i.e. coefficient k in Appedix E.II.
[2] Difference with respect to baseline in percentage points.
Source: Multimod simulations.

GRAPH E.2: **Effect on price level of a 5% price shock in France**

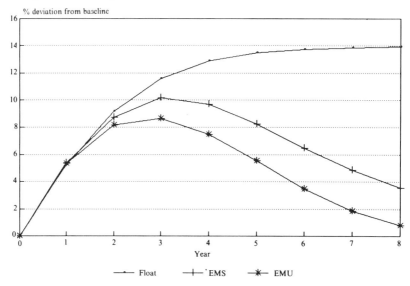

Source: Multimod simulations.

Box E.2: EMU, expectations and wage and price discipline

An analytical example with a two-country, two-period model may illustrate the effect of fixed exchange rates on expectations and therefore on wage and price discipline, compared to a situation of free float. The model used resembles that of Begg (1990), albeit without taking account of fiscal policy, and follows in broad lines that of the Multimod model in the way it was used to compare different exchange rates regimes in this Annex.

The model is entirely written in deviations from a baseline, such that all exogenous variables disappear. Lower case letters denote logarithms of variables except for the nominal interest rate, r, which is in levels.

There are two prices in the model, the output price p and the absorption price $[\mu p + (1-\mu)e]$ which is a weighted average (with μ the share of GDP in [GDP + imports]) of the output price and foreign prices converted into domestic currency through the nominal exchange rate e (since foreign prices are exogenous, they are not shown). The output price equation is a reduced form of a wage-price block with overlapping contracts, cf. Masson et al. (1988), and gives the growth rate $(p - p_{-1})$ of output prices as a partial adjustment to expected future (absorption price) inflation $[\mu(p_{+1} - p) + (1-\mu)(e_{+1} - e)]$, together with an effect of the deviation of output from baseline, y (proxy for Phillips curve effect). Hence, there is perfect price indexation with a lag due to overlapping contracts:

$$(1)\ (p - p_{-1}) = (1 - \varphi)(p_{-1} - p_{-2}) + \varphi[\mu(p_{+1} - p) + (1-\mu)(e_{+1} - e)] + \tau y + u$$

The last term in the output price equation, u, represents a temporary price shock.

Output y is determined by a number of exogenous variables which are not shown since they do not change relative to baseline, by a negative effect from the real interest rate (with forward-looking inflation), and by a positive effect from the real exchange rate $(e - p)$:

$$(2)\ y = -\beta(r - [\mu(p_{+1} - p) + (1-\mu)(e_{+1} - e)]) + \eta(e - p)$$

The nominal exchange rate in terms of local currency per foreign currency is determined by uncovered interest parity:

$$(3)\ e = e_{+1} + r^* - r$$

The monetary policy rule, which may be derived from monetary targeting with an inverted money demand equation, specifies that nominal interest rates increase if inflation or output are above their baseline levels:

$$(4)\ r = \alpha_1[\mu(p - p_{-1}) + (1-\mu)(e - e_{-1})] + \alpha_2 y$$

In equations (1) to (4), all parameters are assumed to be regime-independent, except α_1 and α_2 in the monetary policy rule (4).

In EMU, they will typically be smaller than in a float. The second element which changes between float and EMU is the foreign interest rate r^*. When the country forms an EMU with the foreign country, they will have a common monetary policy. Therefore, in EMU, the foreign and domestic interest rates are equal, whereas the foreign interest rate is assumed to be exogenous in float:

$$(5)\ r^* = (1 - \sigma)r \qquad \sigma = 1\ (\text{Float})$$
$$\sigma = 0\ (\text{EMU})$$

For the analysis of the effect of EMU on wage and price discipline, assume for the moment that the future output price p_{+1} and exchange rate e_{+1} are given. After some tedious but straightforward calculations, the system of equations (1) to (4) may then be solved for the price level p in terms of past and future price levels, past and future exchange rates and the shock u:

$$(6)\ p = \pi_1 p_{-1} + \pi_2 p_{-2} + \pi_3 p_{+1} + \pi_4 e_{-1} + (1 - \pi_1 - \pi_2 - \pi_3 - \pi_4)e_{+1} + \Theta u$$

Independent of the expressions for the parameters, the important feature of this equation is that the long-run price level is homogeneous of degree one in the exchange rate, i.e. in the long run the real exchange rate is constant (this is due to the fact that the shock, u, is temporary). In a two-period framework, it may therefore be assumed for simplicity that $p_{+1} = e_{+1}$, such that the equation may be rewritten (deleting lagged variables which do not differ from baseline) as:

$$(7)\ p = (1 - \pi_1 - \pi_2 - \pi_4)e_{+1} + \Theta u$$

In a float, the short-run effect of a price shock u is determined by the size of the parameters π_i and Θ (which all depend on α_1, α_2 and σ), and by the expected depreciation $e_{+1} > 0$. In EMU, the expected depreciation, and therefore expected price level, is zero: $e_{+1} = p_{+1} = 0$. The difference in the effect of a temporary price shock between EMU and float is therefore:

$$(8)\ [dp/du]_{EMU} - [dp/du]_{FLOAT} = \Theta_{EMU} - \Theta_{FLOAT} - (1 - \pi_1 - \pi_2 - \pi_4)[de_{+1}/du]$$

This expression implies that sufficient conditions for wages and prices to decrease faster in EMU than in a float after an inflationary shock $(du > 0)$ are:

$$(9a)\ \Theta_{EMU} - \Theta_{FLOAT} < 0$$

$$(9b)\ (1 - \pi_1 - \pi_2 - \pi_4) > 0$$

The proof for (9b) is straightforward, and simply requires the substitution of the expressions for the π_i's. Condition (9a) is not necessarily valid, however, the size of the two Θ's being dependent on the α's. In EMU, the first-period effect of a price shock on inflation may therefore be stronger than in a float. Since the Θ's represent a once-and-for-all shock to prices, their effect will die out over time in a multi-period framework, whereas the effect of the expected depreciation continues to have an upward effect on the price level in a float relative to EMU.

In a float, the price level may remain high because the depreciation compensates the effect on the real exchange rate, which is zero in the long run. In EMU, the price level will have to return to the baseline level because this is the only way to have the real exchange rate unchanged in the long run, given the fixed nominal exchange rate. In terms of inflation, this implies that in a float inflation will be positive after a price shock and then return monotonically to zero. In EMU, inflation will also be positive, then turn negative (due to the return of the price level to the baseline) and eventually return to zero. The average inflation level after a price shock will therefore be higher in a float than in EMU. Secondly, the return of inflation to the baseline level (and below, in EMU) after the initial shock will be faster in EMU due to the effect of expectations on future exchange rates.

Exchange rate expectations therefore may be said to enhance the wage and price discipline in EMU.

The previous arguments are illustrated by a simulation with the above theoretical model in Graph E.3, giving a price shock $du = 0,05$, setting long-run values $e_{+T} = p_{+T} = 0,115$ in the case of float (steady state from an initial simulation with T large and long-run values equal to zero), using the parameter values $\varphi = 0,5$, $\mu = 0,8$, $\tau = 0,5$, $\beta = 0,25$, $\eta = 0,2$, $\alpha_1 = 2$ (0,5 in EMU) and $\alpha_2 = 0,4$ (0,1 in EMU).

GRAPH E.3: **Effects of a 5 % price shock in float and EMU, theoretical model**

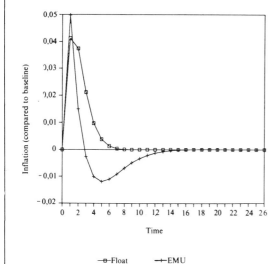

—□—Float   —+—EMU

Solution of the model

Equation (5) implies that $r - r^* = \sigma r$. Using this result, substitute equation (3) in equations (1), (2) and (4):

(1') $(p - p_{-1}) = (1 - \varphi)(p_{-1} - p_{-2}) + \varphi[\mu(p_{+1} - p) + (1-\mu)\sigma r] + \tau y + u$

(2') $y = -\beta(r - [\mu(p_{+1} - p) + (1-\mu)\sigma r]) + \eta(e_{+1} - \sigma r - p)$

(4') $r = \alpha_1[\mu(p - p_{-1}) + (1-\mu)(e_{+1} - \sigma r - e_{-1})] + \alpha_2 y$

Next, solve equation (4') for the interest rate r:

(4'') $r = [\alpha_1\mu(p - p_{-1}) + \alpha_1(1-\mu)(e_{+1} - e_{-1}) + \alpha_2 y]/\Omega$

with $\Omega = 1 + \alpha_1(1 - \mu)\sigma$.

Substituting (4'') in (1') and (2'), solving for p and rearranging terms gives equation (6):

(6) $p = \pi_1 p_{-1} + \pi_2 p_{-2} + \pi_3 p_{+1} + \pi_4 e_{-1} + (1 - \pi_1 - \pi_2 - \pi_3 - \pi_4)e_{+1} + \Theta u$

where the π's and Θ are defined as:

$\pi_1 = [2 - \varphi + \alpha_1\mu\{\Sigma\Gamma - \varphi(1 - \mu)\sigma\}/\Omega]/\Phi$

$\pi_2 = -(1 - \varphi)/\Phi$

$\pi_3 = \mu[\varphi + \Sigma\beta]/\Phi$

$\pi_4 = \alpha_1(1 - \mu)[\Sigma\Gamma - \sigma\varphi(1 - \mu)]/[\Phi\Omega]$

$\Theta = 1/\Phi$,

with as auxiliary symbols:

$\Gamma = \beta + \sigma[\eta - (1 - \mu)\beta]$

$\Sigma = [\tau\Omega + \sigma\varphi(1 - \mu)]/[\Omega + \alpha_2\Gamma]$

$\Phi = 1 + \tau\mu/\Omega + \Sigma(\mu\beta + \varphi) + \alpha_1\mu\Sigma\Gamma/\Omega$.

Using these definitions, the proof of (9b) follows straightforwardly:

(9b) $(1 - \pi_1 - \pi_2 - \pi_4) = 1 - [2 - \varphi + \alpha_1\mu\{\Sigma\Gamma - \varphi(1 - \mu)\sigma\}/\Omega]/\Phi$

$+ (1 - .\varphi)/\Phi$

$- \alpha_1(1 - \mu)[\Sigma\Gamma - \sigma\varphi(1 - \mu)]/[\Phi\Omega]$

$= [\varphi\mu + \Sigma(\mu\beta + \eta) + \alpha_1\varphi(1 - \alpha)]/[\Phi\Omega]$

$> \quad 0$

4. Methodology of stochastic simulations

4.1. General methodology [12]

To describe the methodology, it is assumed that the model can be written in linear form as

$$(9) \quad y = A\, y(-1) + B\, x + C\, y^e + u$$

Current endogenous variables y depend on values for the previous period, $y(-1)$, as well as on expected values for the following period, $y^e = E(y(+1)/I)$, where I is the information available in the current period. The vector of errors may include some that are identically zero, in particular for equations that are identities. The stochastic simulations are performed by repeatedly replacing the error vector u by a draw from its observed statistical distribution; therefore an estimate of the co-variance matrix of the u's is needed. This is complicated by the fact that y^e is unobservable.

In Multimod, equations with expected variables were estimated using McCallum's (1976) instrumental variables method. Therefore, errors from the first stage regression should capture the expectations errors. If the expectations errors are called $v = y(+1) - y^e$, the equation residuals may be decomposed into two parts: the structural residuals u and the expectations errors v:

$$(10) \quad y = A\, y(-1) + B\, x + C\, y(+1) + u - C\, v$$

In practice, autoregressive time series were fitted for the variables for which the model has expectations (except for the exchange rate equations, see below); the forecasts from these equations — say $yfit(+1)$ — were substituted into equation (9) in place of y^e. The structural residuals were calculated residually as

$$(11) \quad u = y - [A\, y(-1) + B\, x + C\, yfit(+1)]$$

A second problem concerns the serial correlation of the residuals u, which was not taken into account in the estimation of the model due to the estimation techniques (e.g. time series/cross-section estimation). Therefore, autoregressions of the following form were fitted to the u's calculated by equation (11):

$$(12) \quad u = \varphi\, u_{-1} + a + b\, t + \varepsilon$$

The ε vector then constitutes the innovations or 'shocks' in the model. In simulation, the model constituted by equations (9) and (12) was solved together, given a draw for the vector ε of shocks. Shocks therefore have persistent effects both through the u's and through the dynamics of the model. Solution to the model in period t replaces y^e by the value calculated for $y(+1)$, given information available at t (call it $yhat(t,t+1)$), which itself depends on $x(+1)$ as well as on $y(+2)$, (which in turn is replaced by its model solution, $yhat(t,t+2)$, etc.). Some terminal condition is imposed on $y(+T)$. The effects in future periods are thus assumed to be correctly anticipated; however, future shocks are not anticipated before they occur. This implies that the forward-looking simulations have to be redone for each time period in which a new shock is applied, so that, for instance, $yhat(t+1,t+2)$, $yhat(t,t+2)$ and $y(t+2)$ may each have different values. This greatly increases the number of simulations needed.

In practice, residuals calculated for the period 1973-84 [13] were used to estimate the parameters of equation (12) and the 98×98 co-variance matrix describing the ε vector. A distinction was made between exchange rate shocks and shocks to other behavioural equations. For the latter, a first-order autoregression plus a time trend was estimated for each of the residuals u. The approach for the former is described below. These residuals ε were then correlated, giving a co-variance matrix V. Table E.6 presents the estimated standard errors of the ε's, save for the exchange rate, which is treated below. The table also excludes shocks to short-term interest rates, since they act as a predictable policy variable.

The stochastic simulations were run by making repeated draws from a random number generator, given standard normal variates w, where

$$E(w) = 0$$

$$E(ww') = I$$

A Cholesky decomposition [14] was performed on the matrix V, yielding a lower triangular matrix D such that

$$D\, D' = V$$

---

[12] This section draws on Masson and Symansky (1990).

[13] This period is determined by the fact that some of the equations contain forward-looking variables up to the period $t+4$. By assuming a chain rule of forecasting (as actually implied by the use of the fitted values of the AR(1) regression), this period could be extended to 1988. For some residuals, however, this resulted in unusually large errors (e.g. the capital stock equation in France).

[14] A special routine was developed to perform the Cholesky decomposition without needing the matrix V to be non-singular.

Table E.6

Estimated standard errors of non-exchange rate shocks, 1973-88

(%)

	D	F	I	UK	USA	Japan	Canada	Smaller ind. coun.	Rest of world
Private consumption	0,6	0,8	1,3	1,0	0,7	0,9	1,0	0,6	1,5[1]
Oil consumption	3,6	2,6	3,2	7,4	2,3	3,0	3,3	2,9	—
Capital stock	0,6	0,8[2]	1,3	1,0	0,7	0,9	1,0	0,6	—
Exports of manufactured goods	2,4	1,8	3,5	2,1	2,9	3,2	4,5	1,9	6,9[3]
Imports of manufactured goods	3,0	1,7	2,5	2,1	2,1	2,9	8,3	3,8	—
Imports of commodities	6,6	5,1	8,6	6,9	6,5	10,3	7,7	5,2	4,7[4]
Money demand	4,1	10,1	6,3	8,2	3,2	1,9	5,1	8,2	—
Long-term interest rate	1,1	1,3	1,8	1,3	1,4	1,2	0,9	1,5	—
GNP deflator	1,0	1,2	1,0	3,3	1,5	1,6	2,5	2,7	—
Export price	1,5	1,6	1,8	2,7	2,4	3,3	3,2	3,0	—
Production capacity	1,2	1,2	2,1	1,2	0,9	1,5	1,3	1,5	—

Estimated standard error of ε in the regression $u = \varphi u_{-1} + a + b t + \varepsilon$.

[1]   Private and public consumption, capital-importing developing countries.
[2]   1973-84.
[3]   All developing countries.
[4]   Exports of primary commodities.

The generated shocks w were premultiplied by D, yielding shocks ε^* with the same properties as the ε's, that is with estimated co-variance V:

$$\varepsilon^* = D w$$

$$E(\varepsilon^* \varepsilon^*) = E(D w w'D') = D D' = V$$

The model was first calibrated to track a smooth baseline. For each year from 1990 to 1999, a draw was made for the ε's; using inherited $y(-1)$, which depends on past ε's, the model is solved forward to the terminal date, which in each case was taken to be 2020. No shocks were applied to the years 2000-20, in order to leave a sufficient period at the end so that the simulations over the period of interest, 1990-99, would not be much affected by the terminal conditions on the expectations variables. This procedure was replicated 43 times, giving a total of 430 draws for the ε's.[15]

4.2. Treatment of exchange rate shocks

The approach for the exchange rate shocks is crucial for the evaluation of EMU. It is also more complicated. Consider the uncovered or open interest parity (UIP) condition used in the Multimod model:

$$(13) \quad e = Ee_{+1} - r + r^* + u,$$

with e the (log of the) exchange rate expressed in domestic currency per dollar, r the domestic interest rate, r^* the dollar interest rate, u a residual and E the model-consistent expectations operator.

Let e^f be the (1 year) forward exchange rate, and e^a_{+1} be the (unobservable) true expectation for e_{+1}. Consider the following definitions:[16]

$fd = e^f - e$	forward discount
$cp = r - r^* - fd$	country premium

---

[15]   One of the issues discussed at the Brookings conference 'Empirical evaluation of alternative policy regimes', 8-9 March 1990, Washington DC, was whether calculating root-mean squared deviations over the complete period 1990-99 would bias the results. Calculating them for the period 1995-99 showed as only major difference for the Community average that the improvement in inflation variability between the float and EMS regime almost became zero.

[16]   These definitions are mainly adapted from Frankel (1989).

$rp = e^f - e^a_{+1}$ risk premium

$ee = e^a_{+1} - Ee_{+1}$ expectational error

$fe = e_{+1} - e^a_{+1}$ forecast error

Hence, the residual u which represents the shocks to the exchange rate equation can be expressed as:

$$(14) \quad u = e - e^a_{+1} + e^a_{+1} - Ee_{+1} + r - r^*$$

$$= (\iota - \iota^* - fd) + (e^f \quad c^a_{+1}) + (c^a_{+1} - Ee_{+1})$$

$$= cp + rp + ee$$

The first term in the above equation is the country premium, the second the risk premium and the third the expectational error. This therefore highlights the three factors contributing to the exchange rate shocks:

(i)   incomplete capital market integration leading to non-zero country premium (i.e. deviation from covered interest rate parity);

(ii)   non-zero exchange rate risk premium arising from aversion towards risk and more generally imperfect substitutability between comparable assets in different currencies;

(iii)   expectational errors arising from differences between the agents' exchange-rate expectations and those represented by the model-consistent expectations $Ee+1$; a major cause for these differences may be changes in hypotheses regarding the long-term equilibrium real exchange rate.

Note that the forecast error $e_{+1} - e^a_{+1}$ does not affect the residual u. Any estimation of u should therefore exclude the forecasting error.

Since Ee_{+1} is not observed, estimation of u requires substituting an estimator $\hat{e}^a_{+1}$ for Ee_{+1} in equation (13), yielding:

$$(13') \quad \hat{u} = e - \hat{e}^a_{+1} + r - r^*$$

Possible solutions are:

(a) $\hat{e}^a_{+1} = e_{+1}$ (observed shocks solution),

(b) $\hat{e}^a_{+1} = e$ ('random walk' hypothesis),

(c)   to use the model to forecast $\hat{e}^a_{+1}$

(d)   to derive $\hat{e}^a_{+1}$ from a partial model.

These four possibilities will each be examined in turn.

Possibility (a): observed shocks

A first possibility is to calculate the residual using the observed exchange rate values in period $t+1$ (i.e. substituting

e_{+1} for $\hat{e}^a_{+1}$ in (13'). The residual $\hat{u}_a$ corresponding to this assumption is simply:

$$\hat{u}_a = cp + rp + fe = e - e_{+1} + r - r^*.$$

The estimated residual therefore includes the forecast error instead of the expectational error. This is not a desirable approach, since the forecast error should theoretically be excluded from the shock because it also depends on news arising in period $t + 1$.[17]

Possibility (b): 'random walk' hypothesis

A second possibility is that taken by Masson and Symansky (1990), and would correspond to the same treatment as for other equations with expectational variables. In this case, it would consist of assuming a random walk to be the best predictor for the exchange rate in period $t+1$ (i.e. $\hat{e}^a_{+1} = e$), which makes the estimated residual u_b of the equation equal to:

$$u_b = cp + fd = r - r^*.$$

In other terms, expected depreciation is always zero, exchange rates follow a random walk, and changes in the forward discount reflect changes in the risk premium. Other sources of error such as the expectational error are removed from equation (14). This is consistent with the empirical evidence put forward by Meese and Rogoff (1983). Nevertheless, it would seem difficult to combine it at the same time with the uncovered interest parity condition in the way Masson and Symansky (1990) do, since the exchange rate remains undetermined in (13) as it drops out of the equation. The correct random walk residuals would be $e_{+1} - e$, the variance of which would probably be very close to that of (a).

Possibility (c): model-consistent forecast

Methods (a) and (b) represent two extreme possibilities: either, as in (a), to assume that all the observed variance of exchange rates is due to deviations from the UIP condition, or, as in (b), to attribute almost all of this variance to 'news' arising in period $t+1$.

A third route would be to use the model itself in forecasting mode to calculate the expectation, at period $t-1$, of the exchange rate in period $t+1$. Inserting this expected ex-

---

17   This is the method originally used for the Multimod stochastic simulations by Frenkel et al. (1989).

change rate in the uncovered interest parity condition gives a residual:

$$\hat{u}_c = e - \hat{e}_{+1} + r - r^*.$$

Given a simulation over $T+1$ periods and a terminal value $\hat{e}_{+T+1}$ for the exchange rate, backward substitution using the simulated interest rate values r_{+i} and r^*_{+i} for periods $t+1$ to $t+T$ expresses the estimated residual as depending on the terminal value and the cumulative simulated interest rate differential: [18]

$$(15) \quad \hat{u}_c = e - \hat{e}_{+T+1} + r - r^* + \sum_{i=1}^{T} [r_{+i} - r^*_{+i}].$$

Though conceptually attractive, this approach also has its problems.

Exchange rate expectations as computed by the model depend obviously on expectations regarding economic policy. In a retrospective simulation, one has to make sure that simulated policy expectations are not confused with observed shifts in policy. Ideally, representation of economic policy should be based on equations representing standard behaviour of the authorities. Monetary policy in Multimod obeys an interest rate reaction function. As a consequence, agents expect interest rates to behave in accordance with this policy rule. However, since the interest rate reaction function comes from an inverted money demand function, it incorporates shifts in the money supply, implying that policy changes were to a large extent anticipated. For fiscal policy, the same kind of problem arises since the fiscal policy stance as measured by budget deficits is partially anticipated.

Possibility (d): long-run equilibrium consistent expectations with a partial model

Given the problems in using a complete model simulation, an alternative method based on a partial model can be designed that would be consistent with long-run equilibrium levels of interest rates and exchange rates. The idea was to retain the basic logic of equation (15), but to make the assumptions regarding economic policy much more transparent. Therefore, a reduced model has been built which consists of the following equations for each of the G7 countries and the smaller industrial countries zone:

$$(16) \quad \tau = \tau_{+1} - R + R^* + u$$

$$(17) \quad R = \mu R_{-1} + (1-\mu)\underline{R} + V$$

$$(18) \quad V = \varphi V_{-1} + \alpha t + \beta + \varepsilon$$

with: τ = log of real exchange rate with respect to dollar
R = real interest rate
R^* = US real interest rate
$\underline{R}$ = long-run equilibrium value real interest rate (2,8 %)
t = time

This model consists of (16), i.e. equation (13) transformed in terms of real exchange rates and real interest rates, and an interest rate reaction function (17), also in real terms, which ensures that all real interest rates converge to the same long-run equilibrium level $\underline{R}$.

The only purpose of equation (17) is to capture a very crude proxy of monetary policy shifts. In order to take sustained shifts in the policy stance into account, equation (18) describing the autocorrelation process and trend movements of the residuals of the interest rate equation is added. Interest rate equation (17) was estimated using pooled time-series/cross-section data for the eight countries over the period 1973-88, and μ has a common value equal to 0,68. The autocorrelation coefficient φ in equation (18) was next estimated for the eight countries separately, having relatively small values (smaller than 0,33 in absolute value).

Equations (16) to (18) were then simulated (with a forward simulator) until the year 2015 ten times, starting from 1979 onwards until 1988. That is, for each year from 1979 to 1988 a separate forward-looking simulation has been run with $u = 0$, taking into account the available information as represented by the initial values of the variables and of the error term ε, to yield a simulated real exchange rate $\underline{\tau}$.

As in equation (15), backward substitution in (16) leads to:

$$(16') \quad \underline{\tau} = \tau_{+T+1} - r + r^* - \sum_{i=1}^{T} [R_{+i} - R^*_{+i}]$$

where τ_{+T+1} is the real long-term equilibrium exchange rate of the baseline simulation and R and R* are simulated real interest rates (using equations (17) and (18) for periods $t+1$ ... $t+T$).

Hence, the estimated residual is:

$$\hat{u}_d = \tau - \underline{\tau}$$

Equation (16') clearly exhibits two major factors affecting exchange-rate expectations: expectations regarding the long-term real exchange rate, and expectations regarding future policy.

---

[18] If it is assumed that the long-term interest rate is related to the short-term interest rate through a perfect term-structure relationship, this result is equivalent to that used by Hooper and Mann (1989) or Koromzai *et al.* (1987), who explain the exchange rate as a function of an equilibrium rate and a cumulative long-term interest rate differential.

Comparison of the results

Table E.7 below gives the measure of exchange-rate shocks derived from methods (a), (b) and (d) (results for method (c) were not judged satisfactory for the reasons spelled out above). Since these methods do not share the same assumptions regarding the underlying exchange rate model, the raw residual results from methods (b) and (d) have been corrected for autocorrelation, trends and for different degrees of integration.

As expected, these methods give clearly different pictures of the stochastic component of exchange-rate unstability. Given the evident limitations of method (a), possible candidates to generate the shocks are methods (b) and (d).

The major problem with method (b) is its reliance on static expectations and the inconsistency of the random walk hypothesis with the UIP condition of the model. [19]

The major problem with method (d) arises from a very crude representation of expectations of future policies. Apart from this admittedly important limitation, however, method (d)

is more satisfying since it takes expectational errors into account in a way which is consistent with the model itself. Method (d) has therefore been chosen for the simulations.

4.3. Stochastic properties of exchange rates under alternative policy regimes

4.3.1. Principles

As outlined above, experiments with alternative policy regimes raise a number of difficult issues.

Strictly speaking, neither coefficients nor statistical characteristics of shocks are invariant with respect to changes in the exchange rate regime. Since these issues warrant more detailed study, a relatively conservative position is justified for the Multimod stochastic simulations: apart from their effect on expectations as represented in a model-consistent way, policy and exchange rate regimes are supposed to be neutral with respect to the internal structure and stochastic properties of the model (leaving aside the exchange rate equation).

This leaves open the choice of parameters for the stochastic properties of exchange rate equations: variance of shocks and co-variance between exchange rate shocks affecting different currencies. In this respect, experience is limited. Since the breakdown of the Bretton Woods regime, the DM and the pound sterling have been floating with respect to the US dollar, together with the yen and the Canadian dollar; the French franc and the Lira have been tightly linked to the DM for most of the period, (even if there was *de jure* floating in 1973-79). Hence, it is not clear from which experience the parameters for generalized floating, EMS or EMU should be drawn.

Since experience is limited and samples are small, the choice has been made to consider, when justified on a priori economic grounds, that national experiences with exchange rate regimes were drawn from the same statistical distribution. An obvious example regards the EMS: both the French and Italian experiences (and also in some respect the German one) are characteristic of EMS performance. It seems therefore valid to derive, for example, the possible stochastic behaviour of the pound after participation in the ERM from the average of German, French and Italian experiences.

Currencies differ, however, by their international role: other things being equal, the DM seems to be a closer substitute to the US dollar than other European currencies. Accordingly, shocks due to portfolio shifts away from the dollar assets

Table E.7

Comparison of exchange rate shocks

Rate	Observed deviation from UIP (a)	'Random walk' + UIP (b)	Model expectations with partial model (d)
USD/DM	17,1	0,7	11,2
USD/FF	17,4	1,1	10,9
USD/LIT	17,7	1,6	10,6
USD/UKL	14,0	2,2	9,7
USD/CAD	5,1	1,2	6,4
USD/YEN	17,0	1,9	16,8
USD/Smaller ind. coun.	13,6	1,3	6,2
FF/DM	5,1	1,3	4,2
LIT/DM	3,7	1,6	2,9
UKL/DM	10,2	1,8	6,5

(a) Observed: the shock is defined as the standard deviation of the residual u_a defined above over the period 1979-88.
(b) 'Random walk': the shock is defined as the standard error of the equation $\hat{u}_b = \varphi \cdot \hat{u}_b$ $(t-1) + a \cdot t + v$, with $\hat{u}_b$ the 'random walk' residual $r-r^*$, t is time and v the shock. Estimated over 1979-88.
(d) Model expectations: the shock is defined as the standard error of the equation $\hat{u}_c = \varphi \cdot \hat{u}_c$ $(t-1) + s \cdot \hat{u}_c (t-2) + a \cdot t + v$, with $\hat{u}_c$ the residual from the partial model simulations as defined in (16). Estimated over 1981-88 with either s = 0 or a = 0.

---

[19] Although early research by Meese and Rogoff (1983) brought some support to the random walk hypothesis, further work by the same authors (1988) brought evidence, contrary to the random walk hypothesis, of an effect of interest rate differentials on exchange rate movements, albeit non-significant. Other empirical evidence against the static expectations hypothesis is brought by Frankel and Froot (1987,1989) on the basis of survey data. Their findings lead to reject clearly the static expectations hypothesis, and to highlight the existence of systematic expectational errors.

would probably in a pure floating rate regime impact more on the DM than on other European currencies. Although hard evidence of clear-cut distinctions among European currencies does not exist, evidence from the floating-rate period tends to confirm this stronger link (Table E.8): the dollar exchange rate variability was higher in 1973-79 for the DM than for other major European currencies, in spite of *de facto* pegging to the DM for the latter.

Table E.8

Observed variability of bilateral dollar exchange rates

				(%)
	DM	FF	LIT	UKL
Standard deviation of three-month logarithmic changes, July 1973-February 1979	5,8	4,8	5,1	4,8

Source: Commission services.

Table E.9 gives an overall qualitative presentation of the methodological choices derived from the above principles. Technical hypotheses are detailed below.

The observed baseline regime (1979-88) can be summarized by four major features regarding intra-ERM exchange rate behaviour and behaviour of the dollar exchange rate for both the ERM members and the pound sterling (Table E.9):

Peg (P) for DM, FF and LIT cross-rates; Joint floating (JF) for DM, FF and LIT dollar rates; Floating with respect to both the other European currencies (F1) and the US dollar (F2) for the pound sterling.

The hypotheses for the simulated regimes are derived from experience with the observed regime in the following way:

(i) In a free float regime, the degree of exchange rate variability within the EC (as measured by shocks) is supposed to be close to that of the pound sterling with respect to currencies of the ERM. With respect to the dollar, the DM would retain the present aggregate variability of ERM currencies and the other currencies that of the pound.

(ii) In the EMS and in EMU, exchange rate variability would be close to that experienced in the ERM, except for fixity within the EC in EMU.

Table E.9

Summary of hypotheses for exchange-rate regimes

	Intra-ERM regime	Regime *vis-à-vis* ROW
Observed regime (1979-88)		
DM, FF, LIT	Peg (P)	Joint floating (JF)
UKL	Floating (F1)	Floating (F2)
Simulated regimes		
Free float		
DM	F1	JF
FF, LIT, UKL	F1	F2
EMS		
DM, FF, LIT, UKL	P	JF
EMU		
DM, FF, LIT, UKL	Fixed	JF

4.3.2. Empirical implementation

The triangular variance-co-variance matrix used to generate the shocks summarizes all information regarding the stochastic features of the simulations. It can schematically be decomposed into four parts:

	Domestic shocks	Exchange rate shocks
Domestic shocks	A	
Exchange rate shocks	B	D C D

Part A

Part A represents the (own and cross-country) variances and co-variances between the shocks other than for the exchange rate. As a consequence of the neutrality hypothesis outlined above, this part is supposed be independent of the exchange rate regime.

Part B

Part B represents the co-variances between the exchange rate shocks and the 'domestic' shocks in different countries. The observed co-variances represent a mixture of the present EMS regime for Germany, France and Italy and a free float for the dollar exchange rates of the other G7 countries. The imposition of co-variances for the different regimes to be simulated which would simultaneously satisfy the restrictions imposed by the regime (e.g. equal co-variances for the currencies participating in the EMU regimes) and economic reality is difficult to realize. [20]

Therefore, in order to avoid any bias through the introduction of largely arbitrary assumptions, the co-variances between the shocks to any dollar exchange rate and any 'domestic' variable have been put equal to zero. While this is not really necessary for the co-variances involving shocks to non-Community currencies, the zero co-variance hypothesis has also been introduced in those cases for want of consistency.

Table E.10

Observed (1981-88) and simulated correlation coefficients for exchange rate shocks

	USD/DM	USD/FF	USD/LIT	USD/UKL
Observed				
USD/DM	1			
USD/FF	0,825	1		
USD/LIT	0,933	0,898	1	
USD/UKL	0,761	0,635	0,750	1
USD/CAD	0,043	−0,101	−0,171	0,026
USD/YEN	0,529	0,678	0,745	0,680
USD/Smaller ind. coun.	0,761	0,820	0,856	0,548
Simulated				
Free float				
USD/DM	1			
USD/FF	0,715	1		
USD/LIT	0,715	0,715	1	
USD/UKL	0,715	0,715	0,715	1
EMS				
USD/DM	1			
USD/FF	0,885	1		
USD/LIT	0,885	0,885	1	
USD/UKL	0,885	0,885	0,885	1
Asymmetric/ Symmetric EMU				
USD/DM	1			
USD/FF	1	1		
USD/LIT	1	1	1	
USD/UKL	1	1	1	1

Part C

Part C represents the co-variances between the exchange rate shocks themselves. Appendix E.V describes more fully the modifications to the observed correlations between the exchange rate shocks in order to obtain appropriate correlations for each of the regimes. Table E.10 below shows the correlation coefficients between the different exchange rate shocks before and after modification. As expected, the original correlation between shocks affecting dollar exchange rates is high inside the ERM, and somewhat lower between the pound and the ERM currencies. Shocks to the Canadian dollar/US dollar exchange rate are uncorrelated to other shocks, while shocks to the yen/ dollar exchange rate are indeed correlated with those affecting European currencies. Finally, the currencies of the (mainly European) smaller industrialized countries appear to be linked to those of the ERM.

Part D

Part D represents the variances of the exchange rate shocks. If V_i is the calculated variance of the exchange rate shock to the dollar rate of currency i, $i = 1,..7$, with the same country correspondences as before, the variances given in Table E.11 are assumed for the different regimes.

Table E.11

Simulated variances for exchange rate shocks

Free float	$(V_1 + V_2 + V_3)/3$	$i = 1$
	V_4	$i = 2,3,4$
	V_i	$i = 5,6,7$
EMS + asymmetric/ symmetric EMU	$(V_1 + V_2 + V_3)/3$	$i = 1,2,3,4$
	V_i	$i = 5,6,7$

V_i is the observed variance of the shocks to the dollar exchange rate of country i.
D = 1, F = 2, I = 3, UK = 4, Canada = 5, Japan = 6, smaller industrial countries = 7.

---

[20] As an example, consider the estimated co-variance between shocks to the USD/FF rate and French private consumption. Due to the presence of the EMS, the shocks to the USD/FF rate are largely determined by those to the USD/DM rate. If the causality of the shocks were entirely from the USD/FF rate in the direction of French private consumption, this co-variance could be used for the free float regime. However, this causality is unlikely in the case of free float, so this approach would be difficult to justify.

For the free float, the same dichotomy as before between the DM as a major international currency and the other three EMU currencies is introduced. The DM shocks are given the average of the calculated variances for the three present EMS members in the model, whereas the shocks for the FF, LIT and UKL receive the calculated variance of the UKL (see Table E.12). The non-EMU variances are assumed unchanged.

For each of the three EMU regimes, the EMU currencies get the (high) variance associated with either the DM as the anchor currency (EMS and asymmetric EMU) or the ecu (symmetric EMU regime).

Table E.12

Standard deviations of exchange rate shocks in the simulated regimes (percentage points)

	USD/DM	USD/FF	USD/LIT	USD/UKL
Assumptions				
Free float	10,9	9,6	9,6	9,6
EMS	10,9	10,9	10,9	10,9
EMU	10,9	10,9	10,9	10,9
PM : Observed	11,2	10,9	10,6	9,6

5. Results from stochastic simulations

The differences, among regimes, in the variability of macro-economic variables in the stochastic simulations can be ascribed to a limited number of factors since the only elements that change between regimes are the exchange rate shocks and the monetary policy rule for the short-term interest rate.

In the model, exchange rate shocks have short-term nominal and real effects. If exchange rate shocks become more symmetric among Community countries, it may be expected that nominal and real variability due to this factor is lower on average in the Community in the EMS regime compared to float, and again lower in EMU compared to EMS. As illustrated by a simple example in Box E.3, this is due to the fact that the variance of intra-Community exchange rates reduces to zero in EMU, therefore eliminating a source of variability.

The effect of the monetary policy rule in the different regimes is twofold. On the one hand, it may restrict national autonomy in conducting monetary and exchange rate policy,

---

Box E.3: Exchange rate shocks and macroeconomic stability

A very simple analytical example may illustrate why the disappearance of intra-Community exchange rate shocks will reduce the variability of macroeconomic variables such as inflation and output.

Suppose the world consists of three countries, say 1 = Germany, 2 = France and 3 = the USA. As an example, consider the effect of exchange rate shocks on prices. Write the semi-reduced form of the price equations for Germany and France as follows:

$$p_1 = \alpha_{11}w_1 + \alpha_{12}(-e_{21} + p_2) + \alpha_{13}(e_1 + p_3) + z_1$$

$$p_2 = \alpha_{22}w_2 + \alpha_{21}(e_{21} + p_1) + \alpha_{23}(e_{21} + e_1 + p_3) + z_2,$$

where (in logarithms and in deviation from the baseline): p_i is the shock to the domestic absorption price level in country i, expressed in local currency, w_i the shock to the domestic output price level (assumed to be equal to the wage level, which in turn is assumed to be fully indexed to the absorption price level, such that $w_i = p_i$), e_{21} is the shock to the log of the FF/DM exchange rate, e_1 is the shock to the log of the DM/USD exchange rate, z_i represents all other shocks in the model, α_{ii} is the share of domestic output in domestic absorption of country i and α_{ij} the share of imports from country j in the domestic absorption of country i ($\alpha_{i1} + \alpha_{i2} + \alpha_{i3} = 1$). These equations explain the domestic absorption price by a weighted average of itself (via

the linkage domestic output price-wage level-indexation to absorption price) and the import prices from the other two countries. For simplicity, it is assumed that the shocks p_3 and z_i are independently distributed, such that for the analysis at hand they may be put equal to zero without influencing the result.

Thus, imposing $w_i = p_i$, $p_3 = z_i = 0$, the two equations may be solved to give the following reduced form:

$$p_1 = e_1$$

$$p_2 = e_{21} + e_1$$

This implies that the arithmetic average of the variance of absorption prices in the Community is equal to:

$$[var(p_1) + var(p_2)]/2 = var(e_1) + [var(e_{21}) + cov(e_1,e_{21})]/2$$

In EMU, the last expression in this equation reduces to zero. If the DM/USD exchange rate variance $var(e_1)$ remains unchanged in EMU (as assumed in the simulations), the average variance of prices in the Community will therefore decline if $[var(e_{21}) + cov(e_1,e_{21})] > 0$, which is the case for the exchange rate shocks used since the correlation between DM/USD shocks and intra-Community exchange rate shocks is small, even though it may be negative due to past tensions in the EMS, when there was pressure on the US dollar.

which may increase macroeconomic variability, as discussed in Chapter 6 and Annex D. On the other hand, the restrictions on exchange rate policy will be incorporated in the behaviour of private agents, which may therefore enhance wage and price discipline, leading to faster readjustment to shocks and therefore to less variability of macroeconomic variables.

The combined impact of these factors on the variability of macroeconomic variables is presented in index form in Table E.13, taking the free float regime as a reference.

The differences in the effects on the individual Community countries are marked by the asymmetric role of Germany in two of the four regimes, where it retains full autonomy in its monetary policy with the other Community countries losing autonomy. The implication is that the float, EMS and asymmetric EMU regime for Germany only differ in terms of exchange rate shocks whose decrease reduces inflation

variability and, to a minor extent, output variability. The big change for Germany occurs with the switch from asymmetric EMU to symmetric EMU. In the latter regime, the German monetary policy objectives for output and inflation only count for one fourth,[21] so that a loss of monetary policy autonomy occurs. Since the common monetary policy reaction function attaches a high priority to low inflation variability, the latter does not deteriorate in EMU compared to the EMS, due to the compensating effect of diminished intra-EC exchange rate shocks. The counterpart of this positive result for inflation variability is an increase in output variability in Germany in EMU compared to each of the other three regimes. This represents a 'worst case scenario', however, since only the role of monetary policy is taken into account, neglecting, for instance, the role of fiscal policy in output stabilization.

---

[21] This weight is model-specific, since only four Community countries are represented.

Table E.13

Stochastic simulations with Multimod: root-mean squared deviations from baseline, float = 100

	Free float	EMS	Asymmetric EMU	Symmetric EMU
Germany				
GDP	100	94	96	108
Private consumption	100	94	93	105
Gross investment	100	96	96	103
Total exports	100	98	99	102
Total imports	100	86	83	84
Absorption deflator	100	91	89	80
GNP deflator	100	96	95	87
Capacity utilization[1]	100	95	95	102
Short-term nominal interest rate[1]	100	91	89	85
Nominal effective exchange rate	100	67	64	67
Exchange rate wrt[2] USD	100	102	99	103
Current account balance[3]	100	98	98	96
Inflation[1]	100	86	83	86
Real effective exchange rate	100	82	80	82
France				
GDP	100	135	104	93
Private consumption	100	154	88	80
Gross investment	100	196	97	86
Total exports	100	90	83	84
Total imports	100	110	67	62
Absorption deflator	100	83	55	51
GNP deflator	100	104	63	60
Capacity utilization[1]	100	115	100	94
Short-term nominal interest rate[1]	100	126	58	56
Nominal effective exchange rate	100	13	0	0
Exchange rate wrt USD	100	65	64	66
Current account balance[3]	100	118	76	75
Inflation[1]	100	98	72	60
Real effective exchange rate	100	68	41	42

Table E.13 *(continued)*

	Free float	EMS	Asymmetric EMU	Symmetric EMU
Italy				
GDP	100	131	114	103
Private consumption	100	147	116	105
Gross investment	100	131	115	109
Total exports	100	99	95	96
Total imports	100	127	107	99
Absorption deflator	100	119	89	80
GNP deflator	100	142	104	93
Capacity utilization[1]	100	126	116	108
Short-term nominal interest rate[1]	100	132	69	67
Nominal effective exchange rate	100	17	0	0
Exchange rate wrt USD	100	81	79	82
Current account balance[3]	100	140	119	114
Inflation[1]	100	125	104	90
Real effective exchange rate	100	81	71	70
United Kingdom				
GDP	100	98	81	80
Private consumption	100	105	97	96
Gross investment	100	125	90	87
Total exports	100	95	94	94
Total imports	100	108	97	95
Absorption deflator	100	97	69	62
GNP deflator	100	112	77	73
Capacity utilization[1]	100	95	79	79
Short-term nominal interest rate[1]	100	194	54	52
Nominal effective exchange rate	100	15	0	0
Exchange rate wrt USD	100	98	93	96
Current account balance[3]	100	83	91	89
Inflation[1]	100	86	75	68
Real effective exchange rate	100	74	61	63
EUR 4 (average)				
GDP	100	109	93	90
Private consumption	100	129	100	96
Gross investment	100	139	102	97
Total exports	100	96	93	94
Total imports	100	112	87	82
Absorption deflator	100	97	71	64
GNP deflator	100	116	81	75
Capacity utilization[1]	100	103	92	90
Short-term nominal interest rate[1]	100	151	64	62
Exchange rate wrt USD	100	83	80	83
Current account balance[3]	100	105	92	91
Inflation[1]	100	96	81	73
Real effective exchange rate	100	75	62	62
USA				
GDP	100	100	99	99
Nominal effective exchange rate	100	100	99	100
Inflation[1]	100	101	101	101
Real effective exchange rate	100	102	100	103

Table E.13 *(continued)*

	Free float	EMS	Asymmetric EMU	Symmetric EMU
Japan				
GDP	100	100	100	100
Nominal effective exchange rate	100	101	101	101
Exchange rate wrt USD	100	99	99	99
Inflation[1]	100	100	99	99
Real effective exchange rate	100	99	98	99

[1] Difference with respect to baseline in percentage points.
[2] wrt = with respect to.
[3] Difference with respect to baseline, % baseline nominal GDP.

For the Community countries other than Germany, significant effects occur between each of the regimes. Comparing the EMS as modelled here to the float regime, inflation variability decreases in France and the United Kingdom, but increases in Italy. In the former two countries, the decrease in intra-EC exchange rate shocks and wage/price discipline effects dominate the loss of monetary policy. In Italy this is not the case, which may be due to the nature of the historical shocks and more backward-looking wage and price behaviour. The loss of monetary policy increases output variability in France and Italy due to the smaller real effects of exchange rate variability reduction. Only in the United Kingdom is the wage and price discipline effect strong enough to reduce output variability slightly. The move from EMS to the asymmetric EMU regime shows a similar pattern for the three countries, with the elimination of intra-EC exchange rate shocks and effects on wage and price discipline having a strong downward impact on the variability of both output and inflation, more than compensating the small additional loss of monetary policy autonomy. When the common monetary policy treats the policy objectives of all EMU members symmetrically, these gains are further strengthened since they regain part of monetary policy control while still enjoying the wage and price discipline effects of the abandoned intra-EC exchange rate instrument.

The picture for the Community average in terms of macroeconomic variability is conditioned by the individual country results. With the EMS as baseline, EMU would reduce output variability on average by some 15-20 %, while inflation variability could be some 25 % lower. As seen above, this result is not uniform for all countries due to the asymmetric position of Germany in the EMS. Due to the high priority of low inflation variability in the monetary policy rule, inflation stability in Germany is guaranteed, however.

To obtain an idea of the actual size of the reductions in variability of macroeconomic variables that can be expected,

the percentage reductions could have been applied to the absolute values of the variations resulting from the simulations (given in Appendix E.VI). These measures of variability are model-dependent, however, and strongly influenced by the choice of similarity of coefficients used for most equations, which could overstate the results. Moreover, there is the problem of choice of baseline. Rather, the reductions should be applied to the observed variability of the growth rate of GDP and the level of inflation (see Box 6.4 in Chapter 6). On that basis, a reduction of output growth variability of 20 % would correspond to a reduction in Member States' output growth variability ranging between 0,3 and 0,7 percentage points, and an inflation variability reduction of 25 % would be equivalent to a reduction in Member States' inflation variability ranging from 0,6 to 1,5 percentage points. It should be noted that all these reductions refer to the variability of output growth or inflation, and not their levels.

6. Caveats and general evaluation

The results of the stochastic simulations presented above are subject to a number of important caveats. Taking these caveats into account is necessary in order to put the results into their proper perspective.

Generally speaking, the methodology used to evaluate the impact of EMU on the variability of macroeconomic variables is well adapted to the problem (for instance, since it meets most of the Lucas critique of policy evaluation with empirical models) and may be considered as being up to date. While this has the advantage that the maximum of empirical information which economic research can deliver on the stability properties of EMU is obtained, this also implies that the results bear the uncertainty associated with a methodology which is still under development.

The Multimod model must be considered a reasonable compromise as regards size and basic assumptions in the class of multicountry models, notably concerning its inclusion of model-consistent expectations and endogenous treatment of exchange rates. Desirable as these features may seem, they also are a possible source of uncertainty since the former could make the results err on the optimistic side concerning the adjustment of variables to expectations, while the latter introduces an element of uncertainty in the floating exchange rate regimes induced by the endogenous modelling of exchange rates, which is known to be a highly fragile exercise. Furthermore, the imposed similarity of most coefficients among countries may underestimate the behavioural asymmetries but overestimate the asymmetries of historical shocks, so that the individual country results should rather be considered as draws from the same population than as precise indications.

The main limitation of the policy regimes introduced in the model is that they focus exclusively on monetary policy and lack a fiscal policy rule. While this has the advantage that the effects of the individual policy regimes are more tractable, it implies a departure from reality. For instance, in the case of Germany, it may be imagined that part of the loss in output variability could be compensated through fiscal policy. Another problem related to the realism of the regimes concerns the way in which the EMS was modeled. Firstly, because there exists no such thing as a 'devaluation rule' in the EMS, and secondly because the EMS is very much an evolving system of which it is difficult to imagine which State could serve as a proper baseline alternative to EMU.

A more intricate problem is related to the monetary policy rule used. As shown in Section 2.3.1, the parameters of the interest rate reaction function should be regarded as a combination of the parameters of the policy-makers' objective function and the multipliers of the model, and should therefore change among regimes since the multipliers are not invariant to regime changes. Nevertheless, the parameters of the interest rate reaction function were kept constant between regimes. Since the parameters chosen correspond to a free float regime, the corresponding rule is not optimal in the other regimes (this is equivalent to saying that the elimination of non-cooperative monetary and exchange rate policies has not been taken into account in the simulations). Removing this obstacle, however, could therefore only increase the gains of EMU in terms of macroeconomic stability.[22]

Some final remarks relate to the generation of the shocks introduced for the stochastic simulations. As discussed above, there exists no standard methodology for the calcu-

lation of exchange rate shocks mainly because of the difficulties in modelling exchange rate behaviour. The present approach was found to give exchange rate shocks which seem a priori acceptable, but departs from the latest IMF methodology (which itself is also evolving). A further difficulty relates to the absence of shocks to exogenous variables (both policy and non-policy), implying that changes to these variables were fully anticipated in the past. Doing so would however have introduced additional uncertainty concerning the distinction between anticipated and non-anticipated changes in these variables. Finally, it was assumed that the observed shocks in behaviour would be the same for all regimes, which again is more instrumental in providing tractable results than necessarily adding to the realism of the model.

Appendix E.I: Overview of the Multimod model

The Multimod model used for the simulations in this Annex was developed at the International Monetary Fund by Masson et al. (1988, 1990). It may be considered as intermediate between purely theoretical and full-scale empirical macroeconomic models. The model links submodels for the four major Community countries (Germany, France, Italy and the United Kingdom), the United States, Japan, Canada, and several 'rest of the world' zones. The country models contain some 10 econometric equations each, and may therefore be considered to be small. An important specific feature of the model is that the labour market has been substituted out, notably in the wage-price block. The nature of the model is such that it hardly has any forecasting abilities, but can usefully be employed for policy simulations around a given baseline.

The theoretical structure of the model is fairly transparent and incorporates both neo-Keynesian and classical features. Forward-looking expectations are combined with wage stickiness, for instance. Furthermore the model is based on intertemporal utility maximization of households but also assumes the existence of liquidity constraints. Forward-looking expectations in the model are equivalent to model-consistent expectations of future variables. Consequently, when a shock occurs, economic agents are supposed to have full knowledge of the state of the economy and notably of the policy rules (as represented by the model). This implies that shocks are unanticipated when they occur, but that their consequences are fully seized. Forward-looking expectations appear notably in the price equation (which is a reduced form equation of the wage-price block), the private consumption equation, the investment equation and the financial block. The latter is not estimated except for a money demand equation (not used in the present simulations); since the

---

[22]   Related to this point is the fact that macroeconomic stability has not been evaluated using an explicit macroeconomic welfare function, but rather on the basis of individual variables. This is only a problem, however, if the variability of output and inflation would move in different directions.

short-term interest rate is determined by a regime-dependent reaction function, the long-term interest rate is determined by a pure arbitrage condition with respect to short-term interest rates and the exchange rate follows uncovered interest rate parity, i.e. the expected change in the exchange rate in period t + 1 with respect to period t equals the interest rate differential in period t.

A specific feature of the model is that economic behaviour is imposed to be highly symmetrical across countries. Economic structures (e.g. as regards the size and geographical composition of foreign trade, the level of public debt etc.) differ among countries, but only statistically significant differences in parameters across countries were maintained, meaning in practice that except for the trade equations and wage rigidity parameter in the price equation most equations have identical parameters. This may underestimate the behavioural asymmetries among the G7 countries, causing them to reappear in the equation residuals in the form of a relatively poor statistical fit and the appearance of more asymmetric shocks than otherwise would be the case for the stochastic simulations through the co-variance matrix.

This point may be illustrated by a simple example. Suppose that there exist two equations estimated separately for two countries, for instance $y_1 = \alpha_1 x_1 + u_1$ and $y_2 = \alpha_2 x_2 + u_2$, with u_i the residuals. When estimated jointly, i.e. imposing a common coefficient α, the equations become $y_1 = \alpha x_1 + e_1$ and $y_2 = \alpha x_2 + e_2$, with the e_i residuals different from the u_i. For a numerical example, take $\alpha_1 = 1$, $\alpha_2 = 3$ and $\alpha = 2$. Suppose that for a particular date the variables have the values $y_1 = 2$, $y_2 = 4$ and $x_1 = x_2 = 1$, such that there is a perfect symmetric shock $u_1 = u_2 = 1$ for the equations with asymmetric behaviour. The shocks to the equation with symmetric behaviour are now more asymmetric, i.e. $e_1 = 0$ and $e_2 = 2$. In terms of co-variances between shocks, this would imply a lower co-variance between the asymmetric shocks.

Appendix E.II: Modifications to Multimod model

In addition to the introduction of explicit currency per Deutschmark equations for France, Italy and the United Kingdom, the Multimod model has been modified in three respects.

1. Tests with price shocks given to the model have pointed to instability problems, i.e. diverging oscillations in prices caused by the asynchronous movement of prices, production capacity and output. The IMF has suggested that this behaviour of the model, which occurs in particular for Italy, might be due to the weak price elasticities of the Italian import

and export equations, whereas it could also be related to the high level of public debt in the baseline and the ensuing contractionary effect on taxes. The solution adopted to avoid this problem of diverging oscillations has been to change the dynamic structure of the price equations for the G7 countries and the zone of smaller industrial countries. In particular, the long-run effect of the degree of capacity utilization has been made instantaneous, without having repercussions in later periods. While this does not change the long-run properties of the price equation, this ensures a better synchronous movement of prices and the degree of capacity utilization towards a long-run equilibium after the occurrence of a price shock.

The original Multimod price equation is as follows:

$$\ln(PY/PY_{-1}) = a + b*f(CU) + k*\ln(P_{+1}/P) + (1-k)*\ln(PY_{-1}/PY_{-2})$$

with PY   − GDP deflator

P   = Absorption deflator

f(CU) = function of degree of capacity utilization.

This equation implies a long-run effect of f(CU) on the rate of inflation of b/k. This equation can be interpreted as being derived from a static equation with a Koyck lag on the expression $(b/k)*f(CU) + \ln(P_{+1}/P)$. The modification consists in assuming that the Koyck lag operates solely on the rate of expected inflation $\ln(P_{+1}/P)$, and leads to the following equation:

$$\ln(PY/PY_{-1}) = a + b/k*[f(CU) - (1-k)*f(CU_{-1})] + k*\ln(P_{+1}/P) + (1-k)*\ln(PY_{-1}/PY_{-2}).$$

This formulation has the same long-run elasticity of prices with respect to the expression in the degree of capacity utilization, but has it frontloaded instead of applying gradually through time according to the geometrical Koyck lag.

2. The second modification to the model deals with the strong effect of endogenous tax rates in response to changes in the debt/GDP ratio, as mentioned above. The response of tax rates with respect to changes in this ratio, which was previously imposed to be equal to 0,3, has, in accordance with ideas of the IMF in this respect, been put equal to a lower value, namely 0,1.

3. The definition of the user cost of capital has a treatment of tax credit which implies that investment is assumed to be 100 % debt-financed. In some circumstances, this could imply that increases in interest rates could decrease the user cost of capital. To avoid this undesirable behaviour, 50 % debt-financing was assumed.

Appendix E.III: Derivation of the nominal GDP targeting rule

A targeting rule involving inflation and output is derived below under the assumption of standard money supply targeting by the authorities.

Let the money demand equation be:

(I) $M_d - p = \mu(aq - bi) + (1 - \mu)(M_d - p)_1 + c$

where M_d is nominal money demand, q is real output, p is the absorption price level, and i is the nominal interest rate. All variables except the interest rate are in log form.

Suppose the monetary authorities have inflation and output level as ultimate objectives, money stock as intermediate target and the (short-term) interest rate as instrument. Let π^*, q^* and i^* be the target values for inflation, output and the nominal interest rate.[23] Assuming the authorities know the money demand function (I), the money target is set at a level consistent with the ultimate targets, i.e.:

(II) $M^* = (p_{-1} + \pi^*) + \mu (aq^* - bi^*) + (1 - \mu) (M_d - p)_{-1} + c.$

Note that output enters the equation in level form, but that only variations in prices (inflation) are taken into account. Monetary authorities target the output level, but there is no memory of past prices. Hence, only inflation is taken into account, instead of price levels.

Putting money demand equal to money supply yields:

$\pi - \pi^* + \mu a (q - q^*) - \mu b (i - i^*) = 0$

where $\pi = p - p_{-1}$ is the inflation rate.

Differentiating with respect to baseline leads to:

$\pi - \pi^b + \mu a (q - q^b) - \mu b (i - i^b) = 0.$

Hence, the associated interest rate reaction function is:

(III) $(i - i^b) = [1/(\mu b)] (\pi - \pi^b) + [a/b] (q - q^b).$

Values of a, b and μ can be derived from the Multimod money demand equation (pooled estimate for the G7 countries, see Masson et al. (1990)): $\mu = 0,21$, $a = 0,94$, $b = 0,024$. Hence,

(IV) $(i - i^b) = 100 [2 (\pi - \pi^b) + 0,4 (q - q^b)].$

---

[23] Alternatively, the target value for the nominal interest rate could be derived from inflation and real interest rate targets.

This equation implies a strong short-term reaction to inflationary shocks since a 1 % rise in inflation implies a 2 % rise in the nominal interest rate. In order to avoid excessive instrument instability in the case of temporary shocks, a partial adjustment mechanism is added to (IV), yielding:

(V) $(i - i^b) = 0.5 [100 (2(\pi - \pi^b) + 0.4 (q - q^b))] + 0.5 [i - i^b]_{-1}.$

Appendix E.IV: Calibration of the parameters of the interest rate reaction function in accordance with recent EMS behaviour

The effective margins of fluctuation vis-à-vis the Deutschmark have already been reduced to 1 % or even less for most participants in the narrow-band ERM (Table E.A1).

Table E.A1

Indicators of exchange rate variability within bands

	1984-87	1987-89
BFR	0,66	0,33
DKR	0,93	0,95
FF	0,68	0,63
IRL	0,92	0,33
HFL	0,25	0,17

Average root-mean square deviation from trend; trends are computed by using exponential smoothing technique.

Source: Calculated using data from the Commission of the European Communities.

Calibration of parameters ß and Θ in (3') allows to combine quasi-linearity for small deviations and strong non-linearity in the neighbourhood of band limits. From the following equation

(3') $(i - i^b) = 100 [\alpha_1 (\pi - \pi^b) + \alpha_2 (q - q^b) + \alpha_3 \{ (e - e^b) + ß (e - e^b)^\Theta \}]$

it appears that:

$[\delta i / \delta e] = 100 \alpha_3 [1 + \Theta ß (e - e^b)^{\Theta - 1}].$

Table E.A2 below gives for $\alpha_3 = 2$, $\Theta = 11$ and $ß = 2.10^{18}$ the values of both interest rate deviations (from (3')) and partial derivative $[\delta i / \delta e]$ for different values of exchange rate deviation.

Table E.A2

Interest rate reactions to exchange rate deviations

Exchange rate deviation (%) = $100(e-e^b)$	$[\delta i/\delta e]^1$	Interest rate deviation (%) = $(i-i^b)$
0,00	2,00	0,00
0,25	2,00	0,50
0,50	2,00	1,00
0,75	2,02	1,50
1,00	2,44	2,04
1,25	6,10	2,97
1,50	27,37	6,46
1,75	120,53	22,36
2,00	452,56	85,92
2,25	1 465,11	303,77

[1] In percentage points.

Appendix E.V: Derivation of simulated correlations among exchange rate shocks

Let R_{ij} (i not equal to j) be the calculated correlation coefficient between the dollar exchange rate shocks of country i and country j, with i,j = 1,..,7 (D = 1, F = 2, I = 3, UK = 4, Canada = 5, Japan = 6, smaller industrial countries = 7). Table E.A3 shows the modifications made to the observed correlation coefficients in accordance with the principles summarized in Table E.9. The modifications to the corresponding co-variances take place via the correlation coefficients that are associated with the variance-co-variance matrix.[24]

For the free float, the correlations between the exchange rate shocks of the four EMS members are assumed to be equal to an average of the calculated correlations between the exchange rate shocks of Germany, France and Italy vis-à-vis the UK. For the correlations between the shocks for the four EMS members and the other currencies, a dichotomy is assumed between the position of the DM and the other three currencies. The DM being more of an international currency than the other three currencies, it is assumed that the correlation of shocks between the DM and the non-EMS currencies can be approximated by the average of the calculated correlations of the DM, FF and LIT with any third-country

currency. The three other EMS countries, France, Italy and the UK, are assumed to be in a similar position with respect to third-country currencies, and therefore all receive the correlation of the exchange rate shock for the UK with respect to each non-EMS currency shock. The correlations among the third-country currency shocks are assumed to be unchanged.

Table E.A3

Simulated correlations for exchange rate shocks

Free float	$(R_{14} + R_{24} + R_{34})/3$	i = 1,2,3,4 j = 1,2,3,4
	$(R_{1j} + R_{2j} + R_{3j})/3$	i = 1 j = 5,6,7
	R_{4j}	i = 2,3,4 j = 5,6,7
	R_{ij}	i = 5,6,7 j = 5,6,7
EMS	$(R_{12} + R_{13} + R_{23})/3$	i = 1,2,3 j = 1,2,3,4
	$(R_{1j} + R_{2j} + R_{3j})/3$	i = 1,2,3,4 j = 5,6,7
	R_{ij}	i = 5,6,7 j = 5,6,7
Asymmetric EMU/ symmetric EMU	1	i = 1,2,3,4 j = 1,2,3,4
	$(R_{1j} + R_{2j} + R_{3j})/3$	i = 1,2,3,4 j = 5,6,7
	R_{ij}	i = 5,6,7 j = 5,6,7

R_{ij} is the correlation between calculated exchange rate shocks relative to the dollar between countries i and j.
D = 1, F = 2, I = 3, UK = 4, Canada = 4, Japan = 6, smaller industrial countries = 7.

For the EMS regime, the correlations between the exchange rate shocks for Germany, France and Italy are taken to be equal to the average calculated correlations. For the correlations between these three countries and the UK, the average of the correlations between the three EMS members is also taken. The correlation between any EMS member and any third currency is assumed to be equal to the average of the correlations between the DM, FF and LIT and that currency. Again, the correlations among the third currencies are left unchanged.

For the asymmetric EMU and symmetric EMU regime, the same correlations as for the EMS regime are used, except that now the correlations for exchange rate shocks between EMU currencies are equal to one.

---

[24] Using the formula cov(x,y) = $R_{xy}*\sigma_x*\sigma_y$, with cov(.) the co-variance, R the correlation coefficient and σ the standard deviation.

Appendix E.VI: Stochastic simulations with Multimod: root-mean squared deviations from baseline

	Free float	EMS	Asymmetric EMU	Symmetric EMU
Germany				
GDP	3,6	3,4	3,4	3,9
Private consumption	3,2	3,0	3,0	3,3
Gross investment	7,4	7,2	7,1	7,7
Total exports	9,5	9,3	9,5	9,7
Total imports	7,3	6,3	6,1	6,1
Absorption deflator	5,7	5,2	5,1	4,6
GNP deflator	5,1	5,0	4,9	4,5
Capacity utilization[1]	4,1	3,9	4,0	4,2
Short-term nominal interest rate[1]	3,5	3,2	3,1	3,0
Nominal effective exchange rate	8,6	5,8	5,6	5,8
Exchange rate wrt[2] USD	18,6	19,0	18,6	19,2
Current account balance[3]	3,4	3,3	3,3	3,3
Inflation[1]	2,3	2,0	1,9	2,0
Real effective exchange rate	6,5	5,4	5,2	5,3
France				
GDP	3,4	4,6	3,6	3,2
Private consumption	6,7	10,4	6,0	5,4
Gross investment	9,1	17,8	8,9	7,8
Total exports	10,2	9,2	8,5	8,7
Total imports	12,9	14,2	8,7	8,1
Absorption deflator	12,1	10,1	6,8	6,3
GNP deflator	10,8	11,2	6,8	6,6
Capacity utilization[1]	3,5	4,1	3,6	3,3
Short-term nominal interest rate[1]	5,4	6,8	3,1	3,0
Exchange rate wrt DM	21,3	2,9	0,0	0,0
Exchange rate wrt USD	28,8	18,9	18,6	19,2
Current account balance[3]	3,8	4,5	2,9	2,9
Inflation[1]	3,2	3,1	2,3	1,9
Real effective exchange rate	10,0	6,8	4,2	4,2
Italy				
GDP	3,5	4,6	4,0	3,6
Private consumption	6,9	10,1	8,0	7,3
Gross investment	13,4	17,6	15,6	14,7
Total exports	9,9	9,8	9,5	9,5
Total imports	10,3	13,1	11,1	10,2
Absorption deflator	9,5	11,3	8,5	7,7
GNP deflator	9,1	12,9	9,5	8,5
Capacity utilization[1]	3,7	4,7	4,4	4,0
Short-term nominal interest rate[1]	4,5	6,0	3,1	3,0
Exchange rate wrt DM	17,5	3,1	0,0	0,0
Exchange rate wrt USD	23,3	19,0	18,6	19,2
Current account balance[3]	2,4	3,4	2,9	2,8
Inflation[1]	3,0	3,8	3,1	2,7
Real effective exchange rate	9,4	7,6	6,7	6,6
United Kingdom				
GDP	6,7	6,6	5,4	5,4
Private consumption	9,3	9,9	9,1	9,0
Gross investment	13,5	16,9	12,2	11,7

	Free float	EMS	Asymmetric EMU	Symmetric EMU
Total exports	8,8	8,4	8,3	8,3
Total imports	7,7	8,4	7,5	7,3
Absorption deflator	12,5	12,2	8,7	7,8
GNP deflator	12,8	14,4	9,9	9,4
Capacity utilization[1]	6,8	6,5	5,4	5,4
Short-term nominal interest rate[1]	5,7	11,1	3,1	3,0
Exchange rate wrt DM	20,7	3,2	0,0	0,0
Exchange rate wrt USD	19,9	19,7	18,6	19,2
Current account balance[3]	4,3	3,6	3,9	3,8
Inflation[1]	5,3	4,6	4,0	3,6
Real effective exchange rate	11,9	8,8	7,3	7,5
EUR 4 (average)				
GDP	4,5	4,9	4,2	4,1
Private consumption	6,9	8,9	6,9	6,6
Gross investment	11,2	15,5	11,4	10,9
Total exports	9,6	9,2	9,0	9,1
Total imports	9,8	11,0	8,5	8,1
Absorption deflator	10,3	10,1	7,4	6,7
GNP deflator	9,8	11,4	8,0	7,5
Capacity utilization[1]	4,7	4,9	4,4	4,3
Short-term nominal interest rate[1]	4,9	7,3	3,1	3,0
Exchange rate wrt USD	3,0	19,2	18,6	19,2
Current account balance[3]	3,5	3,7	3,3	3,2
Inflation[1]	3,6	3,5	2,9	2,6
Real effective exchange rate	9,6	7,3	6,0	6,0
USA				
GDP	2,7	2,7	2,7	2,7
Nominal effective exchange rate	16,3	16,3	16,1	16,4
Inflation[1]	2,3	2,4	2,4	2,4
Real effective exchange rate	12,2	12,5	12,3	12,6
Japan				
GDP	4,1	4,1	4,1	4,1
Nominal effective exchange rate	28,6	29,1	29,0	29,0
Exchange rate wrt USD	33,7	33,6	33,6	33,6
Inflation[1]	4,0	4,0	4,0	4,0
Real effective exchange rate	15,8	15,6	15,5	15,6

[1]   Difference with respect to baseline in percentage points.
[2]   wrt = with respect to.
[3]   Difference with respect to baseline, % baseline nominal GDP.

Note: To obtain convergence, the shocks to the equation residuals were scaled down by a factor of 10. Consequently, the results have been multiplied by 10. Tests have shown that this operation is relatively inconsequential for the results.

References

Begg, D. (1990), 'Alternative exchange rate regimes: the role of the exchange rate and the implications for wage-price adjustment', in *European Economy* (1990).

Bryant, R.C., Hooper, P. and Mann, C. L. (1990), 'The core stochastic simulations: a pre-conference overview', paper presented at the Brookings conference 'Empirical evaluation of alternative policy regimes', 8-9 March, Washington, DC.

Committee for the Study of Economic and Monetary Union (1989), *Report on economic and monetary union in the European Community,* Commission of the European Communities.

De Grauwe, P. (1988), 'Is the European Monetary System a DM-zone?', CEPS Working Document No 39, October.

European Economy (1990), 'The economics of EMU', special issue, forthcoming.

Frankel, J. A. (1989), 'Quantifying international capital mobility in the 1980s', Working Paper No 2856, NBER.

Frankel, J. A. and Froot, K. A. (1987), 'Using survey data to test standard propositions regarding exchange rate expectations', *American Economic Review* 77, pp. 133-153.

Frankel, J. A. and Froot, K. A. (1989), 'Forward discount bias: is it an exchange risk premium?', *Quarterly Journal of Economics,* pp. 139-161.

Frenkel, J. A., Goldstein, M. and Masson, P. (1989), 'Simulating the effects of some simple coordinated policy rules', in Bryant, R. C., Currie, D. A., Frenkel, J. A., Masson, P. R. and Portes R. (eds), *Macroeconomic policies in an interdependent world,* The Brookings Institution, CEPR and IMF, pp. 203-239.

Hooper, P. and Mann C. L. (1989), 'The emergence and persistence of the US external imbalance, 1980-87', *Princeton Studies in International Finance* No 65, Princeton University.

Koromzai, V., Llewellyn, J. and Potter, S. (1987), 'The rise and fall of the dollar: some explanations, consequences and lessons', *Economic Journal* 97, pp. 23-43.

Lucas, R. E. Jr. (1976), 'Econometric policy evaluation: a critique', *Carnegie-Rochester Conference Series on Public Policy,* No 2, pp. 19-46.

Masson, P., Symansky, S., Haas, R. and Dooley, M. (1988), 'Multimod — A multi-region econometric model', Staff Studies, IMF.

Masson, P., Symansky, S. and Meredith G. (1990), 'Multimod Mark II: A revised and extended model', IMF Occasional Paper No 71, July.

Masson, P. and Symansky, S. (1990), 'Stochastic simulation results for Multimod', paper presented at the Brookings Conference 'Empirical evaluation of alternative policy regimes', Washington, DC, 8-9 March.

McCallum, B. T. (1976), 'Rational expectations and the estimation of econometric models: an alternative procedure', *International Economic Review* 17, pp. 484-490.

Meese, R. and Rogoff, K. (1983), 'Empirical exchange rate models of the seventies: do they fit out of sample?', *Journal of International Economics* 14, pp. 3-24.

Meese, R. and Rogoff, K. (1988), 'Was it real? The exchange rate-interest differential relation over the modern floating period', *Journal of Finance* 43, pp. 933-948.

Obstfeld, M. (1988), 'Competitiveness, realignment and speculation: the role of financial markets', in Giavazzi, F., Micossi, S. and Miller, M. *The European Monetary System,* Cambridge University Press.

Sims, C. (1982), 'Policy analysis with econometric models', *Brookings Papers on Economic Activity,* Vol. 1, pp. 107-152.

Van der Ploeg, F. R. (1990), 'Macroeconomic policy coordination during the various phases of economic and monetary integration in Europe', in *European Economy* (1990).

Von Hagen, J. and Fratianni, M. (1989), 'Credibility and asymmetries in the EMS', paper presented at the CEPS/IMF conference 'Exchange rate policies in selected industrialized countries', 12-14 October, Brussels.

Detailed contents

Annexes

List of tables and graphs

Tables

Graphs

Index

Note: specific references to individual EC Member States have been omitted.